ARDS F.C.

Red and Blue HEAVEN

Ivor Edgar

BALLYHAY BOOKS

Published by Ballyhay Books,
an imprint of Laurel Cottage Ltd.
Donaghadee, N. Ireland 2007.
Copyrights Reserved.
© Text by Ivor Edgar 2007.
All rights reserved.
No part of this book may be reproduced or
stored on any media without the express written
permission of the publishers.
Printed by Gutenberg Press Ltd.

ISBN 978 1 900935 64 7

Boys' gate, unreserved, cinder terraces, airport end
Down the Doctor's Lane to join the trekking Old Cross men
Molly Calderwood's sweetie shop,
War Memorial, Canal Row, Castle Gardens
Past the Ulster Transport garage
Who's in goals, who's hurt, who's on from the seconds
O'Connell, Fulton, Walker, Newberry, Moore.
Turnstile puddles on wet Saturdays
Rain streaming, turf greening, tannoy coughing
Standing, whistling, smoking, chewing, cheering

From "Fifties Heavens" by Leslie Adams

For two Ards stalwarts of times past, Hugh Donaldson and Hugh Ritchie

Acknowledgements

A host of people have helped in the preparation of this book and it would be impossible to name them all, but I would like to mention Brian Adams, Leslie Adams, Frank Algie, John Anderson, John Black, Malcolm Brodie, Sam Brown, Addie Donaldson, Chris Edgar, Jonny Edgar, George Glass, Eddie Hanna, Billy Humphries, Davy Lawther, Mick Lynch, Ronnie McAteer, Billy McAvoy, Andrew McCullough, Bishop Gordon McMullan, John Martin, Adrian Monaghan, Ray Mowat, Vera Niblock, Jim Palmer, Brian Rea, Hugh Robinson, Ted Sinnott, Gordon Smith, Bobby Torrance, the staff of Belfast Central Library, and Tim Johnston and Carolyn Scott of Laurel Cottage Ltd. To all of these and to many others I wish to express my grateful thanks. I am especially indebted to George Eastham, who kindly agreed to write the foreword to this book. I am above all thankful to my wife Anne for her support during the long gestation of this project, and to Billy Graham, who first encouraged me to turn a hobby into a history book, and whose skills as the statistician of Ards FC are second to none.

For kind permission to reprint copyright material and to use photographs, acknowledgement is made to: Stevensons Studios, the Newtownards Chronicle, the Newtownards Spectator, the Northern Whig, the Newsletter and the Belfast Telegraph.

Every effort has been made to trace the owners of copyright material used in this book. In the event of omission, the publisher would be glad of notification.

Contents

Foreword

It is indeed an honour and a privilege for me to be able to write the foreword to this much needed book on the history of Ards Football Club. A club for me, where it all began over fifty years ago, and a place which holds such strong and pleasant memories even today.

It was 1953 when my father came home and told us that we were moving to Newtownards in Ireland, where he was to be their new player-manager. I had just finished school and was looking forward to a new 'adventure'.

My mother stayed behind to sell the house, Dad and I took the ferry to Belfast to start a new season in the Irish League. My first memories are of us lodging with a Mr and Mrs Murphy, who were connected with the club and whose hospitality was boundless. The Town Hall in the square which housed three snooker tables where we spent many a happy hour. The small ice cream café (Cafolla's, I think) in the square where I first met my two great friends Harry Murphy and Jimmy Milling – how we understood each other I'll never know. It took me quite a while to get the gist of what was being said. Then there was Castlereagh Park whose ground I still say today was one of the finest playing surfaces I've ever played on, what a pity it had to go. However, the new ground a few hundred yards away will be much more impressive, as all modern stadiums are, but the old one will never be forgotten, certainly not by me.

It's hard to believe that fifty years have passed since I played my first game for Ards v Portadown, it just seems like yesterday. My memories are still very strong

George Eastham

of the Gold Cup Final, surely we are the only father and son to have winners' medals from the same game. I still have them, along with my scrapbook with cuttings from the *Spectator* of some of the games we both played in.

It would be remiss of me not to mention my father, as if ever there was an Ardsman it was he. Even when he lived in South Africa with me, the first result he wanted to know was Ards. He was an amazing man who knew a footballer as soon as he saw him play, he looked to balance, quickness off the mark, and good feet. Once he had seen that he never forgot it, storing it away for a day when he could perhaps have that player in one of his teams. He loved his football simple, played as a team and played fairly; he refused to bend from those principles and as such had unrivalled success, much of it with Ards. As the saying goes in those parts, 'once an Ardsman, always an Ardsman'.

George Eastham

Introduction

I first began watching Ards Football Club in 1957-58: they won the League that year, and I thought it would always be like this. As far as I was concerned Ards was one of the big teams, up there strutting their stuff with the likes of Linfield and Glentoran and Glenavon, the 1956-57 winners of the League pennant. It was not just the Gibson Cup, either. Two years earlier they had won the County Antrim Shield, trouncing the mighty Blues by four goals to one; before that they had brought home the Gold Cup, and at the beginning of the decade, as a small boy, I had been taken to see the team triumphant, atop a lorry, preceded by a band, with crowds lining the streets (I saw them on the New Road, just below the Boyne Bridge) as they displayed the Irish Cup won that very afternoon. It seemed in that era when I grew up the town talked of little else but Ards Football Club. Archie McQuilken, Tommy Forde, Billy Smyth, Davy Lawther: these were the names I eagerly devoured in the sports pages of the *Chronicle* or the *'Spec'* and overheard in the conversations of the grownups who had actually seen these heroes in action. But more than all the other names mentioned were those of the Easthams, old George and young George as they were universally known. It was old George, by now a veteran who nonetheless took the field alongside his precociously, prodigiously gifted son, who had made Ards the talk of the province, as their studied, textbook football attracted spectators and praise in equal amounts. Crowd figures for Irish League matches have always been notoriously hard to discover, with most of my figures in this book based upon gate receipts divided by the price of entry prevalent at the time, but the 1958 Annual General Meeting revealed that the average home attendance in the League-winning season had been 2,748, *not including* OAPs and boys, so presumably in that boom year a remarkable 3000 plus watched Ards on a weekly basis.

Times change: Ards are no longer a power in the land, gates are sadly only a small fraction of what they were in our heyday, the club seems to be in near-perpetual crisis, and does not even have a home to call its own. Yet Ards survive, the support fewer in number but no less fierce in its loyalty. "His beloved —" (insert name of favourite club) has become a truly cringemaking cliché, yet there is an element of truth in it: supporting a football team is a declaration of love, with all its concomitant highs and lows. It is often a one-sided love affair, with hurt and bewilderment when those we admire leave in the hope of bettering themselves. Not everyone stays the course, but for those that do their grief or elation in times of setback or triumph show that devotion to a football team can mirror a real life love affair. Of course supporting a team like Ards is also a statement about the town, about community. Football supporters see things differently. In the 1970s as I worked with colleagues who were Rugby Union men, they would often inquire as to how Ards had done on Saturday, then laugh when I referred to Ards as 'we' or 'us'. It struck me that these muddied oafs, most of whom had played or still did play the 15-a-side game, did not share the same sense of solidarity as those who followed professional football, failing to understand the fierce loyalties that inspired 'us'.

Even when the team is limping through a miserable season there is a camaraderie among Ards supporters that eases the pain and helps to make regular defeat more bearable. Although we can whinge with the best of them, often a gallows humour provokes grim smiles and lightens the mood. Fumbling goalkeepers nicknamed 'Fingers', 'The Snail' as a soubriquet for a striker notably deficient in pace, and 'Whoosh' for a defender whose main aim in life seemed to be to separate his body from the ball by the maximum possible yardage, regardless of his teammates' whereabouts. Or John Irvine's classic crack, delivered in mock-PA announcer style when a dubious decision has gone against Ards, "Is there a referee in the ground?"

Or the stories, like Joe McCormick's when following Ards to Eindhoven for an ultimately disastrous European fixture, when an entertainer in a bar welcomed "our Irish friendsh" to Holland, announced he would sing a number in their honour, and launched into "Climb up on my knee, Danny Boy…."

This book does not claim to be anything other than partisan. It is unashamedly a fan's-eye view of proceedings, and as such revels in the moments of triumph. Readers who support other clubs need not take this too seriously: for a win over the Big Boys was, over the decades, the exception rather than the rule, and from Ards' point of view a big feather in our caps. At the end of the day this is a small town football club. Not for us the easy option of supporting a large, wealthy team, as often as not 'across the water', which is expected to win easily most weeks. How much better it is to be able to offer loyalty to a 'local team for local people', where there is no certainty of victory, and little complacency, and where every single win is cherished.

The familiar, ramshackle ground that we called home lies derelict now. The once immaculate playing surface, (the international referee Arthur Ellis claimed he "was never on a better pitch") is a wilderness. Relegated, Ards play intermediate football for the first time since 1947. Yet the club lives on. Some bright shining day a phoenix will arise from the ashes; a new stadium will witness a return to the big time, and the Newtownards public will return in their numbers to watch the pride of North Down. So long as some of us keep that hope alive, that torch alight, the cynics will be confounded and Ards Football Club will be a power in the land again. Bring it on.

ONE

Prehistory

1900-23

The infant Ards F.C. had a troubled upbringing. Crowd misbehaviour leading to the closure of the ground, results overturned on appeal, the abandonment and then the rebirth of the club: such were the events that littered the early history of Ards Football Club. The team that eventually took its place among the elite in 1923 had fought manfully to survive a score of chequered, often difficult years until its acceptance into the Senior League.

The very first reference to football in Newtownards comes from much earlier, from the Montgomery Manuscripts, which tell us that 'about 1620 the great school of Newton was established', (probably in Movilla Street), where 'golf, archery and football' were introduced. This is the first reference to golf in Ireland, and almost certainly to football. No doubt this 'football' was radically different from anything played in modern times, but it certainly offers Ards the opportunity to lay claim to an ancient lineage. The English Football Association did not appear for another 250 years, until 1863, and it was 1870 when that body legislated for the distinguishing feature of the game as we know it today when it was laid down that 'no player shall carry or knock on the ball', thereby distancing Association Football from the various handling codes. In 1870 there is a reference in the *Irish Football Annual* to 'Newtownards F.C.', its Secretary a Mr. David Caughey. His address is given as the Model School, so presumably this is the Headmaster, a position which then carried with it accommodation in the school. Once again, however, the 'football' referred to is more likely to have been rugby than soccer.

But Caughey's 'Newtownards F.C.' was unrelated to the football club which is the subject of this book. For Ards' beginnings we look to the turn of the century and the last years of the reign of Queen Victoria. At that time Newtownards was rich in sporting activity. Its best-known game was lacrosse, where the local club had been the best in Ireland, so dominant indeed that the predictability of its success is frequently offered as the reason why the sport declined. The Ards Lacrosse Club played at the Recreation Grounds on the Comber Road, which also hosted show jumping. Horse racing took place at Ballyhaft in the annual point-to-point meeting, and also at Ballywalter, while cricket, billiards, cycling, men's hockey and, bizarrely, bicycle polo were all organised sports. The freezing conditions of 1900 and 1901 even saw the revival of curling after a gap of five years, with matches against a Belfast team at Kiltonga Curling Pond. But what of Association Football?

With its thriving industries Newtownards was nothing if not a working class town, and the game of the common man was undoubtedly football. Evidence of its existence in the town in the nineteenth century can still be found. In the late 1890s as many as five clubs from Newtownards competed with others, including some from Comber and Bangor, for the McConnell Cup. The final of this competition, played in May 1899, saw Ards Swifts defeat the 2nd Battalion of the Royal Irish Rifles 6-1. When handing over the trophy Mr. McConnell, the donor, perhaps reacting to some earlier dispute, insisted that the Recreation Society, the official and predominantly middle class owners of the Comber Road complex where the final was played, was not at all hostile to the game of football. Certainly there were no further references to 'the people's game' being denied a welcome at the Recreation Grounds: indeed it was there that Ards would play the majority of their home games for the next twenty years. Ards F.C. per se did not appear until 1900, but a step towards a team representing the town was taken in late August 1899, when a select XI billed as the 'Ards Junior League', apparently drawn from those local teams which had recently competed in the McConnell Cup, drew 3-3 in a challenge match against the Royal Scots.

The breakthrough came on November 17th, 1900, when Castle Gardens F.C. played 'Ards Football Club', a match billed as 'spinners versus weavers', the Ards team originating from Webb's Weaving factory. Mr. W.S. Adams, a manager with Webb's and on whose initiative the team was founded, had seen the successful combination of football and industry in Scotland and thought the idea could be transplanted to Ulster. Further Ards matches, mainly friendlies, took place against Kiltonga, the Industrial School of Belfast, and, as the club's ambition presumably grew, Glentoran II and Linfield Swifts. Competitive games were a rarity, but in December a match lost to Comber seems to have been in the Osborne Cup. Some doubt exists about many of Ards' matches in this era, as newspaper coverage was sketchy, and would remain so throughout Ards' junior days, perhaps a result of the club itself having to submit copy to the *Chronicle*, and the impression gained is that most defeats, and even some victories, went unreported. The football writer called himself 'Spectator', and although only a sporadic correspondent he was nothing if not blunt. Thus he commented on the 5-2 defeat by Linfield Swifts: 'The home team did very well indeed against their experienced opponents, and everyone played up to expectations except Woods in goal, who was simply useless'. Not unexpectedly the unfortunate custodian, to use the language of the day, failed to feature in the very first Ards team to be listed in full in the *Newtownards Chronicle*. The match was a friendly against Distillery West End, who had just won the Steel and Sons' Cup, and it reads: McAvoy; T. Robinson, R. Hedley; S. Robinson, C. Robb. J. Hedley; Carlisle, Harvey, Atcheson, Martin and Francis. By this time it seems that the Ards team was no longer exclusively a Webb's outfit, but rather the pick of the local league, and thus a genuine 'Ards' side. A second XI was also turning out, playing at Kiltonga. All of these matches seem to have been played at home, unless away games did not rate a mention, which seems unlikely. Perhaps the misgivings of the middle class committee which ran the Recreation Grounds, however much Mr. McConnell had denied them, had their roots in the fear of hooliganism, which even at this early stage put in the occasional appearance. 'Spectator' felt obliged to admonish the players after a friendly against local team Boyne Rovers thus: 'It is a great mistake for clubs to indulge in such an amount of feeling and horse play when engaged in a friendly match.' Sadly he did not give details, but felt no such compunction when describing a game played late in May 1901 against Comber, which had to be abandoned after crowd trouble. In the first half several Comber players walked off for a time in protest against rough play and fighting. After the half time break, when the Comber goalkeeper Harrison punched Atcheson in the face with both hands, a free for all ensued, and the crowd invaded the pitch intent on exacting revenge on Harrison, the villain of the piece, who needed an escort in order to reach the safety of the pavilion.

The season 1901-02 saw Ards play competitive football on a regular basis when they entered the Junior League, in practice the second division of the Irish League. The very first match was a home fixture against Cliftonville Olympic, played on August 31st, 1901. The team sheet on that historic day read: W. J. Francis; R. Hedley, T. Robinson; J. Hedley, C. Robb, S. Robinson; S. Carlisle, E. Francis, A. Moore, J. Savage and J. Martin. There was no dream start to report, as Ards lost 3-0, but the next game, against Holywood Swifts, was won 3-0. Once again 'Spectator' felt the need to chastise the Ards followers, advising them that 'chaffing and offensive remarks to visitors should always be avoided'.

Ards FC, 1902-03 – one of the earliest photograhs of an Ards team

The club entered the Steel and Sons' Cup and the Intermediate Cup, losing in the latter to Wesley. There were, however, some fine victories recorded in the League, notably a 4-0 win over Belfast Celtic II played in front of 'a large crowd'. The last fixture of the season was at home against already-crowned champions Glentoran II, followed 'at no extra charge' by a lacrosse match between Down and Antrim. Although no record of Ards' final placing can be traced, it seems to have been a fairly successful beginning, with decent crowds, some good results, and a club well enough organised to be running a second string, who played their home games, still at Kiltonga, in the Newtownards Junior Alliance.

The red and blue colours which give Ards their distinctive strip and this book its title were still a long way in the future, as in the 1902-03 season they are described merely as 'the Reds'. Some dispute also exists as to what the actual name of the club was. Oral tradition persists that 'Old Ards' was their original name, but newspaper accounts from the time make no reference to that name, sticking to the plain and simple 'Ards'. On their revival after the First World War 'Ards Town' alternates with 'Ards', but perhaps this was in an attempt to distinguish the team from the then recently formed Ards United. At the time of their resurrection newspaper comment refers to efforts to revive 'the old Ards club' (note the lower case 'o'), and it may be that this has helped bring about some confusion. At any rate the club, call it what you will, built on a good start in 1902. Still competing in the 12 team Junior League, they held on to 3rd position up to December, defeating Dunmurry, Linfield Swifts and Celtic II by 5-2, but slipped back later in the season to finish in the lower half of the table. In the Steel and Sons' Cup Ards beat Cliftonville Strollers 4-2 in a match where they were accused of 'playing very roughly all through', but lost, perhaps fittingly, to the Strollers' big brothers, the Olympic, in the next round. Late in the season there were two highlights. Initially there was the very first visit to Ards of a team from outside Ireland when the Lancashire Amateur League winners, Liverpool side Old Xaverians, came to play the locals, who defeated them 1-0. The other high spot was the winning, or rather the sharing, of the Junior Charity Shield, after a 1-1 draw with Linfield Swifts. When the team arrived home off the 8.20 train there was a big crowd to welcome them, and the players were conveyed on 'Messrs. Hanna's brake' on a victory parade through the town, preceded by the flute band.

In terms of popular excitement Ards were unable in the 1903-04 season to compete with the major event of the year – the visit of King Edward VII and Queen Alexandra to the town in late July. They got off to a dogged start in the League, drawing most of their matches but losing none in the first half of the season. A 3-2 victory over Glentoran II moved them up to second place, but thereafter results deteriorated and their final placing was less exalted. Nonetheless they were now well established as one of the leading unattached clubs in the Junior League, and had enjoyed their best result of the season in a 3-0 friendly victory over the King's Own Scottish Borderers, then a Senior League team. The Annual General Meeting, which was held in Mr. Apperson's Temperance Hotel under the chairmanship of a Mr. Davis saw the election as Secretary of Mr. J. Freeland and as Treasurer Mr. James Murphy. The meeting heard confirmation of Ards' amalgamation with Windsor F.C., who had earlier in the season 'decided to throw in their lot with Ards and become the second string of that team', to compete in the Ormeau Alliance alongside the likes of Comber and Crusaders.

Presumably the earlier Ards II must have collapsed, and perhaps the Windsor F.C. deal went the same way, for again there was talk of the revival of the Second XI as the 1904-05 season began. It kicked off with a fine 3-0 win over Bangor in an August friendly. The team that turned out that day was: Lavery; Hines, Joe Lindsay; Robb, D. Thompson, Carlisle; Frank Thompson, Campbell, McIvor, Barr and Moore. Despite their success, the team must have changed a great deal as the league campaign, which got off to a reasonable start, wore on, for the Ards side which secured a notable victory by 3-0 over Celtic II, 'in front of a large attendance', showed many changes from that early season team. It read: Ritchie; McPeake, Boal; Robb, Carlisle, Barr; Moore, Runnigan, Campbell, Martin and Totten. After March, when Ards sat 3rd in the table, results must have tailed off, for match reports all but disappear from the local press. One of the handful of exceptions to this came when, after a home defeat to Mountpottinger YMCA, a rowdy crowd obliged the referee to ask for police protection. A happier feature of the year was a good run in the Steel and Sons' Cup, which saw the defeats of Willowfield and Granville and progress as far as the 4th round, when Ards finally bowed out to Dunmurry.

The 1905-06 campaign got off to a wretched start, with Ards one off the bottom of a 14 team competition by mid-November. But things picked up there-after, with a series of wins and a sensational comeback against Forth River, where Ards fought back from 4-0 down to claim a draw, but this turnaround was over-shadowed by justice at last catching up with what appears to have been an unruly following. The match on April 7th, 1906, at home to Dunmurry, was post-poned in view of a sensational statement emanating from the governing body. It read, 'This fixture in the League has been postponed owing to the Irish Football Association having suspended all teams in connection with their association from playing … in Newtownards until 1st November 1906, on account of the conduct of the spectators and the abusive treatment they gave to the referee in the League fixture between Ards and Mountpottinger YMCA.' No details of the nature or the extent of the trouble appear in the newspapers of the time. But given the need for police protection of the referee in the corresponding fixture of the previous sea-son there may well have been a history of trouble between the teams. It must also be said that this was far from the first time spectators at Ards had overstepped the mark, and the closure of the ground could be seen coming from a long way off.

Certainly at the beginning of season 1907-08 Ards F.C. resolved to expel from the ground and refuse further admittance to 'any person participating in rowdyism', and by this resolution the club clearly ate a sufficiently large portion of humble pie to impress the IFA, who eventually agreed to lift the ground closure a month early. The first match at the reopened ground was, fittingly enough, against Dunmurry, the fixture which had been the first to fall foul of the ban. It ended in a 1-1 draw, but more significantly, and even with 'an exceedingly large attendance', without a hint of trouble. It was not a distinguished season on the playing side, with a bottom half finish for Ards, but the goalkeeper, McMillan, gained an Irish Junior cap against Lanarkshire, while a second match against cross-channel opposition ended in a 4-1 victory over Clydevale of Greenock. Once again there seems to be a question mark surrounding a second XI, as at the outset of the season there was yet again talk of playing such a team, but no mention of their results at any stage. Clearly there were persistent difficulties in organising two teams to represent Ards.

Immediately before the 1907-08 season began, a Sports Day was organised by the club, and late in the year a benefit match for Samuel Walker, who had played for Ards for four years, saw the locals defeat Distillery 2-0. Newspaper accounts for this season are sparse in the extreme, but those that do exist single out for praise Charlie Robb and 'Toby' Robinson, 'an energetic half-back'. The most fascinating story of 1907-08, however, concerns the Steel Cup match against Mountpottinger, first won but then lost after an appeal and a replay. Such appeals were then common, with matches forfeited and points regularly lost for teams fielding ineligible players, but the circumstances on this occasion compel attention. McPeake, the Ards player, apparently only signed after the first game had ended, and so was technically ineligible to play. But the forms he signed just too late were professional forms, this being the first hint (coupled with Walker's ben-

Ards FC 1908-09

efit) that at least some of the Ards team were paid for playing. Despite this sign of Ards' ambition, they still only managed to finish in 9th position in the Junior League, and had yet again failed to make a credible challenge for the Robinson and Cleaver Shield, the trophy given to the winners of that competition.

1908-09 was to give Ards their best season yet, although they would still not manage to top the League by season's end. They got off to a flier, winning the first three matches 6-2, 4-2 and 4-2, the last against Linfield Swifts. They headed the table for some time, and held a good position until the turn of the year, but frustratingly reports once again dry up in the latter half of the season, so presumably their early form was not maintained. Ards certainly finished in style, playing Glentoran II in mid-May with a point to prove. They had won the first League encounter with the Belfast side 6-2, but were stymied in the return fixture, for despite winning 4-3 that match was declared void because of the lack of an 'official' referee. In the replay they were winning 1-0 when the game was abandoned, so the eventual 2-0 triumph over the Wee Glens, with goals from Beattie and Newell, was felt to be poetic justice. The players who gave Ards their most successful year since their formation were Douglas in goals, full-backs Boal, Withers or McPeake, half-backs McIvor, Stratton and R. Lindsay, and forwards from Thompson, Russell, McLean, Francis, Waugh, Garrett, Shaw and Hewitt. It was a case of so near yet so far in the Intermediate Cup, as the side reached the fourth round, defeating Glenavon in the third round, but losing to Cliftonville Olympic at the next hurdle. It seems churlish of Ards, to say the least, to have appealed against that defeat on the petty grounds that the match kicked off four minutes late, but this seems to have been an era when many club officials were barrack room lawyers who carried a copy of the rules and regulations in their inside pocket, ready to resort to it at the drop of a hat.

Before the 1909-10 season kicked off Newtownards made the sporting headlines for another reason, when local man Bob Brown became Irish heavyweight champion, knocking out Belfast's Andy Robin in the 5th round of a scheduled 20 round fight! Later in the year he repeated the dose against Sapper Grant to retain his title. On the football front left winger Waugh was selected to play for the Irish Junior team against the Lanarkshire League. The Junior League campaign followed the pattern of so many of these pre-war years, with the Ards side failing to maintain a reasonable start when the pitches became heavier as the season progressed. The real excitement came in a fine run in the Steel and Sons' Cup. In the first round Ards defeated Belgravia with a single goal from Stitt, and secured the same result, this time thanks to a McVicker goal, in the next round. Celtic Strollers, presumably the third string, were easily defeated 5-2, with goals from Stratton (2), Kirk, Thompson and Stitt. The quarter final brought Ards up against Glentoran II. Amidst 'scenes of unparalleled enthusiasm' Ards produced what the *Newtownards Chronicle* described as their 'best performance ever' as they crushed the East Belfastmen 3-0, with goals from Dornan, Kirk and Waugh. The semi-final took the team and a large contingent of supporters to Celtic Park, but hopes of a Christmas morning excursion to the city were dashed as Ards lost 3-0 to Oldpark Corinthians.

These two teams were to meet again the following season in the second round of the same competition. In the first round Ards had defeated the Cheshire Regiment 3-1, and were drawn away to their conquerors of the year before. Ards lost 1-0, but were awarded the tie on the grounds of the appalling behaviour of the Oldpark support, who despite their name seem to have been strangers to the concept of Corinthianism when they assaulted the Ards players during and after the match. In the third round a penalty from Stratton appeared to have secured victory over Barn United, but this time a protest by the Carrickfergus club – it is not clear on what grounds – led to a replay and a 5-0 defeat. Spectator violence, which we perhaps tend to think of as a more recent blight, as already seen, was a recurrent feature in this era. Thus one would have expected the clubs to give their full support to those charged with preserving law and order, yet in 1910 Ards F.C. intervened on behalf of William Meredith, a Newtownards man who appeared before the courts charged with hitting referee McIlwrath after a match at the Recreation Grounds. Ards went out of their way to have him acquitted, with Samuel Foster, a member of the Committee, describing it as only a 'medium blow', and Mr. Alexander Stuart appearing for the plaintiff on behalf of Ards F.C. The clue as to Ards' interest in the case was revealed by Mr. Stuart, who opined that conviction would 'endanger the status of the Ards club, and probably get their grounds suspended.' His plea was ignored, and the defendant was fined ten shillings with twelve shillings costs. There is, however, no record of the football authorities taking any further action against the club.

1910-11 was generally a decent season, with a good start – the first home defeat did not come until December, against Derry Guilds – and a strong finish, a mid-season slump being attributed to a series of new players being introduced into the side. The star performers seem to have been Lowry at centre-half, and right winger Cairnduff, who was a fine crosser of the ball and described as 'a good, clinking forward'. In goals was Jimmy Douglas, later to become a well

James Douglas in his Junior International jersey

known builder in the town, who gained the first of a number of junior caps when selected to play in a Junior Inter-League match against Scottish opposition.

In the 1911-12 season Ards lost their lucrative fixtures against the likes of Linfield Swifts and Celtic II with the formation of a Second Division of the Senior League, specifically for reserve teams. The Junior League was brought up to establishment by the introduction of teams such as Woodburn, Dundela and Lurgan Celtic, but whether this made the competition any easier is open to debate, as during the season, of the fixtures reported in the newspapers, six matches were won, seven lost and six drawn, including a draw against the then League leaders Portadown. Douglas, now the captain, continued to attract rave reviews for his goalkeeping. The grimmest news of the year concerned former half-back and Irish junior international Charlie Robb, who was drowned in an accident at Ardrossan docks.

An attempt to improve facilities came in the summer of 1912, when the ground at the 'Rec' was 'greatly enlarged', and a large room adjoining the 'Ards Dining Rooms' was secured for indoor training purposes. In the absence of any form of floodlighting this gave the players somewhere to work out during the dark winter nights. An almost completely new team started the sea-

Ards FC, 1912-13
Back row (l-r): McAvoy, Lindsay, Johnston, Douglas, Stadius, Carse, Beattie
Middle row (l-r): Murphy, Cairnduff, Robinson, Lowry, McKeag, Rowley, J. McNeilly
Front row (l-r): Russell, S. McNeilly, Vance

Russell and Vance were both killed in World War One

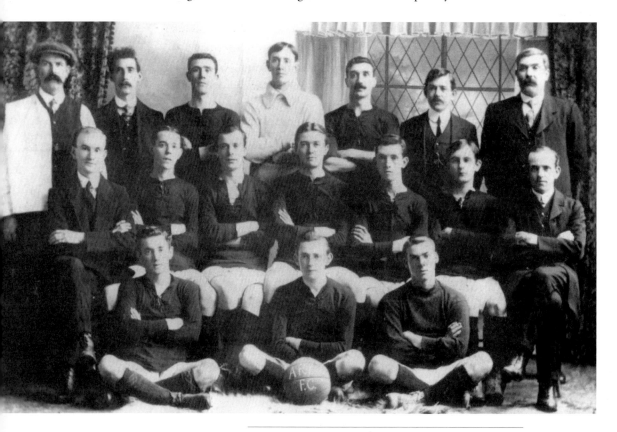

son, with the emphasis on locally-based players. 'Kid' Kearney began to make an impression, and 'Wuffie' Francis represented the Junior League against Lanarkshire. The team did not perform especially well, with what excitement there was centring on Ards II, who battled through to the fourth round of the Junior Cup before falling to Annesboro' by the odd goal in five. Ards' last match of the season had a bizarre ending, when Lurgan Celtic, a goal down and claiming they had a train to catch, left at half time. The *Chronicle* angrily pointed out that most of the Lurgan players in fact came from Belfast, and that the 7 o'clock kickoff allowed them plenty of time to catch the last train, which did not leave until 10 p.m.

The last season before the Great War saw a frustratingly inconsistent Ards side finish in a very respectable 4th position, but excellent results such as the mauling of League leaders Dunmurry by four clear goals were not produced regularly enough. Douglas, who had left Ards for a season, returned between the sticks, but the real backbone of the team seems again to have been centre-half Lowry. Silverware beckoned in the Intermediate Cup as the team fought their way to the 4th round, but defeat at the hands of Broadway after a replay ended their interest in that competition.

The summer of 1914 brought more important matters than football to the fore, and this season was to be Ards' last for a number of years. Even leaving the outbreak of hostilities to one side, Ards did not have their troubles to seek. On July 28th the 800 capacity unreserved stand at the 'Rec' burnt down, the result of arson popularly attributed to Suffragettes. Military demands then meant that the Recreation Grounds as a whole were taken over as a training camp for two infantry battalions. The last match Ards played there was a Junior League game against Glenavon on October 3rd, which the home team won 2-1. Thereafter they played at the Fair Grounds, off the Portaferry Road just behind the Fire Station. Although eight of the regulars went off to the war, those who were left were considered as promising a side as Newtownards had put out in years, yet results were, to put it kindly, mixed. Left-half McKeag received an Irish junior cap, but there were many who felt that it was inappropriate to persist in playing when so many were involved in the life and death business of the War. The *Chronicle* correspondent disagreed, stressing the innocent distraction which football provided in those dark days. At this time provincial papers rarely printed photographs, but whenever a local lad was killed, his picture, in uniform, almost always appeared. The weekly

Irish Junior League—1913-14.

CLUB	P	W	L	D	F	A	Pts.
Dunmurry ..	18	12	2	4	32	15	28
a Forth River ..	19	14	4	1	50	18	29
Ormiston ..	19	12	4	3	51	25	27
Ards ..	18	10	6	2	39	34	22
Queen's Park ..	18	8	6	4	28	17	20
Lurgan Celtic ..	18	9	8	1	29	26	19
Dundela ..	18	7	11	0	27	31	14
Portadown ..	18	6	11	1	35	39	13
Central ..	18	5	13	0	20	30	10
Y.C.V. ..	18	0	18	0	15	73	0

aForth River beat Ormiston in a test game for runners-up position.

The 1913-14 Junior League final table. Four of these teams still exist today display of those stern, accusing faces of young men from East Street, Frederick Street and South Street who would never walk the streets of Newtownards again still has a terrible power to appal even after ninety years, and it is hard to disagree with those who felt that this was no time to expend effort on something as essentially light-hearted as a game of football. The decision to give up was apparently taken, but receives no mention at all in the *Chronicle*. As in so many seasons, coverage simply peters out, but on this occasion, come September, there was no optimistic looking forward to a fresh start. For the record, the last team sheet printed was for a home game against Portadown to be played on May 1st, 1915. It reads: Douglas; McAuley, Russell; Brolly, Montgomery, Rowley; Cairnduff, Vance, Stevenson, Gaw and McLean. The result of the match is unknown.

Many of those who flocked to the colours in 1914 had been persuaded that the war would be 'over by Christmas'. But as the months turned into years and the carnage continued they were disabused of this hope, and during the wearying four years of conflict the disappearance of Ards Football Club seemed to matter less and less. Yet the craving for normality remained, and when at last peace came there were many who expected a revival of the old team. But in Ards' absence a new club, Ards United, had been formed. Setting up their headquarters at Hawlmark Park, better known as the Half Acre, at the bottom of the Crawfordsburn Road, they applied for, and were accepted by the Belfast Combination in 1918. United had immediate success, winning Division 2 and gaining promotion to the top echelon of that League, in which they came second in 1919-20. Ards therefore found themselves on the back foot, but in 1920, spurred on by their indefatigable Secretary James Beattie they regrouped, and like their local rivals entered Division 1 of the Belfast Combination. The Comber Road grounds of the Recreation Society were still required for military use, and so Ards continued where they had left off in 1915, at the Fair Grounds. Their first match after five years in abeyance was in the Steel and Sons' Cup, when they beat Eastmount 4-0. In the next round a 'very large attendance' saw them take on Bangor, but it was the Seasiders who progressed to the next round by a two-goal margin. But it seems that the newly reformed club collapsed in the autumn. Certainly not a single result, let alone a match report, appears in the pages of the *Chronicle* after November. It was certainly not that football was banished from the newspaper's pages, as Ards United continued to attract decent coverage, and indeed it was the younger club which achieved the local football headlines at the tail end of the season, taking 500 supporters with them to the Oval for the Firth Cup Final, which they duly won, beating Mountpottinger 2-0.

The theory that Ards had failed to complete their comeback season gains support from a report at the beginning of the 1921-22 season stating that 'the old

Ards Football Club is going to be revived.' It was, and again the league competition entered was the Belfast Combination, in the same division as Ards United, where the two Newtown teams played against sides such as Calvinville, Sandown Park, Banbridge United, Bangor Rangers and Strandtown. A mainly local squad had what seems to have been a moderately successful season, with the veteran Douglas still between the sticks, and promising performances from the strapping young centre-half William 'Tosher' Burns. But the long-term future of the club seems to have been in some doubt due to the unsatisfactory nature of the Fair Grounds. Oral evidence suggests that this was only a cinder surface, with no grass. If so, there could be no question of it being anything other than a stopgap solution. There was no possibility of a return to the 'Rec', as the Comber Road enclosure had became a training camp for the newly-formed RUC 'B' Specials, and without funds to purchase a ground of their own Ards' only hope was to appeal to the largesse of Lord Londonderry, the leading landowner in the area.

At the outset of the 1922-23 season the club at last made a determined effort to establish itself on a higher plane. New faces appeared on the Committee and an approach to the Marquess of Londonderry produced dividends with the offer of ground situated beside the Long Loaning on the Shore Road. Originally the plan was to take over the adjoining plot, now the home of Ards Rangers, but the existing leaseholder was unwilling to accede to this, and so four acres nearer the town were leased to Ards. In gratitude the club announced that the ground would be named Castlereagh Park, after the Marquess of Londonderry's heir, the Viscount. A series of fund raising events was planned to pay for the building of the new ground, the centrepiece being a Bazaar which eventually raised £375. Small wonder that the *Chronicle* exclaimed that 'the old Ards F.C. seems to have taken a new lease of life'. Playing, for the second successive year, as Ards Town, the side suffered an early setback with the transfer of 'Tosher' Burns to Glentoran. Despite their ambitious plans Ards were, on the field at any rate, the inferior of United, who had done the 'double' over Ards the previous season on their way to winning the League, and who would win it again in 1922-23. The expected rivalry between two teams from the same town continued for the next decade, but if healthy local rivalry sometimes toppled into a deeper-seated hostility it could well have been the result of the side with the better playing record over the past few years being left behind, with the longer established club finding a new ground and moving up into senior football. One hesitates to attribute motives in the absence of written evidence, but it seems very likely that envy played its part in the undercurrents of animosity.

The introduction of partition in 1920 was a blow to the football authorities. The Dublin clubs Shelbourne and Bohemians no longer wished to play in a predominantly Northern League, and in the unsettled atmosphere of the first Troubles Belfast Celtic temporarily withdrew from the League as well. This left a mere five, later six teams in the League, and there was, according to the *Irish News,* a drastic falling off in gate receipts. The Senior League sought expansion, and accordingly 'invited several teams from the provinces to join in the League, so as to keep up interest in the League.' In April 1923 Ards, one of the invitees, decided to apply. In the following month Barn United, Larne and Ards, now dropping the 'Town' part of their name, were formally accepted into the League. Newry Town later joined to make up an even number. Within a week of acceptance Ards Football Club met in Apperson's Commercial Hotel to rubber stamp the move into the Irish Senior League. The office bearers, whose names surely deserve commemoration for their foresight and drive, were Chairman Peter McLean, whose silver tongue had helped persuade the authorities that Ards were worthy of promotion, Vice-Chairman S. J. McDowell, Treasurer James Beattie and Secretary Frank Apperson. Others who played a part in the campaign for senior football included the Chairman's son John, Robert Francis and John Heron. The well-known photographer R. Clements Lyttle was appointed to represent Ards' interests within the League. All that now remained, and of course it was no mean task, was to sign players of the requisite quality and to prepare Castlereagh Park for the forthcoming season. On the playing side Kearney, Nickle and Rowley, already on Ards' books, were considered good enough to sign up for senior football, and new signings included the burly Inter-League player William Reid, who came from Bangor, William Gault from Oldpark Corinthians and full-back John Peden from Glentoran.

TWO

Triumph and Disaster
1923-28

On August 18th, 1923 Viscount Castlereagh, appropriately enough, opened the ground named in his honour. Castlereagh Park was described as having an estimated capacity of 8000, and being 'tastefully enclosed with galvanised iron', a rather startling aesthetic concept. The playing surface was surrounded by wooden palings and a temporary stand stood on the reserved side. The pavilion and much of the ground had been built by voluntary labour, and half of the total costs of £1,000 had already been raised. Although Ards were only the tenants at Castlereagh Park, a purely nominal rent was agreed. The grateful chairman, Peter McLean, invited Viscount Castlereagh to become President of the club, and later in the season presented His Lordship with an illuminated address to commemorate his 21st birthday. The opening day was a gala occasion, with the Ulster Amateur Flute band, and a five-a-side tournament which saw Cliftonville emerge as the first victors at Castlereagh Park when they defeated Distillery 3-2 in the final.

Pleasing though these ceremonies were, the real business of the season now had to be tackled. Achieving senior status had not been easy. Since the end of the Great War there had never been more than eight teams in the Senior League, and there were those who had misgivings about allowing four new provincial clubs to enter the League and increase it by fifty per cent. Ards owed a great deal to the Kirkintilloch-born Peter McLean, who had, as mentioned above, charmed the other delegates into letting the Newtownards team into the League for the 1923-

The historic moment - Ards enter the Senior League. Captains Peden (Ards) and Gee (Barn United), with Mr F Lloyd, referee for the opening match of the 1923-24 season

24 season. Even when they were in, there were those, particularly in the Belfast Press, who hinted that the country clubs were only there on sufferance, and could not hope to make any serious impact. The *Irish News* feared a lack of support for the teams outwith Belfast and prophesied financial difficulties. In this hostile climate it was clearly important to get off to a good start, and thankfully the team did.

The opening match of the season asked Ards to travel to Barn United. There was not at that date a regular bus service to Newtownards (that would not return until the following February when the simultaneous opening of services by the Ards Motor Transport Company Ltd. and McCartney's Bus Service provided a variation on the old adage, namely that you can wait ten years for a bus service and then two come along at once) so two charabancs were hired to bring supporters to Carrickfergus for the game. Amid scenes of great jubilation Ards won by two goals to one, with Weir and Rowley the scorers. The team that represented Ards on that auspicious day was: Diffen, Peden, Gault; Reid, Nickle, McAdam; Weir, Feeney, Munn, Rowley, and Brown. On the following Saturday, September 1st, Ards played their first game at Castlereagh Park and defeated Newry Town 1-0, with Munn scoring in front of an encouraging crowd of 1000. A creditable draw at Cliftonville followed, before defeat, but not disgrace, against both Linfield and Glentoran.

The League programme proved difficult from now on, with only three more wins after the early victories over Barn and Newry. A solid defence, apart from a dispute between club and captain which led to Jack Peden's disappearance from the team in the New Year, remained largely unchanged throughout the season and was clearly not the problem. Held together by burly centre-half Billy Nickle it played well and gave away few goals. Rather it was the forwards, who only managed to score 33 goals in 32 competitive matches, who were the weak link. The pick of them was 13 goal inside-right Feeney, who got some support from outside left James Alexander and the small but tricky inside forward Jimmy Taylor, signed at the end of October. The *Northern Whig* reckoned that Ards' biggest problem was a lack of fitness, as they frequently fell away in the second half of matches. No such problem occurred, however, in late November, when thick fog forced the abandonment of a match at Newry with 35 minutes to go, but, unusually by modern standards, the 1-1 result stood. The highlight of the League programme was undoubtedly the 4-3 win over Linfield in December, where Ards came back from a 3-0 deficit to score the winning goal with two minutes to go!

There was no joy in the cup competitions, with early dismissals from the Gold Cup, the Irish Cup, and worst of all, from the County Antrim Shield at the hands of Irish Alliance club Woodburn. Although the Carrickfergus outfit were defeated finalists in the Steel and Sons' Cup, this loss to junior opposition set a precedent which was unhappily still being followed at the end of the century. After the League ended at the turn of the year, the City Cup took up the rest of the season. Ards got off to a better start in this competition, winning three and drawing three of their first six matches, but then fell away badly, finishing in 6th position, an improvement, at least, on their 9th place in the league.

It had been a difficult season, but at least Ards had got through it, and consolidation in the Senior League was an achievement of sorts. There were some positives in the last few months: Billy Duffy, whom Luton Town wanted to keep after a trial, signed for Ards and looked as if he might solve the centre-forward problem, Jimmy Taylor was selected to represent the Irish Senior League against the Intermediate League, a match in which he scored, and, best of all, Ards had a new skip. When Newry Town took to wearing red in November, Ards, Larne, Cliftonville and Newry, four out of the ten League clubs, were clad in red. In the 1920s, with no such thing as an away strip, something had to be done, and so on Easter Monday 1924, Ards played Linfield in a new kit bought by their supporters. Different from all at the other club colours, the new shirts were red, with large blue hoops. The Red and Blues had been born.

The summer of 1924 saw much activity, both on and off the field. The playing surface, which had not been completely satisfactory, was ploughed up, levelled and re-sown. Committeemen and supporters whitewashed the palings and laid a new cinder track around the pitch. This track was put to good use in July at a children's Sports Day attended by the Duke and Duchess of York, the future George VI and Queen Elizabeth. The royal couple were not the only personalities to visit Newtownards that summer: in August Eric Liddell, the famous athlete and missionary whose story was later told in the film *Chariots of Fire*, was the special preacher at a service in Strean Presbyterian Church. On the Ards playing side two important signings were made. The former Ormiston centre-forward Sandy Patton, who had been playing with Falkirk the previous season, and 'Buster' Brown, a star of the Intermediate League who now wanted to try his hand in the Senior League, both became Ards players. A second team was entered in Division 1 of the Irish Alliance, where it benefited from the experience, both as a player and as a coach, of Billy Nickle.

When the season proper began, Patton scored on his debut, as Ards sensationally beat Linfield at Windsor Park, and in the first round of the Gold Cup the team was unlucky to lose 2-1 to the Blues in a replay. Late in the game Sandy Patton had a goal disallowed when he kicked the ball out of the keeper's hands. Indignantly he argued that it was a fair goal as he had not actually charged the goalie, (shades of George Best and Gordon Banks?). There seems to have been a real feeling of optimism around the club in this season, with decent attendances often entertained by the 1st Old Boys' Silver Band, right-half Billy Reid gaining an Amateur cap for Ireland against England, Patton scoring nine goals in his first eight appearances, and the IIs battling their way to the semi-final of the Steel and Sons' Cup. Results did not entirely warrant this optimism, with a nine match sequence without a win in November and December, and Patton's goals drying up, but just before the barren spell Ards fought back from a two-goal deficit at Belfast Celtic, back in the League for the first time since 1920, to take a deserved draw. Brown's two goals in the match were by all accounts magnificent efforts, and the unlucky Patton (twice) and Gray hit the woodwork. Unhappily Ards could not repeat the dose when they were drawn away to Celtic in the first round of the Cup. Captain Bob Wright won the toss, but disastrously elected to face the wind and the rain in the first half, and Ards lost 3-1.

When the talented James Alexander left Ards in November to sign for Dunfermline Athletic, he was replaced by Tommy Leeman, a Belfast United player who had been sought by several senior clubs. A three-day bazaar held in the Town Hall raised a remarkable £765, the equivalent of attracting a 20,000 crowd. Victories over Newry and Barn United in the two days after Christmas put Ards back on the winning trail, with the local newspaper correspondents commenting that the attempts to play close-passing football on heavy pitches had now thankfully been abandoned. The impetus was not maintained, however, and when the speedy Billy Duffy, a much better player at right-half than he had been up front, suffered a badly broken leg against Larne, it was clear that new signings were needed.

George Shields, the Cliftonville and Ireland full-back, and Louis Kinsler, a Queen of the South player and tax official who had been transferred to Belfast,

ARDS FOOTBALL CLUB

joined the club. The most important signing of this season however, was that of Bob McGee. In September 1923, just turned 20, McGee had been pitched into an Old Firm match on his Scottish League debut when the Celtic centre-forward, Joe Cassidy, whose appearances at training tended to be unreliable, was dropped. Out of position at centre forward, McGee only played one more match for Celtic, and was farmed out on loan to St. Mirren, Stenhousemuir and Dumbarton. Released by Celtic in 1924, he became a stalwart with the Ards club for the next seven years. A centre half who liked to go forward and score goals, he attracted rave reviews even from the partisan Belfast press, and many felt that he would have walked on to the Irish team had it not been for his Mearns birth-place.

Despite the new signings, the season tailed off, but not before Ards achieved two remarkable results. In their final League match they trounced Belfast Celtic 7-1, with three goals from Jack Robinson, two from Reid, and one each from Creaney and Leeman. To be fair to Celtic, their third place in the League was already secure, and only four first-team regulars played, but given the hidings they would administer to Ards many times over the next 20 years, this was a victory to be cherished. Remarkably, in the City Cup, Ards triumphed over the team from Paradise again, and this time against a full-strength Celtic, with a single goal from Bob McGee separating the teams at the finish.

The orignal pavilion at Castlereagh Park

One other match stands out from the tail end of this season, for two very different reasons. On March 7th Ards played out a thrilling 3-3 draw with Glenavon. Three men were sent off: Walker of Glenavon, and Morton and Beattie of Ards. The referee, a Mr Magennis, needed a police escort off the pitch at the end of the game. The other peculiarity of this game was Ards' second goal, scored by Tommy Leeman, It came direct from a corner, something which had allegedly only been done once before in Ireland, by Stanley Mahood of Celtic. To bend the old heavy 'lacer', if that is what Leeman actually did, was an amazing feat and one which would have delighted his grandson, also Tommy, who played for Ards in the 1990s.

The summer of 1925 saw a number of moves designed to build on the improvements of the previous season. In July a Supporters' Club was established under the chairmanship of John Ferris. On the playing side, although Sandy Patton was released and 'Buster' Brown moved to Linfield, two crucial signings were made. Eddie 'Ted' McGuire came to Ards from Shelbourne, and Andy Bothwell was signed from Bangor. Goalkeeper Jack Diffen was allowed to drift away, and eventually signed for Belfast Celtic half way through the season, but he was replaced by Albert McDonald. Ards, under the captaincy of George Shields, were billed as 'the youngest team in the league'.

The youngest team got off to an indifferent start, winning only one of their first seven matches, a 5-3 victory over Queen's Island, but in October they began to click, winning five out of the next seven games. The 3-1 win over Glenavon was the first time that season that the Lurgan men had tasted defeat. Particularly pleasing were the performances of Ted McGuire, who had scored 15 goals by Boxing Day. His exciting form earned him praise as the 'Patsy Gallagher' of local football, after the Glasgow Celtic legend. Bothwell's form was even more exciting. Watched by scouts from a number of clubs, including Liverpool and Everton, he was selected to play for the Irish League against the English League in October and against the Scottish League in the following month, but, best of all, made history by becoming not only the sole Irish League representative on the team which played England but also the first Ards player to represent Ireland at full international level. In the actual match, which was scoreless, Bothwell had a quiet enough game, finding himself starved of the ball by right-half Gowdy and inside forward Irvine, but he had shown enough form to get another chance.

In the first round of the Irish Cup Ards were drawn away to Portadown. Backed by a huge travelling support, and enjoying most of the play, they nonetheless fell to three breakaway goals from the Ports. The following week Ards lost by the odd goal in three at home to Celtic in front of their biggest crowd to date, with gate receipts of £84. These defeats, unlucky as they may have been, heralded another disappointing spell, with only the 5-1 triumph over Newry Town to raise spirits in December and most of January. And yet to complete this topsy-turvy League campaign, the team finished on a high, winning their last four matches, with a 2-1 victory over Glentoran and a sensational 6-1 win over Linfield as the highlights.

In the 1920s there must have been little conception that a reserve team should be a nursery for the first team, for when Ards II were withdrawn from Division 2 of the Intermediate League, the reason given was 'lack of support', with poor gate receipts insufficient to pay for the running of the team. If finance really was the major consideration the withdrawal was all the more ironic, given that in September Ards had been obliged to hold back the kick-off in their match against Portadown to six o'clock, to allow the Steel and Sons' Cup match between the IIs and Ards United to kick off at 3:00 p.m., on the assumption that a much larger crowd would turn out for the junior match. The assumption proved to be spot on. The bigger attendance was no doubt due to the interest in a local derby, but it is unclear at this distance whether the greater part of the spectators was composed of Ards or Ards United followers. Whatever the truth of the matter, it is clear that United were struggling to hold their support now that they had senior rivals within the town. At the end of the 1923-24 season United had turned down a proposed amalgamation, confident they could survive as an independent entity, but the Hawlmark club was under pressure to merge for the remainder of the decade.

The 1925-26 League campaign had been the most successful since Ards' entry into the Senior League. Fourth position was a real achievement, equalling the best ever performance by any club from outside Belfast. With McGuire in top form in front of a regular half-back line of Gamble, McGee, whose performances were described as 'magnificent', and Kinsler, the arrival of left winger Montgomery from Linfield, and the return of Sandy Patton, who in the interim had not in fact signed for any other club, hopes were high for the 1926 City Cup campaign. The opening fixture, against Cliftonville, was, however, a disaster. Not only did Ards lose 1-2, but an element of the crowd disgraced themselves by waiting behind for a full 90 minutes after the game in the hope, presumably, of lynching the referee, who eventually needed a police escort to Conway Square to

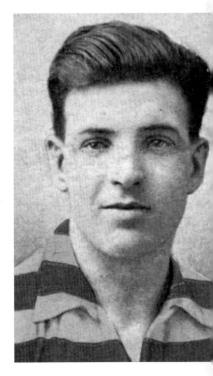

Bob McGee, one of Ards' all time greats. With 74 goals in 279 appearances, surely their greatest-ever centre half?

catch his bus and make good his escape. A sequel to the incident took place at a meeting of the Senior Clubs' Committee, where Mr McDowell, the referee, answering a charge that he had struck a Mr Robert Wightman jr. on the mouth, claimed that he had been kicked during the fracas at the ground. The committee decided to caution both Ards F.C. and the referee.

Only four wins were recorded in the City Cup and Ards finished a disappointing 9th. The highlight of the campaign was another win over Linfield, this time by the margin of 3-1. McGuire's two goals in that match brought his total to 23 for the season, a fine performance, but the inside forward blotted his copybook in May when it was revealed that he had played unofficially and quite illegally for Shamrock Rovers in the Free State League against his former club Shelbourne. After an outstanding season, he never played for Ards again. Goalkeeper MacDonald, on the other hand, did not play for Ards after April 24th for quite different reasons. Unemployed, he decided on an impulse that he could no longer be a burden on his parents, and went off and took the King's Shilling, signing up for the Irish Guards. His decision was so sudden that Ards had to use their outfield player Duff in goals against Larne in the following match. True to the conventions of such crises Duff played solidly between the posts and Ards won 1-0. His near namesake, Billy Duffy, had less luck. Now out of football for over a year with a badly broken leg, Duffy was granted a benefit match, to be played at Celtic Park between teams representing Counties Antrim and Down. Unhappily many of the players selected failed to turn up, and a poor attendance meant that the financial benefit to the unfortunate player was minimal.

Andy Bothwell, on the other hand, continued to shine. Capped against both Scotland and Wales, he had a sparkling game against the Welsh, setting up all three goals in the Irish win. Bothwell also scored both goals against Bangor in the inaugural year of a new trophy.

Outraged at the exclusion of the two North Down clubs from the Belfast Charity Cup, Mr George Tate donated a cup to be competed for annually by Ards and Bangor. The Tate Cup provided a fixture which was eagerly anticipated by both sets of supporters for many years, but after the Second World War the competition took place only intermittently. The trophy eventually disappeared. Last won by Bangor in the 1970s, it was placed on display in a local hostelry, but here the trail goes cold, and its present whereabouts are a mystery. May the Tate Cup, wherever it is, rest in peace.

Taking stock of their progress since entering the League, Ards had good reason to be pleased, having successively finished 9th, 7th and 4th, but the 1926 Annual General Meeting heard that gates had been discouraging. Nonetheless, results had been improving, 'the enclosure had been well banked', and strenuous efforts were being made to strengthen the team for what, it was hoped, would be the most successful season yet. A number of important signings were made. From Forth River came goalkeeper Sam McMullan, and two new full-backs arrived, Harold Risk and John Semple, the latter boasting first team experience at Charlton Athletic. Up front Ards obtained Toby Cleland and, from Belfast Celtic, Andy Smith at centre-forward. Smith would later become the President of the Irish Football League, but obtained his greatest fame as an international boxing referee after the War. With Billy Nickle as the new trainer, Ards got off to a wonderful start. After a 2-2 draw against Distillery at York Park (Grosvenor Park had now been out of action for a number of seasons) a run of six successive victories followed. The most notable was a 2-1 win over Linfield at Castlereagh Park, during which there was a great deal of crowd trouble, Linfield supporters stoning the Ards players until Andy Smith could take no more and fired one of the stones back at the crowd. Sent off for this action, he was fortunate to receive no more than a caution. Unfortunately, despite their excellent League form Ards made their habitual early exit from the Gold Cup, losing 0-1 to Celtic, but attracting a record crowd of 3500 in the process.

The secret of Ards' early season success seems to have been consistency, with the same team turning out unchanged for the first six matches. It comprised McMullan; Risk, Semple; Gamble, McGee, Kinsler; Bothwell, Patton, Smith, Cleland and Leeman. The biggest test yet was a trip to Paradise to play Belfast Celtic, who were two points behind the table-topping Castlereagh Park outfit. Ards maintained the gap with a fine 1-1 draw in front of over 8000. Curran's goal for Celtic was a lucky affair, scored after McMullan kicked more of the ground than the ball at a goal-kick. Even a shock defeat at home to Cliftonville did not dislodge Ards from the top of the League, as their nearest rivals all dropped points. However, a series of blows affected the side thereafter. Semple left to try his luck in the USA, where Ted McGuire had recently resurfaced, starring for Philadelphia, while Risk, Leeman, and Kinsler were forced out of the team with injury. Kinsler's case was by far the worst, with the Scotsman unable to play for the rest of the season. It was a savage blow: he had starred for the Irish League against the English League just before his injury, scoring the local side's only goal from a pass by Bothwell. Although Andy McKeown came from Queen's Island to make the right-back slot his own, partnered for the rest of the season by Tommy Wilson, another new signing, and Sandy McIlreavy also arrived to bolster the squad, the disruptions caused by injury proved too great to overcome, and results in the League tailed off, with only four more wins recorded. Ards' final placing of 5th was respectable, but a sore disappointment after the promise of the autumn. The end of season City Cup campaign brought little joy, with Ards registering only three wins, over Newry Town, Glentoran and Barn United, the last-named producing a 6-4 scoreline. The Tate Cup remained in Ards' possession after a 3-0 win over Bangor. But all of this paled into insignificance compared with Ards' exploits in the Irish Cup, where they became only the 5th non-Belfast team to win the trophy.

The road to Cup glory began in November, with a trip to Newry, where goals by Patton and Campbell secured a 2-1 victory. The second round also saw Ards on their travels, this time to Lurgan, where after a titanic struggle the Newtownards men again triumphed 2-1. A Bob McGee header put Ards into the lead, but after Andrews equalised for Glenavon the Lurgan Blues dominated the game, and Ards had their backs to the wall for most of the second half. The winner, again from McGee, came when he ran the length of the field and exchanged passes with Leeman before crashing the ball home and putting Ards into the semi-finals. The draw paired Ards with Belfast Celtic, with Ards seen as hopeless outsiders, but to the astonishment of the football world the men from Newtownards beat the city club 3-1. In an exhausting match played on a Solitude pitch which was waterlogged in parts, Ards scored two goals late in the first half, via Patton and a McGee penalty, but just on half-time a Curran penalty reduced the lead. Celtic threw themselves at Ards thereafter, but found themselves up against a stalwart defence which gave no quarter, and when Bothwell scored a third goal for Ards it was only a matter of playing out time. And so to the final, which would be played at the Oval against Cliftonville, who had won the Cup on seven previous occasions, although not since the Great War.

The crowd at the Oval on March 26th, 1927 was around 10,000, a respectable attendance, but not as big as had been hoped. The weather, and the forecasts in the Belfast Press of a one-sided match (needless to say, in favour of Cliftonville), were reckoned to have discouraged many neutral supporters. Ards were represented by McMullan; McKeown, Wilson; Smith, Risk, Gamble; Bothwell, Patton, McGee, Croft and McIlreavy. The day was murky, with a hint of rain, and the pitch decidedly on the soft side. In the first half Bothwell probed to some effect for Ards, but it was the Amateurs who took the lead in 25 minutes when Mortished chipped a line of defenders from a free-kick. Worse was to follow just before half-time when Hughes netted a second for Cliftonville following a corner. A two-goal deficit seemed too much to pull back, but Ards had shown great fighting qualities in the earlier rounds of the competition, and got off to the best possible start in the second half, when McGee scored after a pass from Croft, who had only come into the team in time for the semi-final. On 65 minutes McIlreavy equalised after Gardiner could only fist out Bothwell's corner kick. Cliftonville rallied, and the result remained in the balance until the 84th minute, when McIlreavy, effective throughout, cut in from the left, drew his defender, and pushed it to McGee, whose task was easy. The comeback was complete, and Ards had won the Irish Cup. Jubilant fans invaded the pitch to chair their heroes off after the game. It was a triumph that reverberated in circles far beyond those of the Castlereagh Park faithful. The next day, in Newtownards Methodist Church, the Reverend J. W. Stutt based his sermon on the match, taking as his text 'And everyone that striveth in the games is temperate in all things' (I Corinthians, 9, 25). Although it is not recorded, it would seem likely that in their hymns of thanks and praise the Methodists of Newtown sang with more than usual fervour that Sunday.

The transitory nature of success, and of life itself, was brought home all too cruelly to Ards in 1927-28, a season which saw both a diminution in their success, and a genuine human tragedy. Pre-season, however, they could bask in the glory of success in the Irish Cup, the trophy put on display in Carse's shop window in South St. Ground improvements to Castlereagh Park included pulling back the palings at the Pavilion End so as to widen the track, whose surface was improved to allow cycle racing. The admission of Coleraine Olympic and Bangor into a 14 team League meant regular fixtures against their North Down rivals. But for many Ards followers the real local rivalry involved Ards United. It seems a genuine animosity existed between the two sets of supporters, who would attend each other's fixtures, not to offer support, but to root for the opposition. With such a poisonous atmosphere it was not surprising that fresh efforts to amalgamate the two teams failed in the summer of 1927.

Ards got off to a very solid start, going 12 matches without defeat, and winning six of those, the best a 7-1 trouncing of Queen's Island. Goalkeeper Sam McMullan, who shared goalkeeping duties with the exotically named Sylvester Beirne, played behind a solid defence marshalled by McGee, and the pre-season prediction of 'Ben Madigan' in the *Irish News* that Ards would struggle in defence appeared ill-founded. But from Hallowe'en onwards the defence became alarmingly porous, conceding eight goals to Belfast Celtic, the same number in a 4-8 defeat by Linfield, five to Larne, five and later four to Newry Town, seven to Portadown, and, when the City Cup began, five to Glentoran, six to Coleraine and four each to Glenavon and Linfield. Why did a defence which had been giving away on average only a goal a game before the 8-3 hiding by Celtic collapse so spectacularly? Perhaps moving McGee to centre forward fatally weakened the back line, (although he did score 20 goals, one ahead of Ralph Lynas' 19), as did the misfortune which befell Jimmy Gamble, who suffered a broken leg on 26th October. Jimmy was one of those players about whom no one had a bad word. A local preacher, he exerted a quiet and calming influence in the dressing room, and there can be little doubt that his loss was a serious blow to Ards.

A more pleasing memory of the season was Ards' visit to Distillery on November 12th, when they provided the opposition in the first match for seven years at the re-opened Grosvenor Park. Refurbishment was far from complete, with no stand and no dressing rooms, and both teams were obliged to change in the nearby Excise Street School. Distillery's first goal was a penalty, although no one in the ground except the referee thought so. Disgusted at the decision, Gowdy kicked the ball away. An embarrassed Sam McMullan retrieved it, but this time the referee kicked it away, insisting that Gowdy go to get it. The incensed left-half refused, upon which Tommy Wilson brought the ball back and placed it on the spot, and Gowdy escaped further humiliation. Meek scored the penalty, and justice was done. Or not, depending on your viewpoint.

Ards' league position was 11th, and in a miserable City Cup campaign only one match was won and the team finished 13th. What joy there was that season came from cup runs. The defence of the Irish Cup ended at the first hurdle, with a single-goal defeat at Portadown, but in the first half Ards had missed many chances, a Bothwell shot had cannoned off the bar, and after Johnson had scored for the Ports with 10 minutes to go, the Newtownards team missed a penalty. In the Gold Cup Ards trounced Bangor 4-0 in the first round, then drew at Larne. After the match Mr. Cameron, the referee, had to be escorted off the pitch by the Ards players to protect him from their own followers after he had disallowed Bothwell's 'winner' for an alleged offside, and his car was mobbed by the same headcases before he could get away. The eventual 4-2 victory in the replay brought Ards a lucrative semi-final tie against Belfast Celtic, but this time their luck ran out and they were beaten by three clear goals. The team went one stage further in the County Antrim Shield, where they overcame Ormiston after two matches, and secured a splendid victory over Glentoran, 2-1 in the semi-final. In the final, played at Cliftonville, Ards and Linfield could not be separated, with Flynn's goal for Ards cancelling out McCracken's, and Sam McMullan performing heroics in goals to keep the Blues out. But for the replay right winger Thomson failed to turn up, and Flynn went on trial to Preston, apparently unwilling to hold on for one more week. Despite the missing players Ards dominated the first half and scored through Jackson, but Somerset equalised for Linfield in the crucial period just before half-time and the Windsor Park team went on to win 4-2.

But cup runs and leaky defences were as nothing compared with the tragic loss of Andy Bothwell, an event which overshadowed the season and showed Bill Shankly's oft-quoted aphorism about life, death and football to be the crass and unpleasant remark it always was. Capped five times for Ireland (he had added to his tally against England and Scotland in the 1926-27 season) Bothwell was a winger of enormous potential. A direct attacker (he scored 37 times for Ards in 94 appearances) with a fine turn of speed, he was in fact a converted full-back who had played in that position for Cregagh and then Mountpottinger. His talents on the wing were first utilised at Willowfield, then at Bangor, and came to full fruition at Ards. Although he had been 'under the doctor's care' or on the injured list a few times during the previous couple of seasons, his death in February was as unexpected as it was shocking. Admitted into the Royal Victoria Hospital on a Tuesday with abdominal pains, he underwent surgery on Thursday and was dead by Saturday morning. Peritonotis brought on by a burst appendix

The lost hero: Andy Bothwell

seems to have been the cause of death, and in those pre-penicillin days there was little could be done to save his life. The football world beyond Ards was as devastated by Andy's death as was his own club. Of all the tributes paid to the lost hero of the terraces, few were more poignant than the verses which appeared in Belfast Celtic's programme, *The Celt:*

One who was gentle almost to a fault,
Who took a knock and smiled but in return:
One who ran straight and at the final halt
Still smiled awhile and left his friends to mourn.

Eight decades on Andy Bothwell lives on, if only in the memory, as one of Ards' greats.

THREE

The Hungry Thirties
1928-34

The shadow of Andy Bothwell's passing still darkened Ards Football Club as the 1928-29 season opened. To perpetuate his memory public subscription raised enough to purchase the 'Bothwell Cup', to be competed for by junior clubs in the Newtownards area. Briefly Ards had a player coach in the shape of Eli Fletcher, the former England and Manchester City full-back, but he pulled out of the deal and opted instead for non-League Manchester Central. Sandy Patton went to Barrow, but McMullan, McGee, Gowdy and Garrett remained on the books, and they were supplemented by Herbie McCandless, Sam Jackson and Bob Flynn. The most famous name amongst the newcomers was Fred Barrett, the former Chelsea and Belfast Celtic full-back who had been captain of Dundalk in the previous season. In October an even more significant signing was made in the shape of Billy 'Tosher' Burns, the 25 year-old local man and former Ards player who had been with Wolverhampton Wanderers and who was signed in the face of competition from several other Irish clubs. To replace Patton up front the young Alan Davidson was given his chance.

Unfortunately, despite the new blood, the first half of the League proved dismal, with only two wins, 4-0 against Larne and 4-1 against Cliftonville, in the first dozen games. The Gold Cup was a different matter, however. In the first round goals from McGee and Clarke saw off Ballymena, and Newry Town went under by the same 2-0 margin in the following round, the scorers on this occasion being Davidson and Collins. The semi-final, played at Grosvenor Park,

Billy 'Tosher' Burns

pitted Ards against Glentoran, and two goals from Davidson saw Ards through 2-1. The final would not take place until March, so more of that anon. This successful venture in the Gold Cup would not, however, be repeated in the major knockout trophy, the Irish Cup, where Ards suffered the humiliation of losing 2-0 to junior club Broadway United.

There was little to enthuse about in the first half of the league programme, but a few straws were visible to those who wished to clutch them. Burns had settled in very well in the centre of the defence, with McGee moving to right-half, while Barrett's thunderbolt free-kicks and penalties threatened the physical well-being of opposition goalkeepers. Best of all, however, was the form shown by centre-forward Davidson, who was attracting English scouts. His goal against Coleraine in October brought adulation from the press. 30 yards out, with his back to goal, he spun and hit the ball on the turn. It barely rose from the ground as it rocketed into the net. Davidson's amateur cap against England seemed to presage great things in the future.

In December, severe gales lifted the temporary corrugated iron shelter on the reserved side from its moorings, carried it off through the air and deposited it in a neighbouring field. Immediately after this Act of God, Ards' season turned around, although presumably there was no connection. Wins over Bangor, Queen's Island, Portadown, Larne and Newry Town hauled the team up the League. The best win in this successful period was probably the 4-3 victory over Glentoran, when Jimmy Turnbull, who at last was finding form, was one of the scorers, and 'Tosher' Burns was by all accounts the outstanding player on the field. A 5-1 win over Coleraine left Ards in a final position of 9th in the Senior League. If only their form in the first half of the programme had matched that of the second half there could well have been a top three finish. Sam McMullan gained an Irish League cap, but there was local puzzlement that wing-half or inside forward Billy Gowdy, good enough to be selected as a reserve for the full Irish team, was ignored. Once again bias against provincial clubs was cited as the suspected reason.

Inconsistency marred the City Cup campaign, although the final position of 6th was respectable enough, and there were some tremendous results, especially against the Belfast teams. Queen's Island were beaten 5-3, Distillery 7-1, Glentoran 5-2, in front of a packed Oval, and most impressive of all, there was a 2-1 victory over League champions Celtic. Playing at home, Ards went into a first-half lead when Bob Lynn ran three-quarters of the length of the field to lob former Ards' favourite Jack Diffen. Ten minutes after half-time McGee handled the ball: Jackie Mahood's penalty hit the bar, but Sam McMullan was the hero of the hour when he brilliantly saved Curran's shot from the rebound. Curran, however, equalised with 15 minutes to go, and as the match wore on, a draw looked the inevitable outcome. But in the 86th minute Carson crossed from the right and from close in Garrett scored with a fierce drive. His impetus brought him into a collision with Diffen, and both men had to be carried off.

The long awaited Gold Cup final took place on 18th March. Ards went into the game with a weakened team, McMullan and Lynn both injured, and Gordon unavailable due to a death in the family. Although Fred Barrett scored for Ards, Linfield replied with three. Reports of the time claimed that Houston's first goal was clearly offside, that the penalty put away by Moorhead was a very harsh decision, and that when Somerset scored the third three Linfield players were offside. Well, you hardly expected an objective account, did you?

The summer of 1929 saw the signings of the Gough brothers and Vance from Crusaders, but on the debit side Gowdy was transferred to Hull City – a major loss. Fred Barrett acted as player coach, but he was less effective as a defender this season as his pace deserted him, and rumours were rife of friction between Barrett and Sam McMullan. Certainly the defence was poor, and Ards went 10 games without a win in the League until late October, when they beat Cliftonville 2-1. Queen's Island had failed to gain re-election at the end of the previous season, and Ards made their first trip to Derry City, the shipyard men's replacement, in September, gaining a 2-2 draw in front of 5000 spectators. How Ards must have envied such crowds! In December the signing of inside left Devan from Ayr United brought a touch of class and fitness to the side, as well, apparently, as his talents as a dance band vocalist! The Scotsman walked several miles a day to maintain his stamina but the *Chronicle* complained bitterly of the unfitness of many of the rest of the team, hinting darkly at 'all night dances', but offering no further evidence, presumably with one eye on the libel laws. Interestingly, a letter to the *Spectator* many years later, in June 1947, offered an insight into the indiscipline of these pre-war years. Signed by 'Ex-Player', it claimed that training in those days consisted of running four laps of the pitch, possibly some sprinting to follow, occasional skipping, and then a haphazard game of 'shooting in'. The letter contained oblique references to poor discipline on the part of some players, to which a blind eye was usually turned. Mind you, the players then were expected to turn out in conditions which might well lead to a postponement nowadays.

Early in January 1930 Ards were leading Newry 3-2 in a match at Castlereagh Park played in appalling conditions of wind and rain. With 15 minutes to go both of the Gough brothers collapsed and had to be taken from the field. The referee played on for a further five minutes before abandoning the game, but as always seemed to happen in those days, the result stood.

The League performance was poor in the extreme with only six matches won out of 26 and an average of three goals a game conceded. There were early exits from both the Gold and Irish Cups, and although Bangor were thrashed 6-2 in the County Antrim Shield second round, the semi-final saw defeat by Glentoran by the odd goal in three. Ards' luck was summed up in the misfortune of debutant Law, who broke his leg in the Irish Cup match against Newry when Ards were only a goal down. They eventually lost 5-0. With little to cheer at home, Ards supporters were more exercised by the exploits of Billy Gowdy, whose Hull City team battled their way to the semi-final of the FA Cup, defeating First Division Manchester City and Newcastle United on the way. The ex-Ardsman played a prominent role in the Cup run, and finished up in direct opposition to the Arsenal's David Jack in two epic matches before the plucky Humberside team lost the replay by a single goal, and Gowdy was denied his ninety minutes of Wembley fame.

Results in the City Cup helped to explain why many Ards supporters had grey hair. A bright opening brought successive wins over Distillery, Cliftonville and Coleraine, and the team obtained draws away to Belfast Celtic and Glentoran at times when each of those sides was leading the table. But five defeats against 'lesser' opposition brought the season to a melancholy end, and although the final placing of 8th was satisfactory if compared to the earlier part of the season, it was a poor showing for a side which had promised so much in the campaign. One of the few bright spots of the season was the form shown by the Gough brothers, with Billy, bizarrely nicknamed 'Sleepy Valley', scoring 14 goals from the left wing, and 'Silver' adding a further 10 from the opposite flank. In addition, Ards had probably the best goalkeeper in the league in the shape of Sam McMullan, who had played against the English League and the Scottish League. Such was his value that at one stage Linfield offered three decent players in return for the custodian.

There was a greater air of optimism about Castlereagh Park in the summer of 1930 than there had been for some time. Big Fred Barrett went off to coach Celtic II, and Sam McMullan decided to try his luck with Dundalk, but a series of astute signings made good these losses and left Ards with what appeared to be a strong squad for the coming season. To replace McMullan, Albert McDonald returned, as did centre-forward Sandy Patton after two years at Barrow, while the amateur international Jack 'Dot' Doherty would add a touch of class at inside left. But for all the high hopes, the team got off to a poor start, winning only one of their first eight matches, 4-1 against Coleraine. Despite another 4-2 victory over Coleraine, this time in the Gold Cup, from mid-September there was a series of heavy defeats, 3-6 to Ballymena, 1-4 to Glentoran, 2-7 to Linfield, and 3-6 to Belfast Celtic in the semi-final of the Gold Cup. To make matters worse, the normally dependable Bob McGee seemed to be unsettled.

But those who had kept faith in the team would be justified. At last skipper Jack Garrett's team began in to gel, helped no doubt by the introduction of three new players: Totten on the left wing, Duffy, a Scot who had been with Chelsea, and Wilfie Davidson, a centre-forward usually good for a goal or two. Goalscoring was not a problem as Ards roared into form, winning five League games on the trot, and scoring 20 goals in the process! The pick of these were a 6-2 win over Newry, a thrilling 5-4 victory over Bangor, and a 6-1 win over Glenavon in which McDonald saved his fifth penalty of the season. Such astonishing form could not be maintained, however, and four defeats in the next seven matches followed, including a miserable Christmas Day performance when Ards conceded five at Ballymena. But from late December onwards the team refound their form and finished the League programme in style. Their most memorable success was the home match against Linfield, where Ards took advantage of the strong wind to turn around 5-1 up at half-time, also the final score after a goalless second half. 'The goal of the season' was the description of Billy Burns' winner against Newry, a 30-yard scorcher which turned out to be the only goal separating the teams at the finish. Despite the entertainment value which the team was offering this season there were complaints about declining attendances. Nonetheless, the strong finish to the League, with seven points gained from the last four matches, pushed Ards up to 6th position, their best finish for some years, and there were rueful comments that if only they could have clicked earlier they might have been even higher.

The City Cup was something of a let-down after the late flourish in the League, with only three victories in the programme and a 9th place finish. There was another victory over Linfield, this time by 2-1, although during the game Albert McDonald suffered a nasty break to the finger. Ards had exited the Irish Cup to Glentoran on the wrong end of a crazy 4-7 scoreline, the unlucky Davidson scoring all four goals, yet finishing on the losing side. The County Antrim Shield would see a series of battling performances, with two games needed to eliminate Ballymena United, and a further two to get past Larne. But in the semi-final Ards lost to Cliftonville, who had become something of a bogey team for them that season. Barney Duffy's sending off in that match was his second in as many months, and he was released at the season's end.

It had been a season of mixed fortunes, and at this distance it is a little difficult to see why a team which was involved in so many high scoring games should not have attracted higher attendances. The leading scorers had been Patton, Davidson and Doherty, each of whom had scored 18 goals. Despite the low gates Ards reported a profit of £150 on the season, and had now installed baths in the pavilion at Castlereagh Park. (But how did the players clean themselves before these baths were installed?)

To the consternation of the cynics the long-promised stand was finally completed. Officially opened on August 13th, 1931 by Mr Samuel McKee, it had 250 seats in three rows, and 'banking' was erected on either side. The stand was never a beautiful object, and afforded little height to those sitting in it. Its most memorable feature for many was the legend 'Cafolla's For Ice Cream' painted on the roof. The outlay of £300 was a significant sum for a club which rarely attracted the sort of crowds the committee might have wished. Envious glances were cast at Derry City, whose wage bill of £70 per week left Ards' £25 looking decidedly slender. Gate receipts were not helped by some football connoisseurs with an aversion to spending money, who apparently stood on the saddles of their bicycles to see over the corrugated iron fence and obtain a free view. Ards United suffered the same problems, except that in their case freeloaders did not have to perform a balancing act, but could enjoy a more leisurely view from the railway bank overlooking Hawlmark Park. Biggest signings for the 1931-32 season were Sam McMullan, back from Dundalk, left winger James Kelly, who reached double figures as a goalscorer, and Tommy Frame from Linfield, to bolster a leaky defence, with Burns away to Glentoran. Frame's arrival made little difference, with 75 goals conceded in the 23 matches up to the turn of the year. The biggest thrashing came on Boxing Day, with a 9-2 defeat by Cliftonville at Solitude. This was a more than ample revenge for the Amateurs, who had been on the receiving end of Ards' best performance to date, a 6-0 home win in the first round of the Gold Cup. In another heavy defeat at Glentoran, at least Ards had the distinction of scoring the most sensational goal of the game, when Bob McGee rifled home a free-kick from a couple of yards over the halfway line. But it was Davy Jordan who scored most of Ards' goals in the first half the season, with 18 in the bag by

Christmas. Unfortunately he lost his scoring touch after that, and added only two more to his total before the summer. His role as marksman was taken over by the newly arrived Jimmy Gilmour, a Scot who ended the season in style, scoring a remarkable 20 goals in as many games.

With Gilmour's arrival Ards staged a revival of sorts, with three victories in January doubling the number of League wins, but they still had to defeat Belfast Celtic in the final match to avoid the need to apply for re-election. Against a slightly weakened Celtic team they made it, with goals from Gough and Totten producing a 2-1 win. Glenavon, whom Ards leapfrogged with this fine victory, lodged a protest, but to no avail. Salt was rubbed in Glenavon's wounds with a 5-1 victory over the Lurgan team in the City Cup competition, while a Gilmour hat-trick helped Ards to their best result of this competition, a 3-2 victory over Linfield. In the County Antrim Shield Ards beat Cliftonville 4-2, all the goals being scored by the prolific Gilmour, but despite earning a replay with Belfast Celtic in the semi-final, in the second game the team slumped to a 6-1 defeat.

Probably the most famous match of the season was an abandoned match played on 20th February, 1932 against Glentoran. The abandonment was not, as one might expect, the result of weather conditions, but of an incident involving two of the great characters of the Irish League in those pre-war days. At 1-1, Fred Roberts, the Glentoran centre-forward, seeing Sam McMullan catch a high cross from the Glens' winger Lucas, charged at the goalkeeper, as you did. Out of the corner of his eye McMullan saw him coming and sidestepped, tricking Roberts, who charged headlong into the goals, clutched at the net and brought down the post and crossbar, such was his impetus. The referee had no option but to abandon the match, and the draw at 78 minutes stood as the final result.

Sam McMullan, larger than life goalkeeper, and father of the future Bishop Gordon McMullan

1932-33 saw the departure of two Ards stalwarts, Sandy Patton and the long-serving Bob McGee. The latter had been a tremendous servant, and his ability to play with equal facility in the centre of the defence or as leader of the attack was invaluable. In all he appeared 279 times for Ards, scoring 71 goals, many of them as an adventurous centre-half. Alex Vance was also released, and Davy Jordan went to try his luck with Hull City. In their stead Ards looked across the North

Red and Blue Heaven

Channel to Scotland, signing no fewer than seven Caledonians to keep Jimmy Gilmour company. Only three of these imports were retained for any length of time: centre half 'Jock' Niven, full-back, later left-half Alex Tait, and right-half Harry Wilson.

The team got off to a promising start, with two draws and two wins in the first four League matches, but a slump had set in by early September, and 10 League matches in a row were lost. Gilmour was still getting the goals – 12 in his first 11 games – but he found little scoring support from his fellow forwards, with the exception of Joe Kelly on the left wing. The real problem lay with the defence, however, and there were some spectacularly high scoring games in the first half of the season. Ards were beaten 7-5 by Glentoran, 6-5 by Distillery, 6-3 by Larne and 8-2 by Ballymena United. The 4-0 defeat by Ballymena, which began the losing sequence, was followed by rumours, printed in the local press, that several Ards players had been 'at a dance' the night before the game. We were left free to draw our own conclusions as to their state of fitness the next day. After a mediocre campaign, for the second season in a row Ards had to win their last League match to escape the embarrassment of re-election, and with their first win in five matches carried it off with a 1-0 win over Derry City. Artie Sayers, who had been signed from Ards United, scored the winner in the 90th minute, and the club had escaped by the skin of its teeth.

If there were hopes that the Irish Cup might prove a welcome respite, they were dashed, as Ards conceded another six goals away to Distillery in the first round. They defeated Ballymena United to reach the semi-finals of the County Antrim Shield, but then lost 3-1 to Linfield. The Tate Cup match of February (the previous season's game had been belatedly played in early October 1932) saw not only a four goal thrashing for Ards, but also two full-scale free-for-alls in the second half: a lenient referee, however, sent nobody off. The weather that winter was as miserable as Ards' results. A dreadful storm on the last day of 1932 wreaked havoc throughout the town, with windows smashed and chimneys toppled. My people talked of that frightening night when the plate glass shop window in the family business in High Street was blown in. The hoardings around Ards United ground were demolished by the gale, and for once, it seems, neighbourly relations between the two clubs in the town prevailed as United, in their red and green hoops, played out the rest of the season at Castlereagh Park.

The City Cup saw a welcome tightening up of the defence, and the final tally of three wins, five draws, and five defeats represented a plucky, if unspectacular end of season fight. Ards appeared to have found a new goalscorer in centre-forward Fitzpatrick, who scored four goals in his first five appearances, although the honour of scoring the winner in the best result of the campaign, a 1-0 victory over Belfast Celtic, fell to new boy 'Tucker' Parkinson. Sam McMullan was said to have shown 'outstanding' form all year, while full-back Tommy Frame was playing well enough to attract a scout from Manchester United, but no business was done.

The only season in which Ards managed to escape from their own version of the 1930s depression was 1933-34, in which they played themselves into 6th position in the League, and battled their way to the final of the County Antrim Shield. A number of key signings made the difference: Jimmy Buchanan, another Scot, came from Linfield, and 'Tosher' Burns returned from Glentoran. John Mathieson proved an excellent centre half, and the returning Jimmy Kelly bolstered the defence at left-back. Harry Johnstone, the former Irish international, was signed from Portadown halfway through the season, and a further attempt to strengthen the strike force came with the signing of prolific goalscorer Fred Roberts, who may have been over the hill, but had still been capable of scoring six in one match against Ards for Glentoran the previous season. Amongst the departures was Bobby Tait, who had to be released because of his exorbitant signing on demands. Working to a tight budget might have been difficult, but it was necessary, and as proof, despite the travails of 1932-33 the Treasurer reported only 'a slight loss' on that season's working. Various close-season activities helped

Harry Johnstone scores against Larne

fill the coffers, not only cycle racing at Castlereagh Park but also a lucrative Summer League, which provided £150 clear profit for the club.

In the first match of the season 3000 witnessed a thriller against Belfast Celtic. Ards, playing free-flowing football, went 2-0 up thanks to a Fitzpatrick double, but two horrific blunders by McMullan allowed the Belfast team to snatch a draw. Four narrow defeats followed, before an impressive run of four successive victories, which included a 4-0 hammering of Glenavon, and a 5-1 triumph over Newry Town. The veteran Billy Burns held the line together well, on occasions showing that it was not only Bob McGee who could play number five or number nine with equal ease, while Ernie Fitzpatrick, moved out to the right wing, was reckoned to be Ards' best in that position since Andy Bothwell. Billy Neill, captaining the team from right-back, was only the third amateur to captain Ards since they entered senior football, following in the footsteps of John Peden and George Shields. On Christmas Day another barren spell ended with a superb 3-3 draw away to Celtic, and seven further wins followed before the League ended with Ards in a respectable 6th position, the second highest provincial club behind Ballymena United. Sadly the impetus was not maintained in the City Cup, with only two victories, although one of them was a 3-2 success over Belfast Celtic, who had finished second in the league and would go on to dominate Irish football for the rest of the decade. The defeat was Celtic's first in the City Cup, and one in which Fred Roberts made his first appearance in an Ards' shirt. Although he scored the first goal, he then suffered a broken rib and was obliged to go off at half-time, playing only twice more that season. Despite Ards' excellent record against Celtic, there were ominous signs of a crumbling defence as the team lost seven goals to both Ballymena and Glentoran and a further six to Derry City. There was a growing belief that well-meaning committee members were no substitute for a proper manager. Ards were, by this stage, the last remaining team in the league without a manager or player-coach.

The only success in cup competitions so far had been in the one-off Tate Cup match against Bangor, where they had won 3-2, but the County Antrim Shield proved a different story. It didn't appear that way for much of their first match. 3-4 down at Solitude with a mere three minutes to go, Ards fought back sensationally to defeat Cliftonville 5-4 with a last minute 20 yard free-kick from Johnnie Mathieson. The semi-final, against Belfast Celtic II, had to be abandoned after 50 minutes of driving sleet and steadily widening puddles on the Oval pitch. This was fortuitous for Ards, who were two goals down at the time. The replayed match finished at 2-2, and a further replay 1-1. Five weeks after the fixture should have been completed, Ards eventually triumphed 4-2 with two goals from left winger Davidson, and one each from little 'Silver' Gough and from 'Tosher' Burns. The final was played at Grosvenor Park against League champions Linfield, but sadly the newspaper headline told it all: 'Ards Swamped in Shield Final'. Bambrick scored a hat-trick as the Blues ran riot, winning 7-1. Ards were never in the game, five goals down before Gamble scored their consolation effort, and Sam McMullan, who could be volatile at the best of times, was sent off late in the game for striking Cailes, the Linfield winger. It was a disappointing end to a more heartening season, but sadly would be the last taste of success for a long time. At least Ards were on an even financial keel, with an encouraging £200 profit shown over the season.

FOUR

Things Can Only Get Worse
1934-40

Ards fans of a nervous disposition should skip this chapter. The team did not manage a top half finish between 1934 and the Second World War, either in the League or the City Cup. One County Antrim Shield semi-final was as good as it got in the knockout competitions. Yet the history of these years is worth telling. The rough must be chronicled along with its proverbial opposite, (otherwise this book would never have seen the light of day), and the valiant efforts of those who strove to keep Ards going in the face of indifferent results and growing public apathy deserve to be honoured, standing as they do in a long line of similar stalwarts and their efforts to keep the Red and Blue flag flying across many decades and many crises.

Ards began the 1934-35 season with new neighbours, new tenants, and new partners. First the neighbours. For some time Lord Londonderry had been active in trying to secure an airstrip for Newtownards, and the area then known as the Showgrounds was cleared to make way for Ards Aerodrome, with trial flights offered to the public in July. From that time onwards spectators who had lost interest in the proceedings on the field could watch a regular procession of aeroplanes taking off and landing from the neighbouring airport, often idly speculating as to whether an incoming plane would clear the reserved side stand or not. (Well, I have). New tenants came in the shape of near neighbours Bangor, who found themselves temporarily homeless due to their move from Ballyholme to Clandeboye Road. Accordingly, Castlereagh Park was used by Bangor to ful-

---

fil their home fixtures in the early part of the season. Although the agreement proved to be short-lived, and the Seasiders finished up by playing the rest of their matches away from home, Ards had, if only briefly, done the decent thing. The failure of the tenancy agreement to last the season may have had something to do with Ards' new partners, who, sensationally, were old and often bitter rivals Ards United. After turning down a number of proposals for amalgamation over the previous decade, the Hawlmark club finally threw in the towel in July 1934, and asked to be allowed to play as Ards II in the Intermediate League. This duly happened, and Ards United, who had fought gallantly for their autonomy, were no more.

Sam McMullan, for so long a fixture between the sticks at Ards, fell into a dispute with the club, and did not play again, while the invaluable Johnny Mathieson was allowed to go to Larne. New players came and went as experiments to find a winning combination failed. Billy Burns no longer looked the part at centre-forward, and was moved back to his normal centre-half berth, but even he could not single-handedly plug the leaks in defence. Ards would win only one of their first nine League matches, conceding 36 goals during these games. Their effrontery in denying Belfast Celtic full points in the previous season was well and truly punished as Celtic put nine past the hapless McDowell, 'Boy' Martin helping himself to five. In all Ards won only 5 out of 26 League matches, and 2 out of 13 in the City Cup, although they did manage a draw against Celtic in that competition. A 5-2 defeat of Cliftonville in the first round of the Gold Cup was the only other victory before the end of the year. Of the eight victories that season three came against Bangor, the first of them with an astonishing 8-1 scoreline, Gamble (whose 27 goals in the season was a fine effort in the midst of so much mediocrity) scoring four, and the lanky Scotsman Kerr another three. Typically, this result proved a false dawn, with Ards going twelve matches before their next win. For the first time the club had to face the ignominy of seeking re-election. Lack of fitness and lack of enthusiasm were cited as reasons for the poor performances, and increasingly, in the absence of a manager, the Committee had to shoulder the blame. The County Antrim Shield saw Ards drawn at home to Celtic II, but after being offered a guaranteed £50 if they would play at Celtic Park they agreed to forfeit home advantage, losing 2-4 at Paradise. Many saw Ards' action as reprehensible, and the alleged failures of the Committee became the subject of an excited correspondence in the local press, with the *Chronicle's* football correspondent surprisingly vitriolic in his criticisms. Amid rumours of the 2nd XI having to be abandoned because of expense, and increasingly loud calls for the appointment of a manager, 'stormy scenes' took place at the AGM in April. John Heron, the treasurer, reported Ards' worst gates since entering senior football, 40 per cent down on the previous season. R. Clements Lyttle attacked the Treasurer's report, and later resigned to join the board of Glentoran. It proved impossible on the night to persuade anyone to stand for the Committee, and eventually three new members had to be co-opted.

It was not surprising that there was a wholesale clear out of players that summer, or that at last the Committee yielded to pressure from the press and from the public. The job of Player-Manager with Ards Football Club was advertised.

The 1935-36 season proved to be another disaster. Ards' record of five wins and three draws was exactly the same as that of 1934-35, but on this occasion they finished in last position. Only two City Cup games were won, and there were first round exits from all three knockout trophies. Unlike the previous season, where a humdrum mediocrity was the keynote, this time the team would go down in an inglorious blaze of overspending, signings, sackings and wildly over-optimistic predictions of success.

There were 25 applicants for the player-manager's job, which eventually went to Tom Adamson, a native of Scotland whose father had Ulster connections. The 29-year-old former Bury full-back had been player-manager of Stockport County the previous season. He made a series of cross-Channel signings. Half-backs Frank Ryder and C. H. Roy came respectively from Rochdale and from Rhyl Athletic, Pritchard from Partick Thistle, Stevenson from Southend, and Mason from Beith. How good these players were was open to question, with most of them being allowed to go after seven or eight games, Pritchard surviving the longest with seventeen. Adamson, ordered to work to a tight budget, claimed that it was difficult to get decent English or Scottish players at such prices. Funds were raised from what must have been a first for Irish football, when Flight Lieutenant Bryant, the manager of the airport, piloted customers on a 20 minute pleasure flight on a circuit of Newtownards, Ballywalter, Donaghadee and Bangor.

Although three other new signings, Wightman, McAllister and Thompson were released after a single trial game, at least at the outset of the season enthusiasm remained high for the new team, a real League of Nations outfit comprising two Englishmen, two Irishmen, one Welshman and six Scots. What was described as a huge crowd turned up for the opening match, in which Ards defeated Glenavon 3-1, and 400 supporters travelled to Larne for the next game to see Ards lose unluckily by the odd goal in five. But they won only two out of the next eighteen games, with signs of panic as early as late August, the club pleading for more patience from a fickle support, and Adamson flying out to England to hunt for new players after a 7-2 hammering from Newry. Despite a residual belief that there was genuine talent in the team, results failed to go Ards' way. There were rumours of difficulties in paying players' wages, several of the team had to be released, and after a 5-1 defeat at home to Ballymena United, the parting of the ways came between Ards and Tom Adamson. Although it was claimed at the time that he had been sacked, it seems more likely that Adamson resigned. The manager claimed that his hands had been tied financially, and that a section of the Committee had always been opposed to him. What seems indisputable is that he did not have a free hand in team selection, with interference from a number of Committee members who, it should be remembered, had resisted the idea of Ards having an player-manager for a long time, and had only reluctantly bowed to public pressure in relinquishing control of team matters for themselves.

The dismissal of the manager and so many players reduced the wage bill by 50 per cent. At the end of the season it was revealed that Adamson's team had been costing £45 per week, when in practice all Ards could realistically expect to pay was probably around £30. The team went back to being largely home-based, with goalkeeper Dunseith, Jimmy Kelly, back from the Free State, and Tommy Johnston all taking their places on the side. When Andy Pritchard, a playmaker who had looked excellent in the earlier part of the season, walked out on the club, demanding that he be allowed to travel from Scotland every week rather than live in Newtownards, it was clear that a great deal hung on the brilliant No. 11, Danny Laverty. But Laverty lacked support, and results continued to disappoint, to put it mildly. Ironically, Frank Ryder had been by all accounts Laverty's best inside partner, but he was now playing regularly with Port Vale and scoring goals for them. Tyson, Mason and McKeenan were also now featuring regularly in cross-Channel football, yet had failed to produce a winning blend at Ards. An Extraordinary General Meeting had to be held late in February to consider Ards' financial plight, Chairman Peter McLean grimly proclaiming that Ards were 'on the rocks' and that £170 was needed immediately to enable the club to finish the season. Already the football writers in the Belfast Press were clamouring for Ards' expulsion from the League, whether immediately or at the end of the season they did not appear to mind. A wage cut for the players, (accepted without demur), the launch of a subscription list, and a three-day bazaar to raise funds were all proposed and accepted. When the City Cup match against Linfield, which should have been Ards' home game, was switched to Windsor Park for purely financial reasons, there was no repetition of the protests of the previous season when Ards had conceded home advantage to Celtic II. Clearly the crisis was too deep for quibbling. Blame for the whole mess was laid at the doors of Tom Adamson, and of a Committee which had given him too free a hand in financial matters. He was accused of doing nothing to obtain players in the weeks after his appointment, then frantically signing whatever players he could in a last minute rush.

It had been a season of sensations, and Sam McMullan, who had now come back from a spell at New Brighton, was certainly not going to be left out of the fun. Never the most phlegmatic, he took great exception to the award of a penalty to Newry Town in April. All the players stopped after a clear infringement by a Newry player in the Ards penalty area. An Ards defender picked up the ball to place it for the free-kick, only to find the referee had seen no foul, but instead awarded a penalty to Newry for handball. The outraged McMullan made his protest by standing, arms folded, away from the goal as Redfern tapped home the penalty. It may have been an injustice, but at least it was a lighter moment, and heaven knows there were few enough of those in that season.

Danny Laverty

Over the years various pieces of doggerel on the subject of Ards F.C. have appeared in the local press, but far and away the best was penned by the football correspondent of the *Chronicle* towards the end of this appalling season. It is still worthy of being read, and goes like this:

'Twas on a Channel steamer, crossing the Irish Sea,
From Stranraer back to Larne, which is long enough for me;
The season wasn't over, so football was discussed;
Different clubs were mentioned – some smiled, while others cussed.
A smart guy in our company swore that he could trace
The followers of any club by looking at their face.
None of us were punters, but money's hard to get,
So, thinking it a sure thing, we covered up his bet.
The first test we gave him, a youth who strolled around,
One look our guy took at him, then answered "Portadown".
"Right", said this youth, smiling, and believe me if you will,
He named every Celtic follower and those of Cliftonville,
Glentoran, Derry City, why, every team in the news.
Never once he stumbled at Distillery or the Blues.
Our bets looked pretty groggy, this guy knew his stuff:

One more chance we asked for before we cried "Enough".
Then, holding to the handrail, a whey-faced lad we spied,
Stooped and bent with sorrow, weary and hollow-eyed.
"Tell us who he follows", said all of us old diehards.
"Easy", said the wise guy – "that lad follows Ards".
And that's how our bets were saved, sir,
This smart guy lost his trick,
The youth had never followed Ards –
'Twas the sea had made him sick!

In June 1936 a 3-day funfair and fete took place at Castlereagh Park, a huge effort to stop the club from going under. The *Newtownards Spectator's* 'Vigilant', no stranger to purple prose, described it as 'the last desperate throw of the dice which will tell if the old colours will still flutter in the breeze, or be hauled down forever'. The carnival was a financial success, but amazingly the mistakes of the previous season were repeated, not by a manager this time, but by a Management Committee which seemed happy to spend money like a sailor. This Committee would have to shoulder the blame for a disastrous mid-season slump, for despite considering fifteen applicants when the manager's job was advertised, they chose to reject them all and do the job themselves. A series of Scottish signings appeared to wear the red and white quartered jerseys the team would sport that year. Jimmy Tulips and goalkeeper Willie McKay came from St. Mirren, Tommy Wemyss from Dundee, and centre-half Jimmy McKerley from Kilmarnock. Tulips formed a full-back partnership with 'Reeky' Patton, while Tommy Hood and Joe Yates flanked McCurley in the half-back line. The lessons of Adamson's reign seemed to have been forgotten, with the team costing a massive £40 a week, although laudable attempts to bring on local talent were made with the revival of a second XI to play in the Irish Alliance. Certainly the football public of Newtownards was enthused by the new signings, with ten bus loads of supporters travelling to Windsor Park only to see Ards lose 6-1 to the Blues. But by late August a run of three successive victories pushed them to 4th position in the League, a place they held until Hallowe'en. Support remained strong, with sixteen buses going to Bangor for

Goal-scoring winger 'Silver' Gough

the 1-1 draw, and over 1000 Ards supporters travelling to Celtic Park on October 3rd to see Ards suffer their record domestic defeat, Belfast Celtic romping home 10-0. The Jekyll and Hyde nature of the team continued, however, with three successive wins immediately following this reverse, and Ards maintaining their challenging position in the League. But then it all went horribly wrong, with the team failing to gain a single point from November to February, losing sixteen games on the trot. The worst of the defeats were 9-1 at Larne in the League, and another 10-0 trouncing from Celtic, this time in the City Cup.

The running of the club was clearly a shambles. Before the season had begun the Committee had advertised for a new trainer, seen as a slap in the face for Bob Johnston, the existing trainer, and after pressure from supporters he was reinstated. But in November Johnston resigned, taking with him five members of the Committee. It was clear that he was on extremely bad terms with the players, who were bored with unimaginative training routines which apparently consisted largely of lapping the pitch. Ards were described as training three days a week, with sessions in both morning and afternoon, suggesting that these players were in fact full time, and, we are told, typically earning £3 10s a week. Bobby Irvine, a former Portsmouth and Everton star, was finally appointed as the new coach, but within the week left for a job in Leicester without ever meeting the players!

Things went from bad to embarrassing. Sectarian singing, a pitch invasion and the stoning of the Celtic players' coach disfigured the League game in January, (although the sight of a Celtic player holding up five fingers to the crowd to signify the score hardly helped to quell passions), Tulips insisted he was not fit to play when the trainer argued that he was, the 2nd XI was scrapped for the third time in Ards' senior history, McKay and Laverty were suspended sine die by the club and then reinstated, and new trainer Foster walked out after a dispute with the groundsman. Matters came to a head at the end of January, when Tulips, Laverty and John Murphy, the former Oldham player, were all sacked. Joe Yates and Tommy Wemyss, who had been a solitary star in the shambles around him, both left of their own volition.

For the rest of the season Ards struggled on with a largely local team, and to be fair to these lesser names they did put together a late season run which eventually saw the team winning five out of its last nine City Cup games, including a 5-1 defeat of Distillery, while the Easter Monday draw with Derry City was the first point dropped by Derry in the competition, although another nine goals were conceded in a single match, this time to Portadown. By the end of the season the Committee was down to only four or five functioning members, with not enough personnel to man the turnstiles, and Peter McLean resigned as Chairman. Ards' best player, goalkeeper and occasional (and successful) penalty taker Willie McKay, was unsettled, and there were angry and probably justified allegations of Irish League bias against provincial clubs when that body refused Ards and Ballymena United permission to bring forward their final City Cup match in a bid to save each club a week's wages, while simultaneously organising a benefit match against Glasgow Rangers to help Distillery's finances! It was clearly not a happy time, but events have to be put into perspective.

At the beginning of the season, as Artie Sayers and Billy Gamble scored to earn Ards a fine away win at Glenavon, unknown to them back in Newtownards eight people were killed and twenty-seven injured in an appalling crash during the Tourist Trophy race. Among the dead was Sam McAuley, former player and now a kit man for the team. And the TT, which for a decade had been attracting crowds estimated at being anywhere between 250,000 and 500,000, would never take place round the Ards circuit again. The misfortunes of Ards Football Club in the 1936-37 season seem trivial by comparison.

A fraught 1937 AGM, hearing that Ards were in debt to the tune of £500, was obliged to replace Peter McLean with John Heron, and only with difficulty elected a new committee. For the second year in a row Ards appointed a manager, only to have him walk out on the club. This time the phantom boss was ex-Linfield player Billy McCleary. The only retained players were Jimmy McKerley and Willie McKay, whose financial dispute with Ards meant that he would not play at all that season. 'Silver' Gough was released, as, astonishingly, was Billy Gamble, who had scored over 70 goals for Ards in four seasons, and 23 in the one just ended. Portadown manager Tommy Sloan later revealed that he had been preparing to put in a bid for Gamble when Ards made him available on a free transfer. The decision was baffling, all the more so as Gamble continued to score freely with the Ports. The expensive lessons of the previous two seasons had, apparently, been learnt, and McKerley found himself the sole professional in a team of amateur players. The only high profile signings were Bangor's Dickie Gordon, and the returning Jimmy Buchanan, who went on to score 24 goals in the season. There were signs of deterioration in the ground itself. Sharples' Amusements, allowed to use Castlereagh Park in June, left the pitch in poor condition, more cinders were needed to smother the grass growing profusely on the unreserved side, and when the season started there were many complaints on the 'shilling side' (the reserved side) that the turnstiles had been altered in such a way that spectators were unable to bring their bicycles into the ground! The complaint must have been a serious one, since the club responded promptly and took measures to remedy the problem.

Captained by Dickie Johnston, Ards began brightly with a 6-0 home victory over Cliftonville, centre-forward Cowan bagging four. Three out of the next six League fixtures were won, with four goals scored against Ballymena United and six against Newry Town. The right wing pair of Dickie Gordon and Jim Wilson was the inspiration for this promising start, but Wilson proved to be frustratingly inconsistent, and the team as a whole began to struggle, winning only one game between mid-September and mid-January. That solitary victory was over Bangor, with Norman Cochrane, the new left winger, scoring a couple. That victory was preceded by three draws in a row, and this mini-revival was attributed largely to the good form of McKerley and of wing-half Ritchie, a recent signing from Belfast Celtic. Probably the most significant acquisition of the season was another ex-Celtic player, Andy McKeown, an inside forward. 9th position in the League was no great shakes, but an improvement on 1936 and 1937, and at least the team was cheaper. Only three wins were recorded in the City Cup, but oddly enough perhaps the best result was a mere draw. It was achieved against Coleraine, when goals from McKerley, Buchanan, McKeown, and Jimmy Hughes, the well-known broadcaster of later years, pulled back a 1-4 deficit to earn a fighting draw.

Bitter-sweet memories of former players continued to torment supporters throughout the season. Enviously they read of the exploits of Gamble at Portadown, of Jimmy Tulips, a regular at Falkirk, Davy Jordan, who had left Ards five years earlier, at Crystal Palace, and, best of all that season Bobby Tait, now with East Fife, of the Scottish Second Division. The Methil men reached the final of the Scottish Cup in April 1938, where they played Kilmarnock, and by all accounts Tait was the star of the first match, which was drawn in front of 100,000 spectators, and just as prominent in the replay, which East Fife won. Of course there was a feeling of pride in these former players' achievements, but players of this calibre had to be persuaded to commit themselves to Ards on a long-term basis if the club were to become a power in the land again. Probably the answer was to employ a respected professional as player-coach, but having had their fingers burnt in the past, and having at least broken even in the 1937-38 season, Ards would need to be very sure of their man before going down that road again.

After the ignominy of 1935-36, when Ards finished bottom of the table,

Jimmy Buchanan

successive placings of eleventh and ninth represented progress of a sort. In the last season played in peacetime Ards would finish eighth out of fourteen, but more importantly improve on their previous season's total by a good ten points. The difference may have been due to the appointment, at last, of a manager, in the shape of defender Sam Patton. Jimmy Buchanan and his eventual partner Harry Elliott scored nearly forty goals between them, and the defence took on a more solid look with the signing of Wilfy Haire from Linfield. Despite heavy defeats in their first two away matches, Ards beat Bangor, Derry City and Cliftonville to launch an eight match unbeaten run at Castlereagh Park. Before the Derry match 'Neddy' the donkey was paraded around the perimeter track wearing Ards' colours. A more orthodox attempt to improve performances was proposed by club President Viscount Castlereagh, also on the board at Arsenal, who said he would bring the Gunners' manager, George Allison, to Ards to watch the team and pass on his comments. Even without Allison's help, however, the 3-1 victory over Derry City had the *Chronicle* correspondent crowing 'Ards Like Champions'.

Andy McKeown, now on professional terms, was playing well enough to attract cross-Channel interest, as was McKerley, and the team went from strength to strength in September, with wins over Glenavon, Newry Town and Distillery, all by 4-2. Even after successive draws against Larne and Coleraine Ards remained in third place, only three points behind Belfast Celtic. Unlucky at Glentoran, when they missed a penalty, Ards went on to defeat Linfield at home by 4-1, the last 35 minutes of the match featuring in a BBC radio broadcast, with commentary by Raymond Glendenning. Two further draws kept Ards in 4th position, but a disastrous December followed, with only one win in seven. Match reports of the time claimed that Ards were a better team when swinging the ball about, but too often resorted to tip-tap, close-passing football. A crucial factor was the loss of Ernie Fitzsimmons, when the left-half suffered a compound fracture of the arm against Belfast Celtic. The basis of Ards' success in the first half of the League had been the superb play of the half-back line of McKeown, McKerley and Fitzsimmons, and after the loss of the number six the team never regained the same heights for the rest of the season.

At least Ards finished the League campaign with a flourish, winning three out of their last four matches. Their overall form was probably better than their results, decent as they were, suggesting many chances made but not taken, including several penalties, and some rank bad luck, or so the local papers kept claiming anyway. Alex Crooks had made his debut for Ards in December, and the inside forward looked in a higher class altogether, described as 'another Peter Doherty'. Accordingly, hopes were high for a run in the Irish Cup, where Glenavon were the opponents. The first match was drawn 2-2, with visiting keeper Morrison preserving his team's interest in the Cup via a series of brilliant saves. The match was marred by fighting, and a hostile stone-throwing crowd followed the 500 or so Glenavon supporters to the railway station. Some of the Lurgan support were obliged to seek shelter in High St. shops before making the safety of the BCDR. In the replay, thankfully with no trouble, Ards were by far the better side, according to the *Northern Whig,* but lost by the odd goal in five. As had happened all too often in previous seasons, their results nosedived thereafter as the season drew to a close, and only two matches were won in the City Cup. Yet they continued to attract praise for their sparkling football, and often dominated the opposition, only to fail to turn their superiority into goals. Buchanan was seen as the main culprit in terms of misses, but clearly he was not the only one to blaze his chances wide, perhaps subconsciously reacting to the old chant:

Play up, Ards, gie her a blarge,
There's far mair fields than yin.

There were fears that the team which had shown so much promise might break up, as first Jimmy McKerley went to Linfield for £150, and then, at the tail end of the season, Alex Crooks was transferred to Arsenal for a derisory fee, which Ards denied was as low as £750, but was probably not much higher. Turning out for Arsenal's reserve team, Crooks impressed so much that one English scribe referred to him as 'a successor to Alex James'. Time would tell, or rather it might have had the war not intervened. On balance Ards were more than happy with Sam Patton's work, and he was retained as player-coach for the next season. The AGM heard that Ards' deficit had been more than halved, and that the exciting and not unsuccessful brand of football played by the team had nearly doubled gate receipts over the year. It had been the happiest season Ards had spent for some time. As enthusiasm rose within the town the Ards Supporters Club flourished, even boasting its own dance band, 'under the direction of Eddie McMullan and William McCaw'. Hopes were high as the new season approached. Unfortunately 1939 would be a significant year for other, more sombre reasons than the fortunes of a football club.

Ards had only played four matches before war broke out, and from that time on there was an unreal feeling about a season where petrol rationing seriously disrupted public transport and both supporters and players left to join the armed forces. Nonetheless, football in Northern Ireland continued with as full a fixture list as during the pre-war days. Jimmy Buchanan, despite his goalscoring record, was allowed to leave on a free transfer, and was replaced by Donaghadee lad George Bunting. Wilfy Haire, partnered at full-back by 'Murdy' Wright, was appointed as captain. There were concerns, however, about low morale among the players, and the lack of new signings. The blame was placed on Sam Patton, who the committee argued was a full-time appointee. He protested that he was only available to Ards after 6.30 in the evening, but Ards, having taken their case to the IFA, prevailed, and Patton's contract was cancelled.

A now managerless team won only four of their City Cup games (the first time this competition was used as the season's pipe opener), against Cliftonville, Newry Town, Larne and Distillery. Against the Whites they came back from two goals down at half-time to win 5-3, with three goals scored by the promising new right wing combination of Jimmy Todd and Jack Donaldson. At this stage of the season Harry Elliott was in a rich vein of scoring form, and the team was greatly

Ards FC, 1938-39
Back Row (l-r): McMaster,
Fitzsimmons, McKeown,
Corry, McKerley, Haire,
Belshaw
Front row: Smyth,
McLarnon, S. Patton,
Patterson, Buchanan

strengthened by the return of Alex Crooks from Arsenal, his cross-channel career thwarted by the wartime cancellation of English football. In the League programme Ards began brightly, winning four of their first nine matches, with a 7-1 demolition of Larne, a 5-0 defeat of Coleraine, and a 5-2 win over Bangor on Boxing Day. The earlier 3-3 draw at home to Belfast Celtic saw another cracking comeback, Ards retrieving a 0-2 position to gain a point. The odd thing was that this fine mid-season flourish took place despite difficulties in the background. When George Bunting refused to play at outside left he was dropped and did not regain his place for seven matches, rumour suggesting that the professionals on the team had put pressure on the committee to deselect the centre forward. To save money training was cut, temporarily, it turned out, to one night a week, then the players' wages had to be reduced. Disharmony on the committee prompted John Heron to offer his resignation as Chairman, but things were patched up, although when he returned he was obliged to compose a letter to local newspapers appealing for financial help for the club. Once again results deteriorated in the second half of the season, Ards suffering their now traditional first round dismissal from the various knockout competitions, with the County Antrim Shield exit at the hands of Linfield Swifts particularly galling. Donaldson was out with ligament damage, Todd off to Coleraine, and Crooks accused of trying to do too much on his own. The forwards had run out of goals, while keeper John Davidson was making too many errors. Only four of the last seventeen League matches were won, the most notable a 2-1 victory over Glentoran and a thrilling 5-4 win over Portadown in a match where Ards had been three goals behind before coming back to gain a sensational victory via a Crawford penalty. The March game against Distillery was particularly unhappy for Ards. Not only did they lose 4-1, but Jack Donaldson, returning from injury, suffered a compound fracture of the leg. The operation was botched, and young Donaldson, described by 'Tosher' Burns as probably the most promising Newtownards player he had ever seen, would never play again. He had signed for Ards in the face of a persistent campaign by Elisha Scott to lure him to Celtic Park (it was said that Scott had virtually camped out on the doorstep of the Donaldson home in James Street), and he was also a target for Wolves at the time of his injury.

Financial difficulties increased as the season wore on. Crowds dwindled with the unavailability of private hire buses, and no doubt many felt that football was peripheral to their concerns in 1940. To ease the situation the usual extra-curricular activities were tried. A close season carnival the previous summer had produced little revenue but caused serious damage to the drainage system. More successful was a midnight matinee in the Regent Cinema, which featured Richard Hayward and the great Jimmy O'Dea. It was said that 'hundreds' were turned away. The profits from this venture were topped up by a donation of £20 from Miss McKelvey of Cloughey, a generous local benefactress after whom the children's ward of Ards Hospital was later named. The League decision in March to 'cap' players' wages at £1 10s received a warm welcome at Ards and, no doubt, other cash-strapped clubs, but the AGM heard that gate receipts had dropped by one third, and that Ards were £800 in debt. Once again there was difficulty in electing a committee, and it was revealed that members of the outgoing Committee had attended on average only 10 out of the possible 51 meetings. (An honourable exception was Harry Cavan, who had been to nearly all of them, and who would emerge as a key figure in the near future). Of course there was a War on, but pessimism about where the club was going was widespread, and a special crisis meeting was held, advertised by the local papers as 'Is Senior Football doomed in Newtownards?'

FIVE

Don't You Know There's a War On? 1940-47

The gloomy AGM, which had been adjourned, reconvened in a more positive frame of mind late in May 1940. Despite a poor attendance, the meeting elected a number of prominent local businessmen in absentia, and the names of Martin Poots, Hugh M. Donaldson, John J. Black sr., Sam Corry and J. T. Doggart were added to the Committee. It was decided to sell season tickets on the instalment plan, and to re-employ Sam Patton as manager. But then a fresh bout of pessimism took hold when Chairman Poots announced that he had joined the LDV, and felt that football was not important at this time. It was, of course, the summer of 1940, and the news of the fall of France cast a gloom over all else. The *Chronicle,* however, consistent with its sentiments of 1915, contended that workers who were being asked to put in a six or sometimes a seven day week deserved some relaxation, and urged the continuance of football. Swayed by this argument the Ards Committee, which a week earlier had voted for the suspension of the game for the duration, now rescinded that motion.

Even though Ards were now going to go ahead with plans for the forthcoming season they were faced with major team rebuilding as Wright and Crawford decamped to Bangor, Bunting to Glentoran and Doherty and Craig to Cliftonville. Crooks returned to the Arsenal as cross-Channel football got under way again, and McLarnon was allowed his request to leave. At least this time, unlike 1914-18, Ards' ground was not requisitioned for military purposes. The same could not be said for Bangor, Coleraine and Ballymena United, all of

*Ards FC, 1941-42,
with the
Clements Lyttle Cup.
Players, back row (l-r):
Irwin, Crawford, Davidson,
Higginson, Henderson,
McCauley.
Middle row: McCreary,
Todd, Beattie, Rankin,
Hollinger, Crymble, Feeney.
Front: McKnight, Black*

whom found themselves homeless. But a greater blow was yet to come, when in August, with the season's fixtures already published, the big four Belfast clubs announced they were breaking away from the league. The IFA, who could not exist without the support of the city clubs, gave way and sanctioned the setting up of a new competition, the Regional League, consisting of Linfield, Glentoran, Distillery, Cliftonville, Derry City, Glenavon and Portadown, the last two surviving only one year with the big boys. A joint deputation from Ards and Coleraine had their plea to join the Regional League rejected. Booted out by the elite, Ards swallowed their pride and entered the Intermediate League, retaining their senior status for the purpose of the major knockout competitions and therefore playing as Ards II at the lower level.

Despite a 5-0 win over St. Mary's in their first League match, Ards faced a number of setbacks thereafter. A victory over Glentoran II was nullified on appeal. It transpired that Inter-League caps could not play in the Steel and Sons' Cup, and Sam Patton, who featured in the winning team, had represented the Irish League against the Football League in 1934. Expulsion from the Steel and Sons' Cup was estimated, given a decent run, to have cost the club a potential revenue of hundreds of pounds. This loss was one Ards could ill afford, especially as a poorly supported Summer League only brought in a measly £35 that year. On top of this, Sam Patton resigned, citing war work, Basil Higson returned to his first love, rugby, to gain Ulster and Combined Universities caps, and an unsettled McKeown moved to Linfield. Despite these problems, Ards had a decent run in the Intermediate Cup, defeating 30th Old Boys, Command Signals, and Bangor Reserves (their first team, but calling themselves the seconds, like Ards). But in the semi-final the defeat of Glentoran II was again overturned on appeal, the grounds this time being that Ards had played McCartney, a centre-half who was ineligible. The blame for the error was attached to the well-meaning but inexperienced businessmen now running the club. The embarrassed J. T. Doggart resigned as Secretary, replaced on a temporary basis by Hugh Donaldson. At this low point, with meagre gates and the club described as 'almost at the point of collapse', into the breach stepped Norman Boal, who was able to provide a steadying hand on the tiller and steer Ards safely through the perilous seas of the next few years.

Coincidentally, results on the field began to improve from this moment on. Six successive wins were registered in the league, with sixteen goals for and only two against, the pick of the bunch the five goal thrashing of Dundela. The defence was all the steadier for the welcome return from Bangor of centre-half Cecil Crawford. Hopes were high for the Irish Cup, with Ards followers dreaming of a glorious day of revenge against Linfield, who had refused to have Ards in the Regional League. In front of a big gate Ards fought bravely but to no avail, going down 4-1. Spirits did not sink, however, and the good League form continued, with another half dozen victories, only one defeat, against Bangor, and a sharing of the points in a 5-5 draw with Summerfield. The March game against Bangor was a real thriller, one which Ards dominated but lost. By the end of a curtailed season (after the May Belfast Blitz most games were simply cancelled). Ards finished in a creditable 3rd position, and only Bangor, who won the League, and Celtic II took full points from Ards, an excellent recovery given the difficulty of finding a settled team: Ards used as many as forty players in their thirty three competitive games during the season. Regulars on the side were goalkeeper Davidson, full-backs Henderson and Mitchell, left-half Rankin, inside-right Beattie and left winger Ernie Fitzsimmons, who contributed ten goals. Centre-forward Keeley only played eight matches, yet scored six goals, but the find of the season was surely striker Davy Burton, a former York City player, now a serviceman, who netted sixteen goals in eleven games, the highlight a four goal blitz against Brantwood in the Clements Lyttle Cup.

The Regional League had not been a success, with poor gates and a general lack of interest, but when Belfast Celtic proposed winding it up the Chairman of the Irish League ruled their motion out of order. Ards' AGM, on the other hand, was a happy occasion, and the members heard that a profit of £100 had been recorded. The feeling was that if the club had remained in senior football they could not have survived. As Martin Poots quaintly put it, "Our miss was our mercy!"

Although the Intermediate League campaign got off to a shaky enough start in 1941, under Hugh Rankin's captaincy the team displayed better form in the various cup tourneys. The previous season's McElroy Cup had not yet been completed, and in the semi-final Ards fought out an enthralling 4-4 draw with Distillery II. It transpired, however, that the Whites had fielded no fewer than four ineligible players, and so the tie was awarded to Ards. Although their interest in the Intermediate Cup ended after a replayed match against Bangor, in the Steel and Sons' Cup wins over Northern Ireland Paper Mills, Belfast Fire Services and Ballyclare Comrades brought the side a semi-final clash with Celtic II. The

Hugh Rankin

first match, played at Windsor Park, ended in a 2-2 draw. Ards dominated against a Celtic side that included Charlie Tully and the future West Ham and England manager Ron Greenwood, but failed to kill off their more illustrious opponents. Taken to a replay, they had to accept defeat by the odd goal in five. League form began to pick up, and from the beginning of November to the end of January Ards won nine and drew one of their ten matches. Once again Davy Burton was prolific, hitting 23 goals in only 16 starts. Worryingly, however, an Army Council Order of July had cancelled leave for soldiers who wanted to play football. Initially the Order remained a dead letter, but by the turn of the year Burton, Short and Bolton had all disappeared from the team, and for the first time that season Ards fielded an all local side. The losses of Cecil Crawford, who had joined the RUC, and Jimmy Feeney, who was involved in a tug of war between Ards and Linfield before finally joining the Belfast outfit, were additional blows for the Newtownards club.

But a group of young players stepped into the breach and continued the successful run. Local man Walter Hollinger and the precocious 16-year-old Freddie McKnight had been playing well from the start of the season, and they were joined by Jimmy Todd, returning from Ballyclare Comrades, and another 16-

year-old, Harold Black. Unfortunately the crowd seemed keen to demonstrate the Biblical saying that a prophet hath no honour in his own country and gave the Newtownards players McKnight, Hollinger and Black a hard time, something they have been prone to all too frequently in succeeding years. Despite this barracking results continued to be encouraging. Ards made progress in the Irish Cup, bizarrely playing Bangor elevens no less than four times to reach the semi-final. It had been decided to play all the matches on a two-legged basis, and Ards were first drawn against Bangor proper, then against their Reserves. Despite losing 3-2 in Bangor, Ards trounced the Seasiders 5-0 in the second leg to progress to the next round, where they had a facile 8-2 aggregate victory. Glentoran proved too strong in the semi, but Ards acquitted themselves well and were unlucky to hit the woodwork twice.

The packed fixture list meant that Ards' McElroy Cup technical victory over Distillery II in August had not yet been followed up, but at last, in mid-April, the final of the previous year's tournament was decided. The match was at Grosvenor Park, and Ards' opponents were Celtic II. Strikes from Todd and McCreary, who netted twice, were enough to see off the city team, who only scored once, and Ards had won their first major trophy since the Irish Cup in 1927. Nor was this the end of the silverware for the season. In the Clements Lyttle Cup Ards had beaten the Naval XI 6-1, Lurgan Rangers, soon to be expelled from the Intermediate League for crowd disturbances, 4-1, and Distillery II, who included Rowley, the Manchester United centre-forward, 2-1 in the semi-final. In the final, again at Grosvenor, they defeated Aircraft 1-0 with a goal from Black to capture their second trophy of a memorable season. Exhausted by their efforts, they crashed out of the 1941-42 McElroy Cup 6-1 at Ballyclare, perhaps a mercy, since they had already played more matches than any other intermediate or indeed senior club that season. Sergeant Davy Burton's early season tally of 23 goals had not been overtaken by any other player, but Dicky O'Neill, who also found time to play a significant number of games for Celtic, and Harold Black contributed 14 each. Walter Hollinger was lost to Ards, as Celtic stepped in for him, and Hugh Rankin retired from playing, but was asked to run the team. Once again Ards finished in the black, posting a profit of £150, and making further inroads into the elimination of their debts. As the Regional League continued to struggle, Ards could afford to stay solvent and successful in Intermediate football as long as the unusual conditions of the war persisted.

Sam Eadie, who for years performed wonders in selling season tickets, ought to have had an easy task in the summer of 1942, given the twin trophies won the year before. But Ards' success brought the vultures of the bigger clubs flapping around seeking prey. It was not surprising: no fewer than five Ards players had featured in the Intermediate League representative team, a record for a single club, and it was a disappointment but no surprise when Hollinger's departure was followed by those of Beattie to Distillery and McKnight to Linfield, while Feeney was signed for another season by the Blues. Under the rules of the time, however, when they were not playing for their senior club these players could still turn out for an Intermediate team, so Ards must have had mixed feelings about saying goodbye to Hollinger et al. Obviously they wished their former stars well, but guiltily hoped to see them dropped by their big club so as they could at least temporarily come back to Ards! In practice only Beattie was able to play for Ards on a regular basis, and his presence was described as having been 'crucial' to the side.

After a couple of early away defeats in the League Ards hit their stride again. At home they were tremendous, winning all their games up until April, when they finally went down to Bangor. Before that they had claimed the scalps of Glentoran II and Celtic II, and had put eight goals past the hapless Lurgan Rangers, now reinstated in the League. For a long time Ards led the race for the Robinson and Cleaver Shield, but Bangor, with matches in hand, never lost touch with their North Down rivals, and eventually won the trophy. Burton's goalscoring feats of the previous two seasons had been enormously impressive, but he had not been able to play a full season on either occasion. In 1942-43 Ards found another prolific striker. This was Paddy Carroll, who hit no fewer than seven hat tricks in the course of the season, plus a four-goal spree against Glentoran II in a 5-4 win. In all he scored 48 goals in the season, and but for a falling off late in the year would certainly have passed the 50 mark. On a number of occasions Carroll scored by shoulder charging the opposing goalkeeper over the line. Ah, the good old days! Norman Lilley, signed from Distillery, proved a less spectacular but still useful acquisition, and the defence was greatly strengthened when winger Dickie O'Neill moved back to play at number 3, but against that Harold Black was greatly missed when he joined the Fleet Air Arm.

Once again Ards backed up their solid achievements in the League with a number of good cup runs. In the Steel and Sons' Cup they brushed aside Brantwood 4-0 and Aircraft Works 6-0, but surprisingly lost to Victoria Works United by 6-2 in the third round. The pitch was appalling, but a more likely cause of the defeat was the unnecessary tinkering with a winning team, when manager Rankin inexplicably dropped the in form Gorman and Taylor for the game. A first round bye and a 7-1 aggregate victory over the Infantry Training

Centre brought Ards as far as the semi-final of the Irish Cup for the second season running. Once again they found themselves up against Glentoran. 3-0 down at half time, they pulled the tie back to 3-2 and dominated thereafter, but failed to find the crucial third goal, and in the end succumbed 4-2. Interestingly, it was the now only occasional Ardsman Walter Hollinger who saw off Glentoran in the final, scoring the only goal of the game to bring the Cup to Celtic Park. For Ards, however, success would come in the Clements Lyttle Cup for the second successive season. Paddy Carroll scored one of his hat tricks in the 6-3 defeat of Distillery II, and in the second round Ards got past Bangor at the second time of asking, by 3-2 after a 3-3 draw. The semi-final brought a superb performance and a 4-1 victory over Glentoran II, putting Ards in the final with Larne, and at Solitude they triumphed 5-1, with two goals from Malachy Welsh and another three from Carroll.

At the AGM Samuel Corry was able to declare that Ards had now cleared all their debts, helped of course by the cup runs of the last two years. Intermediate football was clearly an attractive proposition for Ards, but it was difficult to hold on to players who were offered the chance to step up to a higher grade of football, and once again they suffered as the season drew to a close, the scheming inside forward Beattie signing this time for Glentoran, and Harry Ledwidge for Belfast Celtic.

The 1943-44 season saw Ards get off to a flying start, winning eight out of their first ten matches. The only defeat was to Distillery II, in a test match postponed from the previous year to decide second place in the McElroy Cup, which had been played, unusually, as a league competition in two sections. Freddie McKnight made a welcome return for the first third of the season, but the *Chronicle* lamented the loss of 'master mind Billy Beattie', while Hollinger only played a handful of matches before being snapped up, this time by Linfield. Beattie, however, reappeared after half the season and once again played an influential part in the team's performances.

Ards' League form was not as good as in the previous couple of years, but they still won twice as many matches as they lost. The highlights were a 5-0 defeat of Bangor, although they lost the away fixture 4-1, a late season 5-0 defeat of Glentoran II, and a 2-1 win at Ballyclare in January, the Steel and Sons' Cup winners' first defeat at Dixon Park that season. In Ards' own Steel Cup venture they were awarded the first round tie against Carrick Rangers when Carrick erred in handing in a team sheet with too many players on it, Ards refused to play the game, waved the rule book at the authorities and had a walkover into round two, where they beat Cliftonville Olympic 4-0. But in the next round, in the midst of a poor run, they were removed from the competition by the only goal of the game by Glentoran II. In the Irish Cup they again defeated Bangor over two legs by an aggregate of 5-3, but came unstuck against Cliftonville, who beat them 3-0 after the first match, played at Solitude, was drawn 2-2. Wins over Ballyclare Comrades, seen at the time as their best performance of the season, and Distillery II, at the second attempt, put Ards into the third round of the Clements Lyttle Cup. But in the semi-final they came a cropper against Celtic II, who defeated them 5-0. The best knockout performance was reserved for the McElroy Cup, reverting to its traditional format, where wins over Aircraft United and Bangor put them into the semi-finals. Here they had a fine win over Linfield Swifts, with Jimmy Todd scoring a hat trick in the 4-0 victory. In the final Ards found themselves up against Celtic II, but they lost 2-1, Billy Beattie's goal counting for nothing against strikes by Burrell and Tully.

The best players of the season were Jock Beattie and right-back Canavan, described as 'outstanding', and Jimmy Todd, who scored 28 goals, outshooting Paddy Carroll, whose 22 goal tally was not as good as his return in 1942-43, but to be fair to the centre forward, he missed a dozen or so Ards matches while playing for Cliftonville. One does not want to harp on about it, but this really was a constant problem for the Intermediate League team, with so many of their best players on the books of Regional League clubs who had first call on their services. To cite an example, on New Year's Day Ards found themselves without a goalkeeper when Joe McNulty opted to play for Glentoran. Into the gap stepped Harold Black, home on leave from the Fleet Air Arm. The ensuing plot line came straight from the pages of the *Wizard,* as Ards, stand in goalie and all, defeated Celtic II by the odd goal in five.

The most bizarre incident of the season came two weeks before Christmas, in a 4-3 defeat at Portadown, when the first goal for the Ports came after a shot from Madill cannoned off the crossbar and rebounded beyond the penalty area. The referee, however, insisted that the ball had bounced back from the back of the net, and was therefore a goal. Clearly nets were made of stronger stuff in those days. An injustice, yes, but not as worrying as another attempt to eliminate Intermediate clubs from the Irish Cup, which seemed about to succeed until an intervention at the IFA meeting by Secretary Norman Boal, who persuaded the delegates to retain the status quo, without which the financial survival of the provincial clubs would have been placed in considerable doubt. Boal was a meticulous and obviously persuasive administrator, but it was nonetheless a surprise when he was also appointed Honorary Manager for the forthcoming season. It remained to be seen whether he could run a team as well as he organised Ards F.C.

In February 1945 the *Chronicle* commented that there had been 'never such interest' in Ards as in that season. The reason was not hard to seek. Norman Boal's team was always in the hunt for the Robinson and Cleaver Shield, and there were yet again good cup runs, but perhaps most pertinently Ards rattled in no fewer than 122 goals: the only surprise being that come May there was no silverware to show for their cavalier approach. Significantly Ards had a fairly settled team for the first time since they were demoted to Intermediate football, a tribute to the authority of Boal, who was determined that the frequent cry offs of the past few seasons should not be repeated. The players who turned out regularly for Ards that year, (wearing blue and white hoops due to the 'war emergency') were Joe McNulty, a Dundalk goalkeeper with an unnerving tendency to dribble the ball far upfield, and full-backs Canavan, McDowell and Baird. The half backs were normally Irvine, Vennard and Corbett, the forwards (eventually) Burrell on the right, Duncan, Carroll, Hollinger and Alex Smyth. The continuity in the line-up partly disguises an unfortunate series

Walter Hollinger

of injuries which prompted some to talk of an Ards' 'hoodoo'. Jimmy Todd was unlucky enough to suffer a snapped ligament in October, and was not discharged from hospital until the New Year. George McKnight played one match, against Cliftonville Olympic, and suffered a broken arm, but most seriously of all Dickie O'Neill was admitted to hospital with heart trouble, a problem that would eventually lead to his premature death.

From the start Ards' ability to hit the net was phenomenal, with 25 goals scored in the first five matches, including nine against Cliftonville Olympic and five against Glentoran II, then a failure to score at Larne in an early exit from the Intermediate Cup, followed by a further seventeen goals in the next five games. On either side of Christmas they hit 27 goals in seven games. In the final third of the season the goals dried up somewhat, but if goals are what attracts crowds it was little wonder Ards' attendances were the best they had been for years. Carroll was back to his best, hitting 40 goals, Alex Smyth, who had played for the club in the 1930s, scored 17, the 20-year-old Gerry Burrell, 'the capture of the season'

George McKnight

when he moved from Celtic, got 15, Walter Hollinger 11 and right-half Irvine 11.

Interspersed with the high-scoring victories, however, were League defeats against Cliftonville Olympic, Linfield Swifts, Alexandra Works and crucially, in the run in for the League, against Larne, Celtic II, and Lurgan Rangers. Nonetheless Ards faced their final match at Dundela knowing that a win would leapfrog them past Celtic II, who had finished their programme, and Dundela themselves. Heartbreakingly they blew it at this last hurdle, going down 4-0 to the Wilgar Park men. It had been a brave, if doomed effort, but if one tries to be objective then it was a failure to kill off the opposition in three or four games in which they dominated which cost them the title, a strange paradox in a year when for most of the time they scored almost at will.

In the Clements Lyttle Cup Ards knocked out Ballyclare Comrades and Glentoran II to reach the semi-final. Against Victoria Works they fought out a 2-2 draw, but lost the replay 2-1. The Steel and Sons' Cup again saw Ards reach the semi-finals, defeating 49th Old Boys, Distillery II and Gallaghers' Ltd. But the Christmas morning final was denied to the Newtownards team as they lost by the only goal of the game to Bangor in a match which drew a crowd of 4000 to Wilgar Park. Yet again Ards faced their seaside neighbours over two legs in the first round of the Irish Cup, and yet again they defeated them, this time by an aggregate score of 6-3. In the second round they played the Infantry Training Centre, and with the advantage of playing both legs at Castlereagh Park triumphed 10-5 over a side which included Dave 'Boy' Martin and a number of cross-channel players. But matched with Linfield in the next round Ards found themselves out of their depth, losing the away leg 8-0 and the home leg 2-0. In the County Antrim Shield they defeated Bangor after a replay, and in the semi-final put up a far better show against top class opposition, only going down to Belfast Celtic by a single goal. Reports of the match suggest Ards were quicker to the ball throughout, but made one defensive slip and thus failed to claim the scalp of the illustrious team from Paradise.

It had been an exciting season, with an industrious Supporters' Club contributing £120 to club coffers and promising to replace the old palings with a concrete wall to upgrade the ground. The only cloud on the horizon was Norman Boal's announcement that he could not continue as Secretary and manager of the team, an understandable decision given that he still had a day job working for the *Newtownards Chronicle*.

Both on and off the field 1945-46 was a year of disappointment for Ards. It seems likely that the resignation of Norman Boal played no small part in the regression that characterised the season. There was a major upheaval in the playing strength of the side. The departures of Jimmy Todd and Paddy Carroll to Crusaders grievously weakened the goalscoring potential, and when Walter Hollinger and George McKnight moved to Coleraine the outlook was bleak. For a time Ben Duncan played well enough to attract the attentions of Huddersfield Town, and he had only played ten matches for Ards when Cliftonville called him into their squad. Some good new players did, of course, break into the Ards team, notably the tall half back Billy Imrie, who received rave reviews throughout the season, Walter Vennard and Joe McNulty, both selected for the Junior Ireland team, while there was a welcome return for full-back Jack Canavan and for Donaghadee lad George Bunting, now a speedy winger and an accurate crosser.

But too many classy players had gone, and results were ordinary enough, despite a promising start which saw eight goals scored in the opening fixture against Lurgan Rangers, four against new boys Ballymoney United, and a 4-0 defeat of Celtic II. Occasionally, and tantalisingly, the team hit top form, such as in the mid-winter defeats of Crusaders by 4-0 and 6-2, and the 8-0 demolition of Glentoran II, but inconsistency seemed to be the name of Ards' game, and after Christmas they won six but lost eleven of their League matches. Certainly Ards had endured seasons far worse than this one, but it was galling to see the high promise of the war years come to nothing just when Ards seemed set to become the leading Intermediate club. Not that they wished to remain in the lower grade of football, of course, now that peace had come, but the prospects of acceptance by the senior clubs looked increasingly unlikely that season. First the IFA decided that Ards and Bangor should no longer be automatically entered into the draw for the money-spinning Irish Cup, then when in December Ards proposed that the Irish League should be reinstated as it was before the War, their motion was rejected by fifteen votes to eight. Undaunted, they appealed, but in February secured support only from fellow underdogs Bangor, Portadown and Glenavon, and the appeal was defeated. Astonishingly Coleraine and Ballymena United voted with the city clubs, or perhaps not so astonishingly, as it was widely believed that the two clubs had received private assurances that they would be admitted to an expanded Regional League in the next season. A seething *Chronicle* correspondent, presumably Norman Boal, wrote that 'the city clubs…determined to rule the roost…are evidently not content with the declaration of the government that the war is over'. But his well-judged sarcasm was scant consolation for the grim reality that Ards could not hope to return to senior soccer for at least another season.

Ards' Steel and Sons' Cup interest ended in the second round after a defeat at Bangor, but they had the last word over those who had slammed the Irish Cup door in their faces via the back door of the Intermediate Cup. Victories over Larne and Coleraine saw them drawn away to Bangor in the fourth round. But the match never took place, Ards claiming that Billy Bradford, who appeared on the Bangor team sheet, was ineligible to play. Their protest was upheld, and so Ards reached the semi-final of the Intermediate Cup, which carried with it automatic entry into the Irish Cup! An incensed Bangor insisted they were in the right, even taking the case as far as the High Court, but they received little satisfaction. Ards found themselves up against the second string of Linfield in the semis, ironically in that they saw Linfield as the main stumbling block to their attempts to regain senior status. Although they held the Swifts to a 2-2 draw, in the replay they went down 3-0. As luck would have it, in the Irish Cup Ards came out of the hat paired with Linfield's first team, the tie to be decided over two legs. In the first match, at Windsor Park, Ards played well despite going down 2-0. Twice they hit the woodwork, and Stanley Vennard had an outstanding game at the heart of the defence. In the return leg Ards played a storming game, coming back from 3-1 down to claim a draw, the first time the Blues had failed to win a match for nearly four months. Tempers ran high as a full-scale fracas developed and Corbett and McCrory were sent off. Interestingly, Ards had grounds for appealing against the overall defeat, as although they had entered the competition as 'Ards II', Linfield's official letter containing their list of players was addressed to 'Ards'. Nothing was done, however, despite the urgings of some supporters, possibly on the grounds that it was time to draw a line under the period of animosity between the two clubs. Such efforts seem to have been in vain, however, for a couple of weeks later Linfield made an attempt to have Ards removed from the County Antrim Shield. Speculation of the time suggested that the ill feeling simmered on because of Ards' persistent fight to restore the old Irish League.

Despite their well organised if fruitless campaign to achieve top grade football, in most other respects Ards verged on the shambolic in the way the club was being run. At the turn of the year the Selection Committee resigned en bloc; in a match played soon after that Ards kept Distillery waiting fifteen minutes before they finally struggled out on to the pitch; and there were loud complaints that the turnstiles on the reserved side did not open until the kick off. For their part the players were complaining of unwarranted abuse from supporters who, they claimed, were simply chasing young or local players away from the club. Overall it had been an unhappy season, with austerity facing both the country and an Ards F.C. unable as yet to achieve its ambition of a return to the top flight.

For the 1946-47 season the Committee, recognising that the last year's results were largely a reflection of the lack of direction from the top, appointed a full time manager. This was Jackie Coulter, the former Belfast Celtic, Everton, and Ireland winger, who had been released by Swansea Town. Coulter brought about wholesale changes in the defence, with Michael O'Connell taking over in goals, Cully and Hamill at full-back, and Cecil Crawford, back once again from Brantwood, at No. 5. Up front Hollinger struck up a wonderful understanding with inside forward Kearney, Ward Fulton partnered Todd on the right, and for all too short a time McCullough proved to be the natural goal grabbing successor to Paddy Carroll.

Nine out of the first ten League matches were won, with six goals scored against Coleraine, seven against Ballymoney United and four away to Portadown. In early September Ards played Glentoran in a friendly to help raise funds to restore the Oval, damaged during the Blitz, and won 2-1, Coulter scoring in one of his only two appearances for his club. Interest from the supporters was sky high, with a run on vice-presidents' and season tickets and 'hundreds' disappointed when post-war shortages meant only two buses were available for the trip to Glenavon. The Clements Lyttle Cup saw Ards coast to the final courtesy of a 4-0 win over Portadown, a 5-1 victory over Bangor and a 4-1 defeat of Newry Town. But in the final itself they disappointed, losing 3-1 to Linfield Swifts. The inside forwards were blamed for their slowness and their inability to involve their wingers sufficiently. In the Intermediate Cup Ards played out an epic series of four matches with Bangor before going out of the competition. In the first of these games they scored twice in the last ten minutes to draw level, and were even denied a winner when everyone but the referee thought the ball had crossed the line. Over 10,000 spectators watched the four games, such was the interest in professional football in North Down at that time.

In October George Bunting was snapped up by Linfield. He scored a hat trick for the Blues on his debut, but was sorely missed by Ards. A further blow occurred when Michael O'Connell broke his thumb, but a replacement was found in Reid, signed from Bury. Coulter strove to strengthen the team, with the return of the big Scot Jimmy McKerley from the Army. Andy McKeown also made a welcome return to Castlereagh Park, inside forward Mulholland was transferred from Bangor, and to replace Bunting Douglas came in from Glentoran. Ards' unbeaten League run only came to an end in spectacular fashion in early December with a 6-1 thrashing by Newry Town. In the next game Ards threw away a 2-0 lead over Brantwood, missed two penalties at 2-2, but still managed a 3-3 draw. The fear was that a decline was about to set in, but the ship was steadied, and the team won eight out of their next nine matches. Four double-decker bus loads of Ards fans made their way to Larne on Boxing Day, and this, it must be remembered, was in the Intermediate League! The victory over Glentoran II in mid-February was particularly thrilling, Ards, 2-0 down after 80 minutes came back to win 3-2 with goals from Kearney and one from Wade. But the events immediately after that game would have been worthy of inclusion in the 'What Happened Next?' round of A Question of Sport. Unbelievably, with Ards top of the League, Jackie Coulter was sacked! The official line taken by the Committee was that the club's 'present financial position' did not warrant employing a manager. Whatever the truth, and one suspects that there was more to it than this, the timing was appalling. Ards won five and lost eight during the run in for the championship, and finished in fifth position after heading the field for so long. They reached the semi-final of the Clements Lyttle Cup, but lost heavily, 6-2 to Bangor, in front of 5000 spectators. To be fair, Ards were badly hit by injuries for the latter half of the season, but the collapse in form must have also been in large part due to the loss of the manager's inspiration.

But just after Coulter's dismissal another issue arose to grab the headlines and take the heat off a Committee which had acted in such a crass manner. In January it was proposed, at long last, that a 12-team Irish League should be reinstated, with Ards, Bangor, Glenavon and Portadown joining the existing eight Regional League clubs. Ards were wary, and a special meeting heard that it would take £1000 to make the necessary preparations for re-entry. There were those whose bitterness at Ards' exclusion from the Regional League led them to argue that the offer should be turned down, but this dog in the manger attitude was only held by a minority. It would have been interesting to hear the views of Peter McLean, who had played such a large part in Ards' promotion to the senior ranks a quarter of a century earlier, but ironically this great servant of Ards F.C. had died just as the debate began. The decision to go ahead was approved, but what exactly was the £1000 for? Harry Cavan sternly pointed out that over the past seven years, since Ards entered Intermediate football, only £20 had been spent on the ground. Now new and extra turnstiles were needed, the pavilion needed upgrading, and despite supporters' club promises the old rotten palings still fenced in the ground. Metal fences were the club's first choice, but pipes were in such short supply that concrete blocks were adopted as a second best option. A new skip would also be needed: Ards had been playing in a variety of colours; red, blue and green had all recently been used, and none of it of decent quality in the constrained economic circumstances of the time. To raise the necessary finances the 'Back to Senior Football" fund was put in the capable charge of Sam Eadie, and had raised £700 by May. A final decision before the summer countdown to the big time was to appoint Harry Cavan as full time Secretary and groundsman!

SIX

"I Like Ike!"

1947-53

There were, during the war, many who felt that Intermediate football was not far behind the quality of the senior game, and certainly Ards were able to make use of several of the players who had served them well during the 1946-47 season when they re-entered the top division. Dickie Corbett, Billy Imrie, Walter Hollinger and Tommy Hamill went on to hold regular places in the team; O'Connell, McKerley, McKeown and Cully featured in many games; while Hughie Couser, signed from Intermediate football with Bangor, played regularly for half the season. For those seeking further proof of the quality of wartime Intermediate football, former Ards players who would hold down places in cross-Channel teams that season included Ben Duncan at Airdrie, Gerry Burrell at St. Mirren, and local boy George McKnight, who made a name for himself at Blackpool.

While Ards supporters were spending the close season relaying the cinder track and building a perimeter wall at Castlereagh Park, all the excitement was taking place at Donaghadee, where thousands gathered to welcome back Nottingham man Tom Blower, who had just become the first person to swim the North Channel. Blower's triumphant return to the seaside town was, apparently, greeted with 'scenes of popular delirium', and one can only hope that the writer of that newspaper headline was exaggerating. Nonetheless, in those heady post-war days a generation which had been starved of entertainment now flocked to greyhound races, cinemas, speedway tracks and football grounds, and Ards F.C.

shared in the surge of popularity which Association Football enjoyed. On many occasions, especially during the first half of the season, Ards saw crowds of two and three thousand, and not just against big Belfast teams either. On the second Saturday of the season, when Ards had to travel to Portadown, over one thousand fans turned out at Castlereagh Park to watch the Seconds defeat Bangor Reserves 7-0, and a couple of weeks after that the Ards Committee had to enforce a ban on bicycles being taken into the ground as they were causing 'congestion'. The big attractions on the team were former Shelbourne right winger Leo Maher, and Ronnie Dellow, a 33-year-old centre-forward with 150 games and 50 goals for a number of English League clubs, but mainly Tranmere Rovers, behind him. The team started the new season with a return to the red and blue hoops first seen in 1924, but abandoned for red and white in the 1930s, while for the first time a regular match programme was produced, costing 3d.

After a heavy defeat by Belfast Celtic in the opening City Cup match Ards embarked on a run which saw them lose only two of their next ten games in the competition. Particularly impressive were the 1-1 draw at Windsor Park, achieved despite a penalty miss, and defeats of Bangor and Derry City where Ards scored five goals and six goals respectively. The team finished 5th in the competition, the highest placed provincial club, and Dellow scored 12 goals in as many matches. Dickie Corbett and Albert Currie were both playing well, Maher was being closely watched by Bolton Wanderers, and after a long running dispute with the club Billy Imrie re-signed. Dellow was such an inspiration that he was appointed player-coach, and all looked set fair for a successful League campaign.

But in practice it did not happen. Wins over Cliftonville and Bangor were the only two in Ards' first 15 matches, and Derry City gained revenge for their 2-1 defeat in the Gold Cup by eliminating Ards from the Irish Cup in the first round by the same score. On Boxing Day Ards contrived to miss their 6th penalty of the season, against Glenavon, while the 6-2 defeat by Derry City on the following day drew the despairing but historically inaccurate comment from the *Chronicle* correspondent that this was the 'worst Ards team ever'. Three wins in a row in February, the best of them a 2-1 defeat of Linfield, were as close as Ards got to a revival. Morale within the team was low. Couser was released, and Dellow, Maher and Currie were rumoured to want away, Currie getting his wish in March, transferred to Linfield for 'several hundred pounds'. A single win in the last four matches condemned Ards to a bottom half finish. Eighth place was respectable, but a real disappointment after the promise of the City Cup campaign. In the County Antrim Shield Ards reached the semi-final stage by defeating Cliftonville, but failed to make further progress, losing to Ballymena United. Many considered the team to be too long in the tooth, and there were calls for more young players are to be tried. On the bright side Billy Imrie was on top form, gaining an Irish League cap and attracting the attention of scouts from Wolves and Aberdeen.

In May Ards played against an English League team for the first time, defeating visitors Luton Town 2-1. Guesting and scoring for Ards were Bangor's prolific Billy Bradford, and Peter Doherty, the former Manchester City inside forward, now playing with Huddersfield Town. At the outset of his career Doherty had reportedly been recommended to Ards, who had him watched, but decided that he was not worth it. The committee had shown a similar lack of foresight in leaving the unreserved side open to the elements, but now, after a mere quarter of a century, conceded that perhaps they ought to put a shelter on what had once been the 'tanner' side, but was now the 'bob' side. To be fair to the committee of 1947-48, at least they were apparently taking steps to remedy the long-standing problem, and they had kept the club solvent. Although it had not been a particularly distinguished season on the pitch, off it the Treasurer was pleased to report a profit on the season of over £500, while the AGM ensured a steady hand on the tiller by re-appointing Harry Cavan as full time Secretary of the club.

For the 1948-49 season Ards lost one classy player and gained another. The loss was that of Ronnie Dellow, contracted to a Dutch team over the summer, but constantly promising that he would be available to play for Ards soon. Well, quite soon. Eventually he did come back, but it was only to play three matches, and then he was gone for good. The gain was the signing of John Connor from Carlisle United. The centre forward had played fifty English League games, and looked a classy player from the word go. Also signed that summer was former Norwich player Leslie Dawes, whose time at Ards was short, but who would go on to become a familiar face as a reporter for UTV.

The team got off to a wretched start, losing its first five games. Criticisms were levelled at a committee which did not have a decent scouting system in place, and in the course of the ensuing debate it emerged that the club was in the habit of using cross-channel papers to advertise for new players! Ards had offered their supporters a glimmer of hope with the performance against Linfield, going 2-0 up before succumbing to defeat, and this hope became reality from mid-September, with four wins and a draw in the ensuing five matches. When trouncing Coleraine 5-2 Ards had no less than four goals disallowed, and in a 3-3 draw with Belfast Celtic, Celtic's last minute equaliser was the result of a series of defensive howlers, when first Hamill's free-kick was mishit and went straight

Ards FC 1948-49
Back row, (l-r): Cavan,
(Secretary), Maher,
Gillespie, Imrie, O'Connell,
Davis, Hamill, McKimm
(trainer).
Front row (l-r): Wright,
Maginnis, Robinson, Smyth,
Kearney

to Campbell, whose shot appeared to be well covered by O'Connell until Bob Dunn rushed in to divert it into the net. But this was the only point dropped in five matches, and Dellow's return made a huge difference to the team. But he soon returned to Holland on a permanent basis, and his departure from the club was a blow. More worrying was the need for a public appeal to members and vice-presidents to pay for their season tickets immediately, as Ards were in serious financial difficulties. Two defeats rounded off the City Cup campaign, and Ards finished in 6th position.

Local boy Tommy Dorman and new signing Dickie Horner were drafted into the side for the League campaign, but apart from a 2-1 win over Glentoran in the second match of their programme the team broke little ice until just after Christmas. But on Christmas Day, even though the team lost the traditional fixture with Bangor, they had a new centre-forward. John Connor had been unable to find accommodation for his wife and family in Ulster in an era of housing shortage, and was unhappy. When Rochdale came in with a bid, Connor was keen and Ards reluctantly let him go. He went on to have a distinguished career in the lower divisions, with over 200 goals to his credit, and I remember as a boy seeing him on BBC Television in his Stockport days, representing the 3rd

Division North against their Southern counterparts in the annual fixture. The fee paid by Rochdale was only £650, far below the prolific scorer's true value, but the makeweight in the deal was Norman Case, a replacement centre-forward who had not yet broken into Rochdale's first team. Case was that rare breed, an attack leader with great ball skills, described by one veteran observer as 'the best footballing striker Ards ever had'. Case made an immediate impact, scoring both Ards' goals in the Christmas Day defeat against Bangor, and repeating the dose two days later in the return fixture, which Ards won 3-2. The Englishman continued to shine for the rest of the League campaign in which Ards won only five more matches while losing nine. He scored four in the 8-0 drubbing of Ballymena in February, which Ards followed up a fortnight later with a 7-0 defeat of Coleraine. When the team travelled to Celtic Park in the first half of the League they had squandered a 3-0 lead and lost the game, and in the return fixture they blew their chances even more spectacularly, this time being pulled back from 4-0 up to a 4-4 draw. To strike a melancholy note, this would be the last ever League fixture against Belfast Celtic, who chose to go out of football a few months after the notorious Boxing Day match against Linfield which ended in a riot, a match, incidentally, refereed by former Ards boss Norman Boal. They would play Celtic once more, losing to them in the second round of the County Antrim Shield. There was no success for Ards in the other knockout competitions, with first round exits at the hands of Ballymena United in the Gold Cup and Bangor in the Irish Cup. Although the team's record was almost identical to that of the year before, with only two points difference, the League finish was much more disappointing, with a drop from 8th place to 11th and the need for re-election.

1949 saw the birth of a new competition, the Ulster Cup, and Ards almost became its first winners. In the first round of what was then a knockout competition, they defeated Bangor 3-1, then Dundela 5-2, and in the semi-final Coleraine 4-2. Willie Maginnis, who had only recently broken into the team, scored two goals against each of these sides. The final was against Linfield, but Ards flopped completely, losing 3-0, to a hat-trick from Billy Simpson. 'Vigilant' in the *Spectator* described the team as 'a clatter of lazy workmen on their notice, just punching in the time of their last half-day'. Clearly not an entirely satisfied customer.

The sad demise of Belfast Celtic meant, of course, the break-up of their team. Harry Walker, who had played a handful of games for Ards many years earlier, was appointed as the team's new player-coach, and he brought with him from Paradise Morgan and Peter O'Connor. Tommy Dorman had gone in the other direction, joining Celtic on their final fling, a US tour, and had the distinction of setting up the first Celtic goal in their famous victory over the full Scottish international XI. When he came home he went to Glentoran, and Sam Gillespie left for Ballymena, but the arrival of the ex-Celtic men and the prospect of Norman Case leading the line whetted the appetite of the Ards football public. They were not disappointed. A cracking start to the City Cup campaign saw Ards travel to Coleraine and win 9-1, with Case scoring five, and the following week defeat Distillery 4-2. Three further wins followed, against Cliftonville, Portadown and Glentoran. Not only were the team top of the City Cup table with full points, but Walker made an astute signing in the shape of Dundalk's John Matthews, a centre-half who had gained an Eire cap the previous season. Despite a first round defeat by Glenavon in the Gold Cup, and a more mundane performance in the concurrently run Ulster Cup, Ards' form was nonetheless extremely promising. Norman Case represented the Irish League against their Scottish counterparts in Glasgow, scored, and attracted the interest of Leicester City, while right-back Savage, a Comber boy, was watched by both Blackburn Rovers and Huddersfield Town. The half-back line of Imrie, Robinson and Corbett was playing superbly, but pessimists detected a weakness at inside forward, and defeats at Derry, Linfield and Glenavon dropped Ards to a final position of third in the City Cup. The most serious loss to the team, however, and the probable explanation of their failure to keep winning in the run-in, was the transfer of Norman Case. So good was his form that when Sunderland bid £3,500 for him, far and away the biggest sum ever offered for an Ards player up to then, the club could do little but accept, and their best forward was gone.

To replace Case and further strengthen the team for the League campaign, Ards allowed Leo Maher to go, but brought in Bangor's Hugh Cunningham, Bernard and Eamonn McDaid, two brothers from Donegal, and at centre-forward Fitzgerald, a former St Patrick's Athletic player. After a 2-0 victory over Portadown in the opening league fixture, Ards went through December without a win. On the final day of 1949 they put up a tremendous fight in a thriller at home to Glentoran, only losing 4-3 after being 3-0 down at half-time. Fitzgerald turned out to be no substitute for Case, but the veteran Walker was playing very well, and Johnny Matthews showed exceptional form on the heavy winter pitches. The centre-half had come on a free transfer when Dundalk hit financial difficulties and were obliged to release all their professionals. He played centre half for the Irish League against both the English League and the League of Ireland, in the latter match playing superbly and receiving generous applause from the

Dalymount crowd. But he showed feet of clay in March, missing two penalties in the 1-0 defeat by Glenavon. Towards the end of the campaign Ards lost the McDaid Brothers, suspended for playing Sunday football, and experimented with a number of young players like White and McCague, the former scoring half a dozen goals in his 11 appearances. In a fairly mediocre League campaign Ards managed only seven wins out of their 22 games. In 1948-49 the same seven wins had left them seeking re-election, but in 1949-50 the gaining of four extra draws hoisted them up to a respectable position of 6th.

The Irish Cup saw Ards drawn away to Banbridge Town, for whom local boy Winston Orr was playing. Nineteen buses and a train (the BCDR was still in operation, but only just – the last train from Newtownards to Donaghadee was a mere three months away) brought a big following from Ards to swell the crowd to 2500. Orr was probably the pick of Banbridge's forward line, but got very little change out of John Matthews, and goals from Hollinger and Maginnis brought Ards safely past a potential banana skin. The second round was a difficult away tie to Derry City. Ards went 2-0 down to a double strike from Hermon, but early in the second half they seemed to have given themselves a fighting chance when Cunningham put the ball in the net. The keeper had only been able to push out a Fitzgerald shot, but when Cunningham followed up to score the referee disallowed it for offside, even though former Ards player Jimmy Kelly was standing on the goal line. It was a disgraceful decision, and manager Walker, criticised for carping at referees too much, for once had solid grounds for his complaints.

Despite Ards' somewhat mixed record the supporters had great faith in Harry Walker. Not only a fine player (two fine end-of-season victories over Crusaders and Derry City were put down largely to his return after injury) but a superb motivator, he seemed the player-manager for whom Ards had been crying out for many years. But disquieting news was leaking out from the Management Committee. It seemed they were reluctant to meet Walker's terms for another season, and it was believed that the influential Harry Cavan did not get on with Walker. In an unprecedented move, in late April a public meeting was held in a packed Town Hall to urge the apparently reluctant Committee to sign a fresh contract with the manager. A deputation consisting of Messrs. Tate, Murphy and Campbell was sent from the Town Hall across the square to the Devonshire Arms to make this request to a meeting of the committee which was being held there: they returned with the news that Ards' terms had been accepted by Walker, and all was apparently well. But two weeks later the shock news broke that Walker would instead go to manage Glenavon, who had made him a financial offer he could not refuse. The supporters were outraged. Whether the fault lay with

Walker or with the committee, it was clear that the fans in the Town Hall had been hoodwinked, and the whole affair left a nasty taste.

The omens for 1950 were not good. The release of the veteran Peter O'Connor was probably justified, but the case of Walter Hollinger, allowed to go to Distillery, was more debatable, and even though Glenavon's transfer fee of £1,150 for the unsettled John Matthews was a good piece of financial business, it severely weakened the team. Ards' failure to find a replacement player-manager for Harry Walker in time to sign up new players was most serious of all. Chairman Billy McMillan was obliged to carry out tasks that really belonged to a manager or coach, making judgements on whether players were worth signing or releasing. Eventually John Reid, an English goalkeeper with an Irish background, was signed as player coach, but his appointment did not survive the season. For the opening game Ards had only four professionals on their books, the veterans Billy Imrie, Tommy Hamill, Dickie Corbett and Jackie Robinson. But the Ulster Cup games seemed to have unearthed a natural goalscorer in the shape of Winston Orr, now back with his home town club, whose hat-trick defeated Bangor in the opening match. He scored two goals in the easy 5-2 victory over Dundela, while a fighting draw against Glentoran, with Dan Feeney scoring twice, gave Ards joint top place in their section. Unfortunately goals by Sammy Hughes and Billy Bingham saw Glentoran win the play-off. 2-0. The City Cup campaign was dreadfully disappointing, with a solitary win over Cliftonville as the only victory, although the 1-1 away draw to Distillery, where Ards had only 10 men for most of the game, was a brave performance. On October 21st a crowd of over 4000 saw Ards share the points with Linfield in an exciting 3-3 draw, but the historic significance of this game was not so much the result as the fact that Ards were wearing numbered jerseys for the first time in their history. Despite the run of poor results attendances remained high until Christmas, with three double deckers needed to take the Ards support to Crusaders for the match immediately following the Linfield draw.

In defence Savage, Corbett and O'Connell were playing well, the goalkeeper receiving an Irish League cap against the English League in October, while Jimmy Moore, from the moment he first stepped on to the field, looked like a fine full-back. The team's problems seemed to lie with a young and inexperienced forward line. The Management Committee took the flak for the poor results. It was all very well, said their critics, to play a young, largely amateur team, but any money saved thereby was going to be lost as gate receipts shrank. An experienced forward was signed in time for the beginning of the League campaign, in the shape of Bobby Bogan, a right winger from Stirling Albion, who scored on his opening appearance as Ards defeated Portadown 3-2. 1950 was the first year the giant Christmas tree appeared in front of the Town Hall, but if Ards supporters were seeking any festive cheer they would have to seek it in Conway Square rather than at Castlereagh Park, where the weeks went by without any sign of another League victory. The whole thing became embarrassing as Crusaders beat Ards 8-1, while in the 5-3 defeat by Distillery the rejected Hollinger tortured Ards throughout the 90 minutes. Panicking, Ards went to Scotland to sign three new players, Murphy, Anderson and McIlwaine. The three featured in a bizarre February match at Portadown, where Ards kicked off on four inches of snow with only eight players, the Scotsmen having missed the bus, only arriving and able to take the field with fifteen minutes already gone. The eventual 1-0 defeat was, all things considered, not too bad. Things got no better, however, and after the 7-2 defeat at the Oval in late February Ards announced that they would appoint a manager. But when only one candidate applied, no appointment was made and the matter had to be adjourned. The 3-2 win over Portadown (Bogan's first match) had taken place on 25th November, and it would be the first week of March before Cliftonville succumbed 3-0 to give the local team only their second win of the League. A third victory, over Bangor, followed on St Patrick's Day, but that was it. Three wins and two draws was a quite awful performance, and bottom of the table Ards were obliged to go cap in hand to the League to apply for re-election.

Briefly, in this wretched season, Ards fans clung to the hope that an Irish Cup run might provide some compensation. Drawn away to Glenavon, for whom Harry Walker was now playing, they managed a fine 2-2 draw, with goals from Orr and Anderson. The Wednesday replay against the high-flying Lurgan team saw Ards triumph 3-1, with Lawther scoring twice and Bogan once. 'Scenes without parallel' followed the match, as the crowd invaded the pitch and chaired the Ards team off the field. There was enormous enthusiasm for the second-round game at Portadown, where a massive crowd of nearly 5000 saw Ards fight gallantly but lose by the only goal of the game.

1951 was Festival of Britain year, and to celebrate Ards decided to play a continental team. Controversy arose over whether memories of the war were too recent to allow the team to play a German side, and in the end this did not happen. Instead the Dutch side EDO Haarlem were invited, and on May 15th, in front of over 2000, Ards and EDO played out a goalless draw.

The match against foreign opposition was one of the few highlights of this season. The committee, allegedly riven by dissension, had still not got round to building the long promised shelter on the unreserved side, and had presided over probably the worst season on record, but they recognised what was wrong, and were well aware that a strong man was needed to take charge if Ards were to get out of this trough. The right decision was made, and former Cowdenbeath and Linfield player Isaac McDowell was appointed as the new player-manager.

The sort of people who seek signs in the sky were probably gibbering with excitement in September 1951 at the finest displays of the Aurora Borealis which had been seen for decades. Did the Northern Lights presage something significant for Ards that season? Luckily there were more concrete signs of progress available to Ards' fans than those favoured by the crystal ball fraternity. Work began to enlarge the pavilion and install new bathrooms, for the first time refreshments were made available on the unreserved side of the ground, while the distribution of season tickets, members' tickets and vice Presidents' tickets was to be completely overhauled. The new ticketing arrangements aroused some hostility, but at least it was clear that after the fiasco of the previous season much was being done to try to kick-start the club back into life. Encouraged by all this, the Supporters' Club, although, like McNamara's band, small in number, was working hard to raise £250 to help build a stand on the popular side.

New boss Ike McDowell was an inspired choice and an inspiring manager. In his efforts to strengthen the team he in brought in Tommy Walker from Crusaders, Archie Norman from Portadown, and former Celtic and Coleraine player Jimmy Tucker. For one year only, the Ulster Cup was scrapped to make way for the similarly-styled Festival (of Britain) Cup, which asked Ards to play both Bangor and Glentoran home and away. Winning two and losing two of these matches, the club failed to make further progress. Briefly Ards shone in the City Cup. Defeats of Coleraine and Cliftonville and a draw against Distillery saw them top the table, but a depressing series of defeats, broken only by the 2-0 win over Derry City, saw them slide down the table, and only a late burst which produced five points from three matches helped them finish in sixth position. The 6-0 thrashing by Glenavon was described by the *Chronicle* as a 'fiasco'. A promising Gold Cup run, which saw a 4-3 victory over Ballymena, ended as Ards went out 6-2 to Linfield after a drawn match. McDowell was well aware of the need to strengthen the side, and Johnny Thomson, the former Alloa Athletic player who had lately been plying his trade in France was brought in at inside-right, and soon afterwards Jimmy Tucker would drop back to right-half to replace the long-serving Billy Imrie.

The changes brought little immediate success. The opening League match saw Ards humiliated at the Oval, losing 8-1, and only one draw, 0-0 against Linfield, was achieved in the first nine games. Depressing though this run was, one match against eventual champions Glenavon would demonstrate the fighting qualities that McDowell had instilled in his side. 4-0 down against the Lurgan men Ards rolled their sleeves up, and urged on by a crowd of 2500 clawed their way back into the game with a hat-trick from Davy Lawther, but could not find an equaliser. Late in the year Ards' fortunes at last turned round. With Mick O'Connell, who had been in dispute with the club, persuaded back into goals by McDowell, the 4-1 victory over Ballymena United began a sequence in which Ards lost only one out of fourteen. The crowds began to flock back to Castlereagh Park as Ards showed that for them this was indeed an League of two halves, and their eight wins and four draws eventually raised them to seventh place, a huge improvement on their performance last time out. Tucker, Robinson and Corbett had been holding the team together in the first half of the campaign, with the forwards taking the blame for the poor run of results. Lawther's introduction into the team added fighting spirit but the centre-forward position remained problematical throughout, with Gorman losing his place to Bobby Brown, signed from Bangor, he in turn replaced by Billy Drake, the former Cliftonville and Glenavon player.

Ike McDowell

It was in the Irish Cup that Ards would taste glory for the first time in a generation. Drawn at home to Larne in the first round, the team won 2-1, with goals from McDowell and Black. A Lawther goal was enough to see them through at Brantwood in the second round, and Ards found themselves up against Ballymena United in the semi-final. Twenty double-deckers were hired to bring supporters to Windsor Park, where they saw Ards triumph 3-1. Johnny Thomson and Davy Lawther added to an Eric Trevorrow own goal, as Ards made a series of attacks down both Lawther's and Walker's flanks, and Jimmy Tucker and Thomson dominated midfield.

Cliché or not, the final produced a match never to be forgotten. Opponents Glentoran were clear pre-match favourites, the *Belfast Newsletter* opining 'Ards … are not in the same class as Glentoran'. But McDowell had ingrained fight and confidence in the side, and there was no question of them being intimidated by the opposition or the occasion. Playing in blue, Ards lined out with the following team: O'Connell; Moore, Hamill; Tucker, Robinson, Corbett;

Lawther, Thomson, Drake, McDowell and Walker. 23,000 were at the match, and as time went on the neutrals in the crowd began to cheer for Ards, and in a second half which fairly sizzled with excitement, 'roar after roar rent the Windsor air' *(Ireland's Saturday Night)*. The first half, which finished scoreless, was relatively even, but after the break Ards dominated the East Belfast side, besieging their goal but missing a series of chances through misfortune or inept finishing. The only goal of the game eventually came in the 63rd minute, and was scored by Scotsman Johnny Thomson, whose proud parents were watching in the stands. At the time of the goal Ards were down to ten men, with Lawther off the field for treatment. Every man jack played his part that day, but the player who stood head and shoulders above everyone else on the park was the same man who had brought the team together. Isaac McDowell was a giant, 'everywhere and always in the right place', prompting his players and setting a captain's example. The same *Newsletter* correspondent who had written off Ards' chances before the final was generous in his praise after the match, singling out Dickie Corbett for his effort and goalscorer Thomson for his ball-playing ability.

The celebrations in Newtownards on that April night have remained in the

Irish Cup winners, 1951-52
Players: Back row (l-r):
Robinson, O'Connell,
Hamill, Corbett
Middle row (l-r): Lawther,
Thomson, McDowell,
Drake, Walker
Front row (l-r): Tucker,
Moore

memory of all who were there. The Cup was paraded around the town in an open topped lorry, accompanied by the Silver Band, the Dr. Wright Memorial Band and the CLB Flute Band. Crowds five and six deep, chanting 'We like Ike!', a slogan borrowed from the Presidential campaign of President Eisenhower, thronged pavements to cheer the conquering heroes. The *Chronicle* captured the mood thus: 'Newtownards was 'bust' wide open on Saturday night. Wildly cheering, cup-crazy, surging, handshaking gleeful thousands of people gave the Ards team the most tempestuous and joyous welcome ever given any organisation in the town'. It was indeed a defining moment for a provincial club which had rarely achieved high regard in Northern Irish football circles, and brought a surge of pride to many who were not necessarily football fans themselves. Leslie Adams, whose poem gives this book its title, was not at the match. Too young to be allowed to go, he went instead to the Regent Cinema where a Bowery Boys feature was playing shortly before 5 o'clock. Without warning the film ground to a halt and the screen went dark. The usual cat calling, booing and foot-stamping broke out, along with the routine cries, offered more in hope than expectation, of "We want our money back." The darkness was broken as the blank screen lit up, and there, pushed in front of the projector lens, was a scrap of gel bearing the legend, 'Irish Cup final – Ards 1 Glentoran 0'. Pandemonium broke out as the inhabitants of the stalls cheered, bounced on the seats and ran excitedly up and down the aisles. Order was eventually restored, but no one was interested in the film any more. The events in this tale took place over fifty years ago, but Leslie Adams recounts them regularly. And I encourage him to tell the story, just as regularly.

Not unnaturally, optimism was sky-high after the heady triumphs of the second half of the 1951-52 season. All of the key players were retained, and financially Ards received a boost first from their £700 cut from the Cup Final receipts, then in October £1,250 as their share of the pooled Ulster Cup gate money. In that competition, after losing the opening match at Portadown, Ards went six matches without defeat. They drew 2-2 at home to Linfield and won the return fixture 1-0 thanks to a Thomson penalty, but subsequent defeats by Portadown and Distillery kept them well away from the silverware. In the City Cup they got off to a flying start, a draw with Coleraine being followed by three successive wins, and for the crunch fixture against Glentoran nearly 8000 people packed into Castlereagh Park. The 5-1 defeat by the Glens was a bitter disappointment, and it would be another ten matches before Ards recorded their next win, 3-0 against Derry City on Boxing Day. A 2-2 draw at home to Linfield was the best moment in this barren spell, but to modern eyes this match was more notable for being the 17th match Ards had played in the season, yet the first to feature a local referee, Tommy Mitchell of Lurgan. Throughout much of the 1950s and 1960s English referees were regularly flown in to take charge of Irish League matches.

Ards' lack of scoring power was seen as the root of their problems, and although Spike O'Neill found his way on to the team he was not the prolific scorer so badly needed. The major disruption to the team was an injury to Jackie Robinson, which necessitated a cartilage operation, and he was replaced at centre half for the rest of the season by Walter Kane. There seemed little chance of young players graduating from the IIs. Twice in successive months Ards II turned up for a match with only seven players. The first time, at Derry, a full complement was eventually achieved when Derry provided three players and committeeman Rex Cavan gamely joined the fray. To sort out this shambles Hugh Rankin returned to Ards to oversee the reserve team.

The Boxing Day victory over Derry represented something of a turning point in Ards' season. Wins over Portadown and Coleraine followed rapidly, and the team fought out a 1-1 draw with Linfield at home. Ugly scenes followed what many took to be a premature final whistle, and Ards lodged a protest with the Irish League after a pitch invasion and an attempted assault on the referee by some of the Linfield following. But January 1953 is remembered for something much more sombre, as it was in this month that the *Princess Victoria* foundered off the Copeland Islands. Among the dead were Jackie Robinson's brother Ivan, and the local M.P. Sir Walter Smiles, who was a vice-president of Ards F.C.

The team got off to a good start in defence of the Irish Cup, trouncing Distillery 6-2. 4000 spectators saw a hat-trick from Billy Drake, who had struggled for most of the season but was at last finding his true form, two goals from Thomson and one from Walker. Ironically the second round draw brought together Ards and Glentoran, the two finalists from the year before, of course. Ards' form in the weeks before the tie gave little cause for optimism, with yet another slump in progress, but for the second time that season an expectant crowd of 8000 packed the Portaferry Road ground to the rafters to witness a thriller. Ards should have won the match. They put on a scintillating display in the first 45 minutes, but missed a bagful of chances, while in the second half Kane's injury reduced them to 10 men for a good quarter of the game. In the end it was a case of 'so near, yet so far' as Ards lost 5-4. Results in the league were mixed but at the end of the campaign Ards had done well to recover from a poor start to the season to finish 7th for the second year in a row. The team reached the semi-final of the two remaining knockout competitions. After a scoreless draw, a fine 5-1 victory over Ballymena United in the County Antrim Shield, with three goals from O'Neill, put them into the semi-final, while victories over Bangor and Ballymena in the Gold Cup got them to the same stage of that competition as well. But in each case Ards were thwarted by Linfield, losing 2-1 in the Shield, and putting up a brave but eventually futile struggle in the Gold Cup, going to extra time but losing 3-2.

Crowds and expectations had remained high throughout the season, with the football club acting as a focus for community pride. But even the diehards were forced to recognise that too many Ards players were approaching the end of their careers. Clearly McDowell would have to undertake a major rebuilding of the team for the next season. But he was not to do so. To Ards' astonishment and fury McDowell, who had already intimated that he could no longer combine the functions of player and manager, left Ards to take up an offer to manage Linfield Swifts. His contract was not yet up and Ards' protest led to Linfield being fined 50 guineas, but this was small compensation for the loss of such an inspirational manager. Hugh Rankin took over in the short term, but made it clear he was not willing to carry on indefinitely. The team broke up, as Robinson, Bogan and Imrie were all released. The discontented Lawther had already gone to Distillery, and now Billy Drake decided to emigrate to Canada. Rankin's successor, whoever he might be, would clearly have to build a team from the ground up.

SEVEN

Rock 'n' Roll Football
1953-59

When the Ards Management Committee got over their anger at the loss of McDowell, it was time for cool heads as they sought their next supremo. Once again they opted for someone who could both play and manage the team, and they found him in the former Bolton, Blackpool and Brentford inside forward George Eastham. With a record of 250 League games and one English cap, he was certainly experienced, although at the age of 39 it did not seem likely that he could contribute a great deal on the field. This opinion was misguided, Eastham's guile and perception more than making up for his lack of 'legs'. But it was as a manager that George Eastham excelled. Single-minded to the point of obstinacy, he knew the type of player he wanted and the type of football his teams should play. A visionary, he saw that keeping the ball was the most crucial thing in the game. When his teams were criticised, as they often were, for playing possession football across the halfway line he never wavered, but stuck to his belief in what he regarded as the purity of his style.

Recognising the need for new blood, the manager signed centre-forward James Baker from Ballymena, and Tommy Forde, also a centre-forward, from Glenavon, while Ward Fulton, who had played with Ards during the war, was brought back from Bangor. The most exciting newcomer was Eastham's son, also George, who was pitched into the team at the beginning of the season, playing half a dozen matches before he turned 17. But in League terms this was hardly a distinguished season. Mind you, the opening match was sensational. Playing at home to Portadown, Ards found themselves 3-1 down after 74 minutes, but tore the Ports apart in the final stages of the match to win 5-3, with a hat-trick for Baker and two goals for Johnny Thomson. Thereafter the team's results fluctuated, although they proved hard to beat, drawing five out of their ten Ulster Cup group matches, including a defeat of Linfield by 2-1, with goals from Thomson and Joe Hedley. In that match, played in late September, to combat the fading light in the closing stages of the game a white ball was used for the first time in the Irish League. The City Cup campaign was largely unsuccessful, with only three wins recorded, over Derry City, Glenavon and Bangor, where Hedley hit a hat-trick in the 6-2 victory. It was clear that the team desperately needed a centre forward. Baker had been released, and although Tommy Forde was plainly not a natural number 9, Ards persisted with him in that position until the middle of the winter.

The League programme began brightly with a defeat of Crusaders and an away draw at Coleraine, but the team lost five in a row after that, before recovering to win four out of six at the turn of the year. The match against Distillery was settled by a single goal, scored by Forde after only ten seconds. In January Mick O'Connell was injured and Tony Murphy took his place in goals. Generally Murphy played well, but earned the nickname 'Mr. Presents' from the *Chronicle* after the 4-3 defeat by Glenavon. To solve their scoring problems Ards tried Willie McIntosh, signed from Walsall, at centre forward, but his best days had probably been at Preston North End five or six years earlier, when he was capable of scoring a goal in every other game, and at the end of the season he was released. A solitary win against Portadown was all Ards could manage in the League from February onwards, and they only escaped having to apply for re-election by a single point.

Once again Ards had to look to the cup competitions for the real excitement of the season. A comfortable 4-0 win over Carrick Rangers gave them a second round Irish Cup tie at home to Glentoran. Over 6000 watched a match in which Ards were easily defeated 4-0, while in the County Antrim Shield the team got no further than the second round, where they lost to Distillery. The Gold Cup was another matter, however. In the first round Ards won a high scoring game against Cliftonville 5-4, and in the second round went to Linfield and won 2-0. Not only did the two Easthams play, but father and son each scored, the only time this ever happened. At the semi-final stage two goals from Hedley and one from Forde saw Ards defeat Portadown with a scintillating display of soccer. In the final, played at Seaview in front of an attendance of 6000, Ards fell behind to a Johnson goal for Distillery, but in the second half Eastham junior set up Tommy Walker for the equaliser, and it was 'Old' George who belied his years

when with 20 minutes to go he was first on to a through ball to drive home the winner. Ards held on to win, despite Dobbs missing a penalty for the Whites in the very last minute of the match. The Gold Cup became increasingly devalued in later years, but in the 1950s it was still seen as a major achievement, and Ards had become only the third provincial club to win the trophy since 1912. The scenes which followed the Cup victory that night were reminiscent of those of two years earlier, when Ards had brought home the Irish Cup. Joyous crowds thronged the pavements to see the Gold Cup paraded round the town, with the team resplendent in their new green blazers, another Eastham innovation. With their cup triumph Ards' mediocre performances across the season were forgotten in one heady night of triumph.

The Annual General Meeting heard of a £700 loss on the season, with attendances slightly down, and the club had to bid farewell to Dickie Corbett, off to start a new life in Chicago after eleven seasons with Ards. But at least the Committee had got two things right: the appointment of George Eastham as manager would prove to be far-sighted and successful, and at long last, after many years of unkept promises, a shelter was erected on the unreserved side. However slowly, Ards appeared to be moving into an new era.

The winners of the Gold Cup, 1954
Players: (Middle row): Johnston, Hunter, McCafferty, Hamill, Fulton, Tucker
Front row (l-r): Hedley, Forde, Eastham (player/manager), Eastham jr, Walker. Inset: Newberry
At extreme right of back row of committee members: Moore

A number of old faces disappeared from the Ards team in the early part of the 1954-55 season. Michael O'Connell was released, Tommy Hamill lost his place after October, Walter Kane moved to Portadown, and Johnny Thomson was transferred to Ballymena United for a 'very nominal' sum. McCafferty, Hunter and Newberry, who had all broken into the team in the latter stages of the previous season, became fixtures in the defence, while Billy McRory took over on the right wing and Jim Neill led the forward line. The ground itself took on a new appearance, with terracing built on the unreserved side and a 'tubular safety stand' beside the existing stand on the reserved side. The new stand was not a success, its roof blown away in gales in September, and the small number of patrons using it insufficient to meet the costs of its hire. This was a season which saw the mushrooming of the supporters' movement. Supporters' clubs sprang up across the town, with the foundation of the Tower, North End, South End, and Movilla Star clubs, in addition to two clubs in Comber and Killinchy..

The Ulster Cup saw wins over Portadown and Distillery, and a goalless draw against Linfield, but the other two matches were lost. The City Cup campaign was disappointingly unsuccessful. Only two matches were won, and Ards finished up one off the bottom of the table. Defending their Gold Cup, Ards lost by the odd goal in seven away to Crusaders, while the Tate Cup, played on a two-legged basis, ended with an aggregate score of 3-3, and Bangor, as holders from the previous season, retained the trophy. Ards were certainly not hitting the high spots in a season where developments outwith the football club were grabbing all the headlines. After playing the Royal Festival Hall in London South Street girl Ottilie Patterson rocketed to fame as Britain's leading female jazz vocalist, while just over the fence from Castlereagh Park Ards Aerodrome became one end of the Silver City Airways air ferry to Castle Kennedy, near Stranraer. Taking only 17 minutes for the journey, the Bristol 170 planes used by the company could carry up to five passengers and, more surprisingly, three cars.

But these outside events concerned Ards less than their own poor form. They had won only 5 out of their 21 matches up to the beginning of the League campaign, and clearly needed to turn their season around. They started brightly enough with a win against Derry City and draws with Cliftonville and Portadown. In the Portadown game Eastham junior, whose form had already earned him an Irish League cap against Western Command, played a 'blinder', scoring two goals and skimming the bar with a fierce shot to end a mazy run in which he had beaten no less than five defenders. Ards' form really took off in

January, with successive wins over Ballymena United (5-3 after being 1-3 down), Distillery and Crusaders. The team scored eleven goals in those three games, and another six against Coleraine the following month, with Eastham continuing to show his precocious brilliance and Joe Hedley in top goalscoring form. After the Coleraine game Ards were handily placed in 3rd position. Despite the improvement efforts were still being made to strengthen the team, with manager Eastham embarking on a fruitless journey to England. The main problem lay with the difficulty of getting work permits, then compulsory in Northern Ireland for cross-Channel footballers. Perhaps Eastham was right not to get carried away by the run of successes, as the team immediately lost three in a row, including a second round exit from the Irish Cup at the hands of Glenavon. Ards had beaten Bangor in the first round in an amazing match witnessed by 4000 spectators packed into Clandeboye Road. After taking a pounding for most of the first half Ards turned the match on its head, with Forde and Eastham junior the stars as Ards won 4-1, young George scoring a wonder goal when he beat four men, then waltzed around keeper Hinton before planting the ball in the back of the net. It was no wonder that he was chaired off the pitch at the end. A fortnight earlier he had scored a similar goal against Crusaders, on this occasion beating five men and then lobbing the goalkeeper. By this stage of the season he was playing in the inside left position, but earlier in his Ards career, regardless of the number on his back he was used down the right side, despite being left footed, in the manner of Tom Finney at Preston. As he dazzled both defences and crowds through-

Ards' greatest ever inside-forward trio? The formal kickoff versus Leeds United watched by George Eastham sr., John Charles and Young George

out the Irish League it was no surprise that Newcastle United were in the hunt for the youngster.

By the time of the second round of the Cup Ards had a new goalkeeper, former Inter-League and international player Billy Smith, signed from Distillery. A huge Ards travelling support formed part of the 6500 crowd at Mourneview Park, but they were bitterly disappointed by the narrow 1-0 defeat. When Stuart Campbell

went down in the penalty area Ernie Moss was considered to have tripped him, and the resultant penalty was put away by Jimmy Jones. Campbell was a player of impeccable sportsmanship, and would not have gone down deliberately, but many observers felt that he had simply tripped over the ball. Nonetheless the damage was done, and Ards were out of the Cup. Although Jim Neill had scored 14 goals in 20 appearances, he was not considered a success, and was released, as Ards still searched in vain for the centre-forward they needed. The team went on to win five more League matches, the best of them 4-0 and 3-1 wins over Distillery and Glentoran respectively, to finish, in the days when goal difference did not count, equal third, a very decent performance. Humiliation would come, however, in the County Antrim Shield, where they lost to Amateur League side East Belfast.

At the end of the season there appeared to be dissent on the committee. Ards had suffered financially from a 30 percent reduction in their allocation of the Ulster Cup gates, and from having to pay five weeks' extra wages the previous season due to the extended nature of the Gold Cup campaign, while there had been a drop of £750 in gate receipts over the season. Harry Cavan claimed that Ards faced "a struggle for existence in the near future", but William McMillan denied this, claiming "we have nothing to worry about". A more pleasing feature of the end of the season was the appearance of Leeds United at Castlereagh Park. In a friendly played in May the Yorkshire club defeated Ards 8-1, the home team's only goal being scored by Bangor player Johnnie Neilson. John Charles, 'the gentle giant', scored three for the visitors, and was so taken with his welcome (and with the state of the pitch, which always attracted high praise) that he returned to Ards to guest for them in a friendly against Cliftonville played for Tommy Hamill's benefit. This time the big Welshman scored three for Ards. The photograph that shows Ards about to kick off the match with an inside forward trio consisting of the two Easthams flanking John Charles is one to make every Ards fan of the right vintage salivate. If only!

Before the 1955-56 season Ards bade a fond farewell to Tommy Hamill, an outstanding servant whose £300 benefit cheque was richly deserved. Jim Wilson, the Distillery utility player, arrived at the club, where he would play at left-back and later at left-half, and the fair-haired inside forward Archie McQuilken was signed from Larne. But the most significant signing was that of a young amateur who had been on Glentoran's books. This was Billy Humphries, who went straight into the first team, and even today the memory of Humphries playing in the same forward line as Eastham junior is one to make the pulses race. It was indeed a 'classy young Ards forward line', as the *ISN* put it, but the crying need for a goalscoring centre-forward remained, and the team was short of fire-power for all its excellent football.

In the Ulster Cup Ards won two, drew two and lost one of their games. The 5-0 win over fierce 1950s rivals Glenavon was a joy to behold, and the 1-1 draw with Linfield attracted over 7000 to Castlereagh Park. In the City Cup Ards won five and lost six of their games. Although Jim Jordan scored nine goals in this competition he soon lost his place to a new centre-forward. Tony Gildea, who came from Bray Wanderers, was a remarkable figure. The 22 year-old was missing half of one arm, but Tony made up for his disadvantage with battling, physical performances which endeared him to the home crowd. Yet despite Gildea's arrival the League programme got off to a shaky enough start, with only two wins recorded out of the first six matches. Then in the New Year Ards at last hit their stride, chalking up successive wins over Distillery, Ballymena United, Portadown and Crusaders, with fifteen goals scored in those four matches.

The scene appear to be set for a genuine bid for the League, especially when Ards signed Liam Munroe, a Shamrock Rovers player who had been capped for Eire. 'Mousey', so called for his diminutive stature, was a tricky little player with an eye for goal who added real fizz to the Ards forward line. But in practice, despite good wins over Cliftonville and Distillery Ards' bid for the League was stillborn, with a 4-0 win over Portadown the only remaining occasion Ards could claim full points in their last seven matches. Once again it would have to be Cup runs which would be needed to enthral the fans, and enthral them they did.

The Irish Cup would bring Ards and Glenavon into opposition again. The first round match, which drew 5000 to Castlereagh Park, saw Tommy Walker's goal for Ards cancelled out by Chapman. In a fast, action-packed thriller Munroe hit the post in the very last seconds of the game, but with stalemate after 90 minutes it was off to Lurgan for a replay. The following Wednesday witnessed another nail-biter, with 4000 in attendance this time, but for all their efforts neither side could manage a goal. The second replay took place at Grosvenor Park, the first ground in Northern Ireland to install floodlights. So great was the interest, from both the supporters of the two teams involved and neutrals fascinated by the epic nature of the struggle between the two provincial teams, that Grosvenor Park was packed for the game An official attendance of 15,249 witnessed the game, and some reports talked off 'thousands' locked out when the gates were closed before kick-off. The game itself lived up to all expectations, with Ards at last defeating their rivals 4-2. Goals from Jimmy Jones and Wilbur Cush could not daunt an irrepressible Ards team, for whom Walker scored a brace of goals, and Eastham senior and Gildea one each. Word spread throughout Newtownards of the victory, and as the buses and cars returned to the town that night they were greeted by housewives in Church Street cheering and banging their pots and pans for all they were worth. The heady excitement of that evening was as far as it would go, however, for after the first round struggle Ards surrendered tamely to Cliftonville in the second round, and all the Cup dreams were dashed.

The County Antrim Shield was Ards' last hope of silverware that season. They received a bye in the first round, beat Crusaders 3-1 in the second, and overcame Distillery in a replayed semi-final. Ards' opponents in the final would be Linfield, League champions by a distance who, with two previous successes against Ards in Shield finals before the war, appeared to have the Indian sign over the County Down side as regards the competition. Both pundits and bookmakers had written off Ards' chances before the match, but they got off to a tremendous start with an early penalty from Tommy Walker. Linfield equalised through Tommy Dickson in the crucial moments just before half-time, and when the second half began the match appeared to have swung decisively in Linfield's direction. For 20 minutes they overran Ards, piling shot after shot at Smith's goal. But Ards held out, began to come to grips with Linfield in the middle of the park, and got through the period of intense pressure without conceding a goal. In the last quarter of the game they ran riot, scoring three times, with two from Tony Gildea and one from Liam Munroe. It had been a triumph against all the odds, and for the third time in less than five years it was carnival time in Newtownards as the team brought home another trophy. For the record, the team which won was: Smith; Moore, Hunter; Forde, Newberry, Wilson; Munroe, McQuilken, Gildea, Eastham junior and Walker.

With the County Antrim Shield, Conway Square, 1956 Front row (l-r): Tony Gildea, George Eastham jr, Harry Cavan, Rab Newberry, 'Mousey' Munroe

It was increasingly obvious as the season wore on that Ards could not hold young George Eastham much longer. Sought after by Wolves, Arsenal, West Ham, West Brom and Newcastle United, the boy was obviously destined for grander stages than Seaview, Shamrock Park and the Brandywell. Guesting for a Distillery side which beat S K Sturm in January, he had been the outstanding player on the team, but it was his performance against the English League which made his reputation once and for all. The match between the Irish League and the English League was usually more of an exhibition game than a genuine contest. In the long history of the fixture the local men had only won twice, and up against a team containing the likes of Jimmy Armfield, Roger Byrne, Ronnie Clayton, Albert Quixall, Tommy Taylor and Johnny Haynes it was assumed that the Irish players were only there to make up the numbers. But in the Mother Of All Upsets the part-timers of the Irish League won, with goals from Tommy Dickson (2), Syd Weatherup, Jimmy Hill (no, not that one, our one) and Eastham, whose cracking volley crowned a match in which the scribes were unanimous that he was the best player on the park. The bigger the occasion, it seemed, the more this nerveless teenager revelled in his audacious dribbles and body swerves which left defenders helpless in his wake. It was inevitable that he would go on to far greater things, but to this day Ards fans remain proud that 'Young George' first shone in the colours of Red and Blue.

It was one of the great coincidences of football that brought together in the summer of 1956 two men who in their very different ways changed the face of the game. Bill McCracken was the Newcastle and Ireland full-back who had famously been responsible for the change in the offside law in the 1920s. McCracken realised that it was a simple task to thwart the opposition by stepping up and playing the attacking forwards offside when the laws of the game demanded that there should be three players between an attacker and the goal line. So effective was the tactic that in 1925 the law was changed and from henceforth only two defenders were required for a player to remain onside. After his retirement from the playing side McCracken took up scouting, and as chief scout for Newcastle United had watched George Eastham on a number of occasions. His recommendations led to the long-prophesied transfer of young George to the North East club for £9,000. Eastham played 124 games for Newcastle before becoming disillusioned with them and asking to be placed on the transfer list. Newcastle refused, and the Eastham case became a *cause célèbre,* with a High Court action required before the player won his freedom. The abolition of the 'retain and transfer system', the iniquitous practice by which players were bound to a club in spite of their own wishes, was therefore down to George Eastham, supported by the P.F.A, and together with Jimmy Hill's successful challenge to the maximum wage regulations it introduced a new era of freedom of trade for the professional footballer. Eventually transferred to Arsenal, George Eastham played 207 games for the Gunners and was capped 19 times for England, where as an influential midfielder he became what Chris Freddi called 'Alf Ramsey's first playmaker'. Moving to Stoke City in 1966, he played almost 200 games for the Potteries club, crowning his distinguished career with the winning goal in the 1972 League Cup final.

So as he left for Tyneside Ards had to come to terms with the fact that the brilliant young inside forward had gone. In addition, Tony Gildea was released, as was the long serving Tommy Walker, a fine player who over the years had scored many more goals than a winger was entitled to. To fill the gaps manager Eastham went for experience as he built a team for the 1956-57 season. From Blackburn came Bobby Langton, with almost 400 games, 87 goals and 11 England caps behind him. Unfortunately Bobby's youth was also behind him, and although he was influential at times during the season, at the age of 37 he was no longer the player he had been in his pomp. Full-back Jimmy Feeney, whom Eastham had played alongside at Swansea, another player who had seen it all, returned to the club he had been with as a young man. The opening Ulster Cup match saw Ards defeat Derry City 3-2, and there were wins over Crusaders, Glenavon, Portadown and Cliftonville in the competition, in which Ards finished 4th. The team looked promising, and attracted the interest of a widening public: where only two years previously there had been one Ards supporters club there were now nine

The League campaign go off to an amazing start. 3-0 down after only 20 minutes at home to Bangor, Ards recovered to win a sensational match 5-4. There were to be some other excellent results before the end of 1956: Ards did the double over Derry City, held Linfield to a 2-2 draw, put five goals past Ballymena and hammered Distillery 8-1. Bobby Langton had moved inside to allow Jim McDonnell to take over on the left wing, and Liam Munroe was doing the bulk of the goalscoring. (By season's end he had accumulated 37). Nonetheless Ards struggled to find a satisfactory centre-forward. Quee, Jordan, Smith and Lawther were all tried, with Davy Lawther probably the best of them, enormously enthusiastic and indefatigable in his work, but prone to miss too many chances. There were some defeats as well, of course, but far more seriously by November a behind-the-scenes row came into the open. The transfer of players was one of the issues involved, but Hastings McGuinness, a Newtownards man who wrote for the *ISN*, saw it as a battle of wills between Eastham on the one hand, and senior committee members Harry Cavan, Billy MacMillan and J.B. Gordon on the other. McGuinness advised them to count their blessings, get their heads down together and fight for Ards Football Club, and no doubt most of the supporters agreed. But at a special meeting on 28th November, where a number of speakers were howled down in a rowdy atmosphere, and some members walked out in disgust, when the Committee asked for a vote of confidence the motion was lost. Five days later the Management Committee resigned en bloc. There were financial worries as well, which might have been solved when Bury tried to buy Dessie Hunter and Liam Munroe, but Ards' asking price of £10,000 killed off any possible deal. Petrol rationing in the wake of the Suez crisis meant that buses to away matches became impossible to obtain, and gates both home and away began to suffer as well. But at least the boardroom struggle appeared to be resolved in January with a crushing victory for George Eastham, when the manager was offered a new two-year contract.

After the New Year Ards took another point off Linfield, drew 3-3 with Glentoran, and had big wins over Coleraine, Cliftonville and Portadown, to finish the League in a highly satisfactory 4th position. In the Irish Cup a Munroe hat-trick helped demolish Crusaders 4-1, but Ards lost away to Derry City by three clear goals in the next round. In the City Cup the side won four out of their first six games, with Munroe scoring prolifically from his inside-right position. By this stage John Smith had taken over as centre forward, but adopted a deep-lying role in the manner of Don Revie at Manchester City. It was yet another example of Eastham's love of innovative experiment. Earlier in the season he had ordered the groundsman to make a mark halfway along the six-yard line to assist the goalkeepers' positioning, but referee Sam Carswell would not condone this breach of regulations, and insisted the line be eradicated before the game could start. Back in the City Cup, a revenge victory over Derry City, wins over Bangor and champions Glenavon, and an amazing 5-5 draw at Crusaders brought the competition to a conclusion, with Ards finishing third.

The benefit match for Jimmy Moore brought Dublin club Drumcondra to Castlereagh Park. Ards won 8-0, with some help from guest players, notably the legendary Newcastle United centre-forward Jackie Milburn. The great Geordie was nearing the end of his career in England, and perhaps Ards had hoped that because of the George Eastham junior connection he might be persuaded to come to Ulster. Indeed he was, but not to wear the red and blue of Ards, rather the blue shirt of Linfield, with whom he became a free-scoring sensation who drew the crowds wherever he went.

1956-57 had been by any standards a successful one for Ards F.C. Although no trophies had been won, the team had rattled in 128 goals and was playing a brand of football which enthralled fans throughout the League, and not just Newtownards, 'the most soccer minded town in Ulster' *(ISN)*. To win some silverware, and mount a credible challenge to double winners Glenavon, most believed that some fine tuning was all that was needed. But in fact a drastic remodelling of the team was undertaken. Billy Smith, seen quite simply as too old, was replaced by Tommy Moffatt, the exciting young Cliftonville goalkeeper, and Ronnie Diffen was brought in as centre half to replace Rab Newberry. Ralph McGuicken took over at left-back, Jackie Cummings, the future broadcaster, played in front of him at left-half, and in the forward line Hugh Lowry came from Bangor, and veteran George Richardson from Linfield. Hugh Forde, Tommy's brother, was allowed to move to Glenavon, Archie McQuilken to Distillery and Bobby Langton, whose weekly air fares were considered prohibitively expensive, was eventually transferred to Wisbech Town. This was not so much a delicate tinkering, more major surgery, but Eastham had found the magic blend. With one more crucial addition later in the season this team of largely unregarded players would surprise Irish football by winning the League. They would do it dressed in style. The Belfast Ards Supporters Club, based in Willowfield, bought the team a new skip. Gone were the old hoops, and in came a 'continental-style' shirt in red, with blue sleeves and a blue V-neck. Ards bought a new minibus, another relatively novel concept, to transport the team, and the club was the only one in Ulster to boast a dedicated canteen, an idea Harry Cavan had copied from Kilmarnock. The question now was, could Ards match their progress off the field with trophies on it?

The opening Ulster Cup campaign saw them finish on even par, with two wins, two losses and a draw. A Hugh Lowry hat-trick saw Ards ease past Bangor in the first round of the Gold Cup, Ballymena were beaten 5-3 in the next round, but in the semi-final, played in early November, Ards lost 2-1 to Glenavon. Oddly enough, it was only after that defeat that Ards clicked into gear properly. Up to that moment, their City Cup form had been in and out, with only three wins out of their first eight matches in the competition, and there were many complaints that Ards were far too slow. But with wins over Bangor, Crusaders and, best of all, Glenavon, by five goals to two, the side at last hit form. Ronnie Giffen became a regular at pivot to replace Harry Murphy, and Liam Munroe began to find his touch again. 'Mousey', far and away the previous season's leading scorer, had been at first reluctant to re-sign for Ards, missing the entire Ulster Cup campaign, and seemed slow to get into his stride. But by November he was performing in his old style, perhaps due to the fact that he had been allowed to move back to inside forward. Before that he was asked to play at centre-forward, a position Ards were still struggling to fill. In the first half of the season they tried McCaffrey, Lowry, Olohan, Richardson, Jordan and Fulton in the No. 9 position, as well as Munroe, soon to leave the club, of which more later. Before the season was out they would experiment further, with Lawther, McCrory, Coll and Quee. I make that ten players, a remarkable statistic: a team that could not find a centre-forward nonetheless winning the League!

That League opened with a much easier victory over Glentoran than the 1-0 scoreline suggests, but a 4-3 home defeat to Coleraine was disappointing. Happily it proved only a temporary blip, with successive wins over Crusaders, Portadown, Bangor, Glenavon and Derry City taking Ards triumphantly to the top of the League at the New Year. The match against Linfield on the 4th January was, many still feel, the finest game Ards played that season. In front of 12,000 people Ards pulled back a 1-4 deficit, with goals from Lawther and Lowry, and two from George Richardson, to come home with a 4-4 scoreline. An away draw with Ballymena followed, and a slightly unconvincing Irish Cup win over Glentoran II, before Eastham pulled off a masterstroke. Jim McDonnell was a decent enough left winger, but even good teams need strengthening, and when Alex Boyd was made available by Distillery, Ards stepped in and bought him. Boyd scored in his first match, a win at Coleraine where the referee was snowballed, and produced a breathtaking performance in his home debut, when he scored four cracking goals against Glentoran in a 5-1 rout. The Glentoran keeper was helpless as Boyd dribbled round baffled opponents and crashed shots into the back of his net with abandon. *Ireland's Saturday Night* rhapsodised 'What polish, Ards!' Alex Boyd was extravagantly talented, a ball-player supreme, but off the field his life was a mess, and he never fully fulfilled his enormous potential. Nonetheless, he was a crucial ingredient, signed at just the right time for the run-in to the League.

Ards remained undefeated until late March, twice being held to draws by Distillery, but beating Crusaders, Portadown and Bangor until they lost a thrilling match to nearest challengers Glenavon 3-4. But by now some felt that Ards were only a shadow of their earlier selves, and the last stages of the League were nerve-shredding. On April 5th a Davy Lawther goal was enough to beat Derry City, and it was little Lawther again, scoring a hat-trick to defeat Linfield on Easter Tuesday in front of a crowd of 8000. Linfield had by far the bulk of the play, but Ards had the cushion of an early two goal lead, and just after the hour Lawther ran through from the halfway line, shrugging off the challenge of Linfield centre half Hamill to make a mockery of his reputation as one who squandered rather than took chances, and slotted home to secure the points. Two fixtures were left.

Ards with the League trophy in 1958.
Back row (l-r):
Eastham, Giffen,
McGuicken, Moffatt,
Cummings, Forde,
Hunter
Front row (l-r):
Humphries, mascot,
Richardson (capt.),
Lawther, Lowry, Boyd

On 12th April a nervous Ards scraped home 4-3 against bottom of the table Cliftonville, but played with far more confidence at home to Ballymena, winning 3-0 and gaining revenge for their earlier Irish Cup exit at the Showgrounds, where they had lost 1-3 to Alex McCrae's team. Ards' League programme was finished. They had 36 points, but Glenavon, with 34, had a match in hand. That match was at Ballymena, and quite a number of Ards fans made their way north to cheer for Ballymena United that night. The gods smiled on Ards. Ballymena won 3-2 but Ards were the real victors. For the first time the Gibson Cup had come to Newtownards. It was a tremendous achievement, arguably a greater one than that achieved by the four trophy team of 1973-74, in that the 22 match League was probably the hardest contest of all to win. Moffatt, Hunter, McGuicken, Forde, Giffen and Cummings, the regular defence, had provided a solid and often classy platform at the back. Among the forwards Alex Boyd had shone in the latter stages, but Billy Humphries, by now a transfer magnet for a number of teams, had been a revelation throughout this season. At the end of the day Davy Lawther's grit had helped see Ards home, and Hugh Lowry's 30 goals in the season had proved invaluable. Geordie Richardson, the captain, was a phenomenon. He was considered by many to be well past his sell-by date, indeed he was the first player about whom I heard the old joke 'I've seen milk turn quicker', but he made up for his lack of pace with his positioning, his regular goals and an ability to bring the ball down and deliver an accurate and frequently telling pass all in one movement. Richardson's form that season was recognised when he was capped by the Irish League, as were Forde, Humphries and Boyd.

By a happy coincidence Newtownards was already bedecked with flags and bunting for the forthcoming visit of the Queen Mother to lay the foundation stone of the Queen's Hall, when the victory celebrations took place. Thousands turned out (the crowds in Regent Street were six deep) to watch a parade with several bands and the triumphant team bearing the Gibson Cup, which had been officially presented to Ards in the afternoon during Jimmy Tucker's benefit match against Shelbourne. And to cap a joyous season, Ards II, who had already won the George Wilson Cup, went on to top the 'B' Division, winning 15 out of their 19 matches.

But it would not have been Ards if the 'clash of personalities', a euphemism for the animosity between Harry Cavan and George Eastham, resurfaced even at what should have been a time of celebration. Earlier there had been a tug-of-war around Liam Munroe. In the first weeks of the season the Committee were prepared to sell the 23 year-old striker until Eastham stepped in to veto any deal, and a previously hesitant Munroe then made a public statement claiming that he was perfectly happy at Ards. When he regained form in November and December, however, and when Bristol City came in with a very modest bid of £1,500, the little man was sold, presumably against the manager's wishes. And now, at the end of the season, George Eastham wrote a letter to the *Chronicle*, asking why Ards had failed to get a grant of £500 which, he claimed, had been given to every other club. "Why leave Ards out", he protested, "especially when we have IFA member Mr Cavan there to state our case? ... I can only hope that Mr Cavan sees fit to thrust these points home to the IFA". But for the vast majority of Ards supporters, such issues were irrelevant. Regardless of the sniping behind the scenes, the team had performed brilliantly, and Ards at last were top of the tree. Hallelujah!

I can still remember my sense of outrage when the *Spectator* urged us to enjoy Ards' League triumph, because 'it may never happen again'. As a schoolboy I looked forward confidently to further glory for my home town team. It would not happen, of course, but it was not only naive youngsters who must have been taken aback by the precipitous decline in Ards' fortunes. A number of the fringe players were allowed to leave the club, although these men had all played a major part in making Ards II the top team at their level! McCrory was transferred to Derry City for £500, McDonnell went to Crusaders, and Jim Jordan and Ward Fulton to Bangor. Jackie Cummings, a constructive and reliable wing-half, was allowed to join Glenavon. The McCrory transfer, and the way it was carried out, so angered Treasurer David Caughey and Assistant Treasurer David Irvine that they resigned. Manager Eastham refused to comment on the affair, but once again the feuding that was going on beneath the surface had erupted into public view. The major new signing was 34-year-old Norman Lockhart. The Irish international outside-left, who had been playing English football for over a decade, had been targeted by a number of Irish League clubs, and it was considered a feather in Ards' cap to obtain him. Wing-half Davy Fletcher was obtained from Linfield, but on the debit side it was clear that Billy Humphries would not remain in Irish League football for long, with several clubs jostling for his signature. The team started brightly enough, with successive Ulster Cup wins against Bangor, Glenavon and Distillery, but a heavy 6-2 defeat by Linfield kept Ards out of the later stages of the tournament, and a single goal defeat by Cliftonville ended their chances in the Gold Cup.

But until their defence of the Irish League title, Ards were probably less concerned about the early season competitions than their first round tie against Rheims in the European Cup The town was agog at the prospect of competing against a team which had reached the final of the competition in 1956, and which contained seven French internationals, including Jules Fontaine, the leading goalscorer in that summer's World Cup. Competitive European football was still a novelty in Northern Ireland and Ards was only the second club to play in Europe, Glenavon having blazed the trail against Aarhus of Denmark the previous season. Accordingly a huge crowd assembled at Windsor Park for the floodlit match. Officially the attendance was 21,000, but many believe it to have been closer to 30,000. For half an hour the part-timers of Ards, minus the injured George Richardson, more than matched the French champions, but in the end Rheims' class and fitness told, and they won 4-1. Fontaine lived up to his reputation as a goal scorer by banging all four, and Hugh Lowry gained a consolation for Ards in the 86th minute. Malcolm Brodie, the doyen of Irish soccer writers, was full of praise for the Ards performance as he described 'a full blooded fighting display ... with clever football which just failed at the final vital moment in front of goal.... A first-class effort... we can feel proud of them.'

Buoyed by their good performance, Ards won their next two City Cup games, but lost Billy Humphries, the exciting winger transferred to Leeds for £5,000.

His brilliant attacking play would be sorely missed by Ards, not only in the second match against Rheims, but over the whole season. Humphries was not the only Ards player in the news, as Tommy Forde, temporarily playing at centre half, was selected in that position to play for Ireland against Spain.

The party for the European Cup return leg in France consisted of 23 people, and the local press felt that this was an inflated number, given that the cost of the trip would come to over £800 even before the official blazers etc. were purchased, the *Spectator* sneering at what it called a 'spree'. The match itself was played in Paris. Ards lost again, 6-2, with Lawther and Quee the Ards scorers. Film of the match existed once upon a time – I was there when Harry Cavan showed it to a church group – but seems to have disappeared. The Shelbourne game at which the Gibson Cup was handed over was also committed to film, but is also untraceable today.

Even before the match in Paris, the sensational news had broken that George Eastham was on the short list for the Accrington Stanley manager's job. Appointed, despite a contract with Ards which ran to the end of the season, he left to return to his native Lancashire. It was a disappointing end to a managerial career which had made Ards one of the top clubs in Ulster, and he had, unfortunately, chosen badly, as Accrington were in irretrievable decline which would see their financial collapse and disappearance from the Football league within a few seasons.. In the interim Jimmy Tucker, who had been running the reserve team, took over as Ards manager, but he was powerless to turn round the fortunes of the team. After the second Rheims match Ards lost nine in a row, and the signings of the popular Albert Corry from Bangor and George Cupples from Linfield did nothing to improve their fortunes. When a win did come it was in remarkable fashion. Playing at home in mid-December, Ards went 3-0 down to Coleraine within 30 minutes, but fought back superbly to win 5-3. On

The first venture into Europe. An itinerary for the trip to Paris to play Rheims

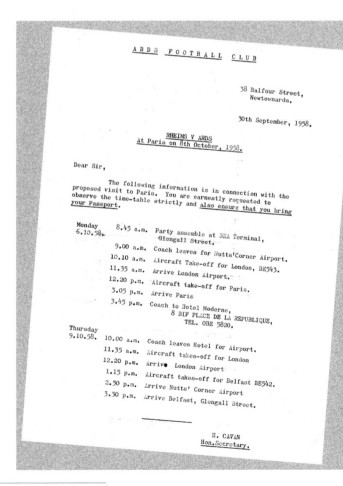

Christmas Day they similarly overcame a two-goal deficit to beat Bangor 3-2. For a fortnight in the New Year it looked as if Ards might have a new manager in the shape of Wally Fielding, an inside forward with Everton for 12 years, but a 'will he, won't he' saga ended when Fielding went to Southport instead.

It was ironic that in the Eastham era, when three trophies were won, Ards had always struggled to find a centre-forward, whereas now, with a greatly weakened team, they found the ideal frontman in Billy Harding, who came from Banbridge Town. Harding not only scored in each of his first eight matches, but found the net at a phenomenal rate, with eighteen goals in those eight games. Inspired by the prolific No. 9, Ards won five League matches in a row, and defeated Bangor in the first round of the Cup. In the second round they travelled to Windsor Park with high hopes, but despite a valiant fight went down 4-2. Nonetheless they won three more League matches before the end of the season, to finish in 7th position. In the County Antrim Shield they walloped Glentoran 4-0, but lost in the semi-final to Bangor.

This season was, of course, an anti-climax, but the European Cup adventure and Harding's amazing goalscoring record at least gave Ards fans some happy memories. It was in this season that the North End Ards Supporters Club inaugurated their Player of the Year award, which went to Tommy Forde, three times capped for Ireland that season. As recriminations about Eastham's departure continued, some felt that a streamlining of the Committee was necessary, with the numbers cut by half. A published response from Mr. C. McManus, the secretary of the Transport ASC, argued that the eighteen man Committee, far from being unwieldy, had moved Ards forward off the field, with two new stands, a new frontage for Castlereagh Park, a new laundry, extra turnstiles and a minibus. The thrust of his positive argument was that Ards was a progressive club, and rather than harking back to the glories of the Eastham era, should be looking ahead for fresh successes.

EIGHT

Graham, Ewing and Neilson
1959-64

Jimmy Tucker had never been seen as anything more than a stop-gap replacement for George Eastham, and he was probably as relieved as anyone when Ards appointed a full-time manager in May 1959. The new boss was Len Graham, capped 14 times for Ireland and a Doncaster Rovers and latterly Torquay United player of many years' standing. Graham preached a youth policy, and jettisoned Richardson, Lockhart, Lawther, Quee and Lowry. Eastham returned to Ireland to take the manager's job at Distillery and lured Jim Conkey to the Belfast club. The club's major new signing was Willie Forsyth, the former Falkirk and Ballymena United inside forward, and the most obvious product of Graham's predilection for young players was the introduction at right-back of 16 year-old John Patterson. There were only two wins in the six team Ulster Cup section, and more disappointingly only two in the City Cup, although one of them was a 2-1 victory over Glentoran. Half way through the City Cup programme Graham caused a minor sensation by importing a Scottish inside forward trio of Murray, Nelson and Kerr, but all three disappointed and the match against Ballymena was the only one they were involved in. The penultimate match in the competition saw Ards concede five goals to Crusaders (nicknamed The Hatchet Men) in an extremely physical game where Ards finished up with nine men on the field of play, having at one stage been down to seven. Finding the net was a problem, in large part due to one of the great mysteries of the late 1950s – the loss of form of Billy Harding. The man who had scored 21 goals in

119

only half a season the year before played a dozen or so games for Ards in 1959-60, but only scored once before disappearing for good.

Youth policies do not, unfortunately, produce winning teams overnight, and in the light of Ards' poor results Len Graham decided to enter the transfer market before the League began. The prize catch was Billy Humphries. Although he had played 25 games for Leeds United he was not happy, feeling that the lack of decent coaching at Leeds was holding him back, and when he decided to return to Ireland Ards snapped him up for £2,000. Also signed were Jimmy Welsh from Third Lanark, and Tommy Ewing, who had spent five seasons at Doncaster where he had played alongside manager Graham. To make way for the newcomers Forsyth, Harding, Fletcher and Fred Patterson, who had not impressed despite early season high hopes, were all placed on the transfer list at nominal fees. For a brief time the spotlight moved on to Ards II, who defeated Crusaders Reserves to reach the final of the Steel and Sons' Cup, but on Christmas morning they were defeated 1-0 by Larne. The team included such rising stars as John Patterson, Billy McCullough and Sammy Hatton as well as the old stager Jimmy Tucker.

A solitary victory over Derry City was Ards' only League success during the remainder of 1959, but in January things began to look up. Tommy Ewing got among the goals, as did Billy McCrory, now returned from Derry, while the defence was held together by the reliable Ronnie Reynolds, recognised by Ireland at amateur international level. Five wins in seven matches saw Ards climb the

Billy Harding

League table, and, favoured with an easy Irish Cup draw, they progressed by beating Dundela 8-0 on a dreadful wintry day, when Alex Boyd tortured the Dundela defence, and Ewing snapped up four goals. In the second round an away fixture to Portadown Reserves resulted in a 4-2 victory, with Ewing scoring a hat-trick. Despite this run of success there was talk of a liquidity crisis at the club, with a letter appealing for financial assistance published in the *Chronicle*. On the field the team's League form subsided again, with only two wins in the last eight matches, but the Cup was another matter. The semi-final paired Ards with Derry City, and in a match described as having 'little cup-tie atmosphere' Ards nonetheless won with a single goal from Ewing. The Cup run at least give some relief to Len Graham, who was having a difficult time both on the pitch and off it. An advertisement in the local press placed by local solicitors Alex. Stewart and Sons offered £25 for information relating to 'scurrilous anonymous letters' which Graham had received. No other details ever appeared in the public arena.

On a happier note the Cup Final attracted 17,000 spectators to the

Oval on a glorious spring day, but Ards' performance did not match the weather. The headlines told the story: 'Letdown for Supporters as Ards are Trounced', and 'Boredom in the Sun as Ards Flop Dismally', as Linfield brushed aside Ards' feeble challenge to win 5-1. The scorer of the Ards goal was Jimmy Welsh. The defeat led to frustration throughout the Ards camp. McCrory, Corry, Cummings, who had returned from Glenavon earlier, and Charlie Hamill, the Scotsman who had taken Cummings' place at left-half late in the season, were all released. Tommy Ewing and Alex Boyd, who despite making up one third of the team's complement of classy players (the others, arguably, were Moffatt, Patterson, Forde and Humphries) were none the less transfer-listed. The Committee was in a dilemma over Graham's own future. He was undoubtedly a good coach, who had taken charge of the Ireland 'B' squad during the season, but he was seen as expensive and had not produced the goods, although one season was a desperately short time in which to expect him to arrest Ards' decline. By nine votes to seven the Management Committee decided to part with Len Graham. Harold Black had voted with the minority. "Ards never had a better manager to work with than Len Graham", he said, "I feel he did not get a proper chance". Graham himself said that his sacking was a 'personal' issue. If so, he was not the first Ards manager to suffer in that respect.

Tommy Ewing in action against Coleraine in the City Cup, November 1961

An aggrieved Len Graham eventually became trainer-coach with Stoke City, and Ards made the decision to replace him with Tommy Ewing, at 25 the youngest manager the club had ever had. But there was no similar reprieve for Alex Boyd, who was transferred to Crusaders. The £100 which changed hands for the player was derisory, given his great talent, but no one ever harnessed it properly again. When Tommy Forde asked for a transfer, the rumour mill anticipated that he was on his way to Bangor as player-manager. Ards asked for £750, Forde appealed, and the IFL reduced the fee to £500. Almost immediately he was selected to play for Ireland against England, which made a laughing stock of the League's reduction in his valuation. Eventually he made up his differences with Ards, and remained to add a touch of class to Ards' midfield for the rest of the season, gaining two further international caps, against Scotland and West Germany. Billy McVea was signed from Glentoran, and £100 brought Mick Lynch from Ballymena United.

Ewing's revamped team showed real improvement on the previous season, and played an exciting brand of football which caught the imagination of the fans. Ards finished third in their section of the Ulster Cup, with only one defeat, against Linfield, and enjoyed a satisfactory City Cup campaign, when their five wins and three draws gave them 5th place. In the Gold Cup Ards again played Linfield, drawing 1-1 at Windsor Park, where there was trouble after the match, but flopped at home, losing 5-3. The squad was strengthened with the signing of Ivan McAuley, a 21 year-old who had spent four seasons at Burnley, and could play either at inside-right or on the extreme wing. Ards were full of goals, with 54 scored by the end of November. The team got seven against Cliftonville, five against Derry City and eight against Coleraine during the City Cup campaign. The strike force of Lynch and Ewing was phenomenal. Ewing was a wonderful header of the ball, and Lynch's thunderbolt shooting soon became the talk of the League.

Michael Anthony Lynch, to give him his full name was, to put it mildly, a man of many parts. He played rugby for Palmerston and St. Mary's, and at one stage coached Wanderers. He played Gaelic football for Cavan, was the

Tommy Ewing, Ralph McGuicken, Billy Humphries, Mick Lynch and Tommy Moffat at North End ASC.

middleweight boxing champion of Connaught, and had played basketball for the Gardai. His sense of fair play had led him to set up a players' union in the Republic, with the assistance of Jimmy Hill, and as an entertainer he had formed a double act with Cecil Sheridan, 'The Rogue with a Brogue', and toured in pantomime with Johnny McEvoy. When the Ards players organised a fund-raising concert at the Queen's Hall, bringing the Cecil Sheridan Show to the town, Lynch's own act brought the house down. On the field he was a larger-than-life character. He wore gloves on cold days, probably the first Irish footballer to do so, and once played for five minutes against Bangor without his boots. A born entertainer, he enjoyed taking the mickey out of crowds, and in those days, when shoulder charging goalkeepers was still allowed, he was the terror of the men in the polo-neck sweaters. Lynch says that when he began his career at Shamrock Rovers, Paddy Coad taught him always to give the goalkeeper a good 'dunt' at the first corner. Even though a free kick might be awarded, at every subsequent corner the goalkeeper would have to divide his concentration between the ball and the attentions of Big Mick. His penalties were something to behold. A stuttering run-up and a feint often sent the goalie diving vainly the wrong way, but it was his shooting power from 18 yards, and even further out, which earned him 40-odd goals in each of two successive seasons, and made him the idol of the terraces. Many observers believed that he should have played international football for the Republic, but he was never selected, perhaps, some felt, because he was playing his football in the north.

The League campaign got off to a flying start, with Billy Humphries, who had been out of sorts for some weeks, back in top form. In the first match Ards dropped a point when they allowed Linfield to score two goals in the last 10 minutes, but then they went on to defeat Cliftonville 6-3, Bangor 6-1, and Derry City 5-1. The Boxing Day match at Glenavon was the most exciting I can ever remember Ards playing. 5000 fans witnessed a thrilling comeback from Ards, who were 3-1 down with 18 minutes to go, but went on to overrun the Lurgan men and snatch a 4-3 victory. Lynch scored two, and Humphries and Ewing supplied the other two goals to send a huge travelling support into raptures. The following day, in front of 6000, a record League attendance for two provincial teams, Ards were held to a 1-1 draw by Ballymena United. (For Alfie Stevenson, making his Ards debut in that match was only part of an eventful week. On Christmas Eve his wife had given birth, on 27th December he played in the top of the table clash with the Braid men, and within two more days he was in hospital with appendicitis.) In the New Year there were defeats against Distillery and Portadown, but otherwise the team kept on winning until the end of February, tucked in just behind Linfield in the race for the League. The return match against Glenavon turned out to be another epic encounter. Ards fell behind twice, and for more than half the game Stevenson was no more than a passenger, but Lynch scored twice in the second half to give Ards a 3-2 victory. Sammy Hatton and Billy McCullough had now progressed from the IIs to become regular fixtures in the half-back line, joined by Vinny Maguire and eventually Jimmy Lowe, two Southern wing halves who exuded class.

Ards' progress in the Cup proved a difficult struggle. After being restricted to a 2-2 draw by Coleraine in the first round, the trip to the North West looked too difficult, but Ards were unfazed by the journey and triumphed 4-1. In the second round a brilliant goal from Billy Humphries equalised Glenavon's effort from Jimmy Jones, but this time an away replay proved a step too far, as Ards lost 4-0.

In April Ards still had a real chance of repeating their League triumph of three years earlier. A defeat away to Glentoran hurt their prospects, but with fixtures against the other main contenders in successive matches Ards' fate was in their own hands. On April 8th they travelled to Portadown, where a combination of a below par performance and the brilliance of Peter Gillespie saw Ards go down to a 3-1 defeat. There had been a very big crowd at Shamrock Park, but the following week Castlereagh Park was absolutely packed for Ards' 'last chance saloon' shootout with Linfield. The gate receipts were a record £774, representing an attendance of around 8000. On the day Ards just did not perform, losing 4-1. Tommy Ewing played only after four injections, was largely a passenger, and finished up in plaster after the game. Wins in the last two games proved irrelevant, and Ards finished in 3rd place, but only a point behind the top two, who had to play off for the title. The absence of the injured Tommy Ewing from crucial games in the run in certainly did not help, but it had been a valiant effort, and the team had played some thrilling football, but their form and possibly their nerve had deserted them at the last minute.

And it had been done economically. Team expenses were down by nearly £2000, and a loss of £4000 had been turned into a small profit. Harold Black, on the other hand, working virtually full-time for Ards as Chairman and talking about giving it up, claimed Ards' best amateurs had been unofficially approached by bigger clubs trying to lure them away with tempting offers. Already Billy McCullough had been snapped up by Glentoran, and it was feared that Hatton and Patterson would soon be on their way also. Ards' response was dramatic. Stating that there seemed little point in running a reserve team only as a nursery for other, bigger clubs, Ards announced that their IIs would cease to exist. Black's plan was for a 16-man squad consisting entirely of professionals.

There was disquiet among some supporters at the abandonment of the second eleven, but in an open letter Harold Black defended the decision, citing the loss of promising young players, first McCullough and now Hatton, who went to Linfield, as reason enough. It would save £1000 a season, he claimed, and there was little point in bringing on the youngsters if Ards were only going to act as a nursery for bigger clubs. No, he said, in the future Ards would have an all-professional first team squad, and there would be no turning back from a decision already made. Financial worries meant that there were no big signings before the 1961-62 season began, but at least Jackie Patterson, the other target for the big boys, re-signed, and Albert Corry and, eventually, Ferris Lunn were both brought in on a trial basis. Some believed that Ards would do a deal with Comber Rec., using the junior club as a IIs by proxy, but Messrs. McCaughey and Thompson, on behalf of the Comber side, denied that anything other than 'cordial relations' would exist between the two clubs. In the days before substitutes one of the main problems of doing without a reserve side was that players not selected for the team could grow rusty with the lack of match practice. The main victim would be reserve keeper Ken Savage, who faced most of a season having to watch rather than play. Not surprisingly he was very unsettled, and after a campaign to secure his release eventually went to Glentoran in February. Ards had now no one to fall back on if Moffatt were injured, except for the redoubtable Mick Lynch, who, it almost goes without saying, claimed goalkeeping as one of the many strings to his bow, having in the past played between the sticks for Bohemians.

There was enormous interest in the opening Ulster Cup fixture, away to Bangor. Under manager Ike McKay the Seasiders had spent heavily, bringing over half a dozen Scots. In the first half of the match they tortured Ards, inspired by John Hume and Willie 'Puskas' Harvey, and went two goals up. But these Scotsmen were mostly veterans, and when their legs went after the break Ards swept them aside, Ewing scoring a hat trick as Ards won 4-2. This was the game when Lynch, having lost a boot a few minutes before half time, threw the other away and played on in sock soles. Unfortunately this was Ards' only win in the Ulster Cup. They lost the remaining four, most notably the home match against Linfield. As a crowd which eventually exceeded 5000 filed in, the gale-force wind, the tail end of Hurricane Debbie, blew a section of corrugated iron from high on the unreserved stand on to the terraces. In a spirit far removed from today's compensation culture, when such an event would have led to cancellation of the match and probable removal of the offending barn, the game went ahead regardless. Ards lost 2-1. As results continued to disappoint there were rumours of rifts within the team, with one story referring to fist fights with the manager in the dressing room. But the City Cup saw a gradual improvement, Ards securing five wins by the end of the competition. The most remarkable of these came on November 25, when Ards went to the Oval and annihilated Glentoran to the tune of 9-1. Lynch scored five that day, and Humphries grabbed a hat trick. The little winger was certainly on song, representing the Irish League against their English and then their Italian counterparts. He was even called into the Irish squad when Billy Bingham was forced to drop out, but did not get a game. Jackie Patterson was also starring, and Albert Corry proved a fine centre-half, although his penchant for dribbling his way out of trouble within his own penalty area sometimes caused palpitations.

Ards hit the ground running as the League campaign began. In the 5-1 defeat of Cliftonville Ewing hit his three goals in the 46th, 47th and 48th minutes, surely the fastest hat trick in Ards' history. Wins over Ballymena and Glenavon saw them enter the holiday games on top of the League. The 2-1 win at Ballymena was soured by events after the match, when police only just managed to hold back a mob which was attempting to storm the dressing-rooms to 'get' Mick Lynch. When the Ards players eventually managed to get away it was with Lynch lying full length on the floor of the minibus to hide him from the view of the hooligans. On the Saturday before Christmas Ards dropped a point after leading Distillery 2-0 with three minutes to go, when Ken Hamilton twice hit the byline before producing devastating crosses from the left wing. Over 4000 saw that game, but this was overshadowed by the 12,000 at Windsor Park on Christmas Day itself. Despite a brace of goals from the old firm of Lynch and Ewing, Ards lost 3-2. Two more wins and two draws, including a super comeback from 2-0 down at Portadown, kept Ards at the top as other results continued to go their way. The Shamrock Park game was an over-physical affair, with some of the blame levelled at referee Mitchell, who was hurt at the end of the game when he was attacked by a Portadown mob. But joint top arguably flattered Ards, and when they lost heavily at Crusaders the pessimists said that this defeat could be seen coming from a long way off. Probably there was too much reliance on Ewing, Lynch and Humphries, and Ferris Lunn and Ivan McAuley were out of sorts, but to be fair to the side it pulled itself together after the Seaview debacle and went on to win five and draw two of the next seven matches, including a 4-1 revenge victory over Crusaders. Tommy Ewing was offered a two year extension to his contract, and accepted.

Sadly this was virtually the last good news of the season. In the Cup Ards welcomed a distinguished spectator in the shape of Labour Deputy Leader George Brown, but even his presence failed to inspire the home team against Coleraine as they went down to two goals from the Bannsiders' Fay Coyle. Successive defeats at the hands of Glenavon and Glentoran seriously weakened Ards' League

prospects, but they were still in with an outside chance on Easter Tuesday, when 8000 fans crammed into the ground to see Ards play Linfield. In an unhappy echo of the crunch fixture the season before, walking wounded Tommy Ewing emerged from hospital only an hour before the game, but despite this Ards were two goals up per Humphries and McAuley when Vinny Maguire disastrously put the ball into his own net, and the Blues went on to win the match 4-2, and eventually the League.

Throughout the season Billy Humphries had been outstanding, and was for the second time in his career the subject of feverish transfer speculation. A further Irish League cap against the League of Ireland and a game for the full international side against Wales increased the interest in the little winger. In March he turned down a move to Coventry City, then Watford came in with a bid of £5000. But in the end Billy moved to Coventry. Manager Jimmy Hill was determined to get his man, and assiduously courted the Humphries family. After Hill brought him over to visit the Third Division club Humphries was persuaded that he should give English football another go, and Ards lost their best player. They did benefit to the tune of £6000, a welcome financial boost after Harold Black had revealed a £2000 overdraft in March despite Ards' big gates. The real

Ards FC 1960-61
Back row (l-r): McAuley,
T. Forde, Lynch, Moffatt,
McGuicken, Maguire,
Hunter, Hatton
Front row (l-r): Humphries,
Ewing, Lowe, McCullough

problem had to be faced. Could the club really support a fully professional side, or would they have to cut their cloth, bring back the IIs and make do with a blend of professional and amateur players?

The exciting Ards team of the early Sixties was said by critics to depend too much on the talents of Tommy Ewing, Mick Lynch and Billy Humphries. The proof, or otherwise of the theory would be put to the test in the 1962-63 season, when all three players left the club. Humphries played over 100 games for Coventry over the next three seasons, scoring 23 goals in the process. From Coventry he would move to South Wales, to appear in 150 games for Swansea Town before returning home. Mick Lynch, who was living in Northern Ireland but could not secure a work permit, went south again, sold to Waterford for a paltry £250. Ewing's position came under pressure as early as June when the committee passed a vote of 'no confidence' in him for his failure to bring new players to the club. In Ewing's defence, he had visited Glenavon's Syd Weatherup no fewer than 15 times before persuading him to join Ards. Jimmy Small, the centre-forward, joined the team from Ballymena United, local boy Ray Whiteside from Crusaders, and ex-Portadown inside forward Harry Robinson from Corby Town. But there were still more gaps appearing in the team. Tommy Moffatt, a dashing figure and an exciting goalkeeper capable of breathtakingly spectacular saves, emigrated to South Africa. He eventually found another club there and Ards received a very satisfactory £1,500. Tommy Forde, a commanding figure at wing-half with over 250 appearances under his belt also left the club. The previous season he had shared a benefit with Dessie Hunter, the biggest event of which was a match at Windsor Park against Wolverhampton Wanderers. A disappointing crowd saw Ards lose 4-1, although Vince Maguire's goal, a 25-yard drive into the roof of the net in the teeth of a gale, even inspired applause from Wolves' goalkeeper Finlayson. The Benefit Fund netted only £200 for each of the long-serving players, and the Irish international Forde moved on to Distillery. To complete this sorry tale of the break-up of what Mick Lynch insists was the happiest squad he had ever been involved with in any sport, Chairman Harold Black finally carried out his long threatened resignation, and Jack McMorran took over.

It came as no surprise that the Ulster Cup campaign was unsuccessful, with only one win, against Bangor, and a draw with Linfield. But halfway through the competition Tommy Ewing was suspended as manager of Ards F.C, the Committee expressing 'grave dissatisfaction with the player manager'. Supporters seem to have been split on the issue, but Ewing was first sacked and then trans-fer-listed, and went to Bangor for £500. Ivan McAuley was the next to leave, although replacements appeared in the shape of goalkeeper Sam Kydd from Portadown, and the return of former goalscoring hero Liam Munroe. But Munroe's best days were past, and in his dozen matches with Ards he scored only once. Ards' troubles became a major talking point in the football pages. Bill Ireland, normally the most sensible of commentators, felt that since neither Ards nor Bangor were 'up to senior standard' they should amalgamate! Some weeks later it was argued by the *ISN* that Ards' troubles all stemmed from their aban-donment of a 2nd XI, and sneered at Ards' reliance on 'other clubs' discards'. But Harry Cavan, by now not only President of the IFA, but a vice-president of FIFA, defended Ards' unwillingness to content themselves with a lowly place in the Irish League food chain in his pithy comment, "Developing talent? What for – somebody else?"

Even without Lynch and Ewing Ards scored 31 goals in their eleven match City Cup campaign. Unfortunately they also conceded 40, and finished near the bottom of the table. The 'goals for' column was boosted by a 7-2 victory over Cliftonville, and a 9-0 thrashing of Bangor, for whom Tommy Ewing's hapless brother played in goals. The League campaign saw Ards lose their first five matches. On Christmas Day Maguire, Munroe and Lowe failed to turn up for the game against Distillery. Staying overnight in Bangor, they claimed their car had broken down. They were reprimanded, and before the end of the season Lowe and Maguire followed Tommy Moffatt to South Africa. A mini-revival began on Boxing Day with a 2-1 victory over Coleraine. Jimmy Small had hit top scoring form, with 'Humpy Sid', as Weatherup was affectionately known, playing well on the left wing. Fred Patterson returned after his spell at Derry City to play at inside forward, but for the rest of the season Ards managed only four more victories, two over Bangor and one each over Glenavon and Cliftonville, to finish the League in 10th position, their lowest since 1951. Since Ewing's sacking a committee had been selecting the team, but in February Hugh Rankin was appointed as a caretaker manager, although Rankin quickly recognised that there could be no quick fix for the club's travails. In the Irish Cup Ards defeated Portadown Reserves, but then lost away to Distillery, and in the County Antrim Shield the embarrassment of a draw against Cliftonville Olympic was redeemed with a 9-2 victory in the replay, but in the ensuing round a 5-3 loss to Crusaders ended Ards' interest in the competition. In the autumn Ards had lost heavily to Shamrock Rovers in the North-South Cup, going down by an embarrassing 2-10 aggregate. Two matches against Crusaders aroused the ire of the supporters late in the season. On Easter Monday, in the County Antrim Shield semi-final Ards finished with only seven fit men after a bruising encounter in which they had led 3-1 until their injuries, and on April 29th, in the last match of the season, Crusaders carried on where they had left off on Easter Monday. Referee Mitchell was unable to control what newspapers of the time tended to call a 'robust' game, in which Ards led 1-0 until recent signing Eric Sterritt was concussed. Crusaders won 2-1, and an angry crowd gathered to hurl abuse and worse at their players after the game.

Ards found themselves in court twice that year. Tommy Ewing lost his case for wrongful dismissal, but Judge Hanna said that his sacking was nonetheless unwarranted. Allegations of Ewing's failure to train properly and about a cashed cheque in the name of his landlady, a Miss McCutcheon, were bandied about during the unsavoury proceedings. In his case Tommy Forde won £170 against Ards. After 10 years with the club, he had asked for a transfer after being dropped for the big clash against Linfield at Easter 1962. Listed at £200, he claimed he was told by Harold Black that any fee received would be added to his benefit fund. Ards denied that such an agreement existed, (the case was clouded by the replacement of Harold Black by Jack McMorran at a crucial time), but Forde was supported by the court and was awarded his claim in full. It was a sour and a sad way to end Tommy Forde's distinguished career at Ards.

Johnny Neilson

The job of reconstructing the Ards team fell to Scotsman Johnny Neilson. Appointed in June 1963, Neilson was a PE instructor who had experience at Aberdeen, Clyde and Bradford City, but was best known from his days at Bangor. Despite Ards' loss of over £1,600 in the previous season Neilsen went for it and signed a trio of Scots: John Walker, George Brown and Jimmy McMillen, but lost gentle giant Albert Corry, who followed the well-beaten trail of Ards players to South Africa. Although Ards only gained three points from their five Ulster Cup games, they had looked good leading Bangor 2-0 in the opening game when Ralph McGuicken was injured and they went down to a 4-2 defeat, but hopes remained high, and in the only win of the campaign, 3-2 over Distillery, the big crowd was described as being 'in ecstasies'. The City Cup campaign was encouraging, with four wins and three draws leaving Ards in 7th position. John Walker was a battling, never say die centre-half, while left-half George Brown, who had played for

Heart of Midlothian, although by no means a ball-winner was constructive and elegant in everything he did. With Bertie Campbell sparkling on the right wing, Ards were beginning to look like a team again. They fought back from 2-0 down to gain a point at Linfield, and put four goals past both Ballymena and Bangor.

When the League campaign began Ards opened with a thrilling 4-3 victory over Derry City. At one stage 3-0 down, the Maiden City team fought back to level the game, but with two minutes to go McMillen scored the winner. The following week saw more excitement, with Ards, 3-0 behind at Ballymena after 25 minutes, fighting back to gain a share of the spoils, Campbell's equaliser coming in the 84th minute. A happy Christmas saw Ards score ten goals without reply in their two matches, and register a victory over Linfield in early January, raising them to 4th in the league. To those who were there, the Linfield match will always be known as Jimmy McMillen's game. The big Stranraer man was a titan, scoring two of Ards' goals and holding up the ball to take the pressure off his defence in heroic fashion as Linfield vainly tried to fight back towards the end of the game. The other scorer that day was Eric Priestley, a former hockey player who scored a couple of goals for Ards, but was considered too slow. Johnny Neilson's efforts received general acclaim, and he was rewarded with a three-year contract, the first ever given to an Ards manager. Unfortunately the new contract coincided with the beginning of a run of thirteen matches without a win, a sequence only alleviated in April when a hat-trick of wins lifted Ards out of the re-election zone towards a mediocre 10th place. Few blamed the defence, which attracted praise all season, but the forwards were generally seen as poor. Best of them was Eric Sterritt, whose 26 goals constituted almost a third of all the goals scored by the side that year.

The most heartening moments of the latter part of the season came in an epic first round Irish Cup encounter with Glentoran. The first match, a thriller, ended 1-1, with Ards' equaliser a gem from 15 year-old Ray Mowat, a local boy who was a product of Earle Hawkins' Ards Boys' stable. The replay at the Oval, played coincidentally on the same day that Cassius Clay defeated Sonny Liston to win the world heavyweight title, produced another draw, this time 2-2. In memory the match was distinguished by the treatment meted out to Bertie Campbell by former Ards' favourite Billy McCullough, now a star of the Oval team, but the last laugh was with Ards, as Campbell scored and McCullough put the ball into his own net to give Ards another chance. But the chance was not taken, and Glentoran, who would win the League that season, eventually showed their class by crushing Ards 4-0 in the second replay.

NINE

Eastham: The Second Term
1964-70

To combat waning interest and to bolster the strike force Ards turned to Mick Lynch again at the beginning of the 1964-65 season. Along with Lynch from Drumcondra came little Ray Keogh. Scottish full-backs Walters and Stevenson joined the club, as did Kenny Coulter and, from Distillery, John Anderson. On their way to Linfield, for a fee of £800, went Bertie Campbell and Jackie Patterson. The chunky full-back, solid and dependable, had gained Youth, Amateur and Inter-League caps while with Ards, and would be difficult to replace. The Ulster Cup was not a success for Ards. A draw, 3-3, against Bangor brought them their only point, but there was hope of better things in the performances of Ray Keogh, an absolute revelation in his first match, where the Distillery crowd rose as one in admiration when the little man went off for the half-time interval. But the City Cup campaign saw more misery, with no victory until late September, in the eleventh match of the season, when Ards hammered Cliftonville 7-1. Eric Sterritt, unhappy at losing his place to Lynch, demanded a move, and soon left for Linfield, but the irony was that Mick Lynch himself did not stay for long. He was criticised for poor form, yet managed six goals in his eight appearances. Lynch himself said he was simply unhappy at the club, finding a very different atmosphere to the one which had prevailed in his glory days, and he moved on to Drogheda. Into the team came Peter Boylan, from Shamrock Rovers, to partner the fiery John Kennedy at full-back. Manager Neilson was coming under increasing pressure, but perversely enough it was in the immediate wake of a fine 5-2 victory over Glenavon that he was sacked. He was asked to resign, but refused to do so, bitter that he had not been given enough time to rebuild the team. Jimmy Tucker took over pro tem, but the team continued to lose, with only three wins in the City Cup and a final placing of 11th.

When a permanent appointee was announced, the new man in the hot seat was once again George Eastham, lured away from Distillery for his second spell in charge at Castlereagh Park. Could he turn base metal into gold in the Sixties just as he had done in the previous decade? Eastham himself said that it would take a good two years, and that everyone would have to show patience. First victim of the new regime was Gordon Shellard, a workmanlike wing-half who felt hard done by, claiming that chairman Harold Black, now back at the helm, had assured him that he was still required by the club. Victories were like gold dust in this miserable season. For the record, Ards defeated Cliftonville twice, Portadown twice, and Glenavon, and that was it. In the Irish Cup they played Glenavon three times before losing 2-0 in a second replay, having gone out to the Lurgan club, again after initially drawing, in the Gold Cup. In the County Antrim Shield the scorers in a 4-2 victory over Cliftonville included a new name, that of 16 year-old Billy McAvoy, who joined Ray Mowat and regular centre half Rowley Houston as local boys on the Ards team. (Houston's grandfather, Charlie Rowley, was the one who had not only played for Ards when they entered a League in 1923, but also scored in the first match against Barn United.) Mowat's form was tremendous that year. He played with a maturity that belied his years, scoring nearly 20 goals, representing Amateur Ireland and the Irish League, and attracting the attentions of Preston manager Jimmy Milne, but when a bid for the youngster's services was finally made, Ards rejected it as inadequate.

Apart from the promise of the young locals, and the hope that Eastham would prove to be a messiah, there was precious little to cheer about that year, when Ards did even worse than the previous season, and were obliged to apply for re-election. And yet there was one incandescent moment from the 1964-65 season that deserves immortality. On January 2nd Ards lost heavily at home to Coleraine, conceding five goals in the process. Ray Keogh, who, when he was good, was very, very good, with trickery that would have graced any stadium, scored Ards' consolation goal. He collected the ball just inside his own half, turned and lost the floundering centre half with one movement, and found himself with a clear run on goal from the halfway line. But there was no need to run. Keogh saw Vic Hunter slightly off his line and chipped the goalkeeper from fully 40 yards. The phrase 'a goal to remember' has become hackneyed, but to those who witnessed it this was a unique piece of effrontery and skill. I remember nothing about the rest of the match, but despite all the intervening years I can still see that goal as if it were yesterday.

1965-66 proved to be another transitional year for Ards. Although results were poor enough, a late season flurry gave some hope for the future, and among the players brought into the team that season were some who would form the backbone of a much more successful side in the future. Jimmy Herron, a right winger with an attitude and an eye for goal joined the club, as did Bangor man Dickie Sands, while Charlie Brown played wing-half regularly during the season, George Russell, an 18-year-old full-back was signed from Motherwell, and Joe Menary came from Portadown. Eastham had long been seeking an old head to control the game in midfield. He failed in his bids to capture Stuart Campbell and Tommy Dickson, so instead turned to Billy Nixon, who had been plying his trade with Shrewsbury Town, but had suffered two leg breaks, in consequence

Ards FC 1965-66
Back row (l-r): Eastham,
Stewart, Kydd, H. Forde,
Kennedy, C. Brown, Mowat
Front row (l-r): Anderson,
Nixon, Menary, Keogh,
Hamilton

of which his career was generally considered to be over at the age of 24. As an inside forward, Nixon was not a great success before Christmas, but when he was moved back to left-half he was a revelation, a superb tackler, but also a supreme midfielder to whom the team looked to turn defence into attack. Hugh Forde returned to Ards after a decade away, but only to play a dozen matches, as it turned out.

The Ulster Cup campaign was mediocre. With only three matches won, Ards finished in 10th position. When the League began in September, they won two out of their first three games before a disappointing draw against Cliftonville. A win against Portadown in early November proved to be the last for a long time, and it was late January before a single goal victory over Distillery gave Ards fans anything further to cheer about. From time to time the team flattered to deceive, with such a moment in the Gold Cup match at Coleraine, where goals by Nixon and Herron gave Ards a fine 2-0 win, inflicting on Coleraine their first home defeat in eight months. But once again Cliftonville put a spoke in Ards' plans, defeating them in the second round, and results continued to disappoint, the blame being placed largely upon an inept forward line. Ards faced a hostile reception at Derry when they played there in early December. Harry Cavan was, in the eyes of Derry City fans, the villain of the piece when the Brandywell was ruled to be unsuitable for European football. At one stage there was a call for a boycott of the match, but in the end there was only a token demonstration, and no signs of ill will in the boardroom. Tactfully, Cavan himself discovered that he had another appointment on the day and could not travel to the North West.

Ards' League finish of 10th was a poor enough effort, but there were still the Irish Cup and the City Cup to come. In the Cup Ards scored a thrilling 3-2 victory over Portadown, with a late winner from Joe Menary galvanising a big crowd which included Conservative MP Reginald Maudling, seen to applaud the winning goal vigorously. Crusaders, however, put an end to all Cup hopes with a 3-1 victory at Castlereagh Park. The City Cup campaign got off to a much better start. Since Mick Lynch's departure the team had never had a really satisfactory centre-forward, and every fresh face only had to score a goal or two to be hailed as 'The Answer'. The latest 'Answer' turned out to be Cecil Newell, a mop-haired striker who came from Glentoran and who made an immediate impact, scoring in each of his first nine matches. An unbeaten run of five matches brought Ards up to third place in the table after Easter, but a single win in the last four saw them slip down the table again. Bangor were defeated in the second round of the County Antrim Shield, but in the semi-final Ards lost to Ballymena. Billy McAvoy, still only 17, was now back in the team, as was a new full-back, George Crothers, who had replaced George Russell. McAvoy, Stewart, Anderson, Sands and Nixon would all join Ray Mowat and Sam Kydd in a more successful team three years down the road. But for the moment, Ards fans, not being clairvoyant, could see not a rosy future, but only a depressing and cloudy present.

The poor season on the pitch was reflected at a doleful 1966 AGM, where a loss of £1,350 was announced. Although gate receipts had risen by almost £1,000, this was due to increased admission charges rather than bigger crowds. Harold Black was critical of the poor response to the club's appeal for funds to buy Castlereagh Park outright, the old lease having expired. He was also unhappy that so few supporters had volunteered to help renovate the new Ards Social Club, to be located in the former Down County Welfare offices at the bottom of Movilla Street. Black held out the threat of Ards having to drop into the 'B' Division, but proposed that a better way forward was to abandon the club's traditional structure, where members elected a Committee, and replace it with a limited company of shareholders and a Board of Directors to run affairs. He found backing from Harry Cavan, who also rang the alarm bells and insisted Ards had to adopt a change of direction. On a cheerier note a carnival held in June produced over £1,000 profit for the club, and would pave the way for other non-football events. On the playing front full-back Jim McGurk soon displaced John Kennedy on the team, but a more interesting signing was that of Joe Elwood, an Irish Under-23 international, from Leyton Orient. Elwood, prematurely bald, looked older than his 26 years, but gave Ards a certain amount of guile and 14 goals from his position out on the left.

1966-67 was a season of two halves. For once Ards got off to a good start, defeating Derry City 5-1, then winning 3-0 at Linfield. As the Ulster Cup progressed they scored four against Bangor, five against Distillery and six against Cliftonville. The penultimate match of the competition, against Glentoran, probably the best team in the country at that time, resulted in a 1-1 draw, with Ards' play described as 'sheer poetry'. The following week witnessed a breathtaking match with Crusaders, although this time Ards finished on the wrong end of a 5-3 score line. But this had been an encouraging beginning, Ards finishing 6th in the table, and Cecil Newell taking up where he had left off the previous season by scoring nine goals in his first eight matches. When the League campaign began Ards won four and drew four of their opening nine matches, holding on to 4th position or thereabouts in the table. The side attracted a great deal of praise for its cultured football, based on a sweeper system which utilised John Anderson at the back, while Ray Mowat was playing well enough to come under the scru-

Only 15 when he made his Ards debut, the incomparable Ray Mowat went on to play a record 671 times for the club.

tiny of Manchester United's Jimmy Murphy. Unhappily the 1-0 win over Coleraine on November 5th was Ards' last until mid-January, and only a couple of victories late in their programme against Derry and Distillery raised them up to 8th position in the league. By that stage Herron and Kennedy had both been transferred to Bangor, and Howard McCurley had joined the club from Portadown. The City Cup saw Ards' slump continue. Only two matches were won, and in a wretched spell they failed to score in six of their eleven matches.

Once again it was clear that if Ards were to gain anything that season, it would have to be via knockout competitions. In the autumn they had defeated Portadown 3-1 in the Gold Cup, earning a semi-final tie against Crusaders. The first match was drawn 1-1, a replay finished 2-2, but in the New Year the Crues at last overcame Ards 4-2. Ards IIs enjoyed a fine run in the Steel and Sons' Cup. Defeating Bangor Reserves 4-0 in the quarter-final, and Chimney Corner 4-2 in the semi, they reached the prestigious Christmas morning final. A crowd of 8000 turned up to see them play Glentoran II, but after centre half Davy Trolan suffered a knee injury which saw him take no further part in the game it was all one-way traffic, and the Oval side ran out 4-0 winners. The IIs team which reached the final was: Miskelly, Gordon, Menary; Lindsay, Trolan, Patton; Sloan, McAvoy, McConnell, Mills and Feeney. Gaining a place in the County Antrim Shield by virtue of having reached the Steel Cup final, the IIs distinguished themselves by managing a first round win, defeating Cliftonville 1-0, with a goal from Colin McConnell.

The Irish Cup match played on February 18th, 1967 was perhaps the most controversial ever played by Ards F.C.. On a filthy day Coleraine took advantage of the gale-force wind and driving rain at their backs to establish a 2-0 lead, with goals from Curley and Halliday, by half-time. But in the second half, with the conditions in their favour, Nixon was pushed forward and Ards laid siege to the Coleraine goal. With the big crowd packed under cover roaring them on, Ards went into the lead with two goals from Mowat and one from Anderson. When Ards scored their third goal, with 14 minutes to go, a number of Coleraine players collapsed, apparently from exposure. Referee Jack Adair, acting within his right to 'suspend (my italics) or terminate the game', called a ten minute break. Ards resumed the field at the end of the ten minutes, but Coleraine refused to come out. They claimed they were acting on their club doctor's advice, and chairman Jack Doherty said his players were already in the bath, and that he believed the referee had said that the game had been abandoned. The match was not completed that afternoon, and the IFA Senior Clubs' Committee ordered the match to be replayed in full. Malcolm Brodie expressed a general feeling of disbelief when he wrote of 'a travesty of natural justice'. Ards were furious, and Harold Black wanted the club to forfeit the tie rather than face the unfairness, as he saw it, of a replay. It took two meetings of the Management Committee before Ards reluctantly decided to play, claiming that they were doing so 'under protest', and that the decision set a 'dangerous precedent'. 'It is (now) possible', read Ards' official statement, 'for a team to ignore the instructions of the referee without fear of disciplinary action being taken'. Harry Cavan resigned from the Senior Clubs' Committee, and Jack Adair, whose report was ignored and who was not called upon to speak to the IFA Committee withdrew from refereeing a Coleraine match on the following Saturday. The replay eventually took place 10 days after the first match, and, almost inevitably, Ards lost 2-0. To this day I can remember the feelings of misery, helplessness and anger as we watched the nightmare scenario unfold. Any faith we had in natural justice was destroyed that bleak Wednesday afternoon.

On the same February day as the Castlereagh Park game ended in confusion the Irish Cup match at Bangor, five miles away, was completed without incident. During the ten minute adjournment in the Ards match five Ards players did not retire to the shelter of the dressing rooms, but chose to keep supple by kicking a ball around in front of the main stand on the reserved side. The referee and linesmen, older and presumably not as fit as the professional footballers, endured the same weather conditions, yet were prepared to complete the match. These are the facts that stick in the mind, and even today, when Ards are playing Coleraine, voices can be heard from some supporters who may have lost their hair and their teeth, but not their memories, politely enquiring as to whether the weather is to the taste of the Coleraine players. Lord knows what they, presumably not as well versed in the ancient quarrel, make of it.

Life has to go on, and Ards made their plans for the future. In February the Social Club opened, and from the start provided a much-needed injection of finance for the club's coffers. An Extraordinary General Meeting of the club was held on 16th May 1967, where by 44 votes to 9 it was decided that Ards should become a limited liability company. 5,000 shares were to be issued at £1 each, the resultant capital providing, it was hoped, for Ards' future financial stability.

George Eastham had always maintained that it would take two years to rebuild the team, and by 1967-68 his prediction looked an accurate one, with Ards making a strong showing in two out of the three league competitions, in addition to reaching a final and a semi-final in the knockouts. There were only a few changes in the Ards team at the beginning of the season. Ronnie McFall came from Dundee United to make the left-back position his own, and Johnny Cochrane, a busy midfielder, was signed from Distillery. Cochrane was one of a trio of diminutive players – the others were John Anderson and Dickie Sands – who worked tirelessly in midfield and whose passing game epitomised the type of football Eastham cultivated. Billy McAvoy became a regular in 1967, and young Warren Feeney, son of the former Ards player Jimmy Feeney, who now was managing the IIs, broke into the team. The Annual General Meeting confirmed the decision taken at the earlier EGM to turn Ards into a limited company, and heard that gates had gone up the previous season by £1,750. Oddly enough, Ards' biggest ever attendance occurred that summer, when 9000 paid their way into a midsummer dusk to dawn pop festival at Castlereagh Park, where the top attraction was the Tremeloes. Fears that serious damage would be done to the playing surface proved unfounded, and the event proved a profitable one for Ards.

The team finished 6th in the Ulster Cup, with a 7-0 victory over Cliftonville, and a 3-2 win over deadly rivals Coleraine as the highlights. Cecil Newell had, however, lost his golden scoring touch, and Ards' lack of punch underlined the perennial quest for a centre-forward of the calibre of Mick Lynch. But there was plenty of promise elsewhere in the team. Billy Nixon was capped against the Scottish League, and in the Gold Cup a Mowat goal saw Ards overcome John Colrain's Glentoran team, undefeated since January of the previous season, and shortly to match the mighty Benfica in two European Cup games before going out on the away goals rule. The victory over Glentoran gave Ards a second round tie against Glenavon, and after a 0-0 draw, Ards won the replay 2-0, McAvoy scoring both goals. The semi-final saw a drawn match again, this time against Derry City, but a Cochrane goal settled the issue in the replay, and Ards were through. The final itself took place at the Oval in late November, but Linfield proved too strong on the night. Goals by McAvoy and Mowat were not enough, and Ards went down to a 3-2 defeat.

The team hit the ground running in the League campaign, winning five out of their opening six fixtures, the only point dropped that in a creditable 1-1 draw away to Linfield. Billy Stewart and Billy Nixon were playing exceptionally in defence and up front McAvoy and Mowat were strutting their precocious stuff and attracting scouts from across Scotland and England. But from mid-November onwards Ards hit a sticky patch, losing six of twelve games, including a

6-1 hammering by eventual champions Glentoran in front of a huge Castlereagh Park crowd. Although some wanted him back, Newell's goals had dried up and he did not regain his place in the team. Instead Ards turned to Scotsman Billy Faulds, who had experience with St. Mirren and had latterly been playing French football with Boulogne. Although Faulds was not a prolific scorer, he held the forward line together better than anyone else that season, and Ards won their last four League games to finish in 4th position. It was generally considered that they could have done much better had they been capable of putting away all the chances created. As a result of the team's improvement George Eastham was offered a new three-year contract. Ards were continuing to plan ahead, with an £18,000 scheme launched to rebuild the pavilion and canteen complex.

Whoever wrote the scripts for the Irish Cup in those days must have had a strongly developed sense of drama, for the first round draw brought together Ards and Coleraine, in a re-run of the infamous match of the previous season, which had left a sense of simmering resentment still keenly felt twelve months on. Coleraine were a fine team in that era, with top-four League finishes every year bar one between 1963 and 1971. Ivan Murray and Bertie Peacock provided their engine room, but Eastham's master tactic was to put Joe Elwood in an unaccustomed man on man marking role to nullify the threat from Peacock. Elwood played what many thought was his best game in an Ards shirt, following Peacock over every inch of the ground. Ards had much the better of the play throughout the game, but with 15 minutes to go and the match still scoreless, Coleraine must have felt that they were on course for a replay. But it did not happen. When McAvoy put Ards into the lead after 75 minutes, the floodgates burst and Ards ran rampant to achieve as glorious a win as Castlereagh Park has ever seen. Warren Feeney scored on 79 minutes, and Joe Elwood on 81. Although Peacock pulled the score back to 1-3 with a penalty, Billy McAvoy scored a fourth goal in the 89th minute to give Ards victory and vengeance all in one. Those last 15 minutes were unbelievable, and I have never seen an Ards crowd show such jubilation. An away trip to Ballyclare in the second round was, by definition, anti-climactic, with a stuttering Ards performance and a 1-0 victory. In the semi-final, however, two goals from Sammy Pavis helped Linfield to a 2-1 victory, and Ards' hopes of the Irish Cup were over for another year.

After the fine wine of the cup it was back to the flat beer of the City Cup, where Ards ran out of ideas, goals and ultimately points, with only two wins recorded in the competition. The side was also involved in two new competitions that year, the first being the Top Four trophy, in which they lost in their first outing to Coleraine. The other was the brainchild of Harold Black. The Blaxnit Cup was the first sponsored football competition in Ireland, and brought together the top clubs from north and south. Ards were drawn at home to Shamrock Rovers, but by that stage of the season they were out of steam. They had already played 55 matches, and had failed to score in their last three City Cup games, so it was no surprise when Rovers give them a footballing lesson and strolled home 3-0.

In the summer of 1968 Ards made their most significant signing for many a year when the 31 year-old Billy Humphries returned from Swansea Town. There were those who believed that Humphries' best years were behind him, but the sheer ability of the little man and a fitness level which belied his age made a mockery of the doubters, and would do for many years yet. There were other new faces in the team as well. At the tail end of the previous season Ards had introduced Don Johnston, signed from Carrick Rangers, at right-half, and he went on to form a full-back partnership with big George Crothers throughout the season. The apparently never-ending search for an effective centre-forward brought the veteran Eamonn Gorman from Portadown, but he was not a success, and Ards had to persist with Billy McAvoy in a position which was not his natural one for much of the season. Ards won four and drew four in the Ulster Cup, finishing 5th. There was a fine 3-2 victory over Glentoran, and in the 3-1 win over Ballymena United there was that unusual event, a Billy Nixon hat-trick. 'Ducky' Johnston received rave reviews for his performances, and was talked of as a transfer target. He stayed with Ards, but a man who did go was the highly promising Warren Feeney, transferred to Linfield, although as the reciprocal part of the deal Ards got the speedy right winger Tommy Shields.

When the League began the team assembled by Eastham almost looked like the finished article, the 'almost' referring specifically to the perennial lack of an orthodox No. 9. But for two glorious months Ards topped the League, winning six and drawing one of their opening seven games. The studied football, so infuriating to many because of its supposed negativity that it led to a demonstration against Eastham after the Gold Cup defeat to Glenavon, now won the plaudits of the crowd as Ards brushed aside all opposition. Billy McAvoy scored a hat-trick in the 5-2 win over Portadown, and the 1-1 away draw to Glentoran saw the young Greyabbey man score yet again. Even the loveable full-back George Crothers got in on the act, with an 18-yard winner against Derry City scored with four minutes to go. A few hiccups came in mid-November. The team lost by three goals to Linfield, an unhappy Gorman returned to Portadown, and Don Johnson was dropped after missing training. To steady the ship Scottish wing-half Alan Bell was brought in, initially on trial, but then on a permanent basis. The team recovered, winning three and drawing three of their next six matches. The 3-3 draw at Coleraine, where the young Ronnie McAteer made his mark with two goals, was described as 'the best match seen for years'. But another 3-3 draw on Christmas Day, this time against lowly Cliftonville, was less impressive, and Ards went into a tailspin, losing four in a row before righting themselves again with a 4-1 victory over Ballymena. At the end of this schizophrenic campaign Ards finished in 5th position. In the City Cup they had victories over Glenavon, Bangor, Portadown and Cliftonville, predictable wins in that their victims had been the bottom four in the league. It might have been thought that this was yet another season where a promising start had fizzled out, but that was not the case. There was still the Irish Cup.

The 'Answer' Ards had craved for so long looked to have been found when Barry Brown, who had plied his trade in the USA as well as with local clubs, was obtained from Ballymena. His signing meant that McAvoy could now play off a striker, instead of foraging for himself up front, although it must be conceded that it did not seem to matter where McAvoy played that season, he seemed to score almost at will. Inevitably the goal that knocked Portadown out in the first round came from McAvoy, and that win brought Ards face-to-face with Crusaders in round two. Stewart, Nixon and Bell kept winning possession for Ards, and Humphries, lying deep, probed the Crusaders defence incisively. When a Brown

Billy McAvoy in the first, drawn game against Distillery in the 1969 Irish Cup Final

header came off the bar in 20 minutes, McAvoy had a simple task to score, and after half-an-hour a Mowat penalty put Ards in the driving seat. The same two each scored again in the second half, and a convincing Ards had won 4-1. By that time the semi-final against Coleraine came round, the third time in successive seasons that these two teams had met in the Irish Cup, McAvoy had already scored 37 goals, but his

winner with eleven minutes to go was arguably the most important he had scored yet. The other heroes on the day for Ards were in the defence, with Billy Nixon outstanding and Sammy Kydd keeping a fine goal. There were less than 4000 at the semi-final, a poor attendance which some put down to the counter-attraction of the Grand National on television.

The final brought together Ards and Distillery. Given that neither of the Big Two were involved, the 17,000 crowd was a very good one, but it was poorly served by a disappointing game on a rock-hard Windsor Park pitch. Neither team ever really looked like scoring, the closest Ards coming being a penalty claim when McAvoy went tumbling in the box under a challenge from Distillery centre half Conlon. If the first game was a disappointment, the replay more than made up for it. For this game Ray Mowat replaced Johnny Cochrane, but the night belonged to Billy McAvoy, whose reputation was immortalised with a classic performance in which he scored all four goals as Ards triumphed 4-2. In a tense first half Distillery took the lead through Gerry McCaffrey, but early in the second McAvoy pounced on a poor Rafferty back-pass to equalise. Ards had it all to do again when Conlon headed home from a corner, but on the hour McAvoy scored after good work by Sands and Humphries. At ninety minutes the teams were still level, and it was down to extra-time. While Jimmy McAlinden gathered his players around him in a huddle, Eastham sat calmly in the stand, still confident in his game plan. After ten minutes of extra time it was still 2-2, but in the

With the Cup, May 1969
Back row (l-r): Eastham,
Bell, Nixon, Crothers, Kydd,
Stewart, Johnston, Shields.
Front row (l-r): Cochrane
Sands, Humphries, McAvoy,
McCoy.

last period of the game McAvoy ran amok, scoring in the 105th and 107th minutes, the last goal a brilliant effort where he collected a pass from Brown, slipped past a lunging defender and swivelled on the ball to crack home. Only the width of the bar prevented Billy Mac gaining a fifth before the final whistle went. It was a breathtaking performance, and fully deserves its place in the folklore of Ards F.C.. But it takes eleven men, or in this case twelve, as substitutes were now allowed, to win a match, and for the sake of posterity the Ards team was: Kydd, Johnston, Crothers, Bell, Stewart, Nixon, Shields, McAvoy, Brown, Humphries and Mowat. Sub: Sands for Shields.

The two matches which constituted the final earned Ards £1,500, and as a reward for the players they went by aeroplane to Limerick for the Blaxnit Cup first round match. I, less impressively, hitch-hiked my way down, and saw Ards lose 2-1. But the Cup triumph had validated Eastham's football, almost painstaking at times, but based upon possession, passing and movement into space. He had at last found the players who could play to his blueprint, and one of them, Billy McAvoy, was honoured as Ulster's 'Footballer of the Year'.

Enoch Powell's famous dictum that all political careers end in failure is also applicable to football managership. Regardless of previous successes, once results begin to go awry, as inevitably they will, the manager usually becomes the sacrificial victim. For the second time in his career at Ards George Eastham would part company with the club when he was dismissed early in 1970, but Ards' form had not slumped to any serious extent, and the team which had won the Irish Cup the previous season looked set fair to push for other trophies in the immediate future. To this day the sacking seems unjust: its causes an enigma.

Despite the Cup success Ards had lost over £2,500 in 1968-69, and hopes that the share issue would be fully subscribed had been cruelly dashed, with less than 2000 of the 5000 on offer actually sold. To be fair, as the troubles gripped the province interest in football was falling away everywhere, and Ards were not the only club to suffer in this climate. The major loss of the close season was that of Raymond Mowat, who was off to Distillery, but in return Ards brought in Jim Burke and Roy Welsh, the latter a long-term Eastham target. The three pre-season friendlies played by Ards were notable for a number of things. First of all, the combined attendance was not far short of 10,000, a heartening total. Second of all, the results were excellent, with a 2-1 victory over Stoke City, a 2-0 win over Mansfield Town and a 2-2 draw with Lincoln City. To be fair, Ards benefited hugely from the temporary return of George Eastham junior, who changed teams to score both goals against Stoke. Lastly, one of the Lincoln scorers was the haunting figure of Alick Jeffrey, the former Doncaster Rovers striker, one of the most promising of his generation, who had tragically broken his leg playing for the England Under-23 team, a break so bad he had been out of the game for seven seasons. Jeffrey squeezed half a dozen more years out of his career, but was never able to fulfil his youthful promise.

When the season proper began Ards' start was ordinary enough, with only two victories in the Ulster Cup, Roy Welsh disappointing in his early games and Billy Nixon tending to get caught in possession too often. Football struggled to carry on as usual against a background of growing civil disorder and anarchy, and the away match to Distillery was postponed until the end of the season, as it turned out, due to Grosvenor Park's proximity to the flashpoint areas. There was even concern that Ards' European Cup Winners' Cup opponents, Roma, might not be prepared to play in Ulster, and at one stage the match looked like being switched to Old Trafford. Thankfully that did not happen, and the Ards-Roma game went ahead at the Oval, albeit with a 5:00 p.m. kick-off on the orders of the authorities. Ards put up a tremendous performance, defending in depth and denying the Italians more than a handful of opportunities. Indeed, it was Ards who should have taken a lead from the first leg, with McAvoy and Crothers both missing good chances. But the most disappointing aspect of the game was the poor crowd. A mere 3000 turned up, and with gate receipts of only £600 Ards were faced with a prospective heavy loss on the tie. An appeal for £2,500 was launched to offset travel expenses, but only a fraction of the sum was actually raised. The half-expected heavy defeat in the Olympic Stadium did not materialise, and Ards put up another brave performance, only going down 3-1, with George Crothers grabbing the Ards goal. Helenio Herrera, the Roma manager, singled out Dickie Sands for praise. In both matches Sands came on as a substi-

The much-loved Geordie Crothers, seen here in action against Coleraine in the infamous 1967 Irish Cup game

tute, worked non-stop and played a major part in preventing the Italian team overrunning Ards in midfield.

Encouraged by the performances in Europe, Ards performed better in their section of the City Cup, defeating Distillery and Portadown, and only losing once, to Linfield. In that match, at Windsor Park, Sammy Pavis took advantage of Billy Nixon's error of judgment, when the big defender, trying to get on with the game, caught a ball that was floating harmlessly away for a goal-kick to Ards. Unfortunately, he caught it before it crossed the goal line, and the result was a penalty to Linfield, from which Pavis scored. With former Ards Boy Davy McCoy now joining McAvoy and McAteer as a regular in the team, full-back Jim McGurk was redundant and was allowed to leave for Portadown, and Alan Bell, whose form had been particularly disappointing after his heroics during the Cup run, was released.

Ards got off to a tremendous start in the League campaign. Driven on by the tireless performances of John Anderson, a player at the peak of his form, the team gained victories over Crusaders and Ballymena United that set them off on a thirteen game undefeated run which kept them at the top of the League right into the New Year. Billy Humphries was in outstanding form, and together with Billy Nixon was chosen to represent the Irish League against the Scottish League. After one of the most impressive performances of this fine run, a 4-0 win over Derry City, Malcolm Brodie commented of Ards' play, "Here is the material of champions!" Ards' biggest home attendance of the season saw them confront Glentoran in January 1970, but goals from McAvoy and McAteer were insufficient to prevent a 3-2 defeat, and the following week the big travelling support was hugely disappointed by a poor performance at Coleraine, where once again the team lost. The rest of the campaign fizzled out, with only two victories in the last seven games. Nonetheless, thanks to their tremendous form in the first half of the League, Ards still managed to finish in third position. Their downfall seemed to be down to that old failing, a lack of punch, but it was also blamed on Humphries' move out to the wing, where he had less opportunity to run the game, and on Jim Burke's frequent need to turn back and to get the ball on to his right foot if he were to deliver a cross from his left wing position. But even a combination of these factors, which, as flaws in the selection of the team, could be blamed on the manager, was surely insufficient to explain Eastham's sacking. The official reason given was some trivial nonsense about Eastham failing to appoint a scout, but clearly there was something more in the background. There were proud, even stubborn men at Ards in those days, and perhaps the irreconcilable differences between Eastham and his enemies could only have had one result. Nevertheless, the timing of the sacking was shocking. The manager had put together a team including Nixon, McCoy, Stewart, Humphries, McAvoy, Johnson, McCoy and McAteer, all excellent players, and at this distance it seems incredible that a mere blip in their form could have led to the manager's downfall. George Eastham deserves to be remembered in Newtownards. He had brought success to the team in both his spells in charge, and put the town on the football map in a way no one else had. His football was ahead of its time: he understood the need to retain the ball, and disdained the hopeful long ball which usually handed possession back to the opposition. The pure football he championed was true to the concept of the 'beautiful game'. We didn't always recognise it at the time, impatient of the tactics, but it needs to be said – Eastham was right and we were wrong.

Fortunately for Ards, despite their cavalier treatment of Eastham, they had a ready-made replacement in Billy Humphries, who would take the squad on to even greater triumphs in years to come as their player-manager. In the short term Billy could do little to turn around Ards' League form, but he did lead them through a marathon County Antrim Shield campaign. It was possible to win the County Antrim Shield by playing as few as three games, assuming a bye in the first round, but Ards in 1970 managed to play nine games in the competition without actually winning the Shield. It took three matches to get past a robust Chimney Corner team, after which Crusaders were comfortably beaten in the second round, 3-0. Ards' finest performance of the second half of the season was the 3-1 semi-final win over Linfield, played at Windsor Park because the authorities refused the use of Cliftonville and tossed a coin to decide which of the two teams should have home advantage. In that semi-final Roy Welsh scored twice and the recalled Frank Gillespie once. The final became a mini-series all on its own. Played against local rivals Bangor, the tie went to four matches before the deadlock was broken. Billy McAvoy, sent off in the victory over Crusaders, was forced to sit out the finals, which finished 1-1 on three successive occasions, before Bangor finally triumphed 3-2 and ended Ards' hopes of silverware for a second successive season.

TEN

Days of Heaven
1970-74

The Treasurer's report for 1969-70 made for gloomy reading. Gate receipts had dropped by nearly £4000, and the European venture had lost £1200, with the club posting an overall loss of £3000 on the season's workings. More welcome news was the signing of Syd Patterson, a full-back also able to play up front if required. Against that, however, the excellent Ronnie McAteer was transferred to Linfield. His loss, coupled with the absence for all but ten games of the injured Billy McAvoy took away the strike force which had contributed over forty goals the previous year. Such a crippling blow would have damaged even a side with money to spend on new players, which clearly Ards had not. Even their one major signing, Patterson, was able to play only seven games before injury kept him out for the next four months.

The home-grown Frank Gillespie took on the mantle of chief goalscorer. His eight goals in the Ulster Cup included a hat-trick in the 5-3 defeat of Portadown, a match in which Ray Mowat marked his welcome return to the club with a debut goal, but that win was one of only three gained in the competition. The final match, against Glentoran, saw the opening of the new £10,000 pavilion, much of the funding coming from the Special Efforts Committee. At the same time Sammy Kydd was rewarded for his years of sterling service to the club. A fine goalkeeper, his Irish Cup medal of 1969 was an apt reward, as he had played in so many mediocre Ards teams in the mid-sixties, but consistently shown fine form, recognised when Glentoran took him to the USA for their famous stint as the Detroit Cougars. His testimonial cheque was thoroughly deserved, but unhappily, on the same evening, the poor man's car was stolen.

Ards competed in the Texaco Cup, but lost 4-1 to Shamrock Rovers in the first round. In the Gold Cup Derry City were beaten 4-1 in round one, but playing midweek matches with afternoon kick-offs was gate receipt poison, and for the second round Ards forfeited home advantage to play under the Oval lights, where they lost 2-1 to Glentoran. The City Cup campaign opened brightly, with victories over Portadown, Glentoran and Crusaders, and a draw against Cliftonville. After those four matches Ards were level top of the competition, alongside Bangor. But a 2-1 defeat at Derry City in a match where they had completely dominated the second half began a slump in form which would see them fail to win any of their last seven matches, finishing 8th in a competition won by Bangor. Ards showed some promise when the Irish League began, defeating Glenavon and Portadown and drawing with Glentoran, Bangor and Crusaders. But the team was chronically short of goals, failing to score in four of the opening seven games, and not surprisingly snapped up the chance to use Barry Brown,

Billy McAvoy

home on leave from the RAF, who played four matches and scored in the 2-1 defeat of Linfield in January. But in the following match a two-goal advantage over Cliftonville was squandered, and a 3-3 draw was the eventual result. Worse was to follow in the Irish Cup. Ards had been drawn away to Chimney Corner and, although the Antrim club gave up home advantage, they still managed to embarrass their hosts by winning 2-0. Only a late surge in the season, which saw Ards win four out of eight, brought them up to the respectable final position of 6th.

The bright spot of the season was provided by Ards II, who progressed to the final of the Intermediate Cup by defeating Glentoran II 4-1, with two goals from Paul Donaldson and two from McAvoy, returning from his long-term injury. In the final Ards drew 1-1 with Chimney Corner, but in the replay Davy Lawther's team did what their senior counterparts could not do, and handsomely defeated Corner 4-1, the goalscorers Rooney, Lindsay, and Porter (2). In early April Ards gave a trial to a League of Ireland player billed as A. N. Other. He turned out to be the Scotsman Tommy Henderson, and made such an impression on the right wing that his transfer from Sligo Rovers was rapidly secured. But when one door opens, another closes, as Sammy Kydd had discovered in the autumn. On this occasion the closed door was a quarrel between Earle Hawkins and Ards, with Hawkins' announcement that Ards Boys would sever their links with the senior club after Ards released seven of the team that had just won the Intermediate Cup. Ards Boys had been a remarkably successful feeder club, and Hawkins took exception when Ards jettisoned so many of his protégés. It was a melancholy end to Billy Humphries' first season in charge.

Cheered by a £770 profit, their first for a number of years, Ards made preparations for what would turn out to be a very successful season. John Anderson went to Glenavon, but in return Ards signed Albert Macklin, and although Frankie Gillespie moved to Portadown, Ards obtained a replacement striker in the former Crusaders centre-forward Danny Hale, signed from Derry City for 'a substantial three-figure fee'. The long-serving Sammy Kydd was controversially released, and in his place came Tom Coburn from Larne. Also joining Ards that season was Davy Graham, a real terrier and one of the unsung heroes of the team for the next few years. The 1960s experiment of doing without a reserve team had been expensive and self-defeating, and under Billy Humphries' guidance Ards now intended tapping into local talent rather than seeking expensive players from other clubs. In the 1930s Ards United, when they folded, had become Ards II, and history repeated itself when Ards Olympic, who played a mere goal kick down the road, merged with Ards to provide a 3rd XI. The disappointments of the previous season had left many supporters disillusioned, and friendlies against Sheffield Wednesday, Greenock Morton and Dunfermline Athletic together produced precisely half the gate receipts of 1970. But the doubters were proved wrong, Ards having their most successful season for a long time, finishing third in the league, and reaching three finals and one semi-final. The key once again seems to have been continuity, with virtually the same team performing week in, week out. Coburn, Patterson, Nixon, McCoy, Humphries, Mowat, Johnston and McAvoy played so regularly that among them all they only missed a couple of dozen games, seven of those due to McAvoy's early-season absence in America.

The Ulster Cup campaign saw Ards finish in a mid-table position, winning five and losing six of their matches, but in the City Cup the team really clicked. In their section Ards beat Portadown, Distillery, Glenavon and Bangor, and drew with Linfield. The value of McAvoy to the team was immense. Without him for most of the previous season, Ards had struggled, but once he returned from the USA, with the tricky Henderson to supply him with plenty of opportunities, Billy scored seven goals in the City Cup. As winners of Section A, Ards went on to the Oval to play Ballymena United. Humphries was unable to play in the final, and an injured Nixon had to go off after 20 minutes. Ards' bad luck did not end there, as McAvoy and Graham both hit the post as the team went down 1-0.

When the Irish League began Ards got off to a winning start against Crusaders, and drew their next match at Coleraine, where the home side fortuitously equalised direct from a corner in the 87th minute. 'Bad light stopped play' is a phrase more usually associated with cricket, but that was what happened at Solitude on 20th November, when with 10 minutes to go and Ards leading 2-0, the visibility became so poor that the game had to be abandoned. The result, however, stood. In their next match Ards were far the better team against Linfield, but only managed a 1-1 draw, and for a time could not recapture their earlier form, winning only one out of their next four games. Billy Stewart, who had lost his centre half position, first to his brother Jim, and then to Davy McCoy, handed Ards a transfer request, claiming, to everyone's surprise, that he had been unhappy at Ards 'for a number of years'. Ards' fortunes rose again in January, with four wins and another draw against Linfield. In the 4-1 win over Distillery, McAvoy scored all Ards' goals, repeating his Cup final feat of two years earlier, and going on to bag another four in the 8-1 trouncing of Cliftonville the following week. But the Troubles overshadowed everything that season, and Henderson's reluctance to travel to the province led to his release. Not that Ards were the only club affected. Distillery were forced to play their home matches at Seaview, and Derry had to up sticks to Coleraine, while crowds everywhere dwindled alarmingly.

Ards' League form continued to be impressive, although on February 12th they lost to Distillery in controversial circumstances. 3-1 down at half-time, they had pulled back to 3-2 and were awarded a penalty. McAvoy's spot kick went through the net, as even Distillery's players conceded, but referee Malcolm Wright refused to give the goal and the Whites went on to win 4-2. But after that Ards won successive matches against Derry City and Glentoran. At this stage in they were in 4th position, but only two points behind leaders Portadown. In a thrilling game against the Ports in late March, Ards won 4-3 in a match where they had been two goals down after only nine minutes, but crucially they lost 4-0 the next week to Crusaders when in joint first, which effectively cost them the League and consigned them to a third place finish. This was a disappointment after hopes had risen so high, but the knockout competitions brought continuing excitement to Castlereagh Park. In the Irish Cup a Mowat goal had seen Ards past Bangor in the first round, and the team were then drawn away to Crusaders. The first match resulted in a 1-1 draw, but in the replay Ards put on a superb performance, winning 3-0 in a match where Crusaders lost the plot when they went two down in 21 minutes and resorted thereafter to rough-house tactics. The semi-final, against Coleraine, again went to two matches. In the first Ards drew 1-1, Mowat again providing the goal, but in the replay they succumbed to a Jennings goal.

In the Gold Cup Ards received a bye in the first round, then trounced Glenavon 5-0 in the second, and handsomely defeated Distillery 4-1 in the semi-final. The final paired Ards with Portadown, and with security worries precluding a Belfast venue, the match was played at Lurgan. In front of a 5000 crowd Davy Graham starred for Ards, but the game finished in a goalless draw. The replay, also at Lurgan, a decision Ards found harsh, to put it mildly, was goalless after 90 minutes. In extra time Vic Fleming put the Ports ahead, Billy McAvoy equalised, but McGowan scored a winner for the Mid-Ulster side and Ards had failed in their gallant bid to bring the Gold Cup home for the first time since 1954. But success would come in the County Antrim Shield. In the second round of the competition Billy Humphries scored a sensational 20-yard winner against Glentoran with only 30 seconds to go. The semi-final, played over two legs against Ballymena United, saw a 2-0 away win for Ards, and a 1-1 draw at Castlereagh Park, so on aggregate Ards won through with something to spare to meet Crusaders in the final. Again the match was played over two legs. At home Ards won comfortably, with goals from McCoy, McCaughtry and Patterson making the away leg a formality. Or so Ards thought. At Seaview too many players had an off day, and Crusaders took a 2-0 lead. Coburn, who had had a fine season, then suffered a dreadful lapse of concentration and let a high ball from Liam Beckett drop over his head and into the net. 3-3 at the end of the two legs, the match now went to penalties, and Coburn made amends by saving Crusaders' fourth penalty, ironically taken by Beckett. McAvoy, Patterson, McCoy, Humphries and Nixon all scored from the spot and Ards had won the Shield.

1971-72 is a season which has been overshadowed by the triumphs which followed two years later, but it should not be undervalued. Although only one trophy was won, Ards had been realistic contenders for every trophy except the Ulster Cup. McAvoy's return to full fitness was crucial, as he was responsible for 39 of the 100 plus goals the team scored. Billy Humphries pulled off two particularly astute moves that year, dropping Mowat back to a more defensive midfield role, and installing McCoy, who had initially been a full-back, at centre half. But when apportioning praise for the resurgence in Ards' fortunes, no one could overlook the contribution on the field of the player-manager himself. Humphries had been in superb form, and was deservedly named by the Northern Ireland Football Writers' Association as their Player of the Year.

The team of 1971-72 was so nearly the finished article that in the close season only minor adjustments were felt necessary. Custodian Tom Coburn was allowed to leave, replaced by West Gillespie, and Russell Peacock was signed from Coleraine. Despite a £700 drop in gate receipts, caused predominantly by the unhappy political climate, Ards recorded a profit of £1,300, largely thanks to £900 as compensation from UEFA for having been forced to play Roma with a late afternoon kick-off.

The new season began with the innovative Carlsberg Cup, in which there was no offside except within 18 yards of the goal line. Ards began with a bang, defeating Ballymena United 6-0 to reach the semi-final. There they beat Bangor 4-1, but lost the final by a 3-0 margin to Portadown, although they might have made more of a fight of it had McAvoy not missed a penalty which would have made the score 2-1. Generous sponsorship meant prize-money of £500 for the runners up, and Ards went on to receive £1000 compensation for the Texaco Cup, which did not include Irish League clubs that year due to the Troubles. The side got off to a tremendous start in the Ulster Cup, winning their first four matches and scoring 18 goals in the process. The 5-0 victory over Derry City was, in retrospect, a melancholy affair, as Derry would drop out of the League in October, and this would be the last time that the two teams would ever meet. On a more cheerful note, Don Johnson was playing superbly at this stage, but it was McAvoy who took the eye, scoring no fewer than 15 goals in his first eight matches. But a surprise defeat at Bangor began a series of four defeats to balance out the four wins, and Ards finished the Ulster Cup in a mid-table position. Davy McCoy was not playing well, and Humphries moved to bolster his squad by signing Maxie Patton from Glenavon. The team was also strengthened when McAvoy and McCoy both signed professional forms, and by the capture of Dennis Guy, the former Glenavon centre-forward. There was, as ever, a crying need for a number 9, and Ards had been forced to utilise a series of unsuited players in that position since the beginning of the season. Guy had a proven track record, but many felt that the Mid-Ulster man was over the hill. The *Chronicle* was aghast that money had been spent on Guy, sneering 'many ... may even say that Ards need their heads examined'. Guy was certainly slow to find his feet in the team, but once he did, he became a regular goal machine. In the short term, however, the performance in the City Cup was nothing to write home about, with only two wins out of their five sectional games.

Ards played their part in creating a little bit of history on November 25th, 1972, when they became the first opponents of Larne, who, as Derry City's last minute replacements, were making their first appearance in the Irish League since 1940. Ards lined up to applaud Larne and their captain, Howard McCurley, on to the field, but there the courtesies ended, and Ards won comfortably by 2-0. Wins over Crusaders and Ballymena followed, and although the team lost at home to Glenavon, they then embarked on a series of successive 1-1 draws over Christmas and the New Year. Gillespie's goalkeeping had been causing some alarm, and he was blamed for two of Glenavon's goals in the 3-1 defeat, on one of those occasions throwing the ball directly to Boyle, then failing to move to cut out his lob. Humphries went public to condemn the barracking that Gillespie received from the crowd, but moved to solve the problem, signing Dennis Matthews from Carrick Rangers. Matthews went straight on to the team, to join the re-signed Tommy Henderson, making a welcome return. After a 3-2 defeat to Glentoran Ards embarked on a successful winning run of six matches, scoring seven against Cliftonville and four against Portadown in a match where their form was described as 'brilliant'. They became 'free to concentrate on the League' after going out of the Cup at the first time of asking to high-flying Crusaders. Placed second in the table with two matches in hand in late March, and with only seven matches to go, Ards looked handily placed to take the League pennant for the first time in fifteen years. But in early April they suffered two grievous blows, with defeats against Linfield and league leaders Crusaders. Both matches were played away from home, but critics at the time said that Ards were far too defensively minded at Crusaders, especially with a team that played so much better going forward. The side recovered from the setbacks, going on to win four of their last five matches, including a last gasp win against Glentoran with an 88th minute McAvoy goal. Ards conceded only one goal in those five games, in a 1-1 draw with Linfield. It had been a titanic effort, but at the end of the day Ards lost the League to Crusaders by a single point. It is, as the proverb has it, no use crying over spilt milk, but the sequence of draws in December and January, and a failure to take numerous chances in the two Linfield matches seem to have cost Ards the title.

The Gold Cup was played in May, and Ards had a good run, defeating Coleraine in round one, and Cliftonville, after two attempts, in the semi-final. The final was played at the Oval against Linfield, but there they lost 3-1. Ards returned a profit of £6,000 over the season, with a major contribution coming from the Social Club. On the field the team had performed very creditably, and to make up for the disappointment of so narrowly losing the League, their second place ensured them a place in the UEFA Cup in the following season.

The 1973-74 season was truly Ards' *annus mirabilis*. Never before had a provincial club won four trophies in a single season. The Ulster Cup, (Ards would have to wait 27 years to win another league competition), the Gold Cup, the All-Ireland Blaxnit Cup, and the Irish Cup-Billy Humphries' team won a string of trophies which eclipsed anything previously achieved by Ards and made them household names in Irish football. Even more praiseworthy was the accomplishment of all this by a squad of a mere 13 players who saw duty in the overwhelming majority of the games that season.

The pre-season Carlsberg Cup provided a foretaste of the glory to come. A 5-0 thrashing of Ballymena, and victories against the Big Two, 4-2 over Glentoran and 3-1 over Linfield, saw Ards make spectacular progress into the final, but they disappointed at Windsor Park, losing 3-0 to Crusaders. Nonetheless, their path to the final was a harbinger of later success, and the astute signings of Dessie Cathcart and the return of former favourite Ronnie McAteer from Linfield provided key links in a winning team. Between them the two newcomers would score 51 goals and provide invaluable support for existing strikers Guy and McAvoy. In the first competition proper of the season, the Ulster Cup, Ards won ten out of their eleven matches, the crucial victory being a 2-0 home win over Linfield, whom they eventually headed by a single point. There were other victories to savour: a 6-0 win over Coleraine, 8-0 over Cliftonville in a match where, due to Don Johnson's late cry off, Ards had to play the first 20 minutes with only 10 men, a 2-0 win at the Oval, and a 4-1 victory over Portadown. Ards only needed a point in their last match at home to Crusaders to clinch the trophy, and with a 1-1 scoreline they achieved it. An anti-climax of sorts, but a thoroughly deserved Ulster Cup for the Castlereagh Park team, who had scored a heady 38 goals in their eleven games, with Ronnie McAteer netting 11 of them, and Billy McAvoy and Dennis Guy 9 each. Denis Matthews played superbly throughout the competition, and 16-year-old left-back Ronnie Cromie looked good enough to attract the attention of a number of English clubs.

In the middle of the euphoric Ulster Cup run Ards achieved what many would see as their greatest triumph of this magnificent season. Entered in the UEFA Cup by virtue of their runners up position in the League the previous year, they were drawn against crack Belgian outfit Standard Liège. The Liège men, unlike a number of teams in the previous two seasons, were undaunted by the Troubles, and had no problems in travelling to the strife-torn province, where their appearance in the centre of Newtownards on an image-building stroll around the shops drew spontaneous and admiring applause from onlookers. But on the Wednesday night in September, when they entered the cauldron that was Castlereagh Park they found that Ards' hospitality had vanished, as the part-timers rocked them with a display of guts and skill that left them reeling. The 5000 crowd was silenced five minutes into the game when Liège centre-forward Bukal scored from eight yards, although some thought he was offside. Ards equalised in an incisive move typical of their football that season when the ball travelled from Mowat to Humphries to Guy and, as the defence was wrong-footed by a dummy run from McAvoy, Guy slid the ball through to Cathcart, who scored. Four minutes later, when Guy was fouled inside the box,

Matthews pulls off a brave save from a Standard Liège forward

McAvoy scored the resultant penalty, but on the half hour the Yugoslav Bukal scored his second to equalise for the Belgians. It remained 2-2 at the break after a breathtaking first half, but many felt that the superior fitness of the full-timers would tell as the match wore on. Nothing of the sort happened, as Ards took the lead in 54 minutes when McAteer scored a disputed penalty after Cathcart went over in the box. Billy McAvoy tells how he went to take the spot kick only to have Ronnie McAteer seize the ball, claiming that the Liège keeper might have got his hand to the first penalty, but that this time he wouldn't see it, let alone get a touch! 3-2 up, and thereafter Ards were comfortable, dominant in midfield, where Mowat and Humphries were outstanding, and sound in defence, where the veteran Billy Nixon was a giant whenever the Belgians attacked. No one realistically expected Ards to hold on when they travelled to Belgium, and this time Liège made no mistakes, winning 5-1, with another four goals for Bukal, but it had been a gritty performance from the local team, whose win at home had kept the Northern Ireland football flag flying.

The City Cup campaign was entertaining enough, with Ards scoring 15 but conceding 16 in their five matches, and unsurprisingly they failed to make further progress. But the Gold Cup was another matter. In round one they trounced Cliftonville 6-1, then drew 1-1 away to Glentoran in the semi-final. Cool heads were required, and Ards kept theirs, winning the penalty shoot-out 5-4 to progress to the final. For that match they once again travelled to the Oval, this time to play Bangor, and with two goals from Dennis Guy, and one each from

Ronnie McAteer and Dessie Cathcart they won 4-1 to take their second trophy in as many months. There was hardly a weak link on the team at this stage of the season, but Maxie Patton, in particular, was superb. His form described as a 'a revelation', Maxie was an excellent utility player, but was to my mind at his best as an attacking full-back, where his long-striding runs up the line panicked opposing defences and thrilled the crowd. Ards' attendances had held up well, not surprising in this of all seasons, but it was a genuine reason to be cheerful given that Irish League crowds in general were collapsing. Before the end of the season a Cliftonville-Glentoran match would attract a £20 gate, and a Distillery-Glentoran match played at Seaview a mere £8.

The League campaign was, frankly, disappointing, with Ards winning only nine matches and finishing in 8th position. Up to the New Year things were not too bad, with three wins, three draws and only one defeat. In that defeat, 4-3 by Crusaders, what looked a perfectly good goal by Ronnie McAteer was rubbed out by referee Smyton with the score at 3-3. But the defence was not playing as well as it had earlier in the season, with too many moments of hesitation as players waited for a colleague to do the needful. In January a slump began, with something of a goal drought and one win in six, and only a partial recovery towards the end of the programme, with five wins out of their last nine games, prevented Ards finishing even lower in the table. But this was not one of those seasons, all too prevalent in the history of Ards, where a bright start was dissipated in a disappointing finale. In the Irish Cup Ards stumbled through the first round, drawing away to the juniors of Ballyclare Comrades before winning the replay 4-2, with a hat-trick from Guy. The second round game against Bangor was a humdinger. The Ards support in the 3500 crowd at Castlereagh Park was sunk in gloom after an hour, when Bangor went 2-0 up, but in a fighting performance Ards scored four times in the final 25 minutes to reach the semi-finals. Their opponents were Glenavon, and after McAvoy had scored twice in three minutes to put Ards in the driving seat after 37 minutes, the result looked cut and dried. But a Hall goal for the Lurgan side took some of the gilt off Ards' tremendous first-half performance, and when the same player equalised 10 minutes into the second half the match could have gone either way. But it was to be Ards' day, a goal from Syd Patterson and a brilliant header from Dennis Guy seeing them safely into the final against Ballymena United.

On a glorious, sunny day in front of 7000 (a bus strike may have done something to limit the crowd) Ards' stars were McCoy, Mowat, Nixon and Guy. The centre forward had said that he would score a goal in every round of the Cup, and after fifteen minutes he made good that promise, three minutes after he had seen a headed effort disallowed by the referee. A Cathcart corner from the right wing was headed back across goal by McAvoy, and there was Guy to nod it over the line. Ards continued to dominate the first half, but failed to add to the scoreline, and with almost an hour gone John Sloan, a replacement for the suspended Paul Kirk, equalised for Ballymena. But eight minutes later McAvoy took a pass from McAteer, raced 35 yards and took the ball round goalkeeper Bobby McKenzie before stroking it into the net. It was a wonderfully cool finish from the striker, although Ballymena vehemently protested that McAvoy was offside. That goal turned out to be the clincher, and a jubilant Ards had won the cup.

Their season was not yet over. Ards were awarded a County Antrim Shield tie against Glentoran II, who would not agree to any of the dates offered them, and found themselves up against Bangor Reserves in the semi-final. They duly won 3-1, but, probably exhausted, failed to take advantage in the final, where they lost 2-1 to Larne. The fourth trophy came in the Blaxnit Cup, where Ards first defeated Finn Harps 3-1, then Drogheda United on penalties after a 3-3 draw. The final brought a repeat of the Irish Cup final, a Windsor Park clash with Ballymena United, and once again Ards triumphed, with goals from Cathcart,

The all-conquering team of 1973-74. Back row (l-r): Patton, Nixon, Matthews, McCoy, Patterson, Tucker. Front row (l-r): Cromie, Cathcart, McAteer, Humphries, McAvoy, Graham, Mowat

McAteer in action against Finn Harps

McAteer and Patterson helping defeat Ballymena 3-1. No one could accuse Ards of failing to provide value for money in that breathtaking season. In 57 matches they scored 149 goals and conceded 97, something close to a 3-2 average. For once, McAvoy, despite his 30 plus goals, was not the leading goalscorer. That honour fell to Dennis Guy, whose 44 goals set a new Ards record in senior football. Shareholders who attended the AGM were greeted with a glass of champagne, and news of a surplus of £1200, half of that coming from the profit on the Liège games. With the four trophies on show it was indeed a happy occasion.

Yet there was a poignant tinge to this year of triumph. Billy Stewart, a linchpin of the defence for so long, had been discontented for some time, and was transferred to Larne, before moving to George Eastham's Glentoran by Christmas. Don Johnston would miss Ards' greatest season, or at least most of it, as he failed to turn up for the Bangor League game in November, and was suspended for four weeks before being offloaded to 'B' Division Carrick Rangers for a reported 'four-figure fee'. With the greatest respect for the Carrickfergus team, Johnston was far too good for that grade of football. Just as talented in attack as in defence, he probably did not take his football seriously enough to fulfil his potential. Never the greatest attender at training, he had missed the first eight matches of the season due to work commitments, and had spent most of September and October as substitute before going AWOL at Bangor. But the greatest loss that season was of Chairman Harold Black, who had given so much time, commitment and hard cash to the club over many years. His fellow directors tried in vain to persuade Harold to stay on, but in late November he called it a day for 'health and business reasons'. George Eastham, who might have been forgiven for being less than enamoured of the man who had sacked him in 1971, was fulsome in his admiration. In a letter written to John Anderson many years after he had parted company with Ards he referred to Sammy Moore and Harold Black as 'two of the most distinguished men I have ever had the pleasure of working with in football'. Generous in every way, Black had been a driving force in building Ards up to the eminent position they now occupied, and one hopes that some part of the new ground will be named after this great servant of Ards F.C.

ELEVEN

After the Sunshine
1974-80

The rain fell steadily on Ards throughout the 1974-75 season. The team won only 14 out of their 45 games that season, and although the prolific McAvoy scored 38 goals his colleagues could only muster another 28 among them. Signs of unease were evident even before the season began, as Ronnie McAteer packed his bags for Crusaders, Cathcart's financial demands set him at loggerheads with the club, and Maxie Patton received a six week suspension for illegally playing summer football. The IFA decided that Billy Humphries, who had been on the Board at Ards since the spring, could not, as a professional player, also serve as a Director. Denis Matthews remained unsigned for a time, but one improvement was that his replacement, Bobby McKenzie, the former Ballymena goalkeeper, found himself playing in front of a new shelter which ran the length of the airport end. A new striker, Ian Hay, arrived from Crusaders, and he scored in the first match, a 2-0 victory over Larne in the Ulster Cup. Although Ards gained a creditable draw at Linfield in the next match, their record in the competition was poor, the only other victories being over Glenavon and Cliftonville. Drawn against PSV Eindhoven in the Cup Winners' Cup, Ards suffered humiliation, losing 10-0 in Holland, where the biggest cheer of the night was reserved for the state of the art Philips' scoreboard, when for the first time it had to display double figures. The home leg, in which McKenzie was the undoubted star of the show, produced a more respectable 1-4 scoreline, but an early kick-off combined with Ards' poor form to attract a mere 1500 to the match. The £2,000 loss on

An Ards team of 1975
Back row (l-r): Gillespie,
Johnston, Miskelly, Nixon,
Crothers, McCoy
Front row (l-r): Humphries,
Mowat, Sands, Cochrane,
Anderson

the tie made this Ards' most ill-starred venture into Europe to date. Only two out of the five City Cup games were won, despite the welcome reappearance of Dessie Cathcart, who had settled his differences with the club. But McCoy was out of form, and Humphries was not dominating midfield in his usual fashion. Even worse, the unsettled Dennis Guy and Maxie Patton, who claimed they had 'travelling difficulties', were transferred to Glenavon. It was a poor deal for Ards, with the two players and an unspecified amount of cash given in return for Jim Hall, the Glenavon centre-forward. Hall played 17 games that season, yet only scored four goals, a wretched return for Ards' investment.

On Christmas Day, by which time Ards had won only a single League game, Billy McAvoy was sent off for disputing a penalty award, which Bangor went on to miss. The match finished 1-1, although Ards thought they had it won when Cathcart scored in 86 minutes, only for Stewart to equalise for the Seasiders three minutes later. McAvoy would later receive a dreadfully harsh four-week suspension for the sending off. By this stage Hay, who had only scored once, had walked out on the club, and Ards' lack of firepower became even more desperate. Billy Nixon had also had a raw deal from the authorities, receiving four weeks' suspension for his sending off against Portadown, despite it being his first dismissal in 17 years! Gates were plummeting as results showed no improvement, the North End ASC bus to a late January game at Crusaders reported as being 'the first for several weeks'. In the Irish Cup, despite two bites at the cherry against Cliftonville, Ards managed to exit the Cup courtesy of a 3-2 defeat at Solitude. In the League they eventually managed to win seven matches, and finished 9th, and although they defeated the amateurs of Lisburn Rangers 5-1 in the County Antrim Shield, they lost in the second round to Bangor.

The losses of Patton, Guy and McAteer were crucial, and it was clear that Ards would have to rebuild if they were to get among the trophies again. A massive deficit of over £5,000 was reported at the end of the season, and Jimmy Tucker decided to retire as trainer. Tucker had trained teams under Eastham, Graham, Neilson and now Humphries. He had won an Irish Cup medal in 1952, and even had a brief spell managing the team. His retirement was a sad affair, but was as nothing compared with the shocking news of the death, at the age of only 46, of George Richardson, Ards' captain when they won the League. That was nearly two decades before: little did any of us realise that the same period of time would have to elapse before any further silverware was draped in Red and Blue.

The losses of the previous season meant that belt-tightening was now the order of the day, but this appeared to be an even more difficult task given a summer decision by the football authorities. The Yom Kippur War and the ensuing oil crisis of 1973 had brought galloping inflation in its wake, and as a result the wages of semi-professional footballers rose by 50% from £6 a week to £9. Ards suffered other pre-season blows in the summer of 1975 as Syd Patterson sought his release from the club and Dessie Cathcart yet again dithered about resigning. He would eventually return, but failed to regain his place on the team. On a brighter note Joe Kinkead, the Former Glenavon goalkeeper, took over the running of the IIs, while Jimmy Todd, dismissed as the Carrick Rangers manager, made a welcome return to his wartime haunts, becoming chief scout and bringing with him the talented and much missed Don Johnston. 'Ducky' would feature regularly in a back four with the promising Tom Ferguson, Davy McCoy and John Flanagan, with the reliable Denis Matthews still behind them in goals.

Billy McAvoy received a well-deserved testimonial, appropriately scoring a hat-trick in a pre-season 3-1 victory over Drogheda United. But McAvoy could not carry the forward line on his own, and after a 3-3 draw against Larne in the opening Ulster Cup fixture the team only managed seven goals in their next eight matches, securing only three wins, over Ballymena United, Distillery and Crusaders in the eleven match City Cup competition. The disappointing Jim Hall was offloaded to Bangor, but with youngsters McCormick, Woods, Watson and Polly now in the team Ards were playing neat football, although they still suffered from a lack of punch in front of goal and tended to fade towards the end of games, something perceived at the time as the result of a lack of stamina on the part of the youngsters. But signs of betterment appeared in the City Cup. In successive games Ards beat Portadown 4-3, shared the points in a thriller with table-topping Bangor, and thrashed Glenavon 5-0, McAvoy scoring five goals in those three games. Although Billy Humphries was now beginning to show his years, and Billy Nixon was now playing more with the IIs than the first team, Alan Larmour was a real powerhouse in midfield, and was voted the Football Writers' Association Player of the Month for November.

Ards' scoring problems were finally addressed with the signing of Tommy Armstrong from Dundalk, and he eventually proved to be McAvoy's best striking partner since Dennis Guy. Thus the League campaign began fairly well, with two wins a and a draw in the opening four games, and even after the Christmas Day defeat at home to Bangor, then top of the League, Ards remained in a respectable 7th position. January 10th, 1976 was a red letter day for Ards, when a McAvoy hat-trick which capped a brilliant Ards display knocked Coleraine off the top of the League. But this splendid win was not followed up, and Ards' inconsistency culminated in a shaming 4-2 defeat to bottom-of-the-table Portadown. Tommy Armstrong's best days in an Ards shirt were yet to come, and the team depended too much for scoring power on Billy McAvoy, whose 30 goals in the season represented nearly half Ards' total. Only three matches were won after January, typically in this season of baffling inconsistency including a 3-2 victory away to high-flying Glentoran.

The knockout competitions brought little joy. In September interest in the Gold Cup ended with the first round defeat at Coleraine, and although Linfield Swifts were defeated in the first round of the County Antrim Shield, Distillery triumphed 1-0 at the next stage to end Ards' hopes. A difficult Irish Cup draw against Linfield produced a fighting Ards performance, when they bossed the first half, scored one goal and had two disallowed, but were too casual after the break and were taken to a replay. The midweek match at Windsor Park was a disaster, with Ards conceding seven goals. To add insult to injury, in the League match at Castlereagh Park nine days later Ards not only lost but could only watch help-lessly as an element of the Linfield support sprayed graffiti all over the new canteen and then attempted to burn it down. There was further late season gloom when Ronnie Cromie and Denis Matthews, neither at that stage able to gain a place on the team, sought transfers. Nonetheless, Ards' final league position of seventh was an improvement of two places on the previous season, and despite disappointing gates the AGM was informed of a profit on the year's workings of well over £4,000. Most of this was thanks to the remarkably successful Golden Goals competition, which had raised a more than healthy £6000. Once again the hard work of those diehard Ards supporters who had cajoled their friends, family and workmates into contributing to the cause had helped saved the day: a story repeated down the years for the Newtownards club.

In the 1976-77 season Old Father Time finally caught up with Billy Humphries, who, it transpired, had played his last match, against Crusaders, the previous March. Billy Nixon continued playing with the IIs, turning out on only a handful of occasions for the first team. Alarm bells briefly rang when Billy McAvoy toyed with the idea of a job in Scotland, but luckily for Ards the prolific scorer decided to stay in Northern Ireland, although his eventual total of 17 goals for the season represented a meagre return by his high standards. Don Johnson once again failed to turn up for training, and was later released, and Denis Matthews was transferred to Glentoran. For a few matches Phil Rafferty took his place in goals, then for the rest of the season Bobby Brown. Billy Kennedy came in from Glentoran, Ronnie Cromie regained his place at left-back, and Frankie McArdle, the former Crusaders man who had come home from Australia in the previous season, continued to play wide on the right.

The season began most promisingly with a 3-1 victory over Ballymena United, a 3-2 win over Crusaders, and, best of all, a single goal triumph against Glentoran, the only blot on this otherwise unblemished record a sensational match where Ards lost 5-3 to Bangor. But this fine start was not maintained, and Ards failed to win any of their seven remaining Ulster Cup games. In their section of the Gold Cup the team drew three but won none of their matches, and with a failure to score in five of their last nine matches before the League began the prospects were not good. A stuttering start saw an away defeat to lowly Ballymena, who thereby gained their first win in 18 matches, but after that Ards defied the doomsayers and hit a run of spectacular form which saw them win five matches in a row, including a fine 3-1 victory over Linfield. The goal scorers in that win included Jimmy Todd's son Brian, just signed from Larne. Todd had played against Ards in the 1974 Irish Cup Final, and his acquisition, together with that of Davy 'Dee' Graham from Linfield, give an impetus to the side which saw them in go into the New Year sitting on top of the League. But a 3-0 defeat to Glentoran began a barren patch where Ards won only one of their next six matches as the forwards ran out of goals. Only three more victories followed in the League campaign, and the team ended miserably with a run of five defeats in a row, to finish 7th. The Irish Cup campaign saw an epic first round series of matches against Bangor, with the first two drawn. In the first replay, although Ards had Flanagan and McAvoy sent off in the 65th minutes, the nine men went on to dominate the rest of the match, but could not find the net. The third match was played at Windsor Park, and this time Ards made no mistake, defeating the Seasiders 3-1. But in the second round, drawn at home to Linfield, they were humiliated 6-0 in front of a huge crowd. Many considered that the more physical Brian Todd, dropped that day, should have played against the Blues, but it is hard to see how his presence could have made much of a difference in such a one-sided game.

What little success there was that year came from Ards II, who reached the Steel and Sons' Cup Final via a 2-1 semi-final victory over Albert Foundry. But in the final it was Brantwood who triumphed by 2-0, and despite gate receipts of £1,200 there were complaints of a lack of atmosphere at this match. The team which represented Ards on Christmas Day was; A. Wright; Gibson, Houston; Mowat, Greer, R Walker; McGuicken, Keyes, Sheppard, McCormick and Eastwood. The substitute was McCartney. Entered into the County Antrim Shield as a result of their Steel and Sons' Cup exploits, the IIs defeated Ballymena United 2-1, with goals from Welsh and McDermott, but there the heroics ended when they lost 5-2 to Larne in the next round.

There were other achievements on and off the field that season. Both Billy Nixon and Ray Mowat played their five hundredth matches for Ards, and McAvoy's brace of goals against Bangor in the Cup brought him to the 300 mark, achieved in less than 400 games. Harry Cavan was awarded the OBE, and Billy Nixon appointed Chairman of the P F A. On the debit side Ards played with indiscipline all year, with far too many sendings-off, two each in the cases of Graham and, out of character, McAvoy. Despite the presence of McAvoy, Todd and Tommy Armstrong, the last eventually voted Ards Player of the Year, there was a lack of punch about the team. In late November a 'clear the air' meeting was held between the directors and representatives of the various supporters' clubs. The poor performances, especially the lack of goals, and a lack of liaison between the club and their supporters saw some full and frank exchanges, as they were euphemistically described, but eventually the meeting passed a vote of confidence in the Board. Yet again this season ended on a sad note for reasons other than those of football, when Laurence Sheppard, only 17, who had played in the Steel and Sons' Cup Final, was killed in a car-crash.

Throughout the 1970s football had been taking place against the grim background of the Troubles, and the general breakdown in law and order was now working its way into football. Despite a general decline in the numbers attending Irish League matches, (crowds were described in the local press as 'dreadful' and 'a mere handful'), enough hooligans turned up to make this a troubled season for the Castlereagh Park club. During a 1-1 draw with Portadown in early October a pitch invasion by Portadown fans was serious enough to lead the referee to threaten an abandonment; later in the month, after they had seen their team lose to Ards some Glentoran fans rampaged through the town and broke a number of windows; the club seemed powerless to prevent young rowdies moving from the unreserved to the reserved section of the ground; in November two Ards fans were jailed after abusing Alan Gracey, a black Glenavon player; in February seats were ripped out in the stand during a Linfield game; and to end this sorry story there were

Roy Walker

a number of arrests in the March game against Portadown, when serious damage was also done to the stand at the Airport End. The town of Newtownards also suffered in these grim times, with the burning down of the Town and Country Inn and the Regent Cinema, which had been entertaining locals since 1938.

But this was also a season when Ards made strenuous efforts to cope with the new financial stringencies. Before the season began the Special Efforts Committee handed over perimeter advertising hoardings to the club, and at a cost of £80,000 a new Social Club was opened within Castlereagh Park. At the time this appeared to be a sensible move towards rationalisation, but the new club was never as successful as the more centrally located Movilla Street premises which had served Ards well for nearly a decade. On the field manager Humphries made strenuous efforts to cut costs as well, fielding a team consisting predominantly of youngsters who had come through the club's junior ranks. Martin Halliday in goals, George Gibson, Roy Walker, Steve Allen, Frankie Houston and Russell Welsh played regularly in the 1977-78 season alongside longer-serving players like Ray Mowat, Davy McCoy and Ronnie Cromie, all of whom had begun their senior footballing careers with Ards. The home-grown talent certainly made up for the loss of Brian Todd and Frank McArdle, who had both moved on, but their departures

Ards FC 1978-79
Back row (l-r): Graham, Armstrong, Halliday, Cromie, Houston, McCoy, Rollins.
Front row (l-r): Allen, Walker, Welsh, Mowat, Gibson

were small potatoes beside the sensational loss of a discontented Billy McAvoy, who moved to Ballymena United in October. There are many who contend that he was the finest striker to pull on an Ards shirt. Although not especially tall he timed his jumps superbly, and he had the knack, crucial among the best goalscorers, of finding space just at the right moment to cause maximum discomfort to a defence. Some, perhaps reasonably, felt he was irreplaceable, but cometh the hour, cometh the man, the man in this case being Tommy Armstrong, who valiantly tried to take the place of Ards' most natural goalscorer since the war. Tommy hit 32 goals in this season, only one less than the League's leading goalscorer, Warren Feeney, himself a former Ards player. Armstrong's exploits even saw him called up to the Northern Ireland squad for the end of season home internationals, although disappointingly he was never selected to play.

In the opening competition of the season, the Ulster Cup, Ards finished 8th. They won four matches, including a defeat of Glentoran, but perhaps their best result was the 3-3 draw with Ballymena United, given that they were 3-0 down at half-time, before goals from Gibson, Welsh and Houston earned them a share of the spoils. In their Gold Cup section Ards at least proved hard to beat, drawing three but winning none of their five matches. When the League proper began in late November they got off to no more than a modest start, winning only two of the seven matches played before the turn of the year. In January Ards signed

George Falloon from Ballyclare Comrades in an attempt to add some punch to the attack. The 23 year-old usually played wide on the right, although many felt he was a better performer in midfield. Despite the new signing there was little improvement in results until March, when a late flurry brought successive victories over Portadown, Bangor and Crusaders, a draw at home to Glentoran and a final victory over Coleraine. Tommy Armstrong's contribution to this late run was immense, as in the last 19 matches of the season he scored 21 goals. Right-back Tom Kennedy was steady throughout the season, his consistently good form bringing him selection for the Northern Ireland Under-21 team to play against the Republic. Ards' final League position of 7th was respectable enough, given the inexperience of many of the players. But the team disappointed in both knockout competitions, and even before the end of the season there were changes at the top. Billy Humphries was moved upstairs to become Secretary-Manager of Ards F.C. and of Ards Football Sports and Social Club. Joe Kinkead was put in charge of the first team, and the long-serving Billy Nixon took over the IIs. It remained to be seen if the new management team could lift Ards from the mid-table mediocrity which had remained their lot since the heady days of the four trophies.

At the beginning of the 1978-79 season the new regime, under the chairmanship of Willie McCully, tried to deal with the hooligan problem by banning the carrying of flagpoles, often used as weapons, into the ground, but although there was thankfully no repetition of the violence of the previous season, pitch invasions, usually celebratory rather than threatening, continued to plague the club. On a more positive note January would see the first sponsorship of an Ards match, the League game against Coleraine attracting the support of Isaac C. Reid and Co. But on the playing side there were early season grumbles that Ards had failed to buy another striker to support Tommy Armstrong, and with the exception of Joe Keyes, brought into the team to replace Armstrong during his four-match suspension, and defender Harry Greer, the team remained much the same as it had been the year before.

Despite the encouragement of a pre-season victory over Crewe Alexandra Ards got off to a poor start, with only one win, over Bangor, in the first 17 matches. But statistics can be deceptive, for nine of the 17 were in fact drawn, including the Ulster Cup matches against Glentoran and Coleraine, the latter after Ards had fought back from two goals down. For a team which finished second bottom of the Ulster Cup table it was remarkable that Ards could provide no less than three players to represent the Irish League against the Scottish League: Tom Kennedy, Ronnie Cromie and Tommy Armstrong. Ray Mowat, a veteran in terms of experience if not years, was in outstanding form all this season. Ards' main problems were that they dominated many games, but still lacked scoring power, and were prone to concede crucial late goals. But whatever the retrospective gloss we can now put on Ards' poor start, at the time supporters were disillusioned, and attendances continued to plummet. Even an attractive friendly against NASL team Tulsa Roughnecks (yet another draw!) failed to attract a decent attendance, and by October the North End Supporters' Club was expressing doubts as to whether it could continue to provide buses to away games.

But after the frustrations of the early months Ards' season was about to turn round in spectacular fashion. When the League proper began on November 25th, the team fought out a thrilling 4-4 draw with Glentoran and went through December undefeated, with victories over Linfield, Portadown, Cliftonville, Bangor and Distillery. In the Glentoran match Ards went two goals up in 12 minutes thanks to a brace from Russell Welsh, but in the second half found themselves 4-3 down, with George Gibson sent off after an incident with former Ards player Barry Brown, but the ten men fought back to equalise through Tommy Armstrong. What brought about this astonishing winter upsurge in the team's fortunes? Credit must go to the Ards board and to Joe Kinkead, named Manager of the Month for December. Recognising that Ards' lack of punch was a major problem, the club had signed two forwards: Gary Reid from Linfield and Lawrence Kennedy from Distillery, with George Falloon going to the Whites as part of the deal. In seven matches during their unbeaten run Ards scored 22 goals, with six coming from Reid and five from Patterson. The other key factor was the signing of Billy Irwin, taken on loan over the Christmas period from Washington Diplomats. Replacing Frank McKenna, the former Bangor goalkeeper showed tremendous form, the shame being that he was only a short-term stop-gap. The upshot of this fine sequence was that Ards entered 1979 on top of the Irish League, not bad for a team which had won only once before December!

But the impetus was lost a in a dreadful January, when heavy snow around the New Year, followed by weeks of frost, led to the postponement of no fewer than five matches during the month. When hostilities resumed, after a draw against Coleraine, Ards struggled to find their pre-Christmas form. Four matches in a row were lost, including a home defeat to Portadown in the first round of the Cup. In February Ards' goalkeeping problems were addressed once again, with the signing of the excellent Peter McCarren from Cromac Albion, but at the same time news came that a £10,000 fee had been agreed with San Diego Sockers for Tommy Armstrong. A year earlier this would have been a devastating blow, but the striker had not always been on top of his form this season, so perhaps the transfer fee was in the end the better option. Despite defeats to Cliftonville and Bangor, the team returned to its winning ways, with Reid and Patterson continuing to score freely. By late April Ards were back in contention for a second place finish in the League after a superb 3-0 demolition of Glenavon, who had gone 11 matches undefeated to that date. The match on 21st April, at home to Ballymena United, was crucial, with a win required to clinch second place and entry into the UEFA Cup. But sickeningly, in front of an inexplicably poor attendance, Ards could only draw 3-3, and their chance had gone. A third place finish was good, but the thought of what might have been was the bitter emotion at the time. The County Antrim Shield almost provided a glorious last fling for Ards. In the first round they trounced Glentoran 4-0 at the Oval and in the second round, drawn at home this time, they defeated Linfield 3-0. But there the excitement ended, and the team went out by the odd goal in five to Cliftonville to end a roller-coaster of a season which, despite the disappointments, at least held out hope of Kinkead's squad going on to greater things the next season.

Tom Cullen

The lack of fire power for much of the previous season led Ards to sign Glentoran's Paul Kirk for 1979-80, but they were disappointed when Tommy Armstrong, whose brief sojourn in America took him from San Diego to San Jose and then home again, opted for Glenavon. Despite the arrival of Kirk the inability to take chances persisted, and this failing in front of goal, coupled with an unfortunate habit of easing off for crucial spells in the match meant that Ards only won 5 out of their opening 27 matches. A fine away win at Waterford in the Tyler All Ireland Cup led to a home draw against Drogheda United, but the match was lost 1-3 when Ards failed to capitalise on a half hour period of almost complete domination. There were only three wins in the Ulster Cup campaign, against Coleraine, Portadown and Larne, but the young Philip Maxwell, a Comber boy, was showing excellent form wide on the left, attracting interest from Coventry, Aston Villa, Luton Town and Fulham, where he spent a week on trial. But even Maxwell's sparkling form could not disguise the poor performances of the team. Crowds were again poor, and angry letters to the local press complained of poor management of the club. For the Drogheda match only three turnstiles were open: the ground, it was alleged, was crumbling while the social club received all the attention. "Are we a football club or a drinking club?" was the pertinent question of correspondent Mr W. Graham.

In the opening match of Ards' section in the Gold Cup the team was humiliated by Linfield, who scored seven goals without reply. The situation could not continue, and Joe Kinkead was sacked. Billy Nixon became caretaker manager, and immediately began to ring the changes. The disappointing Paul Kirk was offloaded to Waterford, and replaced by Jim Martin, signed from Glentoran. There were some encouraging signs for Nixon: Maxwell continued to sparkle, and Tom Cullen, his counterpart on the right wing, was now hitting top form. When Ards advertised for a manager the short list consisted of four applicants, of whom Billy Sinclair was the hot favourite, but the Scotsman was pinched from under Ards' noses by Glenavon, who were prepared to give better terms to Sinclair and who did not hang about, actually offering him the job during the interview. Rather then go through the whole process again, Ards decided to offer the job to Billy Nixon on a permanent basis. His first match in charge had seen a fine 4-1 victory over Distillery, but after that bright beginning the team failed to win any of its next dozen matches.

An improvement in fortunes only appeared in January, with successive wins over Coleraine, 4-1, Larne, 3-0, and Glenavon, 3-0. New goalkeeper Peter Craig, a signing from Larne, proved a safe pair of hands, and was voted the Guinness Player of the Month for January. Cyril Hewitt, who had spent some time at Middlesbrough, was brought in from Linfield, although this was something of a gamble, as he had not played serious football for a year. On the debit side Tom Kennedy, as fine a right-back as Ards had seen for many a year, was discontented and asked for a transfer. Against the wishes of many supporters Billy Nixon acceded to his request, also listing Gary Reid and Lawrence Patterson, neither of whom had succeeded in matching their form of the previous season. Kennedy and Reid both went to Bangor, and in came former centre-forward Jim Hall. After the flurry of wins in January Ards claimed only one more victory in the League, by 4-1 at home to Portadown in late March. With a miserable record of only four wins in the League campaign it was inevitable that they would face the ignominy of applying for re-election. Further humiliation came in the cup competitions, where even with home advantage Ards contrived to lose to 'B' Division RUC, who trounced them 4-0, and in their final match Ards were knocked out of the County Antrim Shield, 4-2, by Linfield Swifts.

It had been a miserable season all round. Ards II were supposed to be pursuing a youth policy, but on a number of occasions had been forced to play Billy Nixon, Alfie Wright and Billy Humphries, who, almost inevitably, had been the best players on the pitch. An edict from the authorities meant that the pitch had to be fenced in, obstructing the view of the majority of spectators. The Annual General Meeting heard of a loss of £26,000, compared with £5,000 the year before. The previous year's credit balance of £8,000 from transfer fees had become a £9,000 deficit, and the wage bill was up by £4,000 over the year, yet most of the newcomers, especially Martin, Hewitt, Hall and Connor had not been successes. To add to the misery it was clear that major work would have to be undertaken to clear blocked drains, which in February had reduced the pitch to near quagmire conditions. It seemed that it was not only the pitch, but the club itself which was in danger of subsiding as the '80s dawned.

TWELVE

The Old Order Changeth
1980-85

A rds made one of their most significant signings of the dawning decade in the close season that preceded 1980-81. The long-serving full-back Ronnie Cromie went to Portadown, and in return there came Jim Campbell, a defender when he arrived, but one who would soon be switched to centre forward with devastating effect. Also joining the Castlereagh Park club was Billy McCoubrey from Bangor, swapped for goalkeeper Peter McCarron, whose place was taken initially by Peter Craig. After three opening defeats in the Ulster Cup, Ards beat Coleraine 2-0, and then played out a thrilling draw with Ballymena United, when goals from McCoubrey and Campbell in the last seven minutes secured a point. In that match centre half Davy McCoy reached the landmark of 500 games for Ards, but he had been reluctant to sign and clearly wanted to move, even walking out only half an hour before the kick-off in a match against Cliftonville after a row over expenses. McCoy eventually left later in the winter, signing for RUC. An excellent centre-half, he had given Ards great service, and his premature death in the 1990s caused sadness to all those who remembered his sterling displays at the heart of the defence. That victory against Coleraine proved to be Ards' only success in the Ulster Cup. One of the most disappointing results of this barren period was a 2-1 defeat at home to Glentoran when Ards led through a Hewitt goal with only two minutes to go before succumbing to two goals from Gary Blackledge. At the end of the Ulster Cup Billy Nixon admitted defeat and resigned as manager, going back to manage the IIs. Billy Humphries

Jim Campbell

returned to the tiller as caretaker manager, but with no immediate success, a 2-1 win over Distillery in the Gold Cup giving Ards their only points in that competition. Crowds were still disappointing – the North End Supporters' Club bus reappeared for a trip to Distillery only because of the novelty of the Whites' new Ballyskeagh Stadium, but once again the valiant efforts of the supporters' clubs helped keep Ards afloat, with contributions totalling £2,000 from North End, Movilla and the Special Efforts Committee. (John Martin, for many years the driving force behind the North End club, estimates that during its existence the NEASC contributed £200,000 to Ards' coffers). It was clear that as many as half a dozen new players were needed, and Sammy Galway was brought in from Larne, as was ex-Ballymena goalkeeper Bobby Brown, while Ray Mowat, who had only re-signed in mid-September, made a welcome return to the team for the League campaign.

With Galway, Brown and Mowat playing regularly alongside the excellent George Gibson, prospects look a little brighter, more so when Humphries secured Newtownards man Alex Robson, a stalwart with Glentoran for many years, to replace Davy McCoy. Certainly results in the Irish League represented an improvement on the dire early season form. There were successive wins over Crusaders and Coleraine, then over Bangor and Portadown. The Christmas Day match against Bangor, which was won 4-3, saw 17 year-old Sean Armstrong add a goal to a hat-trick from Jim Campbell, now playing up front. With goals more plentiful there were wins over Distillery and Larne, but in mid-February the team suffered a terrible hiding at Seaview, going down 8-2 to Crusaders. Two matches later Ards beat Coleraine 4-2, then failed to win any of their next four matches, before finishing the season strongly with a fine draw against Glentoran, and wins over Distillery and Larne. In an astute swap Ards gave Cyril Hewitt to Distillery, gaining the excellent left sided Jim Cowden in return. The team now had much more shape and purpose and its final position of equal 4th was witness to a fine recovery in the second half of the season. In the Irish Cup Ards had begun with a facile 3-0 victory over Ballyclare Comrades, but were unable to overcome Glentoran in the second round. The County Antrim Shield saw the team progress as far as the semi-finals, defeating first Distillery 4-1 and then Cliftonville 1-0, but they found Linfield too much for them in the penultimate round, losing 1-4 even with home advantage.

Billy Humphries had done well with a limited pool of players, although technically he was still general manager of Ards F.C., but this was remedied in late May when he was appointed team manager as well. Steady, reliable and often underrated, sweeper Roy Walker was deservedly named Ards' Player of the Year. Although crowds had not reached the levels of previous years, there was more enthusiasm about at the end of the 1980-81 season. The Hartford ASC handed over £900 to the club, and for the first time in years Ards scarves were once again on sale. A cynic might have wondered if they would be worn regularly on Saturdays or stowed, forgotten, in the back of the wardrobe in a few months' time.

There were, I am afraid, few opportunities for scarf-twirling, flag-waving or indeed any other form of exuberant celebration in the 1981-82 season. Willie McCully's resignation as Chairman, in which position he was succeeded by Hugh Owens, was a blow, and it was soon apparent that both George Gibson and Philip Maxwell wanted to leave the club. In addition, Jim Campbell did not turn up for pre-season training, and although he eventually reappeared, he missed the first eight matches of the season. Little did we know that this disappearing trick would become a signature of the lanky striker's career at Ards, but, to be fair, his chef's hours did not always lend themselves easily to the demands of professional football. Nonetheless Ards began the season reasonably promisingly, with three successive draws, the last of which, 3-3 against Linfield, saw them come back from 2-0 and 3-1 down. Tom Cullen, now pushed further forward than in his largely defensive role of the previous season, scored two blinding 20-yard goals against the Blues, and in the following match, against Distillery, he scored four in a 5-2 thrashing of Distillery. At the end of August Cullen was the surprising leading scorer in the Irish League. Attempts to persuade George Gibson to stay failed, and he eventually moved to Linfield, with full-back Frankie Parks moving to Castlereagh Park as part of the deal, but in the short term young Ronnie Mudd proved a more than satisfactory centre half. Philip Maxwell moved to Glenavon for £2,000, while Russell Welsh and Eddie Coulter became regular fixtures on the team.

But after August the team won only twice more before Christmas, 2-1 in the final match of the Ulster Cup against Larne, and 3-0 against Portadown, their only victory in the Gold Cup. Ards' poor form was all the more frustrating given that the latter victory brought to an end a Portadown eight game unbeaten run. Even with Campbell up front, Ards struggled to score goals, drawing a blank in eight out of their first twenty matches. In mid-December the Smirnoff Irish League match against Linfield (this was the first season when the distilling company sponsored the premier competition) was postponed after a heavy snow fall, while the following day a rapid thaw led to severe flooding, as the pitch, and indeed much of the town found itself under water. There was severe damage to the social club, with £7,000 worth of damage caused. Ominously, an unnamed Supporters' Club spokesman told the *Belfast Newsletter* that his body was not prepared to offer financial help to the stricken club. Relations between the board and the supporters' clubs had plummeted in the last year, the same spokesman suggesting that some directors were more interested in a successful social club than in a winning team. To be fair, Ards' worries paled into insignificance when one considers that the estimated bill for flood damage in the town as a whole would run to £2 million. On the playing side things went from bad to worse, with successive 9-1 and 7-1 defeats to Coleraine and Glentoran, although in the very next match Ards surprisingly secured a 3-2 victory over Larne, with two goals from Russell Welsh.

The only good news of this depressing spell came from Ards Colts, who defeated Carnmoney in the Barry Cup final, when they overcame a two-goal deficit to score through Young and Miskimmon and take the match into extra time. With the Ards youngsters now in the ascendant it was no surprise when Miskimmon capitalised on a goalkeeping error to slot home the winner. But a fresh blow left Ards reeling on February 12th, 1982 when Billy Humphries was sensationally sacked as General Manager of Ards. Technically he was made redundant, as was the steward of the Social Club. Although no official statement was made, leaks suggested that falling revenue meant that the club could no longer afford a GM, but Humphries protested vehemently, pointing out that over the five years he had been general manager Ards had substantially reduced a £70,000 overdraft in addition to spending £46,000 on ground improvements. "I don't think this could be termed failure in these tough economic days," said an upset Humphries. Ex-Chairman McCully, obviously disillusioned with the whole affair, resigned from the board shortly after. Bizarrely, Humphries was asked to stay on as team manager, which he did, but League results did not improve, and after that late January victory over Larne Ards won only two more League matches, late in the season, when goals from Russell Welsh secured crucial single-goal victories over Bangor and Larne, which allowed Ards to leapfrog the East Antrim club and avoid the embarrassment of applying for re-election. Although Ards' defence was, on occasion, prone to collapse like a house of cards, the chronic inability to find the net was even more worrying, with only 18 goals scored in the 26 match League campaign.

Despite these frailties Ards battled their way to the Irish Cup semi-finals, taking an astonishing six matches to do so. Drawn against juniors Chimney Corner in the opening round, Ards drew the first match 2-2, the replay 1-1, and finally won the second replay at the Oval thanks to a Parks penalty. Distillery proved just as stubborn opponents in the second round. After 2-2 and 0-0 draws, Ards once again had to go to the Oval where goals from Ronnie Mudd and Russell Welsh saw them through to a semi-final against Linfield. Given that they had lost their last League match against Linfield by 5-0, it looked a pushover for the Blues. But in the end Ards only lost by the odd goal in three. McKeown gave Linfield the lead, but Ards battled back to equalise through Roy Walker, and at 1-1 both Welsh and Eddie Connor were clean through when tripped just outside the penalty box. In those days there was no automatic red card for such a foul, and Ards failed to profit from the resultant free kicks. With Ards pressing for a winner, McGaughey scored a winner against the run of play, and gallant Ards had failed to make the final. Disappointingly there was a poor local turnout for such a big game, and although just before the end of the season they stepped in to sign John O'Connor from Cliftonville, there was continuing disquiet among supporters, culminating in a demand for an Extraordinary General Meeting of Ards F.C., something that had never happened before in their history as a limited company.

Rationally we know that nothing on this earth can last for ever. But the disappearance of the familiar is still disconcerting, all the more so when we lose people or institutions that have been landmarks for all our lives. 1982 was a year when much of old Newtownards became no more than a memory. This was the year that both Glasgow's and the Co-op would close their doors forever. On top of the final closure of the Gasworks the year before came the devastating news that nearly 200 jobs would be lost with the closure of the Crepe Weavers. And closer to home for our story, the unthinkable happened in the 1982-83 season when Billy Humphries, who had been part of the Ards story for nearly a quarter of a century, was summarily dismissed. And even 40 years' service to the club, never mind the 25 years from Humphries, apparently counted for nothing when one considers the sensational events of June 1982 and the treatment of Harry Cavan.

For some time, as we have seen, relations between the Board of Directors and the various Supporters' Clubs had been at rock bottom. The latter's refusal to help out when the Social Club suffered flood damage was merely symptomatic of the impasse between the two bodies, as was the organised boycott of a home match in January, when only 62 supporters came through the turnstiles to support Ards. The upshot of all this was a boardroom coup, when Bob Gibb, Sammy Moore, Billy Humphries and Harry Cavan were ousted and a new board headed by Hugh Owens, Harold Black, Billy Coey and Ken Lowry took over. Harry Cavan, now summarily rejected, was not only the pre-eminent administrator in Irish football but one of the most respected in the world, but this did not save him. Harry could be difficult, but one who worked alongside him in the running of Ards Football Club said "He didn't always say a lot, but when he did, everything he said was measured, and thoughtful, and, my goodness, you listened!" At least Cavan was not completely cast out into the wilderness, but promoted upstairs to become club President, a position he held until his death.

Billy Humphries' new title was 'Senior Manager', while Lawrence Walker became first team coach. An attempt to re-organise the club right down to its grass roots saw the formation of Ards Foals, an U-13 side. For the second time in recent seasons Ards looked to a veteran centre-half to organise the defence and inspire the team. This time they turned to the former Linfield stopper Peter Rafferty, and for the first third of the season it looked as if he could lead them back to former glories. Too often Ards had struggled at the opening of a season, only to find form about November or December, but on this occasion they began with a bang before fizzling out as the year wore on. There was real continuity in the side, with 9 players appearing in at least 42 of Ards' 45 games. These regulars were Bobby Brown in goals, Jim Cowden, the young Alan Dornan, Frankie Parks, Roy Walker, John O'Connor, Jim Campbell, teenager Colin O'Neill and Kel McDermott, just released by Manchester United.

In the Gold Cup, the opening competition, Ards got off to a flyer, with wins over Glenavon, Bangor and Portadown, and a draw against Distillery. Rafferty certainly proved the hoped-for inspiration, scoring in each of the first three games. The final group match, at home to Linfield, attracted nearly 4000, Ards' biggest gate for many years. A win was needed, but Ards could only draw 1-1 with the Blues, who went on to win the section on goal difference. But hopes had been raised, and in the Ulster Cup Ards continued to make the headlines, extending their unbeaten run to 12 matches, with four goals scored against Bangor, and a fine victory over Linfield, thanks to two goals from McDermott. The crunch game came against fellow high-fliers Glentoran, but in front of 3000 the Glens won embarrassingly easily by five goals to nil. The bubble had burst, and it would be half a dozen games before the team would win again: nonetheless there was a genuine prospect of Ards returning to the big time, with Jim Campbell now getting into his stride and finding the net regularly. But the season had a nasty shock looming just below the horizon.

In early December, the morning after a 4-2 defeat to Cliftonville, Billy Humphries received a phone call from Hugh Owens, informing him he had been dismissed. Humphries, along with most supporters, was staggered. He had been appointed for a one-year term only six months earlier, the team had challenged strongly for the Ulster and Gold Cups, they were still undefeated away from home, and had lost only 3 out of their 18 matches, so how could 'results' be cited as a reason for his dismissal? A later statement from the Board referred to 'dissatisfaction with certain aspects of his team management', which was far too unspecific to throw any light on the real reasons for the sacking. Billy Humphries still remembers the phone call in detail, from the 'shaky' voice of an obviously uneasy Chairman, to his own gradually dawning realisation that this was it, that there would be no face to face meeting, but that his quarter of a century with Ards would come to an end in this humiliating way. Humphries insists that he left a club in rude good health all the way down to the Foals, and to underline his point Ards Colts won the Youth Cup, defeating Glenavon's third string 4-2. Included the team were future stars Brian Strain and, scoring one of the goals from his striking position, future Republic of Ireland central defender Alan Kernaghan!

Lawrence Walker was now appointed manager, with Jim Martin, whose career

Ards FC 1983
Back row (l-r): Walker, Dornan, Welsh, Brown, Campbell, Parks, Humphries, Murphy
Front Row (l-r): Galway, McDermott, O'Neill, Rafferty, Walker, O'Connor, Cowden

Alan Dornan

had been ended by injury, as coach. Under the new management team Ards continued their promising form, with Jim Campbell striding the pitch like a colossus, netting 18 goals in 13 games between Christmas and early March, including hat tricks against Ballymena and Glenavon. But when Campbell failed to find the net, Ards struggled. He scored two in a 5-1 trouncing of Bangor and three to defeat Larne in the final match of the League, but he found little support from the rest of the side when it came to goals-scoring. The over-reliance on Big Jim was worrying, especially given the disappointing form shown by the returned Tommy Armstrong, but there were other compensations. The Red and Blue Shop, John Martin's Aladdin's cave of vintage football programmes, was beginning to make its regular contributions towards club coffers, Ards were promised £10,000 as their share of Northern Ireland's profits from the World Cup, Peter McCusker, a clever right winger, joined from Ballymena United, and the IIs won the George Wilson Trophy and the IIIs the Dunmurry Youth League.

The first team reached the semi-finals of the two major knockout competitions. In the County Antrim Shield the RUC and Dundela were each defeated by a single goal before Glentoran brought Ards' run to an end. In the Irish Cup two goals from Campbell and one from Porter saw off Dungannon Swifts, then another couple from Campbell helped Ards beat Larne 2-1 to reach the penultimate stage, where for the second year in a row their opponents were Linfield. Once again a poor crowd followed Ards that day, caused in part by the televising of the League Cup Final from England, but it is hard to excuse a mere two buses from Newtown for an Irish Cup semi-final. The injured Rafferty was badly missed as Ards lost 2-1. They probably deserved a draw, but were crucially denied a penalty when referee Poucher gave a free outside the box when all of Ards swore that McDermott had been tumbled over inside the area.

On the field it had been a decent season, capped by Jim Campbell's selection as Player of the Year by the NIPFA, and the memories of Ards' 12-match run at the start of the year, but the treatment of Harry Cavan and then Billy Humphries left a sour taste that did a lot to harm Ards' reputation as a friendly small town club.

For the 1983-84 season some of the old guard were moved on. Colin O'Neill went to Larne, and Tommy Armstrong and Russell Welsh to Bangor, but into the side came Tony Bell from Cliftonville and Ron McCreery from Portadown. Off the field the new regime was forced to close the boys' gate because of what they described as 'continuous abuse' by those seeking to gain admittance on the cheap, and it was decided to close the curtains in the Social Club to force its denizens out on to the terraces if they wanted to see the match. The other main problem the new men in charge had to deal with was to cloak their embarrassment at seeing Harry Cavan, the man they had kicked upstairs, still respected enough in wider circles to act as President of the IFA.

Results in the opening competition, the Gold Cup, were mixed. Ards beat Bangor twice, and Newry Town once, but lost both games against Glentoran, and failed to qualify for the knockout stages. In the Ulster Cup they showed improvement, winning their first three matches and their last two, but stumbled in a defeat against Bangor, a match in which Norman Porter was sent off, and in the end they only failed to reach the semi-finals by a goal difference of one. Jim Campbell, in outstanding form, had already reached double figures, and Alan Dornan was attracting rave reviews. With John O'Connor and Roy Walker playing well and young David Dugan establishing himself in the team as a striker of some ability there was quiet confidence about Ards' League prospects, a confidence boosted when Laurence Walker chose to stay with Ards rather than take over the vacant manager's post at Portadown.

Jimmy Todd

Sadly the optimism was not fully borne out by results. Certainly Ards defended well, losing only six of their twenty six games (the extra fixtures a result of the admission of Carrick Rangers and Newry Town into the League), but drew eleven of the remainder. The failure to kill off the opposition was largely due to the over-reliance on Campbell and Dugan for goals: only seven of Ards' total League tally of thirty two were scored by anyone other than those two. One of the best of the drawn matches was in early December away to Glentoran, a real thriller which swayed one way and then the other. Ards went two goals ahead through O'Connor and Dugan, Glentoran came back to make it 2-2, Campbell put Ards back in the lead, but a Dixon goal meant that the points were shared. The best wins of the campaign were a 3-0 victory over Ballymena United and a 4-0 defeat of League novices Newry Town. Towards the end of the season Eddie Dinsmore, who had come from East Belfast, broke into the team. He arrived too late to have any effect on Ards' Irish Cup involvement, which saw a first round 1-0 win over Coleraine, a John O'Connor goal separating the teams, but they went out by the same scoreline to Cliftonville at the next stage. In the County Antrim Shield a 2-2 draw with Ballymena United meant a penalty shootout which Ards lost 5-4.

It was an anonymous enough season, but the Colts had won the Dunmurry Youth League, so there was always the hope that some of these young players would come through, and Jimmy Todd made a welcome reappearance on the Ards' scene when he was engaged as a scout. The usual consolation for lack of success could be held out that there was always next season.

If in 1984-85 Ards were to improve upon their performance of the previous season they would have to reduce their over-reliance on Campbell and Dugan to provide all the goals, maintain their miserly defensive performances and strengthen the playing staff. None of these aims was achieved, and the season proved a mediocre one. When O'Connor went to Portadown Ards received Jim Gardiner and Raymond Hill in return: the former disappointed, scoring only one goal in fifteen appearances, happily the latter proved to be a defensive stalwart. But they could ill-afford to lose players of the calibre of O'Connor and Peter McCusker, who moved back to Cliftonville, where he turned in regular quality performances for the Reds. Jim Campbell, suffering a niggling injury, was able to start in only a third of the first fifteen matches, and Ards averaged little more than a goal a game during this period, while the defence, although generally sound, was prone to off days.

Norman Porter in action against Glentoran

The opening game raised everyone's hopes as Ards beat Bangor 4-1, with Norman Hayes scoring a brace of goals, but a solitary victory over Newry Town

was the only other success in their section of the Gold Cup. In the Ulster Cup there were three wins, the best a 4-0 defeat of Bangor which included a Dugan hat trick. The League programme got off to the worst possible start, with four successive defeats firmly anchoring Ards to the foot of the table. The defeat by Carrick Rangers, the first since the County Antrim team had entered senior football, came after Ards had thrown away a two goal lead and were still 2-1 ahead after 87 minutes. Manager Walker was so unhappy with the team's efforts that he went public in his criticism of the attitude of 'certain players', holding back from naming names but nonetheless incurring a rebuke from the PFA. He may have had a case, but the spectacle of the offloaded O'Neill, Welsh, McCusker and O'Connor all doing well at other clubs put a question mark against Ards' judgement.

The turnaround in fortunes which was just around the corner had something to do with the return from suspension of big Norman Porter. Over-enthusiastic to a fault, Porter vowed to turn over a new leaf, but after a massive 16 week suspension he could say little else. Surprisingly Ards' first win in seven came against Glentoran, when goals from Campbell, only his second of the season, Cowden and Hayes brought them a fine 3-1 win. The confidence engendered by this win gave Ards a real boost, and they went on to lose only twice in the next ten League matches. This run through December and January peaked with the 4-1 win over Portadown and the 3-1 success over Ballymena. But unhappily their form plummeted again, and in the remaining eleven matches the only victory came against second bottom Bangor. Eleventh place out of fourteen teams was certainly a major setback, and only in the Cup competitions did Ards raise their long-suffering followers' hopes as the season wore to a close.

A January snowstorm threatened the first round Irish Cup match against Bangor, but all morning fans shovelled snow from the pitch to gain the referee's go ahead. Centre back Ronnie Mudd was the star of the show as Ards triumphed 3-0, with a 30-yarder from Norman Porter the pick of the goals. A 2-0 win over Ballymoney United saw Ards into the third round, but here they met their match with a single goal defeat at the hands of Ballymena United. A fortnight later Ards gained their revenge over the Braidmen in the County Antrim Shield with a 2-0 win, and drawn against junior opposition in the next round they beat Killyleagh YC 3-2. This, however, was their last fling, for by the same score they lost to Glentoran in the semi-final. By this stage Laurence Walker had gone. In mid-March the manager resigned, accepting that the team had gone backwards in the last year. Originally the Board wanted a player-manager, but instead fell back on appointing Roy Walker as chief coach, and calling on Jimmy Todd to take over as manager. Some eyebrows were raised at the appointment of a man who had starred for Ards as long ago as the war, and whose managerial peak at Seaview, when he took the Crues to the title, was now more than decade away. Only time would tell if experience would prove a better investment than youth.

THIRTEEN

False Dawns

1985-90

The new manager acted swiftly to build a new team. Out went Bobby Brown, Ron McCreery, Norman Hayes, and, more surprisingly, David Dugan, who was allowed to join Ballymena despite his couple of dozen goals in the previous season. Jim Cowden had asked away in the spring, and come September he was transferred to Glentoran for an unsatisfactory fee. When Ards signed Cowden from Distillery they had paid more than £9000, but now, despite an improvement in his form without which a big team like the Glens would hardly have been interested, a League Tribunal decided that he was only worth £8500. To fill the gaps Todd brought in 'Towser' McDowell in goals, Alan Dornan's brother Reggie from Bangor, Tommy Kincaid from Crusaders, and centre-backs Ian Brown and Damien Byrne, the latter a former Dundalk and Drogheda player who had more recently been with Crusaders. Up front former Linfield man Davy McClurg, who held his place until Jim Campbell recovered from an ankle injury, was partnered by a lanky young unknown called Stephen Baxter.

Jimmy Todd admitted to being 'depressed' about the early results, when Ards won only one of their Ulster Cup games and crashed out of the County Antrim Shield at Carrick Rangers. But brand new teams take time to gel, and in the Gold Cup Ards began to put it together. Baxter found the target eleven times in thirteen games, and Ards held Linfield to a draw, beat Portadown 3-0 and overcame table-topping Glentoran 2-0 despite the sending off of Tim Kelly. With two matches to go Ards looked set for a top four playoff slot, but then came a cropper at home to Coleraine. Even though they managed a last gasp win over Cliftonville with a 92nd minute Baxter winner, the draw secured by Crusaders meant that the Shore Road side secured the last place in the knockout stages on goal difference.

When the League proper began Ards won two and lost three of their opening fixtures before embarking on an undefeated run of ten matches in January and February 1986. In the last match before this run began they had been a goal ahead at the Oval when Jim Campbell, at last returned from the sidelines, was sent off after retaliating against Tommy Leeman, and Ards were unable to hold out, conceding two goals in the last 20 minutes. But the clear signs of improvement were there, and six wins and a draw saw them climb to 3rd in the table. The win at Coleraine was clinched in the 90th minute when Tim Kelly scored after a quickly taken free by Leo Flanagan, recently signed from Drogheda, while that over Linfield, 2-0, with Campbell and Mudd the scorers, was only Ards' second victory in a League match at Windsor Park since the war. Campbell was now scoring regularly, which was just as well, as Baxter was out with damaged tendons, probably the result of the abuse he was taking from defenders, and the form of Damien Byrne was such that he was being touted as the best player in the League. Despite this, he was inexplicably omitted from the Irish League team to play the League of Ireland, although Alan Dornan and Jim Campbell were both selected. In the Cup Ards also made progress, overcoming Newry Town at the second time of asking, then Crusaders 4-1 on a snowbound pitch when the famous orange ball had to be used. In the third round, drawn away to Carrick Rangers, Ards scored a single goal victory in astonishing fashion. From the kick off Baxter tapped the ball to Campbell, who utilised the wind to score with a dipping shot from the halfway line. The official version was that the goal was scored in 8 seconds, but many felt that this official time was a copout, with 4 or 5 seconds being a more likely figure. Despite the rest of the match being forgettable, Ards had reached the semi-finals, where they played Coleraine at Ballymena Showgrounds, a choice of venue which Ards bitterly protested. But on the day Coleraine strolled home 2-0, with a desperately disappointing Ards failing to compete, failing to produce a single shot on goal in the 90 minutes. That inability to score was symptomatic of Ards at this period of the League, when they drew a blank in no fewer than five out of their last nine games. But the defence held firm, and a series of draws and narrow wins kept Ards in a creditable 3rd place. The final match of the season saw Ards once again beat Linfield, this time by 2-1. To be fair, the Blues had already won the League and had not much

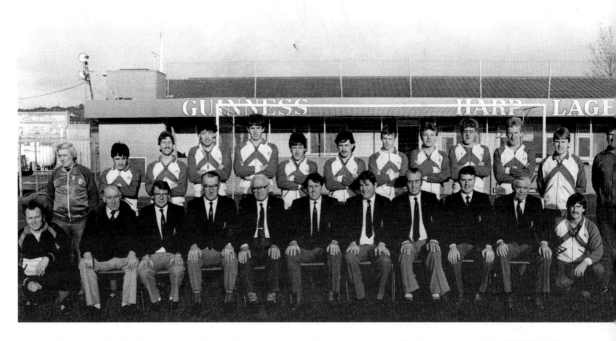

to play for, but for Ards to have taken a draw and two victories from their three games against Linfield was a real feather in their cap.

Prospects for the future also looked bright given that Ards Colts had won the IFA Youth Cup. Included in the team were Paul Kee in goals, Philip Mitchell and Rab Campbell, who scored two of the three goals, the other coming from Murphy. But if it was one thing discovering promising young players it was another holding on to them. As the season came to a close Ards complained that Baxter had been the subject of an illegal approach and a 'fabulous offer', Alan Dornan asked for a transfer and Ronnie Mudd went to Linfield. In addition, the old stand at the Portaferry Road end of the reserved side was declared unsafe, and since Ards could not afford the £3000 needed to improve it, was closed until further notice.

Ards FC 1986-87
Players: Back row (l-r):
B. Kincaid, R. Dornan,
Brown, Baxter, T. Kincaid,
Kelly, McClurg, A. Dornan,
McDowell, Byrne, Hill.
Kneeling: Galway

Alan Dornan followed Mudd to Linfield after a rancorous struggle over the transfer fee. Ards rated their captain at £20,000, but were initially only offered £7000. In the end the Blues got their man for £9000, a bargain in the light of the great service he eventually gave Linfield. A further blow came when Ian Brown's work took him to England and out of the team for all but a handful of games, and Ards had lost two centre-halves. Into the squad came Marty McCoy, bought from Newry Town for £2500, the hard-tackling Tom Pearson from Carrick Rangers, and, returned from his wanderings and still only 25, Philip Maxwell.

This year the Irish football authorities rang a few changes. The season would open with the County Antrim Shield, the League running from late August and to February, and the Gold Cup to close the season. For the first time in domestic competition two substitutes were allowed, the practical implications of which were that a bigger squad of potential first team players was required. Ards did well in the first two rounds of the County Antrim Shield, defeating Dundela, then Crusaders, before going out to Glentoran in the semi-final. In their section of the Ulster Cup they won only one of three, and made no further progress. When the League began Ards took a point at Portadown after squandering a two goal lead, then found themselves up against Linfield in a match played out against a background of accusations of Linfield having 'tapped' Dornan and Mudd, accusations angrily denied by Blues Chairman David Campbell. With the game poised at 1-1 in the 89th minute Simpson played a gem of a pass to give Maxwell a run on goal. The former Linfield man outpaced McKeown before drawing Dunlop and slipping the ball home to give Ards a very satisfying win. Man of the match was goalkeeper McDowell, who had kept his side in the match with a string of superb saves. Three victories, including a 3-1 defeat of eventual runners up Coleraine, and only one defeat, by Bangor, shot Ards up to second position, but this was followed by a spell leading up to Christmas when only three wins were recorded in twelve outings, the most pleasing results the Boxing Day victory over Bangor by four clear goals and a 1-1 draw at home to Glentoran. Jim Campbell was not as prolific as in previous seasons, but Byrne, McCoy and McDowell were all in tiptop form. Jimmy Todd, whose job was reportedly and unfairly under threat after a 5-0 humiliation at the hands of Larne, who went second as a result of the win, moved to strengthen the team with the signing of the shaven-headed schoolteacher Norman McGreevy from Crusaders.

But in an almost uncanny repeat of the previous season, Ards moved into top gear after the New Year. They won eight and drew one of their last nine matches, by far the best result a 3-2 win at the Oval, and a 2-1 revenge victory at Larne. The third place finish was commendable, especially given the crucial losses of Dornan, Mudd and Brown. In the Irish Cup Ards had to travel to 'B' Division Omagh Town, and won 2-1, but in the second round had to bow out to Larne, who triumphed 2-1. In their section of the Gold Cup Ards beat Distillery, Glenavon, Bangor and Portadown, losing two matches on the way, and thus progressed to the semi-finals, but here they lost 2-1 to Linfield after extra time.

On the field it had been a good campaign, but the crowds were not returning as one might have hoped, something revealed in a spat between Jim Palmer of the *Chronicle* and Secretary Ken Lowry. Palmer had criticised a number of perceived failings of Ards F.C.: specifically Harry Cavan's dismissive attitude to the suggestion that Ards might make use of an £8000 IFA grant to install floodlighting, the 'appalling' press facilities, and the need to secure the future by signing new deals with key players well in advance of the expiry of existing contracts. Lowry's reply, despite its patronising tone, was nevertheless revealing as to the financial constraints the club was operating under. The Secretary's letter claimed that, over the last 15 matches, and even though these included games against the Big Two, the average attendance was only 419. This was hardly a solid base on which to build for the future, and Ards suffered a further blow when they proved powerless to prevent their best talent decamping to a wealthier club. This time it was Stephen Baxter, whom Linfield had been chasing for some time. Unfortunately he was not a professional, so Ards received nothing for a player who had netted over a score of goals as well as performing as an excellent target man, all the more galling in that he turned down a move to Dundee United which would have earned Ards £20,000 and kept Baxter out of the hands of their League rivals. It was a serious blow to Ards' playing strength, but Jimmy Todd at least committed himself to the club when he signed a fresh two-year contract.

Damien Byrne receiving his Player of the Year award from Mervyn Brown, Secretary of the Irish League

Easily the biggest blow of the close season was Damien Byrne's decision, once his contract ran out, to return to playing in the League of Ireland. The big centre-half had become worn down by the travelling involved in a weekly round trip of 200 miles from his Malahide home, and Ards had lost the linchpin of their defence and one of their most popular players of the last 25 years in one sickening moment. The news did not improve with the onset of the 1987-88 season: first of all Ron McCreery walked out on Ards to join Glentoran, then Reg Dornan cracked his ribs in the opening fixture, and Jim Campbell suffered what turned out to be a hairline fracture of the ankle in the opening minutes of the Ulster Cup match against Glentoran. Ards went into the lead in that game, per Tommy Kincaid, but were unable to build on it and register a second win in a row, and no further progress was made in the competition. In the Gold Cup Ards won only one game, against Bangor. Marty McCoy and striker Earl Aiken had

Rob Campbell

now joined the injured list, Ricky Simpson was sold to Ballymena United for £4000, and despite their small squad Ards also tried to sell Philip Maxwell to Larne, but the player refused to go.

Not surprisingly coach John Reaney was under some pressure, but he was handed a lifeline when Ards, against all the odds, defeated big-spending Portadown in the opening match of the League. Goals from Maxwell and Rob Campbell gave the home team the result of the day, and they followed it up with a Roadferry League Cup win at Distillery, in the first match to be played at New Grosvenor under the new floodlights. (Ards, who, like all the Irish League clubs, were installing floodlights of their own, were criticised for their apparent tardiness in getting the lights up and running). The return of Ronnie Mudd, who had spent a brief sojourn at Carrick Rangers after his time at Windsor Park, raised spirits further, and a decent spell continued with wins over Bangor, Cliftonville and Distillery, and a draw against Glenavon. In that match, after Kincaid's glanced header from Maxwell's cross secured an equaliser, Ards appeared to have secured a winner when with three minutes to go Beattie's header was about to find the net when it was handled on the line, but the referee failed to see the incident the way everyone else did, and Ards had to be content with one point. There was also a draw with Coleraine, who complained bitterly about what they saw as Ards' negative tactics, given their home advantage in the match. This added an extra piquancy to the League Cup semi-final between the two teams, played at Clandeboye Road because the floodlights, as many had predicted, were not ready. The match was tied at 1-1 after extra time, but the unlucky Tommy Pearson missed his penalty and Ards lost the shootout 5-4.

Paul Kee was now playing superbly, and Ards were showing a welcome determination to hold on to promising players when they signed Robert and Brian Campbell on professional forms. The lights were at last switched on for a friendly between Ards and the Down Area League in mid-December, but after five minutes of the second half the threatening fog finally descended, and the match had to be abandoned. Going into the Boxing Day fixture at the Oval Ards were second in the League. They secured a good draw, with goals from Hill and new striker Noel Hamill, signed from Craigavon AFC. But that was about it as far as success in the League went. There were no more League wins for ten games, when in early February Glenavon were beaten 1-0, thanks to a goal from debutant striker Glenn Ferguson, but there was nothing further to cheer the fans until the last match of the season, when Ards completed the double over Portadown with a 3-2 victory. Their home form was wretched, with no wins in their last ten League games at Castlereagh Park. Even the welcome return of Jim Campbell could make no difference. Ards beat Bangor 4-2 in the Irish Cup, with a brace from Campbell, and one each from Hamill and Black, but despite a valiant fight they lost at Lurgan in the ensuing round. Reaney's position was untenable, with many feeling that his persistence with a 4-4-2 formation was unsuited to Ards' strengths, or perhaps, more realistically, their weaknesses. It was inevitable that he would be removed, and in February he was replaced as coach by Ian Russell. Jimmy Todd remained as a general manager, but the local press was full of letters demanding that the Board should invest their own money in the team or take themselves off.

After warning Jim Campbell for a final time about his attitude to training, Todd lost patience with the big forward and transfer listed him. He sold Johnny Black to Coleraine for £4000 and released Philip Maxwell. Paul Kee also went as part of a lucrative deal with Oxford United. At least, many long-suffering supporters hoped, the money raised at the end of the season could be used to rebuild a team in obvious need of strengthening.

Towards the end of the 1988-89 season a plaintive letter appeared in the *Chronicle*. It listed the players who had recently been on Ards' books but were now starring elsewhere. The litany of the lost included Alan Dornan, Robert Strain, John O'Connor, Jim Campbell, Stephen Baxter, Jim Cowden, Philip Maxwell, Ray Hill and about two dozen others. Sam Brown, the author of the letter, who had been watching Ards since before the War, was making the point that Ards had either let good players go or were powerless to stop them going if a bigger club beckoned. The result of this weakness, or misjudgement, call it what you will, was that Ards were suffering their worst season ever, a season in which they won only a miserable six matches, one of those only after a penalty shootout.

Oddly enough the year began in a flurry of excitement as Ards made their record signing. Chairman Hugh Owens had swooped decisively to snap up Mark Caughey from Motherwell for £10,000 when he spotted a story in a Scottish newspaper stating that Caughey had been listed. Earl Aiken had been released, Philip Maxwell had gone to Bangor, and Paul Kee had gone, but in came Mark Donnelly, Stevie Allen and Mark Patterson, and Neil Murphy was later signed from Harland and Wolff Welders as support for Caughey. Caughey scored two in the opening fixture away to Coleraine: the Bannsiders went on to win 3-2, but it was a promising start. But in the ten matches Ards played in the Ulster and Gold Cups they won only once, a 2-1 victory over Distillery. Caughey scored five and Tommy Kincaid four in this period, but 25 goals were conceded, a harbinger of things to come. On an unseasonably hot October day Ards defeated Chimney Corner on penalties in the League Cup, but crashed out 5-2 to Crusaders in the next round. Bertie McMinn, who scored in that defeat, had been bought from Distillery for £3000, but the team was weakened when Raymond Hill was allowed to go to Bangor. In the light of this dreadful run Jimmy Todd, who had been in charge for over four years, was sacked. The Board's intention was now to sign someone who would be in absolute authority, to bring to an end the ambiguity surrounding the relative positions of Todd and his coaches, formerly John Rainey, now Ian Russell. The job was given to former Linfield star Peter Dornan, who was appointed on a non-contractual basis, in practice a handshake and a gentleman's agreement. Happily, Jimmy Todd, universally regarded as a hard-working and decent man, stayed on to act as a most successful Commercial Manager, a position which he held for many years.

That there was still a public for football in Newtownards was shown in the 2000 plus who attended a schoolboy international against France on Hallowe'en night, but Ards had now only 300 seats in the original stand, the stand at the Portaferry Road end having lost its seats, turned into a mere shelter, and a pretty unsatisfactory one at that, too far back and with a lack of camber. In the League campaign Ards had to wait until their ninth match for a win, 2-1 over Larne. By this time they had unearthed a new keeper, the highly promising Alan Fettis, but had lost Ronnie Mudd, who fell victim to meningitis. Jimmy Campbell, forgiven and embraced by Ards yet again, called off desperately late for a game in late November. Dornan was not prepared to accept what others had tolerated, and the hero of the terraces, who had nonetheless failed to hit the back of the net in six appearances that season, was transfer listed. The 30-year-old, who had been with Ards eight seasons, and was a former players' Player of the Year in Northern Ireland, went to Bangor. He was a naturally gifted goalscorer, and it was a great pity that no one had been able to reconcile his twin roles as footballer and chef, which had always proved conflicting. Even though one Campbell had gone, there was no shortage of the clan at Ards, with the three Campbell brothers from Dundonald, Robert, Brian and Paul representing the club against Distillery.

The win over Larne on Boxing Day was quickly followed up by victories over Crusaders and Newry, and briefly hope flickered, but despite the arrival of Laurence Stitt to take over from Mark Donnelly at centre-half, and the purchase of Bobby Kincaid, Tommy's brother, from Ballyclare Comrades for £3000, that hope was extinguished, as the team embarked on a barren spell of twelve

League games without a single win. The duck was broken with a 2-0 victory over Crusaders, but with only two matches left it was clearly a case of too little, too late. In the Budweiser Cup Ards showed better form, drawing twice with Coleraine and only losing on the away goals rule, but the ultimate humiliation came in the Irish Cup, when despite a home draw, Ards lost 1-0 to the juniors of Cromac Albion.

There were few grounds for optimism as the season mercifully ended, but the discovery of Alan Fettis, even though he had temporarily lost his place to new signing Andy McLean, was one, as was the form of a new striker, the young Glenn Ferguson, who was beginning to show his scoring touch. The hard-working, tough-tackling Tommy Pearson was deservedly chosen as the Ards Player of the Year, and Peter Dornan, who was offered the chance to stay on and get a fair chance at turning round the club's fortunes, agreed to continue as manager.

There was much to report during the close season before the 1989-90 session began. A £16,000 loss on the previous year's workings was announced, despite a contribution of over £7000 from the various Supporters' Clubs. Against their wishes both Ronnie Mudd and Tom Pearson were allowed to leave Ards, but in came Brian McCarroll and John McAuley from Cromac Albion, and Craig McCandless from the RUC. Disturbingly these signings were made by Commercial Manager Jimmy Todd, and not by the manager or the Chairman, both of whom had chosen to take their holidays in July, a period normally seen as crucial for the recruitment of players and preparation for the looming kick off. There were those who wondered who was actually steering the Ards ship at such an important time, and Dornan came under scathing attack in the *Chronicle,* which questioned his commitment. The paper also reported that Assistant Manager Drew McFall was the subject of 'disquieting rumours that the players don't relate to him too well'. Better news was that in the absence of Joao Havelange, who was ill, Harry Cavan acted for a time as the President of FIFA. This was the highest honour in football, and one which brought a great deal of prestige to the Ards President, but one for which Cavan, as was often the case, received insufficient local credit.

Mark Caughey was suspended by the club for a breach of training discipline. Apparently he refused to run up Scrabo Hill

Alan Fettis

Paul O'Neill

when asked to do so. With unpleasant memories of similar instructions during cross-country runs at Regent House I had every sympathy, but then Caughey was a professional footballer, and it was no real surprise when the striker, who had failed to solve Ards' goalscoring problems, was sold to Bangor for a handy £9000. Two newcomers appeared from the Republic: the rangy centre-half John Mullen and midfield hard man Paul O'Neill. O'Neill had numerous Schoolboy and Youth caps, had spent four years as a full time professional at Shamrock Rovers, and although he was now playing with juniors Park Villa was still only 26, and indeed went on to become a ball winner in the middle of the park such as Ards had lacked for some time.

'Spike' Ferguson began the season with a bang, scoring in each of Ards' Ulster Cup games, where they defeated Ballymena and secured an exciting 1-1 draw with Linfield. In the Gold Cup a similar record of one win, one draw and one defeat denied Ards a place in this competition's knockout stages as well. The opening League fixture was a personal triumph for Glenn Ferguson, who scored four goals in a 5-0 thrashing of Distillery. He went on to score a further three in an embarrassingly one-sided League Cup game against UUJ, who were hopelessly out of their depth, and lost 12-0. Bertie McMinn was another who got a hat trick that night, having come on as a substitute! Ards were less impressive against another team from a lower league in the next round, where they had to rely on a penalty shootout to get past Ballyclare Comrades, but in the quarter-final they travelled to Coleraine and came away with a fine 2-1 win, with goals from Kincaid and Rab Campbell. The semi-final was at Seaview, but this time Ards lost to Glenavon after extra time.

But the lesser Cup competitions, although a welcome and often entertaining distraction, could not disguise Ards' grim League form. After a 3-0 win over Crusaders just before Hallowe'en, the team did not win another League match for three months. Up to November the side was praised for its never-say-die spirit, with O'Neill, Mullen and McCandless leading the way, but this attitude pertained more to away matches. At home Ards' form was dreadful, with only three wins out of a dozen games at Castlereagh Park by the end of January. A lightening of the gloom came courtesy of a cushy Irish Cup draw, when Ards travelled to 'B' Division Omagh Town and defeated them 3-0. Successive League wins over Crusaders and Cliftonville followed, but it was a false dawn. Despite home advantage Ards exited the Cup, beaten 2-0 by Larne, and a week later came ignominy, with Ards only scrambling a draw in the County Antrim Shield at home to East Belfast, then losing the penalty shootout 4-5. When Ards were put out of the Cup it was reported that Peter Dornan's proferred resignation had been turned down by the Board, but after the East Belfast game there was an explosion of anger, and shameful scenes took place, with a group of protestors breaking in to the pavilion. Some damage was done, and for the manager it was the breaking-point in more ways than one. Dornan resigned, claiming in the Sunday press that "the players let me down". Hugh Owens described Dornan as "not hungry enough". It was claimed that he did not spend sufficient time at the football club, and was said to be largely inaccessible to the local newspapers. Marty Beattie, speaking on behalf of the players, condemned Dornan's "carping… negative" attitude. Yet this image of an uncommitted dilettante does not sit entirely comfortably with the facts. Dornan turned down summer wages and paid bonuses out of his own pocket. Just before his resignation he made another astute signing (as with Paul O'Neill) when Tommy Leeman, who had decided to come home from Australia, joined Ards. Glentoran tried to stall the deal, claiming that they had an arrangement by which the full-back could only join them, but this seems to have been mere bluster, and 'Leeper' went on to become a firm favourite at Castlereagh Park.

When the dust over Dornan's departure settled, Bertie McMinn was given a chance to take over as manager. He signed Alan Fettis, soon to be selected for the Northern Ireland U-23 squad and for the Irish League, on professional forms, was relieved to hear that the talented little winger Tommy Kincaid would stay on now that there had been a regime change, but lost Tommy's brother Bobby, Ards' Player of the Year, off to Australia. But there was little McMinn could do to stop Ards' slide in what was left of the season, and there was only one more win, surprisingly against Glentoran, where Leeman scored against his old club in a 2-1 victory.

FOURTEEN

Happy Days Are (Temporarily) Here Again 1990-95

In January 1990 Ards had unveiled plans for a new 600 seater stand, utilising £30,000 from the Football Trust and hoping to raise the rest of the estimated £40,000 themselves. A ten year season ticket, guaranteeing a stand seat, was offered for a bargain £100, but these tickets moved surprisingly slowly, and it was almost Christmas before the club claimed that they were 'nearly all' gone. The new stand was supposed to be ready by October, but was delayed, and in the meantime Castlereagh Park had no seats at all. In the close season Ards tried to address their lack of punch by signing proven goalscorer Sammy Shiels, a centre back in the shape of Fred Scappaticci, right sided midfielder David Eddis from Bangor, and in September, utility defender Allen Morrison from Coleraine. The team got off to a reasonable start, with a draw against Cliftonville, a win against Omagh Town, now promoted to senior ranks along with Ballyclare Comrades, and a narrow 1-0 defeat by Linfield, in a game where Tommy Leeman was red carded. A draw against Coleraine in a match Ards had dominated followed, but then came nine games without a win. Shiels had begun to find the target regularly, but he had little support from the others. A scapegoat was duly found, and Bertie McMinn was shown the door after barely six months in the job. It was hardly a fair length of time to prove himself, and if he was simply not up to the job the question must be put as to why he was appointed in the first place.

Perhaps the answer was that Ards had a bigger managerial name waiting on the sidelines. Roy Coyle, who in fifteen years at Windsor Park had guided Linfield to 31 trophies, had a few months earlier parted company with the Blues, and he now became Ards' manager. He promised to stay for the full term of his contract, and was quoted as saying "If I'm not here at the end of three years it will be because of Ards' choice, not mine". It is fair to say that Coyle's appointment galvanised the club. Attendances went up, there was talk of fresh faces on the Board, and although it took a few weeks, Ards eventually got their act together on the field of play. There were signs of better things to come in the Budweiser Floodlit Cup match against Portadown, but the eventual outcome was particularly disappointing. Ards led 2-1 with 12 minutes to go: Kincaid broke through but was too slow to get a clean shot in, the Ports grabbed a late equaliser and went on to score two more goals in extra time. Coyle recognised that the team needed fresh players, and was given the wherewithal to recruit Winston 'Winky' Armstrong, a big centre-forward signed from Carrick Rangers. £5000 changed hands to bring Brian McLoughlin from Glenavon, and a similar sum was paid to Larne for the excellent defender Tommy McDonald. In the New Year central defender Noel Mitchell moved to Ards from Coagh United. The new players began to make a difference, and after Armstrong's goal brought Ards a fighting draw at home to Linfield, a seven match sequence began which saw Ards win six and draw the Boxing Day fixture against Crusaders.

League results faltered somewhat in January, but by now Ards were showing good form in the knockout competitions. In the League Cup there were wins over Ballinamallard United and Queen's University (3-0 on a gale-lashed night which was as cold as anything I can remember), and a fine 4-0 victory over Larne in the quarter-final. The semi-final was played at Shamrock Park, the opponents Omagh Town, and Ards tore the County Tyrone side apart with goals from Armstrong (2), Campbell and McLaughlin in a 4-1 win. Meanwhile the Irish Cup saw Ards beat Dungannon Swifts 4-1 before being drawn against the progressive junior club Donegal Celtic. There were always likely to be sectarian undertones to such a game, and sadly the match was marred by a series of incidents, with stones and an iron bar thrown from the Ards side, four arrests after fighting between rowdy elements and the RUC, and some disgraceful spitting at the Donegal Celtic subs. It was clear that the no go area meant to keep rival fans apart was inadequately policed, but even though those involved were by common consent strangers to matches at Castlereagh Park the events were shaming to Ards. On the field they failed to score against dogged opponents, and the match finished scoreless. Immediately fears were expressed about the likelihood of further violence in a West Belfast replay. The RUC said they would not consent to a rematch on the Tuesday, but Ards announced that they were perfectly happy to travel. In the end Donegal Celtic decided to end the impasse by withdrawing from the Cup, and Ards progressed in a less than satisfactory manner. In a move to avert similar trouble in the future the Ards Board announced that in future no flags other than Ards flags could be brought into the ground, but then those intent on violence would be merely inconvenienced by this, not dissuaded.

In the quarter-final Ards were drawn at home to Linfield, a tie heavy with symbolism for Roy Coyle. On the day, in front of a huge and passionate crowd, Ards won a classic cup tie 3-2, with Tommy Kincaid's third goal for the homesters a delight, as he latched on to McKeown's slip like lightning and deftly slipped the ball into the net with two perfect touches, to send the big Ards support into raptures. Linfield pulled one back and subjected Ards to a real battering as the minutes ticked away, but Coyle's men held out for a glorious win and entered the semi-finals. A week and a half later Ards faced Glentoran in the League Cup Final. The match was originally scheduled for Bangor, but sensibly the venue was later changed to Windsor Park, where the wisdom of the change of mind was witnessed in the Ards support filling the South Stand, still outnumbered by Glentoran fans. What might have happened at Clandeboye Road with such a big attendance hardly bears thinking about. On the night the Glentoran side was simply too good, and two goals from Gary McCartney saw the men from East Belfast win 2-0. There was still the Irish Cup proper, however, and here Ards found themselves up against Portadown, for whom Frazer and Cowan were then in their pomp, and it was two goals from the latter which saw the Ports home by two goals to one. The season ended disappointingly for Ards, with a shock exit from the County Antrim Shield at the hands of Dundela, and a series of League defeats only redeemed by a late flurry of three wins and a draw in the last four matches.

Nonetheless there was a definite buzz around the club in Coyle's first season. A final and a semi-final had provided genuine excitement, and the Ards club had self-belief again. The new stand had opened in January with a friendly against Everton. There was an excellent crowd of 6000, and Everton won 5-2, with Peter Beagrie pleasing the fans not so much with his two penalties as with his trademark handspring celebration, a novelty in those days. Harry Cavan performed the opening ceremony, and Malcolm Brodie quite rightly campaigned for the stand to be named after him, but nothing was done, and the stand remained anonymous until its demolition.

Never drop your guard, for as sure as Monday follows Sunday fate will sneak up on you and strike a blow just when you least expect it. As Ards looked back with some satisfaction on the season just ended, anticipating the imminent return of the good old days, came the bombshell that Roy Coyle, only six months into his contract, had gone to Derry City as their new manager. The club and the fans were first dumbfounded, then furious. But anger and bitterness would not solve immediate concerns, and the Ards Board, vowing that they would be seeking maximum compensation from Derry, went about the business of appointing a new manager. At least the new man would have the advantage of taking over a team which was on the up. An arrangement was almost reached with Glentoran stalwart Billy Caskey, but at the last minute he pulled out, so instead Ards turned to the 38-year-old Paul Malone, the Larne manager. Pointedly Ards did everything by the book when approaching Malone, and secured their new boss on a five-year contract after shaking hands on a compensation deal agreed by both clubs.

Malone, seen as a tough, no nonsense boss, did not waste any time in getting to work. The 20-year-old Alan Fettis became the second Ards goalkeeper to be transferred across the water in as many years. He had spent three and a half years at Ards, having been persuaded to join the club by the perceptive Jimmy Todd, and now earned Ards £40,000 from Hull City as soon as he had reached a quota of first team games and been picked to represent his country. O'Neill

Darren Erskine, Ards' most prolific goalscorer since Jim Campbell

and Mullen were transfer listed as too expensive to carry, a decision that seemed short-sighted. John Mullen went back to St. Francis, to be replaced by Crystal Palace target Joe Kerr from Donegal Celtic, but eventually Paul O'Neill was re-signed to add some steel to the Ards midfield, where he was joined by Ian Bustard, who had played under Malone before, and who joined from Glenavon for £5000. Winky Armstrong expressed a desire to leave, and Sammy Shiels, a decent enough player but criticised for being too slow, was allowed to go. To replace these strikers Ards turned to a junior player, Darren Erskine of Ards Rangers, who was joined by Armagh Gaelic footballer Ger Houlahan, and shortly after the season got under way Ards splashed out on another striker in Portadown's Marty Magee, spending a club record £15,000 on the little forward. John McAuley had announced that he had to study for exams and would consequently be unavailable for the season, but he reneged and signed for Glentoran instead.

The AGM heard of a profit of £52,000, with gates having doubled during Coyle's stint at Castlereagh Park. Ards demanded £26,000 as compensation from Derry for the balance of Coyle's contract, but were disappointed when an international tribunal only awarded them £7500. In addition, £30,000 was still owed on the stand, and the club was also obliged to fork out £18,000 to tarmac the rough areas that had provided ammunition for the hooligan element at the Donegal Celtic match, for which misbehaviour Ards were fined £750.

Malone's team failed to register a win in their three Ulster Cup group games, although in the first of these they actually led Portadown 2-0 before losing 4-3. There was one win in the Gold Cup, a splendid 5-2 away victory at Coleraine, where John Smith, who had come from Ards Rangers along with Erskine, scored twice. In the League proper Ards had very mixed fortunes, but were certainly moving in the right direction, winning six and losing three up to Christmas. Their best results were a 4-1 win at Bangor, a rousing 2-1 home defeat of Portadown, and a 6-1 trouncing of Ballymena United in mid-December which propelled them up to 4th place. Of the drawn matches in this period, none was more sensational than the Distillery game in mid-October. From 4-1 up Ards were pegged back by the Whites, but real controversy surrounded referee Loughins' denial of what looked like two clear cut penalties to Ards, and his subsequent sending off of Assistant Manager Jimmy Brown and blameless team attendant John Wilton. After the festive season Ards' league form slumped, and it was late February, ten matches later, before they put together another win. In that barren spell probably their best result was a 1-1 draw at the Oval, where Ards would have won but for Glentoran keeper Alan Patterson, who produced half a dozen incredible saves to keep his side in the hunt. In the meantime the team progressed to the semi-final of the County Antrim Shield after a 5-0 defeat of Comber Rec. and a 3-1 win at Ballyclare. By this stage another young goalkeeper was starring for Ards. Stephen Vance, on loan from Glenavon, had replaced David Crooks, but he was badly exposed in the semi-final against Crusaders at Ballyskeagh. Ards won the toss but elected to face the gale force wind, only to find themselves two down after five minutes, both goals the result of Vance misjudging the ball in the high winds. Crusaders went on to reach the final after scoring a third goal.

In another knockout competition Ards brushed aside Queen's and Ballyclare to reach the quarter-final of the League Cup, but here they lost 2-0 to Portadown. This was revenge for the Ports, whom Ards had beaten just over a fortnight earlier in the League, probably the best result that season. 2-0 down after 28 minutes, Ards hit back to level the scores after Mickey Keenan had been sent off at 2-1. In the 91st minute Rab Campbell swivelled to crash home a twelve yard volley and Ards had won. Campbell came in for high praise from the watching Tommy Docherty shortly afterwards when Ards held Linfield to a 2-2 draw, a match in which Noel Mitchell also attracted the former Manchester United boss's commendation. The League campaign finished well as Ards went unbeaten through their last four games, by which time Harry McCourt had joined the club from Omagh Town for £15,000, joined by midfielder John Crilly who cost a similar sum. Ards exited the Irish Cup at Glenavon, but there was trouble in the Glenavon Social Club after the game, and Ards supporters had to shoulder the blame for instigating the violence. The club took firm action, confirming the de-affiliation of one Supporters' Club. It was only one of a number of times that season that the fans misbehaved. When Joe Kerr opted to stay away from Ards late in the season it was alleged that this was the direct result of abuse he had received, again in a Social Club, after the County Antrim Shield defeat.

It had not been a spectacularly successful season, but after the shock defection of Roy Coyle at least the ship had been righted. A minor trophy came Ards' way in the McEwen Sixes at the Dundonald Ice Bowl, when they won the tournament. A small competition, yes, but one which thanks to its TV coverage brought Ards more publicity than even the best of their wins in 'proper' football. Such is the power of television: such should be the lessons of self-promotion by Irish football. Harold Black's 'Three Score and More' club, formed exclusively of veteran supporters, was now running smoothly and contributing regularly to Ards F.C.. Most interesting of all, a small group of supporters began the fanzine known as *We're All Going Down to Davy Lee's*, which specialised in robust, frequently scurrilous support for the team, and abuse for rivals, especially near neighbours Bangor. Their song, sounding vaguely like *Will your anchor hold?* gave Ards their own unique song for a few years, and has been revived in a version played in the build-up to Ards' home games.

1992-93 was a season in which Ards reached two cup finals, attained their longest unbeaten run, yet finished with nothing more tangible than the wistful longing for what might have been. From a year that promised so much yet delivered so little there are still the memories of little Andy Beattie flying down the wing and delivering pin-point crosses for Darren Erskine, of the ball-playing striker Harry McCourt, of David Jeffrey and Noel Mitchell standing tall at the heart of the defence, and of the heartache of the Cup Final defeat to Bangor.

For some time Robert Campbell had been attracting the interest of Linfield, and after some hard bargaining a deal was done which took Campbell to Windsor Park in return for £18,000 and vastly experienced centre-half David Jeffrey, whose crunching tackles were a legend in the Irish League. Andy Beattie was a late developer, a 26-year-old who had never played above 'B' Division level, but whose speed from a standing start took him past his marker time and time again, and who proved a more then adequate replacement for Campbell. Other new signings included Gareth Davies, the young William Murphy, Conor McCaffrey and the Nottingham Forest youth team keeper, the 18-year-old Mark Smith, later to achieve dubious celebrity when he was sent off in record time, under 20 seconds when playing for Crewe Alexandra.

Harry McCourt scores against Bangor in the 1993 Irish Cup final, game one

The pre-season was distinguished by a 1-1 draw with Sheffield Wednesday, and the omens continued to look good as Ards went through their Ulster Cup section with full points. They beat Portadown, despite going behind and then missing a penalty, Distillery and Ballymena United, who were hammered 6-0, with Harry McCourt grabbing a hat trick. In the quarter final Ards and Omagh Town were still locked at 1-1 after extra time, but in a thrilling penalty shootout, when Omagh's Coyle was allowed three attempts before scoring, Mark Smith emerged as the hero of the hour as Ards went through 3-1. Paired with Glenavon in the semi-final Ards took the lead thanks to another McCourt goal, but were unconvincing thereafter and had to hold on for dear life as the Lurgan Blues dominated but failed to score. The final was played against Linfield at the Oval in front of a crowd of 5000, but Ards, although they began each half brightly, went down 2-0. The first goal was a disaster for Smith, who kicked the ball against, of all people, Robert Campbell, and the former Ards player scored inadvertently, while the goalkeeper was blamed by some for Linfield's second, scored by Johnston. In the meantime Ards had experimented with another on loan player in the Gold Cup. Darren Cairns came from Hull City, but his Ards' career lasted barely half an hour when he was sent off for a ferocious tackle on Glenavon's Michael McKeown, who also saw red for his retaliation. The final straw for Ards in that match came with a last minute equaliser for Glenavon which left the score at 1-1. Another fascinating 'might have been' loan was the projected appearance in an Ards shirt of hard man Steve McMahon, but when he came back into favour at Manchester City that plan fell through. The Ards shirt that he almost wore was, however, not one which found much favour with the fans, the Lotto designs coming in for much criticism, especially the version which can only be described as white with red splodges. Not surprisingly promises were made that Ards would revert to a more traditional red and blue, but it was a roundabout route to a settled strip: the match against Distillery on November 28 saw Ards turn out in their eighth different shirt that season. But never mind the bewildering array of kit, it was the form of the team that was causing more serious concern. The League campaign got off to a mediocre start, with two particularly dismal performances against Glentoran and Portadown, who respectively scored three and six goals without reply. There was also considerable disquiet at tactics which appeared to miss out midfield in favour of getting the ball up to the front men as quickly as possible.

Changes had to come. The Board apparently discussed Malone's future, but sensibly took Ards' good start to the season into account as well as the recent blip, and he was enabled to stay and rejig the team. Marty Magee, however, was allowed to go. The record signing had been a huge disappointment, but in fairness to the little striker he was obliged to play wide rather than in his preferred central position. Paul O'Neill, after much speculation, finally went to Newry Town. Back came Tommy Leeman, who had been away on loan, and in came Mick Kavanagh from Dundalk, and Dave Connell from Shamrock Rovers. Now 30, Connell was a teak-tough midfielder who had represented the League of Ireland and had been Rovers' Player of the Year in each of the last two seasons. Results began to improve from Hallowe'en, with three wins out of four, and a Budweiser Cup quarter-final victory over Cliftonville in which Tommy McDonald lived up to his nickname of 'Hammer' with two spectacular goals, the first from 20 yards, the second from 30! Unhappily Portadown knocked Ards out at the next stage, by 4-2 at the Oval, while the County Antrim Shield adventure came to a halt at the same venue in the second round, this time at the hands of Glentoran. But that defeat, nine days before Christmas, turned out to be the last until the end of February, as the team embarked on a record equalling run of fourteen matches without defeat.

Spurred on by the never say die example of Dave Connell in midfield, and fuelled by Erskine's goals (15 out of the 37 scored during the undefeated spell), Ards shrugged off the lingering injuries of Harry McCourt and the departure of Assistant Manager Jimmy Brown to take over at Ballyclare Comrades to enter 1993 as the form team of the Irish League. On Boxing Day they outfought and eventually outplayed League leaders Crusaders 2-0, continued with victories over Omagh, Coleraine and Cliftonville among others, and secured a share of the points against Portadown and Glentoran. Andy Beattie's speedy forays down the flanks provided much of the ammunition for Darren Erskine, while David Jeffrey and Noel Mitchell were steadfast in repelling and snuffing out opposition attacks. But winning sequences have to end sometime, and as bad luck would have it the team to stop Ards in their tracks and prevent a new record of fifteen unbeaten matches in a row had to be Bangor. In a Clandeboye Road thriller they won 4-3, the discarded Marty Magee ironically scoring twice. The Bangor defeat turned out to be a turning point, at least in League terms, as Ards struggled thereafter, only gaining one more victory in their last seven games.

But as the League campaign sputtered and died, Ards had other fish to fry in the shape of Cup runs. In the Irish League Cup they brushed aside Banbridge Town, with Beattie securing a hat trick in the 4-0 win, then squeezed past Distillery at the second time of asking in a match which went to extra time before Erskine and Morrison clinched a semi-final place. But an Ian Bustard goal proved insufficient against Coleraine, and Ards exited the competition.

Ards' cup form certainly kept them busy: the team would go on to play an exhausting 56 games before season's end. In the Irish Cup, drawn at home to junior side Loughgall they had an easy passage, winning 3-0, then made a trip to East Down, where, although not on top form, they beat Drumaness Mills 4-0. With home advantage, Ards nonetheless failed to score against Distillery, but in the replay got rid of their gremlins with a storming performance and a 4-1 victory, the highlights of which were the first goal, an acrobatic overhead kick from Erskine, and the second, a stunning 25-yarder from Ian Bustard. On then to the Oval and a semi-final with Cliftonville, with the atmosphere on the terraces going beyond the red-hot to, at times, the ugly. Harry McCourt was only passed fit to play an hour before kickoff, but it was his skill which propelled Ards into an apparently unassailable lead. The first goal came after a scintillating run down the left from McCourt: he looked up and found Beattie, who scored from eight yards. In the second half McCourt embarked on a dazzling run which took him past several defenders before he calmly sidefooted into the net. It looked all over, but Cliftonville fought bravely, and McFadden gave them some hope when he hit the post on the hour. With only seventeen minutes to go Vance failed to claim a corner, and Donnelly shot home from close in. Ards were visible fraying at the edges, and five minutes after the Reds' first goal Morrison lost possession 25 yards out, Vance failed to hold the resultant low cross, and McFadden scored the equaliser. It looked sickeningly inevitable that Cliftonville would find a winner, if not now then in extra time, but astonishingly it was Ards who came back from the dead. In the 90th minute Morrison hit a low and seemingly harmless cross into the box from the left. In a comedy of errors two Cliftonville defenders miskicked horribly, goalkeeper Rice also missed his kick, even though he had not been given a back pass and could have gathered the ball, and there was McCourt, able to tap home from six yards. Despair became jubilation, and Ards had reached the Irish Cup final for the first time since 1974.

Their opponents were Bangor, the first time the two clubs had met in the major final. The media went to town, as the novelty of a Bangor-Ards Cup Final gripped North Down and tickets sold like the proverbial hot cakes. Amid the enthusiasm, however, the more cautious noted that Ards' goalscoring form had dried up since the quarter-final, with a mere seven goals coming in eight games. Against that, on the other hand, a fortnight before the big match, Ards had secured a good 1-1 draw at Crusaders, albeit against ten men, thereby denying the League title to the Seaview side. When the long-awaited day came Ards whipped up the atmosphere by driving the team round the town on the Saturday morning to ensure a rousing send off, and a crowd which looked in excess of 10,000 rather than the official figure of 8,500 turned Windsor Park into a sea of noise and colour. The match itself failed to catch fire until the very end. A dour and cautious affair, it looked to be heading towards a replay when with only four minutes left Ards took the lead. McDonald freed the speedy Beattie, he made good ground down the right and his cross was headed in off the underside of the bar by Harry McCourt, who had now scored in every round of the Cup, and had apparently brought the trophy home. But it was not to be. A free kick to Bangor two minutes later was taken by Paul Byrne, and full-back Glendinning's looping header broke Ards' hearts and secured a replay for the Seasiders.

Perhaps neither side deserved to win a disappointing game, and Ards' complaints about a lack of luck have to be balanced against their last minute good fortune in the semi-final, but it was Ards who were now on the back foot, and they who had to pick up for the rematch, a week hence. They could not have got off to a better start. McDonald's free kick was flicked on by McCourt, and Darren Erskine dived full length to head home. But Bangor fought back to level matters, again courtesy of a looping Glendinning header. Unlike the first match, extra time was played when neither team had added to the score after 90 minutes, but it made no difference, and a second replay was needed. After this game Bangor manager Nigel Best stoked up the local rivalry when he accused Ards of being too defensive. "They have bored the tripe out of everyone for two games", he claimed. Certainly Ards played it carefully, but then I didn't see Bangor throw caution to the winds either. The lack of excitement may also have been due to the hard and bumpy Windsor pitch: another reminder to those who clamour for summer football that Irish League players struggle to play flowing football on rock-hard surfaces. But by this time most of the media had simply dismissed the 'best of three' series as a bore, blaming the teams rather than the pitch, and the IFA said that never again would the final be allowed to go to a third game.

The second replay need not detain us too long. Both teams had chances: both defences played well, but in the very last minute Paul Byrne scored from the edge of the penalty area to finish Ards off. Byrne was voted Man of the Match, taking into account all three games, but this did scant justice to Tommy Leeman, who had effectively shadowed the talented midfielder throughout most of the five hours of play, even sitting down beside him on the pitch when the Celtic-bound player needed attention from the trainer! Leeman's anguish was obvious at the final whistle, but it was a massive disappointment for all of the players, not only to have lost the tie, but to have gained nothing after such a gargantuan effort across 1992-93. Perhaps they were, to some extent, victims of their own success, looking more and more jaded as their marathon season reached its final month. For the record, the players who appeared in the series of finals were: Vance, McDonald, Leeman, Mitchell, Jeffrey, Bustard, Beattie, Connell, Erskine, McCourt, Davies, Brian Campbell and Kavanagh. They may not have won any silverware, but my goodness they gave us a year to remember.

Despite the disappointment of the Irish Cup Final, Paul Malone was not one to cry over spilt milk, and before the 1993-94 season he set about honing his team. The talented Marty McCann was signed from Derry City, and from the same source came former Linfield full-back Paul Mooney for a fee of £5000. But Dave Connell's move to Drogheda for £2500 took the steel out of an Ards midfield which had benefited from Connell's and Paul O'Neill's presence over the previous few seasons. At the time the major acquisition was reckoned to be the

All-time fans' favourite Marty McCann

former Linfield striker Martin McGaughey, now nearing the end of an illustrious career but hoping for an Indian summer with Ards. The AGM heard of a profit of £10,000, with £20,000 coming from sponsorship and perimeter advertising, largely the work of the indefatigable Jimmy Todd. Once upon a time Ards had raised money through special efforts like funfairs and bazaars, now they had moved into promoting easy listening concerts, with evenings featuring Daniel O'Donnell and Dominic Kirwan producing healthy profits. Ominously, however, on the horizon was a cloud no bigger than a man's hand, with a Touche Ross warning that the Inland Revenue was turning its attention to

football clubs who were often less than assiduous about their income tax contributions. Swindon Town had already been successfully prosecuted for 'defrauding the Revenue', and it was no secret that Irish League clubs were next on the list for investigation.

But results on the field were of more pressing concern as the big kick off came, and Ards could not have foreseen the nightmare start to 1993-94, with only two wins in the first fourteen games. A lack of punch was the big problem, with the team failing to score in no fewer than seven of those fourteen matches. McCourt's groin injury prevented his playing more than half a dozen matches before mid-January, and Martin McGaughey did not hit the net until late October. What seemed a major capture, the exotically named Ken Petit de Mange, who had played a dozen games for Liverpool and had two caps for the Republic, simply did not work out. De Mange could certainly pass a ball accurately, but he failed to run the midfield the way that might have been expected, and he left for Bohemians before Christmas. The goalkeeping position was another area giving rise to concern. Stephen Vance, once seen as a natural successor to Kee and Fettis, was now badly out of form, and Ards experimented first with Craig Robson, Alex's son, then Brendan Kennedy, brought on loan from Bohemians. Even more worrying than the poor run was a frightening incident in September, when a mob forced open the doors of the Ards bus and attempted to drag Darren Erskine out when the vehicle was stopped at a red light near the Cliftonville ground. It is hard to imagine that the 5-1 defeat which followed was unrelated to the assault.

In spite of Paul Malone's insistence that he would not quit, the choice was not really his, and early in October he parted company with Ards, supposedly amicably. Surprisingly, in view of the venomous atmosphere which surrounded his departure for Derry City eighteen months earlier, Roy Coyle again became persona grata and the new manager of Ards F.C.. There was no immediate miracle, however, and after a particularly incompetent display at Coleraine in a 4-0 defeat Coyle lost patience and declared that he would listen to offers for any of the Ards squad. The threat was little more than that, and there was no wholesale clearout, although de Mange was allowed to go and at one stage Ards were believed to have offered Tommy McDonald and Marty McCann to Cliftonville in return for Jim McFadden. Mercifully this proposed swap never took place. The shakeup in the team came via the influx of Southern players Ken Blood, Karl Wilson and Christian Bowes, all signed on loan. Although all three made a difference, it was the speedy Bowes who had the greatest impact. Marty McCann had never, and would never be a ball-winner in the midfield, but he had tremendous vision and could deliver a defence-splitting pass of weight and precision. In Christian Bowes he found the ideal partner, someone whose pace enabled him to run on to Marty's threaded passes, as often as not inside the full-back. And so, as the days were at their shortest Ards began to pick up speed.

A 4-1 win over Glentoran in the County Antrim Shield saw the side at its sparkling best, with McGaughey scoring a couple as he at last began to recapture his old form. In the next round Ards had to go to extra time, but eventually defeated Distillery 2-1. Between these games they enjoyed their all-time record League win, 9-0 against Newry Town, with Bowes claiming a hat trick, and McCann's goal, the last, an audacious lob from twenty yards when he raced through, stopped, put his toe under the ball and simply lifted it over the bemused keeper. The Budweiser Cup saw Ards sail through to the final. A forty-yard chip from McGaughey made the long midweek trip to Omagh worthwhile, and in the second round Larne were despatched 3-1. The semi-final, played at Windsor Park, was one of the most astonishing games most of us have ever witnessed. Against a Cliftonville team reduced to ten men Ards nonetheless found themselves 2-0 down at half-time, and in the second half they showed precious little improvement. With both substitutes already used and Karl Wilson stretchered off, it looked like

Roy Coyle, manager of Ards

one of those nights, until, in the 88th minute Ken Blood headed home a Puckrin cross from the left. It seemed no more than a consolation effort, but Ards persisted, and in the 90th minute, in a goalmouth scramble former Ardsman Joe Kerr, under pressure from the hovering Erskine, put into his own goal. Ards had played poorly but got out of jail, and we all settled back in our seats to wait for extra time. But extra time was not needed. Two minutes into injury time Ards were awarded a free kick 35 yards out. With the wind at his back Paul Mooney lined it up, and somehow we now knew that the gods were with Ards that night. Sure as fate Mooney's shot sailed high and handsome past the bemused Brujos and into the net, and the South Stand went berserk. Three goals in four minutes in a match where they had been outplayed for most of the 93 minutes surely constitutes Ards' greatest ever fightback. Sadly, from an Ards point of view, there is less to talk about when it came to the final. At the Oval Linfield simply outplayed Ards. Inspired by a superb display from Raymond Campbell the Blues won 3-0 to take the trophy.

Ards' League form now began to pick up. The day after Boxing Day they won what the papers usually describe as a Christmas cracker, defeating Bangor 5-3 in a game where Erskine scored three. They only lost by a desperately late goal to Linfield, and beat Ballymena 3-0. That match was distinguished by a McCann goal scored in the gathering gloom when he waltzed round three defenders before striking a fierce cross-shot past the despairing Smyth. By this stage Ards seemed to have, at least temporarily, solved their goalkeeping problem, as Paul Kee returned home on loan from Oxford United, and immediately brought a fresh stability to the defence. In the Irish Cup Ards should have killed off Glentoran with a scintillating display in the first half, but they failed to put away their chances and had to be content with a 2-2 draw. The replay, at the Oval, was probably lost when Ards inexplicably opted to face the rain and gale in the first half. They went three goals down, and although they pulled the tie back to 3-2 they were unable to add to that scoreline and duly made their exit from the competition. Meanwhile, however, they had defeated hot favourites Glenavon in the semi-final of the County Antrim Shield, by 2-1, and faced Crusaders in the final. That match, which saw yet another trip to the Oval, was a real advertisement for Irish League football. On a raw February night, watched by a crowd of 4000, Ards went in at halftime a goal up, thanks to an eight yard strike from Bobby Browne, just signed from Shelbourne. The game really exploded in the second half. Ards looked to have the Shield in their possession when Karl Wilson was on the end of a slick passing movement involving Bustard and Brown. But with only eighteen minutes left Browne, hitherto immaculate in his work, hesitated over a clearance and

Happy days are here again: the County Antrim Shield winners

in the ensuing scramble Kirk Hunter got the last touch as the ball crossed the line. Ards wobbled for a spell before the young David Stranney, who had come on for McCourt, only just recovered from injury, was set up by Browne. He hesitated for what seemed like an awfully long time, but eventually rolled the ball into the net, and Ards had re-established their two goal lead. It looked as if it was only a matter of playing out time, but the words 'Crusaders' and 'lying down' never occur in the same sentence, and a brilliant volley by Roddy Collins in the 80th minute put the result in doubt again. It's never over until it's over, as they say, and the final twist of this pulsating match was the best yet. As desperation set in and Kee was forced into a couple of blinding saves the minutes ticked away as Crusaders hurled themselves at Ards. Then, in the 90th minute, Erskine put Stranney in the clear just over the halfway line. The youngster might have been offside, but he sensibly played to the non-existent whistle, raced through the inside-right channel, shimmied round McKeown and knocked the ball home. It was a stunning goal to win a thrilling match, and Ards had won their first trophy for twenty years. The suspended Andy Beattie had missed the final, but in a fine gesture Paul Kee, about to return to Oxford, gave the little winger his medal.

Ards might have been excused for easing off and playing out the remainder of the season some way below their peak, but this proved far from the case. In the League Cup they thrashed an outclassed QUB 9-2, then went on to win their next seven matches to equal their best ever winning sequence. The best of the League victories were a 1-0 defeat of Glentoran, and home and away wins over Glenavon, 4-1 and 3-2. Interspersed with these was a successful League Cup run where they followed up the easy win over Queen's with defeats of Bangor and Distillery, but in the semi-final they lost 2-1 to Coleraine. By that time the record-equalling run had come to an end, in the tenth match, surprisingly at the hands of lowly Ballyclare Comrades, when they went down to a single goal ironically scored by ex-Ards player John Johnston. But they finished the season on a high, with three wins in the last three matches, to finish in sixth position, a remarkable achievement considering that Ards had been one off the bottom of a sixteen-team League when Roy Coyle took over. Late in the season £4000 had changed hands with Shelbourne for the experienced defender Kevin Brady, and Ards pulled off a coup when they obtained Paul Dunnion on a free from Omagh Town. The player should have cost several thousand pounds, but due to an over-sight Omagh had failed to offer him a new contract when his old one expired, and he became a free agent. Paul Kee returned on a permanent basis, but Martin McGaughey, who had failed to live up to expectations, was released.

For some time the bigger clubs had grown restive with a sixteen team league format. They felt that there was little interest in matches against the Carrick Rangers and Ballyclares of this world, and craved what they believed would be the continuous excitement of 'big' games involving top teams every week. Thus the Irish League voted to split itself into two leagues of eight, the makeup of each division to be decided by average placings over two seasons, last season and this one. Accordingly 1994-95 would be a crucial season. A lower half finish would mean that Ards would be condemned to an existence among the also-rans.

At the beginning of the campaign a number of players moved on. Karl Wilson returned South, Tommy Leeman was sold to Distillery for £2000, and the promising full-back Glenn Puckrin went off to do his two years' Mormon missionary work. Noel Mitchell went back to Coagh United, where he eventually became the manager. Mitchell was a strong central defender who was adept at tidying up, but this more often than not this involved a pass back to his goalkeeper, and with the ban on goalies picking up the ball in those circumstances his effectiveness waned. In came John Sayers from Derry City, although doubts over his training schedule in Londonderry soon saw him on his way, the veteran Glentoran midfielder Raymond Morrison, and a new centre-half, Paul McBride, signed from Larne. The team would now have the benefit of a completely refurbished changing room, which along with the Social Club benefited from a £30,000 grant from the Football Grounds Improvement Trust. This brought the amount spent on Castlereagh Park over the previous six seasons to the surprising figure of £250,000.

Even with the new signings Ards got off to a wretched start in 1994. They lost their first six matches, and by the middle of November, by which time they had played sixteen, they had managed to win on only two occasions. In the second match of the League campaign, against Glenavon, Ards suffered a particularly harsh refereeing decision when Ferguson was allowed to retake a saved penalty on the dubious grounds that he had not placed the ball correctly on the spot. Thus reprieved, he scored, and Glenavon got a draw. But there were no such excuses when, a fortnight later, Omagh Town, reduced to nine men, secured a draw at Castlereagh Park. The only good news during this depressing period was the international call up of Paul Kee, who played so well for Northern Ireland in Austria that he was awarded Nat Lofthouse's old sobriquet of 'The Lion of Vienna'. But nothing could take away from the poor form of the team in this early part of the season. A year earlier a similar start had led to the removal of Paul Malone, but Roy Coyle did not suffer the same fate, despite the growing threat of Ards having to play in the lower division two years down the line. Nine points from the opening ten fixtures certainly pointed that way, and there was a small but noisy demonstration against the Board after a 4-1 defeat at home against Carrick Rangers, but thankfully results began to turn around as the winter drew on. One of the reasons for the upturn was the arrival of two newcomers from the League of Ireland, Gary O'Sullivan and the excellent Paul Cullen, as Bobby Browne was released. Seven wins in ten League games pushed Ards up the table, as Darren Erskine found his shooting boots, Kevin Brady revealed his true form when switched from full-back to centre-half, and the side consistently gained full points against the lesser teams, something higher placed clubs could not always do. The most prestigious win in this good run was a 3-1 defeat of Linfield. Ards also twice defeated high-flying Crusaders, in the League and in the County Antrim Shield, although Linfield would end their interest in the latter competition in the next round, even though the game went to extra time and Ards only lost 4-3.

It was a blow when Harry McCourt, a terrace favourite despite occasional inconsistency, asked for his release and was allowed to go, albeit for a handsome £10,000, to Derry City. But at least Ards profited from this deal, unlike the case of Tommy McDonald, who went to Cliftonville for nothing when Ards had failed to do the necessary paperwork to retain him as a professional. 'Hammer' was probably worth £15,000, money which Ards could ill afford to lose if they had to forfeit the use of the player, yet despite the gravity of this error, no one resigned. But in spite of these losses Ards continued to prosper on the field. In the knockout tournaments they enjoyed a good run in the Irish Cup, favoured by a draw which allowed them to ease past Chimney Corner and Brantwood. In the quarter-final they defeated Glenavon 3-2, scoring all their goals in a thrilling seven minute spell. In the League Cup they beat Dungannon Swifts on penalties after a 3-3 draw, but in mitigation they finished the match with only nine men, Beattie ands McBride having been sent off, then went on to beat Omagh by the odd goal in five, Ballyclare Comrades 4-2, and reached the final when they knocked out Bangor by a score of 2-1, where the decisive goal was a thirty yard screamer from O'Sullivan. By this stage David Jeffrey, out of the side, had moved on to Larne to become their Assistant Manager, and Ards had gained two new strikers, in the shape of Derry City's Gary Heaney and Warren Patmore, a strong target man, on loan from Yeovil Town. And a young Michael Owen had played at Castlereagh Park, scoring the only goal of the game from the penalty spot as England's U-15 side beat Northern Ireland, in front of a healthy attendance of 2000.

Come April Ards' attentions were divided, as their need to retain a position in the top flight had to be balanced against their cup ambitions. First would come an Irish Cup semi-final with Linfield. The tie went to two games, the first a goalless draw, the replay a much better affair once it exploded into life in the second half. As tempers rose on the field Ards rose to the challenge and moved up another gear. Denied what supporters to this day argue was a clear penalty for a push on the hard-working Patmore, they could consider themselves unfortunate to finish on the wrong end of a 2-1 scoreline. Ards' other cup interest was, of course, the final of the League Cup. Played against Cliftonville at Windsor Park, the game was, frankly, dire. At the end of 90 minutes, and even after an extra half hour neither side had managed to score. For Ards Patmore had, as ever, shown enthusiasm and enterprise, and it was a surprise when he was substituted, but the official Man of the Match, ironically, was Tommy McDonald, now a Cliftonville player. The game had to be decided on the night, and so everything was down to a penalty shootout. Cliftonville's record in such tie breakers had been dreadful in recent times, and sure enough they blew it, failing to score even once, although Kee's save from Ron Manley was superb. Ards, on the other hand, scored twice, via Erskine and Mooney, and duly won the League Cup. At the finish Andy Beattie, who had suffered a serious injury at Larne a week earlier, discarded his crutches to dance around in delight as Ards collected their second trophy in as many years. The unlucky Beattie had missed both of the finals, yet had played well all season, as had the unspectacular but effective Morrison, who added solidity to midfield.

The run in for the League saw Ards coast to fourth position with four wins in their last four games, with an aggregate goal tally of 10-0, but it was the very last game which sticks in the memory. The legislators had, you will remember, opted for the sixteen teams dividing in two on the basis of average places rather than the simpler 'points obtained' method. This led to the embarrassment of a final match at Castlereagh Park, when Bangor came to Ards knowing that a win would condemn them to relegation. So long as Ards won Coleraine, Bangor's nearest challengers, would fail to make the cut. (Are you still with me? No, me neither.) Anyway, against the spirit of football and presumably against the rules, Bangor merely went through the motions, blasting well wide of the goal when, in the second half, Ards also appeared to stop trying and allowed Bangor to threaten their goal. Some were embarrassed, some were angry, I remember being merely amused as the big Bangor following cheered Cullen's second and clinching goal for Ards, and a large proportion of the crowd stayed behind to listen to commentary on the last five minutes of the Ballymena-Coleraine game, with Bangor cheering for Ballymena and Ards for Coleraine. They say it could only happen in Ireland; perhaps that ought to be refined to read 'It could only happen in the Irish League'.

FIFTEEN

From Bad to Worse

1995-2000

Ards entered the newly-named Premier League in 1995 with some trepidation. Those who supported the idea of an elite league argued that every match would be a big one. But this was a flawed concept. A league programme has a natural rhythm, with a number of run of the mill games building up to The Big One. By definition every match cannot be a top of the table clash, and sooner or later ennui will set in and be reflected in gates. Ards' particular fears concerned survival. With one team out of eight being relegated, a club with little money to spare would probably struggle. Ards found themselves in that position, and the season was punctuated with manager Coyle's complaints that financial constraints were tying his hands. Interestingly, in a pre-season interview with the *Chronicle,* chairman Hugh Owens claimed that gate receipts were only providing around a fifth of expenditure, and that sponsorship, social club profits, perimeter advertising etc. had to make up the shortfall. In the autumn the AGM would hear that Ards had made a £16,000 loss in the previous season, and that a big tax bill, not as yet finalised, would soon face the club.

Prospects were not improved with the losses of Ards' best defender and of their most prolific forward. Sweeper Kevin Brady, tired of the travel, returned south to join Bohemians, while Darren Erskine was transferred to Linfield for what a tribunal eventually decided should be £35,000. Brady's loss was to some extent nullified as Paul McBride came of age as a central defender, but the lack of a striker was only temporarily solved by players brought in on loan from across the water. To bolster the defence Michael Kelly was brought from Ballyclare, and Brian Campbell returned after a year out of football. Gary O'Sullivan moved permanently to the club, joined by the enthusiastic Dubliner Dwayne Shanley, while up front Michael Boyle, who also played Gaelic football for Antrim, and would prove a regular goalscorer in a team crying out for goals, and Paddy Flannery, on loan from Greenock Morton, strengthened the squad. The most exotic signings of the close season were Steve Elliott and Richie Breza, two Americans who, alas, did not make the grade.

Ards' League Cup run did not get beyond the second round, but the team came good in their section of the Ulster Cup, winning all three matches. The home fixture against Linfield was a clinker, with a big crowd and a tremendous atmosphere and Darren Erskine, on his return, seeing his penalty saved by Paul Kee, while Paddy Flannery made a sensational debut with a brace of goals as Ards won 2-0. But in the quarter final Ards lost to Portadown, and ten days before that had suffered a 7-3 mauling, also at the hands of the Ports, in the final match of the Gold Cup. Coyle demanded some of the Erskine fee to strengthen an obviously shaky squad, and bought the veteran Barney Bowers from Glentoran for £5,000. No other big-money signings were made, although Andrew Hawkins came on a short-term loan from Dunfermline, and Scotsman Paul McLoughlin, a robust full-back, was signed from Derry City. Best of all, Marty McCann settled his financial differences with Ards, and returned to pull the strings in midfield.

Paul Cullen

The predictions of doom seemed justified as Ards reached their eighth match in the League before securing a win, 3-0 over Cliftonville. In the games against the Big Two there was a tendency to self-destruct. Paul Kee came racing out of his box to deal with a breakaway attack from Glentoran after Ards had pulled back to within a goal of the Glens and were pressing for an equaliser, handled, and was sent off. Against Linfield Raymond Morrison instinctively handled a shot on the line after half-an-hour, and was similarly despatched. This time Kee became a hero as he saved Fenlon's penalty, but referee Frank McDonald insisted that he had not given the go-ahead, and Fenlon scored with his second attempt, the second year in a row when a referee had appeared to favour an unsuccessful penalty taker to an extraordinary extent. Ards' disciplinary record was further tarnished when Michael Kelly was sent off in an otherwise encouraging 1-1 draw with Portadown. A 2-1 win over high-flying Crusaders was the only other success before the turn of the year, but the 3-1 victory over Distillery in the County Antrim Shield saw two sensational goals, McLoughlin's free-kick from the halfway line which left the keeper grasping at air, and a 30 yarder from McCann which would have graced *Match of the Day*. From mid-January onwards Ards at last give their long-suffering supporters something to enthuse about. For the most part these were Cup victories, with a comfortable 5-0 aggregate win over Larne in the Coca-Cola Cup, and a 2-1 win at Glenavon in the next round before a defeat in the semi-final at the hands of Cliftonville. In the Irish Cup Ards went into double figures against Cookstown United, Paul Cullen scoring four, then beat Larne 1-0, thanks to a Ray Morrison overhead kick which belied his years, to reach the quarter finals. The run ended at Portadown, however, with a 2-1 defeat. The surge in form was at least partly due to the arrival of a new centre-forward. Although Paddy Flannery had scored eight goals, he was clearly losing form and was allowed to return to Morton in late December. His replacement was Richie Barker, brought on loan from Sheffield Wednesday. Strong enough to hold the ball up, with a decent turn of speed, it was Barker's couple of months at the club which inspired their best spell of the season. In February Ards travelled to table-topping Portadown and beat them

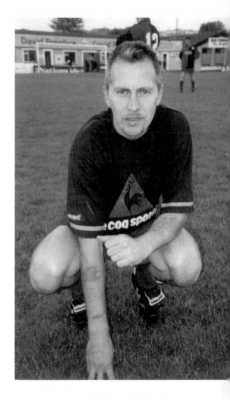

Raymond Morrison

3-1 in a game run by Marty McCann at his imperious best. Barker scored two cracking goals in a second half played in a blizzard, and memorably celebrated his late clinching goal by diving forward and sliding fully 20 yards through the snow to greet the ecstatic Ards support. Two wins over Bangor pretty well sealed the Seasiders' fate, with Paul McLoughlin scoring a memorable free-kick in the first of those victories. Way out on the right, a dozen yards from the goal line, he drove a searing free-kick across the goal and into the top corner of the net where it lodged amid a temporary silence before the crowd realised what had happened.

But in the last quarter of the season things went very wrong. The dependable full-back John Wills returned to England, Michael Kelly suffered an appalling knee injury which put him out for the season, and Sheffield Wednesday recalled Richie Barker. A solitary win over doomed Bangor was the only victory registered in the last nine League matches, and Ards finished one off the bottom. The end of the season was less than harmonious, with Roy Coyle hesitating over a belatedly-offered new contract, while a tedious series of boardroom changes culminated in rumours, denied by the chairman, of Hugh Owens' resignation. A bizarre feature of these changes was the apparent desire of local entrepreneur

Norman Carmichael to join a board unwilling to take him on. The conviction that Ards, one of the minnows of the new Premier League, would struggle, had sadly been all too accurate.

Their financial constraints put Ards at a disadvantage compared with almost all their rivals, and in 1996-97 the worst fears became reality, with the team finishing second bottom after a disastrous run in destroyed the good work of much of the rest of the season. The odd thing is that, looking at the squad, there were many decent players on the books that year, but the fighting qualities needed to stay up were only sometimes evident. It must have been difficult, however, for players to ignore the turmoil in the background, with bickering and resignations in the boardroom, and unrest within the Supporters' clubs. The return of Harry McCourt for the start of the season was widely welcomed. His transfer fee was part funded by North End ASC, thus bringing to a temporary end the standoff between the Board and the supporters' club, which had been unhappy about how their significant cash input was being spent. Other newcomers were Martin Tighe, a midfielder from Hamilton Academicals, and from the Republic Roy Fox and Matt Britton. Both players were sourced from St. James' Gate, who were obliged to offload many of their professionals when their sponsor withdrew his support. From the same club therefore came Damien Maher, a tall central defender, and former Arsenal striker John Bacon, whose name was a gift to sub-editors across the land, or at least would have been had he scored more often. The final product of the harvesting of the St James' Gate F.C. playing staff was goalkeeper Stephen Henderson, brought in to replace the out-of-form Paul Kee, and in October the all-action midfielder Sean Collins came from Glenavon in a swap for Paul Mooney. Also leaving Ards were Andy Beattie, back to Dundela for £2000, the skilful Marty McCann, whose contract was up and who returned to the North West to Finn Harps, and Dwayne Shanley, as honest and committed a performer as we are ever likely to see.

After a couple of wins over lesser opposition in the League Cup and the Ulster Cup, Ards' form nosedived. They failed to win a game in September or October, although they were unlucky to lose 1-0 at Coleraine in the opening League fixture, forfeited a 2-0 lead the next week to lose 3-2 to Portadown, and collapsed most spectacularly of all in the Ulster Cup quarter-final against Glentoran. 3-0 up after 23 minutes, they still enjoyed a 3-1 lead with ten minutes to go, but still managed to go down 4-3. Matters were not helped when a full month without a home game led to cash flow problems, and the 3-0 defeat at Ballymena was lashed by manager Coyle as 'an embarrassment and disgraceful'. A long overdue win came courtesy of a 35-yard Michael Kelly thunderbolt at Clftonville, and the following week Ards reversed the earlier score between the two clubs when they defeated Glentoran 4-3. This time it was Ards' turn to come off the ropes, when Morrison equalised from 30 yards with ten minutes to go, and McCourt scored the winner in the 90th minute. A Bacon penalty gave Ards their only other success in 1996, against Portadown, but from New Year's Day things began to look up.

For the rest of the season a series of young English players were brought in on loan. Paul Kee's stint in England had established cordial relations with Oxford United, and Ards secured Mark McGregor, Mark Stevens, Todd Lumsden and Paul Powell through that link, plus Mark Pemberton from Oldham Athletic. The short duration of these loans did not allow for continuity, but while they were there McGregor and Pemberton had a real impact. Apart from defeating Bangor over two legs in the first round of the Coca-Cola Cup, Ards now embarked on a seven match unbeaten run in the League. They held front runners Crusaders and Coleraine to draws, and scrambled a point at home to Portadown despite having Henderson dismissed when 2-1 down. The run reached its peak with a 4-1 defeat of Linfield at the beginning of February. The Blues, now managed by David Jeffrey, were no great shakes at the time, but to defeat them was still an achievement. In the Linfield match the speedy Pemberton scored the third of his four goals in a six match loan period. But although Ards were sixth out of eight, the teams below them were also picking up points, and it proved impossible to shake anyone off and reach safety. Worse, behind the scenes things were deteriorating fast. Long-time Secretary Ken Lowry left the Board, which before the end of the season had only four members. When Jack Irwin resigned he hit out at what he claimed was a lack of leadership, and warned that Ards could 'go to the wall'. The turmoil centred on a financial restructuring plan which seemed to split the Board. A crucial defeat at Solitude to fellow-strugglers Clifonville was the result of a harsh penalty decision with only five minutes to go, but Ards picked themselves up to beat Glentoran 3-0 and fight out a thrilling 3-3 draw with Coleraine. After that game a furious Kenny Shiels fiercely attacked an Ards team which he claimed "didn't create one chance in the whole match, had no pattern of play and [just] humped the ball up the field." Coyle dismissed the opinion of the excitable Shiels, laconically pointing out that if Harry McCourt had been on song he should have scored a first half hat trick. One last loan signing had arrived just before this managerial spat. He was the exciting Lee Feeney, who could not get on to Linfield's first team, and he added devil to the front line with his clever ball skills and darting runs.

There was still everything to play for. With half a dozen matches left it was still very possible that Ards could escape the playoffs, but in the early spring it all went horribly wrong. Two hammerings, 5-0 at Portadown and 5-1 at home to Crusaders, rocked them back on their heels, and only one point from the two succeeding matches meant that the home game against Cliftonville would effectively decide who would finish bottom. A draw would not do Ards, but as the final whistle approached that was what seemed the likely result, the two sides cancelling each other out. But in the 94th minute Tim McCann scored a winner for the Reds and Ards knew they were doomed. A large proportion of the crowd just stood there at the end, lost in depression and despair, sickened by the late season collapse. One man who did not stay on was Chairman Hugh Owens. Nor did he leave. He had opted out of what was billed as Ards' most important match for years, choosing instead to travel to England to watch Liverpool play Manchester United. Regardless of his reasons, it was a remarkably ill-judged decision, and his stock with supporters, already teetering after recent events, never recovered.

Ards had to regroup and raise themselves to play two games which might decide if the club lived or died. Relegation to the First Division (do these people not know that 'premier' means 'first'?) was not the same as relegation in England. There would be no healthy crowds amongst the lower orders, no Linfield or Glentoran coming to Newtownards with their army of supporters to gladden the Treasurer's heart. And in Ards' especially difficult financial straits their prospects of survival were problematical, to say the least. The playoff matches against Bangor were therefore of the utmost importance. The supporters rallied round, with a couple of thousand at the home leg, and Ards won both matches, each by a single goal. It was The Great Escape, and fans being eternal optimists, the professional performances in the playoffs (although Bangor caused a few frights in the Clandeboye Road game) gave rise to optimism that lessons would be learned, and that the next season not only could, but would be better. McBride and Murphy had both had sterling years, and if Lee Feeney could be retained his promise would be a good foundation for a better time ahead. Little did we know!

It showed real chutzpah to finish last in the League yet enter a European competition, but that was precisely what Ards did in the summer of 1997, when they applied for, and were nominated to compete in, the Inter-Toto Cup. The likelihood of reaching the last three and finding themselves in the UEFA Cup was remote, but the games would provide experience for the players, a guaranteed income from UEFA even if gate receipts disappointed, and see Ards back in Europe for the first time in over twenty years. In the event Ards struggled to make any sort of an impact. In the first match, at home to Royal Antwerp, Morrison was sent off for an instinctive handball, and the resultant penalty went in. For the rest of the game Ards battled bravely with ten men, Feeney showing some good touches. The next match involved an away trip to Cyprus, to play Nea Salamina. Here Ards scored their only goal of the tournament, a penalty from Barney Bowers, but were well beaten. They were very unfortunate in the game, losing goalkeeper Patterson after only five minutes, Winky Murphy taking over in the absence of a substitute keeper, and then Bowers, who had missed most of the previous season due to injury, broke his arm. Ards' cup of woe finally spilled over when Kelly was sent off at 1-0, and the Northern Irish representatives collapsed, losing 4-1. Against the big guns of Auxerre thay fought well until new signing Colin Beggs was sent off on the hour, but then fell away to lose 3-0. The final match was at the Olympic Stadium in Lausanne, where a predominantly youthful team played gamely, but lost 6-0 to the Swiss outfit. At least Ards finished this one with eleven men!

Apart from this venture matters were still miserable. The £10,000 which would have brought Darren Erskine back to Castlereagh Park could not be afforded, John Bacon failed to turn up for the Lausanne game and was allowed to leave, and Matt Britton, a good defender, went to Shamrock Rovers for nothing courtesy of the Bosman ruling. This was a measure designed to extend player

A 1997-98 Ards team pictured in their new away strip. Back row (l-r): Barker, Wilton, McBride, McCourt, Henderson, Hegan, Dyson, Johnston, O'Neill, Brown, Gregg
Front row (l-r): Yeo, Feeney, Lawless, Morrison, Lynch, Larmour, Bird

freedom, but it proved a savage blow to small clubs like Ards dependent on transfer fees. Winky Murphy left for Linfield, Paul Cullen went to Finn Harps, and Michael Kelly joined Omagh Town without any money changing hands, despite his estimated value of anywhere up to £15,000. The matter went to a tribunal, where it transpired that once again Ards had been lax about offering terms to Kelly, who thus became a free agent. The long established and generous North End Ards' Supporters' Club wound itself up, and when Treasurer Robert Boyle resigned Ards had only three directors left. To compound the misery the club was fined £2500 for its poor disciplinary record in the Inter-Toto.

Looking to the incoming season, Ards signed Peter Hinds, a big striker who had played for Dundee United, and Colin O'Neill, who had started with Ards as a teenager, but who had not played since suffering serious injury in the Scottish Cup Final of 1991! Aaron Lynch arrived from Shamrock Rovers, and Hugh Sinclair from Carrick Rangers. With the greatest respect to these newcomers, the balance sheet of players lost and players gained suggests that if Ards had just about survived with the squad they had the previous season, they had little or no chance this one. In the opening match of the League, Peter Hinds was sent off against Linfield, whose winning goal was scored by Richie Barker, back in the Irish League but wearing blue this time. With the season barely begun Hugh Owens decided it was time to go, and resigned after twenty years as Chairman. He was succeeded by Geddis Dunn, but more significantly for those who had been campaigning for change, local restaurateur and publican Norman Carmichael, along with Billy Hardy, joined the Board at last. John Wills returned to Ards, and for a short time centre-forward Simon Yeo looked promising, but then returned to England, claiming work commitments. His subsequent signing for Coleraine, just a couple of weeks later, left a bitter taste. In the 4-3 defeat to Glenavon Henderson was sent off for handling the ball outside the box, and in the game against Cliftonville McCourt was red carded for using foul and abusive language to the referee when Ards were 2-1 up: they went on to lose 3-2. Supporters were stunned by a series of blows in the autumn. It was revealed that Ards were £500,000 in debt, the biggest creditors being the Inland Revenue and the VAT people, and the club only just survived a winding up order. To save money Assistant Manager Jimmy Brown was dismissed, but returned shortly afterwards, his wages being paid by a group of supporters. Angry letters in the press were highly critical, not just of the Board, but now of the manager as well, and it transpired that Ards II had not been entered for the Steel and Sons' Cup. On the field there was no relief either: after a 2-0 Gold Cup win over Distillery Ards went eight games without a victory, then defeated Omagh Town 4-2 before going another five without a win. The disciplinary record was appalling: when

Paul McBride was sent off against Coleraine he was the third Ards player to be dismissed in successive matches.

Something had to give, and in late November Roy Coyle moved to Glentoran to replace the sacked Tommy Cassidy. In the short term George Bowden took over, and the side enjoyed a mini-revival, with two draws and two wins in his first four matches in charge. In the first of those wins Sean Collins, one of the few playing well at the time, scored Ards' winner against Glenavon with a peach of a shot, an 18-yard half-volley which fairly flew into the corner of the net. In a bewildering series of changes to the team striker Dave Maynard and central defender Lee Dyson, both Englishmen, had joined Ards, but Lee Feeney had moved back to Linfield. Five former directors who had left the Board, including Hugh Owens, now rejoined it, but by this stage Norman Carmichael had gone. He claimed that during his brief period in charge he had managed to reduce Ards' weekly wage bill from £3000 per week to £1700, but the comings and goings in the boardroom inspired little confidence. The team's revival ended, a home defeat in a stormy post-Christmas game against Omagh seeing McCourt and Johnston both sent off. By this stage Ards had a new manager, Tommy Cassidy completing the swap for Roy Coyle by moving to Castlereagh Park. Unlike his predecessor, Cassidy was only part time, another financial saving for the impoverished club. He made two early and important decisions, the first to move Harry McCourt on to Cliftonville, the second to re-employ groundsman Billy Johnston, whose dismissal had been in the interests of cost-cutting but which had led to a marked deterioration in a pitch which was once the pride of the Irish League. He also brought in the little Scotsman John Kerr, formerly with Linfield, but for all his endeavour John was not a goalscorer on a regular enough basis. To be fair to Kerr, no one on the side seemed capable of hitting the net on any sort of a consistent basis, with Ards scoring on average only once in every two games after the New Year, failing to win a single game after January 10. For all the fight that they showed on occasion, this lack of goals would prove fatal to Ards' diminishing chances of avoiding relegation.

A poor season became a humiliating one, with embarrassing exits from two cup competitions in a nightmare four day spell. First of all Ards were dismissed from the Irish Cup, at Castlereagh Park, by the juniors of Institute, then from the Mid-Ulster Cup by AFC Craigavon, despite going two goals up in as many minutes! Worse was to come. Despite the signing of Greenock Morton midfielder Barry Mason, Scots striker Derek Cook and the on loan Jonathan Prizeman from Glenavon, the First Division now beckoned. The last ray of hope was a fighting draw with table toppers Cliftonville, but on Easter Monday the 1-0 defeat by Portadown confirmed what had seemed inevitable for a long time, and officially

Ards were now down. In the last third of the season they had at last shown fighting qualities allied to greater discipline, but a chronic inability to put away the chances they created was a handicap too great to overcome.

Off the field the news was no better. The long-delayed 1997 AGM at last took place in January: the North End ASC had said they were only prepared to reconstitute themselves if a number of major changes took place. These were not forthcoming, but the status quo was only temporarily maintained, with a show-down expected at an Extraordinary General meeting to be held in late March. When that meeting took place the Board had openly conceded that Castlereagh Park would have to be sold. Offering this scenario as the basis of their plans to save Ards F.C., the Board fought off another attempt by Carmichael's consortium, as they became known, to take the club over and rescue it while retaining Castlereagh Park as Ards' home. As the ground where Ards had played since 1923 was offered for sale, the growing crisis had now exploded into the open, and from now on the struggle for survival would become desperate.

Tommy Cassidy

The line between success and failure can be frustratingly slender. The 1998-99 season was to prove a classic example, as Ards got off to a flier, led the race to gain a place in the Premier League by a distance at Christmas, yet folded when the crunch came, and had to contemplate another season down among the dead men. Perhaps the fault lay with a lightweight side which could not cope with the heavy and often sub-standard pitches as the winter rains came, perhaps it was the inability to match more physical 'up and at 'em' opponents, perhaps it was the comparative youthfulness of the Ards team, perhaps it was a loss of confidence as results began to go against them, perhaps a combination of all of these. The bottom line was that the red-hot favourites for promotion collapsed spectacularly when the chips were down, and were bested by Distillery as champions of the First Division.

Behind everything lay the ongoing power struggle and the knowledge that Ards' days at Castlereagh Park were numbered. The Carmichael group had been outvoted at the EGM, but made it clear they would not go away, arguing that the support for the existing Board expressed at the meeting was based upon unsubstantiated promises regarding a new venue. So as well as watching their backs Owens and co. still had to secure a site for the new ground.

Worryingly, although the old Scrabo School grounds and Hamilton Park were mooted as possible venues, both proved cul-de-sacs and as the season wore on there was still no word of a new home. As regards the playing staff, although Ross Hegan went to Distillery, Philip Dykes was signed in return, and in came the veteran Portadown keeper Micky Keenan, teenager Barry Reid from Glentoran: Jonny Wright was signed from Glenavon, and Andy Beattie returned to the club, as did Darren Erskine, despite worries about long-term injury problems.

Yet another administrative faux pas marred the opening of the season, this one costing Ards £1000 and the Ulster Cup. This competition, now confined to First Division teams, was in Ards' grasp as they recovered after losing two of their first three games. They would have finished in top position had not John Kerr, who should have been serving a suspension, played against Bangor in the opening fixture, which although won 2-0 by Ards, was now awarded to Bangor. The three forfeited points meant that Ards lost the Ulster Cup by a mere one point. Off the field the storm clouds continued to hover. There was talk of an approach to the local council, and even of a ground share with Bangor. As the search for the new ground continued fruitlessly, former manager Coyle lodged a claim for unpaid wages totalling £16,000, Department of Economic Development officials seized Ards' business records (Hugh Owens denied that there was anything to hide, and claimed a dirty tricks campaign against the club), and Jimmy Todd stood down as Commercial Manager. Against such a background it was a wonder the players could function at all, and yet they carried on with an excellent run which saw only one League defeat in the first ten games, including two victories over Distillery and one over Bangor, Ards' joint challengers for promotion. Their efforts were recognised when they were named as Smirnoff Team of the Month for November, and Tommy Cassidy as Guinness Manager of the Month. But there the good times stopped, as the winning run came to an end with a heavy 4-1 defeat at home to Carrick Rangers. It was not quite as surprising a result as it now seems. Ards had, towards the end of the month, been winning without looking convincing, and Carrick's physical, no nonsense approach would prove a match for Cassidy's more studied football each time the teams met over the rest of the season.

Sensibly the squad was added to in the shape of striker Alan Campbell and midfielder Jackie Coulter, but despite a 3-0 win over Limavady a week before Christmas the loss of both holiday games, victims of the weather, meant that lost impetus had to be built up again. Although Larne were beaten at the turn of the year, successive defeats to Distillery and Ballyclare followed, and suddenly a Division which the press had declared to be all over bar the shouting was alive again. To be fair, Ards probably deserved a draw in the Distillery game, while

Ballyclare's victory came through a poor penalty decision and a deflected shot in a match where Ards enjoyed overwhelming possessional superiority. Modest success in the various cups was perhaps a distraction from the all-important promotion push. Nonetheless seven goals were scored against AFC Craigavon in the Mid-Ulster Cup, and in a poor game Ards made hard work of easing past next door neighbours Ards Rangers by a single goal in the Irish Cup. The best of the Cup victories came in the Coca-Cola Cup, where a seesawing game saw Ards 3-2 down to Bangor with three minutes of extra time left, only for two late goals from Sean Collins and Barry Reid to snatch a breathtaking victory. The man who turned the game, even though he only came on as a sub in the 74th minute, was Rory Ginty, a new signing who had played half a dozen games for Crystal Palace, on one occasion coming off the bench to replace the great Attilio Lombardo. But Ards' interest in the Irish Cup and the Coca Cola ended in successive defeats at Carrickfergus, while another League defeat at Bangor halved their lead to just six points. 'Just' six points. In other circumstances that would have been a healthy cushion, but in the winter mud and with confidence at rock bottom Ards were about to go into freefall. Another defeat by Bangor in mid-February allowed Distillery to take over at the top. Ards clearly lacked a midfield general, Keenan had lost form and the confidence of his defence, and there was a lack of physical presence, greatly needed in the lower league. Ards attempted to arrest the slide with a series of signings. Goalkeeper David Henry came on loan from Linfield, strikers Donal McCourt and Paul Lynch were signed, and reserve Brian Hylands broke into the team. But all to no avail. Of the remaining nine League matches three were won but five lost, and only a 5-1 defeat of Larne in the last game secured second place and a playoff against the second bottom team in the Premier League.

The only bright spot of the late season was a shock defeat of Portadown in the semi-final of the Mid-Ulster Cup, when after a 2-2 draw Ards kept their heads better in the penalty shootout, Hylands scoring the decider in a 5-4 win. The final had to be played at the home of opponents Glenavon, and although Ards lost 3-1, they put on a tremendous display, with John Kerr, always a hard worker, having probably his best game in a red and blue shirt. But the last chance promotion saloon now beckoned in the shape of a home and away playoff against Cliftonville. At Newtownards Kerr again excelled, but Ards were thwarted by Reds' keeper Ingham and their own ineptitude in front of goal, and they went down to a goal from Down GAA star Peter Withnell. At Solitude Withnell almost beat Ards single-handedly, scoring a hat trick before being sent off in the closing stages. 'Nuts' Morrison scored a couple, but Ards lost 4-2 and had to resign themselves to another season in the lower division, this after enjoying a twelve point lead at Christmas.

Norman Carmichael's consortium, meanwhile, was still working to take over the club. They pointed to the spiralling losses of the last few years, from £12,000 in 1995 to a staggering £132,000 in 1998, and hammered home the devastating truth that for all the brave talk Ards had sold their ground yet still had nowhere to build a replacement. Confronted by these awkward truths, struggling to keep the club afloat and faced with hostility from a majority of supporters, the beleaguered Board finally caved in late May. A new Board, consisting of Messrs. Carmichael, Ferguson, Ennis, Irwin, Orr and Armstrong took over. It was a heady moment for those who had campaigned for change for so long, but even in the hour of their triumph there were warnings from the new incumbents that Ards' survival still hung by a thread. Clearly the fight to save the club was still very much on.

Sean Collins

The new Directors opened the 1999-2000 season with a real coup, when they persuaded a big name to join them. This was boxing promoter and bookmaker Barney Eastwood, whose self-confessed lack of intimate knowledge of local football mattered less than the reflected glory of having such a celebrity on board. Over the summer a great deal of work was carried out to revamp Castlereagh Park, and the Board still talked optimistically of securing a fresh deal with new owners Morrison's. Recognising the failures of the previous campaign, Tommy Cassidy had to replace Darren Erskine, who finally admitted defeat in his struggle against injury, and Philip Dykes, who moved to Bangor. The trouble with the host of newcomers was that although they brought vast experience and ability, with the exception of Mark Magill, who moved from Linfield, they were none of them in the first flush of youth, with consequent worries about their stamina, especially as the inferior pitches of the First Division became heavier. Old favourite Sammy Shiels and Robert Campbell returned, along with Tom Cleland from Linfield, centre-forward Shane McQuillan and Stephen Young from Coleraine, and Scottish hard man Gary Peebles from Portadown. Peebles was signed on a trial basis, and was not retained for long, but a greater loss in the midfield was that of Raymond Morrison, who had just been the deserved recipient of a benefit season.

With only one win in their first three matches, Ards did not get off to the flying start many would have hoped for, but a fine 3-1 victory over promotion rivals Omagh Town began a four game League run which saw full points gained. The first round of the Gold Cup brought a 2-1 win at Bangor, although Shane McQuillan seemed very hard done by when he was to all intents and purposes the victim of an assault, did not retaliate, yet was sent off for 'fighting'. After that victory Ards went off the boil, winning only one of their next six matches in the League, and fell behind new leaders Omagh. They exited the Gold Cup at the hands of Glentoran, but put up a brave fight and only lost to an 89th minute winner from Rainey. But behind the scenes there were big changes afoot. Newry businessman Joe Rice had left his home town club and came to Ards to join the Board, bringing with him former Newry and Linfield manager Trevor Anderson. Tommy Cassidy, after just short of two years in charge, was the unfortunate sacrificial victim of the arrival of Rice and Anderson. Perhaps he should have been given more time, but the parlous financial position of the club did not allow for patience and a medium term rebuilding. An essentially decent man, Cassidy himself found it difficult to accept his removal, describing himself as "gutted, totally numb".

Anderson had to act quickly to get the team back on the winning trail. Although it emerged that Ards had approached the Council with a view to buying back the ground, and had applied for an Administrator to oversee a financial rescue, there were also disquieting rumours that the overall debt was continuing to rise, and that a number of Directors were contemplating resignation. Many regretted the departure of Paul McBride to Distillery, but his replacement as a central defender was the Derry City stopper Paul Curran, hugely experienced, and, as time would tell, a fine clubman. Shortly before Christmas Alan Hall, a left-back, came from Newry Town to rejoin his former boss, and John McGrath was taken on loan from Linfield. Despite a crucial loss to Omagh in Anderson's second match in charge, Ards went through November and December undefeated, but frequently failed to kill off their opponents, drawing as many games as they won. In the County Antrim Shield they defeated Premier League Distillery at New Grosvenor, goals from Curran and Cleland edging out the Whites. On their travels again in the second round, Ards easily accounted for Ballyclare Comrades to the tune of 5-1, but in the semi-final Glentoran were simply too good and won 4-1. The first match of the new millenium witnessed a vital 2-1 win at Omagh, a result which narrowed the gap at the top to a mere three points. The winner came with four minutes to go, and the following week a draw was achieved at a similar late stage. In both cases the scorer of these crucial goals was Tom Cleland, who although now a veteran (he was 30) embarked on a fine run of games in which he scored eight goals in nine games. But neither Cleland nor anyone else, for that matter, could score in 210 minutes of Irish Cup action against Dungannon Swifts, and Ards lost 1-0 in a replay, forfeiting much-needed revenue from any future rounds.

League form continued to disappoint. Too many draws were interspersed with the victories, and Limavady proved to be Ards' bogey team, defeating them in late January and late April. There was a major clearout in February, with no fewer than nine players allowed to go, among them Colin Beggs, Andy Beattie, Rab Campbell and Barry Reid. The saving to the wages bill was reported to be in the region of £1000 a week. Although for the first time that season Ards had a settled team in the spring, there was no prospect of them catching Omagh after the second Limavady defeat and a sharing of the points when the leaders took a 1-1 draw from Castlereagh Park. Indeed, the last two matches in the League had to be won to keep Ards ahead of Bangor to retain second place and another playoff game. Those two matches were duly won, 2-1 at home to Ballyclare and a much more confident display at Carrick Rangers, where they ran out 4-1 winners. The hard-working and enthusiastic McQuillan found the net more regularly towards the end of the season, but against this Shiels was now struggling, and goals were often hard to get. Once again Ards' opponents in the playoff were Cliftonville, and although both games were hard-fought and the results closer than the year before, there was no disputing the Reds' superiority over the two legs, and in the end they won 3-0 on aggregate.

For the second year in a row April had proved the cruellest month for Ards, as they failed to capitalise on a good start and were unable to gain automatic promotion. And yet there is an element of huffiness about regarding another second place finish as failure. Ards had no God-given right to spring back into the top flight, but in our hurt pride we believed they were a 'big' team, the biggest fish in a small pond, and as such the natural choice to go up. We paid too little heed to the fact that after the home tie against Cliftonville Ards would be homeless, dependent on the largesse of other clubs, and that our financial position was perilous in the extreme. Walter Lismore and Co. were now the Administrators, no longer merely advisers to Ards F.C., and alarmingly it became evident that a delay in securing planning permission for the redevelopment of Castlereagh Park could mean that the second instalment of the payment for the ground, just over £1m, might no longer be available. In such circumstances the failure to go up was indeed serious, the fans' disappointment less a matter of hurt pride and more a question of survival. As a depressing footnote to the season, the deaths of those two old adversaries, Harry Cavan and George Eastham, took place within a month of each other. It was now staring us in the face that the football club to which they had brought fame and glory could soon be gone as well.

SIXTEEN

Postcards from the Edge
2000-2007

Extinction appeared uncomfortably closer in the summer of 2000. Although Ards had received £400,000 as a down payment for Castlereagh Park, a narrow window of one year had been set for the receipt of planning permission, and as this period had now expired, purchasers Morrison's were under no obligation to pay the balance of more than £1m, but were free to renegotiate, obviously from a position of strength. With an overall debt of £500,000 the prospect for Ards was indeed bleak. The homeless club looked around for temporary lodgings, and found them in Solitude, courtesy of Cliftonville, whose generosity in Ards' hour of need should not be forgotten. But only a hard core of Ards support, hardly ever more than two hundred, was prepared to make the journey to North Belfast, and with poor gates and a weekly wage bill of £2500 for the first team alone additional sources of income were clearly needed. Hopes of a return to the boom years when the Social Club was in the middle of Newtownards were briefly raised with the agreement to rent the former Scrabo Inn in Mary Street, but problems in obtaining a licence meant that the scheme was stillborn.

Trevor Anderson allowed John Kerr to go to Distillery and soon Sean Collins, basically too good for First Division football, left to join Glenavon. In came another batch of players, including Brian Donaghy, the speedy Peter Lowry, Donal O'Brien, Darren Parker, and Stuart McLean. Goalkeeper Henderson returned south, to be replaced by former Queen's Park keeper Neil Inglis. The most debatable newcomer was Dessie Gorman, once upon a time a peerless striker, but now 35. In fact Gorman showed that even in the twilight of his career he still had an eye for goal, and his contribution over the season was to confound the critics. The revamped team got off to an excellent start, remaining undefeated in the League until mid-November. Eight matches were won and four drawn, with Gorman netting seven times in as many games during a purple patch. The 1-1 draw against Bangor saw O'Brien score after only ten seconds, while the 'home' 3-3 draw against Distillery was achieved after Ards had gone 2-0 down. This would be a season with an unusually large number of postponements. Most were due to the weather and were therefore unavoidable, but Ards were left seething when Limavady United called off a late September fixture, citing the selection of two of their players for a junior international. The North West club was within its rights, but for Ards it would mean a rearranged fixture in midweek, a costly, logistically awkward and financially unrewarding exercise.

Institute brought Ards' undefeated run to an end with a 3-1 victory, and immediately Anderson moved to strengthen the midfield, securing the hard-tackling Shane Reddish, an experienced campaigner with nearly 150 Football League appearances behind him, from Newry Town. After that Institute match Ards bounced back to win the next two, the second an important 3-1 victory over Distillery, but in early December suffered another dip in form, failing to score in a home draw with Limavady, then losing heavily to Armagh City. Fears that yet another pole position would be squandered were dissipated, however, with a 3-0 win over Carrick Rangers, where all three Ards goals, two from young Declan Divin and a 25-yard effort from Reddish, were out of the top draw-er. But successive postponements on Boxing Day and the following Saturday allowed Distillery to close the gap at the top, and on New Year's Day Institute yet again frustrated Ards, claiming a draw at Solitude. The next three games saw Ards obtain only two points, dropping to 2nd place after losing 3-2 to ten-man Distillery despite having home advantage. Cup exploits interrupted Ards' quest for promotion throughout February: they were obliged to play their Irish Cup home match against the RUC in Larne when Cliftonville were also drawn at home and Bangor were unwilling to help. The eventual 1-0 victory brought a tie at Linfield where Ards put up a determined rearguard action to draw 0-0, only to lose 5-0 in the replay. In the Coca Cola League Cup they travelled to Distillery to win 2-0, and to Premier League Ballymena United to secure a fine 2-1 victory. Eventually Ards lost 2-0 at Omagh in the third round, hitting the bar in the 90th minute before conceding two goals in extra time.

But by this stage everything had changed off the field, with a steadily brightening glimmer appearing at the end of the tunnel. Before the start of the season a group of directors and fans, with the support of Strangford MP John Taylor, had hit upon the idea of a demonstration outside the Belfast offices of Morrison's Developments Ltd. This not only drew media attention towards Ards' plight, but also cast the club in the role of innocent victims in a major financial game. But best of all, it seems to have broken the stalemate and led to talks between the developers and Ards. The upshot of all this was the astonishing news that Ards were to return to Castlereagh Park! Although the reprieve was only a temporary one, which would have to come to an end as soon as work on the site commenced, the announcement was more than welcome. Ards had not settled in at Solitude, winning a mere five of their thirteen matches played there: their League position owed a great deal more to excellent away form, while if they could remain promotion favourites there would surely be a surge in gate receipts with the return to Newtownards. And this was not all: at the turn of the year Ards District Council agreed to lend the football club £400,000 to help fund a new ground. Jimmy Crothers and Ronnie Ferguson deserved great praise for their successful lobbying, not only of the Council, but also of Morrison's, the IFA and a number of other bodies which could in any way help Ards F.C.

The first game back at the Park attracted a big crowd, although Ards were unconvincing in a 1-0 win over Dungannon Swifts. Already three matches behind schedule in late February, they lost two more games to the weather and to the foot and mouth outbreak of 2001. The consequence was that they faced a demanding final lap of the League which required them to play nine games in less than a month. It was to the team's credit that they took this gargantuan task on board and came through on top. By this stage David Rainey had joined Ards from Glentoran to add width down the left, offering balance to the right-sided Adrian Larkin, brought in earlier from Newry Town. Shane McQuillan, a strong, battling target man, had suffered a serious double leg break while Ards were still playing at Cliftonville, so to bolster the forwards for the run in Anderson brought in Andy Moran, a former Tranmere Rovers centre-forward who had more recently been with Derry City and had scored a baker's dozen for them. It was Moran's two goals which secured the points at Institute, although the day was clouded by a dreadful cruciate ligament injury to Shane Reddish when a combination of an appalling tackle and a referee who appeared out of his depth left the midfielder writhing in agony and out of

John Bailie

the game for nearly a year. The win at Institute was the first of four in a row, as Moran and Rainey chipped in to take the striking pressure of Gorman, and Armagh, Dungannon and Ballyclare were all despatched.

A goalless draw at New Grosvenor left Ards a point behind the Whites with two games in hand, but the final week of the season would be testing, with the title resting on a punishing schedule of four games in eight days. The home match against Limavady was won comfortably, 3-0; the crucial Monday night game at Bangor resulted in a 2-0 win, the match goalless with fifteen minutes to go until strikes from Gorman and Lowry. Ards expected to go up in style three days later, when a big crowd in carnival mood turned up to see the back-to back Bangor game. In the end they were left with a feeling of anti-climax. Barring two cricket scores on the last day of the season, Ards got the point that would see them return to the top flight, but a goalless draw was an inglorious way to round off their home fixtures. Perhaps this is carping: a tired team did what was required, but how much happier would we have been with a clear triumph over the old enemy! The final match, at Armagh, saw a fatigued Ards side lose 2-1 to the home team, but the result was irrelevant. The big travelling support ignored the scoreline to celebrate the bottom line – Ards had won the First Division despite having to ground share until March, despite the ludicrous schedule imposed on them during the last month of the season, and despite the ongoing financial battle for survival.

That battle now appeared to be won, with the announcement that a new deal had finally been agreed over the sale of the ground. Morrison's agreed to pay Ards £750,000 plus two future instalments of £150,000 each. A bonus of £25,000 was to be paid in the event of promotion, and, wonder of wonders in the light of the strained relations of the past year or so, the developers would sponsor Ards to the tune of £25,000 in the following season! All these events,

Peter Lowry lifts the league trophy at Holm Park

and more, were now regularly reported on Ards' website. A few years earlier an Ards Hotline had proved popular and lucrative, but in the shambolic late 90s had simply been allowed to lapse. Now Andrew McCullough began to produce a site that was informative, up to date and attractive, and which has continued as essential cyberspace for Ards fans in the ensuing years.

To allow an expansion of the Premier League in the following season, the football authorities decided that there should be no automatic relegation in 2001-02. As Ards attempted to consolidate their restoration to the top flight this was, assuming a worst case scenario, welcome news, the more so given their misfortune regarding injuries. Shane Reddish was sidelined all year, McQuillan's leg refused to knit despite the insertion of a rod, while a broken jaw sustained in the penultimate game of the previous season thankfully did not keep Bailie out of football, but meant that he would have to spend nine months with a plate in his jaw. As if these long-term casualties were not enough, McLean, Curran and Massey (yes, all three of the central defence) missed a significant number of games through injury, as did left-back Alan Hall, and later David Rainey. As regards squad changes, Dessie Gorman was allowed to leave for Banbridge Town, and was replaced by Paul Millar, more of an orthodox target man but another player closer to the end of his career than the beginning. The other major signing of the close season was Ian Young, a midfielder or defender who came from Linfield. For the moment Ards were able to use Castlereagh Park, but they were on borrowed time there, and would soon have to go on their travels again. They tried to make the most of their limited spell back home, with half-time entertainment on a regular basis, sometimes a schoolboy match, sometimes the Ards Pumas, an enthusiastic cheerleading and dancing group.

Marty McCann came back to haunt Ards in their first match in the Premier League, scoring the only goal of the game for Omagh Town, then Ards had to play Linfield twice. The League match produced a blinding goal from Millar before Ards went down 4-2, but in the League Cup O'Brien's dismissal after a mere three minutes hardly helped, and they lost heavily, 4-0. An Ian Young goal gave them their first win, 1-0 at Newry, and towards the end of September there were successive 2-1 victories against Cliftonville and Coleraine. The former match saw Paul Curran break an ankle, while the latter, a fighting victory which owed much to the tremendous display of the injured Young as a stand-in centre-back, was nonetheless Ards' last League victory until February. After half a dozen defeats in a row Trevor Anderson was removed upstairs, his official title now

Paul Curran

Director of Football, and his assistant Frankie Parks, a full-back with the club many moons earlier, took over responsibility for the team. Midfielder Gary Sliney came in from Newry, as did Andy Morrow, a striker who had been with Northampton Town.

Ards were bumping along just one place off the bottom, but under Parks they at least began to pick up the odd point with gritty draws, two scoreless ones against Cliftonville and Glenavon, and a run of three on either side of Christmas, the best of them a 2-2 result against Linfield. The penultimate day of 2001 was, for many, the most heart-breaking day in Ards' one hundred and one years of existence. They lost 4-0 to Glentoran on a snow-covered pitch, but the result, for once, did not seem to matter. The end of the calendar year brought to an end Ards' tenure of Castlereagh Park. This time there was no reprieve, no temporary arrangement by which they could stretch out their use of the old ground for a few more weeks or months. At the end of the game the tannoy boomed out the chimes of Big Ben, followed by Auld Lang Syne, and it was all over. Malcolm Brodie's account movingly recalled the great days and the memories of "this incomparable, immaculate pitch". His elegy ended "The demise of the old stadium is one of Irish League football's great tragedies. May a Phoenix arise from the ashes".

For the rest of the season Ards were obliged to play their remaining games away from home. They fought a determined rearguard action to take a point away from the Oval, defeated Crusaders 2-1, Glenavon 1-0, thanks to a last-minute goal from Rainey, and Newry Town 2-1. The unfortunate Paul Curran fractured a cheekbone in the defeat at Seaview, and was penalised for his part in the incident, yet the Crusaders players, to their great credit, refused to take advantage of the goalscoring opportunity and simply tapped the free kick to Neil Inglis. In late March Ards almost pulled off the shock of the day on a Saturday in late March. They were leading 1-0 at Glentoran with the supporters already whistling for the final whistle when Curran, returned from his injury, cleanly tackled Glendinning, who fell over in the process. Not a single Glens player appealed, yet the referee, to general disbelief, awarded them a penalty, and the match was drawn. In the Irish Cup Ards defeated Limavady United 2-1 before going out to a Glentoran team which on this occasion was irresistible, Ards losing 5-0. Oh, and just in case you thought that the litany of injuries had mercifully come to an end, in the last game of the season, against Glenavon, reserve goalie Ciaran McLoughlin played throughout with an undiagnosed broken leg.

The Premier League had been just as tough as everyone had feared, but at least Ards were still in it, and found a home for the next season with Carrick Rangers when negotiations with Bangor failed to reach a satisfactory conclusion. The way forward was spelt out with the launch of plans for a 5000-seater stadium modelled on Livingston's ground, complete with conference and banqueting facilities, an hotel, a fitness centre and offices. It was hoped to build this ground just down the road, beyond the Airport. But in the meantime, it was off to Carrickfergus.

So for 2002-03 Ards played their home matches at Taylor's Avenue. It was clear that the club could not survive on gate money alone, for beyond the Big Two only Portadown brought a decent travelling support, and the experience of the last few seasons showed that precious few Ards supporters were prepared to make the journey to any ground other than the one down the Portaferry Road. All the more credit, therefore, to the diehards who stuck by Ards during their years 'on the road', whether in North Belfast or Carrickfergus, or, eventually, Bangor, to the handful who worked valiantly to raise money through selling programmes or ballot tickets, and to the members of the Board who beavered away behind the scenes to keep the club afloat and to continue negotiations to obtain the necessary planning permission and grant aid to fund a new ground for Ards Football Club.

Frankie Parks had to remould the team of the previous year before the beginning of the 2002-03 season. Gary Sliney moved on to Dublin City, (the new identity of Home Farm), Neil Inglis to Berwick Rangers and Ian Young to Newry Town. In their stead came the former Glentoran central defender Alastair McCombe, the vastly experienced Raymond Campbell from Crusaders, and David Young, a midfielder who had 25 Scottish Youth caps and who had played for a number of years for the Rangers U-21 team, in practice the Glasgow team's reserve XI. A number of youngsters who were surplus to the existing requirements of various cross-channel clubs were signed on extended loans. From Derby County came the big defenders Sean Cleary and Gareth McKeown, from Aston Villa striker David Scullion, from Ayr United another striker, Aidan McVeigh, and from Wimbledon full-back and local boy David Murphy. Not a newcomer, but making a welcome return from his career-threatening cruciate ligament injury was combative midfielder Shane Reddish. An unscheduled signing was that of the ex-St. Johnstone and more recently Clydebank goalkeeper Stephen Robertson, secured whenever the unlucky Ciaran McLoughlin suffered his second leg break in as many years. Robertson was a real discovery, voted Ards Player of the Year at the end of the season, and in the opinion of many the best keeper in the Irish League.

The programme for the season was unusual, in that the twelve teams in the League would play each other three times, then split in two, like the Premier League in Scotland, with the final five games played against the clubs in either the top or the bottom half, depending on where you finished. The decision to go down this road was bizarre in that this was always going to be a one-off, with an enlargement of the League to sixteen teams planned for the following season, and an already planned abandonment of the split! The only other league competition was the CIS League Cup, in which Ards drew with Distillery and Bangor, and lost a thriller to Linfield by 4-3. In the League proper Ards suffered all season from an inability to score, a drought which sadly was not reflected in the growing number of matches called off because of heavy rain and consequent flooded pitches. The number of cancellations was probably a record, and Ards not only suffered loss of revenue by having to play the rearranged fixtures on less lucrative midweek dates, but also lost the rhythm built up by regular games and were obliged to scramble to complete their fixture list in a hectic end of season rush.

An opening draw against Crusaders was followed by a single goal defeat at Distillery where Craig McCracken missed a penalty, the first of a hat trick of such misses by Ards players in the early weeks of the season. A 2-1 win against Newry raised hopes, but it was merely the prelude to a sequence in which the best they could manage in their next six games was a scoreless draw against Cliftonville. The best performance during this depressing sequence was a 2-1 defeat against Glentoran, where Ards went ahead through McCracken, Scullion missed a one-on-one chance at 1-0, and the game remained poised at 1-1 until Darren Nixon was sent off. Improvement came in October, when a difficult trip to surprise early leaders Omagh Town resulted in a 1-0 win, a cracking volley from John Bailie separating the teams at the finish. Another spectacular goal, this time an overhead kick from the unlikeliest of sources, centre-half Paul Curran, came in the 3-0 defeat of Institute. A victory over Crusaders and a point at Glenavon completed a good month's work which saw Ards in a comfortable 8th place, not only climbing away from the lower depths of the table, but playing good, on the carpet football into the bargain. Paul Curran, an inspirational player whom many saw as managerial material with Ards, was offered such a position at Dundalk by Trevor Anderson, and opted to go to the border club. Only two more wins, against Newry and Distillery, came before Christmas, but there was a heart-warming defensive display at Portadown, where wave after wave of attacks from the Ports was repelled until the last minute of the game, when McAreavy's goal denied Ards a victory they thought Reddish's early strike had won.

Ards must have believed the much-discussed midwinter break had finally been decided upon when unplayable pitches meant they lost out on no less than four successive matches, leaving them with no fixtures between December 28th and January 18th, when they were finally able to play again, ironically in a torrential downpour at Moyola Park, their opponents in the Irish Cup. Ards had taken advantage of the transfer window, a new concept, to sign the much-travelled Garry Haylock, the scourge of defences North and South of the border, and another youngster, Mark Magennis, who had spent time with Coventry City. It was Haylock who scored both the goals against Moyola which saw Ards through to face junior kingpins Killyleagh YC, who almost embarrassed them before Rainey scored desperately late in the game to see Ards safely into the quarter-finals. Meanwhile there was merely a solitary win over Distillery in the League in January, while in the defeat by Linfield early the next month they lost Reddish and Lowry after only 22 minutes of the game, the latter's injury keeping him out for seven matches. Glentoran were too good for a spirited Ards side in the Cup, winning 1-0, and as the spring approached there was some disquiet at the prospect of playing the remaining eleven games in seven weeks.

We need not have worried. Despite the continuing lack of scoring power (although he led the line well Haylock had not scored as many as might have been hoped, and he soon returned to Dundalk for the start of the FAI's experimental summer season) the team finished the year in something like style, winning five and drawing three of these last eleven matches. The decisive goal against Institute came when Rainey ghosted past two defenders before unleashing a powerful cross-shot, and in his last game for Ards Haylock scored a winner from 20 yards against Newry while the bench had already reached for his number as they waited for an opportunity to sub him! Although they did not make the cut, this was a mixed blessing for Ards, as although they were denied the bigger gates a top half finish would have produced, they had a much easier run in, and eventually finished in 7th position, the best of the rest, thanks to a couple of goals from Gary Kennedy, a close season signing from Kilmore Rec. who had missed most of the League through injury.

The balance sheet of the season's activities gave some cause for quiet satisfaction. For a team without a home to call their own Ards had done remarkably well. Although they could not yet compete on equal terms with the best sides, their mid-table performance had suggested that the road to recovery had begun. Parks' side had usually played the game the way it should be played, shunning the long ball approach often adopted by lesser lights, and the nucleus of a good team seemed to be there. Above all, in spite of the travails of the last few years, Ards were still alive. The superhuman efforts of Ronnie Ferguson and Jimmy Crothers had ensured survival, and these two now found others to share the load when Sinead Fitzgerald, the first female director of an Irish League club, joined the Board.

The 2003-04 season brought the most sensible solution to Ards' homelessness, when at long last a deal was done with Bangor which would allow Ards to use Clandeboye Road for their home fixtures. (The arrangement was cemented with the presentation of the awkwardly titled Chronicle and Spectator Newpapers Cup, an annual pre-season contest between landlord and tenant.) Why was this logical course not achieved much earlier? The answer seems to lie with personal animosities. Thus what is a happy arrangement for AC Milan and Internazionale was, it seems, not good enough for those mighty rivals, Ards and Bangor. But that was all now in the past, and a happier era of co-operation between the North Down near neighbours dawned. How long would the new arrangement have to last? Not long now, we were told. Although further grants for the projected new ground remained to be finalised, Stadia Scotland was forging ahead with a £9.5m scheme which would place Ards' new ground at the centre of a leisure and hotel complex. Chairman Ferguson went off to inspect Dunfermline's new plastic pitch, another Stadia project, and hopes were high that soon our own club might enjoy state of the art facilities which would make them the envy of the Irish League. On the playing front Frankie Parks brought in David Williamson, a local man with Hong Kong international caps, former Linfield and St. Johnstone front man George O'Boyle, and Lee Feeney, whose mercurial talent had never completely been harnessed. The biggest and most important signings, as it turned out, were the Glentoran pair of striker Darren Fitzgerald and midfielder Marty Hunter, the nephew of fifties' favourite Dessie, and the classy full-back Ronan Scannell, transferred from Cliftonville.

The early season League Cup saw Ards installed, along with Coleraine, as favourites to go beyond the group stages, and successive wins over Crusaders and Limavady in the opening matches portended well, but four points from the next three games left the team needing to defeat Coleraine at home to make sure. Alas, they froze on the day, lost too many crucial headers, and went down 4-1 to allow Crusaders to sneak past into the quarter-finals. In the Premier League Ards stumbled to three draws and two defeats in the opening five fixtures: clearly the team was not playing as well as it ought, but Frankie Parks' dismissal after a savage 4-0 beating by Linfield was still a surprise to most. Taking the side over when they were at rock bottom the previous season, he had done wonderfully well to steady the ship, but patience with under-performing teams is notoriously thin, and Parks left, angrily denying the Board's suggestion that he had left by mutual consent, and complaining that five League matches was far too short a time in which to make a judgement. The tough decision was that so many big names had been added to the playing strength that only a position near the top was acceptable, and the likeable Frankie was gone, his successor Ards' former player Shane Reddish, who had been acting as Trevor Anderson's managerial assistant at Dundalk.

As so often happens, the change at the top proved a catalyst, with three wins out of the next four League games. In the 2-0 defeat of Crusaders Feeney's first was a gem, when he first nutmegged Livingstone before chipping the bemused keeper from 35 yards out. The only defeat of Reddish's honeymoon period was at home to Glenavon, when a 2-0 half time lead was squandered, at 2-1 Feeney missed a penalty, and two late Glenavon goals meant a 4-2 defeat in a game where Ards appeared incapable of defending set pieces, a tendency that was to become a persistent feature over the next few seasons. But in the very next match Ards triumphed by 4-1 at Omagh, Gary Kennedy claiming the first Ards hat-trick against senior opposition since Raymond Morrison in 1995. Kennedy's form was more than matched by that of Darren Fitzgerald, who by year's end had over a dozen goals to his credit, and by the often majestic performances of Marty Hunter. Reddish had certainly fired up the team, who in early December matched and eventually outfought Glentoran in a hard physical contest, their first win over the East Belfast men in six years. Even better, on the Saturday before Christmas goals in the last ten minutes from Fitzgerald and Rainey toppled league leaders Portadown in a real Clandeboye thriller. The Boxing Day game at Larne attracted a big Ards following, many home for the holidays, but to the despair of the regulars the visitors were left shaking their heads and wondering what all the fuss was about as Ards conceded five goals to a team well below them in the table.

The transfer window saw the disappearance of the disappointing O'Boyle, and of loyal servant Darren Nixon, while in came Padraig Gollogley, a gangling centre-half who had twice in three seasons been Drogheda United's Player of the Year, and the talented midfielder Paddy Quinn. Results continued to go well after the hiccup at Larne, with only one defeat in January. An in form Ards also looked to have a genuine chance of silverware in the knockout competitions. In the autumn they had coasted past Carrick Rangers and Ballyclare Comrades in the County Antrim Shield, and now, in February, a Scannell goal was enough to ease them past Ballymena United and into the final. In the Irish Cup they had gone into double figures against juniors Donard Hospital, with Fitzgerald hitting five and Kennedy three. With reports that work on the new ground would begin at Easter everything seemed set fair for Ards' renaissance. But every silver lining has its cloud, and for Ards that cloud burst in the first week of February with the news of the collapse of the Stadia Investment Group. Up to thirty stadium projects were jeopardized as Gavin Masterson's company hit rough waters, but, in our insular way, we were only concerned that the new Castlereagh Park had lost its backer. What did not become clear to the man on the terraces was that Stadia had been subsidising Ards for some time, and the sudden loss of this income would lead to a cash flow crisis before season's end.

Such matters did not immediately seem to faze the team, who disposed of Ballyclare Comrades in the 5th round of the cup, and gained a draw at Windsor Park, having led 2-0 with eleven minutes to go, but thereafter the season fizzled out. Some would blame the infamous Curse of the Manager of the Month Award, with Reddish's side winning only one of their last nine fixtures after he received the accolade for February, but a more likely cause was a lack of goals, Ards failing to score in eight of their 20 matches in 2004, compared with a mere four out of 23 before the turn of the year. The manager himself complained of a lack of effort on the part of the players as the season wound down. Before that the high point had been the County Antrim Shield Final, where a big Ards support watched a game of crunching tackles where Quinn, Raymond Campbell and Gollogley all played well, but had to accept that Linfield were the better team on the night. In the first half Andrew Fox, in for the injured Robertson, gave away and then brilliantly saved a first half penalty. But in the 69th minute Marty Hunter, attempting to cut out a Picking cross, headed in to his own net. Ards did not lie down, and with three minutes to go Fitzgerald appeared to have put the match into extra time, only to have his effort ruled out for offside. Within a minute came the double whammy, as Linfield scored again to secure the game.

Four days after the final Ards had to pick themselves up, dust themselves down, and lose all over again. What should have provided a relatively straightforward path into the Irish Cup semi-finals proved a step too far as Omagh Town snatched an away win by the odd goal in three, and our season was as good as over. Ards took revenge in the League fixture against Omagh the following week, but it was poor consolation, and, indeed, proved to

Raymond 'Soupy' Campbell

be the last win of the year, as the team managed only two points and a miserable two goals from the last six matches. Towards the end of this depressing run the Board issued a statement that the players had agreed to defer their wages, clearly not paid up to date, until after the last match of the season. Only a few items of cheer remain to be recorded: Ronan Scannell was voted best left-back in the Irish League by Radio Ulster listeners; a Sports Auction proved a good fund-raiser for the club; and a white tie dinner dance and Player of the Year function, meant to be the first of many, was held in the Clandeboye Lodge. An Extraordinary General Meeting held in May generated much heat but not a lot of light, as Chairman Ferguson said he had six interested parties who wanted to take over the building of the new ground from Stadia, but could not disclose their identities at that stage. In the meantime the Bangor groundshare would continue, and 30,000 £1 shares were to be issued to help fund a football club with no ground to call its own.

Nails were bitten down to the quick during 2004-05, with survival as a senior club in serious doubt early and late season. But during the summer break things had begun to look more positive. A fortnight after the 2003-04 season ended came rumours that one of Ronnie Ferguson's potential developers was a consortium with links to the new Dundalk dog track, with plans to build a football stadium-cum-greyhound track in Newtownards. The rumour mill had it that the late season wages crisis had only been rectified courtesy of a £45,000 injection of cash from this group. After Ards councillors had been taken to a night at the races at Dundalk, a heated debate took place in the Council, with an anti-gambling faction opposing the idea of Council land being used for such purposes. The debate was continued at length in the correspondence columns of the local press, where those who had moral objections to gambling were joined by others who felt dog racing to be inherently cruel. At the key Council debate in early summer Ronnie Ferguson, a Councillor himself, argued passionately that the very existence of the football club was at stake. If the project went ahead one hundred jobs would be created, and Newtownards would enjoy not only a modern stadium but a brand new conference centre as well. At the end of a heated argument the Council voted in favour of the development on Council-owned land on the Portaferry Road, with Ards holding a 99 year lease at a rent to be decided (eventually £55,000 p.a., with the possibility of a higher bill if the greyhound track were added). As the smoke generated by the dog track controversy cleared more facts began to emerge. The developers, known as Ards Stadia

Management, and fronted by architect Paul Monaghan, (the actual developer was named in the local press as Jersey-based Tom Wilson) had apparently already funded Ards to the tune of £120,000, which seemed to shed further light on the wages crisis of April and its resolution. And while we're talking about narrow escapes, a few weeks earlier the club had found itself facing the prospect of relegation, after the AGM of the Irish League had debated demoting the club because of its homeless status, before confirming that there was nothing in its statutes to prevent groundsharing.

On the playing front the young full-back Kris Pike, surplus to Glentoran's requirements, was signed, as was Larne's Derek Delaney, and David Reeves, a big centre-forward who had scored 70 goals for Chesterfield. A promising start to the League Cup, with two victories and a scoreless draw at Windsor Park was, however, brushed to one side by the happenings of early September. Perhaps the warning signs could have been read in the resignation of Sinead Fitzgerald from the Board during the previous month, although she claimed she lacked the time due to pressure of work. The storm broke when Ronnie Ferguson announced not only his own resignation, but the closure of Ards F.C. "within days". He claimed he was "not happy with the direction the club is taking", surely one of the great understatements of all time. The entire squad was asked to take a pay cut: reputedly the weekly wages bill was £6,500, if true a ludicrous overspend which could only be funded by average gates of well over 1000, closer to 2000 if other sources of income dried up. Ronnie Ferguson denied being a director any more, claiming he had resigned weeks before, and Jimmy Crothers was left to make a desperate appeal for a backer to appear to save the club from imminent demise. More details began to emerge, with stories of debts and bouncing cheques in the *Chronicle,* and the team which played, and lost at Loughgall had apparently agreed to turn out for nothing. Unpaid rental on the Social Club brought the possibility of eviction from its Fire Authority premises. An 11-man Management Committee, its leading figure Brian Adams, but officially still headed by Ferguson, now a director again, was set up to keep the club ticking over, and succeeded in thrashing out a deal with Paul Monaghan by which running costs (to be greatly reduced) were met, but there was still the question of huge debts, reported at the time as being £115,000. Cost-cutting measures were taken: Reeves, who was far too costly and not particularly effective, was released, although his signing on fee was lost for good, Lee Feeney had already gone to Glenavon, and the players were offered a new deal which would reduce their wages by 40%. Paddy Quinn and Darren Fitzgerald refused the cuts, and Quinn moved to Portadown, Fitzgerald to Ballymena. (The IFA said they could not play for their new clubs until the January transfer window, so Fitzgerald agreed to help Ards in the short term). Glenavon, in the shape of their Vice-Chairman, demanded Ards be thrown out of the League, but after a meeting with the club the IFA proved less vindictive, agreeing to Ards' continued status after certain financial assurances were given. Members of the Management Committee and ordinary supporters proved extraordinarily generous in their contributions: one anonymous pensioner gave £2200 to pay Ards' shirt manufacturers, and a '100 Club' was set up to ask fans for £100 each, with great success. By mid-October Ards' debts had been halved, and a £20,000 income tax bill, potentially the most life-threatening, paid. Against this, the local MP, Iris Robinson, attacked the greyhound track/ground proposals as a "disastrous development".

Against this volatile background Reddish and his players had to carry on with their weekly fixtures. Although only two League Cup matches had been won, Ards nonetheless qualified for the knockout stages, but an injury-ravaged team went down at Cliftonville, taking the home team to extra time. The following Saturday Gary Kennedy scored a hat trick as Ards gained glorious revenge with a 3-0 win at the same venue, and chalked up victories over Crusaders, Limavady and Omagh within the next seven weeks. The team which won at Limavady had no fewer than six teenagers on the field by the final whistle. When these victories are added to three draws, including a 2-2 scoreline against Linfield, no one could dispute that Ards had, on the field if not off it, few problems, as they climbed the table to 5th by mid-November. In addition, the form of the energetic young midfielder Aidan Watson had attracted a lot of interest, and he was capped for the Northern Ireland U-19 team against both France and Italy. But on the debit side Padraig Gollogley's sending off when he queried Coleraine's third goal, a goal which was palpably offside, as television replays showed, was the beginning of a wretched period for the big central defender. Padraig was a whole-hearted enthusiast, by no means a dirty player, yet a series of bookings, coupled with the extraordinary disciplinary code in the Irish League, which worked on an increasingly punitive scale rather than wiping the slate clean when an offender had served his suspension, meant that he was banned for 14 games altogether. Nor was he alone in enforced absences, as Sean Cleary missed 15 games. There was a regrettable lack of self-discipline among Ards players that season, with seven players sent off, not to mention a series of missed penalties, and the more far-sighted could perhaps see trouble looming.

They were right. A side that had been 5th on November 20th would not win another League game until late March, a total of 16 matches without a win. In the first six games of this depressing run only one goal was scored. The nadir came on New Year's Day, when Ards lost 7-0 at Dungannon. In the middle of the slump came the news that former player David Young had received 'thousands' in a settlement of his claim for unpaid wages, swallowing up the £2000 Ards supporters had raised via a sponsored walk to Bangor for the game against Portadown. New faces appeared in January: David Ward, a striker from Dundalk, Ricky Cathcart, a big central defender from Ballinamallard, and David Fairclough, who had experience with Tranmere Rovers and Bohemians, and who could deliver a curling dead ball. Delaney was allowed to go, as was David Murphy. But it was all to no avail, as the defeats kept on mounting up. The only solace was in the Cups. While they were still winning, back in the autumn, Ards had slipped past Dundela, 2-1, in the County Antrim Shield, but lost comprehensively, 3-0, to Crusaders in the next round. In the Irish Cup, again drawn favourably against lower division opposition, they took two attempts to get past Ballyclare Comrades, a Marty Hunter goal in the replay Ards' ticket into the 5th round. This time a brace of goals from Gary Kennedy, the second in the fourth minute of injury time, produced a fine victory at Institute. But the quarter-finals brought defeat at home to Portadown, a Vinny Arkins overhead kick separating the teams at the finish. On top of the Cup exit came continued financial pressure, as yet another unpaid debt was settled with a payment of 'several thousand pounds' to former player John Kennedy.

And so the grim fight against relegation continued. Ards seemed unable to concentrate for the full 90 minutes, as Glentoran's winning goals came in the 90th and 92nd minutes, and Crusaders' equaliser was scored in the last minute of the game. But at least Ards appeared to be fighting hard as they flirted with the relegation zone, and an invaluable away point at Ballymena, thanks to a Rainey strike, was followed by a victory at last. Amazingly, it was at Portadown, and appeared unlikely, to say the least, when Ards found themselves 2-0 down. But they fought back tenaciously, and scored through Kennedy and Rainey before a sensational winner from new boy Andrew Waterworth, who beat two defenders as he turned and chipped across the keeper for the most unlikely win of the season. The win took the pressure off Shane Reddish, but only temporarily, as three defeats followed: the performance at Loughgall one to make even the most optimistic despair. The manager watched his team lose one more time, at home to Dungannon, and then, with two matches to go in which to save Ards' Premier status, resigned. The timing seemed ill-chosen, coming either too late, or prematurely, in view of the desperate need for points. In the emergency the team was placed under the control of a triumvirate of Charlie Murphy, Reddish's assistant, Soupy Campbell and John Bailie.

The penultimate match was at Larne, where a real crackerjack ended two apiece. A big Ards following saw the team cope with a physical Larne outfit to gain a crucial point with a fighting display, Gollogley, returning from suspen-

sion, a real giant, and both teams were applauded off the pitch by an appreciative crowd. And so it was on to Bangor, for the make or break game with Newry
City. Only a win, coupled with a defeat for Crusaders, would suffice if Ards were
to avoid the playoffs, which few thought they could win. On the day sizeable
numbers turned out, and, glory be, for once Ards didn't freeze in front of the big
crowd. The star of the show was Davie Rainey, always potentially a match winner, but a player whose form could be frustratingly inconsistent. On the day he
was superb, scoring a hat trick, to which Gary Kennedy added two more, as Ards
romped home by 5-1. Crusaders duly lost to Glentoran, and Ards had escaped
by the skin of their teeth. But then it had been that sort of a season. Continued
existence as a football club had been an achievement in itself, never mind staying in the top flight. As if to confirm The Great Escape, an EGM in early April
had elected a new Board, consisting of the eight man Management Committee,
and headed by Brian Adams. The meeting revealed that when the crisis broke in
September Ards owed over £200,000, much of which had now been paid. The
following month Ards District Council approved revised plans which visualised
a football ground, a restaurant, and at a later date, a greyhound track. For the
moment things looked more promising than they had done for some considerable time.

After the narrow escapes of the previous term, Ards' objectives for May 2006
were clear. First, avoid the twin spectres of bankruptcy and relegation, and second, ensure that a start was made on the new ground. The latter did not happen,
but this was a situation out of the club's control, with everything depending on
the developer. As regards potential financial ruin, at long last Ards appeared to be
working within a strict budget, but this in turn impinged on the strength of the
squad, with drastic consequences for their playing record. The wage restrictions
were more than a number of players could stomach, and an exodus took place
which left Ards rebuilding the team on a minimal budget, although, to be fair,
one that was no tighter than those operating at many other Irish Premier League
clubs. When the dust settled Kennedy, Cleary and Scannell had all gone to
Solitude, and Robertson, to whose wages had to be added weekly air fares, found
a new berth at Airdrie United. Gollogley, who had only been sent off once, had
another ludicrous 11-match suspension to serve at the start of the new season,
and was allowed to go.

The manager who had to find players who could replace those lost was to be
George Neill, the former Glentoran full-back, and latterly Harland and Wolff

Welders boss, where his experience in achieving results with limited resources was felt to be appropriate to Ards' straitened circumstances. Presumably happy to work with players whose strengths he knew, Neill plundered his former team's ranks, bringing David Henry, Marc Roy, Ian McGrath, Gordon Hillis and Chris Towell from the Welders, and adding Mark Parker and Gary Wray from Larne, Brian Adair from Loughgall, and former Ards stopper Ross Hegan from Distillery. Of those nine players only the last three played regularly, and Adair would rejoin Loughgall in the New Year. A much better signing was Jason Hill, a busy midfielder released by Glentoran, but against that the highly promising Aidan Watson chose to go to Ballymena, while Davie Rainey, whose late season form had done much to keep Ards up, was negligently allowed to leave for Crusaders after he had started pre-season training with Ards. With Andrew Waterworth's early season injury against Limavady ruling him out for six weeks the signs that this would be a struggle were not long in manifesting themselves.

The League Cup results were not altogether bad, with Ards doing the double over Loughgall and picking up a point at Limavady, and Hill hitting the net four times during the tourney, but few others appeared capable of scoring, and the 7-0 home defeat to Linfield revealed a chasm in class. Worse, in the same match Pike was stretchered off and needed surgery, an injury serious enough to keep him out for the rest of the season. With 22 players used in the opening six games, the omens were poor, and when the League began Ards' form

Ards captain Aaron McKee

was simply awful. The first nine matches were all lost and only five goals scored. Luck was certainly absent, as goalkeeper Henry was the next casualty, with a broken hand, and the 3-2 defeat at Portadown came after a 2-1 lead held as late as the 85th minute, but too many chances were missed, none of the custodians Ards experimented with seemed confident, and defending in general was sub-standard. To address the lack of punch Ards brought in Avun Jephcott, formerly with Coventry City but currently out of contract. He played eight times and scored three goals, but it was not enough. A more interesting prospect was Tom Bates, from the same source, but his promising handful of midfield appearances, when his astute passing suggested he could be a playmaker of genuine class, came to an end as he secured new employment which prevented weekend travel. A win came at last, when Jephcott and Marty Hunter scored to defeat Limavady, and there were two other wins on either side of Christmas, at home to Loughgall and away to Cliftonville, on each occasion the teams separated by an Andrew Waterworth goal. The County Antrim Shield had afforded Ards a crumb of comfort, when they cruised past former neighbours Ards Rangers, but they came horribly unstuck in the second round, again conceding seven goals at home to Linfield.

The January transfer window saw the arrival of Brendan Ward, a rugged, hard-working centre-half, striker Paul McDowell and Aaron McKee, an Ulster exile newly returned from Australia. The return of Ciaran McLaughlin in goals was widely welcomed, offering a goalie with real authority in his box. In the same month the Chairman announced that Ards had paid off almost all the debts inherited by the current Board, a considerable feat of fund-raising, and a symptom of the Board's scrupulous approach to doing business. The Social Club, however, despite a temporary stay of execution, would have to close its doors at the end of April, and Adams conceded that finding suitable premises for its replacement would not be easy. Hopes of a decent cup run were dashed when Ards were drawn away to Glentoran, not the force they had been at this particular juncture, but still a desperately difficult tie. Yet Ards almost confounded everyone, with a squad of fourteen which included seven teenagers. When their fighting performance was capped by an excellent Waterworth equaliser it seemed odds on a replay, but a Melaugh winner in the 93rd minute broke Ards' hearts and gave Glentoran a victory they scarcely merited.

Despite the promise shown against the Glens and on occasion in other games League results did not improve, with six defeats on the bounce after the win at Solitude. Sure, luck did not go their way, with a dreadful penalty decision a major influence on the Glenavon game, and a 93rd minute winner for Portadown, but the series of late goals conceded must have said something about Ards' fitness, or their ability to concentrate for the whole 90 minutes, or their loss of nerve when in an unwonted strong position, or some fault, in short, that lay not in the stars, but in themselves. Not that they couldn't have used a little fortune off the pitch. When UTV filmed a piece with Paul Monaghan, the developer, although unable to offer a firm date for beginning the build, confirmed his continuing strong interest in constructing a new ground. Unfortunately, the piece was dropped from the schedules when the more exciting story of Roy Coyle's sacking by Glentoran came up, and an opportunity for some positive publicity was denied the club. Worse, Ards Council now withdrew their offer of a lease for the new ground, able to do so because the plans involved commercial development, and not merely a football stadium and dog track. It appeared that the Councillors had tired of trying to pin down Paul Monaghan to a definite timetable: their patience had run out as they claimed that he had failed to reply to a series of letters. The only good news to come out of this imbroglio was that Mr. Monaghan continued to show good faith by his financial input into Ards F.C..

As if this crisis were not enough, George Neill, who had been facing mounting criticism as the team bumped along at the bottom of the League, finally resigned, succeeded, at least in the short term, by his assistants Raymond Morrison and Gary Hillis. Some signs of life were now detectable in what many saw as a moribund team. A decent draw was obtained at Ballymena, but the following week a Jason Hill penalty miss right at the death denied Ards another draw, this time against Distillery. Another late penalty went a-begging at Limavady, the culprit McKee, and another point gone. Early April offered a tantalising glimpse of unlikely escape, with a 3-3 draw against Dungannon (although Ards led three times, and ought to have held on) and a decision to award the points to Ards for the match against Glenavon, who had fielded an unregistered player. But much as one understood those who listened anxiously for the results of our fellow strugglers, the chances of escaping relegation, even surviving as far as the playoffs, were never realistic. All that could be hoped for was a last hurrah, and it came at Loughgall, with a fine 3-2 win on Easter Tuesday, when the rapidly emerging Jay Magee, a centre-back of real presence, replaced the injured Ian Lester in goals and performed heroics for a quarter of the game to keep Ards' mathematical hopes alive. But the following week, at home to Newry Town, ironically now managed by Roy Coyle, whose arrival in the 1990s had done so much to rejuvenate spirits, a 3-1 defeat formalised what had been inevitable since the autumn, if truth be told. Ards' relegation was, in some ways, worse than the drop of 1997. Unlike then, they were now homeless, and, for the first time since 1946-47, would be playing intermediate, not senior football, where there are no referee's assistants, no reserve teams, few floodlights, and minimal crowds.

But it was no one's fault but their own. If a team finishes bottom it deserves to go down, and the seeds of the demotion to Division 1 were undoubtedly sown during the various spells of financial profligacy over the past decade and a bit. The loss of Castlereagh Park, and the consequent decline in attendances, the over-reliance on outside funding, the need for drastic cutbacks, the uncertainty over the new ground – all these were part of a downward spiral which has left Ards down, if not quite out, overtaken by smaller clubs and obliged to borrow a ground to play at a lower level.

But to accentuate the positives from 2005-06, throughout a miserable year there were often fine performances from Marty Hunter, from the evergreen 'Soupy' Campbell, and late in the season from Jay Magee, Alan Murray, and, most of all, the precocious Ryan Tumelty. Slight of build but brimful of skills, Tumelty's finest hour came in the very last game of the season, at Coleraine. Already down, Ards could have merely gone through the motions, but instead a predominantly young team played its part in a game of all out attacking football which they eventually won 4-2. Tumelty tortured his marker throughout, and the 16-year-old Gary Sharratt scored coolly on his debut. The travelling Ards support was ecstatic. For that suspended moment the heartbreak of the season was forgotten: at the final whistle players and fans bonded to celebrate not just a victory, but one achieved with fluency and style. Despite the euphoria of that day, however, the reality that was relegation to intermediate football was now upon us.

In addition to the lack of linesmen etc., it also transpired that fixture lists for Division I matches were only revealed a month at a time because the Steel and Sons' and Intermediate Cups took priority. There were some consolations: derbies with Bangor, developer Paul Monaghan's continued funding of the club, and the optimistic belief that Ards would be among the high fliers of the Division, in contrast to the traumas of the previous two seasons. Gary Hillis and Raymond Morrison were given the chance to continue in charge, but had to accept the losses of the influential Marty Hunter, Andrew Waterworth and Ryan Hill. Raymond Campbell decided to call it a day, while controversially John Bailie was allowed to return to his first club, Bangor. To fill the gaps the managerial team brought in a number of experienced players, something of a gamble as Justin McBride, Philip Major and Jeff McNamara were, with the best will in the world, no longer in the first flush of youth, but encouragingly most of the young prospects from 2005-06, notably Tumelty, Magee and McKee, chose to stay on. Kris Pike had almost recovered from his cruciate ligament operation, and Glentoran's Ian Mannus, a promising goalkeeper, came on a year-long loan.

There were high expectations for the early season Carnegie League Cup, but optimism proved ill-founded as Ards crashed to defeat in their away games at Portstewart, Lurgan Celtic and Carrick Rangers, where the home side won convincingly by three goals to nil. Midfield was seen as the problem area, with the team lacking a ball-winner, something that was too often the case during the season. Ards did play neat enough football but often found themselves outmuscled by less skilful but more direct, physical opponents. To be fair, good football was often difficult on surfaces that were at times of a poor standard. In the Steel and Sons Cup, where the draw kept them away from the bigger names, Ards made progress, albeit unconvincingly, scraping home by a single goal against Lisburn Rangers, and taken to penalties by both Newcastle and Albert Foundry.

When the League proper began there were wins against Ballinamallard and, slightly fortuitously, Banbridge, but Ards' reality check came in a 2-0 defeat at promotion favourites Institute. Further knockout action interrupted the

League campaign, most entertainingly at Dollingstown in the Intermediate Cup, where the home side's neat little pitch turned out to be in the middle of a farm, approached past byres and down a lane, complete with all the appropriate barnyard sounds and smells. Ards won 5-0, with a brace from Justin McBride, easily the most successful of the veteran signings, but exited the competition at the next time of asking at the hands of Bangor. Defeat in the County Antrim Shield at Premier League Distillery nonetheless saw a fighting performance, while a decent 3-0 win over Orangefield OB saw Ards into the Steel and Sons' semi-final. But successive defeats to Harland and Wolff Welders and Carrick Rangers saw them slipping out of League contention, and clearly much hung on reaching the Christmas morning final. Playing the Welders for the second time in ten days, Ards made and missed many chances before and after the speedy Alan Neill scored, but when the Welders equalised their more determined approach made them look the more likely. When their winner came it was, not for the first time that season, a defensive mess, the ball going directly into the net from a corner. With eight out of Ards' seventeen matches to date lost, Hillis and Morrison bit the bullet and resigned.

The new manager was to be Tom Kincaid, the popular little winger who had played for Ards in the late 80's, now in charge at East Belfast but with a record of success in achieving promotion to the Premier Division. He immediately brought in Craig McMillan, a tricky and combative winger who added a new sense of urgency to Ards' attacks. Performances picked up and the team embarked on a ten-match unbeaten run. On Boxing Day Ards defeated Bangor 3-1, the clinching goal, when Bangor had pulled one back and were threatening to snatch a late point, a gem from Ryan Tumelty when he ghosted past two defenders before curling a wonderful shot into the net in front of the massed ranks of jubilant Ards fans. At this stage Ward and Magee were looking solid at the back, Johnny Shaw and Kris Pike were capable of going forward to launch attacks from the back, Aaron McKee at his best was a cultured playmaker and the burly Ricky Billing put himself about to good effect. Despite the lateness of Johnny Roy's equaliser Ards looked far the better team at high-flying Carrick, and the 2-0 win over Moyola Park pushed Ards into 3rd.

In the Irish Cup Ards needed two matches to defeat a tenacious Dundela, and were then drawn at home to Linfield in Round 6. A crowd of 2000 pleased the Treasurer, but it was the end of the Cup road for Ards, 5-0 down at half time to a Linfield team that looked in a different class, although the home team fought bravely in the second half to prevent any addition to the score. Before the Cup exit, despite McBride equalising twice against Institute, the North West club got away with a point when Ards needed three, crucially there was another draw when the team travelled to play a very physical Ballinamallard, and in a final blow to Ards' promotion aspirations in a game they dominated they lost to a Dundela winner that looked yards offside. Three good wins followed, but there was no realistic hope of going up, especially during a disappointing run in that only saw two wins out of five, and an Easter derby where Bangor gained revenge for the Boxing Day defeat.

Disappointing though a 5th place finish was, at least there was no repeat of the struggles of the previous two seasons, and the promise of many of Ards' youngsters augured well for the future. The lack of a second XI means that replacements come direct from the U-18 team, giving a chance of rapid promotion to young talent, more of whom will undoubtedly emerge via the conveyer belt of the excellent Ards Youth setup. Although it does not always come off, the team persists in the tradition set by George Eastham of playing football with a sense of style. The financial problems of the club are being addressed, with the opening of a Sports Club back in in Regent Street in the town centre, and continuing support from the club sponsor, Huw Worthington, still showing his faith in Ards' future despite the setback of relegation. Best of all, there is now a real possibility of the club moving back to Newtownards, as tenants of a new Council-built stadium just down the road from Castlereagh Park. Support remains, perhaps surprisingly, buoyant, and there can be little doubt that it will continue on the rise if and when a new ground appears. As Kevin Costner put it in his baseball movie, "If you build it they will come".

Those who fill the ground for the first match back home should remember the band of brothers who have kept the faith at Solitude, Taylor's Avenue and Clandeboye Road, and the sleepless nights and the financial sacrifices of those who have kept Ards alive in the face of almost insuperable difficulties. All of us, former, occasional or diehard Ards supporters, even if we are not always conscious of it, should cherish a heritage that stretches back over a century of triumph and disaster, that acts as a focus for the pride of a community, that will live on when we are long gone, and is enfolded in the old colours of Red and Blue.

SEVENTEEN

Final Standings

AIC	Tyler's All-Ireland Cup	INL	Intermediate League
BC	Blaxnit Cup	IPL	Irish Premier League
BWC	Budweiser Cup	ITC	InterToto Cup
CaC	Carlsberg Cup	1LC	Carnegie League Cup
Cas	County Antrim Shield	LC	League Cup
CC	City Cup	McC	McElroy Cup
CCC	Coca Cola Cup	MU	Mid-Ulster Cup
CCT	Cawood's Chalice Trophy	NSC	North-South Cup
ChC	Belfast Charity Cup	PLPO	Premier League Play Off
CLC	Clements Lyttle Cup	SL	Senior League
EC	European Cup	SSC	Steel and Sons' Cup
ECWC	European Cup Winners' Cup	TC	Tate Cup
F	Friendly	TexC	Texaco Cup
FBC	Festival of Britain Cup	TF	Top Four Competition
GC	Gold Cup	UC	Ulster Cup
IC	Irish Cup	UEFA	UEFA Cup
INC	Intermediate Cup		

For games played before 1947 some scorers have been untraceable

Final positions, season 1923-24

League: 9th   P 18   W 5   D 4   L 9   F 18   A 30   pts 14
City Cup: 5th   P 9   W 3   D 3   L 3   F 11   A 11   pts 9

	Date	Comp.	Venue	Opponents	Result	Goalscorers
1	Aug 25	SL	A	Barn United	W 2-1	Weir, Rowley / Murray
2	Sept 1	SL	H	Newry Town	W 1-0	Munn /
3	8	SL	A	Cliftonville	D 1-1	Feeney / Simpson
4	15	SL	A	Linfield	L 0-2	/ McIlveen, Wilson
5	22	SL	H	Glentoran	L 1-2	Rowley / Elwood, Allen
6	Oct 6	SL	H	Glenavon	D 1-1	Feeney / Neill
7	13	SL	A	Distillery	L 0-4	/ Dalrymple 2, Garrett, Blair
8	27	SL	H	Queen's Island	L 1-2	Feeney / Croft, Cowan
9	Nov 3	SL	H	Larne	W 2-0	Feeney, McGregor /
10	14	GC[1]	H	Cliftonville	L 2-4	Taylor, Feeney / Kane, Gault, Grey 2
11	17	SL	H	Barn United	D 0-0	
12	24	SL	A	Newry Town	D 1-1	Bowers / Bradley
13	Dec 1	SL	H	Cliftonville	L 0-2	/ Robinson, Ballantine
14	8	SL	H	Linfield	W 4-3	Feeney 2, Taylor, Bowers / Scott 3
15	15	SL	A	Glentoran	L 0-2	/ Duff, Keenan
16	22	SL	A	Glenavon	L 1-2	Jackson / Weir, McLeeve
17	25	SL	H	Distillery	W 1-0	Alexander /
18	26	SL	A	Queen's Island	L 0-2	/ Burns 2
19	29	SL	A	Larne	L 3-5	Feeney 2, Rowley / Meneilly, M. McKinney, J. McKinney 3
21	Jan 5	F	H	1st Lincolns	W 7-3	Duffy 4, Diffen, Alexander, Patterson / Betts 3
22	12	CAS[1]	A	Woodburn	D 1-1	Duffy / Curran
23	16	CAS[1R]	H	Woodburn	L 0-1	/ Armstrong
24	26	IC[1]	H	Distillery	L 0-1	/ McIlvenny
25	Feb 2	CC	H	Glenavon	W 1-0	Alexander /
26	16	CC	H	Barn United	D 1-1	Feeney / Gregretski
27	Mar 8	CC	H	Larne	W 2-0	McCormick 2 /
28	22	CC	A	Newry Town	D 1-1	Taylor / Cochrane
29	Apr 5	F	H	Falls League	W 4-0	Feeney, Taylor, Gault, Alexander /
30	12	CC	A	Queen's Island	D 2-2	Feeney, Taylor / Kennedy 2
31	19	CC	A	Cliftonville	W 1-0	Feeney /
32	21	CC	H	Linfield	L 1-2	Feeney / McAnally 2
33	26	CC	A	Glentoran	L 1-3	McCormick / Meek 3
34	May 3	CC	H	Distillery	L 1-2	McCormick / McIlvenny, Harrison
35	5	ChC[1]	A	Bangor	L 0-1	/ Clarke

Final positions, season 1924-25

League: 7th   P 22   W 7   D 4   L 11   F 39   A 41   pts 18
City Cup: 8th   P11   W 3   D 3   L 5   F 19   A 9   pts 9

	Date	Comp.	Venue	Opponents	Result	Goalscorers
1	Aug 23	SL	A	Linfield	W 1-0	Patton /
2	27	GC[1]	H	Linfield	D 0-0	
3	30	SL	H	Cliftonville	W 2-1	Patton 2 / Lynas
4	Sept 2	GC[1R]	A	Linfield	L 1-2	Patton / McAnally 2
5	6	SL	A	Glentoran	L 1-2	Patton / Keenan, Rainey
6	13	SL	H	Glenavon	W 2-0	Alexander, Duffy /
7	20	SL	A	Newry Town	L 3-4	Patton 3 / Moore 2, Crothers, Campbell
8	27	SL	A	Barn United	L 0-1	/ Kelly
9	Oct 4	SL	H	Portadown	W 1-0	Patton /
10	18	SL	A	Distillery	D 1-1	Creaney / Rush
11	25	SL	A	Belfast Celtic	D 2-2	Brown 2 / Smith, J. Mahood
12	Nov 1	SL	H	Larne	L 0-3	/ Slowey, McKinney, Walls
13	15	SL	A	Queen's Island	L 1-2	Tester / Kennedy, Cowan
14	22	SL	H	Linfield	L 0-2	/ McIlreavey, Shaw
15	29	IC[1]	A	Belfast Celtic	L 1-3	Brown / Smith, Moore, J. Mahood
16	Dec 6	SL	A	Cliftonville	L 0-3	/ Relph, Mortished, McCracken
17	13	Cas[1]	H	Cliftonville	L 1-3	Patton / McCracken , Mortished 2 (1 pen)
18	25	SL	A	Glenavon	L 2-5	Robinson, Gault (pen) / Weir 2, McCourt 2, Carroll
19	26	SL	H	Newry Town	W 4-0	Patton, Brown 2, Blackwood /
20	27	SL	H	Barn United	W 4-0	Brown 3, Leeman /
21	29	SL	H	Glentoran	L 0-3	/ Burns, Vance 2
22	Jan 3	SL	A	Portadown	L 0-1	/ Kane
23	10	SL	H	Distillery	W 3-2	Leeman, Morton, Gault (pen) / White, Thompson
24	24	SL	A	Larne	L 4-5	Leeman, McGee, Robinson, Blackwood / Walls 2, Kane, Magee, Lindsay
25	31	SL	H	Queen's Island	L 1-4	Robinson / Cowan, Scott, Holmes, Robertson
26	Feb 7	CC	H	Cliftonville	W 1-0	Leeman /
27	19	SL	H	Belfast Celtic	W 7-0	Robinson 3, Reid 2, Creany, Leeman /
28	21	CC	A	Queen's Island	D 0-0	
29	Mar 7	CC	H	Glenavon	D 3-3	McGee (pen), Leeman, Patton / Weir, McCourt, Carroll
30	14	CC	A	Linfield	L 0-3	/ Andrews 2 (1 pen), McIlreavey
31	28	CC	H	Newry Town	W 4-1	Stewart, Reid, Leeman 2 / Moore
32	Apr 4	CC	A	Barn United	L 1-2	Blackwood / Reid o.g., Matheson
33	11	CC	H	Belfast Celtic	W 1-0	McGee /
34	13	CC	A	Distillery	D 1-1	Leeman / Rushe
35	14	CC	A	Glentoran	L 0-4	/ McKeague, Burns, Rainey (pen), Meek
36	18	CC	H	Portadown	L 0-3*	Chambers, A.N. Other o.g. Ballentine
37	23	ChC[1]	H	Bangor	L 0-1	/ Armstrong
38	25	CC	H	Larne	L 1-2	Gault / Somerset, Walls

* abandoned result stands

Final positions, season 1925-26

League: 4th   P 22 W 11 D 4   L 7   F 56   A 42 pts 26

City Cup: 9th   P 11 W 4   D 1   L 6   F 18   A 19 pts 9

	Date	Comp.	Venue	Opponents	Result	Goalscorers
1	Aug 22	SL	A	Queen's Island	W 5-3	McGuire 2, Shields, Stuart 2 / Burns, Fergie, Burns
2	26	GC[1]	A	Belfast Celtic	L 2-3	McGee, McGuire / Curran 2, Tolan
3	29	SL	H	Distillery	L 1-2	McGuire / Blair, Dalrymple
4	Sept 5	SL	A	Belfast Celtic	L 0-2	/ Smith, Mahood
5	12	SL	H	Portadown	D 3-3	Leeman 3 / Ferguson 2, Carragher
6	19	SL	A	Newry Town	D 3-3	McGee, Bothwell, Reid / Carroll 2, Pitt
7	26	SL	H	Larne	L 1-2	McAnally / Walls 2
8	Oct 3	SL	H	Glenavon	W 3-1	Leeman 2, Moore / Carroll
9	10	SL	A	Cliftonville	W 2-0	Leeman 2 /
10	17	SL	A	Glentoran	L 2-4	McGuire 2 (1 pen) / Meek 3, Armstrong
11	31	SL	H	Barn United	W 3-1	McGuire 2 (1 pen) , Moore / Gregretski
12	Nov 7	SL	A	Linfield	L 0-1	/ McIlreavy
13	14	SL	H	Queen's Island	W 4-2	McGuire , Moore 2, Leeman / Roberts, Turnbull
14	21	SL	A	Distillery	W 5-2	Moore 2 (1 pen), McGuire 3 / Burnison 2 (1 pen)
15	28	IC[1]	A	Portadown	L 0-3	/ Carragher, Cochrane, Withers
16	Dec 5	SL	H	Belfast Celtic	L 1-2	McAnally / Mahood 2
17	12	SL	H	Newry Town	W 5-1	McGuire 2, Moore, McAnally, Bothwell / McGinn
18	19	SL	A	Portadown	D 2-2	McAnally, Patton / Ferguson 2
19	26	SL	A	Larne	L 1-4	McGuire / Wilson (pen), McCambridge, Ward, Walls
20	Jan 2	Cas[2]	A	Cliftonville	D 2-2	McGuire 2 (1 pen) / Woodrow, Quinn
21	6	Cas[2R]	H	Cliftonville	L 2-4	Gault, McGee (pen) / Mortished 2, Jones, Webb
22	9	SL	H	Cliftonville	D 1-1	Montgomery / Addis
23	23	SL	A	Barn United	W 4-3	McGee, Montgomery, Bothwell, Gamble / Palmer, Campbell 2
24	30	SL	A	Glenavon	W 2-0	McGuire, Montgomery /
25	Feb 6	CC	H	Cliftonville	L 1-2	Montgomery / Mortished, J. Jones
26	20	SL	H	Linfield	W 6-1	McGee 3, Patton 2, Montgomery / Andrews
27	27	SL	H	Glentoran	W 2-1	McGuire, Gilliland / Walker
28	Mar 6	CC	H	Glenavon	W 4-1	Patton, McGee, Bothwell, Montgomery / Hedley (pen)
29	20	CC	A	Glentoran	L 2-3	McGuire, Bothwell / Devlin, Armstrong 2
30	Apr 3	CC	H	Newry Town	L 1-2	Gilliland / Cochrane, McGreevy
31	5	CC	A	Barn United	W 1-0	McGuire /
32	6	CC	H	Queen's Island	L 0-1	/ Roberts
33	10	CC	A	Distillery	D 1-1	McGee / McGrath
34	17	CC	A	Belfast Celtic	L 3-4	McGee, Bothwell, Knocker / McGrillen, Curran 3
35	24	CC	H	Portadown	L 1-4	Blair / Carragher, Jackson, Cochrane, Bradley
36	May 1	CC	H	Larne	W 1-0	Leeman /
37	6	TC	H	Bangor	W 2-0	Bothwell 2 /
38	8	CC	A	Linfield	W 3-1	Parker, McGuire 2 / Holmes

Final positions, season 1926-27

League: 5th   P 22   W 9   D 7   L 6   F 42   A 42   pts 25
City Cup: 7th   P 11   W3   D 3   L 5   F 22   A 22   pts 9

	Date	Comp.	Venue	Opponents	Result	Goalscorers
1	Aug 21	SL	A	Distillery	D 2-2	Smyth 2 / Harrison, Morrow
2	28	GC[1]	H	Belfast Celtic	L 1-2	Bothwell / McGrillen, Curran
3	Sept 4	SL	H	Linfield	W 2-1	Leeman, Cleland / Ferguson
4	11	SL	A	Queen's Island	W 3-2	Bothwell, Leeman, Smyth / Armstrong, Murdough
5	18	SL	H	Newry Town	W 4-2	Smyth 3, Cleland / Byrne, Lyness
6	25	SL	A	Portadown	W 3-0	Cleland, Smyth, Bothwell /
7	Oct 2	SL	H	Larne	W 2-1	Cleland, Foster / Houston
8	16	SL	A	Belfast Celtic	D 1-1	Robertson / Curran
9	23	SL	H	Cliftonville	L 0-1	/ McGuire
10	30	SL	H	Glenavon	L 0-1	/ Andrews
11	Nov 13	SL	A	Barn United	W 3-1	McIlreavey, Bothwell, Hayes / Ward
12	20	SL	A	Glentoran	D 2-2	Cleland, Bothwell / Dinnen, Geary
13	27	IC[1]	A	Newry Town	W 2-1	Patton, Campbell / Cochrane
14	Dec 4	SL	H	Distillery	W 3-0	Leeman, Bothwell 2 /
15	11	SL	A	Linfield	L 1-4	Bothwell / Moorhead, McCracken 2, McGaw
16	18	SL	H	Queen's Island	D 1-1	Bothwell / Turnbull
17	25	SL	A	Newry Town	D 0-0	
18	27	SL	H	Portadown	D 3-3	Adams 2, Bothwell / Doyle, Jackson, Johnston
19	Jan 1	SL	A	Larne	L 1-5	McIlreavey / Crooks, Houston 2, McCambridge 2
20	8	SL	H	Belfast Celtic	L 1-6	Adams / Mahood 2, McGrillen, Ferris, Hanna, Curran
21	15	IC[2]	A	Glenavon	W 2-1	McGee 2 / Andrews
22	22	SL	A	Glenavon	D 2-2	McGee, Leeman / Andrews, Risk o.g.
23	29	SL	H	Barn United	W 4-1	McGee 2, Patton, Bothwell / Rainey
24	Feb 5	IC[SF]	N	Belfast Celtic	W 3-1	Patton, McGee, Bothwell / Curran (pen)
25	12	CC	H	Portadown	L 2-5	McGee 2 / Johnston 3, Doherty 2
26	19	CC	A	Linfield	L 1-2	Bothwell / McCracken 2
27	23	Cas[1]	H	Distillery	W 3-2	Smyth, Leeman, Gamble / Creaney, Halliday
28	28	SL	A	Cliftonville	L 1-4	Cobley / Ferguson, Gowdy 2, Hughes
29	Mar 12	CC	A	Queen's Island	D 2-2	McGee, Bothwell (pen) / Blair 2
30	19	CC	H	Newry Town	W 5-0	McIlreavey, McGee 2, Risk, Croft /
31	26	ICF	N[2]	Cliftonville	W 3-2	McGee 2, McIlreavey / Mortished, Hughes
32	Apr 2	CC	A	Cliftonville	L 1-3	McGee / Mortished, Hughes 2
33	9	CC	A	Glenavon	D 1-1	McGee / McCourt
34	13	Cas[SF]	N	Dunmurry	L 2-3	Bothwell (pen), Patton / Roy, Gunning 2
35	16	CC	H	Larne	L 1-2	Bothwell / Burns, Houston
36	18	CC	A	Belfast Celtic	L 0-2	/ Curran 2
37	19	CC	H	Distillery	D 2-2	Patton, Croft / Harrison, McKenzie
38	23	CC	A	Glentoran	W 4-2	Smyth 2 (1 pen), Croft 2 / Moore, Bambrick
39	28	TC	A	Bangor	W 3-0	Smyth, Bothwell, Croft /
40	30	SL	H	Glentoran	W 3-2	Smyth, Bothwell 2 / Moore, Bambrick

41	May 7	CC	H	Barn United	W 6-4	Bothwell, Patton 3, Smyth, Croft/Gregretski, McCafferty, Weir, Cunningham
40	19	CC	H	Distillery	D 2-2	Patton, Croft / Harrison, McKenzie
41	28	TC	A	Bangor	W 3-0	Smyth, Bothwell, Croft /

N = Solitude

N^2 = Oval

Final positions, season 1927-28

League: 11th   P 26   W 8   D 5   L 13   F 54   A 69   pts 21

City Cup: 13th   P 13   W 1   D 4   L 8   F 21   A 39   pts 6

	Date	Comp.	Venue	Opponents	Result	Goalscorers
1	Aug 20	SL	H	Bangor	D 1-1	Lynas / McKinney
2	27	SL	A	Glentoran	D 0-0	
3	29	GC[1]	A	Bangor	D 2-2	Bothwell, Jackson (pen) / McKinney, Morrow
4	Sept 3	SL	H	Queen's Island	W 7-1	Lynas 3, Jackson 2, Cleland, Bothwell / Morton
5	7	GC[1R]	H	Bangor	W 4-0	Lynas 2, Jackson, Cleland, /
6	10	SL	A	Barn United	W 3-1	Cleland, Patton, Lynas / Baxter
7	14	GC[2]	H	Larne	D 0-0	
8	17	SL	H	Larne	L 1-2	Lynas / Houston 2 (1 pen)
9	24	SL	A	Cliftonville	W 2-0	Bothwell, Ferguson /
10	27	GC[2R]	A	Larne	D 1-1	Gamble / Houston
11	Oct 1	SL	H	Newry Town	D 0-0	
12	5	GC[2RR]	H	Larne	W 4-2	Bothwell 3, Ferguson / Houston 2
13	8	SL	A	Glenavon	L 0-2	/ Graham 2
14	15	SL	H	Coleraine	L 0-1	/ Dunlop
15	26	GC[SF]	N	Belfast Celtic	D 2-2	Jackson (pen), Lynas / Curran 2 (1 pen)
16	29	SL	A	Belfast Celtic	L 3-8	Bowden o.g., Lynas 2 (1 pen) / Curran 5, McCullough, Ferris, Mahood
17	Nov 5	SL	H	Portadown	W 3-1	Patton, McGee, Lynas / Johnston
18	12	SL	A	Distillery	L 0-2	/ Meek (pen), Anderson
19	15	GC[SFR]	N	Belfast Celtic	L 0-3	/ Gallagher, Curran, Ferris
20	19	SL	A	Linfield	L 4-8	Patton 2, Ferguson 2 / Bambrick 5, Houston, Millar, McCaw
21	26	IC[1]	A	Portadown	L 0-1	/ Johnston
22	Dec 3	SL	A	Bangor	L 3-4	Lynas, Patton, Garrett / Magee 2, Wilson, McCarroll
23	10	SL	H	Glentoran	W 5-2	Patton, Lynas 2, Ferguson, McGee / Geary, Moore
24	17	SL	A	Queen's Island	L 0-3	/ Finlay, Hutchinson, Turnbull
25	24	SL	H	Barn United	W 3-1	McGee 2, Gowdy / Armstrong
26	26	SL	A	Larne	L 2-5	McIlreavy, McAuley (pen) / McCambridge, Houston 2, Silcock, Fergie
27	27	SL	H	Cliftonville	W 3-1	McGee 2, Ferguson / Ruddy
28	31	SL	A	Newry Town	L 3-5	Bothwell, Ferguson 2 / Turley, Wilson, Carroll 2, Lyness

29	Jan 7	SL	H	Glenavon	W 4-3	Bothwell, Gowdy, Lynas,McAuley (pen) / Rushe 2, McBride
30	14	SL	H	Linfield	D 1-1	Bothwell / Somerset
31	21	SL	H	Belfast Celtic	L 1-4	Wilson / Mahood 2, Curran, McCullough
32	28	SL	A	Portadown	L 2-7	McGee 2 / Allen 2, Johnston 2, Doherty 3
33	Feb 11	SL	H	Distillery	D 3-3	McGee 2, Lynas / McAdams 2, Howard
34	20	CC	A	Coleraine	L 4-6	McGee 2 (1 pen), Cleland, McIlreavy / McGrath, Mathieson 2, Kelly 2, White
35	25	SL	H	Newry Town	L 2-4	Patton, Cleland / R. Lyness 2, W, Lyness 2
36	29	Cas^2	A	Ormiston	D 2-2	Patton, Jackson / Gallagher, Miller
37	Mar 3	CC	A	Belfast Celtic	L 1-4	McGee / Gallagher 3, Weir
38	5	Cas^{2R}	H	Ormiston	W 4-1	McGee 3, Jackson / Thompson
39	10	SL	A	Coleraine	L 0-3	/ O'Connell, McLaughlin, Mathieson
40	14	Cas^{SF}	N^2	Glentoran	W 2-1	Lynas 2 / Moore
41	17	CC	H	Larne	D 2-2	Patton, Cleland / White, Houston
42	24	CC	A	Glentoran	L 2-5	McGee, Jackson (pen) / Geary, Mercer 2, Moore 2
43	31	CC	A	Portadown	L 1-3	Jackson / Gilmore 2, Johnston
44	Apr 7	CC	A	Barn United	D 2-2	McGee 2 / Davidson, Wilson o.g.
45	9	CC	H	Cliftonville	D 0-0	
46	10	CC	A	Coleraine	L 4-6	McGee 2 (1 pen), Cleland, McIlreavy /
47	14	CC	H	Glenavon	L 3-4	Garrett 2, Jackson / McCourt 3, Moore
48	21	CC	A	Linfield	L 0-4	/ Bambrick 4 (1 pen)
49	24	Cas^F	N^2	Linfield	D 1-1	Flynn / McCracken
50	28	CC	H	Queen's Island	W 2-1	Gowdy, Rowley / Hutchinson
51	May 2	Cas^{FR}	N^2	Linfield	L 2-4	Jackson, McGee / Somerset, Bambrick 2, McCracken
52	5	CC	A	Bangor	L 0-3	/ Stewart 3
53	12	CC	H	Distillery	D 2-2	Clarke, Murphy / McAdams, McCarroll

N = Solitude
N^2 = Oval

Final positions, season 1928-29

League: 9th	P 26	W 9	D 5	L 12	F 55	A 64	pts 23
City Cup: 7th	P13	W6	D1	L6	F36	A30	pts 13

	Date	Comp.	Venue	Opponents	Result	Goalscorers
1	Aug 20	SL	A	Bangor	L 0-3	/ Stewart 3
2	25	SL	H	Linfield	L 2-4	Gowdy 2 / Matthews, McCracken, Bambrick, Adams
3	Sept 1	SL	A	Glenavon	L 2-3	Flynn, Adams / McCourt 2, McBride
4	5	GC^1	H	Ballymena	W 2-0	McGee, Clarke /
5	8	SL	H	Ballymena	L 1-2	Barrett / Shiels, McCambridge
6	15	SL	A	Queen's Island	D 4-4	Davidson 2, Flynn, Collins / Hall 2, Lyner, Abraham
7	19	GC^2	H	Newry Town	W 2-0	Davidson, Collins /
8	29	SL	H	Portadown	L 1-2	Barrett (pen) / Kimlin 2

9	Oct 6	SL	A	Belfast Celtic	L 0-3	/ Gallagher 2, J.Mahood
10	10	GC^{SF}	N	Glentoran	W 2-1	Davidson 2 / McKeague
11	13	SL	H	Larne	W 4-0	Davidson 2, Collins, Jackson /
12	20	SL	A	Coleraine	D 2-2	Davidson, Barrett / Nelis, Gilmour
13	27	SL	H	Newry Town	D 1-1	Garrett / Nicholson
14	Nov 3	SL	H	Cliftonville	W 4-1	Jackson 3, Davidson / Halliday
15	14	SL	A	Glentoran	L 1-3	Burns / Geary 2, Roberts
16	17	SL	H	Distillery	L 0-1	/ Walker
16	14	SL	A	Glentoran	L 1-3	Burns / Geary 2, Roberts
17	24	IC¹	H	Broadway Utd	L 0-2	/ Ringland 2
18	Dec 1	SL	H	Bangor	W 2-1	McGee, Davidson / Arlow
19	8	SL	A	Linfield	L 1-6	Carson / Bambrick 3, Gallagher 2, McCracken
20	15	SL	H	Glenavon	D 1-1	Davidson / Tillie
21	22	SL	A	Ballymena	L 2-4	Barrett, Garrett / Shields 2, Clarke 2
22	25	SL	H	Queen's Island	W 3-2	Gowdy 2, Jackson / Croft, Ferguson
23	26	SL	A	Portadown	W 4-1	Gowdy, Carson, Gordon 2 / Carragher
24	29	SL	H	Belfast Celtic	L 2-6	McGee, Lynn / Gallagher 2, S.Mahood, J.Mahood, Weir, McCullough
25	Jan 5	SL	A	Larne	W 3-2	Jackson, Carson 2 / White, Houston
26	19	SL	A	Newry Town	W 2-1	Turnbull, Garrett / Hanna
27	23	Cas¹	H*	Linfield	L 0-2	/ Houston, Bambrick
28	26	SL	A	Cliftonville	D 1-1	Turnbull / Millar
29	Feb 2	SL	H	Glentoran	W 4-3	Edwards, Turnbull, Barrett, Jackson / Roberts 2, Allan
30	20	SL	H	Coleraine	W 5-1	Burns, Gordon 3, Carson / Murphy
31	9	SL	A	Distillery	L 3-6	Turnbull 3 / McMullan 2, McAdams 3, Blair
32	16	CC	A	Bangor	W 5-0	Garrett 3, Gowdy, Gordon /
33	Mar 2	CC	H	Linfield	L 1-4	McGee / McCaw 2, Somerset 2
34	16	CC	A	Ballymena	L 0-3	/ Shiels 3
35	18	GC^F	N²	Linfield	L 1-3	Barrett / Houston, Moorhead (pen), Somerset
36	23	CC	H	Belfast Celtic	W 2-1	Lynn, Garrett / Curran
37	Apr 1	CC	A	Portadown	L 1-2	Gowdy / H. Johnston 2
38	2	CC	H	Glenavon	D 2-2	Lynn 2 / Turkington, Tillie
39	6	CC	H	Coleraine	W 2-1	Clarke, Burns / Doherty
40	13	CC	A	Larne	L 2-4	Lynn, Garrett / White, Kinsella 2, Rafferty
41	20	CC	H	Cliftonville	L 3-4	Lynn, Carson, Turnbull / Wishart 2, McConkey, Mitchell
42	27	CC	A	Glentoran	W 5-2	Burns, Clarke, Lynn, Turnbull, Jackson / Roberts 2
43	May 4	CC	H	Distillery	W 7-1	Clarke 2, Turnbull 2, Burns 2, Edwards / Wallace
44	11	CC	A	Newry Town	L 1-3	Clarke / Carroll, Hobbs 2 (2 pens)
45	15	CC	H	Queen's Island	W 5-3	Lynn 2, Turnbull, Garrett, Clarke / Munn, Hall, Neill

H* = Grosvenor Park
N = Grosvenor Park
N² = Solitude

Final positions, season 1929-30

League: 12th   P 26   W 6   D 6   L 14   F 47   A 77   pts 18

City Cup: 8th   P13   W5   D3   L 5   F 22   A 22   pts 13

	Date	Comp.	Venue	Opponents	Result	Goalscorers
1	Aug 20	SL	H	Distillery	D 1-1	Barrett / McAdam
2	24	SL	A	Bangor	L 0-2	/ McKinney, Viney
3	28	GC[1]	H	Glentoran	L 0-3	/ Roberts 2, Geary
4	31	SL	H	Glentoran	L 1-5	Lynn / Roberts 4, Croft
5	Sept 7	SL	A	Portadown	D 1-1	Garrett / Edwards
6	14	SL	H	Ballymena	L 0-2	/ Hanna 2
7	21	SL	A	Derry City	D 2-2	W, Gough, R. Gough / Hilley, Curran
8	28	SL	H	Belfast Celtic	L 1-2	McGee / Davey 2
9	Oct 5	SL	A	Newry Town	L 1-3	Turnbull / Carroll 2, Hobbs
10	12	SL	A	Linfield	D 2-2	McGee 2 / McCracken, Bambrick
11	26	SL	H	Cliftonville	W 2-1	Burns (pen), McGee / Quinn
12	Nov 2	SL	A	Glenavon	L 1-4	McGee / McCourt 2, Tillie, Maginness
13	9	SL	H	Larne	W 2-1	R. Gough, McGee / Blair
14	16	SL	A	Coleraine	L 1-6	R. Gough / Smith 3 , Nelis 3
15	23	SL	A	Distillery	L 3-6	McGee 2, Garrett / Harrison, McAdams 2, Wallace 2, Rafferty
16	30	IC[1]	A	Newry Town	L 0-5	/ Carroll 3, Lyness, Rushe
17	Dec 7	SL	H	Bangor	D 4-4	R. Gough, W.Gough, McGee, Ellis o.g. / Maloney 2, McKinney, Salisbury
18	14	SL	A	Glentoran	L 1-6	Devan / McNeill 3, Hutchinson, Geary, Crooks
19	21	SL	H	Portadown	W 4-2	W. Gough 3, Clarke / Johnston 2
20	25	SL	A	Ballymena	W 3-1	Devan, Turnbull, R. Gough / McCambridge
21	26	SL	H	Derry City	L 1-2	W. Gough / Senior 2
22	28	SL	A	Belfast Celtic	L 1-6	Turnbull / J. Mahood 2, S. Mahood 2, Ferris, Gallagher
23	Jan 4	SL	H	Newry Town	W 3-2	Burns 2, Devan / Dennett, Lyness
24	11	TC	A	Bangor	L 1-3	W. Gough / Maloney 3
25	13	Cas[2]	H	Bangor	W 6-2	Adams 2, R. Gough, W. Gough 2, Turnbull / McKinney, Moloney
25	18	SL	A	Cliftonville	W 3-2	Devan, Mitchell, Barrett (pen) / Moore, Mortished
26	22	SL	H	Linfield	L 1-3	Garrett / Meharg, Sloan, Bambrick
27	25	SL	H	Glenavon	L 3-5	R.Gough, Adams, Burns (pen) / Bingham 3, McCourt, Kerr
28	Feb 8	SL	A	Larne	D 3-3	R. Gough 2, Burns / Small 2, Kelly
29	13	Cas[2]	H	Bangor	W 6-2	Adams 2, R.Gough, W.Gough, Turnbull 2 / McKinney, Maloney
30	15	SL	H	Coleraine	L 2-3	Garrett, Burns / McGinnigle 2, Gilmour (pen)
31	22	CC	H	Distillery	W 3-0	Adams 2, Garrett /
32	Mar 8	CC	A	Cliftonville	W 3-1	Devan, R. Gough, Garrett / Moore
33	12	Cas[SF]	N	Glentoran	L 1-2	Garrett / Geary, Crooks
34	15	CC	H	Coleraine	W 2-1	W. Gough 2 / Mitchell

35	22	CC	A	Linfield	L 1-2	McGee / Bambrick, McGaw
36	Apr 5	CC	H	Ballymena	W 2-0	Wishart, W. Gough /
37	12	CC	A	Portadown	L 1-3	W. Gough / Lappin 2, Blair
38	19	CC	A	Belfast Celtic	D 1-1	Garrett / McColgan
39	21	CC	H	Newry Town	L 2-3	W. Gough, Garrett / Dennett 3
40	22	CC	A	Glenavon	L 2-5	Clarke, W. Gough (pen) / McCourt 2, McCahill, Madill, Garrett o.g.
41	26	CC	H	Derry City	W 2-1	R.Gough, Taggart / Curran
42	May 3	CC	A	Glentoran	D 1-1	W. Gough / Montgomery
43	7	CC	H	Bangor	D 1-1	Devan / McKinney
44	10	CC	A	Larne	L 1-3	W. Gough / McGuffie 2, Aiken

N = Solitude

Final positions, season 1930-31

League: 6th   P 26   W 11   D 4   L 11   F 64   A 69   pts 26

City Cup: 9th   P 11   W 3   D 5   L 5   F 23   A 27   pts 11

	Date	Comp.	Venue	Opponents	Result	Goalscorers
1	Aug 21	SL	A	Belfast Celtic	L 2-3	Lyness, Doherty / Coulter 2, Carroll
2	23	SL	H	Cliftonville	L 2-3	Doherty, Patton / McCaw, Reynolds, Millar
3	30	SL	A	Distillery	L 0-1	/ McAdam
4	Sep 4	GC[1]	A	Coleraine	W 4-2	Patton 2, Doherty, Lyness / Smith, Lynn
5	6	SL	H	Coleraine	W 4-1	Patton 2, Lyness 2 / Mears
6	13	SL	A	Portadown	D 0-0	
7	20	SL	H	Ballymena	L 3-6	Patton 2, Lyness / Turkington 3, Murphy 3
8	27	SL	H	Glentoran	L 1-4	Burns / Callaghan 2, Burke, Geary
9	Oct 4	SL	A	Linfield	L 2-7	Gough, Lyness / Bambrick 3, McCleery, McCaw 2, McCrory
10	11	SL	H	Newry Town	W 6-2	Totten 3, Burns, Patton 2 / Nicholson, Carroll
11	15	GC[SF]	N	Belfast Celtic	L 3-6	Gough, Davidson, Doherty / Carroll 4, Mahood, McCullough
12	18	SL	A	Derry City	W 1-0	McGee /
13	25	SL	H	Glenavon	W 6-1	Davidson, Doherty, Murray, McGee, Patton 2 / Kerr
14	Nov 1	SL	A	Larne	W 2-1	Doherty 2 / Agnew
15	8	SL	H	Bangor	W 5-4	Doherty 3, Davidson, Burns / McKinney 2, Henson, Shimmon
16	15	SL	H	Belfast Celtic	L 1-3	Murphy / Carroll, Canavan, Frewen
17	22	SL	A	Cliftonville	L 2-5	Patton, Harrison / Millar 4, McQuillan
18	29	IC[1]	A	Glentoran	L 4-7	Davidson 4 / Geary, Roberts 2, Mitchell (pen), Crooks 2, Burke
19	Dec 6	SL	H	Newry Town	W 3-1	Duffy, Totten 2 / McAdam
20	13	SL	A	Coleraine	D 3-3	Patton, Doherty, Gough / Nelis, Menlove, Smith
21	20	SL	H	Portadown	W 5-4	Davidson 3, Harrison, Gough / Weir, Johnston, Sayers, Edwards (pen)

22	25	SL	A	Ballymena	L 1-5	Duffy (pen) / Cassidy, Gilmour 4
23	26	SL	A	Glentoran	L 2-4	Doherty 2 / Roberts 4
24	27	SL	H	Linfield	W 5-1	Harrison, Gough 2, Davidson, Patton / Grice
25	Jan 3	SL	A	Newry Town	W 1-0	Burns /
26	17	SL	A	Glenavon	W 4-3	Burns, Gough, Davidson 2 / Wallace, Kerr, Moorehead
27	24	SL	H	Larne	D 0-0	
28	28	Cas[1]	A	Ballymena	D 1-1	Doherty / Dalrymple
29	31	SL	A	Bangor	D 3-3	Gough 2, Davidson / McKinney 2, Henderson
30	Feb 2	Cas[1R]	H	Ballymena .	W 4-1	Davidson, Patton, Doherty, Burns / Turkington
31	7	CC	H	Belfast Celtic	D 2-2	Gough, Harrison / Pollock , Mahood
32	14	CC	A	Cliftonville	L 2-4	Patton, Fergie / McCaw 2, Millar 2
33	24	Cas[2]	A	Larne	D 1-1	Duffy / McGuffie
34	26	Cas[2R]	H	Larne	W 5-3	Doherty 3, Patton, Davidson / McGuffie, Magill, Turnbull
35	28	CC	H	Derry City	L 0-1	/ Curran
36	Mar 7	CC	A	Bangor	D 1-1	Murray / McKnight
37	11	Cas[SF]	N	Cliftonville	L 0-4	/ Hume, Mitchell, Millar 2 (1 pen)
38	14	CC	A	Portadown	W 3-2	Gough, Burns, McGee / Blair, Johnston
39	21	CC	H	Ballymena	D 3-3	Davidson 2, Patton / Howard 2, Murphy
40	Apr 4	CC	A	Distillery	L 2-3	Harrison, Davidson / Sinnamond, Mitchell (pen), Hutchinson
41	6	CC	A	Linfield	W 2-1	Gough 2 / Jones
42	7	CC	H	Newry Town	W 4-2	Patton, McGee, Davidson, Burns / Richardson, Connolly
43	11	CC	A	Glentoran	L 1-4	Burns / Roberts 2, McNeill, Geary
44	18	CC	H	Coleraine	D 0-0	
45	25	CC	A	Glenavon	D 1-1	Davidson / Gallagher
46	May 2	CC	H	Larne	L 2-3	Parke, Totten / Brownlees, Glover, McGuffie

N = Windsor Park

Final positions, season 1931-32

League: 12th   P 26   W 7   D 4   L 15   F 52   A 82   pts 18
City Cup: 9th   P 13   W 4   D 3   L 6   F 25   A 34   pts 11

	Date	Comp.	Venue	Opponents	Result	Goalscorers
1	Aug 20	SL	H	Distillery	W 3-1	Doherty 2, Gough / McAdam
2	22	SL	A	Glentoran	L 2-6	Jordan, McGee / Borland 3, Roberts 2, Morgan
3	24	GC[1]	A	Cliftonville	D 2-2	McGee, Gough / Millar, McCaw
4	29	SL	H	Derry City	L 1-2	Doherty / Kelly, McDaid
5	Sept 3	GC[1R]	H	Cliftonville	W 6-0	Jordan 3, Gough, Kelly, McGee /
6	5	SL	A	Portadown	W 3-2	Doherty, Jordan 2 / Cochrane, McDonnell
7	12	SL	H	Cliftonville	D 2-2	Jordan, Kelly / Wallace, Millar
8	16	GC[2]	A	Ballymena	L 1-3	Jordan / Cox, Cameron, McCandless

9	19	SL	A	Ballymena	L 2-6	Jordan, Fergie / Barr 2, Cox, Cameron, Stoddart 2
10	26	SL	H	Linfield	L 2-5	Gough, Jordan / McCleery, Bambrick 2, Hewitt, Pollock
11	Oct 3	SL	A	Larne	L 4-5	Jordan 2, McGee, Doherty / Gilmour 3, Aiken 2
12	10	SL	A	Newry Town	L 0-4	/ Hutchinson, Inglis 2, Donnelly
13	24	SL	H	Coleraine	L 3-4	McGee, Gough, Jordan (pen) / Chambers 2, Pringle, Devan
14	31	SL	A	Glenavon	L 2-3	Moorhead o.g., Patton / Crone, Kerr, Morgan
15	Nov 7	SL	H	Bangor	D 2-2	Doherty 2 / Salisbury, Gibson
16	14	SL	A	Belfast Celtic	L 0-3	/ Firth 2, Tierney
17	21	SL	A	Distillery	D 1-1	Jordan / McCartney
18	27	IC[1]	A	Coleraine	W 3-2	Jordan, Doherty, Connell / Williamson 2
19	Dec 12	SL	H	Glentoran	W 3-2	Jordan 2 (1 pen), Doherty / Borland (pen), P. Doherty
20	19	SL	A	Derry City	L 3-6	Jordan, Kelly, Patton / Kelly 3, Johnston 2, Irvine
21	25	SL	H	Portadown	L 3-4	Mitchell, Doherty, Jordan / Johnston, Curran, McClure (pen), Blair
22	26	SL	A	Cliftonville	L 2-9	Gough, Davidson / McCaw 4, Millar 3, Watson, McClelland
23	28	SL	H	Ballymena	D 1-1	Kelly / Stoddart
24	Jan 2	SL	A	Linfield	L 1-4	Doherty / Bambrick 2, McCracken, Houston
25	9	IC[2]	A	Linfield	L 2-5	Gough, Connell (pen), / Bambrick 4, McCracken
26	14	SL	H	Larne	W 4-1	Kelly 3, Gough / Aiken
27	16	SL	H	Newry Town	W 2-0	Doherty, Jordan
28	22	SL	A	Coleraine	L 0-4	/ McClelland, Devan, Lyness, Pringle
29	27	Cas[1]	H	Distillery	D 1-1	Davidson / McAdam
30	30	SL	H	Glenavon	W 4-1	Gilmour 3, Kelly / Silcock
31	Feb 1	Cas[1R]	A	Distillery	W 2-0	Flack o.g., Jordan /
32	6	SL	A	Bangor	L 0-3	/ McKnight, Moore 2
33	13	SL	H	Belfast Celtic	W 2-1	Gough, Totten / Corrigan
34	17	Cas[2]	A	Cliftonville	D 2-2	Jordan, Patton / Bell, Watson
35	20	CC	H	Glentoran	D 1-1	Patton / Roberts
36	22	Cas[2R]	H	Cliftonville	W 4-2	Gilmour 4 / McClelland, Hume
37	27	CC	A	Larne	D 1-1	Gough / Coulter
38	Mar 5	CC	H	Glenavon	W 5-1	Gilmour 3, Gough, Davidson / Jones
39	12	CC	A	Derry City	L 0-4	/ Irvine, Kelly 2, Ferguson
40	16	Cas[SF]	N	Belfast Celtic	D 1-1	Connell (pen) / Martin
41	19	CC	H	Cliftonville	L 0-3	/ McCaw 2, Millar
42	28	CC	A	Distillery	D 2-2	Gilmour, Frame / Thompson 2
43	29	CC	A	Linfield	W 3-2	Gilmour 3 / McCaw, Donnelly
44	Apr 2	CC	H	Newry Town	W 4-1	Gilmour, Kelly 2, Patton / Rooney
45	6	Cas[SFR]	N	Belfast Celtic	L 1-6	Gilmour / Coulter, Mahood 2, Martin 2, Tierney
46	9	CC	A	Ballymena	L 1-4	Connell (pen) / Haddow 3, Cameron
47	16	CC	H	Portadown	W 3-1	Patton, Gough, Totten / Johnston
48	23	CC	A	Belfast Celtic	L 1-4	Patton / Donnelly 2, Coulter, Frewin
49	30	CC	H	Bangor	L 2-3	Gilmour 2 / McKnight, Kilpatrick 2
50	May 7	CC	A	Coleraine	L 2-7	Gilmour 2 / Priestley 2, Nesbitt, Pringle 3, Williams (pen)

N = Grosvenor Park

Final positions, season 1932-33

League: 12th   P 26 W 6 D 5 L 15 F 51 A 83 pts 17

City Cup: 9th   P 13 W 3 D 5 L 5 F 14 A 21 pts 11

	Date	Comp.	Venue	Opponents	Result	Goalscorers
1	Aug 20	SL	H	Portadown	D 1-1	Byrne / Brown
2	25	SL	A	Bangor	W 4-1	Gilmour 3, Kelly / Casey
3	27	SL	H	Belfast Celtic	D 1-1	Kelly / Coulter
4	Sept 1	GC1	H	Glentoran	L 1-3	Gilmour / Coats, Roberts, Geary
5	3	SL	A	Cliftonville	W 4-3	McMeekin, Gilmour 3 / Mitchell, Over, Doherty
6	10	SL	H	Ballymena	L 0-4	/ McClelland, Lee, McPherson, McNinch (pen)
7	24	SL	A	Glentoran	L 5-7	Gilmour 3, Grainger, Kelly / Roberts 6, Lucas
8	Oct 1	TC*	H	Bangor	L 2-3	Gilmour 2 / Wemyss, McKnight, McGee
9	8	SL	H	Coleraine	L 1-2	Gough (pen) / Pringle, Lyness
10	15	SL	A	Glenavon	L 1-2	Gilmour / Torrence, Jones
11	22	SL	A	Newry Town	L 1-4	Kelly / Flanagan, Morrow, Cunningham, Agnew
12	27	SL	H	Larne	L 2-3	Gilmour 2 / Smith 2, Coulter
13	29	SL	A	Linfield	L 0-6	/ Houston 3, Priestley, Bambrick, Jones
14	Nov 5	SL	H	Distillery	L 5-6	Gough 3 (1 pen), Kelly, Niven / Storer 3, Kirby, McAdam, Wallace
15	12	SL	A	Derry City	L 0-2	/ Ferguson, Forster
16	19	SL	A	Portadown	L 2-3	Gough (pen), Gilmour / Stewart 2, McCart
17	26	SL	H	Bangor	W 2-1	Kelly, Gough / Bell
18	Dec 3	SL	A	Belfast Celtic	L 0-4	/ Martin 3, Mahood
19	10	SL	H	Cliftonville	D 2-2	Kelly, Gough / Mills, Smith o.g.
20	17	SL	A	Ballymena	L 2-8	Gilmour, Bowers / McElfatrick 5, Patterson, Lee 2
21	24	SL	H	Glentoran	D 4-4	Gough, Bruce 2, Gilmour / McNeill, Roberts, Lyttle (pen), Doherty
22	26	SL	A	Coleraine	L 0-5	/ McDaid, Pringle 3, Devan
23	27	SL	H	Glenavon	W 3-2	Sayers 2, Gough (pen) / Jones, Davidson
24	31	SL	H	Newry Town	W 6-0	Wilson, Gough, Frame, Kelly 2, Gilmour /
25	Jan 7	SL	A	Larne	L 3-6	Sayers, Gilmour 2 / Elliott, McGuffie 5
26	14	IC[1]	A	Distillery	L 0-6	/ Kirby (pen), McLarnon, McCartney 3, Sinnamon
27	21	SL	H	Linfield	D 1-1	Bruce / Bambrick
28	28	SL	A	Distillery	L 0-5	/ Sinnamond, Storer 2, Kirby, McCartney
29	Feb 4	SL	H	Derry City	W 1-0	Sayers /
30	11	TC	A	Bangor	L 0-4	/ Bell 3, Russell
31	16	CC	H	Belfast Celtic	W 1-0	Parkinson /
32	25	CC	H	Distillery	L 0-2	/ McAdam, Jones
33	27	CC	A	Cliftonville	L 1-2	Kelly / Cooke 2
34	Mar 2	Cas[2]	H	Ballymena	W 1-0	Bruce /
35	4	CC	A	Coleraine	W 2-1	Gilmour 2 / Devan
36	11	CC	H	Portadown	D 2-2	Sayers, Gilmour / Johnston, Smith
37	18	CC	A	Ballymena	D 1-1	Sayers / Surgeoner
38	25	CC	A	Glentoran	L 1-2	Sayers / McNeill, Roberts

39	29	Cas^{SF}	N	Linfield	L 1-3	Gough / Bambrick, Maynes, Houston
40	Apr 1	CC	H	Linfield	L 0-2	/ Jones, Bambrick
41	15	CC	A	Newry Town	D 1-1	Fitzpatrick / Sturgeon
42	17	CC	H	Derry City	W 1-0	Fitzpatrick /
43	18	CC	A	Glenavon	L 0-4	/ Walker 2, Jones, Suddick
44	22	CC	H	Larne	D 3-3	Fitzpatrick, Sayers, Gilmour / Coulter, McCartney, Stewart
45	29	CC	A	Bangor	D 1-1	Fitzpatrick / Inch

N = Solitude

TC* = 1931-32 competition

Final positions, season 1933-34

League: 6th   P 26 W 11 D 5 L 10 F 47 A 46 pts 27
City Cup: 12th   P 13 W 3 D 2 L 8   F 22 A 42 pts 8

	Date	Comp.	Venue	Opponents	Result	Goalscorers
1	Aug 21	SL	H	Belfast Celtic	D 2-2	Fitzpatrick 2 / McCullough, Walker
2	23	SL	A	Distillery	L 1-2	Patterson / Kirby 2
3	26	SL	H	Glentoran	L 0-2	/ Duncan 2
4	Sept 2	SL	A	Portadown	L 0-1	/ Bullick
5	7	GC[1]	H	Cliftonville	L 0-2	/ Mathieson o.g., Hewitt
6	9	SL	H	Glenavon	W 4-0	Burns 3, Gough /
7	16	SL	A	Cliftonville	W 2-0	Fitzpatrick 2 /
8	23	SL	H	Newry Town	W 5-1	Gough 3 (2 pens), Buchanan, Fitzpatrick / McAdam
9	30	TC	H	Bangor	W 3-2	Graham 2, Buchanan / Wemyss, Clint
10	Oct 7	SL	H	Larne	W 1-0	Gough /
11	19	SL	A	Derry City	L 0-2	/ Shearer, Smith
12	21	SL	H	Linfield	L 1-4	Graham / Bambrick 3, Donnelly
13	28	SL	A	Ballymena	D 2-2	Buchanan, Graham / Williamson, McCormick
14	Nov 11	SL	A	Bangor	L 2-3	Davidson, Fitzpatrick / Inch, Coates 2
15	18	SL	A	Coleraine	L 1-2	Davidson / McDaid, Martin
16	25	SL	A	Belfast Celtic	D 3-3	Johnstone 2, Gough (pen) / Martin 2, McCullough
17	Dec 2	SL	H	Distillery	W 3-2	Gough, Burns, Johnstone / Wallace, Rorrison
18	9	SL	A	Glentoran	L 2-6	Davidson, Johnstone / Duncan, Fitzsimmons 3, Leathem 2
19	16	SL	H	Portadown	W 2-0	Gough, Graham /
20	23	SL	A	Glenavon	L 1-2	Hodder / McGill, Burns
21	25	SL	H	Cliftonville	W 3-2	Buchanan 2, Johnstone / Neill o.g., McCaw
22	26	SL	A	Newry Town	D 1-1	Johnstone / Chambers
23	30	SL	A	Larne	W 3-1	Johnstone 2, Small o.g. / McGuffie
24	Jan 6	SL	H	Derry City	D 2-2	Gough, Graham / Kelly 2
25	13	IC[1]	H	Portadown	L 1-2	Gough (pen) / Smith, Johnston

26	20	SL	A	Linfield	L 0-5	/ Bambrick 4, Baird
27	27	SL	H	Ballymena	W 2-1	Fitzpatrick 2 / McIlroy
28	Feb 3	SL	H	Bangor	W 2-0	Davidson, Fitzpatrick /
29	10	SL	H	Coleraine	W 2-0	Buchanan 2 /
30	17	CC	A	Portadown	L 1-4	Burns / Harte 3, Smith
31	24	CC	H	Bangor	L 0-1	/ Coates
32	28	Cas[2]	A	Cliftonville	W 5-4	Gough 2 (1 pen), Gamble 2, Mathieson / Millar,"Smyth" 2, Laverty
33	Mar 3	CC	A	Ballymena	L 2-7	Davidson, Gamble / McIlroy,McCormick 3, Shiels, Mahood, Williamson (pen)
34	17	CC	A	Glentoran	L 2-7	Gough, Fitzpatrick / Kerr 4, McKnight 3
35	22	CC	H	Belfast Celtic	W 3-2	Roberts, Smyth, Gough / Murray, Feenan
36	24	CC	H	Coleraine	D 3-3	Buchanan, Gamble, McKittrick / Donnelly 2, Byrne
37	28	Cas[SF]	N	Belfast Celtic II	D 2-2	Gamble, Burns / Kelly, O'Boyle
38	31	CC	A	Glenavon	L 1-2	Gough (pen) / Lynn, Andrews
39	Apr 2	CC	H	Cliftonville	W 3-2	Gamble, Burns, Gough / Ferguson, Hewitt
40	3	CC	H	Linfield	L 1-2	Burns / Bambrick 2
41	7	CC	A	Newry Town	L 1-4	Davidson / Cassidy 2, Hall, Syddall
42	11	Cas[SFR]	N	Belfast Celtic II	D 1-1	Gamble / Kelly
43	18	Cas[SFR]	N	Belfast Celtic II	W 4-2	Burns, Davidson 2, Gough / Kelly, McGivern
44	21	CC	H	Larne	W 3-1	Roberts, Johnstone, Davidson / Sullivan
45	25	CC	H	Derry City	L 1-6	Burns / Brown, Pringle 3, Ferguson, M. Doherty
46	28	CC	A	Distillery	D 1-1	Johnstone / Forrest
47	30	Cas[F]	N[2]	Linfield	L 1-7	Gamble / Caiels 2, Mackay 2, Bambrick 3

N = Oval

N[2] = Grosvenor Park

Final positions, season 1934-35

League: 13th   P 26   W 5   D 3   L 18   F 45   A 91   pts 13

City Cup: 12th   P 13   W 2   D 3   L 8   F 22   A 36   pts 7

	Date	Comp.	Venue	Opponents	Result	Goalscorers
1	Aug 18	SL	A	Portadown	L 1-5	Burns / McAllister 3, Moore, Fitzsimmons
2	23	SL	H	Larne	L 1-2	Gamble / Dodds 2
3	25	SL	A	Belfast Celtic	L 0-9	/ Murray 2, Brown, McCullough, Martin 5
4	Sept 1	SL	H	Cliftonville	L 2-5	McKittrick, Smith / Millar 4, McCaw
5	6	GC[1]	H	Cliftonville	W 5-2	Gamble, McKittrick, O'Neill 2, Johnston / Billingsley, Hewitt
6	8	SL	A	Glentoran	L 0-6	/ Tyson 2, Kerr 3, Smith
7	15	SL	H	Coleraine	W 2-0	Burns, Watson /
8	22	SL	A	Glenavon	L 0-1	/ Hughes
9	29	SL	H	Ballymena Utd.	D 2-2	Gough, Kerr / Campbell, McGowan
10	Oct 6	SL	A	Linfield	L 0-6	/ Baird 2, Bambrick 3, McCormick
11	13	SL	H	Newry Town	W 5-2	Kerr, Gamble 3, Mailey / Redfern, Roberts

12	27	SL	A	Distillery	L 1-2	Gough / McCartney, Firth
13	Nov 3	SL	H	Bangor	W 8-1	Buchanan, Gamble 4, Kerr 3 / Hanna
14	7	GC[SF]	N	Belfast Celtic	L 1-3	Gamble / Moore, Martin 2
15	10	SL	H	Derry City	L 0-3	/ McLeod, Kelly, Doherty
16	17	SL	H	Portadown	D 4-4	Mailey, Gamble 3 / McAllister 2, Hyslop, Elliott
17	24	SL	A	Larne	L 0-3	/ Henderson (pen), McGuffie, Dodds
18	Dec 1	SL	H	Belfast Celtic	L 1-4	O'Neill / Geoghegan 2, Martin 2
19	8	SL	A	Cliftonville	L 2-8	Gamble, Buchanan / Over 5, McCaw 2, Gibb
20	15	SL	H	Glentoran	L 3-4	Gough 2 (1 pen), Buchanan / McNeill 2, Leathem, Goodwin
21	22	SL	A	Coleraine	L 0-3	/ Craig 2, Donnelly
22	25	SL	H	Glenavon	D 2-2	Mailey 2 / Hughes 2
23	26	SL	A	Ballymena Utd.	L 1-5	Burns / Mitchell, Campbell 2, Hargreaves 2
24	29	SL	H	Linfield	L 0-4	/ Baird 3, Mackay
25	Jan 5	SL	A	Newry Town	W 3-2	Gamble 2, Burns / Redfern 2
26	12	SL	H	Distillery	L 1-3	Burns / Bell 2, Firth (pen)
27	19	IC[1]	A	Glentoran	L 1-3	Gamble / Tyson 2, McNeill
28	26	SL	A	Bangor	W 4-1	Buchanan, Gamble, Burns, Gough (pen) / Thornton
29	Feb 2	SL	A	Derry City	L 2-4	Gamble 2 / Duffy 3, Kelly
30	9	CC	H	Derry City	L 4-5	Davidson, Gamble 3 / Kelly 2, Duffy 2, Smith
31	16	CC	A	Larne	L 1-2	Burns / Byrne, Lyness
32	20	Cas[2]	A	Belfast Celtic II	L 2-4	Buchanan, Mitchell / McAlinden 2, Whiteside 2 (1 pen)
33	27	CC	H	Glentoran	L 1-4	Beck o.g. / Smith, McNeill 3
34	Mar 2	CC	A	Portadown	L 2-3	Gough, Buchanan (pen) / Fitzsimmons, McAllister, Laing
35	9	CC	H	Newry Town	D 2-2	Gough, Gamble / Tracey, Redfern
36	16	CC	A	Linfield	L 1-2	Gamble / Allison, Jones (pen)
37	23	CC	A	Distillery	L 1-3	Burns / Weldon 2, Storer
38	30	CC	H	Coleraine	D 3-3	Clarke, Burns 2 / Olphert, Creelman, McCready
39	Apr 13	CC	A	Ballymena Utd.	L 0-3	/ Mitchell 2, Hargreaves
40	20	CC	H	Glenavon	W 1-0	Gamble /
41	22	CC	A	Cliftonville	L 2-7	Burns, Gough /Cooke 2, Over 2, Smith 2, McCaw
42	23	CC	H	Belfast Celtic	D 1-1	Gamble / McIlroy
43	29	CC	H	Bangor	W 3-1	Burns, Gough, Davidson / Parkinson

N = Grosvenor Park

Final positions, season 1935-36

League: 14th   P 26   W 5   D 3   L 18   F 44   A 94   pts 13

City Cup: 13th   P 13   W 2   D 2   L 9   F 18   A 48   pts 6

	Date	Comp.	Venue	Opponents	Result	Goalscorers
1	Aug 17	SL	H	Glenavon	W 3-1	McKeenan, Lowry 2 / Fitzpatrick
2	20	SL	A	Larne	L 2-3	McKeenan, Ryder / Dodds 2, McLeod
3	24	SL	H	Belfast Celtic	L 0-3	/ Kernoghan, McCullough, McKnight
4	31	SL	A	Newry Town	L 1-7	Lowry / Cassidy, Redfern 4 (1 pen), Wilkin, Cromie
5	Sept 5	GC[1]	H	Belfast Celtic	L 1-3	Pritchard (pen) / Feenan (pen), McKnight, Geoghegan
6	7	SL	H	Distillery	L 2-7	Ryder, Laverty / McLarnon, McNally 4, McCartney, Patton (pen)
7	14	SL	A	Derry City	L 1-8	Pritchard / Kelly, Shearer 4, Smith, Grant 2
8	21	SL	H	Bangor	W 5-1	Gamble 2, Laverty 2, Pritchard (pen) / Hamilton
9	28	SL	A	Portadown	L 3-4	Gamble, Laverty 2 / Hamilton 2, Walsh, Brown
10	Oct 5	SL	H	Ballymena Utd.	L 1-5	Gamble / Mitchell 4, Olphert
11	12	SL	A	Cliftonville	L 0-6	/ Over 3, McCaw 2 (1 pen), Scott
12	26	SL	A	Linfield	L 1-5	Gamble / McCormick 3, Baird 2
13	Nov 2	SL	H	Coleraine	W 2-1	Laverty, Pritchard / Tickle
14	9	SL	A	Glentoran	L 6-9	Johnston 3, Pritchard, Gamble, Laverty / McCrea 5, McNeill, Miller (pen), Aicken 2
15	16	SL	A	Glenavon	L 1-3	Laverty / Kennedy o.g., Johnston, Kelly
16	23	SL	H	Larne	D 3-3	Johnston, Pritchard, Bennett / Dodds, McLeod 2
17	30	SL	A	Belfast Celtic	L 1-2	Gough / McPhee, McGivern
18	Dec 7	SL	H	Newry Town	L 2-3	Laverty 2 / Redfern 2, Wilkin
19	14	SL	A	Distillery	L 0-4	/ McNally 3, Prentiss
20	21	SL	H	Derry City	L 0-2	/ Smith, Renfrew
21	25	SL	A	Bangor	W 3-0	Johnston 2, Gough /
22	26	SL	H	Portadown	D 2-2	Gough 2 (1 pen) / McIlroy, Elliott
23	28	SL	A	Ballymena Utd.	D 1-1	Gamble / Wallace
24	Jan 4	SL	H	Cliftonville	L 2-3	Gamble, Mathieson / Over 2, Gibb
25	11	IC[1]	H	Glentoran II	L 2-3	Laverty 2 / Boyd 2, Loughlin
26	18	SL	H	Linfield	L 0-4	/ Houston 3, McCleery
27	25	SL	A	Coleraine	L 0-6	/ Tickle 2, Duncan 2, McIlroy, Lyness
28	30	Cas[1]	A	Distillery	L 0-3	/ McLarnon 2, Patterson
29	Feb 1	SL	H	Glentoran	W 2-1	Laverty, Gamble / McNeill
30	8	CC	H	Cliftonville	L 2-4	Parkinson, Gough (pen) / Over 3, McNeill
31	15	CC	A	Belfast Celtic	L 0-7	/ Feenan (pen), Kelly 4, Kernoghan, Geoghegan
32	22	CC	H	Glentoran	L 2-7	McAllister, Laverty (pen) / McNeill, McIndoe, McCrea 2, Gray, Loughlin, Blaney
33	29	CC	A	Bangor	D 1-1	Laverty / McPherson
34	Mar 7	CC	H	Larne	W 3-2	Laverty 2 (1 pen), Gamble / McGuffie, Richmond
35	14	CC	A	Glenavon	L 1-3	McAllister / Rosbotham, Kelly, Burns
36	21	CC	H	Coleraine	W 3-1	McAllister, Gamble 2 / McIlroy
37	28	CC	A	Distillery	L 0-4	/ Prentice, Gibson 3
38	Apr 11	CC	H	Linfield	L 3-5	Gough, Laverty 2 / Ruddy 2, McCleery, McCormick 2
39	13	CC	A	Newry Town	L 0-4	/ Wilkin, Redfern (pen), McIvor, Peters
40	14	CC	A	Ballymena Utd.	L 1-4	Kennedy / Fisher 3, Mitchell
41	18	CC	H	Portadown	D 2-2	Gamble, McAllister / Martin 2
42	25	CC	A	Derry City	L 0-4	/ Kelly, Hughes 2, McLeod

Final positions, season 1936-37

League: 11th   P 26 W 8 D 2 L 16 F 42 A 74 pts 18
City Cup: 9th   P 13 W 5 D 1 L 7   F 26 A 48 pts 11

	Date	Comp.	Venue	Opponents	Result	Goalscorers
1	Aug 15	SL	H	Linfield	L 2-6	Rice 2 / Hume 3, McCormick, Baird, Dornan
2	20	SL	A	Coleraine	W 2-0	Laverty, Shaw o.g. /
3	22	SL	A	Distillery	L 1-2	Laverty / Whiteside (pen), McDaid
4	26	GC[1]	A	Linfield	L 0-5	/ Hulme 3, Dornan, McCormick
5	29	SL	H	Ballymena Utd.	W 6-1	Gamble 4, Hughes, Hood / Moore
6	Sept 5	SL	A	Glenavon	W 2-1	Sayers, Gamble / Connor
7	12	SL	H	Cliftonville	W 3-1	Gamble 2, Hood / George
8	19	SL	A	Bangor	D 1-1	Laverty / Barnard
9	26	SL	H	Derry City	L 4-5	Sayers, Yates, Gamble, Tulips (pen) / McLeod 2, Kelly, Lambie, Clarke
10	Oct 3	SL	A	Belfast Celtic	L 0-10	/ Turnbull 6, Kernaghan 3, McAlinden
11	10	SL	H	Larne	W 5-0	McKerley, Gamble 4 /
12	17	SL	A	Portadown	W 1-0	Gamble /
13	24	SL	H	Glentoran	W 2-0	Tulips, Gough /
14	Nov 7	SL	A	Newry Town	L 1-4	Tulips (pen) / Redfern 3, McIvor
15	14	SL	A	Linfield	L 1-3	Hood / Bowden, Baird, Richardson (pen)
16	21	SL	H	Coleraine	D 1-1	Yates / Andrews
17	28	SL	H	Distillery	W 3-1	Smyth, Tulips (pen), Laverty / McDaid (pen)
18	Dec 5	SL	A	Ballymena Utd.	L 1-4	Crowther / Brown 3, Lingwood
19	12	SL	H	Glenavon	L 0-4	/ Kelly, Rosbotham (pen), Holbeach, Pringle
20	19	SL	A	Cliftonville	L 2-4	Murphy, Gough / McCaw 2, Banks 2
21	25	SL	H	Bangor	L 0-1	/ McGurk
22	26	SL	A	Derry City	L 1-3	Laverty / Duffy, Carlyle (pen), McLeod
23	Jan 2	SL	H	Belfast Celtic	L 0-5	/ Kernaghan, McIlroy 3, Turnbull
24	9	IC[1]	A	Ballymena Utd.	L 1-5	Gamble / Fisher 3 (1 pen), Buckley, Moore
25	16	SL	A	Larne	L 1-9	Murphy / Mitchell 3 (1 pen), McKerley o.g., McGown 4, Keenan
26	23	SL	H	Portadown	L 1-3	Finlay / Elliott 2, Cochrane (pen)
27	27	Cas[2]	A	Distillery	L 0-4	/ Ruddy 3, Doherty
28	30	SL	A	Glentoran	L 1-2	Smyth / McKay, McNeill
29	Feb 6	SL	H	Newry Town	L 0-2	/ McCart, Whitehouse
30	13	CC	A	Belfast Celtic	L 0-10	/ Turnbull 5, McIlroy 2, Bruce, Walker, McAlinden
31	20	CC	H	Coleraine	L 1-4	Gamble / Dougherty 2, Kilpatrick 2
32	27	CC	A	Glentoran	L 2-7	Sayers, Crowther / Lavery, Stitt 3, Williamson, Rigby 2
33	Mar 6	CC	H	Bangor	L 1-3	McKay (pen) / Cooke, Bernard, Couser
34	20	CC	H	Larne	W 4-3	McKay (pen), Smyth, Sayers, Gamble / Donaghy, Black, Campbell
35	27	CC	A	Linfield	L 1-3	Gamble / Hulme, McCormick (pen), McMurray
36	29	CC	H	Derry City	D 0-0	
37	30	CC	A	Distillery	W 5-1	Gamble 2, Gough 3 / Patton

38	31	CC	A	Newry Town	L 1-5	Hughes / Redfern, McCart, Thompson 2, Whitehouse
39	Apr 3	CC	H	Cliftonville	W 5-2	Gamble 2, Hood, Hughes 2 / Martin, Shannon
40	17	CC	A	Portadown	L 1-9	Crowther / Pierson 3, Kerr 2, McGurk, Cochrane (pen), Fitzsimmons 2
41	24	CC	H	Glenavon	W 2-0	Gamble, J. Wilson /
42	May 1	CC	H	Ballymena Utd.	W 3-0	Gamble, Donnelly, Hughes

Final positions, season 1937-38

League: 9th   P 26   W 7   D 4   L 15   F 43   A 66   pts 18

City Cup: 11th   P 13   W 3   D 2   L 8   F 19   A 45   pts 8

	Date	Comp.	Venue	Opponents	Result	Goalscorers
1	Aug 21	SL	H	Cliftonville	W 6-0	Cowan 4, Buchanan, McDowell /
2	23	SL	A	Portadown	L 0-2	/ Gamble, McGivern
3	26	SL	H	Bangor	W 2-1	Scott 2 / Clayton
4	28	SL	A	Glentoran	L 0-2	/ John (pen), Griffith
5	Sept 4	SL	H	Derry City	L 2-5	McKerley 2 (1 pen) / Kelly 2, McLeod 2, Duffy
6	11	SL	A	Ballymena Utd.	W 4-1	Hughes, Cowan 2, Scott / Bailie
7	14	GC[1]	A	Larne	L 1-4	Hughes / Newberry 3, Boyce o.g.
8	18	SL	H	Newry Town	W 6-2	Lappin, Gordon 2, Wilson, Buchanan 2 / Peters, McKenna
9	25	SL	A	Belfast Celtic	L 0-6	/ McAlinden 2, Kernaghan, Bruce 2, McKerley o.g.
10	Oct 2	SL	A	Distillery	L 1-3	Hughes / Clark 3
11	9	SL	H	Glenavon	L 1-3	Scott / Murray, Halliday, Henderson
12	16	SL	A	Coleraine	L 1-3	Gordon / Stewart, Boyle, Kilpatrick
13	30	SL	H	Linfield	L 0-3	/ Grant 2, Graham
14	Nov 6	SL	A	Larne	D 1-1	Buchanan / Pierce
15	13	SL	A	Cliftonville	D 1-1	Buchanan / McCaw
16	20	SL	H	Portadown	D 2-2	Buchanan, Wilson / McGivern, Lightbody o.g.
17	27	SL	A	Bangor	W 3-1	Buchanan, Cochrane 2 / Morrow
18	Dec 4	SL	H	Glentoran	L 3-4	Blaney o.g., Buchanan 2 / Brown 3, Rigby
19	16	SL	A	Derry City	L 0-3	/ Carlyle (pen), Duffy, McDaid
20	18	SL	H	Ballymena Utd.	L 1-3	Ritchie / Wallace 2, Moore
21	25	SL	A	Newry Town	L 1-4	Buchanan / Barlow 2, McIvor, Dempsey
22	27	SL	H	Belfast Celtic	L 1-4	Gordon / Leathem, Walker 2 (1 pen), O'Neill
23	Jan 1	SL	H	Distillery	D 1-1	Dornan / Bradford
24	8	IC[1]	A	Newry Town	L 0-3	/ Whitehouse, Barlow, Thompson
25	15	SL	A	Glana	L 1-4	Scott / McKnight, Halliday 2, Harrison
26	22	SL	H	Coleraine	W 2-1	Stewart, Scott / Tracey
27	26	Cas[2]	A	Linfield	L 1-8	Buchanan / Donnelly, Grant 3 (1 pen), McCormick 2, Gibb, Pringle
28	29	SL	A	Linfield	L 0-6	/ Grant, McDowell, Thompson, McCormick 2, Donnelly
29	Feb 5	SL	H	Larne	W 3-0	Buchanan 2, Ritchie /

30	12	CC	A	Cliftonville	W 3-2	Buchanan 2, Gordon / Banks, Over
31	19	CC	H	Larne	L 2-5	Buchanan, Gordon / McLarnon 3, Mitchell 2
32	23	CC	A	Linfield	L 0-7	/ McAllister 3, Walker, Marshall 2, Todd
33	Mar 5	CC	H	Coleraine	D 4-4	McKerley, Buchanan, McKeown, Hughes / Boyle, Johnston 2, Foye
34	12	CC	A	Distillery	L 1-4	McKeown / Clarke, Newberry 3
35	19	CC	H	Glenavon	W 2-1	McKeown, Gordon / Craig
36	26	CC	H	Ballymena Utd.	L 1-2	Buchanan / Sclater, Brand
37	Apr 2	CC	A	Belfast Celtic	L 2-5	McKeown, Buchanan / McIlroy, Turnbull 3, Shannon
38	16	CC	H	Newry Town	W 2-1	Buchanan 2 / Barlow
39	18	CC	A	Derry City	L 2-7	Buchanan 2 / McLeod 2, Rigby, Carlyle, Kelly, Duffy, Holbeach
40	19	CC	H	Glentoran	D 1-1	Buchanan / Browne
41	23	CC	A	Bangor	L 0-4	/ Clayton (pen), Robinson, McCartney, Graham
42	30	CC	H	Portadown	L 0-2	/ Dowling 2

Final positions, season 1938-39

League: 8th   P 26   W 11   D 6   L 9   F 63   A 66   pts 28
City Cup: 12th   P13   W 1   D 1   L 10   F 14   A 42   pts 5

	Date	Comp.	Venue	Opponents	Result	Goalscorers
1	Aug 20	SL	A	Portadown	L 2-6	Buchanan, Patterson / McNally 2, Gordon, Simpson, Black (pen), Allen
2	22	SL	H	Bangor	W 2-0	Irwin, Patton (pen.)
3	25	SL	A	Belfast Celtic	L 1-8	McLarnon / Turnbull 4, McAlinden 2, McIlroy, Kernoghan
4	27	SL	H	Derry City	W 3-1	Peden, McKeown, McLarnon / Kelly
5	Sept 3	SL	A	Ballymena Utd.	D 1-1	McMaster / Moore
6	10	SL	H	Cliftonville	W 5-2	Peden, Buchanan 2, McLarnon, Patton / Lyttle, Johnston
7	14	GC[1]	A	Ballymena Utd.	L 3-5	Buchanan 2, Patton / Grant, Moore 2, Sclater 2
8	17	SL	A	Glenavon	W 4-2	Smyth 3, Buchanan / Craig 2
9	24	SL	H	Newry Town	W 4-2	Fitzsimmons, McLarnon, Patton (pen), McMaster / Myers, Gibb
10	Oct 1	SL	H	Distillery	W 4-2	Buchanan, McLarnon, Patton, McKeown / Bradford 2
11	15	SL	A	Larne	D 2-2	Patterson, McLarnon / McFarland, Johnston
12	22	SL	H	Coleraine	D 4-4	Elliott 3, Smyth / Foye 2, Shiels 2
13	29	SL	A	Glentoran	L 1-2	McAllister / Taylor, Todd
14	Nov 5	SL	H	Linfield	W 4-1	McLarnon, Smyth, Elliott, Pedlow / Ferguson
15	12	SL	H	Portadown	D 3-3	Smyth 3 (1 pen) / McNally (pen), R. Black, Mitchell
16	19	SL	A	Bangor	D 1-1	Elliott / Couser
17	26	SL	H	Belfast Celtic	L 2-3	McMaster, Elliott / McAlinden 2, Kernoghan

18	Dec 3	SL	A	Derry City	L 0-5	/ Shearer, Kelly 3, Duffy
19	10	SL	H	Ballymena Utd.	L 2-6	Elliott 2 / Sclater 6
20	17	SL	A	Cliftonville	L 3-4	Crooks, McKerley, Patton / Ritchie, Roden 3
21	24	SL	H	Glenavon	W 4-2	Buchanan 2, McLarnon 2 / Reid, Holbeach
22	26	SL	A	Newry Town	D 1-1	Hood / O'Hara
23	27	SL	A	Distillery	L 0-2	/ Thompson 2 (2 pens)
24	31	SL	H	Larne	W 3-2	Buchanan 2, Peden / Bell 2
25	Jan 7	SL	A	Coleraine	W 5-2	Buchanan 2, Elliott 2, McLarnon / Montgomery 2
26	14	SL	H	Glentoran	W 2-1	Elliott, Buchanan / Taylor (pen)
27	21	IC[1]	H	Glenavon	D 2-2	Elliott, McLarnon / Burns, Craig
28	25	IC[1R]	A	Glenavon	L 2-3	Buchanan, Elliott / Craig 2, Burns
29	28	SL	A	Linfield	L 0-1	/ McDonald
30	Feb 1	Cas[1]	A	Glentoran	L 2-3	McLarnon, Cowan / Taylor 2 (1 pen), Connor
31	4	CC	A	Linfield	L 1-5	Elliott / Robertson, Marshall, Rosbotham, McCormick 2
32	11	CC	H	Larne	L 3-5	Buchanan, Patton, Elliott (pen) / Craigie (pen), Taylor, McPeake 2, Girvan
33	18	CC	H	Portadown	L 1-5	Buchanan / Mitchell, Black 2, Wright, McNally
34	25	CC	A	Glentoran	L 0-1	/ McCandless
35	Mar 4	CC	H	Newry Town	D 2-2	Elliott, Bailie / Gibb, Wall
36	18	CC	A	Derry City	L 0-4	/ Kelso 2, Shearer 2
37	25	CC	H	Ballymena Utd.	W 3-2	McLarnon 2, Howard / Moore, Sclater
38	Apr 1	CC	A	Belfast Celtic	L 1-8	Bailie / Pierce 4, O'Connor 3 (1 pen), Leathem
39	8	CC	H	Bangor	W 1-0	Howard /
40	10	CC	A	Glenavon	L 1-3	S. Patton / Holbeach, Brand, Craig
41	11	CC	H	Distillery	L 0-1	/ McIntyre
42	15	CC	A	Cliftonville	L 0-2	/ Thompson, Wright o.g
43	22	CC	H	Coleraine	L 1-4	Buchanan / Bowden 3 (1 pen), Creelman
44	28	TC	A	Bangor	D 2-2	Buchanan, Donaldson / Couser 2 (1 pen)

Final positions, season 1939-40

League: 9th	P 26	W 9	D 2	L 15	F 49	A 72	pts 20
City Cup: 12th	P13	W4	D1	L 8	F 23	A 31	pts 9

	Date	Comp.	Venue	Opponents	Result	Goalscorers
1	Aug 19	CC	H	Ballymena Utd.	L 1-2	Bunting / Sclater, Moore
2	23	CC	A	Cliftonville	W 3-0	Bunting 2, McKeown /
3	26	CC	H	Newry Town	W 2-0	Bunting, Rankin /
4	Sept 2	CC	A	Derry City	L 1-4	Bailie / Gilmour 2, Kelso, Morton
5	6	CC	H	Coleraine	D 0-0	
6	9	CC	A	Belfast Celtic	L 0-6	/ O'Connor 3, Kelly 2, Kernoghan
7	12	GC[1]	A	Distillery	L 2-4	Bunting, McLarnon / Carroll, Lonsdale 3
8	16	CC	H	Linfield	L 2-3	Bunting, McLarnon / Bell, McCormick 2 (1 pen)
9	23	CC	A	Glenavon	L 1-2	Elliott / Haire o.g., Brand (pen)
10	30	CC	H	Portadown	L 1-2	Elliott (pen) / Russell 2

11	Oct 7	CC	A	Glentoran	L 3-5	McLarnon 2 (1 pen), Bunting / Douglas 2, Lavery, Smyth 2
12	14	CC	H	Distillery	W 5-3	Todd 2, Bunting 2, Donaldson / Lonsdale 2, Burns
13	21	CC	A	Bangor	L 0-3	/ Hanratty, McCandless, Couser
14	28	TC	H	Bangor	W 4-2	Elliott 2, McLarnon, Donaldson / Atkinson 2
15	Nov 4	CC	A	Larne	W 4-1	Donaldson, McKeown, Elliott, Moore o.g. / Kane
16	11	SL	H	Cliftonville	W 3-1	Elliott, Donaldson, Todd / Over
17	18	SL	A	Derry City	L 2-6	Elliott, McLarnon / Kelly, Kelso 3, Doherty, Clark
18	25	SL	A	Newry Town	L 0-2	/ L.. Hughes, J. Hughes
19	Dec 2	SL	H	Belfast Celtic	D 3-3	Todd, Elliott 2 / McIlroy, O'Connor, Kernoghan
20	9	SL	A	Portadown	L 1-3	McLarnon / Black, McCartney, McIntyre
21	16	SL	H	Larne	W 7-1	Bunting 3, Crawford, Doherty, McLarnon, McKeown / Kane
22	23	SL	A	Distillery	W 2-1	McLarnon 2 / Wilton
23	25	SL	H	Coleraine	W 5-0	Todd 3, Bunting, McLarnon /
24	26	SL	A	Bangor	W 5-2	Doherty 2, Crawford, Crooks, McKeown / Couser, Bradford
25	30	SL	H	Linfield	L 2-3	Bunting, Crawford (pen) / Lyness, McKennan, Baird
26	Jan 6	SL	A	Glenavon	L 1-5	Todd / Robinson 2, Craig, Holbeach, Duffy
27	10	Cas[1]	H	Linfield Swifts	D 2-2	Todd 2 / Douglas, Hume
28	13	SL	H	Ballymena Utd.	L 0-2	/ Sclater 2
29	15	Cas[1R]	A	Linfield Swifts	L 0-3	/ Hume, Harvey, McIlroy
30	20	IC[1]	A	Larne	L 0-3	/ Kane 3
31	27	SL	A	Glentoran	L 1-8	Bunting / McMillen 2, Grice 2, Lavery, Smith 2, Robinson
32	Feb 3	SL	A	Cliftonville	W 3-1	Bunting, King 2 / Crosby
33	10	SL	H	Derry City	L 1-3	Crawford / Kelly 2, Gilmour
34	17	SL	H	Newry Town	D 1-1	Bunting / McCaul
35	24	TC	H	Bangor	L 1-5	Doherty / Bradford 5
36	28	SL	A	Belfast Celtic	L 0-3	/ Kernoghan 2 (1 pen), Leathem
37	Mar 2	SL	H	Portadown	W 5-4	Howard 2, McLarnon 2, Crawford (pen)/ McCartney, Wright, Gaughran, Russell
38	9	SL	A	Larne	L 0-4	/ McFarlane, Barr, Girvan, Crofts
39	16	SL	H	Distillery	L 1-4	Doherty / O'Neill 2, Lonsdale, Barr
40	23	SL	A	Coleraine	L 1-3	Gordon / McDonald 2, Stannex
41	25	SL	H	Bangor	W 3-1	Higson, Gordon, Doherty / McCandless
42	26	SL	A	Linfield	L 0-4	/ McIlroy, Peden, Baird (pen), Walsh
43	30	SL	H	Glenavon	L 0-1	/ Craig
44	Apr 13	SL	H	Glentoran	W 2-1	Gordon, Bunting / Smith
45	24	SL	A	Ballymena Utd.	L 0-5	/ Grant 2, Sclater 3

Final positions, season 1940-41

League: 3rd   P 23   W 16   D 1   L 6   F 51   A 33   pts 31

	Date	Comp.	Venue	Opponents	Result	Goalscorers
1	Aug 31	INL	H	St. Mary's	W 5-0	Irwin, Fitzsimmons 3, Beattie /
2	Sept 6	CLC[1]	A	Glentoran II	W 5-2	McKeown, Higson 2, Johnston, Fitzsimmons / Coulter 2
3	14	Cas[1]	H	Glentoran II	L *	
4	21	INC[1]	H	30th OB	W 6-1	Fitzsimmons, Johnston 2, Williams 2, Higson / Magowan
5	28	INL	A	Crusaders	L 1-4	Fitzsimmons / Croft, Evans, Bell, A. N. Other
6	Oct 5	INC[2]	H	Comm. Signals	W 2-0	Johnston, Higson /
7	19	CLC[2]	A	Larne Olympic	L 0-2	/ Smyth, McCreery
8	26	INC[3]	H	Bangor Res.	W 3-1	Johnston, Fitzsimmons, Rankin / Birch
9	Nov 2	INL	A	Bangor Res.	L 0-2	/ McCandless, Mailey
10	9	INL	H	Larne Olympic	W 1-0	Beattie /
11	16	INL	H	Summerfield	W 2-1	Keeley, Crawford / O'Hara
12	23	INL	A	Celtic II	L 0-6	/ Dinnen 6
13	30	INC[SF]		Glentoran II	L *	
14	Dec 7	INL	H	Celtic II	L 1-3	McCormick / Horner, Keenan, Nelson
15	21	INL	A	Ballyclare Com.	L 1-2	Short / Cowan 2
16	25	INL	H	Brantwood	W 3-2	Cochrane 3 / Cummings, Houston
17	28	INL	A	Dundela	W 5-0	Keeley 3, Williams, Simpson /
18	Jan 4	INL	H	Cliftonville Oly.	W 1-0	Fitzsimmons /
19	11	INL	H	Crusaders	W 2-0	Rankin, Goss /
20	Feb 1	INL	H	Distillery II	W 3-0	Burton 2, Keeley /
21	15	INL	H	Linfield Swifts	W 2-0	Crawford, Moore /
22	22	IC[1]	A	Linfield	L 1-4	Short (pen) / Sheen 2, Baird, McKeown
23	Mar 1	Cas[1]	H	Bangor Res.	W 4-1	Hollinger, Burton, Short (pen), Fitzsimmons / Bradford
24	8	INL	A	Brantwood	W 5-0	Burton 3, Hollinger, Crawford (pen) /
25	15	INL	H	Glentoran II	W 2-1	Burton, Hollinger / Smyth
26	20	Cas[2]	H	Distillery	L 0-5	/ Lyness, Embleton 2, Prout, Brownlow
27	22	INL	H	Bangor Res.	L 0-1	/ Frith
28	29	INL	A	Distillery II	W 4-1	Beattie, A. N. Other o.g., Craig 2 / Kane
29	Apr 3	McC[1]	A	Brantwood	D* 0-0	
30	5	INL	A	Summerfield	D 5-5	Moore 2, Craig 2, Fitzsimmons / Orr 3, Barr, O'Hara
31	12	McC[1R]	H	Brantwood	W 6-1	Burton 4 (1 pen), Beattie 2 / Hood (pen)
32	14	INL	A	Larne Olympic	W 5-3	Burton 2, McCormick, Fitzsimmons, Beattie / Hughes 2, A. N. Other
33	26	McC[2]	H	Bangor Res.	W 2-0	Beattie, Burton /
34	May 3	INL	A[#]	Cliftonville Oly.	W 3-1	Moore, Burton 2 / Williamson
35	10	INL	A	Glentoran II	W w-o	
36	17	INL	H	Ballyclare Com.	P	
37		INL	A	Linfield Swifts	C	

INL result (v St. Mary's (A)) untraceable
L* = ties lost on appeal before k.o.
D* = abandoned after 80 mins.
C = cancelled
P = postponed

A[#] = Castlereagh Park
w-o = walkover

Final positions, season 1941-42

League: 3rd   P 22   W 14   D 3   L5   F 70   A 35   pts 31

	Date	Comp.	Venue	Opponents	Result	Goalscorers
1	Aug 23	INL	H	Bangor Res.	W 2-0	Burton 2 /
2	27	McC[SF]	N	Distillery II	D 4-4	Burton 3 (1 pen), McCormick / Parker, Davis 2, Cochrane o.g.
3	30	INL	A	Ballyclare Com.	L 1-2	Dinnen / Stokes, Short
4	Sept 6	INL	H	Naval XI	W 8-2	Dinnen 3, Burton 3, Hollinger 2 / de Heer, Best
5	20	INL	A	Larne	L 2-5	Burton, Short / Stannex 3, Hill, Bell
6	27	SSC[1]	H	NI Paper Mills	W 2-0	R. Beattie, McMullan /
7	Oct 4	INC[1]	H	Bangor Res.	D 2-2	Burton 2 / McCandless, Graham
8	8	INC[1R]	A	Bangor Res.	L 2-4	Burton (pen), R. Beattie / R. Walsh 2, M. Walsh 2
9	11	SSC[2]	H	Belfast Fire Ser.	W 5-1	Burton, McMullan, McKnight, Rankin, Hollinger / Craig
10	18	INL	H	Larne	L 0-1	/ Gamble
11	Nov 1	INL	H	Cliftonville Oly.	W 6-5	O'Neill 2, Hollinger 2, Burton, Buchanan / Baker 3, Ford 2
12	8	SSC[3]	A	Ballyclare Com.	W 2-1	Burton, Beattie / Legg
13	15	INL	A	Naval XI	W 5-0	Burton 4, O'Neill /
14	22	INL	A	Distillery II	W 3-2	Duke, Bolton, Johnston / Sergeant, Duff
15	29	INL	H	Ballyclare Com.	W 5-0	Duke, Bolton, O'Neill 3 /
16	Dec 6	SSC[SF]	N[2]	Belfast Celtic II	D 2-2	Johnston, Burton / Sterling, McDonald
17	10	SSC[SFR]	N[2]	Belfast Celtic II	L 2-3	Burton 2 / McDonald, Sterling 2
18	13	INL	H	Glentoran II	W 3-0	Burton, O'Neill, Duke /
19	20	INL	A	Summerfield	D 1-1	Duke / Logan
20	27	INL	H	Lurgan Rangers	W 6-1	Johnston, Beattie, Black, Maguire 2, Todd / McNally
21	Jan 3	INL	A	Cliftonville Oly.	W 4-2	Holllinger 2, Todd, Beattie / Magee (pen), McCormick
22	10	INL	H	Summerfield	W 4-0	McLernon, Black 2, Todd /
23	17	IC[11L]	A	Bangor	L 2-3	McLernon, Black / Bruce, Lennox, Couser
24	24	IC[12L]	H	Bangor	W 5-0	Johnston 2, Todd 2, O'Neill /
25	31	INL	H	Aircraft Utd.	W 5-2	O'Neill 2, Todd 2, Johnston / Russell, Taylor
26	Feb 7	INL	A	Bangor Res.	D 2-2	Todd, O'Neill / McCandless, Bradford
27	21	IC[21L]	A	Bangor Res.	W 4-1	Beattie, Hollinger 2, Johnston / Ritchie
28	28	IC[22L]	H	Bangor Res.	W 4-1	Hollinger, Johnston 3 / McCandless
29	Mar 14	INL	A	Lurgan Rangers	W 4-2	Todd 2, Duke, Johnston / McBride, McKnight o.g.
30	21	IC[SF]	N	Glentoran	L 0-2	/ Barrie, Keddy
31	28	INL	A	Aircraft Utd.	L 0-2	/ Millar 2
32	31	Cas[2]	A	Belfasr Celtic	L 2-5	Todd, Black / Sterling, Kernaghan, McAlinden 2, O'Connor
33	Apr 6	CLC[1]	H	Naval XI	W 6-1	Black 2, McCreery 2, Todd, Hollinger / Leedell
34	18	McC[F]	N[3]	Belfast Celtic II	W 3-1	Todd, McCreery 2 / Best

35	25	INL	H	Distillery II	W 2-1	Black, Todd / Rowley
36	May 2	INL	A	Belfast Celtic II	L 0-3	/ Cairns 2, Lavery (pen)
37	9	INL	A	Glentoran II	W 5-1	Todd, Black 2, Duke, Beattie / Walsh
38	14	McC[1]	H	Naval XI	W 4-1	Todd 2, Black, McKnight / Snow
39	16	CLC[2]	A	Lurgan Rangers	W 4-1	Todd 2, Black 2 / Dowey
40	23	CLC[SF]	N	Distillery II	W 2-1	Beattie, O'Neill / Davidson (pen)
41	26	CLC[F]	N[3]	Aircraft Utd.	W 1-0	Black /
42	29	INL	H	Belfast Celtic II	D 1-1	Todd / Erskine
43	30	McC[2]	A	Ballyclare Com.	L 1-6	Beattie / Harvey 2, Dinnen 4

N = Solitude
N[2] = Windsor Park
N[3] = Grosvenor Park

Final positions, season 1942-43

League: 2nd   P 22   W 16 D 1   L 5   F 66   A 40   pts 33

	Date	Comp.	Venue	Opponents	Result	Goalscorers
1	Aug 22	INL	H	Aircraft United	W 4-3	McLean, Todd, Carroll, Black / McIlroy, McCune, Lunn
2	29	INL	A	Larne	L 0-2	/ Thompson, Williams
3	Sept 5	INL	H	Ballyclare Com.	W 5-2	Carroll 3, Todd 2 (1 pen) / Dinnan, Cunningham
4	19	INL	H	Distillery II	W 4-3	McLean 2, Carroll, Todd / Wickham, Tucker 2
5	26	INL	A	Lurgan Rangers	L 1-4	Todd / McMaster, McCourt 3
6	Oct 3	SSC[1]	H	Brantwood	W 4-0	Carroll 2, Johnston 2 (1 pen) /
7	10	INC[1]	A	Naval XI	L 3-4	Carroll, McLean, Black / Hutchinson, Thomas (pen), A. N. Other, Kilbride
8	17	SSC[2]	A	Aircraft Works	W 6-0	McKnight, Taylor, Black, Carroll 2, Meharg /
9	24	INL	H	Cliftonville Oly.	W 4-0	Carroll 3, Richer /
10	31	INL	A	Cliftonville Oly.	W 4-1	Todd, Carroll 3 / Brady
11	Nov 7	INL	H	Larne	W 3-2	Johnston, Smyth, Carroll / Girvan, Craigie
12	14	SSC[3]	A	Vic. Works Utd.	L 2-6	Johnston 2 (1 pen) / McIlroy 2, Walsh, Burrell, Fryers 2
13	21	INL	H	Lurgan Rangers	W 8-0	Carroll 3, Todd, Lilley 2, Black 2 /
14	28	INL	A	Distillery II	W 4-2	Carroll 2, Todd 2 / Downey 2
15	Dec 5	INL	H	Portadown	W 4-1	Carroll 3, Todd / West
16	12	INL	H	Belfast Celtic II	W 2-1	McKnight, Todd / Elliott
17	19	INL	A	Glentoran II	W 5-4	Todd, Carroll 4 / Sherry, Ferguson 3
18	Jan 2	INL	A	Ballyclare Com.	W 2-1	Graham, Beattie / Dinnen
19	9	INL	A	Alexandra Wrks.	W 4-3	Todd, Cunningham, Carroll 2 / Stannex 2, Magee
20	16	INL	H	Glentoran II	W 1-0	Carroll /
21	30	INL	A	Aircraft United	L 0-2	/ Sloan, Collins
22	Feb 6	CLC[1]	H	Distillery II	W 6-3	Carroll 3, O'Neill, Lilley, Todd (pen) / Smyth 2, Campbell
23	13	INL	A	Belfast Celtic II	W 2-1	Lilley, Carroll / McAuley
24	20	IC[11L]	H	25th ITC	W 2-1	Todd, McIlroy / Weir
25	27	IC[12L]	H	25th ITC	W 5-0	Carroll 2, Crawford, Lilley, Graham /

26	Mar 6	INL	A	Portadown	W 5-1	Graham, Carroll 2, McNeilly, Todd / Reid
27	13	CLC[2]	H	Bangor	D 3-3	Carroll, Todd, McNeilly / Bradford 2 (1 pen), Rae
28	20	CLC[2R]	A	Bangor	W 3-2	Beattie, Todd, McNeilly / McCandless, Bradford
29	27	IC[SF]	N	Glentoran	L 2-4	Crawford, J. A. Graham / Kelly 2, Wright 2
30	Apr 3	INL	H	Bangor	L 0-2	/ Bradford 2
31	7	Cas[2]	H	Linfield	L 2-3	Graham, Carroll / Cochrane 2, Rae
32	10	McC	H	Alexandra Wrks.	W 6-1	Carroll 2, Todd 4 / Farmer
33	17	INL	H	Alexandra Wrks.	L 2-3	J. A. Graham 2 / Fleming, Gray (pen), Bruce
34	30	CLC[SF]	N	Glentoran II	W 4-1	Carroll, O'Prey, Todd 2 (1 pen) / Ferguson
35	May 4	McC	A	Cliftonville Oly.	W 1-0	Todd (pen) /
36	15	INL	A	Bangor	D 2-2	Beattie, Todd (pen) / McBurney, Crowther
37	20	CLC[F]	N[2]	Larne	W 5-1	Walsh 2, Carroll 3 / McIlroy
38	22	McC	H	Distillery II	D 2-2	O'Prey, McNeilly (pen) / Smyth 2
39	27	McC	A	Bangor	W 3-1	McKnight 2, McNeilly (pen) / Elliott
40	29	McC	A	Ballyclare Com.	L 1-5	Black / Harvey, Russell 2, McKnight, Dinnen

N = Grosvenor Park
N[2] = Solitude

Final positions, season 1943-44

League: 4th P 25 W 15 D 2 L 8 F 67 A 44 pts 32

	Date	Comp.	Venue	Opponents	Result	Goalscorers
1	Aug 21	INL	H	Ballyclare Com.	W 5-0	McKnight, Todd 3, Hollinger, Carroll /
2	26	McC*	A	Distillery II	L 0-3	/ Campbell, Smith 2
3	28	INL	A	Glentoran II	D 2-2	J. A. Graham, Todd / Battersby, Kane
4	Sept 4	INL	H	Lurgan Rangers	W 5-1	Carroll, Todd 2, J. Graham, J. A. Graham / Treanor
5	18	INL	H	Victoria Works	W 2-1	Todd 2 / McLaughlin
6	25	INL	H	Distillery II	W 4-2	Hollinger, Carroll 3 / Smyth, Campbell
7	Oct 2	SSC[1]	A	Carrick Rgrs.	W w.o.	
8	9	INC[1]	A	Bangor Abbey	W 4-0	Carroll, Corbett 2, McKnight /
9	16	INL	A	Distillery II	W 2-1	Corbett, J. A. Graham / Smyth
10	23	SSC[2]	H	Cliftonville Oly.	W 4-0	J. A. Graham, J. Graham, Carroll 2 /
11	30	INC[2]	A	Belfast Celtic II	L 2-5	J. A. Graham 2 / Collins, Russell 2, Megarry, McBurney
12	Nov 6	INL	H	Victoria Works	L 1-2	McKnight / Hayes 2
13	13	SSC[3]	A	Glentoran II	L 0-1	/ Nimmick
14	20	INL	A	Alexandra Wks.	L 3-5	Beattie, Carroll, Todd / A. N Other, Sloan 2, Hunsdale, McCrudden
15	27	INL	H	Bangor	W 5-0	Carroll 3, Todd, Corbett /
16	Dec 4	INL	A	Larne	D 3-3	Beattie, Ledwidge 2 / Wilson 2, A. N Other
17	11	INL	A	Portadown	L 3-4	Todd (pen), Carroll, Corbett / Madill, Hanna, Gilpin, Kirkwood (pen)
18	Jan 1	INL	H	Belfast Celtic II	W 3-2	J. Graham, McMullan, Carroll / Burrell, McGarry

19	8	CLC[1]	A	Ballyclare Com.	W 2-1	Todd 2 / Blair
20	15	IC[11L]	A	Bangor	L 2-3	Thompson, J. A. Beattie / Moreland 2, Bunting
21	22	IC[12L]	H	Bangor	W 3-0	Todd (pen), J. Graham, Carroll /
22	29	CLC[2]	A	Distillery II	D 2-2	J. A. Graham 2 / Lynas 2
23	Feb 5	CLC[2R]	H	Distillery II	W 2-1	J. A. Beattie, W Beattie / Johnston
24	12	IC[2]	A	Cliftonville	D 2-2	Carroll, McMullan / Graham, McCausland
25	19	IC[2R]	H	Cliftonville	L 0-3	/ Wilson 2, Green
26	Mar 4	INL	A	Bangor	L 1-4	Todd / Bradford 3, McCandless
27	11	INL	H	Larne	W 2-1	Todd (pen), J. A. Graham / Andrews
28	18	INL	H	Linfield Swifte	W 2-1	J. A. Graham, Todd / McMorran
29	25	Cas[2]	H	Distillery	L 0-3	/ Jones 2, Lonsdale
30	April 1	INL	A	Ballyclare Com.	W 2-1	Hayes, Todd /
31	6	CLC[SF]	N	Belfast Celtic II	L 0-5	/ Roden 2 o.gs., others unknown
32	8	INL	H	Aircraft Utd.	L 1-3	McCready / Dinnen, Baun, O'Prey
33	13	INL	H	Cliftonville Oly.	W 2-1	Todd 2 / Johnston
34	15	INL	A	Lurgan Rangers	W 3-0	Todd, Roden, Hayes /
35	21	McC[1]	H	Aircraft Utd.	W 3-2	Todd 2, Hayes / Baun 2
36	24	INL	A	Cliftonville Oly.	L 1-2	Spence / Not known
37	27	McC[2]	H	Bangor	W 2-1	Carroll 2 / Bradford
38	29	INL	H	Portadown	W 4-1	J. A. Graham 2, Carroll, Todd / Hanna
39	May 6	INL	A	Aircraft Utd.`	L 1-4	Carroll / Best 2, Smyth, Russell
40	11	INL	A	Belfast Celtic II	D 1-1	Carroll / Tully
41	13	INL	H	Glentoran II	W 5-0	Todd 2, J. A. Graham, Carroll 2 /
42	19	McC[SF]	N	Linfield Swifts	W 4-0	Todd 3, Carroll /
43	23	INL	A	Linfield Swifts	L 0-1	/ Parkes
44	26	McCF	N	Belfast Celtic II	L 1-2	W. Beattie / Burrell, Tully
45	27	INL	H	Alexandra Wks.	W 4-1	W. Beattie 2, J. A. Beattie, Graham / Russell

N = Grosvenor Park

w.o = walkover

McC* = playoff for 2nd in section, 1942-43 competition

Final positions, season 1944-45

League: 4th   P 26   W 16 D 3   L 10   F 75   A 47   pts 35

	Date	Comp.	Venue	Opponents	Result	Goalscorers
1	Aug 19	INL	H	Cliftonville Oly.	W 9-1	Hollinger 2, Carroll 5, Smyth 2 / Wade
2	26	INL	A	Ballyclare Com.	W 4-3	McCausland, Carroll 3 / Blair 2, Magee
3	Sept 2	CLC[1]	H	Ballyclare Com.	W 4-3	McCausland, Carroll, Todd 2 / Drain, Cowan 2
4	16	INL	H	Dundela	W 3-1	Todd, McCready, Smyth / Brown
5	18	CLC[2]	A	Glentoran II	W 5-0	Hollinger, McCausland 2, Todd, Carroll /
6	23	INC[1]	A	Larne	L 0-3	/ Brown, Girvan 2
7	30	SSC[1]	A	49th Old Boys	W 5-1	Smyth 2, Hayes, Carroll 2 / Stewart
8	Oct 7	INL	A	Portadown	W 2-1	Smyth, Duncan / Hanna
9	14	SSC[3]	A	Distillery II	W 3-2	McCausland, Smyth, Beattie / Brennan, Lonsdale
10	21	INL	H	Celtic II	D 4-4	Smyth, Carroll 3 / Denver 3, Currie

11	28	INL	H	Victoria Works	W 3-2	Carroll 2, Smyth / Atkinson, Redpath
12	Nov 4	INL	A	Cliftonville Oly.	L 0-1	/ Russell
13	11	SSC[4]	A	Gallagher's Ltd.	W 7-3	Hanna 3, Carroll 2, Smyth, Irvine (pen) / McCormick 2, Hamilton
14	18	INL	A	Linfield Swifts	L 1-2	Duncan / Kelly, Vennard o.g.
15	25	INL	H	Portadown	W 5-1	Irvine 4, Hanna / Stewart
16	Dec 2	SSC[SF]	N	Bangor	L 0-1	/ Campbell
17	9	INL	H	Linfield Swifts	W 5-2	Carroll 2, Hollinger 2, Duncan / Kelly, Brown
18	16	INL	A	Victoria Works	D 3-3	Carroll 2, Burrell / Watson, Hayes 2
19	23	INL	H	Ballyclare Com.	W 3-0	Smyth, Hollinger 2 /
20	30	IC[1L1]	A	Bangor	W 3-2	Irvine 2, Burrell / Russell, A. N. Other
21	Jan 6	IC[1L2]	H	Bangor	W 3-1	Duncan, Burrell, Carroll / Bradford
22	13	IC[2L1]	A*	ITC	W 5-3	Burrell 2, Smyth 2, Hollinger / Daykin, Martin 2
23	Feb 3	IC[2L2]	H	ITC	W 5-2	Burrell, Carroll 2, Smyth 2 / Martin, Brockhurst
24	10	IC[3L1]	A	Linfield	L 0-8	/ Walsh 3, Robinson, Liddell 2, Cochrane 2
25	17	IC[3L2]	H	Linfield	L 0-2	/ Cochrane 2
26	24	INL	H	Glentoran II	W 3-2	Burrell 3 (1 pen) / O'Mahony, Mahon
27	Mar 3	INL	A	Alexandra Wrks	L 0-1	/ Kerr
28	10	INL	H	Alexandra Wrks	W 3-0	Irvine 2, Hollinger
29	17	Cas[1]	A	Bangor	D 0-0	
30	21	Cas[1R]	H	Bangor	W 2-1	Carroll 2 / Campbell
31	24	INL	H	Lurgan Rgrs.	W 5-1	Carroll 3, Corbett, Irvine / Hand
32	29	CLC[SF]	N	Victoria Works	D 2-2	Carroll, Baird (pen) / McKean, Douglas (pen)
33	31	INL	H	Distillery II	W 3-1	Burrell, Smyth, Carroll / Ewing
34	Apr 3	CLC[SFR]	N	Victoria Works	L 1-2	Carroll / A.N.Other, Hayes
35	6	McC[1]	A	Distillery II	D 2-2	Corbett 2 / Lyness, Davidson
36	10	McC[1R]	H	Distillery II	L 0-1	/ Lonsdale
37	14	INL	A	Larne	L 1-3	Hollinger / McMorran 2, Cairns (pen)
38	19	Cas[SF]	A	Belfast Celtic	L 0-1	/ McGarry
39	21	INL	H	Larne	W 4-2	Burrell, Duncan, Smyth, Hollinger / McCormick, McMorran
40	25	INL	A	Glentoran II	W 4-0	Burrell, Corbett 2, Duncan /
41	28	INL	A	Celtic II	L 1-6	Burrell / McHugh 3, Denvir 2, Kernaghan
42	May 5	INL	A	Lurgan Rgrs.	L 1-3	Irvine / Kane 2, McCourt
43	10	INL	A	Distillery II	D 1-1	Burrell / A. N Other
44	16	INL	A	Bangor	W 3-1	Corbett, Burrell 2 (1 pen) / Campbell
45	24	INL	H	Bangor	W 3-1	Carroll 3 / Bradford
46	Jun 1	INL	A	Dundela	L 0-4	/ Harvey 2, Wade, A. N. Other

A* = Castlereagh Park

Final positions, season 1945-46

League: 10th   P 32   W 14 D 4   L 14   F 82   A 62   pts 32

	Date	Comp.	Venue	Opponents	Result	Goalscorers
1	Aug 18	INL	H	Lurgan Rangers	W 8-2	Todd 2, Jackson 3, Mahon, Graham, McKeown / Burns 2

2	25	INL	A	Brantwood	D 2-2	Graham, Todd / Reid, Graham
3	Sept 1	INL	H	Ballymoney Utd.	W 4-2	Irvine 2, Graham 2 / Moffett, Doherty
4	8	INL	A	Dundela	L 0-2	/ Walsh, Harvey
5	14	INL	A	Distillery II	W 1-0	Duncan /
6	22	INC^1	H	Larne	D 0-0	
7	26	INC^{1R}	A	Larne	W 4-0	Irvine 2, Graham 2 /
8	29	SCC^1	A	Cliftonville Strlr	W 7-0	Bunting 3, A.N.Other o.g., Irvine 3 /
9	Oct 6	INL	A	Glenavon Res.	L 1-2	Graham / Lunn, McCann
10	13	INL	H	Celtic II	W 4-0	Mahon, Graham, Corbett, Irvine /
11	20	SCC^2	A	Bangor	L 2-3	Irvine, Beattie / Hamilton, Bradford 2
12	27	INL	A	Linfield Swifts	D 1-1	Graham / Bell
13	Nov 3	INC^3	H	Coleraine	W 2-1	Bunting 2 / Crossan
14	10	INL	H	Linfield Swifts	L 0-2	/ Hughes, McBennett
15	17	INL	H	Glenavon Res.	W 5-1	Hughes o.g., Duncan, Sloan 3 / Kennedy
16	24	INL	A	Crusaders	W 4-0	Morgan, Graham 3 /
17	Dec 1	INC^{SF}	N	Linfield Swifts	D 2-2	Mahon, Sloan / Hughes, Kelly
18	5	INC^{SFR}	N	Linfield Swifts	L 0-3	/ Hughes, Nelson, Russell
19	8	INL	H	Cliftonville Oly.	W 6-2	Sloan 2, Corbett, Bunting 2, Atkinson / Carroll, O'Neill (pen)
20	15	INL	A	Portadown	L 1-2	Burns / Cowan, Proctor
21	22	INL	H	Crusaders	W 6-2	Carroll 4, Bunting, Beggs / Keenan, A.N.Other
22	24	INL	A	Glentoran II	D 2-2	Atkinson, Morgan / A.N.Other, Matier
23	29	INL	A	Newry Town	L 1-3	Graham (pen) / Hook, Parkin, McCleary
24	Jan 5	INL	H	Distillery II	L 1-3	Atkinson (pen) / Fulton 2, Kavanagh
25	12	INL	A	Ballymoney Utd.	L 3-4	Beggs, Bunting, Carroll / Wallace, Kidby, Kirgan 2
26	19	INL	H	Brantwood	D 3-3	Atkinson, Carroll, Hollinger / Wright 3
27	26	INL	A	Ballyclare Com.	W 2-0	Atkinson, Bunting /
28	Feb 9	CLC^2	A	Portadown	W 2-1	McFarland, Carroll / A.N.Other
29	16	IC^{11L}	A	Linfield	L 0-2	/ Russell, McCrory
30	23	IC^{12L}	H	Linfield	D 3-3	Fulton, Hollinger, Atkinson (pen) / Bryson (pen), Nelson, Walsh
31	Mar 2	INL	H	Ballyclare Com.	L 2-3	McFarland, Bunting / Davidson 2, Wilson
32	9	CLC^3	A	Larne	L 0-1	/ Fenton
33	16	Cas^1	A	Dundela	L 1-5	Graham / Beck 2, Campbell 3
34	30	INL	H	Glentoran II	W 8-0	Bunting 3, Hollinger 2, Bennett 3 /
35	April 6	INL	A	Bangor	L 0-2	/ Frampton, Doherty
36	13	INL	H	Larne	W 2-0	Bennett 2 /
37	22	INL	A	Celtic II	L 1-3	Atkinson / McMorran, Regan, A.N.Other
38	May 1	McC^2	A	Dundela	L 2-4	Hollinger 2 /
39	4	INL	H	Dundela	L 1-5	Bennett / Burrell 2, Campbell 3 (1 pen)
40	7	INL	H	Coleraine	L 1-3	Hollinger / Currie, McKnight, Haslett
41	11	INL	H	Portadown	W 2-0	Bunting 2 /
42	18	INL	A	Coleraine	L 3-5	Atkinson, Hollinger, Bunting / Dixon, Haslett, McKnight, Laughlin, McIntyre
43	21	INL	H	Bangor	L 0-1	/ Bradford
44	25	INL	A	Larne	W 2-1	Hollinger, Bunting / Duddy (pen)
45	28	INL	A	Cliftonville Oly.	L 1-2	Kearney / McDonald 2
46	June 1	INL	A	Newry Town	W 4-2	McFarland, Atkinson 3 (1 pen) / McStay, Preston

N = Celtic Park

Final positions, season 1946-47

League: 5th   P 34   W 21   D 2   L 11   F 93   A 58   pts 44

	Date	Comp.	Venue	Opponents	Result	Goalscorers
1	Aug 17	INL	H	Coleraine Res.	W 6-0	McCullough 2, Bunting, Hollinger 2, Kearney /
2	24	INL	A	Glenavon	W 3-2	McCullough, Kearney, Bunting / Thompson, Morrow
3	29	CLC[1]	H	Portadown	W 4-0	Kearney, McCullough, Bunting, Hollinger /
4	31	INL	H	Celtic II	W 4-1	McCullough 2 (1 pen), Kearney, Hollinger / McIlveen
5	Sept 7	INL	A	Ballymoney Utd.	W 7-1	McCullough 3, Hollinger 2, Bunting 2 / Padino
6	14	INC[1]	H	Bangor	D 2-2	Bunting, McCullough / McCandless, Imrie o.g.
7	18	INC[1R]	A	Bangor	D 0-0	
8	21	INL	H	Ballymoney Utd.	W 2-0	Hollinger, Kearney
9	23	INC[1R]	H	Bangor	D 2-2	A.N.Other o.g., McCullough / Mulholland, Frampton
10	26	INC[1R]	A	Bangor	L 1-3	Bunting / McCandless, McCarroll, Horner
11	Oct 5	INL	A	B'Mena Utd.Res	D 1-1	Darragh / Anderson
12	12	CLC[2]	H	Bangor	W 5-1	McKerley 2, Corbett, Kearney 2 / Horner
13	19	SSC[2]	H	Cliftonville Strl.	W 5-0	Kearney, Martin 3, Hollinger /
14	26	INL	A	Portadown	W 4-0	Milliken 2, Kearney, Darragh /
15	Nov 2	SSC[3]	H	Crusaders	L 0-1	/ W. Smith
16	9	INL	A	Distillery II	W 3-0	Smith 2, Hollinger /
17	16	INL	H	Dundela	W 2-1	McKerley 2 / Stannex
18	23	CLC[SF]	N	Newry Town	W 4-1	McKerley 2, Kearney, O'Prey / Chambers
19	30	INL	H	Cliftonville Oly.	W 4-1	Smith (pen), McKerley 2, Kearney / Millar
20	Dec 7	INL	A	Newry Town	L 1-6	Kearney / Chambers 2, McStay 2, D'Arcy, Fearon
21	14	INL	H	Brantwood	D 3-3	Smith (pen), Hollinger, Coulter / Jackson, Cully o.g., Graham
22	21	INL	H	Bangor	W 1-0	Kearney /
23	26	INL	A	Larne	W 1-0	Cathcart o.g. /
24	28	INL	A	Glentoran Res.	L 0-3	/ Ferran, Stewart 2
25	Jan 1	CLC[F]	N[2]	Linfield Swifts	L 1-3	Bunting / Beck, Simpson, Kelly
26	4	INL	H	Larne	W 4-1	Martin, Douglas, Todd, Cully / Cairns
27	11	INL	H	Glenavon Res	W 3-0	Mulholland, Douglas, McKeown /
28	18	INL	A	B'Mena Utd.Res	L 0-4	/ Mulgrew 2, Agnew, Hughes
29	25	INL	H	Ballyclare Com.	H 5-1	Wade 2, Imrie, Todd, Douglas / Magowan
30	Feb 1	INL	H	Distillery II	W 3-1	Kearney 2, Mulholland / Jones
31	15	INL	H	Glentoran Res.	W 3-2	Kearney 2, Wade / McConville, Jones
32	22	INL	A	Coleraine Res.	W 3-1	Mulholland, Todd, Douglas / Beare
33	Mar 28	INL	A	Celtic II	L 0-1	/ Jones (pen)
34	Apr 8	INL	A	Bangor	L 1-2	Todd / Nelson, Gillespie
35	12	McC[2]	A	Linfield Swifts	W 4-0	Mulholland 3, Mills /
36	26	INL	H	Portadown	W 3-0	Todd, Douglas, Bunting /
37	29	INL	A	Cliftonville Oly.	W 7-1	Mulholland 5, Todd 2 / A. N. Other
38	May 3	INL	A	Ballyclare Com.	L 2-3	O'Prey 2 / J. Davidson, Smyth, S. Davidson
39	7	McC[3]	A	Brantwood	W 2-1	Mulholland, Todd / Mahood

40	10	INL	A	Linfield Swifts	L 2-4	Mulholland, Hollinger / Hughes, Conn, Kelly, Melville
41	17	INL	H	Crusaders	L 2-3	O'Prey, Hollinger / Weir 2, Hunter
42	23	McC[SF]	N[2]	Bangor	L 2-6	Corbett, Hollinger / Bradford 3, Couser 2, Cunningham
43	27	INL	H	Newry Town	W 5-1	McKeown, Hookes o.g., O'Prey, J. McKeown, Taggart / Preston (pen)
44	31	INL	H	Linfield Swifts	W 4-2	J. McKeown 2, Douglas 2 / McKee, Cully o.g.
45	June 2	INL	A	Brantwood	L 3-7	J. McKeown 2, O'Prey / Malone (pen), Hood, Fulton, Green, Smyth 2, Mahood
46	7	INL	A	Dundela	L 1-2	Corbett / Campbell 2
47	14	INL	A	Crusaders	L 0-3	/ Unknown

N = Solitude
N[2] = Grosvenor Park

Final positions, season 1947-48

League: 8th	P 22	W 7	D 4	L 11	F 37	A 54	pts 18
City Cup: 5th	P 11	W 5	D 3	L 3	F 22	A 16	pts 13

	Date	Comp.	Venue	Opponents	Result	Goalscorers
1	Aug 16	CC	H	Belfast Celtic	L 0-5	/ Jones 3, Bonnar, Tully
2	23	CC	A	Portadown	W 3-1	Couser, Frazer, Dellow / White
3	28	GC[1]	H	Derry City	W 2-1	Couser, Dellow / Kelly
4	30	CC	H	Ballymena Utd.	D 1-1	Dellow / McStay
5	Sept 3	GC[2]	A	Distillery	L 3-5	Couser 2, Dellow / McLoughlin, Ewing 2, Mitchell, Lonsdale
6	6	CC	A	Linfield	D 1-1	Maher / Russell
7	13	CC	A	Glenavon	D 1-1	Dellow / Kelly
8	20	CC	H	Glentoran	L 1-3	Hollinger / McCormack 3
9	27	CC	H	Bangor	W 5-1	Dellow 2, Maher 2, Currie / Bradford
10	Oct 11	CC	A	Cliftonville	W 2-1	Maher, Graham o.g. / Crawford
11	18	CC	H	Coleraine	W 2-0	Dellow, Maher /
12	25	CC	H	Derry City	W 6-1	Maher, Douglas, Couser, Dellow 3 / Donaghy
13	Nov 1	CC	A	Distillery	L 0-1	/ Walker
14	8	IL	H	Belfast Celtic	L 2-5	Maher, Dellow / Tully 3, Campbell, Jones
15	15	IL	A	Coleraine	D 1-1	Maher / Doherty
16	22	IL	A	Cliftonville	W 4-3	Dellow, Couser, Hollinger, Corbett / Preston 2 (1 pen), Graham
17	29	IL	H	Distillery	L 1-2	Dellow / Mitchell, Ewing
18	Dec 6	IL	A	Portadown	L 2-4	Couser, Dellow / Mullett 3, Tolan
19	13	IL	A	Linfield	L 1-3	Dellow / Brown 2, Thompson
20	20	IL	H	Ballymena Utd.	D 2-2	Hollinger 2 / Walsh 2
21	25	IL	A	Bangor	W 2-1	Currie, Dellow / Bradford
22	26	IL	H	Glenavon	L 2-4	Dellow, Corbett / Kelly 2, Cronin 2

23	27	IL	A	Derry City	L 2-6	Imrie (pen), Douglas / J. Kelly 2, H. Kelly 3, Lynch
24	Jan 3	IL	H	Glentoran	D 1-1	Maher / McKnight
25	10	IL	A	Belfast Celtic	L 0-6	/ Jones 3, Denvir, O'Neill, Montgomery
26	17	IL	H	Coleraine	W 3-2	Dellow, Maher, Douglas / Clarke, McDowell
27	24	IC[1]	A	Derry City	L 1-2	Dellow / Hirrell, Wright
28	31	IL	H	Cliftonville	L 1-3	Dellow / Armstrong, Gillespie o.g., Beggs
29	Feb 7	IL	A	Distillery	L 0-2	/ McKechnie, Kirkpatrick
30	21	IL	H	Portadown	W 3-0	Maher, Dellow 2 /
31	28	IL	H	Linfield	W 2-1	Maher, Corbett / Simpson
32	Mar 6	IL	A	Ballymena Utd.	W 1-0	Dellow /
33	13	IL	H	Bangor	L 1-2	Imrie (pen) / Bradford 2
34	20	TC	A	Bangor	L 0-1	/ Bradford
35	27	IL	A	Glenavon	D 1-1	Maher / Silcock
36	30	IL	H	Derry City	W 4-1	Maher, Hollinger, Cully, Douglas / McGahey
37	Apr 3	IL	A	Glentoran	L 1-4	Maher / Lavery, Coffey, McKnight 2
38	13	Cas[1]	H	Cliftonville	W 3-1	Chambers 2, Douglas / Graham
39	24	Cas[SF]	N	Ballymena Utd.	L 1-4	Hollinger / McDonald, Spalding, McCormick, McNally (pen)

N = Grosvenor Park

Final positions, season 1948-49

League: 11th   P 22   W 7   D 2   L 13   F 46   A 49   pts 16

City Cup: 6th   P 11   W 4   D 1   L 6   F 22   A 23   pts 9

	Date	Comp.	Venue	Opponents	Result	Goalscorers
1	Aug 21	CC	A	Glenavon	L 1-2	Evans / Doran, Kelly
2	25	GC[1]	H	Ballymena Utd.	L 0-2	/ Williamson, McCormick
3	28	CC	H	Cliftonville	L 0-2	/ Preston. McGarry
4	Sept 4	CC	A	Derry City	L 1-2	Maher / Carlyle, Honey
5	11	CC	H	Linfield	L 2-3	Agnew, Connor / McDowell, Thompson, Campbell
6	18	CC	H	Distillery	W 3-1	Agnew, Lonsdale o.g., Robinson / Harris
7	25	CC	A	Bangor	W 2-1	Connor, Robinson, / Bradford
8	Oct 2	CC	A	Coleraine	W 5-2	Connor 3, Maher, Dellow / McFaul, Clarke
9	16	CC	H	Belfast Celtic	D 3-3	Booth, Connor, Corbett / Bonnar 2, Campbell
10	23	CC	A	Ballymena Utd.	W 3-2	Maher 2, Connor / Dobbin, McDonald
11	30	CC	A	Portadown	L 1-2	Robinson / Arthur, Brown
12	Nov 13	CC	H	Glentoran	L 1-3	McCarthy o.g. / Lavery 2, Corbett o.g.
13	20	IL	A	Linfield	L 1-5	Imrie (pen) / Russell 2, Lavery, Bryson (pen), Thompson
14	27	IL	H	Glentoran	W 2-1	Imrie (pen), Dorman / Feeney
15	Dec 4	IL	A	Coleraine	L 1-4	Connor / Fulton, Clarke 3
16	11	IL	A	Cliftonville	L 2-3	Robinson 2 / Gillespie o.g., Bell 2
17	18	IL	H	Portadown	D 2-2	Corbett, Connor / Louden 2

18	25	IL	H	Bangor	L 2-4	Case 2 / Bradford 2, Taylor, Bunting
19	27	IL	A	Bangor	W 3-2	Case 2, Horner / McMillen, Bradford
20	Jan 8	IL	A	Derry City	W 3-2	Dorman, Case, Hollinger / McLaughlin, Kelly
21	15	IL	H	Distillery	L 0-1	/ Dodds
22	22	IC[1]	H	Bangor	L 0-3	/ Bradford 2, Taylor
23	29	IL	A	Belfast Celtic	L 3-4	Case 2, Smyth / Walker 3 (1 pen), Campbell
24	Feb 5	IL	H	Linfield	L 0-4	/ Russell, McDowell, Simpson 2
25	12	IL	H	Ballymena Utd.	W 8-0	Maher, Smyth 2, Case 4, Dorman /
26	19	IL	A	Glentoran	L 0-2	/ Feeney, McFarlane
27	26	IL	H	Coleraine	W 7-0	Case, Smyth, Dorman, Maginnis 2, Imrie, Maher/
28	Mar 5	IL	H	Cliftonville	L 1-2	Maher / Beggs, Irwin
29	12	IL	A	Portadown	L 1-2	Maginnis / Allen, Smiley
30	19	IL	A	Glenavon	W 2-1	Case, Maginnis / Parkes
31	26	IL	H	Belfast Celtic	D 4-4	Maginnis 2, Smyth, Case / Denvir 2, Bradford 2
32	Apr 2	IL	H	Glenavon	L 0-2	/ Cush, Stone
33	5	Cas[2]	H	Belfast Celtic	L 1-2	Maginnis / Morgan, Robinson o.g.
34	9	IL	A	Ballymena Utd.	L 0-1	/ McDonald
35	19	IL	H	Derry City	W 3-1	Maher 2, Kearney / Gilmartin
36	27	IL	A	Distillery	L 1-2	Smyth / Kirkpatrick, Dodds (pen)
37	May 3	UC	H	Bangor	W 3-1	Imrie (pen) , Maginnis 2 / McMillen
38	10	UC	A	Dundela	W 5-2	Smyth, Imrie (pen), Maginnis 2, Maher / Sterling 2
39	12	UC	N	Coleraine	W 4-2	Maginnis, Maher 2, Smyth / Montgomery, Robinson o.g.
40	19	UC[F]	N[2]	Linfield	L 0-3	/ Simpson 3

N = Seaview

N[2] = Solitude

Final positions, season 1949-50

League: 6th	P 22	W 7	D 6	L 9	F 34	A 38	pts 20
City Cup: 3rd	P 11	W 7	D 1	L 3	F 30	A 16	pts 15
Ulster Cup: 3rd	P 3	W 1	D 0	L 2	F 4	A 5	pts 2

	Date	Comp.	Venue	Opponents	Result	Goalscorers
1	Aug 20	CC	A	Coleraine	W 9-1	Maher, Case 5, Hollinger 3 / Fitzsimmons
2	27	CC	H	Distillery	W 4-2	Morgan 2, Walker, Case / Lonsdale, Griffiths
3	31	GC[2]	A	Glenavon	L 0-3	/ Falloon 3
4	Sept 3	UC	A	Glentoran	L 1-2	McDonald / Feeney, McFarland
5	10	CC	A	Cliftonville	W 2-0	Case, Hollinger /
6	13	UC	H	Bangor	L 0-1	/ McMillen
7	17	UC	A	Dundela	W 4-2	Case 2, McDonald, Hollinger / Fulton, Cahoon
8	24	CC	H	Portadown	W 3-0	Maginnis 2, Case /
9	Oct 8	CC	A	Glentoran	W 2-1	Hughes o.g., Matthews / Hughes (pen)
10	15	CC	H	Derry City	L 3-5	Morgan, Walker (pen), Maher / Kelly 3 (1 pen), Cannon, Colvin
11	22	CC	A	Linfield	L 0-3	/ Thompson, Dickson 2

12	29	CC	H	Crusaders	W 2-1	Imrie, Maginnis / Haslet
13	Nov 5	CC	A	Glenavon	L 1-2	Walker / McLafferty, Wilson
14	12	CC	H	Ballymena Utd.	D 0-0	
15	19	CC	H	Bangor	W 4-1	Hollinger, Robinson, Walker, B. McDaid / McMillan
16	26	IL	A	Portadown	W 2-0	Fitzgerald, B. McDaid /
17	Dec 3	IL	H	Ballymena Utd.	D 1-1	Robinson / Dorris
18	10	IL	A	Coleraine	L 0-1	/ Clarke
19	17	IL	H	Distillery	D 2-2	Robinson, E. McDaid / Casement, Blackledge
20	24	IL	A	Glenavon	L 0-3	/ Cush, Graham 2
21	26	IL	H	Bangor	D 2-2	B. McDaid, Imrie / Masters (pen), McGahy
22	27	IL	A	Cliftonville	L 0-6	/ Fenton 2, McGarry 2 (1 pen), Drake, McKeown
23	31	IL	H	Glentoran	L 3-4	E. McDaid, Walker (pen), Mulholland o.g. / Feeney, Ewing 2, Hughes
24	Jan 7	IL	A	Crusaders	W 6-2	Robinson 6 (1 pen) / Hamill o.g., Simpson (pen)
25	14	IL	H	Derry City	L 0-1	/ McCreary (pen)
26	21	IC[1]	A	Banbridge Town	W 2-0	Hollinger, Maginnis /
27	28	IL	A	Linfield	L 1-3	Maginnis / McDowell, Currie, Simpson
28	Feb 4	IL	H	Portadown	D 1-1	Feeney / Gilmore
29	11	IC[2]	A	Derry City	L 0-2	/ Hermon 2
30	18	IL	A	Ballymena Utd.	D 0-0	
31	25	IL	H	Coleraine	W 3-1	McCaigue, O'Connor, Matthews / Doherty
32	Mar 4	IL	A	Distillery	W 2-1	McCaigue, White / Mulholland (pen)
33	11	IL	H	Glenavon	L 0-2	/ Parkes, Denvir
34	18	IL	A	Bangor	W 2-1	Feeney 2 / Lawther
35	Apr 1	IL	H	Cliftonville	D 0-0	
36	5	Cas[2]	A	Glentoran	L 2-4	Feeney, White / J. Feeney, McFarlane 2, Bingham
37	8	IL	A	Glentoran	L 1-2	White / Lowry, McCarthy
38	11	IL	H	Crusaders	W 5-2	Cunningham. White 3, Feeney / Freel 2 (I pen)
39	15	IL	A	Derry City	W 3-1	Feeney, White 2 / Hermon
40	29	IL	H	Linfield	L 0-2	/ McDowell 2

Final positions, season 1950-51

League: 12th	P 22	W 3	D 2	L 17	F 28	A 68	pts 8
City Cup: 11th	P 11	W 1	D 3	L 7	F 15	A 33	pts 5
Ulster Cup: 1st=	P 3	W 2	D 1	L 0	F 10	A 5	pts 5

	Date	Comp.	Venue	Opponents	Result	Goalscorers
1	Aug 19	UC	A	Bangor	W 3-1	Orr 3 / Taylor
2	23	GC[1]	H	Glentoran	L 1-3	Hamill (pen) / McFarlane, Feeney, Bingham
3	26	CC	H	Coleraine	L 1-3	Robinson / Milne, Corr, McCormick
4	28	UC	A	Glentoran	D 2-2	Feeney 2 / S. Hughes, Lowry
5	Sept 2	UC	H	Dundela	W 5-2	Orr 2, White, Parkes, Black / Wilson, Tucker
6	9	CC	A	Distillery	D 1-1	White / Dodds
7	16	CC	H	Cliftonville	W 2-1	Hamill (pen), Robinson / Beggs
8	23	CC	A	Portadown	D 1-1	Hamill (pen) / Dobbin
9	30	CC	H	Glentoran	L 1-4	McCarthy o.g. / McFarlane 2, Bingham 2
10	Oct 2	UC[PL]	H	Glentoran	L 0-2	/ S. Hughes, Bingham
11	14	CC	A	Derry City	L 1-3	Feeney / Kelly 2, Walker

12	21	CC	H	Linfield	D 3-3	Feeney, White, Sweeney / Walsh, Smyth 2
13	28	CC	A	Crusaders	L 1-4	White / Brady, Houston 2, Crowther
14	Nov 4	CC	H	Glenavon	L 1-4	Orr / McDaid, Martin 2, McVeigh
15	11	CC	A	Ballymena Utd.	L 2-6	Orr, Kirkpatrick / Murphy, Small, Morrison, Trevorrow, Williamson, Anderson
16	18	CC	A	Bangor	L 1-3	Kirkpatrick / Smith, McGrath, McNeill
17	25	IL	H	Portadown	W 3-2	Bogan, White, Kirkpatrick / Boyce 2
18	Dec 2	IL	A	Ballymena Utd.	L 2-4	Kirkpatrick, Orr / Trevorrow, Small, Williamson, Imrie o.g.
19	9	IL	H	Glentoran	L 1-5	Robinson (pen) / Feeney 2, McFarlane, McCarthy (pen), Dunlop
20	23	IL	H	Glenavon	L 1-2	Orr / Martin, Walker
21	25	IL	A	Bangor	D 1-1	Robinson / Smith
22	26	IL	H	Distillery	L 3-5	Bogan 2, Robinson (pen) / Graham 2, Mulholland 2, McDonald
23	30	IL	A	Linfield	L 0-3	/ Blackledge, McDowell, McMillan
24	Jan 6	IL	A	Crusaders	L 1-8	Kirkpatrick / Coffey 5, Houston, Bradford 2
25	13	IL	H	Derry City	L 1-2	Bogan / Higgins, Madden
26	20	IC[1]	A	Glenavon	D 2-2	Orr, Anderson / Denvir, Walker
27	24	IC[1R]	H	Glenavon	W 3-1	Lawther 2, Bogan / McVeigh
28	27	IL	H	Coleraine	L 1-3	Orr / McCormick, Currie 2
29	Feb 3	IL	A	Portadown	L 0-1	/ Darragh
30	10	IL	H	Ballymena Utd.	D 1-1	Kirkpatrick / Currie
31	12	IL	A	Cliftonville	L 1-3	Orr / Gilmore 2, Reid
32	17	IC[2]	H	Portadown	L 0-1	/ Giffen
33	24	IL	A	Glentoran	L 2-7	Orr, Bogan / Williamson, Ewing, S. Hughes 3, Cunningham 2
34	Mar 3	IL	H	Cliftonville	W 3-0	Murphy, Lawther, Bogan /
35	10	IL	A	Glenavon	L 0-4	/ McGinn 3, Moore o.g.
36	17	IL	H	Bangor	W 3-0	Bogan 2, Lawther
37	24	IL	A	Distillery	L 1-2	Watters o.g. / Mulholland, Dodds
38	27	IL	H	Linfield	L 0-3	/ Thompson, Dickson, Hamill o.g.
39	31	IL	H	Crusaders	L 1-2	Robinson / Bradford 2
40	Apr 14	IL	A	Derry City	L 2-3	Robinson, Lawther / Higgins, Kennedy, Madden
41	18	Cas[1]	A	Glentoran	L 1-2	Kirkpatrick / Cunningham, McFarlane
42	21	IL	A	Coleraine	L 0-5	/ McCormick, Doherty, McConkey, Corr, McCavana

PL = Sectional playoff

Final positions, season 1951-52

League: 7th   P 22   W 8   D 4   L 10   F 43   A 49   pts 20
City Cup: 6th   P 11   W 5   D 2   L 4   F 27   A 26   pts 12
Festival Of Britain Cup: 3rd
                P 4   W 2   D 0   L 2   F 7   A 5   pts 4

	Date	Comp.	Venue	Opponents	Result	Goalscorers
1	Aug 18	CC	A	Coleraine	W 4-2	Walker 2, McDowell, Gorman / Milne, McCormick
2	23	FBC	A	Bangor	L 0-1	/ Gordon
3	25	CC	H	Distillery	D 1-1	McDowell / Dodds (pen)
4	28	GC[1]	A	Ballymena Utd.	W 4-3	Walker, Black 2, Bogan / Lyness, Mitten, Murphy
5	30	FBC	H	Bangor	W 3-1	McDowell, Walker, Black / Leeman
6	Sept 1	CC	A	Cliftonville	W 6-4	Gorman 2, Walker, McDowell 3 / Shiells 2, Davidson, Beggs
7	8	CC	H	Portadown	L 2-3	Walker, McDowell / Allen 2, Ross
8	13	GC[2]	H	Linfield	D 1-1	Walker / Thompson
9	15	CC	A	Glentoran	L 3-4	Black 2, Gorman / Ewing, Lowry, Feeney, Hughes
10	19	GC[2R]	A	Linfield	L 2-6	Robinson (pen), Walker / Dickson 4, Walker, Thompson
11	22	CC	H	Derry City	W 2-0	Gorman, Murphy /
12	29	CC	A	Linfield	L 0-3	/ Dickson, Walker, Thompson
13	Oct 9	FBC	H	Glentoran	L 1-2	McDowell / Feeney 2
14	13	CC	H	Crusaders	D 2-2	Walker, Tucker / Bradford, Casement
15	20	CC	A	Glenavon	L 0-6	/ Denvir 3, Walker 3
16	27	CC	H	Ballymena Utd.	W 3-0	Robinson (pen), Tucker, Walker /
17	Nov 3	CC	H	Bangor	W 4-1	Tucker, Gorman 2, Lunn / Clarke
18	10	IL	A	Glentoran	L 1-8	Gorman / Hughes 4, Lowry, Ferran 2, Ewing
19	17	IL	H	Portadown	L 1-2	Walker / Ross, Giffen
20	24	IL	A	Distillery	L 3-4	Walker, Gorman, McDowell / Gee, McNally, Dodds 2
21	Dec 1	IL	A	Linfield	D 0-0	
22	8	IL	H	Coleraine	L 3-5	Martin 2, Corbett / Doherty 3, Milne, McCormick
23	15	IL	H	Glenavon	L 3-4	Lawther 3 / Denvir, Cush, Forde, Jones
24	22	IL	A	Derry City	L 0-4	/ Lynch 3, Higgins
25	25	IL	H	Bangor	L 1-2	McDowell / Clarke, Leeman
26	26	IL	A	Cliftonville	L 3-4	Corbett, McDowell 2 / McGarry, Shiells, Miller 2
27	29	IL	H	Ballymena Utd.	W 4-1	Black, Walker 2, Kingsmore / Mitten
28	Jan 5	IL	A	Crusaders	W 3-1	Gorman 3 / Mulholland
29	12	IL	H	Glentoran	L 1-3	Walker / Ewing, Williamson, Feeney
30	19	IC[1]	H	Larne	W 2-1	McDowell, Black / White
31	26	IL	A	Portadown	W 2-1	Walker, Black / Ross
32	Feb 2	IL	H	Distillery	D 2-2	Brown, Walker / McNally, Dodds
33	9	IL	H	Linfield	W 3-1	Brown 3 / Minford
34	16	IC[2]	A	Brantwood	W 1-0	Lawther /
35	23	IL	A	Coleraine	W 1-0	Thomson /
36	Mar 1	IL	A	Glenavon	D 1-1	Lawther / Cush
37	8	IL	H	Derry City	W 4-1	Drake, Lawther 2, Thomson (pen) / Kennedy
38	15	IC[SF]	N	Ballymena Utd.	W 3-1	Trevorrow o.g., Thomson, Lawther / Lyness
39	22	IL	A	Bangor	W 3-2	McDowell, Thomson, Walker / Jordan, Deakin
40	29	IL	H	Cliftonville	D 0-0	

41	Apr 5	IL	A	Ballymena Utd.	L 1-3	Lawther / J. Mitten (pen), Lyness, S Mitten
42	12	IL	H	Crusaders	W 3-0	Lunn 2, Drake /
43	14	Cas[2]	A	Distillery	L 0-2	/ Johnston, McNally
44	26	IC[F]	N	Glentoran	W 1-0	Thomson /
45	30	FBC	A	Glentoran	W 3-1	Walker 2, Brown / Hughes

N = Windsor Park

Final positions, season 1952-53

League: 7th	P 22	W 7	D 7	L 8	F 32	A 35	pts 21
City Cup: 7th	P 11	W 3	D 3	L 5	F 20	A 26	pts 9
Ulster Cup: 3rd	P 8	W 3	D 3	L 2	F 11	A 9	pts 9

	Date	Comp.	Venue	Opponents	Result	Goalscorers
1	Aug 16	UC	A	Portadown	L 1-2	Lawther / Ross 2
2	19	UC	A	Glenavon	D 1-1	Corbett / Jones
3	21	UC	H	Distillery	D 3-3	Thomson 2, Drake / McIntosh 2, McEvoy
4	23	UC	H	Bangor	W 3-2	Thomson 2 (1 pen), Drake / McKee 2
5	28	UC	H	Linfield	D 2-2	Drake, Walker / Hewitt 2
6	30	UC	A	Linfield	W 1-0	Thomson (pen) /
7	Sept 4	UC	A	Bangor	W 1-0	Walker /
8	6	UC	H	Portadown	L 0-1	/ Fitzpatrick
9	8	UC	A	Distillery	L 0-1	/ Donaghy
10	13	CC	H	Coleraine	D 2-2	Thomson (pen), McDowell / Cuneen, Doherty (pen)
11	18	UC	H	Glenavon	L 1-3	Walker / Jones 2, Denvir
12	20	CC	A	Distillery	W 3-1	Walker 2, Clarke / McIntosh
13	27	CC	H	Cliftonville	W 4-2	Walker 2, Bogan, Clarke / Rooney, Ferguson
14	Oct 11	CC	A	Portadown	W 2-0	Walker, Clarke /
15	18	CC	H	Glentoran	L 1-5	Walker (pen) / Deakin 2, Hughes 2, Williamson
16	25	CC	A	Derry City	L 0-2	/ Mulgrew, Collins
17	Nov 1	CC	H	Linfield	D 2-2	Bogan 2 / Dickson, Thompson
18	8	CC	A	Crusaders	D 2-2	McDowell 2 / Bradford, Casement
19	15	CC	H	Glenavon	L 2-4	O'Neill, Walker (pen) / Denvir 3, McVeigh
20	22	CC	A	Ballymena Utd.	L 1-2	McDowell / Baker 2
21	29	CC	A	Bangor	L 1-4	O'Neill / Rice, McKee 2, Richardson
22	Dec 6	IL	A	Glenavon	L 3-4	Walker, McDowell, Drake / Jones 2, Cush, Denvir
23	13	IL	H	Ballymena Utd.	L 1-3	Bogan / Baker 2, Johnston
24	20	IL	A	Glentoran	L 0-3	/ Lowry, Ewing, S. Hughes
25	25	IL	A	Bangor	D 2-2	Drake, Tucker / Russell, Milford
26	26	IL	H	Derry City	W 3-0	Thomson, McDowell, Walker (pen) /
27	27	IL	A	Distillery	D 0-0	
28	Jan 3	IL	H	Cliftonville	W 3-1	Walker, Thomson 2 / Weir
29	10	IL	A	Crusaders	L 1-2	Thomson / Hicks, Shields
30	17	IL	H	Coleraine	W 6-4	Walker 2, Drake 2, McDowell, Thomson / Colvan 2, O'Kane, McCormick

31	24	IL	H	Linfield	D 1-1	Walker / Dickson
32	31	IL	A	Portadown	W 1-0	O'Neill /
33	Feb 7	IC[1]	H	Distillery	W 6-2	Thomson 2, Drake 3, Walker / Johnston, Dodds
34	14	IL	H	Crusaders	D 1-1	Thomson / Mulholland
35	21	IL	A	Ballymena Utd.	L 0-4	/ Johnston, Bonnar, White 2
36	28	IL	H	Distillery	L 0-1	/ Johnston
37	Mar 7	IC[2]	H	Glentoran	L 4-5	Thomson 2, Drake, Corbett / S. Hughes, Lowry, 3, Feeney
38	14	IL	H	Glenavon	W 1-0	Walker /
39	21	IL	A	Coleraine	D 2-2	Thomson 2 / McCormick, Doherty
40	Apr 1	Cas[1]	A	Ballymena Utd.	D 0-0	
41	4	IL	A	Linfield	L 0-2	/ McDowell, Walker
42	6	IL	H	Bangor	W 2-1	Thomson, Walker / Irwin
43	7	IL	A	Derry City	W 3-1	O'Neill, McKirdy, Walker / McCaffrey
44	11	IL	H	Portadown	D 0-0	
45	13	Cas[1R]	H	Ballymena Utd.	W 5-1	O'Neill 3, McKirdy, Thomson / Currie
46	18	IL	A	Cliftonville	L 1-2	Bogan / Hollywood, McGarry
47	20	GC[1]	H	Bangor	D 1-1	Drake / Irwin
48	24	GC[1R]	A	Bangor	W 5-2	Thomson 3, Drake 2 / Rice 2
49	May 2	Cas[SF]	N	Linfield	L 1-2	Thomson (pen) / Thompson, Walker
50	5	GC[2]	A	Ballymena Utd.	W 1-0	Trevorrow o.g. /
51	16	GC[SF]	N[2]	Linfield	L 2-3	O'Neill , Murray / Dickson 2 (1 pen), Nixon
52	20	IL	A	Glentoran	D 1-1	Shanahan o.g. / Feeney

N = Oval
N[2] = Solitude

Final positions, season 1953-54

League: 9th   P 22 W 6 D 2 L 14 F 32 A 53 pts 14
City Cup: 7th   P 11 W 3 D 5 L 3 F 18 A 25 pts 11
Ulster Cup: 3rd   P 10 W 3 D 5 L 2 F 17 A 17 pts 11

	Date	Comp.	Venue	Opponents	Result	Goalscorers
1	Aug 15	UC	H	Portadown	W 5-3	Baker 3,Thomson 2 / Wishart 2, Punton
2	18	UC	H	Glenavon	D 1-1	Eastham / Campbell
3	20	UC	A	Distillery	D 0-0	
4	22	UC	A	Bangor	W 3-2	Baker 2, Murray / Forsythe 2
5	26	UC	A	Linfield	L 0-1	/ Walker
6	29	CC	A	Coleraine	L 0-5	/ Doherty 2, Tucker o.g., Colvan, O'Kane
7	Sept 1	UC	A	Portadown	D 1-1	Forde / Kane o.g.
8	3	UC	H	Bangor	D 1-1	Tucker / McKee
9	5	CC	H	Distillery	D 1-1	Baker / McCabe
10	7	UC	H	Distillery	D 4-4	Tucker 2, Thomson, Eastham jr. / McAdam 3, McIntosh
11	12	CC	A	Cliftonville	D 1-1	Eastham jr. / Moss
12	17	UC	A	Glenavon	L 0-3	/ Forsythe, McVeigh, Corr

13	19	CC	H	Portadown	L 1-4	Baker / Wishart 2, Dobbin 2
14	21	UC	H	Linfield	W 2-1	Thomson, Hedley / Maze
15	26	CC	A	Glentoran	L 0-6	/ Feeney 4, Ewing, Cunningham
16	Oct 10	CC	H	Derry City	W 3-1	Walker, Forde, Thomson / Hermon
17	17	CC	A	Linfield	D 1-1	Thomson / Nixon
18	24	CC	H	Crusaders	D 2-2	Thomson, Eastham / Shields 2
19	31	CC	A	Glenavon	W 2-1	Hedley 2 / Denvir
20	Nov 7	CC	H	Ballymena Utd.	D 1-1	Forde / Coll
21	14	CC	H	Bangor	W 6-2	Thomson (pen), Forde, Hedley 3, Walker / Nelson, Innes
22	21	IL	H	Crusaders	W 3-2	Forde 2, Hedley / Tully, Mulholland
23	28	IL	A	Coleraine	D 1-1	Eastham / Buchan
24	Dec 5	IL	H	Ballymena Utd.	L 1-2	Thomson / McMullan, McClure
25	12	IL	H	Glentoran	L 0-4	/ Hughes, Lowry, Feeney, Clugston
26	19	IL	A	Cliftonville	L 2-3	Eastham, Forde / McGarry, Shields, Scott
27	25	IL	H	Bangor	L 1-3	Eastham / Fulton o.g., Neill, O'Neill
28	26	IL	A	Linfield	L 0-4	/ Walker 2, Dickson 2
29	28	IL	A	Bangor	W 2-0	Thomson (pen), Forde /
30	Jan 2	IL	A	Glenavon	L 2-4	Forde 2 / Fulton o.g., Matthews, Corr 2
31	9	IL	H	Distillery	W 1-0	Forde /
32	16	IL	A	Derry City	L 1-6	Thomson / Delaney 3, Young 3
33	23	IL	H	Derry City	W 3-2	McIntosh 2, Thomson (pen) / Delaney, Hunter o.g.
34	30	IL	H	Cliftonville	W 4-2	McIntosh 2, Eastham, Higgins / Fulton, Shiells (pen)
35	Feb 6	IC[1]	H	Carrick Rangers	W 4-0	Walker, McIntosh, Higgins 2 /
36	13	IL	H	Linfield	L 1-2	McIntosh / Richardson, Walker
37	20	IL	A	Distillery	D 2-2	Maze, Thomson (pen) / McEvoy, Cubitt
38	27	IL	H	Glenavon	L 3-4	Forde 3 / Denvir 2, Corr, Jones
39	Mar 6	IC[2]	H	Glentoran	L 0-4	/ Lewis, Hughes 2, Lowry
40	13	IL	A	Portadown	L 0-1	/ Kennedy
41	20	IL	A	Crusaders	L 0-2	/ Haslett, Mulholland
42	24	Cas[1]	H	Linfield Swifts	W 2-1	Forde 2 / Keenan
43	27	GC[1]	H	Cliftonville	W 5-4	Walker, Forde 2, Eastham jr., Moore / Williams 2, Barr 2
44	Apr 3	IL	H	Coleraine	L 1-4	Forde / Cuneen 2, Waterstone 2
45	7	Cas[2]	H	Distillery	L 0-1	/ Wilson
46	10	IL	A	Ballymena Utd.	L 0-2	/ McGuckian, Currie
47	17	IL	A	Glentoran	L 0-2	/ Hughes, Scott
48	20	IL	H	Portadown	W 4-1	Forde 3, Thomson / Biggins
49	26	TC	A	Bangor	L 0-1	/ O'Neill
50	29	TC	H	Bangor	D 1-1	Forde / Duffy
51	May 7	GC[2]	A	Linfield	W 2-0	Eastham jr., Eastham (pen) /
52	11	GC[SF]	N	Portadown	W 3-1	Hedley 2, Forde / Biggins
53	15	GC[F]	N[2]	Distillery	W 2-1	Walker, Eastham / Johnston

N = The Oval
N[2] = Seaview

Final positions, season 1954-55

League: 3rd   P 22   W 9   D 6   L 7   F 53   A 45   pts 24

City Cup: 11th   P 11   W 2   D 2   L 7   F 20   A 30   pts 6

Ulster Cup: P 5   W 2   D 1   L 2   F 6   A 6   pts 5

	Date	Comp.	Venue	Opponents	Result	Goalscorers
1	Aug 21	UC	A	Bangor	L 1-2	Eastham / Neilson, Williamson
2	25	UC	A	Glenavon	L 1-2	Eastham jr. / Jones 2
3	28.	UC	H	Portadown	W 1-0	Forde
4	Sept 4	UC	A	Linfield	D 0-0	
5	8	UC	H	Distillery	W 3-2	McCrory, Hedley (pen), Neill / Parkes, Moore
6	11	CC	H	Coleraine	D 1-1	Neill / McKennan
7	14	TC	A	Bangor	W 3-2	Lester, McMullan, Forde / Beare, Innes
8	18	CC	A	Distillery	L 0-5	/ Parkes 3, Neill, Weatherup
9	20	GC[1]	A	Crusaders	L 3-4	McCrory 2, Neill / McCafferty, Vernon, Tully, Harris
10	23	TC	H	Bangor	L 0-1	/ Parks
11	25	CC	H	Cliftonville	W 5-0	Walker 3, Eastham jr., Forde /
12	Oct 9	CC	A	Portadown	L 0-2	/ Morrison 2
13	16	CC	H	Glentoran	D 3-3	Neill 2, Hedley / Scott, Cunningham, Hughes
14	23	CC	A	Derry City	L 0-3	/ Feeney 3
15	30	CC	H	Linfield	L 0-1	/ Douglas
16	Nov 6	CC	A	Crusaders	W 4-3	Walker, McCrory, Neill 2 / Tully, McMullan, Harris
17	13	CC	H	Glenavon	L 3-5	Neill, Eastham jr., Hedley / Denvir 3, Jones 2
18	20	CC	A	Ballymena Utd.	L 3-4	Hedley, Eastham jr., Neill / Coll, McCormick, Thompson, Rickett
19	27	CC	A	Bangor	L 1-3	Fulton / O'Neill, Neilson 2
20	Dec 4	IL	H	Portadown	D 3-3	Neill, Eastham jr. 2 / Barr, Buchanan, Kane
21	11	IL	A	Cliftonville	D 1-1	McCrory / Hunter o.g.
22	18	IL	H	Derry City	W 4-2	Walker 3 (1 pen), Eastham / Curran, Coyle
23	25	IL	A	Bangor	D 1-1	McCrory / McMurray
24	27	IL	H	Linfield	L 1-3	Eastham jr. / Douglas, Kennedy 2
25	Jan 1	IL	A	Glenavon	L 0-4	/ Denvir 2, Jones, Campbell
26	8	IL	H	Ballymena Utd.	W 4-3	Kingsmore, Walker 2 (1 pen), Hedley / Fearon, Moore, Lawlor
27	15	IL	A	Distillery	W 3-2	Hedley 2, Eastham jr. / Innes, Dodds
28	22	IL	H	Crusaders	W 4-0	Neill, Eastham jr., Walker, Hedley /
29	29	IL	A	Glentoran	L 2-3	Neill, Eastham jr. / Chapman, Humphreys, Johnston
30	Feb 5	IC[1]	A	Bangor	W 4-1	Eastham jr. 2, Neill, Eastham / Neilson
31	12	IL	H	Coleraine	W 6-1	Eastham jr., Hedley 3, Eastham, Fulton / Lowry
32	19	IL	A	Portadown	L 0-4	/ Dobbin 2, Patterson, Newberry o.g.
33	26	IL	H	Cliftonville	L 4-5	Hedley, Eastham jr. 2, Neill / Barr, McGarry 2, Shiels 2
34	Mar 5	IC[2]	A	Glenavon	L 0-1	/ Jones (pen)

35	12	IL	A	Derry City	W 1-0	Tucker /
36	19	IL	H	Bangor	W 5-1	Tucker, Eastham jr. 3, Walker / Neilson
37	23	Cas[1]	N	East Belfast	L 0-1	/ Booth
38	Apr 2	IL	A	Linfield	D 2-2	Eastham jr., Hedley / Dickson, Kennedy
39	9	IL	H	Glenavon	L 0-1	/ Denvir
40	11	IL	A	Ballymena Utd.	D 2-2	Hedley, Kingsmore / Curtis, Lawlor
41	12	IL	H	Distillery	W 4-0	Wilson o.g., Kingsmore 2, Eastham jr. /
42	16	IL	A	Crusaders	D 2-2	Walker, Eastham jr. / Boyd, Braithwaite
43	22	TC	A	Bangor	L 1-3	Stitt / Watson 2, Truesdale
44	25	TC	H	Bangor	W 2-0	Eastham jr., Stitt /
45	28	IL	A	Coleraine	L 1-4	Tucker / Coyle 4
46	30	IL	H	Glentoran	W 3-1	Jordan, Hedley, Eastham / Quee

N = Seaview

Final positions, season 1955-56

League: 7th	P 22	W 9	D 2	L 11	F 44	A 45	pts 20
City Cup: 8th	P 11	W 5	D 0	L 6	F 21	A 26	pts 10
Ulster Cup: 2nd	P 5	W 2	D 2	L 1	F 8	A 4	pts 6

	Date	Comp.	Venue	Opponents	Result	Goalscorers
1	Aug 20	UC	H	Bangor	L 0-2	/ Lowry, Neilson
2	24	UC	H	Glenavon	W 5-0	McQuilken, Liggett o.g, Jordan 2, Eastham jr./
3	27	UC	A	Portadown	W 2-1	Humphries, Wallace / Keenan
4	Sept 3	UC	H	Linfield	D 1-1	Wallace / Kennedy
5	7	UC	A	Distillery	D 0-0	
6	10	CC	A	Coleraine	L 1-3	Jordan / Coyle, Waterstone 2
7	17	CC	H	Distillery	W 4-2	Jordan 2, McQuilken, Eastham jr. / Orr, Johnston
8	24	CC	A	Cliftonville	L 2-3	Jordan, Eastham jr. / Shiells 2, McGarry
9	28	GC	H	Portadown	L 1-3	McQuilken / Brown 2, Boyd
10	Oct 1	CC	H	Portadown	W 2-1	Jordan 2 / McIlroy
11	15	CC	A	Glentoran	L 0-3	/ Quee 2, McConnell
12	22	CC	H	Derry City	W 2-1	Hedley 2 / McQuade
13	29	CC	A	Linfield	L 1-3	Hedley / Weatherup 2, Kennedy
14	Nov 5	CC	H	Crusaders	W 3-2	Hedley, Walker, Jordan / Casement, Linden
15	12	CC	A	Glenavon	L 2-4	Hedley, Walker / McVeigh 2, Denvir 2
16	19	CC	A	Ballymena Utd.	L 1-3	Hedley / McCartney, Watt, Thompson (pen)
17	26	CC	H	Bangor	W 3-1	Jordan 2, Gildea / Smyth
18	Dec 3	IL	H	Cliftonville	W 3-2	Eastham jr., Jordan, Hedley / Small 2
19	10	IL	A	Linfield	L 1-2	Hedley / Richardson, Dickson
20	17	IL	H	Glenavon	W 1-0	Jordan /
21	24	IL	A	Derry City	L 1-3	Gildea / Colvan, Innes 2
22	26	IL	H	Bangor	L 2-4	Eastham jr., Walker / Lindsay, Lowry 2, Smyth
23	31	IL	A	Coleraine	L 0-1	/ McKennan
24	Jan 2	IL	A	Distillery	W 2-1	Wilson, Walker / Orr

25	7	IL	H	Ballymena Utd.	W 4-3	Moss, Gildea, Hedley, Wilson / Watt 2, Thompson
26	14	IL	A	Portadown	W 4-2	Humphries, Eastham jr., Gildea 2 / Boyd, Andrews
27	21	IL	H	Crusaders	W 5-2	Eastham jr., Munroe 3, Wilson / Linden, Mulholland
28	28	IL	A	Glentoran	L 1-2	Walker / Lowry, Hughes
29	Feb 4	IC^1	H	Glenavon	D 1-1	Walker / Chapman
30	8	IC^{1R}	A	Glenavon	D 0-0	
31	11	IL	H	Glentoran	L 2-3	Humphries, Munroe / Lowry 2 (1 pen), Hughes
32	15	IC^{2R}	N	Glenavon	W 4-2	Gildea, Walker 2, Eastham jr. / Jones, Cush
33	18	IL	H	Linfield	L 0-1	/ Weatherup
34	25	IL	A	Cliftonville	W 6-1	Walker 3 (1 pen), Gildea 2, Munroe / Murray
35	Mar 3	IL	H	Distillery	W 3-2	Gildea 2, Munroe / Tadman 2
36	10	IC^2	H	Cliftonville	L 1-2	Gildea / McKeague, Small
37	17	IL	H	Derry City	L 1-2	Hedley / Innes, McGreevy
38	31	IL	A	Bangor	D 1-1	Gildea / Lowry
39	Apr 3	IL	A	Glenavon	L 0-6	/ Corr, Cush, Newberry o.g., Campbell, Jones Denvir
40	7	IL	H	Coleraine	D 1-1	Munroe / Ervine
41	11	Cas^2	H	Crusaders	W 3-1	Jordan, Eastham jr., Walker / Linden
42	14	IL	A	Ballymena Utd.	L 2-3	Humphries, Munroe / Norris, Haslett, McReynolds
43	28	IL	H	Portadown	W 4-0	Gildea, Tucker, Walker, Munroe /
44	30	IL	A	Crusaders	L 0-3	/ Adair 2, Davis (pen)
45	May 3	Cas^{SF}	N^2	Distillery	D 0-0	
46	9	Cas^{SFR}	N^2	Distillery	W 2-1	Eastham jr., Munroe / Humphries
47	12	Cas^F	N^2	Linfield	W 4-1	Walker, Gildea 2, Munroe / Dickson

N = Grosvenor Park
N^2 = Oval

Final positions, season 1956-57

League: 7th	P 22	W 12	D 4	L 6	F 65	A 33	pts 28
City Cup: 3rd	P 11	W 6	D 3	L 2	F 33	A 18	pts 15
Ulster Cup: 4th	P 11	W 5	D 2	L 4	F 21	A 22	pts 12

	Date	Comp.	Venue	Opponents	Result	Goalscorers
1	Aug 18	UC	H	Derry City	W 3-2	Langton 2 (1 pen), McQuilken / Bonnar, McBride
2	21	UC	A	Linfield	L 0-3	/ Ervine, Dickson, Hill
3	25	UC	H	Crusaders	W 2-0	Humphries, Langton /
4	29	UC	A	Coleraine	L 2-3	Humphries, Lawther / Robertson, Young, Coyle
5	Sept 1	UC	A	Glenavon	W 4-3	Munroe 2, McQuilken 2 / Jones 3

6	3	UC	A	Glentoran	D 3-3	Lawther 2, Humphries / Feeney o.g., Hughes, Haslett
7	8	UC	H	Ballymena Utd.	L 1-4	Forde / McCartney 2, Walker, McGhee
8	10	UC	H	Portadown	W 3-0	McDonnell 3 /
9	15	UC	H	Bangor	L 1-3	McDonnell / O'Neill, McMillan, Lindsay
10	22	UC	A	Cliftonville	W 1-0	McDonnell /
11	29	UC	H	Distillery	D 1-1	Humphries / Tadman
12	Oct 13	IL	H	Bangor	W 5-4	Quee 2, Humphries, Munroe, Matier o.g. / Smith 2, Neilson, Lindsay
13	20	IL	A	Glenavon	L 0-1	/ Jones (pen)
14	27	IL	H	Derry City	W 4-2	Lawther 2, Langton, McDonnell / Nash, McBride
15	Nov 3	IL	A	Linfield	D 2-2	Munroe 2 / McCrory 2
16	10	IL	H	Cliftonville	W 4-3	Humphries, Langton, McDonnell, T. Forde / Barr, Small, McGarry
17	17	IL	A	Ballymena Utd.	W 5-0	Munroe 3, McDonnell, Smith /
18	24	IL	H	Coleraine	L 1-2	Munroe / O'Kane, Coyle
19	Dec 1	IL	H	Distillery	W 8-1	Munroe 4, H. Forde 2, Humphries 2 / S.Humphries
20	8	IL	A	Glentoran	L 0-1	/ Mulvey
21	15	IL	H	Crusaders	W 3-1	Langton, Munroe, Humphries / Mulholland
22	22	IL	A	Portadown	D 4-4	Humphries, Smith, Langton 2 / Harris, McClatchy, Semple, Dobbin
23	25	IL	A	Bangor	W 3-0	Munroe, McDonnell 2, /
24	29	IL	A	Derry City	W 2-0	Lawther, T. Forde /
25	Jan 5	IL	H	Linfield	D 1-1	Munroe / Parke
26	12	IL	A	Cliftonville	W 7-0	Lawther 2, Langton 2, Smith, Humphries, Munroe /
27	19	IL	H	Ballymena Utd.	W 2-1	Munroe 2 / McGhee
28	21	IL	H*	Glenavon	L 1-2	McDonnell / Campbell, McVeigh
29	26	IL	H	Coleraine	W 5-1	Lawther, Langton (pen), Munroe 2, Humphries / O'Kane
30	Feb 2	IC[1]	H	Crusaders	W 4-1	Munroe 3, McDonnell / Murray
31	9	IL	A	Distillery	L 1-3	Munroe / Humphries, Boyd, Neilson
32	16	IL	H	Glentoran	D 3-3	McQuilken, Lawther, Humphries / Lowry, Fogerty, Hughes
33	Mar 2	IC[2]	A	Derry City	L 0-3	/ Campbell, Crossan, Nash
34	9	IL	H	Portadown	W 4-1	Quee, McQuilken, Munroe, Smith / Andrews
35	16	CC	H	Coleraine	W 4-1	Munroe 3, Smith / Coyle
36	23	Cas[2]	H	Cliftonville	W 5-0	Humphries, Munroe, Smith 2, McDonnell /
37	30	CC	A	Distillery	W 2-1	Munroe 2 / Neilson
38	Apr 3	IL	A	Crusaders	W 1-0	H. Forde /
39	6	CC	H	Cliftonville	L 3-5	McQuilken, Munroe 2 (1 pen) / Small 2, Barr 2, Davies
40	12	GC[1]	A	Coleraine	L 0-3	/ Barr 2, Coyle
41	20	CC	A	Portadown	W 4-0	Munroe, Langton, Quee, Fulton /
42	23	CC	H	Glentoran	D 1-1	Munroe / Hughes
43	27	CC	A	Derry City	W 3-0	McQuilken, Lawther, McDonnell /
44	29	Cas[SF]	N	Glentoran	L 0-2	/ Thompson 2
45	May 4	CC	H	Linfield	L 3-4	Munroe, Quee 2 / Dickson 2, Braithwaite (pen), Ervine

46	6	CC	H	Ballymena Utd.	D 1-1	H. Forde / Stewart (pen)
47	9	CC	A	Bangor	W 4-0	Lawther, Jordan, McDonnell, H. Forde /
48	11	CC	A	Crusaders	D 5-5	Lawther 3, Humphries, McDonnell / Mulholland 3, Pavis, Beggs
49	18	CC	H	Glenavon	W 3-0	Jordan, Lawther, Humphries /

H* = Grosvenor Park

Final positions, season 1957-58

League: 1st   P 22   W 16   D 4   L 2   F 68   A 32   pts 36

City Cup: 5th   P 11   W 6   D 2   L 3   F 26   A 22   pts 14

Ulster Cup: 4th   P 5   W 2   D 1   L 2   F 15   A 13   pts 5

	Date	Comp.	Venue	Opponents	Result	Goalscorers
1	Aug 17	UC	A	Bangor	W 5-1	McCaffrey 2, McDonnell, Humphries, Richardson / Irwin
2	21	UC	H	Glenavon	D 3-3	Humphries 2, McCaffrey / Jones 3
3	24	UC	H	Distillery	L 1-4	Lowry / Lunn, Shiels, Dougan, Neilson
4	28	UC	A	Portadown	W 6-1	Lawther, McDonnell, Humphries, Lowry 2, Forde / Wallace
5	31	UC	A	Linfield	L 0-4	/ Dickson 3, Milburn
6	Sept 4	GC[1]	A	Bangor	W 3-0	Lowry 3 /
7	7	CC	A	Coleraine	W 4-1	Lawther 2, Richardson, Munroe / Waterstone
8	14	CC	H	Distillery	D 1-1	Lowry / Lunn
9	18	GC[2]	A	Ballymena	W 5-3	Munroe 2, Lowry, Lawther , Humphries / McCrae, Brown, Cubitt
10	21	CC	A	Cliftonville	D 2-2	Lawther, McGuicken / Robinson 2
11	28	CC	H	Portadown	W 3-2	Quee 2, Munroe (pen) / Walker, McGuicken o.g.
12	Oct 12	CC	A	Glentoran	L 2-4	Lawther, Lowry / Thompson 2, Hughes, Lowry
13	19	CC	H	Derry City	W 3-1	Quee, Lawther, McDonnell / James
14	26	CC	H	Ballymena	L 1-4	Lowry / McGhee 2, Egan, McCrae
15	Nov 2	CC	A	Linfield	L 1-3	Munroe / Milburn, Parke 2
16	4	GC[SF]	N	Glenavon	L 1-2	Munroe / Campbell 2
17	9	CC	H	Bangor	W 1-0	McDonnell /
18	16	CC	H	Crusaders	W 3-2	McDonnell, Munroe, Richardson / Hunter o.g., Miller
19	23	CC	A	Glenavon	W 5-2	Richardson, Munroe 3, Humphries / Jones 2 (1 pen)
20	30	IL	A	Glentoran	W 1-0	Richardson /
21	Dec 7	IL	H	Coleraine	L 3-4	Richardson, Munroe, Forde / Coyle 3, McCormick
22	14	IL	H	Crusaders	W 6-1	McDonnell 2, Richardson, McGuicken, Lowry, Munroe / Mulholland
23	21	IL	A	Portadown	W 2-1	Richardson, Lowry / Walker
24	25	IL	H	Bangor	W 5-2	Fulton, Richardson, Lowry, Humphries 2 / O'Neill, Bell

25	26	IL	A	Glenavon	W 3-0	Richardson 2, Fulton
26	28	IL	H	Derry City	W 2-1	Forde, Coll / Crossan
27	Jan 4	IL	A	Linfield	D 4-4	Lawther, Richardson 2 (1 pen), Lowry / Dickson, Milburn, Parke 2
28	11	IL	H	Cliftonville	W 7-2	Lowry 4, Lawther 2, Richardson / Crozier, McConnell
29	18	IL	A	Ballymena	D 1-1	Lowry / Lowry (pen)
30	Feb 1	IC[1]	H	Glentoran II	W 4-2	Leeman o.g., McCrory, Lowry, Richardson / Lowry, Keenan (pen)
31	8	IL	A	Coleraine	W 3-1	Lowry 2, Boyd / Coyle
32	15	IL	H	Glentoran	W 5-1	Richardson, Boyd 4 / Bruce
33	17	IL	A	Distillery	D 1-1	Lowry / Dugan
34	22	IL	A	Crusaders	W 4-1	Boyd 3, McCrory / Mulholland
35	Mar 1	IC[2]	A	Ballymena	L 1-3	Richardson / McGhee 2, Lowry (pen)
36	8	IL	H	Portadown	W 3-2	Humphries, Lowry, Richardson / Wallace, Jennings
37	15	IL	A	Bangor	W 2-1	Lowry, Beattie o.g. / O'Neill
38	22	IL	H	Distillery	D 2-2	Lowry, Boyd / Neilson, Lunn
39	29	IL	H	Glenavon	L 3-4	Lowry, Boyd, Humphries / Jones 3, Hughes
40	Apr 5	IL	A	Derry City	W 1-0	Richardson /
41	8	IL	H	Linfield	W 3-0	Lawther 3
42	12	IL	A	Cliftonville	W 4-3	Lowry 2, Humphies 2 / Crozier, Robinson, Davies
43	19	IL	H	Ballymena	W 3-0	Humphries, Lawther, Lowry /
44	31	Cas[1]	A	Linfield	L 0-3	/ Milburn 3

N = Windsor Park

Final positions, season 1958-59

League: 7th	P 22	W 10	D 3	L 9	F 53	A 51	pts 23
City Cup: 11th	P 11	W 3	D 0	L 8	F 14	A 34	pts 6
Ulster Cup: 2nd	P 5	W 3	D 1	L 1	F 10	A 9	pts 7

	Date	Comp.	Venue	Opponents	Result	Goalscorers
1	Aug 16	UC	H	Bangor	W 3-0	Richardson 2, Lowry /
2	21	UC	A	Glenavon	W 2-1	Humphries 2 / Jones
3	23	UC	A	Distillery	W 1-0	Humphries /
4	27	UC	H	Portadown	D 2-2	Richardson, Allen / Walker 2
5	30	UC	H	Linfield	L 2-6	Allen, Humphries / Milburn 3, Cairns, Braithwaite 2
6	Sept 4	GC[1]	H	Cliftonville	L 0-1	/ Giffen o.g.
7	6	CC	H	Coleraine	L 1-4	Lawther / Coyle, Tully, Crossan, McGuicken o.g.
8	13	CC	A	Distillery	W 2-1	Richardson, Lawther / McCullough
9	17	EC[1]	H*	Rheims	L 1-4	Lowry / Fontaine 4
10	20	CC	H	Cliftonville	W 2-0	Lowry, Conkey /
11	27	CC	A	Portadown	W 3-1	Lawther 2, Quee / Henderson

12	Oct 8	EC[1]	A	Rheims	L 2-6	Lawther, Quee / Piantoni 2, Fontaine 2, Bliard 2
13	11	CC	H	Glentoran	L 1-2	Boyd / Thompson, Calderwood
14	18	CC	A	Derry City	L 0-5	/ Doherty 2, Nash, McCrory, Hewitt
15	25	CC	A	Ballymena Utd.	L 1-5	Quee / McGhee 2, Clarke, Lowry (pen), Russell
16	Nov 1	CC	H	Linfield	L 1-3	Richardson / Ervine 2, Dickson
17	8	CC	A	Bangor	L 0-3	/ Garston o.g., McGreevy, Fulton
18	15	CC	A	Crusaders	L 0-5	/ Weatherup 2, McDonnell, Mulholland, Truesdale
19	22	CC	H	Glenavon	L 3-5	Richardson, Boyd, Conkey / Jones 2, H. Forde, Weatherup, Campbell
20	29	IL	A	Crusaders	L 1-5	Conkey / Weatherup 2, Mulholland 3 (1 pen)
21	Dec 6	IL	H	Distillery	D 1-1	Quee / Munroe
22	13	IL	H	Coleraine	W 5-3	Quee, Richardson 2, Lawther, Boyd / Coyle, Crossan, Barr
23	20	IL	A	Portadown	L 1-6	Boyd / Richardson 3, Walker 3
24	25	IL	A	Bangor	W 3-2	Lockhart, O'Neill o.g., Forde / Morrow 2
25	26	IL	H	Glenavon	L 2-3	Giffen, Lockhart / Denver, Jones, H. Forde
26	27	IL	A	Linfield	L 1-5	Fletcher / Milburn 3, Ervine, Ferguson
27	Jan 3	IL	H	Ballymena Utd.	L 1-4	Harding / Welsh, Russell 2, McGhee
28	17	IL	A	Derry City	W 3-1	Harding 2, Lockhart / Brolly
29	24	IL	H	Glentoran	L 2-3	Allen, Boyd / Bruce, Thompson, Frazer
30	31	IC[1]	H	Bangor	W 3-1	Harding 2, Boyd / Neill
31	Feb 7	IL	A	Glenavon	W 3-2	Harding 3 / Wilson, Jones
32	14	IL	H	Cliftonville	W 7-0	Harding 5, Lawther, Lockhart /
33	21	IL	A	Derry City	W 6-0	Cupples 3, Harding 2, Richardson /
34	28	IC[2]	A	Linfield	L 2-4	Harding 2 / Milburn 2, Dickson 2
35	Mar 4	IL	A*	Cliftonville	W 5-1	Lawther 2, Corry (pen), Richardson, Harding / Williamson
36	7	IL	A	Glentoran	D 1-1	Richardson / Hughes
37	14	IL	H	Crusaders	L 1-2	Harding / McCartney 2
38	21	Cas[2]	H	Glentoran	W 4-0	Lawther 2, Harding, Corry (pen) /
39	28	IL	A	Coleraine	W 2-1	Lawther, Harding / Coyle
40	30	IL	H	Linfield	L 0-3	/ Milburn, Dickson, Cairns
41	31	IL	A	Ballymena Utd.	D 3-3	Forde, Allen, Cupples / Stewart, Forsyth, McEvoy
42	Apr 4	IL	H	Distillery	L 3-5	Forde, Harding, Watters o.g./ Emery, Munroe, McGuicken o.g., Hamilton, Watters
43	11	IL	H	Bangor	W 1-0	Richardson /
44	25	IL	H	Portadown	W 1-0	Allen /
45	30	Cas[SF]	N	Bangor	L 1-2	Lockhart / Dugan, McGreevy

N = Oval
A* = Grosvenor Park
H* = Windsor Park

Final positions, season 1959-60

League: 8th	P 22	W 8	D 3	L 11	F 37	A 47	pts 19
City Cup: 11th	P 11	W 2	D 0	L 9	F 12	A 31	pts 4
Ulster Cup: 3rd	P 5	W 2	D 0	L 3	F 6	A 16	pts 4

	Date	Comp.	Venue	Opponents	Result	Goalscorers
1	Aug 15	UC	A	Bangor	W 2-0	Forsythe, Patterson /
2	19	UC	H	Glenavon	L 1-4	Allen / Magee, Campbell 2, H. Forde
3	22	UC	H	Distillery	W 2-1	Forsythe, Jennings / Munroe
4	26	UC	A	Portadown	L 1-3	Patterson / Galbraith, Gorman 2
5	29	UC	A	Linfield	L 0-3	/ Dickson 2, Ervine
6	Sept 3	GC[1]	A	Portadown	L 0-4	/ Johnston, Casement, Gillespie, Henderson
7	5	CC	A	Coleraine	L 0-2	/ Blair 2
8	12	CC	H	Distillery	L 0-3	/ Lunn, Hamilton (pen), Callender
9	19	CC	A	Cliftonville	W 2-0	Harding, Boyd /
10	26	CC	H	Portadown	L 2-4	Boyd (2 pens) / Henderson 2, Walker 2
11	Oct 10	CC	A	Glentoran	W 2-1	T. Forde, Boyd (pen) / Drennan (pen)
12	17	CC	H	Derry City	L 1-4	T.Forde / Cassidy 2, McCrory, Nash
13	24	CC	H	Ballymena Utd.	L 1-2	McGreevy / Maguire, Barr
14	31	CC	A	Linfield	L 1-4	McGreevy / Stewart, Cairns, Ervine 2
15	Nov 7	CC	H	Bangor	L 1-2	Lennon / Dignam, Carr
16	14	CC	H	Crusaders	L 0-5	/ McDonnell 2, Reynolds o.g., Mulholland 2
17	21	CC	H	Glenavon	L 2-4	Lennon, Welsh / Campbell 2, Jones, Armstrong
18	28	IL	A	Cliftonville	L 0-2	/ Carroll, Delaney
19	Dec 5	IL	H	Ballymena Utd.	D 1-1	McGreevy / Russell
20	12	IL	A	Derry City	W 4-1	Ewing, McGreevy, Corry, Humphries / Smyth
21	19	IL	H	Distillery	L 4-5	Humphries, Ewing,T. Forde, McCrory / Keenan, Meldrum 2, Welsh 2
22	25	IL	H	Bangor	L 1-4	Ewing / Dignam 2, Hunter, McAuley
23	26	IL	A	Glenavon	L 0-4	/ Jones 2, H. Forde 2
24	Jan 2	IL	H	Linfield	L 2-5	Humphries, Boyd / Stewart, Braithwaite 3, Ferguson
25	9	IL	H	Portadown	W 2-0	McCrory 2 /
26	16	IL	A	Glentoran	L 1-5	Lennon / Spiers, Briggs 3, Bruce
27	23	IL	A	Coleraine	W 3-1	Boyd 2, Ewing / McBride
28	30	IC[1]	H	Dundela	W 8-0	Humphries, Ewing 4, McCrory, Boyd 2 /
29	Feb 6	IL	H	Crusaders	W 4-1	Welsh, McCrory, Hamill, Ewing / Forsyth
30	13	IL	H	Cliftonville	W 4-1	Ewing 2, McCrory 2 / Lawther
31	27	IC[2]	A	Portadown Res.	W 4-2	Ewing 3, McCrory / McPolin, Henderson
32	Mar 2	IL	A	Ballymena Utd.	L 1-2	McCrory / Lynch, Barr
33	5	IL	H	Derry City	W 2-1	Humphries, Ewing / Doherty
34	9	Cas[1]	A	Glentoran II	L 0-1	/ Catherwood
35	12	IL	A	Distillery	L 0-3	/ Welsh, Keenan 2
36	19	IL	A	Bangor	L 1-5	Humphries / Dugan 2, Dignam 2, Hunter
37	26	IC[SF]	N	Derry City	W 1-0	Ewing /
38	Apr 2	IL	A	Portadown	D 0-0	
39	9	IL	H	Glentoran	L 1-2	McCrory / Calderwood, Spiers
40	16	IL	A	Crusaders	D 2-2	Welsh, Boyd / Nixon, Mulholland
41	18	IL	H	Glenavon	W 2-0	Hamill, Ewing /
42	19	Il	A	Linfield	L 0-2	/ Milburn, Stewart
43	26	Il	H	Coleraine	W 2-0	Ewing 2 /
44	30	IC[F]	N	Linfield	L 1-5	Welsh / Ferguson, Gough, Milburn 3

N = Oval

Final positions, season 1960-61

League: 3rd	P 22	W 14	D 3	L 5	F 66	A 39	pts 31
City Cup: 4th	P 11	W 5	D 3	L 3	F 37	A 21	pts 13
Ulster Cup: 3rd	P 5	W 3	D 1	L 1	F 13	A 10	pts 7

	Date	Comp.	Venue	Opponents	Result	Goalscorers
1	Aug 20	UC	H	Bangor	W 4-0	Humphries, Lynch, Rosbotham, McVea /
2	23	UC	A	Glenavon	D 2-2	Humphries, Ewing / Dugan, Johnston
3	27	UC	A	Distillery	W 5-4	Lynch, N. Boyd, Humphries, Sleith, Ewing (pen) / Meldrum 3, Lunn
4	31	UC	H	Portadown	W 2-0	Lynch, N. Boyd /
5	Sept 3	UC	H	Linfield	L 0-4	/ Gough, Stewart 2, Cairns
6	10	CC	A	Ballymena Utd.	L 3-4	Lynch, Ewing, N. Boyd / Barr, Clarke, Smyth 2
7	17	CC	H	Linfield	D 2-2	Lynch, Ewing (pen) / Ferguson, Milburn
8	21	GC[2]	A	Linfield	D 1-1	Ewing / Dickson
9	24	CC	A	Distillery	L 1-3	Lynch / Hamilton 2, Meldrum
10	28	GC[2R]	H	Linfield	L 3-5	Ewing, Lynch 2 / Dickson, Ferguson, Milburn 2, Stewart
11	Oct 1	CC	H	Cliftonville	W 7-2	Lynch 2, McVea, Ewing 3, Humphries / McDowell, Hale
12	15	CC	A	Crusaders	D 1-1	Ewing / Boyd
13	22	CC	H	Glenavon	D 4-4	Lynch 2, Ewing, McAuley / Jones, Weatherup, Johnston, Dugan
14	29	CC	A	Portadown	L 1-2	Ewing (pen) / McKenzie, Robinson
15	Nov 5	CC	H	Derry City	W 5-2	McVea 3, Ewing 2 / Campbell, Doherty
16	12	CC	A	Coleraine	W 8-0	Lynch, Ewing 5, Humphries, McVea /
17	19	CC	H	Bangor	W 2-1	Ewing, Lynch / Dignam
18	26	CC	H	Glentoran	W 3-0	Humphries, Maguire, McAuley /
19	Dec 3	IL	A	Linfield	D 2-2	Humphries, McAuley / Cairns, Gough
20	10	IL	H	Cliftonville	W 6-3	Ewing 3, Lynch 2, Maguire / Thompson, McDowell 2
21	17	IL	A	Bangor	W 6-1	Lynch, Ewing 3 (2 pens), Humphries, Forde / Mulholland
22	24	IL	H	Derry City	W 5-1	Humphries 2, Lynch, Maguire, Ewing / Neilson
23	26	IL	A	Glenavon	W 4-3	Lynch 2, Humphries, Ewing / Johnston 2, Jones
24	27	IL	H	Ballymena Utd.	D 1-1	Lynch / Smyth
25	31	IL	A	Distillery	L 2-3	Maguire, Ewing / Ellison, Nixon, Hamilton
26	Jan 7	IL	H	Crusaders	W 2-0	McAuley, Ewing /
27	14	IL	H	Glentoran	W 2-1	Ewing 2 / Doherty
28	21	IL	A	Coleraine	W 3-1	Maguire, Ewing 2 (1 pen) / Nash
29	28	IL	H	Portadown	L 0-2	/ Gorman, Gillespie
30	Feb 4	IL	A	Derry City	W 6-3	Ewing 2, Lynch 4 (1 pen) / Fisher 3
31	11	IL	H	Glenavon	W 3-2	Humphries, Lynch 2 / Dugan, Magee
32	18	IL	A	Ballymena Utd.	D 1-1	Lynch / Neill
33	25	IC[1]	H	Coleraine	D 2-2	Lynch, Ewing / Trainor, Harkin
34	28	IC[1R]	A	Coleraine	W 4-1	Humphries, Lynch (pen), Ewing, Calderwood / Moffatt o.g.

35	Mar 4	IL	H	Distillery	W 3-0	Lynch 2, Humphries /
36	11	IC²	H	Glenavon	D 1-1	Humphries / Jones
37	15	IC²ᴿ	A	Glenavon	L 0-4	/ Jones 2, Campbell, Weatherup
38	18	IL	A	Crusaders	W 2-1	Ewing, Humphries / Whiteside
39	25	Cas¹	H	Brantwood	W 3-2	Bell, Lynch (pen), Maguire / Doherty, Woods
40	Apr 1	IL	A	Glentoran	L 0-2	/ Thompson, Murdough
41	4	IL	H	Coleraine	W 7-2	Doherty 2, Maguire 2, Humphries, Lynch 2 (1 pen) / Harkin, Trainor
42	8	IL	A	Portadown	L 1-3	Doherty / Gorman, Robinson, Gillespie
43	11	Cas²	H	Distillery	L 2-5	Lynch 2 (1 pen) / Keenan (pen), O'Neill 2, Welsh, Meldrum
44	15	IL	H	Linfield	L 1-4	Ewing / Ferguson, Braithwaite, Gough, Dickson
45	25	IL	H	Bangor	W 4-2	Sinclair, Lynch 2 (1 pen), Doherty / Hume, Lowry
46	29	IL	A	Cliftonville	W 5-1	Lynch 5 / Walsh

Final positions, season 1961-62

League: 4th	P 22	W 11	D 5	L 6	F 46	A 38	pts 27
City Cup: 6th	P 11	W 5	D 1	L 5	F 31	A 20	pts 11
Ulster Cup: 5th	P 5	W 1	D 0	L 4	F 8	A 15	pts 2

	Date	Comp.	Venue	Opponents	Result	Goalscorers
1	Aug 19	UC	A	Bangor	W 4-2	Ewing 3, Maguire / Dignam, Harvey
2	23	UC	H	Glenavon	L 2-3	Lynch (pen), Coyne / Campbell, Jones, Griffiths
3	26	UC	H	Distillery	L 1-5	Ewing / Ellison, O'Neill, Meldrum 3
4	30	UC	A	Portadown	L 0-3	/ Gorman, Robinson, McMillan
5	Sept 2	UC	A	Linfield	L 1-2	Lynch / Barr (pen), Braithwaite
6	6	GC¹	A	Cliftonville	D 3-3	Sinclair 2, Doherty / Sykes 3
7	9	CC	H	Ballymena Utd.	L 2-5	Sinclair, Maguire (pen) / Twentyman, Smith, Clarke, Neill, Greenfield
8	11	GC¹ᴿ	H	Cliftonville	W 5-1	Ewing 2, Lynch 2, Humphries / Sykes
9	16	CC	A	Linfield	L 1-2	Ewing / Ferguson, Reid
10	18	GC²	A	Glentoran	L 1-6	Sinclair / Harvey, Thompson 3, Doherty, Bruce
11	23	CC	H	Distillery	W 2-1	Lynch, Ewing / Welsh
12	30	CC	A	Cliftonville	W 7-1	Humphries 4, Ewing, Lynch 2 / Campbell
13	Oct 14	CC	H	Crusaders	L 1-2	Lynch / Spiers, Weatherup
14	21	CC	A	Glenavon	W 2-1	Lunn, Lynch / Campbell
15	28	CC	H	Portadown	L 0-1	/ Gorman
16	Nov 4	CC	A	Derry City	D 2-2	Calderwood, Maguire / Torrens, Wood
17	11	CC	H	Coleraine	W 3-1	Calderwood, Humphries, Lunn / Smith
18	18	CC	A	Bangor	L 2-3	Lunn, Lynch / Hume, O'Neill, Wilson
19	25	CC	A	Glentoran	W 9-1	Ewing, Lynch 5, Humphries 3 / Thompson
20	Dec 2	IL	H	Cliftonville	W 5-1	Maguire, Ewing 3, Lynch / McKeown
21	9	IL	A	Ballymena Utd.	W 2-1	Humphries, Lynch / Small
22	16	IL	H	Glenavon	W 4-3	Lynch 4 / Wilson, Jones, Weatherup
23	23	IL	A	Distillery	D 2-2	Lynch, Ewing / Meldrum, Keenan
24	25	IL	A	Linfield	L 2-3	Ewing, Lynch / Barr, Dickson, Reid

25	26	IL	H	Glentoran	W 4-2	Lynch 2, Borne o.g., Geoghegan o.g. / Smyth, Doherty
26	30	IL	H	Bangor	D 1-1	Lynch (pen) / Moore
27	Jan 6	IL	A	Portadown	D 3-3	Humphries 2, Lynch (pen) / Gorman 3
28	13	IL	H	Coleraine	W 3-2	Lynch 2 (1 pen), Ewing / Coyle 2
29	20	IL	A	Crusaders	L 0-3	/ Dignam, Weatherup, Nixon
30	27	IL	A	Derry City	D 0-0	
31	Feb 3	IL	H	Portadown	W 2-1	Ewing 2 / Mitchell (pen)
32	10	IL	A	Coleraine	W 1-0	Ewing /
33	17	IL	H	Crusaders	W 4-1	Lynch (pen), Maguire, Ewing, Humphries / Dignam
34	24	IC[1]	H	Coleraine	L 1-2	Humphries / Coyle 2
35	Mar 17	IL	A	Cliftonville	W 3-1	Maguire, Lynch 2 / Fusco
36	24	IL	H	Derry City	W 2-0	Humphries 2 /
37	31	IL	H	Ballymena Utd.	D 1-1	Humphries / Hughes
38	Apr 7	IL	A	Glenavon	L 2-5	Maguire, Lynch (pen) / Jones 3 (1 pen), Johnston 2
39	9	Cas[1]	A	Glentoran	L 3-6	Lynch, Maguire, Lunn / Hume 2, Thompson 2, Doherty, Stewart
40	21	IL	A	Glentoran	L 0-1	/ Thompson
41	24	IL	H	Linfield	L 2-4	Humphries, McAuley / Maguire o.g., Dickson 2, Ferguson
42	28	IL	H	Distillery	W 3-1	Lynch 2, Muirhead / Keenan
43	30	IL	A	Bangor	L 0-2	/ Sands 2

Final positions, season 1962-63

League: 10th   P 22   W 5   D 3   L 14   F 30   A 54   pts 13

City Cup: 10th   P 11   W 2   D 2   L 7   F 31   A 40   pts 6

Ulster Cup: 5th   P 5   W 1   D 1   L 3   F 4   A 11   pts 3

	Date	Comp.	Venue	Opponents	Result	Goalscorers
1	Aug 18	UC	H	Bangor	W 2-1	Ewing 2 / McKenna
2	21	UC	A	Glenavon	L 0-3	/ Campbell, Johnston 2
3	25	UC	A	Distillery	L 0-3	/ Meldrum 2, McCaffrey
4	30	UC	H	Portadown	L 0-2	/ Gorman, McMillan
5	Sept 1	UC	H	Linfield	D 2-2	Ewing, Weatherup / Dickson, Braithwaite
6	8	CC	A	Ballymena Utd.	L 2-4	Robinson, Ewing (pen) / McNamara, Halliday, Twentyman, Patterson o.g.
7	15	CC	H	Linfield	L 3-4	Weatherup 2 (1 pen), Small / Reid 2, Dickson, Ferguson
8	22	CC	A	Distillery	L 1-4	Weatherup / Meldrum 4
9	26	NSC	A	Shamrock Rvrs.	L 1-3	Small / Bailham, O'Connell, Mooney
10	28	CC	H	Cliftonville	W 7-2	Small 2, McAuley 2, Weatherup (pen), Robinson 2 / Brolly, Irons
11	Oct 4	GC[2]	A	Derry City	L 1-2	Weatherup / McKenzie, Maguire o.g.
12	6	CC	A	Crusaders	L 1-5	Whiteside / Hale 2, Nixon 2, Spiers

13	10	NSC	H*	Shamrock Rvrs.	L 1-7	McAuley / O'Connell 3, Keogh 2, O'Neill, Fullam
14	13	CC	H	Glenavon	D 2-2	Dugan o.g., Munroe / Watson, McKinney
15	20	CC	A	Portadown	L 1-4	Weatherup / Jones 3, McMillan
16	Nov 3	CC	H	Derry City	D 2-2	Robinson, Weatherup (pen) / Imrie, Torrens
17	10	CC	A	Coleraine	L 0-6	/ O'Neill 5, Vickers
18	17	CC	H	Bangor	W 9-0	Small 3, Munroe, Hunter, Robinson 2, Weatherup, Lowe /
19	24	CC	H	Glentoran	L 3-7	Weatherup, Small 2 / Doherty 2, Mitchell 2, Thompson 3
20	Dec 1	IL	A	Crusaders	L 1-4	Small / Hale 2, McCrory, Weatherup
21	8	IL	H	Glentoran	L 1-6	Maguire (pen) / Stwart, McGuicken o.g., Mitchell 2, Warburton 2
22	15	IL	A	Cliftonville	L 1-4	Small / Irons, Waugh 2, Hidvegi
23	22	IL	A	Portadown	L 0-5	/ Gorman 2, Jones 2, McGuicken
24	25	IL	H	Distillery	L 2-3	Whiteside 2 / Scott, Welsh, T. Hamilton
25	26	IL	A	Coleraine	W 2-1	Small, Patterson / Coyle
26	29	IL	H	Ballymena Utd.	D 2-2	Small, Weatherup / McDonnell 2
27	Jan 5	IL	A	Bangor	W 3-1	Small 2, Weatherup / Ewing
28	12	IL	H	Glenavon	W 1-0	Small /
29	26	IL	H	Derry City	L 1-5	Small / Campbell, McKenzie, Imrie 3
30	Feb 2	IL	A	Glentoran	L 1-2	Maguire / Hume, Doherty
31	16	IL	H	Portadown	D 0-0	
32	23	IC[1]	H	Portadown Res.	W 3-2	Small 3 / Huddleston, Corry o.g.
33	Mar 2	IL	A	Distillery	L 3-5	Maguire (pen), Whiteside, Small / Meldrum 4, Welsh
34	9	IC[2]	A	Distillery	L 2-4	Weatherup, Small / Hamilton 2, Welsh, Meldrum
35	9	IL	A	Linfield	L 1-3	Devanney / Guy 2, Ferguson
36	16	IL	H	Coleraine	L 1-2	Whiteside / Kelly 2
37	23	Cas[1]	A	Cliftonville Oly.	D 1-1	Corry / Stitt
38	28	Cas[1R]	H	Cliftonville Oly.	W 9-2	Patterson 3, Devanney, Whiteside, Weatherup 2, Sterritt, Lowe / Adams, Walker
39	30	IL	A	Ballymena Utd.	D 0-0	
40	Apr 1	IL	A	Cliftonville	W 4-3	Sterritt 2, Weatherup, Carlisle o.g. / Corry o.g., Spence, Allen
41	6	IL	H	Bangor	W 3-0	Weatherup, Whiteside, Patterson /
42	8	Cas[2]	A	Crusaders	D 2-2	Whiteside, Weatherup / Weatherup 2
43	13	IL	A	Glenavon	L 0-2	/ Dugan, McNally
44	15	Cas[2R]	H	Crusaders	L 3-5	Weatherup (pen), Small 2 / Speers 2, Pavis, Weatherup, McCrory
45	16	IL	L	Linfield	L 0-1	/ Cairns
46	27	IL	A	Derry City	L 2-3	R. Cassidy, Sterritt / Torrens, Brown, Young
47	29	IL	H	Crusaders	L 1-2	Devanney / Weatherup, Hale

H* = Grosvenor Park

Final positions, season 1963-64

League: 10th   P 22 W 7 D 3 L 12 F 45 A 58 pts 17

City Cup: 7th   P 11 W 4 D 3 L 4 F 24 A 28 pts 11

Ulster Cup: 5th   P 5 W 1 D 1 L 3 F 11 A 18 pts 3

	Date	Comp.	Venue	Opponents	Result	Goalscorers
1	Aug 17	UC	H	Bangor	L 2-4	Shellard, Campbell / Watterson, Sands 3
2	21	UC	A	Glenavon	L 2-6	Sterritt 2 / Johnston 2, Wilson 3, Campbell
3	24	UC	H	Distillery	W 3-2	Weatherup, McMillan, Cooper / Hunter o.g., Campbell
4	28	UC	A	Portadown	D 3-3	Campbell, Sterritt 2 / Cush 2, Gorman
5	31	UC	A	Glentoran	L 1-3	Weatherup / Curley, McCullough, Hume
6	Sept 7	CC	H	Ballymena Utd.	W 4-2	Weatherup 2, Sterritt, McMillan / Cowan, McDowell
7	9	GC[1]	H	Linfield	L 2-6	Sterritt, Small / Scott 2, Craig, Ferguson, Reid, Parke
8	14	CC	A	Linfield	D 2-2	McMillan, Weatherup / Reid, Parke
9	21	CC	H	Distillery	L 2-3	Lewis, Weatherup / J. Kennedy 2, Cochrane
10	28	CC	A	Cliftonville	L 1-2	McMillan / Thompson 2
11	Oct 5	CC	H	Crusaders	W 3-2	Weatherup 2, Campbell / Hale, Callender
12	19	CC	A	Glenavon	D 2-2	Campbell, Priestley / Watson, Magee
13	26	CC	H	Portadown	W 2-1	Brown, McMillan / Webb
14	Nov 2	CC	A	Derry City	L 0-6	/ Coyle 2, McGeough, Seddon, Doherty, Campbell
15	9	CC	H	Coleraine	D 2-2	Sterritt, Lewis / Halliday, Irwin
16	16	CC	A	Bangor	W 4-2	McMillan, Sterritt 3 / McCoubrey, Wright
17	23	CC	A	Glentoran	L 2-4	Sterritt, Whiteside / Thompson 3, Curley
18	30	IL	H	Derry City	W 4-3	Sterritt 2, McMillan 2 / Coyle 2, McKenzie
19	Dec 7	IL	A	Ballymena Utd.	D 3-3	McMillan, Sterritt, Campbell / Moffatt, Hickson 2
20	14	IL	H	Glenavon	L 2-4	Lewis 2 / Guy, Halliday, Johnston 2
21	21	IL	A	Crusaders	L 1-3	Whiteside / Pavis, Hale 2
22	25	IL	H	Bangor	W 4-0	Weatherup, Brown, Niblock o.g., Sterritt /
23	26	IL	A	Cliftonville	W 6-0	Shellard, Mowat, Campbell, Brown, Sterritt, Rea o.g. /
24	28	IL	H	Coleraine	L 1-3	Sterritt / Halliday 3
25	Jan 4	IL	H	Linfield	W 3-1	Priestley, McMillan 2 / Craig
26	11	IL	A	Glentoran	L 0-2	/ Thompson 2
27	18	IL	H	Portadown	L 0-1	/ Webb
28	25	IL	A	Distillery	L 1-6	Weatherup / Camppbell 3, Cochrane, Meldrum 2
29	Feb 1	IL	A	Linfield	L 2-5	McKeown 2 / Craig, Reid, Scott 3
30	8	IL	H	Glentoran	D 2-2	McKeown, Sterritt / Byrne, Curley
31	15	IL	A	Portadown	L 0-3	/ Webb, Newell, Gorman
32	22	IC[1]	H	Glentoran	D 1-1	Mowat / Pavis
33	26	IC[1R]	A	Glentoran	D 2-2	Campbell, McCullough o.g. / Thompson, Curley
34	29	IL	H	Distillery	D 2-2	Sterritt, Weatherup / Burke, Campbell
35	Mar 2	IC[1RR]	N	Glentoran	L 0-4	/ Brannigan, Thompson, Stewart 2

36	14	IL	A	Derry City	L 1-6	Sterritt / Lindsay, McGeough 2, Coyle 3
37	28	IL	H	Ballymena Utd.	L 2-3	Sterritt, Whiteside / McDonnell 2, Russell
38	30	IL	A	Glenavon	L 0-6	/ Guy 3, Johnston, Halliday, Campbell
39	Apr 4	IL	H	Crusaders	W 4-2	Mowat 2, Sterritt 2 / Hale, McDonnell
40	11	IL	A	Bangor	W 2-0	Sterritt 2 /
41	18	IL	H	Cliftonville	W 5-0	Sterritt, Campbell, McMillan 2, Weatherup /
42	20	Cas²	A	Glentoran	L 1-3	Weatherup / Thompson 2, Brannigan
43	24	IL	A	Coleraine	L 0-3	/ Halliday, Dunlop, Kinsella

N = Solitude

Final positions, season 1964-65

League: 11th	P 22	W 5	D 6	L 11	F 34	A 55	pts 16
City Cup: 11th	P 11	W 3	D 0	L 8	F 20	A 34	pts 6
Ulster Cup: 6th	P 5	W 0	D 1	L 5	F 6	A 13	pts 1

	Date	Comp.	Venue	Opponents	Result	Goalscorers
1	Aug 15	UC	H	Bangor	D 3-3	Mowat, Anderson, Brown / Wright, Gnaulati, Emery
2	18	UC	A	Glenavon	L 0-2	/ Guy, Mulgrew
3	22	UC	A	Distillery	L 1-3	Keogh / Campbell 2. Meldrum
4	26	UC	H	Portadown	L 1-2	Shellard / Shellard o.g., Fleming
5	29	UC	H	Linfield	L 1-3	Lynch / Cairns, Ferguson, Robinson
6	Sept 5	CC	A	Ballymena Utd.	L 3-7	Lynch, Coulter, Mowat / Hickson 4, Thomas 2, Smyth
7	12	CC	H	Linfield	L 1-3	Lynch / Ferguson, Dickson 2
8	14	GC¹	H	Glenavon	D 2-2	Lynch 2 / Johnston 2
9	19	CC	A	Distillery	L 1-5	Lynch / Meldrum 2, Welsh, Black, Hamilton
10	23	GC¹ᴿ	A	Glenavon	L 2-6	Keenan 2 (1 pen) / Watson 2, Campbell, Guy 2, Johnston
11	26	CC	H	Cliftonville	W 7-1	Mowat 2, Herron 3, Keenan, Walker o.g. / D. Walker
12	Oct 10	CC	A	Crusaders	L 1-2	Keogh / Hale 2
13	17	CC	H	Glenavon	W 5-2	Walker, Scott 2, Coulter, Mowat / Guy, Campbell
14	24	CC	A	Portadown	L 0-5	/ Gorman 4, Gilbert
15	31	CC	H	Derry City	L 1-2	Keogh / Seddon, Coyle
16	Nov 7	CC	A	Coleraine	W 1-0	Keogh /
17	14	CC	H	Bangor	L 0-2	/ Woods (pen), Harte
18	21	CC	H	Glentoran	L 0-5	/ Warburton, Thompson, Gillespie, Brannigan, Turner
19	28	IL	A	Cliftonville	W 2-1	Stevenson, Coulter / Walker
20	Dec 5	IL	H	Derry City	D 3-3	Walker, Mowat, Barron / Coyle 2, McKenzie (pen)
21	12	IL	A	Distillery	L 1-2	Mowat / Cochrane 2
22	19	IL	H	Bangor	D 1-1	Keogh / Weatherup
23	25	IL	A	Portadown	W 1-0	Mowat /

24	26	IL	H	Linfield	L 0-1	/ Craig
25	28	IL	A	Glentoran	D 2-2	Coulter 2 / Hall 2
26	Jan 2	IL	H	Coleraine	L 1-5	Keogh / Irwin 2, Davey, Halliday 2
27	9	IL	A	Crusaders	D 1-1	Mowat / Hale
28	16	IL	H	Glenavon	W 2-0	Brown, Herron /
29	30	IL	H	Portadown	W 3-0	Brown, Keogh, Mowat /
30	Feb 6	IL	A	Linfield	D 3-3	Brown, Herron, Anderson / Scott, Sterritt, Ferguson
31	13	IL	H	Glentoran	L 1-4	Herron / Ross, Warburton, Houston o.g., Williams
32	20	IC[1]	A	Glenavon	D 2-2	Anderson, Keogh / Guy 2
33	24	IC[1R]	H	Glenavon	D 1-1	Mowat / Guy
34	27	IL	A	Coleraine	L 1-2	Mowat / Curley, Gaston
35	Mar 6	IL	H	Ballymena Utd.	L 2-3	Coulter, Stewart / Thomas, Smith, Bell
36	8	IC[1RR]	N	Glenavon	L 0-2	/ Magee 2
37	13	IL	H	Crusaders	L 1-4	Brown (pen) / Hale, Weatherup, Campbell, McNeill
38	20	IL	A	Glenavon	L 2-7	Mowat 2 / Johnston 2, Guy 2, Watson 2, Weatherup
39	27	IL	A	Ballymena Utd.	L 1-4	Mowat / Thomas 3, G. Smith
40	Apr 10	IL	H	Cliftonville	W 4-2	Mowat 2, Scott, Brown / Anderson, Walker
41	13	Cas[2]	H	Cliftonville	W 4-2	McAvoy 2, C Brown 2 / Bingham, Oakes
42	17	IL	A	Derry City	L 1-5	Stewart / Gilbert 2, Stewart o.g., Seddon 2
43	19	IL	H	Distillery	L 0-4	/ B. Hamilton 3, Campbell
44	26	IL	H	Bangor	D 1-1	Mowat / McDonnell
45	May 1	Cas[SF]	N[2]	Crusaders	L 0-3	/ Hale, Pavis, Weatherup

N = Oval
N[2] = Grosvenor Park

Final positions, season 1965-66

League: 10th	P 22	W 4	D 6	L 12	F 29	A 54	pts 14
City Cup: 5th	P 11	W 5	D 3	L 3	F 19	A 15	pts 13
Ulster Cup: 10th	P 11	W 3	D 1	L 7	F 17	A 27	pts 7

	Date	Comp.	Venue	Opponents	Result	Goalscorers
1	Aug 7	UC	A	Derry City	L 0-6	/ Doherty 2, Wilson 3, Wood
2	11	UC	H	Linfield	L 1-2	McCully / Scott, Pavis
3	14	UC	A	Glenavon	W 2-0	Keogh, Mowat /
4	18	UC	H	Bangor	D 2-2	McCarroll o.g., Nixon / Light, Farrell
5	21	UC	A	Ballymena Utd.	L 3-7	Herron 2, Nixon / Thomas 4, Russell, McDonnell, G. Smith
6	26	UC	H	Coleraine	L 0-2	/ Doherty, Irwin
7	28	UC	A	Distillery	L 1-2	Herron / Symington, Bailey
8	Sept 2	UC	H	Portadown	W 3-1	Herron 2, Sands / Harley
9	4	UC	A	Cliftonville	W 2-0	Keogh, Kennedy (pen) /

10	8	UC	A	Glentoran	L 2-3	Mowat, Byrne o.g. / Hamilton, Thompson, Stewart (pen)
11	11	UC	H	Crusaders	L 1-2	Mowat / Wilson, Weatherup
12	18	IL	H	Linfield	L 1-3	Keogh / Scott, Pavis, Gregg
13	25	IL	A	Glenavon	W 2-1	Mowat, Kennedy (pen) / Johnston
14	Oct 7	GC[1]	A	Coleraine	W 2-0	Nixon, Herron /
15	9	IL	A	Glentoran	W 3-2	Keogh, Russell, Emerson / Thompson, Stewart (pen)
16	16	IL	H	Cliftonville	D 1-1	Hamilton / Sullivan
17	21	GC[2]	H	Cliftonville	L 1-2	Sands / Larmour, Sullivan
18	23	IL	A	Coleraine	L 1-5	Menary / Jennings 2, Halliday 3
19	30	IL	H	Bangor	L 1-2	Mowat / Rice, Coulter
20	Nov 6	IL	A	Portadown	W 2-0	Keogh, Menary /
21	13	IL	H	Crusaders	D 2-2	Kennedy (pen), Keogh / Weatherup, Hale
22	20	IL	A	Distillery	D 2-2	Anderson, Keogh / Hamilton, Burke
23	27	IL	H	Ballymena Utd.	L 1-2	Mowat / McDonnell, Aiken
24	Dec 4	IL	A	Derry City	L 1-4	Kennedy (pen) / Coyle 2, Wilson 2
25	11	IL	A	Linfield	L 1-5	Kennedy (pen) / Scott, Pavis 3, McCambley
26	18	IL	H	Glenavon	L 1-3	Sands / McManus 2, Guy
27	28	IL	H	Glentoran	L 2-3	Keogh, McCullough o.g. / Gnaulati, Thompson, Conroy
28	Jan 1	IL	H	Coleraine	D 0-0	
2	8	IL	A	Bangor	D 2-2	Menary, Snowden / Campbell, Farrell
28	15	IL	H	Portadown	L 1-4	Mowat / Smyth, Anderson, Wright, Gorman
29	22	IL	A	Crusaders	L 1-6	Kennedy (pen) / Hale 5, O'Halloran
30	29	IL	H	Distillery	W 1-0	Mowat /
31	Feb 5	IL	A	Ballymena Utd.	D 2-2	Kennedy (pen), Herron / McDonnell 2
32	12	IC[1]	H	Portadown	W 3-2	Mowat 2, Menary / Gorman 2
33	17	IL	A	Cliftonville	L 1-2	Snowden / Smyth, Spence
34	26	CC	A	Crusaders	L 1-3	Newell / Pavis 2, Campbell
35	Mar 5	IC[2]	H	Crusaders	L 1-3	Newell / Hale 2, Weatherup
36	10	IL	H	Derry City	L 0-3	/ McConomy, Parke 2
37	12	CC	H	Glentoran	D 1-1	Godbold / Thompson
38	19	CC	H	Cliftonville	W 4-1	Menary, Newell 2, Sands / Fusco
39	26	CC	H	Distillery	W 2-1	Newell, Menary / Hamilton
40	Apr 2	CC	A	Portadown	W 2-0	Newell, Menary /
41	9	CC	A	Coleraine	D 2-2	Newell, Mowat / Dunlop, Kinsella
42	11	CC	H	Derry City	W 3-0	Nixon, Mowat, Newell /
43	12	Cas[2]	H	Bangor	W 4-0	Nixon, Menary 2, Newell /
44	22	CC	H	Glenavon	L 1-3	Nixon / Magee (pen), Johnston, Guy
45	25	CC	A	Linfield	L 0-3	/ Pavis 2, Scott
46	30	CC	H	Ballymena Utd.	D 1-1	Mowat / Cloughley
47	May 2	CC	A	Bangor	W 2-0	McAvoy, Mowat /
48	4	Cas[SF]	N	Ballymena Utd.	L 0-1	/ Cairns

N = Oval

Final positions, season 1966-67

League: 8th   P 22   W 7   D 7   L 8   F 37   A 38   pts 21

Ulster Cup: 6th   P 11   W 5   D 2   L 4   F 30   A 16   pts 12

City Cup: 11th   P 11   W 2   D 2   L 7   F 9   A 18   pts 6

	Date	Comp.	Venue	Opponents	Result	Goalscorers
1	Aug 6	UC	H	Derry City	W 5-1	Elwood 2, Kennedy, Mills, Mowat / Parke
2	10	UC	A	Linfield	W 3-0	Lindsay, Anderson, Mills /
3	13	UC	H	Glenavon	L 0-2	/ Coulter, S. Magee
4	18	UC	A	Bangor	W 4-1	Elwood 2, Mills, Newell / Meldrum
5	20	UC	H	Ballymena Utd.	L 2-4	Newell, Anderson / Cairns 3, McDonnell
6	25	UC	A	Coleraine	L 1-2	Newell / Murray, Curtin
7	27	UC	H	Distillery	W 5-0	Newell, Herron 3, Mowat /
8	Sept 1	UC	A	Portadown	D 0-0	
9	3	UC	H	Cliftonville	W 6-0	Newell 3, Mowat 3 /
10	8	UC	H	Glentoran	D 1-1	Newell / Ross
11	10	UC	A	Crusaders	L 3-5	Newell, Mowat (pen), Sloan / McCullough, Meldrum 3, McNeill
12	17	IL	A	Portadown	L 0-1	/ Caswell
13	24	IL	A	Bangor	W 4-1	Newell 2, Elwood 2 / Clements
14	Oct 1	IL	H	Crusaders	W 3-1	Elwood, Mowat, Anderson (pen) / Trainor
15	6	GC[2]	H	Portadown	W 3-1	Newell 2, Elwood / Conway
16	8	IL	H	Glenavon	D 1-1	Mowat / Guy
17	15	IL	A	Ballymena Utd.	D 1-1	McConnell / Broad
18	29	IL	A	Cliftonville	W 1-0	Cahoon /
19	Nov 5	IL	H	Coleraine	W 1-0	Anderson /
20	12	IL	A	Glentoran	D 2-2	Newell, Mowat / Ross, Thompson
21	19	IL	H	Linfield	D 1-1	Newell / Pavis
22	26	IL	H	Derry City	L 2-3	Elwood, Newell / Seddon 2, Parke
23	30	GC[SF]	N	Crusaders	D 1-1	Newell / Trainor
24	Dec 10	IL	A	Crusaders	L 1-3	Mowat / Meldrum 2, Wilson
25	14	GC[SFR]	N	Crusaders	D 2-2	Elwood 2 / Trainor 2
26	17	IL	H	Bangor	D 2-2	Newell 2 / Farrell, Morrison
27	24	IL	H	Portadown	D 3-3	McAvoy (pen), Nixon, Elwood / Gorman 2, Fleming
28	26	IL	A	Linfield	L 2-6	Sands, Mowat / Thomas 2, Scott 2, Shields, Pavis
29	31	IL	H	Glentoran	L 1-3	Mowat / Thompson, Morrow, Ross
30	Jan 7	IL	A	Coleraine	L 2-4	Mowat, Elwood / Gaston 2, Curley, Jennings
31	11	GC[SFR]	N	Crusaders	L 2-4	Mowat 2 / Meldrum 2, McNeill, McCullough
32	14	IL	H	Cliftonville	W 3-1	Lindsay, Elwood, Mowat / McGucken
33	21	IL	A	Glenavon	L 0-2	/ Guy 2
34	28	IL	H	Ballymena Utd.	L 1-2	Elwood / Crothers o.g., Broad
35	Feb 1	IL	A	Distillery	D 1-1	Smith / Craig
36	4	IL	A	Derry City	W 2-0	Mowat, McAvoy /
37	11	IL	H	Distillery	W 3-0	Mowat, Elwood, Nixon /
38	18	IC[1]	H	Coleraine	* 3-2	(Mowat 2, Anderson / Curley, Halliday)
39	25	CC	H	Crusaders	L 2-3	Nixon, Mowat (pen) / Trainor 2, Law
40	Mar 2	IC[1]	H	Coleraine	L 0-2	/ Curley, Murray

41	4	CC	A	Glentoran	L 0-5	/ Weatherup, Colrain 2, Johnston, Stewart o.g.
42	11	CC	A	Glenavon	W 3-0	Newell 3 /
43	18	CC	A	Cliftonville	L 0-1	/ McGucken
44	25	CC	H	Portadown	L 0-2	/ Conway 2
45	27	CC	A	Distillery	L 0-1	/ Welsh
46	Apr 8	CC	H	Coleraine	D 0-0	
47	11	CC	A	Ballymena Utd.	D 2-2	Sands, Crothers / Aiken, Cairns
48	15	CC	H	Bangor	W 1-0	Mowat (pen) /
49	19	CC	H	Linfield	L 1-2	Sands / Ferguson, Pavis
50	24	Cas²	H	Glentoran	L 1-2	Sands / Stewart, Thompson
51	29	CC	A	Derry City	L 0-2	/ Parke 2

* = abandoned after 76 minutes

N = Oval

Final positions, season 1967-68

League: 4th	P 22	W 14	D2	L 6	F 51	A 34	pts 30	
City Cup: 9th	P 11	W 2	D 3	L 6	F 10	A 13	pts 7	
Ulster Cup: 6th	P 11	W 4	D 4	L 3	F 24	A 20	pts 12	

	Date	Comp.	Venue	Opponents	Result	Goalscorers
1	Aug 5	UC	A	Distillery	D 1-1	Elwood / Rafferty
2	10	UC	H	Portadown	W 3-1	Mowat, Newell 2 / Conway
3	12	UC	A	Cliftonville	W 7-0	Anderson 2, Mowat 2, Newell, Elwood, McFall /
4	16	UC	A	Glentoran	D 1-1	Nixon / Hunter
5	19	UC	H	Crusaders	D 2-2	Mowat, Nixon / McFall o.g., Trainor
6	24	UC	A	Derry City	L 0-2	/ Wood (pen), Parke
7	26	UC	H	Linfield	L 0-4	/ Pavis, Scott, Hamilton 2
8	30	UC	A	Glenavon	W 2-1	Sands, Mowat / McNally
9	Sept 2	UC	H	Bangor	D 3-3	Sands 2, Mowat / Morrison 2, Herron
10	4	GC¹	A	Glentoran	W 1-0	Mowat /
11	9	UC	A	Ballymena Utd.	L 2-3	Cochrane, McAvoy / McDonnell 3
12	16	UC	H	Coleraine	W 3-2	Nixon, McAvoy, Newell / Murray, Dickson
13	23	IL	A	Portadown	W 1-0	Newell /
14	27	GC²	A	Glenavon	D 0-0	
15	30	IL	H	Bangor	W 2-0	Newell, Mowat /
16	Oct 5	GC²ᴿ	H	Glenavon	W 2-0	McAvoy 2 /
17	7	IL	A	Linfield	D 1-1	McCurley / Pavis
18	14	IL	H	Cliftonville	W 5-0	Elwood 2, McAvoy 3 /
19	28	IL	A	Derry City	W 3-2	McAvoy, Mowat, Feeney / Gallagher, Parke
20	Nov 4	IL	H	Ballymena Utd.	W 3-1	Mowat, Cochrane, Elwood / McDonnell
21	7	GCˢᶠ	N	Derry City	D 2-2	McAvoy, Mowat / Parke, Porter
22	11	IL	H	Crusaders	W 2-1	Mowat, Feeney / Law
23	18	IL	A	Glentoran	L 0-3	/ Stewart o.g., McGucken 2
24	23	GCˢᶠᴿ	N	Derry City	W 1-0	Cochrane /
25	25	IL	H	Coleraine	D 1-1	McAvoy / Mullan

26	29	GC[F]	N	Linfield	L 2-3	McAvoy, Mowat / Wood (pen), Shields 2
27	Dec 2	IL	H	Glenavon	W 2-1	McAvoy 2 (1 pen) / Cloughley
28	16	IL	H	Portadown	L 1-2	McAvoy (pen) / Conway 2
29	23	IL	A	Bangor	W 5-1	Mowat, Newell 2, Flanagan o.g., Cochrane / Morrison
30	25	IL	H	Linfield	L 0-2	/ Gregg, Millen
31	26	IL	A	Cliftonville	W 1-0	Sands /
32	30	IL	H	Derry City	W 6-1	McAvoy 3, Magee 2, Mowat / Porter
33	Jan 6	IL	A	Ballymena Utd.	L 1-3	Mowat / Treacy 2, Kay
34	20	IL	H	Glentoran	L 1-6	McAvoy / Hutton, McGuckin 3, Jackson (pen), Johnston
35	27	IL	A	Coleraine	L 1-3	McAvoy / Murray, 2, Mullan
36	31	IL	A	Crusaders	W 5-3	Patterson o.g., Elwood, McAvoy, Faulds, Feeney / Meldrum 3 (2 pens)
37	Feb 3	IL	A	Glenavon	W 1-0	Feeney /
38	10	IL	H	Distillery	W 5-1	Faulds 3 (2 pens), McAvoy, Elwood / Rafferty
39	17	IC[1]	H	Coleraine	W 4-1	McAvoy 2, Elwood, Feeney / Peacock (pen)
40	24	IL	A	Distillery	W 4-2	Feeney 2, McAvoy, Crothers / Lennox, Savage
41	Mar 2	CC	H	Cliftonville	L 0-1	/ Watson
42	9	IC[2]	A	Ballyclare Com.	W 1-0	McAvoy /
43	16	CC	H	Glentoran	L 0-2	/ Gorman 2
44	23	CC	A	Crusaders	L 2-3	Sands, Cochrane / McArdle 2, Trainor
45	30	IC[SF]	N	Linfield	L 1-2	Elwood / Pavis 2
46	Apr 2	Cas[1]	H	Bangor	L 1-3	Feeney / Herron, Morrison, Nelson
47	6	CC	A	Linfield	L 1-2	McAvoy / Scott, Ferguson
48	8	TF	N[2]	Coleraine	L 0-2	/ Jennings, Dickson
49	11	CC	H	Ballymena Utd.	D 1-1	Elwood / Stewart
50	13	CC	A	Coleraine	W 1-0	McAvoy /
51	15	CC	A	Portadown	W 4-1	Feeney (pen), McAvoy, Nixon, Johnston / McFall o.g.
52	16	CC	H	Distillery	L 1-2	Cochrane / D. Meldrum, Pike (pen)
53	20	CC	H	Glenavon	D 0-0	
54	24	CC	A	Bangor	D 0-0	
55	25	CC	H	Derry City	L 0-1	/ Hill
56	May 1	BC	H	Shamrock Rov.	L 0-3	/ Leech 2, Richardson

N = Oval

N[2] = Windsor Park

Final positions, season 1968-69

League: 5th	P 22	W 12	D 5	L 5	F 48	A 34	pts 29
City Cup: 7th	P 11	W 4	D 2	L 5	F 19	A 21	pts 10
Ulster Cup: 5th	P 12	W 4	D 4	L 3	F 24	A 19	pts 11

	Date	Comp.	Venue	Opponents	Result	Goalscorers
1	Aug 3	UC	A	Linfield	L 2-3	Humphries, McAvoy / Hamilton 2, Andrews
2	8	UC	H	Glenavon	W 4-0	Mowat, Gorman, Anderson, Humphries /
3	10	UC	A	Bangor	D 1-1	Cochrane / Pavis
4	15	UC	H	Ballymena Utd.	W 3-1	Nixon 3 / Brannigan
5	17	UC	A	Coleraine	L 2-3	Nixon, Mowat / O'Neill, Reid, Irwin
6	22	UC	H	Distillery	W 4-3	Mowat 2, McAvoy, Anderson / McCaffrey 2, Jess
7	24	UC	A	Portadown	D 1-1	McAvoy / Conway
8	29	UC	H	Cliftonville	D 1-1	Cochrane / Peacock
9	31	UC	H	Glentoran	W 3-2	McAvoy, Nixon, Gillespie / Conroy, Herron
10	Sept 3	UC	A	Crusaders	L 1-2	McAvoy / McArdle, Parke
11	7	UC	H	Derry City	D 2-2	Shields 2 / Doherty, O'Sullivan
12	12	GC[1]	H	Glenavon	L 2-3	Stewart, McAvoy / Guy 3
13	14	IL	A	Distillery	W 2-1	McAvoy 2 / McCaffrey
14	21	IL	H	Bangor	W 2-0	Shields 2 /
15	28	IL	A	Glenavon	W 2-1	Gorman, Mowat / Cush
16	Oct 5	IL	H	Coleraine	W 3-1	Humphries 2, Cochrane / Curley
17	12	IL	H	Cliftonville	W 1-0	Humphries /
18	19	IL	A	Glentoran	D 1-1	McAvoy / Morrow
19	26	IL	H	Portadown	W 5-2	McAvoy 3 (1 pen), Crothers, Sands / Graham 2
20	Nov 9	IL	H	Derry City	W 2-1	McAvoy, Crothers / O'Sullivan
21	12	IL	A	Linfield	L 0-3	/ Cathcart, Scott, Hamilton
22	16	IL	H	Ballymena Utd.	W 4-3	Mowat, McAvoy 2 (1 pen), Cochrane / McDonnell, Martin, Erwin
23	23	IL	A	Crusaders	D 3-3	Mowat, McAvoy 2 / Meldrum, Hume, McArdle
24	30	IL	A	Bangor	W 3-0	Cochrane 2, McAvoy /
25	Dec 7	IL	H	Glenavon	W 4-1	McAvoy 2, Mowat, Humphries / Hughes
26	14	IL	H	Distillery	W 3-1	McAvoy 2, Humphries / McCaffrey
27	21	IL	A	Coleraine	D 3-3	McAteer 2, Mowat / Curley, Jennings, McCurdy
28	25	IL	A	Cliftonville	D 3-3	McAvoy 2 (1 pen), Mowat / Reaney, Peacock, Macklin
29	26	IL	H	Glentoran	L 1-2	McAteer / McParland, Macken
30	28	IL	A	Portadown	L 0-1	/ Fleming
31	Jan 4	IL	H	Linfield	L 1-2	McAvoy / Millen, Ferguson
32	11	IL	A	Derry City	L 0-3	/ O'Sullivan 2, Hale
33	18	IL	A	Ballymena Utd.	W 4-1	Humphries, Cochrane, McAvoy (pen), Johnston / McColl
34	25	IL	H	Crusaders	D 1-1	Brown / McArdle
35	Feb 1	CC	H	Coleraine	L 2-4	Brown, McAvoy / Irwin 3, O'Neill
36	15	IC[1]	A	Portadown	W 1-0	McAvoy /
37	22	CC	A	Glenavon	W 6-3	Shields 2, McAvoy 2 (1 pen), McAteer, Nixon / Guy 3
38	Mar 1	CC	H	Bangor	W 3-0	McAvoy 2, Shields /
39	8	IC[2]	H	Crusaders	W 4-1	McAvoy 2, Mowat 2 (1 pen) / Jamieson
40	15	CC	A	Ballymena Utd.	L 0-3	/ Larmour, Martin, Fullerton
41	22	CC	H	Linfield	D 1-1	McAvoy / Hamilton
42	29	IC[SF]	N	Coleraine	W 1-0	McAvoy /
43	Apr 5	CC	A	Derry City	L 1-2	Humphries / Balmer, Hale
44	8	CC	H	Crusaders	D 2-2	Nixon, Cochrane / Nicholl, Jamieson
45	12	CC	A	Glentoran	L 1-2	Brown / Patterson 2

46	19	IC^F	N^1	Distillery	D 0-0	
47	23	IC^{FR}	N^1	Distillery	W^T 4-2	McAvoy 4 / McCaffrey, Conlon
48	28	BC	A	Limerick	L 1-2	Mowat / Finucane 2
49	30	CC	H	Portadown	W 2-1	Cochrane, Brown / Lunn
50	May 2	Cas^2	A	Glentoran	L 1-3	Brown / Morrow 2, Herron
51	8	CC	A	Distillery	L 0-3	/ McMahon, McCaffrey 2
52	15	CC	A	Cliftonville	W 1-0	Sands /

W^T = AET
N = Oval
N^1 = Windsor Park

Final positions, season 1969-70

League: 3rd   P 22   W 10   D7   L 5   F 41   A 26   pts 27

City Cup: 3rd   P 5   W 2   D 2   L 1   F 11   A 8   pts 6

Ulster Cup: 9th   P 10   W 2   D 2   L 6   F 13   A 11   pts 6

	Date	Comp.	Venue	Opponents	Result	Goalscorers
1	Aug 9	UC	A	Derry City	W 3-0	Sands, Brown, McAvoy /
2	14	UC	H	Linfield	L 1-2	Humphries / McGraw, Hamilton
3	16	UC	A	Glenavon	D 1-1	Nixon / Sloan
4	21	UC	H	Bangor	D 0-0	
5	23	UC	A	Ballymena Utd.	L 1-5	Burke / Herron 3, Ferguson, Martin
6	30	UC	H	Coleraine	L 1-3	Humphries / Dickson, Jennings, Curley
7	Sept 4	UC	H	Portadown	L 2-3	McAteer 2 / Lunn 2, Graham
8	6	UC	A	Cliftonville	L 0-1	/ Lynch
9	9	UC	H	Crusaders	W 3-1	McAteer, Humphries, Brown / McPolin
10	13	UC	A	Glentoran	L 1-3	Burke / Weatherup, Henderson 2
11	17	ECWC^1	H*	Roma	D 0-0	
12	20	CC	A	Portadown	D 1-1	Humphries / Lunn
13	27	CC	H	Distillery	W 2-0	McAvoy, Anderson /
14	Oct 1	ECWC^1	A	Roma	L 1-3	Crothers / Salvori 2, Peiro
15	4	CC	A	Linfield	L 2-3	McAteer, McAvoy / Hamilton, Pavis (pen), McGraw
16	11	CC	H	Glenavon	W 4-2	Stewart, McAvoy, McAteer, Humphries (pen) / Robinson, A. Welsh
17	18	CC	A	Bangor	D 2-2	Brown, McAvoy / Murphy, Crothers o.g.
18	23	GC^1	A	Derry City	D 1-1	McAvoy / Hale
19	25	IL	H	Crusaders	W 2-1	McAvoy, Humphries (pen) / McCamley
20	30	GC^{1R}	H	Derry City	L 1-2	Brown / Doherty, Rowland
21	Nov 1	IL	A	Ballymena Utd.	W 2-1	Johnston 2 / Porter
22	8	IL	A	Glentoran	D 1-1	Burke / Henderson
23	15	IL	H	Coleraine	D 1-1	Burke / Campbell
24	22	IL	A	Cliftonville	W 2-0	Johnston, McAvoy /
25	29	IL	H	Distillery	W 1-0	McAvoy /
26	Dec 6	IL	A	Glenavon	W 2-0	McAvoy, McAteer /

27	13	IL	H	Derry City	W 4-0	Burke, Welsh, McAvoy 2 /
28	20	IL	A	Linfield	D 2-2	McAteer, Hatton o.g. / Hamilton, Matchett
29	26	IL	H	Bangor	W 2-1	McAvoy, Crothers / Nelson
30	27	IL	A	Portadown	D 1-1	McAteer / Hoar
31	Jan 3	IL	A	Crusaders	D 1-1	McAteer / McArdle
32	10	IL	H	Ballymena Utd.	W 4-1	Humphries, Burke 2, McAteer / Cooke
33	17	IL	H	Glentoran	L 2-3	McAvoy, McAteer / McCullough, Weatherup, McCaffrey
34	24	IL	A	Coleraine	L 1-2	McAvoy / Mullan, Dickson
35	31	IC[1]	H	Crusaders	L 0-1	/ Nicholl
36	Feb 7	IL	H	Cliftonville	W 3-1	McAvoy 3 / Lynch
37	14	IL	A	Distillery	D 0-0	
38	21	UC	A	Distillery	W 6-4	McAteer 3, Burke 3 / Mowat, Halloran, Watson, Lennox
39	28	IL	H	Glenavon	L 0-1	/ Macklin
40	Mar 14	Cas[1]	A	Chimney Corn.	D 2-2	McAteer, McAvoy (pen) / T. Craig, S. Craig
41	18	Cas[1R]	H	Chimney Corn.	D 1-1	McAvoy / Craig (pen)
42	21	IL	H	Linfield	L 2-3	Burke, Mills / Millen, Violett, Pavis
43	24	Cas[RR]	N	Chimney Corn.	W 2-1	McCoy (pen), Gillespie / Miller
44	28	IL	A	Bangor	D 2-2	Johnston, Gillespie / Cochrane, McManus
45	30	IL	H	Portadown	W 4-1	McAvoy 4 / Anderson
46	Apr 2	Cas[2]	H	Crusaders	W 3-0	Johnston 2, McCoy (pen) /
47	4	IL	A	Derry City	L 2-3	Johnston, McAvoy / Parke, Wood (pen), Rowland
48	21	Cas[SF]	A	Linfield	W 3-1	Shields 2, Gillespie / Millen
49	May 9	Cas[F]	N	Bangor	D 1-1	Shields / Gregg
50	12	Cas[R1]	N	Bangor	D 1-1	Burke / Gregg
51	18	Cas[R2]	N	Bangor	D 1-1	McAteer / Mulgrew
52	22	Cas[R3]	N	Bangor	L 2-3	Stewart, McAteer / Herron, Mulgrew, McAllister

H* = Oval
N = Solitude

Final positions, season 1970-71

League: 6th	P 22	W 8	D 5	L 9	F 30	A 37	pts 21
City Cup: 8th	P 11	W 3	D 4	L 4	F 22	A 20	pts 10
Ulster Cup: 7th	P 11	W 3	D 4	L 4	F 20	A 23	pts 10

	Date	Comp.	Venue	Opponents	Result	Goalscorers
1	Aug 15	UC	H	Derry City	D 2-2	Gillespie, Burke / Wood, Smith
2	19	UC	A	Linfield	L 1-3	Gillespie / Cathcart, Magee, Millen
3	22	UC	H	Glenavon	W 2-1	A. Welsh, Anderson / Dowd
4	27	UC	H	Ballymena Utd.	D 2-2	Gillespie, Humphries / Martin 2 (1 pen)
5	29	UC	A	Bangor	D 4-4	Johnston 2, R. Welsh, Humphries / Gregg 2 (1 pen), Murphy 2
6	Sept 1	UC	A	Coleraine	L 1-3	McAvoy (pen) / Dickson, Curley, Mullan
7	5	UC	H	Distillery	D 0-0	

8	10	UC	A	Portadown	W 5-3	Mowat, Gillespie 3, R. Welsh / Nicholl, Anderson, Kerrigan
9	12	UC	H	Cliftonville	W 2-1	Gillespie, Humphries / Stewart
10	17	TexC	H	Shamrock Rov.	L 1-4	Rooney / Lawlor 2, Hannigan, Brophy
11	19	UC	A	Crusaders	L 1-2	Gillespie / McPolin, Jameson
12	21	UC	H	Glentoran	L 0-3	/ Cassidy, Morrow 2
13	26	CC	H	Portadown	W 3-1	Anderson 2 (1 pen), Mowat / Kerrigan (pen)
14	30	TexC	A	Shamrock Rov.	W 3-2	Anderson, (pen), Humphries, Gillespie / F O'Neill 2
15	Oct 3	CC	A	Cliftonville	D 2-2	Humphries 2 / Peacock 2
16	8	GC[1]	H	Derry City	W 4-1	Gillespie 3, McCoy (pen) / Hale
17	10	CC	A	Glentoran	W 2-0	Stewart, Mowat /
18	17	CC	H	Crusaders	W 4-2	Mowat, Humphries, Gillespie 2 / Cavanagh, Trainor
19	24	CC	A	Derry City	L 1-2	Burke / Hale, O'Halloran
20	28	GC[2]	H*	Glentoran	L 1-2	Anderson / Magill 2
21	31	CC	H	Linfield	L 1-2	Gillespie / Hamilton, Pavis
22	Nov 7	CC	A	Glenavon	L 4-5	Humphries 2, Shields 2 / Guy 2, Macklin 2, Fleming
23	14	CC	H	Bangor	D 2-2	Shields, Gillespie / Graham, Craig
24	21	CC	A	Ballymena Utd.	D 2-2	Burke 2 / Vincent, Gregg
25	28	CC	H	Coleraine	D 1-1	Burke / Dickson
26	Dec 5	CC	A	Distillery	L 0-1	/ Law
27	12	IL	A	Glenavon	W 3-1	Humphries 2, Anderson / Macklin
28	19	IL	H	Glentoran	D 2-2	Mowat, Gillespie / Jamison, McCaffrey
29	26	IL	A	Bangor	D 0-0	
30	28	IL	H	Coleraine	L 0-2	/ Dickson 2
31	Jan 2	IL	A	Portadown	W 1-0	Davidson /
32	9	IL	A	Crusaders	D 0-0	
33	16	IL	H	Ballymena Utd.	L 0-1	/ Frickleton
34	23	IL	H	Linfield	W 2-1	Gillespie, Brown / Hamilton
35	30	IL	A	Cliftonville	D 3-3	Mowat, Patterson 2 / Peacock 3
36	Feb 6	IL	H	Distillery	L 1-4	Patterson / Savage 2, Brannigan, Watson
37	13	IC[1]	H	Chimney Corn.	L 0-2	/ S. Craig, T. Craig
38	Mar 6	IL	H	Glenavon	W 4-2	Burke 2, Porter 2 / Guy, Fleming
39	20	IL	A	Glentoran	L 0-4	/ Morrow 2, Kirk, Weatherup
40	27	IL	H	Bangor	L 1-2	Mowat / Graham, Matchett
41	Apr 3	Cas[2]	A	Glentoran	L 1-2	Burke / Macken, Magill
42	8	IL	H	Coleraine	L 1-2	Mowat / Gaston, Mullan
43	10	IL	H	Portadown	W 3-2	Gillespie, Anderson, Burke / Conlon, Lunn
44	12	IL	H	Crusaders	D 1-1	Burke / Tuson
45	15	IL	A	Derry City	L 1-3	Humphries / Rowland 2, Ward
46	17	IL	A	Ballymena Utd.	W 1-0	Anderson /
47	20	IL	H	Derry City	W 3-2	McCoy (pen), Nixon, Mowat / Ward, Rowland
48	22	IL	A	Linfield	L 0-3	/ Scott, Cathcart, Magee
49	28	IL	H	Distillery	L 1-2	Porter / McCarroll, O'Neill
50	29	IL	H	Cliftonville	W 2-0	Johnston, Stewart /

H* = home advantage conceded

Final positions, season 1971-72

League: 3rd	P 22	W 12	D 5	L 5	F 49	A 30	pts 29
City Cup: 1st	P 5	W 4	D 1	L 0	F 13	A 6	pts 9
Ulster Cup: 9th	P 11	W 5	D 0	L 6	F 16	A 20	pts 10

	Date	Comp.	Venue	Opponents	Result	Goalscorers
1	Aug 19	UC	H	Linfield	L 2-3	Hale, McAllister o.g. / Patterson, McAllister, Cathcart
2	21	UC	A	Glenavon	L 0-1	/ Malone
3	26	UC	A	Ballymena Utd.	W 2-1	Macklin, Humphries / Aiken
4	28	UC	H	Bangor	W 2-0	Humphries, Mowat /
5	Sept 2	UC	A	Derry City	L 0-2	/ Kilburn, McLaughlin
6	4	UC	H	Coleraine	W 3-2	McCoy, Hale, Johnston / Dickson 2
7	9	UC	H	Distillery	L 1-3	Johnston / O'Neill 2, Welsh
8	11	UC	H	Portadown	W 2-1	Hale, Johnston / Gillespie
9	14	UC	A	Cliftonville	L 0-3	/ Cairns 2, Sands
10	18	UC	A	Glentoran	L 0-1	/ Kirk
11	25	UC	H	Crusaders	W 4-3	Macklin 2, McAvoy 2 / Woods, Pavis, McKenzie
12	Oct 2	CC	A	Portadown	W 3-2	Henderson, McAvoy 2 / Anderson, Morrison
13	9	CC	H	Distillery	W 1-0	Humphries /
14	16	CC	A	Linfield	D 2-2	McAvoy 2 / McAllister, McAteer
15	23	CC	H	Glenavon	W 2-1	Hale 2 / Guy
16	30	CC	A	Bangor	W 5-1	McAvoy 3, Henderson 2 / Craig
17	Nov 6	IL	H	Crusaders	W 1-0	McCoy /
18	13	IL	A	Coleraine	D 1-1	Patterson / Dunlop
19	20	IL	A	Cliftonville	W 2-0	Hale, McAvoy /
20	27	IL	H	Linfield	D 1-1	Hale / Scott
21	Dec 4	CC[SF]	N	Ballymena Utd.	L 0-1	/ Averill
22	11	IL	A	Glentoran	L 1-2	McAvoy / Weatherup 2
23	18	IL	H	Derry City	L 1-2	Henderson / Ward, Johnston o.g.
24	25	IL	H	Bangor	W 3-1	Hale 2, McAvoy / Craig
25	27	IL	A	Portadown	L 1-2	Shields / Morrison, Malcolmson
26	Jan 1	IL	H	Glenavon	W 1-0	Patterson /
27	8	IL	A	Distillery	W 4-1	McAvoy 4 / Watson
28	15	IL	H	Cliftonville	W 8-1	Humphries, Shields, McAvoy 4, Mowat, Hale / Clarke
29	22	IL	A	Linfield	D 1-1	Henderson (pen) / Larmour
30	29	IL	H	Ballymena Utd.	W 1-0	Hale /
31	Feb 5	IC[1]	A	Bangor	W 1-0	Mowat /
32	12	IL	H	Distillery	L 2-4	McAvoy 2 / Donnelly, Malone 2, Savage
33	19	IL	A	Derry City	W 4-0	McAvoy, Humphries, Shields, Munn /
34	26	IC[2]	A	Crusaders	D 1-1	Patterson / Calder
35	Mar 1	IC[2R]	H	Crusaders	W 3-0	McAvoy 2 (1 pen), McCoy /
36	4	IL	H	Glentoran	W 2-0	Munn, Mowat /
37	11	IL	A	Bangor	W 4-2	McAvoy 2 (1 pen), McManus o.g., Patterson / Dornan, Mulgrew
38	18	IC[SF]	N[2]	Coleraine	D 1-1	Mowat / Curley
39	22	IC[SFR]	N[2]	Coleraine	L 0-1	/ Jennings

40	25	IL	H	Portadown	W 4-3	Patterson, Crothers, McAvoy, Humphries / B. Morrison 2, R. Morrison
41	Apr 1	IL	A	Crusaders	L 0-4	/ McQuillan 3, Calder
42	4	IL	H	Coleraine	W 4-2	Munn, McAvoy 2, Humphries / Curley 2
43	8	GC^2	A	Glenavon	W 5-0	Humphries, McAvoy 3, Johnston /
44	12	Cas^2	H	Glentoran	W 1-0	Humphries /
45	15	IL	A	Glenavon	D 2-2	McAvoy 2 / Boyd 2
46	17	IL	A	Ballymena Utd.	D 1-1	McAvoy / Weatherup 2
47	29	Cas^{SF}	A	Ballymena Utd.	W 2-0	Graham, McAvoy /
48	May 3	Cas^{SF}	H	Ballymena Utd.	D 1-1	Crothers / Frickleton
49	8	Cas^F	H	Crusaders	W 3-0	McCoy, McCaughtry, Patterson /
50	11	Cas^F	A	Crusaders	L 0-3*	/ Finney, McQuillan, Beckett
51	15	GC^{SF}	N	Distillery	W 4-1	Mowat, Crothers, Rafferty o.g., Patterson / Malone
52	19	GC^{F1}	N^3	Portadown	D 0-0	
53	24	GC^{FR}	N^3	Portadown	L 1-2	McAvoy / Fleming, McGowan

* = won on penalties 5-4

N = Oval

N^2 = Windsor Park

N^3 = Mourneview Park

Final positions, season 1972-73

League: 2nd	P 22	W 13	D 5	L 4	F 49	A 22	pts 31
City Cup: 4th	P 5	W 2	D 0	L 3	F 8	A 8	pts 4
Ulster Cup: 7th	P 11	W 6	D 0	L 5	F 28	A 21	pts 12

	Date	Comp.	Venue	Opponents	Result	Goalscorers
1	Aug 8	CaC^2	A	Ballymena Utd.	W 6-0	Johnston 2, Peacock, Mowat, Humphries 2 /
2	11	CaC^{SF}	H	Bangor	W 4-1	McAvoy 3 (2 pens), Peacock / Matchett
3	16	CaC^F	N	Portadown	L 0-3	/ Fleming, Anderson 2
4	19	UC	H	Derry City	W 5-0	Humphries, Patterson, McAvoy 3 /
5	23	UC	A	Linfield	W 4-2	McAvoy 3, McCaughtry / Prenter 2
6	26	UC	H	Glenavon	W 4-1	Humphries, Graham, McAvoy 2 / Morrison
7	31	UC	H	Ballymena Utd.	W 5-1	McAvoy 2, Humphries 2, Lowry / Davidson
8	Sept 2	UC	A	Bangor	L 2-3	McAvoy 2 (2 pens) / Madden, Mulgrew, Bailie
9	9	UC	A	Coleraine	L 1-4	Humphries / Dickson 2, McLernon, Curley
10	16	UC	H	Distillery	L 0-1	/ Malone
11	23	UC	A	Portadown	L 1-3	McCaughtry / McAuley 2, Anderson
12	30	UC	H	Cliftonville	W 2-1	McAvoy 2 / Peacock
13	Oct 7	UC	H	Glentoran	W 2-1	Shields 2 / Hall
14	14	UC	A	Crusaders	L 2-4	Mowat, McAvoy / Finney, Fullerton 2, McQuillan
15	21	CC	H	Portadown	L 2-3	McCoy, McAvoy (pen) / Morrison 2, Strain
16	28	CC	A	Distillery	W 3-0	White o.g., Patton, Patterson (pen) /
17	Nov 4	CC	H	Glentoran	L 0-2	/ Kirk, Dickinson

18	11	CC	A	Glenavon	L 0-2	/ Boyle, Morrison
19	18	CC	H	Bangor	W 3-1	Humphries, McAvoy, Guy / O'Halloran
20	25	IL	A	Larne	W 2-0	McAvoy, Guy /
21	Dec 2	IL	H	Crusaders	W 5-2	McCoy, McAvoy 2, Guy 2 / Finney, Fullerton
22	9	IL	A	Ballymena Utd.	W 2-0	Munn, McAvoy /
23	16	IL	H	Glenavon	L 1-3	Guy / Boyle 2, Alexander
24	23	IL	H	Coleraine	D 1-1	McAvoy / Murray
25	25	IL	A	Bangor	D 1-1	Humphries / Larmour
26	30	IL	H	Distillery	D 1-1	Humphries / Watson
27	Jan 6	IL	A	Portadown	D 1-1	McAvoy / McAuley
28	13	IL	H	Glentoran	L 2-3	McAvoy 2 / Anderson, Hall, Feeney (pen)
29	27	IL	H	Cliftonville	W 7-0	Humphries 3, Guy 2, McAvoy, Henderson (pen) /
30	Feb 3	IL	H	Portadown	W 4-0	McAvoy 2, Guy, Humphries /
31	10	IC[1]	A	Crusaders	L 1-3	McAvoy / McKenzie, McPolin, Fullerton
32	24	IL	H	Bangor	W 3-1	Whiteside o.g., Patterson, Guy / Bailie
33	28	Cas[1]	A	Linfield Swifts	W 1-0	Humphries /
34	Mar 10	IL	A	Coleraine	W 1-0	McAvoy /
35	17	IL	A	Glenavon	W 2-1	Guy 2 / Alexander
36	27	Cas[2]	H	Linfield	L 0-1	/ Millen
37	31	IL	H	Ballymena Utd.	W 3-1	Torrington o.g., McCoy, Mowat / Young
38	Apr 4	IL	A	Linfield	L 2-4	McAvoy 2 / Magee, Malone, McAllister,Cochrane
39	7	IL	A	Crusaders	L 1-2	Patterson / Finney, McQuillan
40	12	IL	H	Larne	W 2-0	Patton, Warren /
41	14	IL	A	Glentoran	W 1-0	McAvoy /
42	19	IL	H	Linfield	D 1-1	Guy / Malone
43	21	IL	A	Cliftonville	W 4-0	Guy 2, McAvoy, Bowden o.g. /
44	24	IL	A	Distillery	W 2-0	McAvoy, Guy /
45	May 9	GC[1]	H	Coleraine	W 2-0	McAvoy, Guy /
46	15	GC[2]	A	Cliftonville	D 2-2	McAvoy, Bowden o.g. / Hanna, Cairns
47	17	GC[2R]	H	Cliftonville	W 3-2	Guy 2, McAvoy / Clark, Hanna
48	22	GC[SF]	N[2]	Linfield	L 1-3	McAvoy / Millen 2, McAllister

N = Windsor Park
N[2] = Oval

Final positions, season 1973-74

League: 8th	P 22	W 9	D 4	L 9	F 42	A 37	pts 22
City Cup: 5th	P 5	W 1	D 2	L 2	F 15	A 16	pts 4
Ulster Cup: 1st	P 11	W 9	D 1	L 1	F 37	A 11	pts 19

	Date	Comp.	Venue	Opponents	Result	Goalscorers
1	Aug 4	CaC[1]	H	Ballymena Utd.	W 5-0	Guy 2, McAvoy 2, McAteer /
2	8	CaC[2]	H	Glentoran	W 4-2	McAvoy 3, Patterson / Feeney 2 (1 pen)
3	11	CaC[SF]	H	Linfield	W 3-1	Cromie, Guy 2 / Malone
4	15	CaC[F]	N	Crusaders	L 0-3	/ McQuillan 2, Finney
5	18	UC	A	Larne	W 3-0	McAteer 3 /

6	23	UC	H	Linfield	W 2-0	McAvoy, McAteer /
7	25	UC	A	Glenavon	L 2-3	Guy, McAteer / Alexander 3
8	30	UC	A	Ballymena Utd.	W 4-3	McAvoy 2, Cathcart, Guy / Brown, Todd 2
9	Sept 1	UC	H	Bangor	W 3-2	Mowat, McAteer 2 (1 pen) / Cromie o.g., Reid
10	8	UC	H	Coleraine	W 6-0	Guy, McAteer, McAvoy 2 (1 pen), Humphries, Cathcart /
11	12	UEFA	H	Standard Liege	W 3-2	Cathcart, McAvoy (pen), McAteer (pen) / Bukal 2
12	15	UC	A	Distillery	W 2-1	McAteer 2 / Welsh
13	19	UEFA	A	Standard Liege	L 1-6	Guy / Bukal 4, Gerets 2
14	22	UC	H	Portadown	W 4-1	McAvoy, Guy 2 (1 pen), McAteer / Sloan
15	25	GC[2]	A	Cliftonville	W 6-1	McAvoy 3, McAteer 2, Guy / Cairns
16	29	UC	A	Cliftonville	W 8-0	Guy 3, McAvoy 2, Cathcart 2, Mowat /
17	Oct 6	UC	A	Glentoran	W 2-0	McAvoy, Cathcart /
18	9	GC[SF]	A	Glentoran	W[P] 1-1	McCullough o.g. / Stewart
19	13	UC	H	Crusaders	D 1-1	Guy / Lennox
20	20	CC	A	Portadown	L 4-6	Cathcart, McAteer, Guy 2 / Fleming, Malone 4, Morrison (pen)
21	27	CC	H	Distillery	W 5-2	Cathcart, Guy 2, Mowat, McAteer / Savage, Hewitt
22	Nov 1	GC[F]	N[2]	Bangor	W 4-1	Guy 2, McAteer, Cathcart / Reid
23	3	CC	A	Linfield	L 1-3	Patton / Malone 2, Magee (pen)
24	10	CC	H	Glenavon	D 2-2	Guy, McAteer / Hill, O'Rourke
25	17	CC	A	Bangor	D 3-3	McAvoy, Guy (pen), Graham / Hume, Devine (pen), Reid
26	24	IL	H	Linfield	D 2-2	Guy, Cathcart / Brown, Magee
27	Dec 1	IL	A	Larne	D 2-2	McAvoy 2 / Davis, Rainey
28	8	IL	H	Glenavon	W 3-2	Cathcart, Guy, McAteer / Woods, Alexnder
29	15	IL	A	Crusaders	L 3-4	McAteer, Cathcart, Guy / McQuillan 2, Lennox, Hay
30	22	IL	A	Cliftonville	W 4-1	Guy, Patton, McAteer (pen), Humphries / Bowden
31	25	IL	H	Bangor	W 2-1	McAteer, Guy / Stewart
32	29	IL	H	Coleraine	D 2-2	Guy, Cathcart / Jennings, Murray
33	Jan 1	IL	A	Distillery	D 1-1	Graham / A. Welsh
34	5	IL	H	Portadown	L 0-1	/ Morrison
35	12	IL	A	Ballymena Utd.	L 0-1	/ Erwin
36	19	IL	A	Glentoran	L 0-1	/ Feeney
37	26	IL	H	Larne	W 4-3	Cathcart, Patterson, McAvoy 2 / Platt, Rainey, Baxter
38	Feb 2	IL	A	Glenavon	L 0-1	/ Sands
39	9	IC[1]	A	Ballyclare Com.	D 1-1	Humphries / McKenzie
40	14	IC[1R]	H	Ballyclare Com.	W 4-2	Mowat, Guy 3 / Higgins, D.J. McKenzie
41	23	IL	H	Cliftonville	W 4-1	Guy 2 (1 pen), Patterson, McAteer (pen) / Cairns
42	Mar 2	IC[2]	H	Bangor	W 4-2	McCullough o.g., McCoy, McAvoy, Guy / Stewart, Bailie
43	9	IL	A	Bangor	L 2-3	McAteer, Guy (pen) / Stewart 2, Whiteside
44	16	IL	H	Distillery	W 3-1	McAteer, Cathcart 2 / Scannell
45	23	IC[SF]	N[2]	Glenavon	W 4-2	McAvoy 2, Patterson, Guy / Hall 2
46	30	IL	A	Coleraine	L 0-1	/ R. Peacock
47	Apr 4	IL	H	Crusaders	L 3-4	Guy, Cathcart 2 / Flanagan, Hay 3
48	6	IL	A	Portadown	W 2-1	Guy 2 / Malone
49	9	BC[1]	H	Finn Harps	W 3-1	McAvoy 2, McAteer / Harkin

50	13	IL	H	Ballymena Utd.	W 1-0	McAvoy /
51	15	IL	H	Glentoran	W 3-0	McAteer 2 (1 pen), McAvoy /
52	20	IL	A	Linfield	L 1-4	Guy / Brown 2, Pogue 2
53	27	IC^F	N	Ballymena Utd.	W 2-1	Guy, McAvoy / Sloan
54	May 1	BC^2	A	Drogheda Utd.	W^P 3-3	Guy, McAteer, McAvoy / Trainor, Stevens 2
55	7	BC^F	N	Ballymena Utd.	W 3-1	Cathcart, McAteer, Patterson / Todd
56	13	Cas^1	H	Glentoran II	w-o	
57	15	Cas^2	A	Bangor Res.	W 3-1	Patterson, Whiteside o.g., Guy / McCoy o.g.
58	17	Cas^{SF}	A	Larne	L 1-2	Cathcart / Rainey, Nixon o.g.

W^P = won on penalties
N = Windsor Park
N^2 = Oval
w-o = walkover

Final positions, season 1974-75

League: 9th	P 22	W 7	D 3	L 12	F 28	A 43	pts 17	
City Cup: 3rd	P 5	W 2	D 0	L 3	F 10	A 9	pts 4	
Ulster Cup: 8th	P 11	W 4	D 2	L 5	F 17	A 22	pts 10	

	Date	Comp.	Venue	Opponents	Result	Goalscorers
1	Aug 17	UC	H	Larne	W 2-0	Hay, McAvoy /
2	21	UC	A	Linfield	D 2-2	Steenson 2 / Bell, Magee
3	26	UC	H	Ballymena Utd.	L 1-2	Guy / Barr, Kirk
4	31	UC	A	Bangor	L 1-4	McAvoy / Hume 2, Best o.g., Stewart
5	Sept 5	UC	H	Glenavon	W 2-1	McAvoy 2 / Hall
6	7	UC	A	Coleraine	L 0-5	/ Dickson, Simpson, Murray, Jackson, Jennings
7	12	GC^1	A	Coleraine	L 1-2	McAvoy / Tweed, Dickson
8	14	UC	H	Distillery	D 1-1	McAvoy / Nicholl
9	18	CWC^1	A	PSV Eindhoven	L 0-10	/ van der Kuylen 3, Lubse 3, Kemper, Deikders, Edstrom, van Kraaj
10	21	UC	A	Portadown	L 1-4	Guy / Malone 3, Morrison
11	28	UC	H	Cliftonville	W 4-1	Guy, Patterson 2, McAvoy / Largy
12	Oct 2	CWC^1	H	PSV Eindhoven	L 1-4	Guy / van der Kuylen, Edstrom, Dahlquist 2
13	5	UC	H	Glentoran	L 0-1	/ Jamieson
14	12	UC	A	Crusaders	W 3-1	Guy, McAvoy 2 / McQuillan
15	19	CC	H	Portadown	L 2-3	McAvoy 2 / Strain, Hutton, Murray
16	26	CC	A	Distillery	W 5-1	Cathcart, McAvoy 3, Patterson / A. Welsh
17	Nov 2	CC	H	Glentoran	L 0-2	/ Robson 2
18	9	CC	A	Glenavon	W 2-1	McAvoy 2 / Hall
19	16	CC	H	Bangor	L 1-2	Cathcart / Armstrong, Hutchinson
20	30	IL	A	Linfield	L 1-3	McAvoy / Patterson, Malone 2
21	Dec 7	IL	H	Portadown	D 1-1	Nixon / Bell
22	14	IL	A	Ballymena Utd.	W 2-1	Mowat, Hall / McFall
23	21	IL	H	Larne	L 1-4	McAvoy / Todd 2, Butcher, Rainey
24	25	IL	A	Bangor	D 1-1	Cathcart / Stewart

	Date	Comp.	Venue	Opponents	Result	Goalscorers
25	28	IL	H	Distillery	W 3-0	McAvoy 3 /
26	Jan 1	IL	A	Glentoran	L 0-4	/ Feeney 3, Robson
27	4	IL	H	Cliftonville	W 3-2	McAvoy 3 / Crozier, Hogg (pen)
28	11	IL	H	Glenavon	W 4-1	McAvoy 2 (1 pen), Hall, Cathcart / McVeigh
29	18	IL	A	Coleraine	L 0-2	/ Cochrane, Jennings
30	Feb 1	IL	H	Linfield	L 2-6	Cathcart 2 (1 pen) / Malone 4, Magee, Hunter
31	8	IC[1]	H	Cliftonville	D 0-0	
32	12	IC[1R]	A	Cliftonville	L 2-3	Hall, Humphries / Stevenson, McCurdy, Lavery
33	15	IL	A	Portadown	L 1-2	McAvoy / Strain, Malcolmson
34	22	IL	H	Ballymena Utd.	D 0-0	
35	Mar 1	IL	A	Crusaders	W 3-1	Cathcart, McAvoy 2 / McQuillan
36	8	IL	A	Larne	L 0-4	/ Platt 3 (1 pen), Collins
37	15	IL	H	Bangor	W 1-0	McAvoy /
38	22	IL	H	Crusaders	L 0-1	/ McAteer
39	29	IL	A*	Distillery	L 0-2	/ Hewitt, McMinn
40	31	IL	H	Glentoran	L 1-2	D.J.Graham / Feeney 2
41	Apr 5	IL	A	Cliftonville	W 2-0	Graham, McAvoy /
42	12	IL	A	Glenavon	L 1-3	Hall / Horne 2, Alexander
43	26	IL	H	Coleraine	L 1-3	McAvoy / M. Guy 2, Murray
44	29	Cas[1]	H	Lisburn Rangers	W 5-1	McAvoy 4, Cathcart / Neill
45	May 5	Cas[2]	A	Bangor	L 2-4	McAvoy 2 (1 pen) / Hutchinson, Armstrong, Whiteside, Hume

A* = at Solitude

Final positions, season 1975-76

League: 7th	P 22	W 7	D 5	L 10	F 32	A 43	pts 19
City Cup: 3rd	P 5	W 2	D 2	L 1	F 13	A 8	pts 6
Ulster Cup: 9th	P 11	W 3	D 3	L 5	F 15	A 18	pts 9

	Date	Comp.	Venue	Opponents	Result	Goalscorers
1	Aug 16	UC	A	Larne	D 3-3	Hall, McAvoy 2 (1 pen) / Sloan, Rainey, Turner
2	21	UC	H	Linfield	L 0-1	/ M. Malone
3	23	UC	A	Glenavon	D 2-2	McAvoy, Larmour / Paul 2
4	28	UC	A	Ballymena Utd.	W 1-0	McAvoy /
5	30	UC	H	Bangor	L 0-1	/ Armstrong
6	Sept 6	UC	H	Coleraine	L 0-3	/ Moffett 2, Murray
7	11	GC[1]	H	Coleraine	L 1-3	Johnston / Guy, Moffett, Dickson
8	13	UC	A	Distillery	W 2-0	McAvoy, McMullan /
9	20	UC	H	Portadown	L 1-2	Humphries / Blackledge, Watson
10	27	UC	A	Cliftonville	L 2-3	Keyes, Flanagan / Fleming 2, McConnell
11	Oct 4	UC	A	Glentoran	D 2-2	Larmour, McCormick / Moreland, Dickinson
12	11	UC	H	Crusaders	W 2-1	McAvoy, Polly / Hay
13	18	CC	A	Linfield	L 0-1	/ Hunter
14	25	CC	H	Distillery	D 1-1	Ferguson / Jess (pen)

15	Nov 1	CC	A	Portadown	W 4-3	Watson 2, McAvoy, Mowat / Murray, Watson, Kingon
16	8	CC	A	Bangor	D 3-3	Ferguson, McAvoy, Larmour / Bailie, Hall, Hume (pen)
17	15	CC	H	Glenavon	W 5-0	McAvoy 3 (1 pen), Flanagan, McCoy /
18	22	IL	A	Distillery	W 2-0	McAvoy 2 /
19	29	IL	H	Ballymena Utd.	D 1-1	Armstrong / Averall
20	Dec 6	IL	A	Portadown	L 2-3	McAvoy, Armstrong / Murtagh 2, Clery
21	13	IL	H	Cliftonville	W 4-3	McAvoy 4 / Platt, Quinn
22	20	IL	A	Linfield	L 0-3	/ Malone, Graham, McCurdy
23	25	IL	H	Bangor	L 1-2	Feeney o.g. / Clarke, Jamison
24	27	IL	A	Crusaders	D 1-1	McAvoy / Lennox
25	Jan 1	IL	H	Glentoran	L 0-3	/ Feeney (pen), Craig, Caskey
26	3	IL	A	Glenavon	W 3-1	McGuicken, McAvoy 2 / Harvey
27	10	IL	H	Coleraine	W 3-1	McAvoy 3 / Guy
28	17	IL	A	Larne	L 0-3	/ Todd, Graham, Sloan
29	24	IL	H	Distillery	L 1-2	Flanagan / Kane 2
30	31	IC[1]	H	Dundela	W 1-0	Armstrong /
31	Feb 7	IL	A	Ballymena Utd.	W 1-0	McAvoy /
32	14	IL	H	Portadown	L 2-4	McAvoy, Mowat / Watson 2, Murray, Cleary
33	21	IC[2]	H	Linfield	D 1-1	McAvoy / Bell
34	25	IC[2R]	A	Linfield	L 1-7	Armstrong / Lemon, McCurdy 2, McKee, Malone 2, Magee
35	28	IL	A	Cliftonville	D 2-2	McArdle, McCoy (pen) / Platt, Patterson
36	Mar 6	IL	H	Linfield	L 1-3	Nixon / Malone, Bell 2
37	20	IL	A	Bangor	D 0-0	
38	27	IL	H	Crusaders	L 0-3	/ McDonald, McAteer 2
39	Apr 3	IL	A	Glentoran	W 3-2	Armstrong, Ferguson, McAvoy / Caskey, Moreland
40	15	Cas[1]	A	Linfield Swifts	W 4-0	McAvoy 2, Armstrong, Woods /
41	17	IL	H	Glenavon	D 2-2	Armstrong 2 / Horner, McDonald
42	19	IL	A	Coleraine	L 0-3	/ Cochrane, Dickson, Guy (pen)
43	24	IL	H	Larne	W 3-1	Ferguson, Mullan, Nixon (pen) / Hunter
44	29	Cas[2]	A	Distillery	L 0-1	/ Kane

Final positions, season 1976-77

League: 7th   P 22   W 10 D 1   L 11   F 34   A 39   pts 21
Ulster Cup: 8th P 11   W 3   D 2   L 6   F 15   A 26   pts 8
Gold Cup: 5th   P 5   W 0   D 3   L 2   F 5   A 10   pts 3

	Date	Comp.	Venue	Opponents	Result	Goalscorers
1	Aug 21	UC	H	Ballymena Utd.	W 3-1	W. Kennedy, Flanagan, McAvoy / Martin
2	25	UC	A	Bangor	L 3-5	Armstrong, McAvoy 2 / Davidson, Gordon, Jamieson, Cranston, Maguire
3	28	UC	H	Crusaders	W 3-2	McAvoy, Cathcart, Flanagan / Cooke, McCann
4	Sept 1	UC	H	Glentoran	W 1-0	Gallagher /

5	4	UC	A	Larne	D 1-1	Armstrong / Thompson
6	8	UC	H	Portadown	L 1-2	McAvoy / Lunn, Blackledge
7	11	UC	H	Distillery	L 0-2	/ Higgins 2
8	18	UC	A	Coleraine	L 0-3	/ Cochrane 2, Moffett
9	25	UC	A	Glenavon	D 3-3	Armstrong, McAvoy 2 / Neill, McDonald, Malone
10	Oct 2	UC	H	Linfield	L 0-3	/ M. Malone 2, McKee
11	9	UC	A	Cliftonville	L 0-4	/ Platt 4
12	16	GC	H	Glentoran	L 1-3	McAvoy / Robson, Feeney (pen), Caskey
13	30	GC	H	Portadown	D 1-1	McAvoy / Blackledge
14	Nov 6	GC	H	Bangor	D 2-2	McAvoy 2 / Hume, Jamison
15	17	GC	A	Distillery	L 0-3	/ Patterson, McMinn, Higgins
16	20	IL	H	Distillery	W 1-0	Graham /
17	22	GC	A	Glenavon	D 1-1	McAvoy / McDonald
18	27	IL	A	Ballymena Utd.	L 0-1	/ Kingon
19	Dec 4	IL	H	Portadown	W 2-1	McCoy (pen), Graham / Blackledge
20	18	IL	H	Linfield	W 3-1	Todd, W. Kennedy, McAvoy / Garrett
21	25	IL	A	Bangor	W 2-0	McAvoy, McArdle /
22	27	IL	H	Crusaders	W 2-1	McCoy (pen), W. Kennedy / McPolin
23	30	IL	A	Cliftonville	W 1-0	Todd /
24	Jan 1	IL	A	Glentoran	L 0-3	/ Jamieson, Dickinson, Caskey
25	8	IL	H	Glenavon	L 2-3	Todd 2 / Smith, Harvey, Malone
26	15	IL	A	Larne	L 0-2	/ Rainey, McClenaghan (pen)
27	22	IL	H	Coleraine	W 4-2	Todd, Armstrong, Flanagan, Butcher o.g. / Dickson, Guy
28	29	IL	A	Distillery	D 0-0	
29	Feb 5	IC[1]	A	Bangor	D 0-0	
30	9	IC[1R]	H	Bangor	D 0-0	
31	12	IL	H	Ballymena Utd.	W 2-0	Armstrong, W .Kennedy /
32	16	IC[1RR]	N	Bangor	W 3-1	McAvoy 2, Armstrong / Davidson
33	19	IL	A	Portadown	L 2-3	McAvoy, Armstrong / Lunn, Murray, Penny
34	26	IC[2]	H	Linfield	L 0-6	/ Martin, Bell 3, Nixon, Lemon
35	Mar 5	IL	H	Cliftonville	W 2-1	Graham, Larmour / Platt
36	12	IL	A	Linfield	L 1-3	Rafferty o.g. / Hamilton, Nixon, Martin
37	26	IL	H	Bangor	W 3-2	Armstrong 2, McArdle / Stewart, Hume
38	Apr 2	IL	A	Crusaders	L 3-4	Mowat, McArdle, Rollins / Hanvey 2, Kirby, Gillespie
39	9	IL	H	Glentoran	L 0-1	/ McVeigh
40	11	IL	A	Glenavon	L 1-4	Keyes / Neill 3, McDonald
41	16	IL	H	Larne	L 3-5	Todd, Armstrong 2 / McGarrity, 3, Sloan, McCurdy
42	30	IL	A	Coleraine	L 0-2	/ Dickson 2
43	May 3	Cas[1]	A	Larne	L 0-1	/ McCurdy

Final positions, season 1977-78

League: 7th	P 22	W 9	D 3	L 10	F 38	A 41	pts 21
Ulster Cup: 8th	P 11	W 4	D 3	L 4	F 14	A 16	pts 11
Gold Cup: 6th	P 5	W 0	D 3	L 2	F 6	A 9	pts 3

	Date	Comp.	Venue	Opponents	Result	Goalscorers
1	Aug 20	UC	A	Crusaders	L 0-3	/ Swann, Boyle, Strain (pen)
2	23	UC	H	Ballymena Utd.	D 3-3	Welsh, Houston, Armstrong / Brown 2, Malcolmson
3	27	UC	H	Distillery	L 1-2	McCoy / Higgins, Jess (pen)
4	31	UC	A	Glenavon	W 3-2	Welsh 2, Armstrong / Neill, McDonald
5	Sept 3	UC	H	Larne	L 0-1	/ Bowden
6	10	UC	A	Linfield	L 0-2	/ Hamilton, Martin
7	17	UC	H	Coleraine	D 2-2	Allen, Armstrong / Dickson 2
8	26	UC	A	Bangor	W 2-0	Armstrong 2 /
9	Oct 1	UC	H	Portadown	D 1-1	Armstrong / Campbell
10	8	UC	A	Cliftonville	W 1-0	McCoy (pen) /
11	15	UC	H	Glentoran	W 1-0	McCoy (pen) /
12	22	GC	H	Glenavon	L 1-2	Armstrong / P. Malone, McQuiston
13	29	GC	A	Bangor	D 3-3	Allen, Welsh, Mowat / Cromie o.g., Davidson, Hall
14	Nov 5	GC	A	Distillery	L 0-2	/ Higgins, Kane
15	12	GC	H	Portadown	D 1-1	Tom Kennedy / Blackledge
16	19	GC	A	Linfield	D 1-1	Armstrong / Martin
17	26	IL	A	Distillery	D 2-2	Allen, Houston / McMinn, Jess (pen)
18	Dec 3	IL	H	Ballymena Utd.	W 2-1	Armstrong 2 / Brown
19	10	IL	A	Linfield	L 4-6	Allen, Cromie, Tom Kennedy, McCoy / Malone, Hayes, Walker o.g., Murray, McCoy o.g., Hamilton
20	17	IL	H	Cliftonville	L 1-2	Allen / Martin, Adair
21	24	IL	A	Portadown	L 1-3	McCoy (pen) / Blackledge, Lunn, Gardiner
22	26	IL	H	Bangor	L 0-2	/ McCoubrey, Crawford
23	31	IL	A	Crusaders	W 2-1	Armstrong 2 / Strain (pen)
24	Jan 2	IL	H	Glenavon	W 2-0	Larmour, Armstrong /
25	7	IL	A	Glentoran	L 2-4	Armstrong, Goodall / Walsh, Feeney 2, Moreland
26	14	IL	H	Larne	W 1-0	Houston /
27	21	IL	A	Coleraine	L 0-2	/ Brown, Guy
28	28	IL	H	Distillery	L 1-2	Armstrong / Coulter, Higgins
29	Feb 4	IC[1]	H	Dungannon Sw.	W 5-2	Armstrong 3, Mowat, Allen / Mowat o.g., Morrison
30	11	IL	A	Ballymena Utd.	W 3-1	Armstrong 3 / Sloan
31	18	IL	H	Linfield	L 0-1	/ Hewitt (pen)
32	25	IC[2]	A	Ballymena Utd.	L 0-1	/ McAvoy
33	Mar 4	IL	A	Cliftonville	D 1-1	W. Kennedy / Hewitt
34	11	IL	H	Portadown	W 3-2	Houston, W. Kennedy, Armstrong / Blackledge, Lavery
35	25	IL	A	Bangor	W 2-1	Welsh 2 / Kirk
36	27	IL	H	Crusaders	W 3-1	Armstrong 3 (1 pen) / Barrett
37	Apr 1	IL	A	Glenavon	L 2-5	Armstrong 2 (1 pen) / McDonald 2, Campbell, McQuiston 2
38	8	IL	H	Glentoran	D 1-1	Armstrong / Feeney
39	15	IL	A	Larne	L 1-3	Armstrong / Devine, Sloan, Donaghy
40	22	IL	H	Coleraine	W 3-0	Armstrong 3 /
41	May 1	Cas[1]	A	Crusaders	L 1-4	Armstrong / Barrett 2, McAteer 2

Final positions, season 1978-79

League: 3rd   P 22   W 11   D 5   L 6   F 47   A 34   pts 27
Ulster Cup: 11th   P 11   W 0   D 7   L 4   F 13   A 18   pts 7
Gold Cup: 4th   P 5   W 1   D 1   L 3   F 8   A 14   pts 3

	Date	Comp.	Venue	Opponents	Result	Goalscorers
1	Aug 19	UC	H	Crusaders	D 2-2	Armstrong, Trevor Kennedy / Lennox, Gillespie
2	23	UC	A	Ballymena Utd.	L 1-2	Gibson / McLean, Jackson
3	26	UC	A	Distillery	D 1-1	Trevor Kennedy / Palnoch
4	30	UC	H	Glenavon	D 1-1	Falloon / McCoy o.g.
5	Sept 2	UC	A	Larne	D 2-2	Keyes 2 / Hunter, Sloan
6	9	UC	H	Linfield	L 2-4	Mowat, Armstrong / Martin, Murray 2 (1 pen), Dornan
7	16	UC	A	Coleraine	D 2-2	Gibson, Armstrong / Dickson 2
8	23	UC	H	Bangor	L 0-1	/ McAuley
9	30	UC	A	Portadown	L 1-2	Allen / Lavery (pen), Blackledge
10	Oct 7	UC	H	Cliftonville	D 0-0	
11	14	UC	A	Glentoran	D 1-1	W. Kennedy / Martin
12	21	GC	H	Bangor	W 2-1	Mowat, Armstrong (pen) / Malone
13	28	GC	A	Glenavon	L 2-3	Armstrong, Tom Kennedy / P. Malone 2, McDonald
14	Nov 4	GC	A	Portadown	L 1-2	W. Kennedy / Campbell, Magee
15	11	GC	H	Distillery	D 2-2	Walker, Greer / Brown (pen), McDonald
16	18	GC	H	Linfield	L 1-6	Tom Kennedy / Murray, Mawhinney, Kirk, Dornan, Jamison, Feeney
17	25	IL	H	Glentoran	D 4-4	Welsh 2, W. Kennedy, Armstrong / Cranston, Martin 2, Beattie
18	Dec 2	IL	A	Linfield	W 2-1	Reid 2 / Feeney
19	9	IL	H	Portadown	W 3-0	Reid 3 (1 pen) /
20	16	IL	A	Larne	D 3-3	Greer, Reid, Welsh / O'Kane, Quinn 2
21	23	IL	H	Cliftonville	W 3-2	Patterson 2, Tom Kennedy / Adair, Quinn
22	26	IL	A	Bangor	W 5-2	Patterson 3, Mowat, McCoy / Collins, McCoubrey
23	30	IL	H	Distillery	W 2-0	Ferris o.g., McCoy (pen) /
24	Jan 24	IL	H	Coleraine	D 2-2	Patterson, Walker / Mahon 2
25	30	IL	A	Glenavon	L 1-3	Rodgers / Sheppard, Halliday, P. Malone
26	Feb 3	IC[1]	H	Portadown	L 1-3	Patterson / Campbell, Lavery, Magee
27	10	IL	A	Glentoran	L 0-1	/ Porter
28	17	IL	H	Linfield	L 0-2	/ Koch, Murray
29	21	IL	H	Crusaders	W 3-2	W. Kennedy 2, Maxwell / Barrett, Strain (pen)
30	24	IL	A	Crusaders	L 0-1	/ McKenzie
31	Mar 3	IL	A	Portadown	D 0-0	
32	10	IL	H	Larne	W 3-2	Reid 3 / Graham, McManus (pen)
33	17	IL	A	Ballymena Utd.	W 3-1	Reid, Patterson, Cromie / McQuiston
34	24	IL	A	Cliftonville	L 1-2	Patterson / Platt, McCurry
35	31	IL	H	Bangor	L 1-2	Reid (pen) / Barrett, Dickinson
36	Apr 7	IL	A	Distillery	W 3-0	Maxwell, Patterson, Reid /

37	14	IL	H	Glenavon	W 3-0	Mowat, Patterson, Maxwell /
38	16	IL	A	Coleraine	W 2-1	Reid 2 (1 pen) / Stewart
39	21	IL	H	Ballymena Utd.	D 3-3	Patterson 2, Maxwell / Gibson o.g., McQuiston, Sloan
40	26	Cas[1]	A	Glentoran	W 4-0	Patterson 2, Welsh, Maxwell /
41	May 5	Cas[2]	H	Linfield	W 3-0	Gibson, Patterson, Reid /
42	9	Cas[SF]	A	Cliftonville	L 2-3	Morgan, Walker / Bell 2, McCusker

Final positions, season 1979-80

League: 11th	P 22	W 4	D 5	L 13	F 26	A 39	pts 13
Ulster Cup: 10th	P 11	W 3	D 1	L 7	F 17	A 26	pts 7
Gold Cup: 5th	P 5	W 1	D 2	L 2	F 10	A 16	pts 4

	Date	Comp.	Venue	Opponents	Result	Goalscorers
1	Aug 3	AIC[1]	A	Waterford	W 3-1	Patterson, Mowat, Reid / Keane
2	8	AIC[2]	H	Drogheda Utd.	L 1-3	Reid / Leech 2, Connelly
3	18	UC	H	Glenavon	L 2-3	Patterson, Mowat / Armstrong, Davey 2 (1 pen)
4	21	UC	A	Linfield	L 2-6	Gibson, Kirk / Feeney 2, McCurdy 2, Garrett, Rafferty
5	25	UC	H	Crusaders	L 1-2	Welsh / Graham, Malone
6	28	UC	A	Coleraine	W 3-1	Patterson, Kirk, Reid / Moffett
7	Sept 1	UC	H	Ballymena Utd.	L 0-1	/ P. Malone
8	8	UC	A	Bangor	D 2-2	Reid, Maxwell / McCoubrey (pen), McLoughlin
9	15	UC	H	Portadown	W 3-2	Kirk, Welsh, Gibson / Alexander, Kilburn
10	22	UC	A	Glentoran	L 0-1	/ Martin
11	29	UC	H	Distillery	L 0-2	/ McMinn 2 (1 pen)
12	Oct 6	UC	A	Cliftonville	L 1-4	Patterson / Adair 2, McCurry, McCusker
13	13	UC	H	Larne	W 3-2	Welsh 2, Reid (pen) / McManus (pen), Prenter
14	20	GC	A	Linfield	L 0-7	/ Gibson o.g., Feeney 2, Murray, Dornan, McCurdy, Rafferty
15	27	GC	H	Distillery	W 4-1	McGreevy o.g., Welsh, Maxwell, Kirk / Greer
16	Nov 3	GC	H	Portadown	D 3-3	Kirk 2 (2 pens), Maxwell / Campbell, Gardiner, Kilburn
17	10	GC	A	Bangor	D 3-3	Martin 2, Gibson / McLoughlin 2, McCoubrey (pen)
18	17	GC	H	Glenavon	L 0-2	/ Higgins, Armstrong
19	24	IL	A	Glenavon	D 2-2	Cullen (pen), Maxwell / Quinn, Davey
20	Dec 1	IL	H	Linfield	D 1-1	Cullen (pen) / Rafferty
21	8	IL	A	Crusaders	L 0-2	/ King, Rice
22	22	IL	A	Ballymena Utd.	L 0-2	/ McQuiston 2
23	26	IL	H	Bangor	D 1-1	Gibson / McLoughlin
24	29	IL	A	Portadown	L 0-3	/ Graham 2, Campbell
25	Jan 1	IL	H	Glentoran	L 1-3	Martin / Blackledge, McCreery 2
26	5	IL	A	Distillery	D 1-1	Martin / Kerr
27	12	IL	H	Cliftonville	L 0-2	/ Adair 2
28	16	IL	H	Coleraine	W 4-1	Cullen 2 (1 pen), Martin 2 / Beckett (pen)

29	19	IL	A	Larne	W 3-0	Maxwell, Hewitt (pen), Gibson /
30	26	IL	H	Glenavon	W 3-0	Foster, Martin, Cullen (pen) /
31	Feb 2	IC[1]	H	RUC	L 0-4	/ Bell 3, McCartney
32	9	IL	A	Linfield	L 0-1	/ Rafferty
33	16	IL	H	Crusaders	L 2-5	Foster, Hewitt (pen) / Byrne, Kennedy, King 2, Gillespie (pen)
34	Mar 1	IL	A	Coleraine	L 0-2	/ Dickson, Platt
35	8	IL	H	Ballymena Utd.	L 1-3	Hewitt (pen) / Breen, McQuiston, Malone
36	15	IL	A	Bangor	L 2-3	Martin, Hall / Reid, McCoubrey 2
37	29	IL	H	Portadown	W 4-1	Martin 2, Maxwell 2 / Bell
38	Apr 5	IL	A	Glentoran	L 0-2	/ Blackledge 2
39	7	IL	H	Distillery	L 0-1	/ McIlhenney
40	12	IL	A	Cliftonville	L 0-2	/ McAteer, Alexander
41	19	IL	H	Larne	D 1-1	Cullen (pen) / Adair
42	30	Cas[1]	H	Linfield Swifts	L 2-4	Walker 2 / Murray 2, Garrett 2

Final positions, season 1980-81

League: 5th	P 22	W 9	D 6	L 7	F 35	A 40	pts 24
Ulster Cup: 12th	P 11	W 1	D 3	L 7	F 10	A 23	pts 5
Gold Cup: 5th	P 5	W 1	D 0	L 4	F 2	A 12	pts 2

	Date	Comp.	Venue	Opponents	Result	Goalscorers
1	Aug 16	UC	A	Glenavon	L 2-3	Hewitt 2 / Lemon (pen), Armstrong, Dennison
2	19	UC	H	Linfield	L 0-4	/ Murray, McCurdy 3
3	23	UC	A	Crusaders	L 0-2	/ King 2
4	27	UC	H	Coleraine	W 2-0	Maxwell, Hewitt /
5	30	UC	A	Ballymena Utd.	D 2-2	McCoubrey, Campbell / McQuiston, Malone
6	Sept 6	UC	H	Bangor	D 2-2	McCoubrey, Martin / Campbell o.g., Lennox
7	13	UC	A	Portadown	L 0-4	/ Sloan, Ball 2 (1 pen), Gardiner
8	20	UC	H	Glentoran	L 1-2	Hewitt / Blackledge 2
9	27	UC	A	Distillery	L 0-1	/ Coulter
10	Oct 4	UC	H	Cliftonville	D 1-1	McCoubrey / Alexander
11	11	UC	A	Larne	L 0-2	/ Bryson, Carland
12	18	GC	H	Linfield	L 0-4	/ McCurdy 2, McKee, McKeown
13	25	GC	H	Distillery	W 2-1	Connor, Campbell / McClurg
14	Nov 1	GC	A	Portadown	L 0-3	/ Gracey, Graham, Gardiner
15	8	GC	H	Bangor	L 0-2	/ Millar, Duddy
16	15	GC	A	Glenavon	L 0-2	/ Malone, Tully (pen)
17	22	IL	H	Glenavon	D 2-2	Campbell, Martin / Mawhinney, O'Kane
18	29	IL	A	Linfield	L 0-5	/ Feeney 2, McKee 2, Murray (pen)
19	Dec 6	IL	H	Crusaders	W 2-0	Connor, Hewitt (pen) /
20	13	IL	A	Coleraine	W 1-0	Hewitt /
21	20	IL	H	Ballymena Utd.	L 0-1	/ McCusker
22	25	IL	A	Bangor	W 4-3	Armstrong, Campbell 3 / Dickinson, Allen, McBride
23	27	IL	H	Portadown	W 2-0	Campbell, Gibson /

24	Jan 1	IL	A	Glentoran	L 3-4	Connor, Martin, Campbell / Blackledge, Cleary 2 (1 pen), Porter
25	3	IL	H	Distillery	W 2-0	Mowat, Connor /
26	10	IL	A	Cliftonville	L 0-3	/ Platt 2, Holden
27	17	IL	H	Larne	W 2-0	Campbell, Gilchrist /
28	24	IL	A	Glenavon	D 1-1	McCoubrey / Armstrong
29	31	IC[1]	H	Ballyclare Com.	W 3-0	Connor 2, Robson /
30	Feb 7	IL	H	Linfield	D 1-1	Martin / McKee
31	14	IL	A	Crusaders	L 2-8	Gibson, Martin / Gillespie, Rice, King 3, Mulhall 3
32	21	IC[2]	H	Glentoran	L 1-3	Campbell / Jamieson, Blackledge 2
33	28	IL	H	Coleraine	W 4-2	Armstrong, Martin, Connor, Gilchrist / Brammeld, Healey
34	Mar 7	IL	A	Ballymena Utd.	L 2-3	Gilchrist, Campbell (pen) / McCusker, McQuiston, Fox
35	14	IL	H	Bangor	D 2-2	Robson, McCoubrey / Milburn, Walker
36	28	IL	A	Portadown	L 0-3	/ Gardiner 3
37	Apr 4	IL	H	Glentoran	D 1-1	Maxwell / Blackledge
38	11	IL	A	Distillery	W 2-1	Welsh 2 / Hewitt
39	14	Cas[1]	H	Distillery	W 4-1	Galway, Connor, Martin, Campbell (pen) / Cummings
40	18	IL	H	Cliftonville	D 0-0	
41	20	IL	A	Larne	W 2-0	Campbell 2 /
42	23	Cas[2]	A	Cliftonville	W 1-0	Welsh /
43	30	Cas[SF]	H	Linfield	L 1-4	Martin / McGaughey 3, Gordon

Final positions, season 1981-82

League: 10th	P 22	W 5	D 4	L 13	F 18	A 47 pts 14
Ulster Cup: 8th	P 11	W 3	D 3	L 5	F18	A21 pts.9
Gold Cup: 5th	P 6	W 1	D 0	L 4	F 4	A 10 pts 2

	Date	Comp.	Venue	Opponents	Result	Goalscorers
1	Aug 15	UC	A	Bangor	D 0-0	
2	18	UC	H	Portadown	D 2-2	Welsh 2 / Topley, Gardiner
3	22	UC	A	Linfield	D 3-3	Foster, Cullen 2 / Mowat o.g., Garrett, McGaughey
4	26	UC	H	Distillery	W 5-2	Cullen 4 (2 pens), Foster / Beck, McDowell
5	29	UC	A	Ballymena Utd.	W 2-1	Welsh, Cullen (pen) / Neill
6	Sept 5	UC	H	Crusaders	L 0-1	/ Feeney
7	12	UC	H	Glenavon	L 1-2	Cullen (pen) / Denver, Clarke
8	19	UC	A	Glentoran	L 0-2	/ Robson o.g., Cleary
9	26	UC	H	Cliftonville	L 1-3	Connor / Higgins, McCurry, Galway o.g.
10	Oct 3	UC	A	Coleraine	L 2-4	Maxwell, Campbell / Dickson 2, Brammeld, Mullan
11	10	UC	H	Larne	W 2-1	Robson, Cowden / Mowat o.g.
12	17	GC	A	Linfield	L 0-2	/ Rafferty, Anderson

13	24	GC	A	Distillery	L 1-2	Quinn o.g. / Smyth 2
14	31	GC	H	Portadown	W 3-0	Campbell 2, Martin /
15	Nov 7	GC	A	Bangor	L 1-4	Walker / Bell 2, Lemon (pen), Milburn
16	14	GC	H	Glenavon	L 0-2	/ Clarke, Bell
17	21	IL	H	Ballymena Utd.	D 0-0	
18	28	IL	A	Cliftonville	L 0-4	/ Mills, Alexander 2, Patterson
19	Dec 5	IL	A	Glenavon	D 2-2	Welsh 2 / Craig o.g., Bowyer
20	19	IL	A	Crusaders	L 0-1	/ Brammeld
21	26	IL	H	Distillery	W 2-0	Welsh, Connor /
22	Jan 1	IL	A	Coleraine	L 1-9	Parks / Dickson 3, Healey 3, O'Kane 2, Liddy
23	16	IL	H	Glentoran	L 1-7	Campbell / Kingon, Blackledge 2, Cleary, Jamieson, Manley 2
24	23	IL	A	Larne	W 3-2	Welsh 2, Wilson o.g. / Wilson, Sloan
25	30	IC[1]	H	Chimney Crnr.	D 2-2	Campbell, Welsh / Prenter, Higgins
26	Feb 3	IC[1R]	A	Chimney Crnr.	D 1-1	Walker / Carleton
27	6	IL	A	Ballymena Utd.	L 1-2	Campbell / Sloan, Malone
28	10	IC[1RR]	N	Chimney Crnr.	W 1-0	Parks (pen) /
29	13	IL	H	Cliftonville	L 0-1	/ McCurry
30	16	IL	H	Bangor	W 2-0	Campbell 2 /
31	20	IC[2]	A	Distillery	D 2-2	Welsh, Armstrong / Beck, McMinn
32	24	IC[2R]	H	Distillery	D 0-0	
33	27	IL	H	Glenavon	L 2-4	Connor, Foster / McDonald, Maxwell 2, Glenholmes
34	Mar 3	IC[2RR]	N	Distillery	W 2-0	Mudd, Welsh /
35	6	IL	A	Linfield	L 0-5	/ McGaughey 3, Welsh o.g., McKeown
36	13	IL	H	Crusaders	D 0-0	
37	20	IC[SF]	N	Linfield	L 1-2	Walker / McKeown, McGaughey
38	23	IL	H	Linfield	L 1-2	Welsh / McKee, McKeown
39	27	IL	A	Distillery	L 0-1	/ Smyth
40	30	Cas[1]	H	Killyleagh YC	W 2-0	Welsh, Miskimmin /
41	Apr 3	IL	H	Coleraine	L 0-3	/ Mullan, O'Kane (pen), Healey
42	6	IL	A	Portadown	D 1-1	Campbell / Flanagan
43	10	IL	A	Bangor	W 1-0	Welsh /
44	13	IL	H	Portadown	L 0-1	/ Edgar
45	15	Cas[2]	H	Cliftonville	L 1-5	Campbell / Hewitt, Alexander, Campbell o.g., Mills (pen.), McAlinden
46	17	IL	A	Glentoran	L 0-2	/ Jameson 2
47	22	IL	H	Larne	W 1-0	Welsh /

N = Oval

Final positions, season 1982-83

League: 7th	P 22	W 9	D 4	L 9	F 40	A 41	pts 22
Ulster Cup: 5th	P 11	W 4	D 5	L 2	F 18	A 15	pts 13
Gold Cup: 2nd	P 5	W 3	D 2	L 0	F 8	A 4	pts 8

	Date	Comp.	Venue	Opponents	Result	Goalscorers
1	Aug 21	GC	A	Glenavon	W 3-2	Campbell 2, Rafferty / Bell, Wilson
2	24	GC	H	Bangor	W 2-0	Rafferty (pen), McDermott /
3	28	GC	H	Distillery	D 1-1	Rafferty / Higgins
4	31	GC	A	Portadown	W 1-0	Welsh /
5	Sept 4	GC	H	Linfield	D 1-1	O'Neill / McCartney
6	11	UC	H	Bangor	W 4-0	Cowden, O'Connor, Armstrong, McDermott /
7	18	UC	A	Portadown	D 1-1	Campbell / Kirk
8	25	UC	H	Linfield	W 2-1	McDermott 2 / Murray (pen.)
9	Oct 2	UC	A	Distillery	W 2-0	O'Neill, Campbell /
10	9	UC	H	Ballymena Utd.	D 1-1	Campbell / P. Malone
11	16	UC	A	Crusaders	D 2-2	Campbell, Rafferty / McCurdy 2
12	23	UC	A	Glenavon	W 2-0	Campbell 2 /
13	30	UC	H	Glentoran	L 0-5	/ Jamieson, Manley 3, Neill
14	Nov 6	UC	A	Cliftonville	D 2-2	Campbell, McDermott / McAlinden, Dunlop
15	13	UC	H	Coleraine	L 0-1	/ Bell
16	20	UC	A	Larne	D 2-2	Rafferty, Campbell / Thompson 2
17	27	IL	A	Ballymena Utd.	D 4-4	Armstrong, Campbell 2, Porter / Penney 2, Malone (pen.), McCall
18	Dec 4	IL	H	Cliftonville	L 2-4	Rafferty, Campbell / Brown, Holden, Higgins 2
19	11	IL	H	Glenavon	W 4-2	Willis o.g.., Cowden, Walker, Porter / Denvir, Whitten
20	18	IL	A	Linfield	D 0-0	
21	27	IL	H	Crusaders	W 3-1	Campbell, Rafferty, Porter / Gillespie
22	28	IL	A	Distillery	L 2-3	Campbell 2 / Ferris, McMinn 2
23	Jan 1	IL	H	Coleraine	L 0-3	/ Healy 2, Wade
24	3	IL	A	Bangor	W 2-1	O'Neill, McDermott / King
25	8	IL	H	Portadown	W 3-2	Porter, McDermott, Campbell / Gordon 2
26	15	IL	A	Glentoran	L 1-4	Campbell / Mullan, Morrison, Jamieson, Manley (pen)
27	22	IC[1]	A	Bangor	W 1-0	Campbell /
28	29	IL	H	Larne	W 1-0	Porter /
29	Feb 5	IL	H	Ballymena Utd.	W 4-0	Campbell 3, Porter /
30	12	IC[2]	H	Dungannon Sw.	W 3-0	Campbell 2, Porter /
31	19	IL	A	Cliftonville	D 0-0	
32	26	IL	A	Glenavon	L 3-5	Campbell 3 / Mudd o.g., Denvir 2, Wilson, Whitten
33	Mar 5	IC[3]	H	Larne	W 2-1	Campbell 2 / Maxwell
34	12	IL	H	Linfield	L 0-1	/ McGaughey
35	19	IL	A	Crusaders	D 0-0	
36	26	IC[SF]	N	Linfield	L 1-2	Armstrong / Murray, Dornan
37	31	Cas[1]	H	RUC	W 1-0	O'Connor /
38	Apr 2	IL	H	Distillery	W 1-0	Ferris o.g. /
39	4	IL	A	Coleraine	L 0-2	/ McCoy, McDowell
40	9	IL	H	Bangor	W 5-1	Parks, McCusker, O'Connor, Campbell 2 / Frazer
41	13	Cas[2]	H	Dundela	W 1-0	Cowden /
42	16	IL	A	Portadown	L 1-3	McDermott / McDonnell, Topley 2
43	21	Cas[SF]	N[2]	Glentoran	L 0-2	/ Manley, Cleary
44	23	IL	H	Glentoran	L 1-3	Parks (pen) / Jamieson, Mullan, Manley
45	26	IL	A	Larne	W 3-2	Campbell 3 (1 pen) / Cowden o.g., Thompson

N = Oval
N² = Clandeboye Park

Final positions, season 1983-84

League: 4th   P 26   W 9   D 11 L 6   F 32   A 26   pts 29

Ulster Cup: 2nd   P 7   W 5   D 1   L 1   F 10   A 4   pts 11

Gold Cup, 2nd   P 7   W 3   D 1   L 3   F 12   A 13   pts 7

	Date	Comp.	Venue	Opponents	Result	Goalscorers
1	Aug 20	GC	H	Bangor	W 4-0	Campbell 2, McDermott, McCusker /
2	24	GC	A	Glenavon	L 1-2	Campbell (pen) / Wilson, Johnston (pen.)
3	27	GC	H	Glentoran	L 0-4	/ Blackledge, Manley 2, Bowers
4	30	GC	A	Glentoran	L 2-5	McCusker, Parks (pen.) / Morrison, Manley, Blackledge 2, Neill
5	Sept 3	GC	A	Newry Town	W 2-1	Dornan, Campbell / Doran (pen)
6	6	GC	H	Portadown	D 0-0	
7	10	GC	A	Bangor	W 3-1	Bell, Campbell, Dornan / Armstrong (pen)
8	17	UC	H	Cliftonville	W 1-0	Campbell /
9	24	UC	A	Glenavon	W 2-1	Walker, Bell / Crawley
10	Oct 1	UC	H	Portadown	W 2-1	Campbell, Dugan / Gardiner
11	8	UC	A	Bangor	L 0-1	/ Carson
12	15	UC	A	Coleraine	D 1-1	Campbell / O'Kane
13	22	UC	H	Newry Town	W 1-0	Campbell /
14	29	UC	H	Larne	W 3-0	Montgomery, Dugan, Campbell /
15	Nov 5	IL	A	Ballymena Utd,	L 0-2	/ Smyth 2
16	12	IL	H	Carrick Rangers	W 2-1	Dugan, Campbell / Alexander
17	19	IL	A	Cliftonville	D 1-1	Dugan / McAlinden
18	26	IL	H	Distillery	W 1-0	McCusker /
19	Dec 3	IL	A	Glentoran	D 3-3	O'Connor, Dugan, Campbell / Manley, Blackledge, Dixon
20	10	IL	H	Glenavon	L 0-3	/ Dennison, Reilly 2
21	17	IL	A	Bangor	D 2-2	Dugan 2 / Welsh, McGivern
22	24	IL	H	Coleraine	D 0-0	
23	27	IL	A	Larne	D 1-1	Dugan / Carland
24	31	IL	H	Crusaders	D 1-1	Campbell / Barr
25	Jan 7	IL	H	Linfield	L 0-2	/ McKeown, Jeffrey
26	21	IL	H	Portadown	D 0-0	
27	28	IC¹	H	Coleraine	W 1-0	O'Connor /
28	Feb 4	IL	H	Ballymena Utd.	W 3-0	Hayes 2, Dugan /
29	11	IL	A	Carrick Rangers	W 1-0	Campbell /
30	18	IC²	A	Cliftonville	L 0-1	/ Coulter
31	25	IL	H	Cliftonville	D 0-0	
32	Mar 3	IL	A	Distillery	L 1-2	Campbell / Andrews 2
33	10	IL	A	Portadown	W 2-0	Campbell, Young /
34	17	IL	H	Glentoran	D 0-0	

35	19	IL	A	Newry Town	W 4-0	Campbell 3 (1 pen), Montgomery /
36	24	IL	A	Glenavon	L 1-2	Dugan / Crawley, Hewitt
37	27	Cas[1]	A	Ballymena Utd,	L[P] 2-2	Campbell, Dugan / Smyth, Wright
38	31	IL	H	Bangor	W 1-0	Campbell /
39	Apr 7	IL	H	Larne	W 2-0	Campbell (pen), Dugan /
40	14	IL	A	Coleraine	L 3-5	Campbell 3 (1 pen) / Wade 2, McQuiston 2, McCoy
41	21	IL	A	Crusaders	D 0-0	
42	24	IL	H	Newry Town	W 2-0	Dugan 2 /
43	28	IL	A	Linfield	D 1-1	Dugan / McKeown

L[P] = lost on penalties

Final positions, season 1984-85

League: 11th	P 26	W 8	D 5	L 13	F 32	A 40	pts 21
Ulster Cup: 3rd	P 7	W 3	D 1	L 3	F 9	A 10	pts 7
Gold Cup: 2nd	P 7	W 2	D 3	L 2	F 9	A 7	pts 7

	Date	Comp.	Venue	Opponents	Result	Goalscorers
1	Aug 18	GC	A	Bangor	W 4-1	Young, Dugan, Hayes 2 / Armstrong
2	21	GC	H	Glenavon	D 1-1	Gardiner / Denver
3	25	GC	H	Glentoran	D 0-0	
4	28	GC	A	Glentoran	D 1-1	Dugan / Jameson
5	Sept 1	GC	H	Newry Town	W 2-0	Dugan 2 /
6	4	GC	A	Portadown	L 1-3	Young / Paton, McDonnell, Keane
7	8	GC	H	Bangor	L 0-1	/ Beattie
8	15	UC	A	Cliftonville	W 1-0	Hill /
9	22	UC	H	Glenavon	L 0-1	/ Drake
10	29	UC	A	Portadown	L 1-3	Cowden / Jeffers, McCullough 2
11	Oct 6	UC	H	Bangor	W 4-0	Dugan 3, Hill /
12	13	UC	H	Coleraine	W 2-1	Cowden, Dugan / Mahon
13	20	UC	A	Newry Town	L 0-4	/ Cunningham, Ralph 3
14	27	UC	H	Larne	D 1-1	Hill / Wilson
15	Nov 3	IL	H	Ballymena Utd.	L 1-2	Dinsmore / Crockard, Campbell
16	10	IL	A	Carrick Rangers	L 2-3	Dugan 2 / Richardson 2, Hardy
17	17	IL	H	Cliftonville	L 0-1	/ McCusker
18	24	IL	A	Distillery	L 1-2	Campbell (pen) / Smith, McMinn
19	Dec 1	IL	H	Glentoran	W 3-1	Cowden, Hayes, Campbell (pen) / Manley
20	8	IL	A	Glenavon	D 1-1	Hayes / Murray
21	15	IL	H	Bangor	W 1-0	Campbell /
22	22	IL	A	Coleraine	D 1-1	Dugan / Healy
23	26	IL	H	Larne	W 2-1	Campbell, Dugan / Nicholl
24	29	IL	A	Crusaders	L 1-3	Dugan / Brammeld, Holden 2
25	Jan 1	IL	H	Newry Town	W 1-0	Hayes /
26	12	IL	H	Portadown	W 4-1	Campbell 2 (1 pen), Walker, Dugan / McCullough

27	19	IC[1]	A	Bangor	W 3-0	Dugan 2, Porter /
28	22	IL	A	Linfield	L 0-5	/ McGaughey 2, Crawford, Maxwell 2
29	Feb 2	IL	A	Ballymena Utd.	W 3-1	Dugan, Hayes, Mudd / Harrison (pen)
30	9	IL	H	Carrick Rangers	W 4-0	Campbell 2, Fettis, Walker /
31	16	IC[2]	H	Ballymoney Utd.	W 2-0	Campbell, Dugan /
32	23	IL	A	Cliftonville	L 0-1	/ Tully
33	Mar 2	IL	H	Distillery	D 0-0	
34	9	IC[3]	H	Ballymena Utd.	L 0-1	/ Sloan
35	16	IL	A	Glentoran	L 0-2	/ Bowers (pen), Blackledge
36	20	Cas[1]	A	Ballymena Utd.	W 2-0	Dugan, Burns o.g. /
37	23	IL	H	Glenavon	L 1-3	Dugan / Gardiner 3
38	30	IL	A	Portadown	L 0-1	/ Conlon
39	Apr 6	IL	A	Bangor	W 3-1	Cowden, Fettis, Dugan / Sterling
40	9	IL	H	Coleraine	L 1-2	Campbell (pen) / Wade 2
41	13	IL	A	Larne	L 0-3	/ Sloan, Smyth, Maxwell
42	16	Cas[2]	H	Killyleagh Y.C.	W 3-2	Dugan, Dornan, Young / Cranston 2
43	20	IL	H	Crusaders	D 1-1	Young (pen) / Flanagan (pen)
44	23	IL	A	Newry Town	L 1-4	Dugan (pen) / Morrow, Ralph 2, McInerney
45	27	IL	H	Linfield	D 0-0	
46	May 7	Cas[SF]	H	Glentoran	L 2-3	Campbell, Young / Blackledge 3

Final positions, season 1985-86

League: 3rd	P 26	W 12	D 7	L 7	F 37	A 19	pts 31
Ulster Cup: 3rd	P 3	W 1	D 0	L 2	F 4	A 7	pts 2
Gold Cup: 5th	P 13	W 7	D 3	L 3	F 22	A 16	pts 17

	Date	Comp.	Venue	Opponents	Result	Goalscorers
1	Aug 17	UC	A	Glenavon	L 2-4	B. Kincaid 2 / Drake, Dennison, McCabe, McCann
2	20	UC	H	Glentoran	L 1-3	Hill / Manley, Bowers 2 (1 pen)
3	24	UC	A	Chimney Corn.	W 1-0	McClurg /
4	27	Cas[1]	A	Carrick Rangers	L 0-2	/ McDonnell, Hardy
5	30	GC	A	Newry Town	L 2-4	Hill, Baxter (pen) /Ralph 2, Whitten, Marron
6	Sept 14	GC	A	Linfield	D 1-1	McClurg / Anderson
*7	17	GC	H	Portadown	W 3-0	Simpson, Baxter 2 /
8	21	GC	H	Glenavon	D 3-3	Baxter (pen), B. Kincaid, Dornan / Quinn, Lowry (pen), Drake
9	28	GC	A	Carrick Rangers	W 2-0	T. Kincaid, Baxter /
10	Oct 5	GC	H	Bangor	W 1-0	Baxter (pen) /
11	12	GC	A	Larne	D 1-1	Brown / Smyth
12	19	GC	H	Ballymena Utd.	W 3-1	Baxter, McClurg, B. Kincaid / Hamilton
13	26	GC	A	Distillery	L 0-3	/ McMinn (pen), Ferris, Elliman
14	Nov 2	GC	H	Crusaders	W 2-1	McClurg, Kelly / Totten
15	9	GC	A	Glentoran	W 2-0	Baxter 2 (1 pen) /
16	16	GC	H	Coleraine	L 1-2	Baxter / McQuiston 2
17	30	GC	A	Cliftonville	W 1-0	Baxter /

18	Dec 7	IL	H	Crusaders	L 1-3	Baxter (pen) / Hillis, Holden, Nixon
19	14	IL	A	Carrick Rangers	W 3-0	Baxter 2 (1 pen), Simpson /
20	21	IL	A	Larne	L 1-2	T. Kincaid / Caulfield 2
21	26	IL	H	Ballymena Utd.	W 1-0	T. Kincaid /
22	28	IL	A	Glentoran	L 1-2	Campbell / Mullan, Morrison
23	Jan 1	IL	H	Glenavon	W 2-0	Baxter, McClurg /
24	4	IL	A	Distillery	W 2-0	Campbell, Baxter /
25	11	IL	H	Cliftonville	W 4-0	Campbell, T. Kincaid, Baxter 2 /
26	18	IL	A	Bangor	D 1-1	Campbell / Douglas
27	25	IL	H	Coleraine	W 1-0	Kelly /
28	Feb 1	IC[1]	H	Newry Town	D 1-1	Campbell (pen) / Buchanan (pen)
29	5	IC[1R]	A	Newry Town	W 2-0	Campbell, Hill /
30	8	IL	A	Linfield	W 2-0	Campbell, Mudd /
31	15	IL	H	Portadown	W 3-0	Mudd 3 /
32	22	IC[2]	H	Crusaders	W 4-1	Campbell (pen), Flanagan, Mudd, Hawkins o.g. / Totten
33	Mar 1	IL	A	Portadown	L 0-2	/ Elliot, McKee
34	8	IL	A	Newry Town	L 0-1	/ Marron
35	15	IC[3]	A	Carrick Rangers	W 1-0	Campbell /
36	22	IL	A	Crusaders	L 1-2	T. Kincaid / Holden, McCurdy
37	29	IL	H	Carrick Rangers	W 4-1	Campbell, Flanagan, Dornan, Spiers o.g. / White
38	Apr 1	IL	H	Larne	D 1-1	Mudd / Harrison
39	5	IC[SF]	N	Coleraine	L 0-2	/ Wade, Healey
40	8	IL	A	Ballymena Utd.	L 0-1	/ Speak
41	12	IL	H	Glentoran	D 0-0	
42	15	IL	A	Glenavon	D 0-0	
43	19	IL	H	Distillery	W 4-0	Campbell 3, R. Dornan /
44	22	IL	A	Cliftonville	D 0-0	
45	24	IL	A	Newry Town	D 0-0	
46	26	IL	H	Bangor	W 2-1	Campbell, Mudd / Frazer
47	May 5	IL	A	Coleraine	D 1-1	Baxter / McQuiston
48	9	IL	H	Linfield	W 2-1	Baxter, Mudd / Jeffrey

N = Ballymena Showgrounds

Final positions, season 1986-87

League: 3rd	P 26	W 14	D 6	L 6	F 47	A 31	pts 48
Ulster Cup: 3rd	P 3	W 1	D 1	L 1	F 6	A 7	pts 4
Gold Cup: 2nd	P 6	W 4	D 0	L 2	F 12	A 7	pts 12

	Date	Comp.	Venue	Opponents	Result	Goalscorers
1	Aug 8	Cas[1]	H	Dundela	W 2-1	Kincaid, Baxter / Hanvey
2	12	Cas[2]	A	Crusaders	W 2-1	Maxwell, Simpson / Burrows (pen)
3	16	UC	A	Glenavon	L 2-4	Baxter 2 (1 pen) / Love, Jennings, Smith (pen), Gardiner
4	19	UC	H	Ballymena Utd.	D 2-2	Baxter, Maxwell / Speak 2

5	23	UC	H	Dundela	W 2-1	Baxter 2 (1 pen) / Coey
6	29	IL	A	Portadown	D 2-2	Campbell (pen), Simpson / Smith 2
7	Sept 6	IL	H	Linfield	W 2-1	Dornan, Maxwell / Hanna
8	11	Cas[SF]	A	Glentoran	L 1-4	Baxter / Caskey, Cleary, McCartney 2
9	13	IL	A	Coleraine	W 3-1	Maxwell, Tabb o.g., Love o.g. / McCoy
10	20	IL	H	Bangor	L 0-1	/ Eddis
11	27	IL	A	Cliftonville	W 1-0	Maxwell /
12	Oct 4	IL	H	Distillery	W 1-0	Andrews o.g. /
13	11	IL	A	Glenavon	L 0-1	/ McCann
14	18	IL	H	Glentoran	D 1-1	Baxter / Miller
15	25	IL	A	Ballymena Utd.	L 1-2	Simpson / Pyper, Dougherty
16	Nov 1	IL	H	Larne	L 0-5	/ Huston, McCoy o.g., McLeod, Sloan 2
17	8	IL	H	Carrick Rangers	D 4-4	Maxwell, McCoy, McGreevy, Baxter (pen) / Thompson 3, McCallan
18	22	IL	H	Newry Town	W 4-3	Campbell 2, Baxter (pen), Simpson / Coulter, McCabe, Crawley
19	29	IL	A	Newry Town	D 0-0	
20	Dec 6	IL	H	Portadown	W 3-1	Baxter 2, Campbell / Smith
21	13	IL	A	Linfield	L 0-2	/ McCullough, Murray
22	20	IL	H	Coleraine	L 1-2	Baxter / McCreadie 2
23	26	IL	A	Bangor	W 4-0	Baxter (pen), Campbell, Kincaid, Hill /
24	27	IL	H	Cliftonville	D 0-0	
25	Jan 1	IL	A	Distillery	W 2-0	Baxter (pen), Maxwell /
26	3	IL	H	Glenavon	W 1-0	Byrne /
27	10	IL	A	Glentoran	W 3-2	Hill 2, Simpson / McCartney, Blackledge
28	17	IL	H	Ballymena Utd.	D 1-1	Kincaid / Speak
29	24	IL	A	Larne	W 2-1	Baxter (pen), Maxwell / McLoughlin
30	31	IL	A	Crusaders	W 3-1	Campbell, Kincaid, Maxwell / Hillis
31	Feb 7	IL	A	Carrick Rangers	W 5-0	Baxter 3, Campbell 2 /
32	14	IL	H	Crusaders	W 3-0	Kincaid, McGreevy, Simpson /
33	21	IC[1]	A	Omagh Town	W 2-1	Baxter, Maxwell / Reynolds
34	28	GC	H	Distillery	W 5-2	Baxter, McGreevy, Simpson, McCoy, Byrne / Cochrane, Young
35	Mar 14	IC[2]	H	Larne	L 1-2	Maxwell / Guy 2
36	21	GC	H	Glenavon	W 2-0	Kincaid, Simpson /
37	24	GC	A	Glentoran	L 1-3	Campbell / McCartney 2, Smyth
38	28	RLC[1]	H	Ballymoney Utd.	W 1-0	Campbell /
39	Apr 11	GC	A	Newry Town	L 0-1	/ Foy
40	15	GC	A	Bangor	W 2-0	Baxter, Maxwell /
41	18	GC	H	Portadown	W 2-1	Maxwell 2 / Elliott
42	21	GC[SF]	N	Linfield	L 1-2	Davis o.g. / Doherty, McGaughey
43	24	RLC[2]	A	Newry Town	L 1-2	Campbell / Magee, O'Kane

N = Oval

Final positions, season 1987-88

League: 11th	P 26	W 6	D 7	L 13	F 29	A 38	pts 25
Ulster Cup: 3rd	P 3	W 1	D 0	L 2	F 4	A 7	pts 3
Gold Cup: 7th	P 7	W 1	D 2	L 4	F 5	A 10	pts 5

	Date	Comp.	Venue	Opponents	Result	Goalscorers
1	Aug 15	UC	H	RUC	W 3-2	J. Campbell, Mitchell, Pearson / Ferris, Crawford
2	18	UC	A	Glentoran	L 1-3	Kincaid / Clery, McCartney, Montgomery
3	22	UC	H	Crusaders	L 0-2	/ Stewart, Totten (pen)
4	29	GC	A	Distillery	D 0-0	
5	Sept 5	GC	H	Glentoran	L 1-2	Kincaid / Bowers, Mullan
6	12	GC	A	Glenavon	D 1-1	Mitchell / Drake
7	19	GC	A	Ballymena Utd.	L 0-1	/ Pyper
8	26	GC	H	Newry Town	L 0-3	/ Patterson 2, Hawkins (pcn.)
9	Oct 3	GC	A	Cliftonville	L 1-3	Maxwell / Elliman 2, McDonald
10	10	GC	H	Bangor	W 2-0	Black, Gibson o.g. /
11	17	LC[1]	H	Tobermore Utd.	W 2-0	Dornan (pen.), Maxwell /
12	24	IL	H	Portadown	W 2-0	Maxwell, R. Campbell /
13	31	IL	A	Linfield	L 0-1	/ McGaughey
14	Nov 3	LC[2]	A	Distillery	W[T] 1-0	Mudd /
15	7	IL	H	Coleraine	D 1-1	Whittley / Tabb
16	13	LC[SF]	H*	Coleraine	L[P] 1-1	Kincaid / McCoy
17	20	IL	A	Bangor	W 4-2	Maxwell 2, Kincaid, Black / McKee, Glendinning
18	27	BWC[1]	A	Bangor	L 0-1	/ Frazer (pen)
19	Dec 5	IL	H	Cliftonville	W 1-0	Black /
20	12	IL	A	Distillery	W 3-1	Black, Kincaid, Hill / Cleland
21	19	IL	H	Glenavon	D 1-1	Kincaid / McBride
22	26	IL	A	Glentoran	D 2-2	Hamill, Hill / Manley, Cleary
23	28	IL	H	Ballymena Utd.	L 0-1	/ Dougherty
24	Jan 1	IL	A	Larne	L 0-2	/ McCreadie, Bustard
25	9	IL	H	Crusaders	L 1-2	Black / Lawther, Greer (pen)
26	16	IL	A	Newry Town	L 0-1	/ Ralph
27	20	IL	A	Carrick Rangers	L 1-2	Black / Kirk, McAlinden
28	30	IL	A	Coleraine	L 2-4	Mudd, Kincaid / McDowell, McCreadie, Mudd o.g., Beggs
29	Feb 6	IL	H	Bangor	D 1-1	Maxwell / Mudd o.g.
30	13	IL	A	Cliftonville	D 0-0	
31	20	IC[1]	H	Bangor	W 4-2	J, Campbell 2, Hamill, Black / Mudd o.g., Glendinning
32	27	IL	H	Distillery	D 1-1	Kincaid / Tabb
33	Mar 2	IL	H	Linfield	L 1-2	Hamill / McGaughey 2
34	5	IL	A	Glenavon	W 1-0	Ferguson /
35	12	IC[2]	A	Glenavon	L 1-2	Black / McBride, Drake
36	19	IL	H	Glentoran	L 0-2	/ Cleary 2 (2 pens.)
37	26	IL	H	Larne	L 2-3	Hamill 2 / Hardy, D. Smyth, F. Smyth
38	30	CCT[1]	H	Ballyclare Com.	W 2-0	Hamill, Black /
39	Apr 2	IL	H	Carrick Rangers	L 1-2	Black / Harkness o.g., Hunter
40	5	IL	A	Crusaders	L 0-3	/ Hillis 2, Hunter

41	12	IL	A	Ballymena Utd.	D 1-1	Kincaid / Pyper
42	16	IL	H	Newry Town	L 0-1	/ Hawkins
43	19	CCT^2	H	Dundela	W^P 1-1	Kincaid / Stewart
44	23	IL	A	Portadown	W 3-2	Kincaid 2 (2 pens.), Hunter / McCourt, Millar
45	May 3	CCT^{SF}	A	Glentoran	L 0-1	/ Mathieson

W^P or L^P = match decided on penalties
H* = at Clandeboye Park
W^T = after extra time

Final positions, season 1988-89

League: 13th   P 26   W 4   D 6   L 16   F 26   A 54   pts 18
Ulster Cup: 4th   P 3   W 0   D 1   L 2   F 4   A 6   pts 1
Gold Cup: 7th   P 7   W 1   D 1   L 5   F 7   A 15   pts 4

	Date	Comp.	Venue	Opponents	Result	Goalscorers
1	Aug 20	UC	A	Coleraine	L 2-3	Caughey 2 / R. Campbell o.g., Brown, Workman
2	23	UC	H	Ballyclare Com.	D 0-0	
3	26	UC	A	Ballymena Utd.	L 2-3	Kincaid, Caughey (pen.) / Hardy, Donnelly o.g., Heron
4	Sept 3	GC	A	Glentoran	L 1-4	Kincaid / Beattie o.g., Cleary (pen.), Morrison, McCartney
5	10	GC	H	Distillery	W 2-1	Kincaid 2 / McMinn (pen.)
6	17	GC	H	Glenavon	L 1-2	Kincaid / McCann, Lowry
7	24	GC	H	Ballymena Utd.	D 2-2	McMinn, Murphy / Pyper, Smyth
8	Oct 1	GC	A	Newry Town	L 0-5	/ Ralph 2, Burns, Brannigan, Elliman
9	8	GC	H	Cliftonville	L 1-2	Caughey (pen.) / Maguire 2
10	12	GC	A	Bangor	L 1-2	Caughey (pen.) / Douglas 2
11	15	LC^1	A	Chimney Corner	W^{P}1-1	Murphy / White
12	22	LC^2	H	Glenavon	L 2-5	McMinn (pen.), Caughey / McBride 3 (2 pens), Woodhead 2
13	29	IL	A	Portadown	L 0-2	/ Davidson, Magee
14	Nov 5	IL	H	Linfield	L 1-3	Murphy / Coly, O'Boyle, Baxter
15	12	IL	A	Coleraine	D 1-1	Patterson / Mullan
16	19	IL	H	Bangor	L 2-3	Caughey, Murphy / McKee, Drake, Coulter
17	26	IL	A	Cliftonville	D 2-2	Murphy 2 / Maguire, Armstrong
18	Dec 3	IL	H	Distillery	D 1-1	Kincaid / Purdy
19	10	IL	A	Glenavon	L 0-3	/ McConville, Gardiner 2
20	17	IL	H	Glentoran	L 1-5	Ferguson / Harrison, Hillis, Cleary 2, Morrison
21	26	IL	H	Larne	W 3-1	Kincaid, Caughey, McMinn / McDonald
22	31	IL	H	Carrick Rgrs.	L 0-1	/ Crawford (pen.)
23	Jan 2	IL	A	Crusaders	W 1-0	R. Campbell /
24	7	IL	H	Newry Town	W 4-3	Ferguson, R. Campbell, Patterson, McMinn (pen.) / Ralph 2, Clarke
25	10	IL	A	Ballymena Utd.	L 2-3	McMinn (pen.), Ferguson / Curry (pen), Young, Doherty

26	14	IL	A	Linfield	L 1-2	Caughey / Coly, Baxter
27	18	IL	A	Bangor	L 1-2	Patterson / Eddis 2
28	21	IL	H	Coleraine	L 0-2	/ Wright, Mullan
29	28	IC[1]	H	Cromac Albion	L 0-1	/ Hyland
30	31	BWC	H	Coleraine	D+ 2-2	Ferguson 2 / Wade, Mullan
31	Feb 4	IL	H	Cliftonville	L 0-4	/ Hamill 2, McCullough, McFadden
32	11	BWC	A	Coleraine	D+ 1-1	Caughey / Wade
33	25	IL	A	Distillery	L 0-2	/ Surgeon, Cochrane
34	Mar 4	IL	H	Glenavon	L 1-5	Ferguson / Conville, McLoughlin 2, Blackledge (pen.), Byrne
35	18	IL	A	Glentoran	L 0-1	/ McCartney
36	25	IL	H	Ballymena Utd.	D 0-0	
37	28	IL	A	Larne	D 1-1	R. Campbell / Smyth
38	Apr 1	IL	A	Carrick Rgrs.	L 0-1	/ Kirk
39	13	Cas[1]	H	Newry Town	L 0-4	/ Ralph 2, Fay, Hawkins
40	15	IL	H	Crusaders	W 2-0	Kincaid, Ferguson
41	22	IL	A	Newry Town	L 1-6	B. Kincaid / Ralph 2, McGuinness, Hawkins (pen.), Edgar, Patterson
42	29	IL	H	Portadown	D 0-0	

W^P = won on penalties

+ = lost on away goals

Final positions, season 1989-90

League: 12th	P 26	W 5	D 6	L 15	F 25	A 44	pts 21
Ulster Cup: 2nd	P 3	W 1	D 1	L 1	F 5	A 7	pts 4
Gold Cup: 2nd	P 3	W 1	D 1	L 1	F 4	A 4	pts 4

	Date	Comp.	Venue	Opponents	Result	Goalscorers
1	Aug 19	UC	H	Glenavon	L 1-4	Ferguson / McBride 2, Blackledge, Lowry
2	22	UC	A	Ballymena Utd.	W 3-2	McAuley, Ferguson 2 / Curry, Hardy
3	25	UC	A	Linfield	D 1-1	Ferguson / McAllan
4	Sept 1	GC	H	Glentoran	L 1-3	McAuley / Jamieson, Douglas, Caskey
5	9	GC	A	Carrick Rangers	D 1-1	T. Kincaid / Lavery
6	16	GC	A	Newry Town	W 2-0	McAuley 2 /
7	23	IL	H	Distillery	W 5-0	Ferguson 4, McMinn /
8	30	IL	A	Larne	L 0-1	/ Smith
9	Oct 7	IL	H	Coleraine	L 0-4	/ Mullan, Dougherty 2, McCoy
10	14	LC[1]	H	UUJ	W 12-0	Kincaid 2 (1 pen), Ferguson 3, McCandless 2, McAuley, McMinn 3, Stitt /
11	17	LC[2]	H	Ballyclare Com.	W^P 2-2	Kincaid, McAuley / Tabb, Clarke
12	28	IL	A	Crusaders	W 3-0	Ferguson 2, Kincaid (pen) /
13	Nov 4	IL	H	Cliftonville	L 3-4	McCandless, Kincaid (pen), Ferguson / Hamill 3, O'Kane
14	11	IL	A	Ballymena Utd.	D 0-0	
15	14	LC[3]	A	Coleraine	W^T 2-1	R. Campbell, B. Kincaid / Dougherty

	Date	Comp.	Venue	Opponents	Result	Goalscorers
16	18	IL	H	Carrick Rangers	D 1-1	McCandless / Armstrong
17	21	LC[SF]	N	Glenavon	L[T] 1-3	McCandless / McCann, Blackledge 2 (1 pen)
18	25	IL	A	Glenavon	D 0-0	
19	Dec 2	IL	H	Newry Town	L 1-5	O'Neill / Elliman 4, McConville
20	9	IL	A	Glentoran	D 0-0	
21	22	BWC[1]	A	Cliftonville	L 1-4	O'Neill / Muldoon, Drake 2, Murray
22	26	IL	H	Bangor	L 0-2	/ McCreadie, Campbell
23	30	IL	A	Portadown	L 1-4	O'Neill / Magee 2, Mills, McKinstry
24	Jan 1	BWC[1]	H	Cliftonville	D 2-2	Stitt, O'Neill / McDonald, Muldoon
25	6	IL	H	Larne	L 0-1	/ Kernoghan
26	9	IL	A	Linfield	D 0-0	
27	13	IL	A	Coleraine	L 0-4	/ Wade, McCoy, Tourish 2
28	20	IC[1]	A	Omagh Town	W 3-0	Anderson, Ferguson, T. Kincaid (pen)/
29	27	IL	H	Crusaders	W 3-1	T. Kincaid 2 (2 pens), Anderson / Moore
30	Feb 3	IL	A	Cliftonville	W 2-1	McMinn 2 / Muldoon
31	10	IL	H	Ballymena Utd.	L 0-2	/ Sloan 2
32	17	IC[2]	H	Larne	L 0-2	/ Smyth, Goldsmith
33	24	Cas[1]	H	E. Belfast	L[P] 1-1	R. Campbell / Lamont (pen)
34	Mar 3	IL	A	Carrick Rangers	L 0-2	/ McDermott, Crawford (pen)
35	17	IL	H	Glenavon	L 0-1	/ McBride
36	24	IL	A	Newry Town	D 2-2	O'Neill, Stitt / Lundy, Hawkins (pen)
37	31	IL	H	Glentoran	W 2-1	Leeman, Carleton / McCartney
38	Apr 14	IL	H	Linfield	L 1-2	T. Kincaid (pen) / Spiers, McGaughey
39	16	IL	A	Bangor	L 0-3	/ Campbell 3
40	21	IL	H	Portadown	L 0-1	/ Fraser
41	28	IL	A	Distillery	L 1-2	Tully / Adams 2

W^P or L^P = won or lost on penalties
N = Seaview
W^T = after extra time

Final positions, season 1990-91

League: 9th   P 30   W 12   D 7   L 11   F 47   A 40   pts 43

Ulster Cup: 3rd   P 3   W 1   D 1   L 1   F 3   A 3   pts 4

Gold Cup: 4th   P 3   W 0   D 1   L 2   F 4   A 8   pts 1

	Date	Comp.	Venue	Opponents	Result	Goalscorers
1	Aug 18	UC	H	Cliftonville	D 2-2	Leeman, Kincaid (pen) / Muldoon (pen), Hamill
2	21	UC	H	Omagh Town	W 1-0	Shiels /
3	25	UC	H	Linfield	L 0-1	/ McCandless
4	Sept 1	GC	H	Coleraine	D 1-1	R. Campbell / Donaghy
5	8	GC	A	Ballymena Utd.	L 2-3	Kincaid 2 / Young, Loughery, Pyper
6	15	GC	A	Cliftonville	L 1-4	McAuley / O'Kane 2, Stitt, McFadden
7	22	IL	H	Glenavon	L 1-2	T. Scappaticci o.g. / McLoughlin 2
8	28	IL	A	Glentoran	D 1-1	Shiels / McCartney

9	Oct 6	IL	H	Newry Town	L 1-2	Shiels / Ralph, Crawley
10	13	IL	A	Distillery	D 2-2	Shiels, R. Campbell / Nixon, Hamilton
11	20	BWC[1]	A	Portadown	L 2-4	R. Campbell, Shiels / Doolin, Davidson, Cunningham, Cowan (pen)
12	27	IL	H	Bangor	L 0-2	/ Cunningham, Murphy
13	Nov 3	IL	A	Cliftonville	L 0-2	/ Breslin, Murray
14	10	IL	H	Carrick Rangers	W 2-0	O'Neill, Eddis /
15	17	IL	A	Portadown	L 0-1	/ Magee
16	24	IL	H	Linfield	D 1-1	Armstrong / Curry
17	Dec 1	IL	H	Omagh Town	W 4-2	O'Neill, Kincaid 2, Armstrong / Donaldson 2
18	8	IL	H	Ballyclare Com.	W 4-3	McCarroll 3, Dunlop o.g. / Kirk, Armstrong, Beattie
19	22	IL	A	Coleraine	W 1-0	Armstrong /
20	26	IL	H	Crusaders	D 0-0	
21	29	IL	H	Larne	W 4-1	O'Neill, McDonald, Mullen, Shiels / Hannan
22	Jan 1	IL	A	Glenavon	W 2-1	Kincaid, Armstrong / Ferguson.
23	5	LC[1]	H	Ballinamallard U.	W 4-1	McLaughlin, Kincaid (pen), Armstrong, Shiels / Thompson
24	12	IL	H	Glentoran	L 2-3	Shiels 2 / McCartney 3
25	19	IC[5]	A	Dungannon Sw.	W 3-1	Shiels, Kincaid, McLoughlin / Clarke
26	22	IL	A	Ballymena Utd.	L 1-4	Kincaid / Smyth, Thompson, Candlish, Pyper
27	26	IL	A	Newry Town	L 1-3	Kincaid (pen) / Burns, Lundy, Ralph
28	Feb 2	IL	H	Distillery	W 2-1	R. Campbell, McLoughlin / Adams
29	6	LC[2]	H	Queen's Univ.	W 3-0	McDonald, Armstrong, Morrison /
30	9	IL	A	Bangor	D 1-1	Armstrong / Brown
31	12	LC[3]	H	Larne	W 4-0	Eddis, B. Campbell, Kincaid (pen), Armstrong /
32	16	IC[6]	H	Donegal Celtic	D 0-0	
33	23	IL	H	Cliftonville	D 1-1	Armstrong / O'Kane
34	26	LC[SF]	N	Omagh Town	W 4-1	Armstrong 2, R. Campbell, McLoughlin / Leeman o.g.
35	Mar 2	IL	A	Carrick Rangers	W 5-2	Shiels 2, Eddis 2, McAuley / Montgomery, Thompson
36	5	Cas[1]	H	Cliftonville	W 1-0	McLaughlin /
37	9	IC[7]	H	Linfield	W 3-2	R. Campbell, Eddis, Kincaid / Curry, Magee
38	16	IL	H	Portadown	L 1-2	McLoughlin / Cowan 2 (1 pen.)
39	20	LCF	N[2]	Glentoran	L 0-2	/ McCartney 2
40	23	IL	A	Linfield	L 0-1	/ Spiers
41	26	IL	H	Omagh Town	W 5-1	McLoughlin, Shiels 2, Johnston, Kincaid / Ballard
42	30	IL	A	Ballyclare Com.	L 0-1	/ Thompson
43	Apr 1	Cas[2]	H	Dundela	L 0-1	/ Erskine
44	5	IC[SF]	N[3]	Portadown	L 1-2	Kincaid (pen) / Cowan 2
45	10	IL	A	Crusaders	W 2-0	Shiels, B. Kincaid /
46	13	IL	H	Ballymena Utd.	D 0-0	
47	20	Il	H	Coleraine	W 1-0	Quigley o.g. /
48	27	Il	A	Larne	W 2-0	O'Neill, Eddis /

N = Shamrock Park
N[2] = Windsor Park
N[3] = Oval

Final positions, season 1991-92

League: 7th	P30	W10	D11	L9	F50	A46	pts 41
Ulster Cup: 4th	P 3	W 0	D 1	L2	F 5	A 9	pts 1
Gold Cup: 3rd	P 3	W1	D 0	L 2	F 5	A 6	pts 3

	Date	Comp.	Venue	Opponents	Result	Goalscorers
1	Aug 17	UC	A	Portadown	L 3-4	R. Campbell, Eddis, Erskine / Cowan 2, Magee 2
2	20	UC	H	Coleraine	D 1-1	Houlahan / Quigley
3	24	UC	A	Ballymena Utd	L 1-4	R. Campbell / Pyper 3 (1 pen), Young
4	30	GC	A	Coleraine	W 5-2	Smith 2, McDonald 2, Erskine / Wade, Wright
5	Sept 7	GC	H	Ballymena Utd	L 0-2	/ Candlish, Hardy
6	13	GC	H	Cliftonville	L 0-2	/ Hamill, O'Kane
7	21	BWC[1]	A	Newry Town	W 3-2	O'Neill, Bustard (pen), Magee / Burns, Ralph
8	28	IL	A	Newry Town	W 2-1	Mitchell, Erskine / Ralph
9	Oct 5	IL	H	Glentoran	D 1-1	Magee / Morrison
10	8	BWC[2]	A	Glentoran	L 0-4	/ Hillis, Morrison 2, McCartney
11	12	IL	A	Glenavon	L 0-3	/ McBride, Conville, McCoy
12	19	IL	H	Distillery	D 4-4	Erskine, Leeman, R. Campbell, McLoughlin / Adams 3 (1 pen), Hamilton
13	26	IL	A	Bangor	W 4-1	O'Neill 2, Erskine, Magee / Nelson
14	Nov 2	IL	H	Cliftonville	W 3-0	Magee 2, R. Campbell / Fraser
15	9	IL	A	Carrick Rangers	D 1-1	Eddis / Halliday (pen)
16	16	IL	H	Portadown	W 2-1	Bustard, R. Campbell / Fraser
17	23	IL	A	Linfield	L 2-5	Erskine 2 / McGaughey 2, Doherty 2, Baxter
18	26	Cas[1]	H	Comber Rec.	W 5-0	Erskine, Leeman, O'Neill, Magee 2 /
19	30	IL	H	Omagh Town	W 2-0	Erskine 2 /
20	Dec 7	IL	A	Ballyclare C.	L 1-2	Bustard (pen) / Armstrong, Nixon
21	14	IL	H	Ballymena Utd	W 6-1	Erskine 2, R. Campbell 4 / Heron
22	17	Cas[2]	A	Ballyclare C.	W 3-1	R. Campbell, Erskine 2 / McCullough
23	26	IL	A	Crusaders	L 1-2	R. Campbell / Murray, Greer
24	28	IL	A	Larne	L 0-1	/ McNamee
25	Jan 1	IL	H	Glenavon	L 2-3	Bustard, Morrison / Ferguson, Conville, McBride
26	4	IL	A	Glentoran	D 1-1	Pyper / McBride
27	8	Cas[SF]	N	Crusaders	L 0-3	/ Uprichard, Collins, Burrows
28	11	IL	H	Newry Town	D 2-2	Bustard, Erskine / Fay, Griffin
29	18	IC[5]	A	Bangor	W 2-1	Erskine, O'Neill / Byrne
30	25	IL	A	Distillery	D 1-1	Pyper / Hamilton
31	Feb 1	IL	H	Bangor	L 1-4	R.Campbell / McCloskey, Kerr o.g., Brown, Nelson
32	4	LC[1]	H	Q.U.B.	W 5-0	Bustard, Erskine 2, Eddis, R. Campbell /
33	8	IL	A	Cliftonville	D 0-0	
34	15	IC[6]	H	Dunmurry Rec.	W 3-2	R. Campbell 2, Magee / McCartney 2
35	18	IL	H	Coleraine	L 0-1	/ Wright
36	22	IL	H	Carrick Rangers	W 1-0	Erskine /
37	25	LC[2]	A	Ballyclare C.	W 3-1	Erskine 2, R. Campbell / Flynn
38	29	IL	A	Portadown	W 3-2	McDonald 2, R. Campbell / Cowan 2 (1 pen)
39	Mar 7	IC[7]	A	Glenavon	L 0-3	/ McCoy, McMahon, McBride (pen)
40	14	IL	H	Linfield	D 2-2	R. Campbell, Magee / Beatty (pen), Wade

41	17	LC[3]	H	Portadown	L 0-2	/ Russell, Murray
42	21	IL	A	Omagh Town	L 0-3	/ Kavanagh 2 (1 pen), Gregg
43	28	IL	H	Ballyclare C.	D 0-0	
44	Apr 11	IL	A	Ballymena Utd.	W 2-1	McCourt 2 / Mellon
45	18	IL	A	Coleraine	W 4-1	Bustard 2, McCourt, R. Campbell / Healy
46	21	IL	H	Crusaders	D 1-1	R. Campbell / Parker
47	25	IL	H	Larne	D 1-1	R. Campbell / Barnes

Final positions, season 1992-93

League: 8th   P 30   W 12   D 9   L 9   F 45   A 45   pts 45

Ulster Cup: 1st   P 3   W 3   D 0   L 0   F 11   A 1   pts 9

Gold Cup: 3rd   P 3   W 1   D 1   L 1   F 4   A 4   pts 4

	Date	Comp.	Venue	Opponents	Result	Goalscorers
1	Aug 15	UC	A	Portadown	W 2-1	McCourt, Beattie / Cowan
2	18	UC	H	Distillery	W 3-0	Beattie, Bustard (pen), Magee /
3	22	UC	A	Ballymena Utd.	W 6-0	Davies, McCourt 3, Magee, Jeffrey /
4	26	UC[QF]	H	Omagh Town	W[P] 1-1	Beattie / O'Donnell
5	28	GC	H	Ballyclare Com.	W 3-0	McCourt, Bustard (pen), Magee /
6	Sept 1	UC[SF]	N	Glenavon	W 1-0	McCourt /
7	5	GC	A	Glentoran	L 0-3	/ Bowers, Mathieson, Campbell
8	12	GC	H	Glenavon	D 1-1	Mitchell / Smyth
9	19	BWC[1]	A	Newry Town	W 3-2	Beattie 2, McCourt / P. Magee 2
10	23	UC[F]	N[2]	Linfield	L 0-2	/ Campbell, Johnston
11	26	IL	A	Carrick Rangers	L 2-3	Beattie, Bustard / Cummings, McNamara, Wright
12	Oct 3	IL	H	Omagh Town	D 2-2	McDonald, Erskine / Coyle 2
13	10	IL	A	Ballyclare Com.	W 1-0	Erskine /
14	17	IL	H	Glentoran	L 0-3	/ McCartney 3
15	24	IL	A	Portadown	L 0-6	/ Cowan 2, Casey, Murray, Surgeon, Major
16	31	IL	H	Coleraine	W 3-1	Beattie, Erskine 2 / Cook
17	Nov 7	IL	A	Cliftonville	W 2-1	Kavanagh, Beattie / McCann
18	14	IL	H	Bangor	L 1-4	Erskine / McCallan 3, Brown
19	21	IL	A	Ballymena Utd.	W 4-3	McCourt, Beattie, Erskine, Kavanagh / Speak 2 (1 pen), Loughery
20	24	BWC[2]	A	Cliftonville	W 2-1	McDonald 2 / McCreadie
21	28	IL	H	Distillery	D 1-1	Erskine / Dykes
22	Dec 1	BWC[SF]	N[2]	Portadown	L 2-4	McDonald, Beattie / Fraser 2, Cowan, Gorman
23	5	IL	A	Linfield	L 0-1	/ Campbell
24	8	Cas[1]	A	Bangor	W 2-0	Erskine, Beattie /
25	12	IL	H	Glenavon	L 1-2	McCourt / McConville, Ferguson
26	16	Cas[2]	A	Glentoran	L 1-2	McCourt / Morrison o.g., Caughey
27	19	IL	A	Newry Town	W 3-2	O'Hagan, Campbell, Erskine / Griffen, Lundy
28	26	IL	H	Crusaders	W 2-0	Erskine, Beattie /
29	28	IL	A	Larne	W 3-1	O'Hagan, Hanna o.g., Erskine / McCourt
30	Jan 1	IL	H	Carrick Rangers	W 2-0	Connell, Beattie /
31	2	IL	A	Omagh Town	W 4-1	McDonald 2, Erskine, Beattie / O'Donnell

32	9	IL	H	Ballyclare Com.	D 1-1	Erskine / Gordon
33	16	IL	A	Glentoran	D 1-1	Erskine / Douglas
34	27	IC^5	H	Loughgall	W 3-0	Erskine 2, McCourt /
35	30	IL	H	Portadown	D 2-2	Erskine 2 (1 pen) / Cowan 2 (1 pen)
36	Feb 2	LC^1	H	Banbridge Town	W 4-0	Erskine, Beattie 3 /
37	6	IL	A	Coleraine	W 3-1	O'Hagan, Erskine 2 (1 pen) / Ewing
38	11	LC^2	A	Larne	W 4-2	Jeffrey, Erskine 3 (1 pen) / Barnes, McCourt
39	13	IL	H	Cliftonville	W 1-0	McDonald /
40	20	IC^6	A	Drumaness M.	W 4-0	Jeffrey, McCourt, Erskine, Kavanagh /
41	27	IL	A	Bangor	L 3-4	Erskine (pen), O'Hagan 2 / McCreadie, Magee 2, McCallan
42	Mar 2	LC^3	A	Distillery	W 2-1	Erskine, Morrison / White
43	6	IL	H	Ballymena Utd.	D 0-0	
44	13	IC^7	H	Distillery	D 0-0	
45	17	IC^{7R}	A	Distillery	W 4-1	Erskine, Bustard, McCourt, Kennedy o.g. / Dykes
46	20	IL	A	Distillery	L 1-2	McCourt / Dykes, McAleenan
47	24	LC^{SF}	N^3	Coleraine	L 1-2	Bustard / Donaghy, McLean
48	27	IL	H	Linfield	L 0-2	/ Harvey, Hunter
49	Apr 2	IC^{SF}	N^2	Cliftonville	W 3-2	Beattie, McCourt 2 / Donnelly, McFadden
50	10	IL	A	Glenavon	D 0-0	
51	12	IL	H	Newry Town	W 1-0	Erskine /
52	17	IL	A	Crusaders	D 1-1	Erskine / Burrows
53	24	IL	H	Larne	D 0-0	
54	May 1	IC^F	N	Bangor	D 1-1	McCourt / Glendinning
55	8	IC^{FR}	N	Bangor	D 1-1	Erskine / Glendinning
56	11	IC^{FR}	N	Bangor	L 0-1	/ Byrne

N = Windsor Park
N^2 = Oval
N^3 = Ballymena Showgrounds
W^P = won on penalties

Final positions, season 1993-94

League: 6th	P 30	W 13	D 2	L 15	F 59	A 55	pts 41
Ulster Cup: 3rd	P 3	W 1	D 0	L 2	F 4	A 5	pts 3
Gold Cup: 3rd	P 3	W 0	D 1	L 2	F 1	A 7	pts 1

	Date	Comp.	Venue	Opponents	Result	Goalscorers
1	Aug 14	UC	H	Portadown	L 0-3	/ Smith, Casey, Frazer
2	17	UC	H	Omagh Town	W 4-0	Erskine 3, Mooney /
3	20	UC	A	Ballyclare Com.	L 0-2	/ Leckey, Hanna
4	27	GC	A	Cliftonville	L 1-5	Beattie / Gill 2, Flynn, Hitchcock, McCann
5	Sept 4	GC	H	Linfield	L 0-2	/ Gorman, McConnell
6	11	GC	A	Newry Town	D 0-0	
7	18	IL	H	Linfield	L 0-3	/ Peebles 2, Johnston
8	25	IL	A	Glenavon	L 0-1	/ Kennedy
9	Oct 2	IL	H	Ballymena Utd.	L 1-2	McDonald / McConville, McCabe

10	9	IL	A	Omagh Town	W 2-1	Erskine 2 / Patton
11	16	IL	H	Portadown	L 1-2	De Mange / Cunningham 2
12	23	IL	A	Distillery	L 2-3	McCourt, McGaughey / Cleland 2, Armstrong
13	30	IL	A	Coleraine	L 0-3	/ Carlyle, McWalters 2, Cook
14	Nov 6	IL	H	Carrick Rangers	D 3-3	Bowes, Erskine 2 (1 pen) / Pyper 2, Nicholl
15	9	BWC[1]	A	Omagh Town	W 1-0	McGaughey /
16	13	IL	A	Glentoran	L 0-2	/ Smyth, Hall
17	20	IL	H	Ballyclare Com.	W 2-0	Murphy, Erskine (pen) /
18	25	BWC[2]	A	Larne	W 3-1	Blood, Erskine, McGaughey / Barnes
19	27	IL	A	Cliftonville	L 2-6	O'Hagan, Wilson / McAllister, Shearer, McCann, Strang 2, O'Kane
20	30	Cas[1]	H	Glentoran	W 4-1	Bustard, Erskine, McGaughey 2 / Morrison
21	Dec 4	IL	H	Newry Town	W 9-0	Erskine 2, McGaughey 2, Bowes 3, Beattie, McCann /
22	8	BC[SF]	N	Cliftonville	W 3-2	Blood, Kerr o.g., Mooney / Strang, Shearer
23	11	IL	H	Crusaders	L 2-4	Beattie, Stranney / Collins 2, Burrowes, Hunter
24	14	Cas[2]	A	Distillery	W 2-1	Erskine (pen), Beattic / Allen
25	18	IL	A	Larne	L 1-4	Erskine / Crawford, Barnes, McCourt 2
26	21	BC[F]	N[2]	Linfield	L 0-3	/ Doherty, Haylock, Campbell
27	27	IL	H	Bangor	W 5-3	Erskine 3, McCann, Bowers / Nelson, Glendinning, McAllan
28	Jan 1	IL	A	Linfield	L 1-2	Erskine / Haylock, Gorman
29	8	IL	A	Ballymena Utd.	W 3-0	Blood, Beattie, McCann /
30	11	Cas[SF]	N[2]	Glenavon	W 2-1	Beattie, Erskine / Ferguson
31	15	IL	H	Omagh Town	D 3-3	Erskine, Stranney, Jeffrey / Deery, Donnelly, Kavanagh (pen)
32	22	IC[5]	H	Glentoran	D 2-2	Stranney, Beattie / McBride 2
33	26	IC[5R]	A	Glentoran	L 2-3	Beattie, McCann / McBride, Candlish, McCabe
34	29	IL	A	Portadown	L 0-1	/ Fraser
35	Feb 1	Cas[F]	N[2]	Crusaders	W 4-2	Browne, Wilson, Stranney 2 / K. Hunter, Collins
36	5	LC[1]	H	Queen' Univ.	W 9-2	Wilson 2, Jeffrey, Erskine 3 (1 pen), McCourt 2, Bustard / McCourt, Hanna (pen)
37	12	IL	H	Distillery	W 1-0	Wilson /
38	22	IL	H	Glenavon	W 4-1	Wilson, Erskine (pen) McCourt, Browne / Feehan
39	26	IL	H	Coleraine	W 3-2	McCann, McCourt, Erskine (pen) / Ewing, Donaghy
40	Mar 5	IL	A	Carrick Rangers	W 2-1	Browne, Erskine / Robson
41	8	LC[2]	A	Bangor	W 3-1	Beattie 2, Erskine / Nelson (pen)
42	15	LC[3]	A	Distillery	W 2-1	Beattie, McCann / Baxter
43	19	IL	H	Glentoran	W 1-0	Erskine (pen) /
44	26	IL	A	Ballyclare Com.	L 0-1	/ Johnston
45	Apr 2	IL	H	Cliftonville	L 1-2	Erskine / Strang, Donnelly
46	13	LC[SF]	N[3]	Coleraine	L 1-2	Wilson / Cook 2
47	16	IL	A	Crusaders	L 1-3	Erskine (pen) / Livingstone 2, G. Murray
48	23	IL	H	Larne	W 4-0	Beattie, Erskine 2, (1 pen), Birney o.g. /
49	25	IL	A	Newry Town	W 3-1	Erskine, Stranney 2 / Magee (pen)
50	30	IL	A	Bangor	W 2-0	Wilson, Beattie /

N = Windsor Park
N[2] = Oval
N[3] = Seaview

Final positions, season 1994-95

League: 4th   P 30   W 15   D 5   L 10   F 56   A 42   pts 50

Ulster Cup: 4th   P 3   W 0   D 0   L 3   F 2   A 6   pts 0

Gold Cup: 4th   P 3   W 0   D 0   L 3   F 2   A 6   pts 0

	Date	Comp.	Venue	Opponents	Result	Goalscorers
1	Aug 13	UC	A	Portadown	L 1-3	Stranney / Smith, Doolin, Russell
2	16	UC	H	Coleraine	L 0-1	/ Ferris
3	20	UC	H	Newry Town	L 1-2	Beattie (pen) / Ralph, McBride o.g.
4	26	GC	A	Carrick Rangers	L 0-1	/ Shiels
5	Sept 3	GC	H	Crusaders	L 1-2	McCourt / Burrows, K. Hunter
6	10	GC	A	Glentoran	L 1-3	Browne / O'Brien (pen), McDowell 2
7	17	IL	A	Linfield	D 1-1	Beattie / Fenlon
8	24	IL	H	Glenavon	D 2-2	McCourt 2 / Ferguson 2 (1 pen)
9	Oct 1	IL	A	Ballymena Utd.	W 2-1	Browne, McCourt / Tully
10	8	IL	H	Omagh Town	D 1-1	Erskine / Cullen o.g.
11	15	IL	A	Portadown	L 0-1	/ Ferguson
12	22	IL	H	Distillery	W 2-1	Stranney 2 / Dykes
13	29	IL	H	Coleraine	L 1-2	Erskine / Carlyle, Cook
14	Nov 1	IL	H	Bangor	L 1-2	Morrison / Surgeon 2
15	4	IL	A	Carrick Rangers	L 1-4	O'Sullivan / Robson, Shiels (pen), Crawford, Donaghy
16	12	IL	G	Glentoran	L 2-3	Parker o.g., Erskine / Smith, Kelly, Bowers
17	19	IL	A	Ballyclare Com.	W 4-1	Erskine 2, P. Cullen 2 / Wilson
18	26	IL	H	Cliftonville	L 1-2	Morrison / McAllister, Donnelly
19	29	Cas[1]	H	Crusaders	W 2-1	Stranney, Dunnion / G. Hunter
20	Dec 3	IL	A	Newry Town	W 3-1	Erskine 3 / Ralph
21	10	IL	A	Crusaders	W 2-1	Erskine, Stranney / G. Hunter
22	13	Cas[2]	H	Linfield	L[T] 3-4	Morrison 2, McCann / Peebles 2, Gorman, Haylock
23	17	IL	H	Larne	W 3-1	Erskine 3 (1 pen) / McKinstry
24	26	IL	A	Bangor	L 1-3	Stranney / Batey, Ferguson 2
25	31	IL	H	Linfield	W 3-1	P. Cullen, Erskine 2 / Fenlon
26	Jan 3	IL	A	Glenavon	L 0-3	/ Ferguson 3 (1 pen)
27	7	IL	H	Ballymena Utd.	W 4-1	Erskine 2 (2 pens.), O'Sullivan, Stranney / Patton
28	14	IL	A	Omagh Town	W 3-1	McCann, Jeffrey, P. Cullen / B. McCreadie
29	24	IC[5]	H	Chimney Corn.	W 3-1	P. Cullen, McCann, Erskine / McGurnaghan
30	28	IL	H	Portadown	L 1-4	P. Cullen, / Kee o.g., Russell, Kennedy, Doolin
31	Feb 4	LC[1]	H	Dungannon Sw.	W[P] 3-3	C. Cullen, P. Cullen, Heaney / Smith, Drake, Montgomery (pen)
32	18	IC[6]	H	Brantwood	W 4-1	Heaney, Stranney, P.Cullen, Mooney (pen) / McDonald
33	25	IL	A	Coleraine	D 2-2	Parmore, Mooney (pen) / Gorman, McWalter
34	Mar 4	IL	H	Carrick Rangers	W 2-0	P. Cullen, Patmore /
35	11	IC[7]	H	Glenavon	W 3-2	P. Cullen 2, Mooney (pen) / McBride (pen), Ferguson
36	14	LC[2]	A	Omagh Town	W 3-2	P. Cullen 2, Heaney / Mohan, Donnelly
37	18	IL	A	Glentoran	L 1-4	P. Cullen / Smyth 3, McBride

38	21	LC³	A	Ballyclare Com.	W 4-2	Morrison 3, McCann / O'Connell, Kelly
39	25	IL	H	Ballyclare Com.	W 3-0	Erskine (pen), McCann, P. Cullen /
40	28	LC^SF	N	Bangor	W 2-1	Erskine (pen), O'Sullivan / Spiers
41	Apr 1	IL	A	Cliftonville	L 0-1	/ Manley
42	8	IC^SF	N	Linfield	D 0-0	
43	12	IC^SFR	N	Linfield	L 1-2	Morrison / Fenlon, Haylock
44	15	IL	H	Crusaders	D 0-0	
45	17	IL	H	Newry Town	W 4-0	P. Cullen, Beattie, Murphy, Heaney /
46	20	IL	A	Distillery	W 3-0	Beattie, McCann, P.Cullen /
47	22	IL	A	Larne	W 1-0	Morrison /
48	25	LC^F	N²	Cliftonville	W^P 0-0	
49	29	IL	H	Bangor	W 2-0	P. Cullen 2 /

W^P = won on penalties
N = Oval
N² = Windsor Park
L^T = aet

Final positions, season 1995-96

League: 7th	P 28	W 6	D 7	L 15	F 29	A 43	pts 25
Ulster Cup: 1st	P 3	W 3	D 0	L 0	F 7	A 0	pts 9
Gold Cup: 3rd	P 3	W 1	D 1	L 1	F 8	A 11	pts 4

	Date	Comp.	Venue	Opponents	Result	Goalscorers
1	Aug 12	LC¹	H	Queen's Univ.	W 2-0	Dunnion, Boyle /
2	15	LC²	H	Coleraine	L 1-2	McBride / Beckett, Maloney
3	19	UC	H	Linfield	W 2-0	Flannery 2 /
4	26	UC	H	Larne	W 1-0	P. Cullen /
5	Sept 2	UC	A	Ballymena Utd.	W 4-0	Flannery, P. Cullen 2, Boyle /
6	9	GC	A	Omagh Town	D 2-2	Mooney (pen), Johnston o.g. / McHugh 2
7	16	GC	H	Ballyclare Com.	W 3-0	Flannery, P. Cullen, Boyle /
8	23	GC	A	Portadown	L 3-7	Flannery, P. Cullen 2 / Peebles, Strain, Haylock 3, Casey, Evans
9	30	PL	A	Cliftonville	D 0-0	
10	Oct 3	UC^QF	A	Portadown	L 1-2	Morrison / Peebles, Casey
11	7	PL	H	Glenavon	D 1-1	Flannery / McBride
12	14	PL	A	Portadown	L 1-3	Shanley / Russell, Haylock, Candlish
13	21	PL	H	Crusaders	D 0-0	
14	28	PL	A	Glentoran	L 2-3	Boyle 2 / Smith, Nixon, Cunningham
15	Nov 4	PL	A	Bangor	L 1-2	Maloney / Morrow, Irwin (pen)
16	11	PL	H	Linfield	L 2-3	Boyle, Flannery (pen) / Fenlon 2 (1 pen), Campbell
17	18	PL	H	Cliftonville	W 3-0	P. Cullen 2, McLaughlin /
18	21	Cas¹	A	Distillery	W 3-1	McLaughlin, McCann, Flannery / Brush
19	25	PL	A	Glenavon	L 0-3	/ McBride (pen), Ferguson, McCoy
20	Dec 2	PL	H	Portadown	D 1-1	Mooney (pen) / Haylock

21	6	Cas[2]	H	Crusaders	L 0-1	/ O'Brien
22	9	PL	A	Crusaders	W 2-1	McGreevy, Cullen / K. Hunter
23	16	PL	H	Glentoran	L 1-4	McCann / Finlay, Batey, Smith, McBride
24	Jan 1	PL	A	Linfield	D 0-0	
25	6	PL	A	Cliftonville	L 0-1	/ Donnelly
26	13	PL	H	Glenavon	L 1-2	Boyle / Ferguson, Johnston
27	17	CCC[1]	A	Larne	W 3-0	Boyle 2, Bowers /
28	20	IC[5]	H	Cookstown Utd.	W 10-0	P. Cullen 4, Barker 3, Boyle 2, McCann /
29	23	CCC[1]	H	Larne	W 2-0	Barker, Bowers /
30	27	PL	A	Portadown	W 3-1	Barker 2, Boyle / Evans
31	30	PL	H	Bangor	W 3-0	McLaughlin, Bowers, Morrison /
32	Feb 3	PL	H	Crusaders	L 0-1	/ Baxter
33	6	CCC[2]	A	Glenavon	W 2-1	Murphy, Boyle / McBride
34	10	PL	A	Glentoran	L 1-3	Barker / Coyle, Finlay, Smith
35	17	PL	A	Bangor	W 1-0	P. Cullen /
36	24	IC[6]	H	Larne	W 1-0	Morrison /
37	Mar 2	PL	H	Linfield	L 1-2	Morrison / Johnston, Millar
38	5	CCC[SF]	N	Cliftonville	L 1-3	McCann / Cross, Sliney, Stokes
39	9	IC[7]	A	Portadown	L 1-2	Morrison / Kennedy, Candlish
40	16	PL	H	Cliftonville	D 2-2	McLaughlin, McCann / Donnelly, McCann
41	23	PL	A	Glenavon	L 1-3	McCann / Johnston, Shipp 2
42	30	PL	H	Portadown	L 0-2	/ Kennedy, Haylock
43	Apr 6	PL	A	Crusaders	L 0-2	/ O'Brien, G. Hunter
44	8	PL	H	Glentoran	L 0-2	/ Smith 2
45	20	PL	H	Bangor	W 2-1	Mooney (pen), P. Cullen / Spiers
46	27	PL	A	Linfield	D 0-0	

N = Oval

Final positions, season 1996-97

League: 8th   P 28   W 5   D 10   L 13   F 33   A 50   pts 25

	Date	Comp.	Venue	Opponents	Result	Goalscorers
1	Aug 10	LC[1]	H	Chimney Corn.	W 3-1	Fox, Mooney (pen), McCourt / McAlea
2	13	LC[2]	H	Crusaders	L 0-3	/ Morgan 3
3	17	UC[11L]	A	Carrick Rangers	W 2-0	Murphy, Mooney /
4	24	UC[12L]	H	Carrick Rangers	W 3-0	P. Cullen, Bacon, McCourt /
5	28	UC[2]	H	Glentoran	L 3-4	McCourt 2, Murphy / Kirk 2, Finlay, McBride
6	Sept 7	GC	H	Crusaders	L 1-3	McCourt / Baxter, Hunter 2
7	14	GC	A	Ballymena Utd.	L 0-3	/ Feehan, Murphy o.g., Loughery
8	21	GC	A	Larne	D 2-2	McCourt, Murphy / McKinstry, Collins
9	28	PL	A	Coleraine	L 0-1	/ Brunton (pen)
10	Oct 12	PL	A	Portadown	L 2-3	P. Cullen, Bacon / O'Driscoll, Smith, Haylock
11	19	PL	A	Crusaders	L 1-3	Bacon (pen) / McMullan, Callaghan, Dunne
12	26	PL	H	Linfield	L 2-3	Maher, P. Cullen / McBride o.g, Barker, Collier
13	Nov 2	PL	H	Glenavon	D 0-0	
14	9	PL	A	Cliftonville	W 1-0	Kelly /

15	16	PL	H	Glentoran	W 4-3	McCourt 2, P. Cullen, Morrison / Kirk 2, T.McCourt
16	23	PL	H	Coleraine	L 1-4	Maher / Gaston, Young, Forsberg, Brunton (pen)
17	26	Cas[1]	A	Cliftonville	L 0-1	/ Flynn
18	30	PL	A	Portadown	W 1-0	Bacon (pen) /
19	Dec 7	PL	H	Crusaders	D 0-0	
20	21	PL	A	Glenavon	L 1-2	Bacon (pen) / Glendinning, Williamson
21	26	PL	H	Cliftonville	L 0-2	/ Stokes 2
22	28	CCC[1]	A	Bangor	D 1-1	Morrison / Morrow
23	Jan 1	PL	A	Glentoran	D 0-0	
24	4	PL	A	Coleraine	D 0-0	
25	7	CCC[1]	H	Bangor	W 3-0	McGregor, Sims, C.Cullen /
26	11	PL	H	Portadown	D 2-2	McGregor, Pemberton / Russell, Casey
27	18	PL	A	Crusaders	D 2-2	Collins, Pemberton / Hunter, Baxter
28	25	IC[5]	A	Glenavon	L 0-1	/ McCartan
29	28	PL	A	Linfield	D 0-0	
30	Feb 1	PL	H	Linfield	W 4-1	P. Cullen, Pemberton, Morrison, McBride / Hill
31	8	PL	H	Glentoran	D 2-2	Pemberton, McBride / Glendinning, Grant
32	15	PL	A	Cliftonville	L 1-2	Stevens / O'Neill, Stokes (pen)
33	18	CCC[2]	A	Glentoran	L 0-3	/ McCourt, Hamill 2
34	25	MU[1]	H	Armagh City	W 1-0	McBride /
35	Mar 1	PL	H	Glentoran	W 3-0	Morrison, Feeney 2/
36	8	PL	H	Coleraine	D 3-3	Tighe 2 (2 pens), McBride / Shipp 2, McCallan
37	13	MU[2]	H	Portadown	W 1-0	Feeney /
38	22	PL	A	Portadown	L 0-5	/ Scully, Haylock 4
39	26	PL	H	Crusaders	L 1-5	Powell / Hunter 2, O'Brien 2, Morgan
40	Apr 1	PL	A	Linfield	L 1-3	Murphy / Gorman, McLean (pen), Erskine
41	5	PL	A	Glenavon	D 1-1	McCourt / Grant
42	15	MU[SF]	H	Distillery	L 0-1	/ McDonagh
43	19	PL	H	Cliftonville	L 0-1	/ McCann
44	26	PL	A	Glentoran	L 0-2	/ Hamill, McCourt
45	29	PLPO	A	Bangor	W 1-0	P.Cullen /
46	May 2	PLPO	H	Bangor	W 1-0	Murphy /

Final positions, season 1997-98

League: 10th	P 36	W 6	D 9	L 21	F 30	A 71	pts 27
Gold Cup: 3rd	P 5	W 2	D 1	L 2	F 9	A 13	pts 7
Intertoto Cup:	P 4	W 0	D 0	L 4	F 1	A 13	pts 0

	Date	Comp.	Venue	Opponents	Result	Goalscorers
1	Jun 21	ITC	H	Royal Antwerp	L 0-1	/ Kiekens (pen)
2	28	ITC	A	Nea Salamis	L 1-4	Bowers (pen) / A.N.Other
3	Jul 5	ITC	H	Auxerre	L 0-3	/ Compan, Sibierski, Guivarch
4	12	ITC	A	Lausanne	L 0-5	/ Hanzl, Iglesias, Carrasco, Celestini (pen), Douglas (pen)

5	Aug 9	LC[1]	H	Brantwood	W 7-2	Murphy, Hinds 2, Morrison 2, Sims, Feeney / Hamilton, Clarke
6	16	PL	H	Linfield	L 0-1	/ Barker
7	18	LC[2]	A	Glenavon	L 1-2	Feeney / Patton, Ferguson
8	23	PL	A	Cliftonville	L 0-1	/ Davey
9	30	PL	H	Omagh Town	D 2-2	Hegan, Lawless (pen) / McHugh, Kavanagh
10	Sept 10	PL	A	Crusaders	L 0-4	/ Baxter, Hunter, Arthur 2
11	13	PL	A	Glentoran	L 0-3	/ Hamill, Livingstone, McBride
12	17	GC	A	Bangor	W 3-2	Bird, McCourt, S. Johnston / MacPherson 2
13	20	PL	H	Coleraine	D 0-0	
14	23	GC	H	Distillery	W 2-0	McCourt, Yeo /
15	27	PL	A	Portadown	L 0-1	/ Arkins
16	29	GC	H	Coleraine	L 2-5	Getty 2 / Young, Shipp, McCallion 2, McCallen
17	Oct 4	PL	H	Glenavon	L 3-4	Morrison, McCourt, Smyth o.g. / Smyth, Murphy, Ferguson 2 (1 pen)
18	7	GC	A	Limavady Utd.	D 1-1	McBride / McCallum
19	11	PL	A	Ballymena Utd.	L 1-3	Yeo / Knell 3
20	14	GC	H	Linfield	L 1-5	Yeo (pen) / Larmour 2, Gorman, Cleland, Doherty
21	18	PL	A	Linfield	L 0-4	/ Cleland, Larmour, Gorman, Kerr
22	25	PL	H	Cliftonville	L 2-3	Feeney (pen), Hinds / Dyson o.g., McAtee, O'Connor
23	Nov 1	PL	A	Omagh Town	W 4-2	Maynard, Morrison, Dyson, Feeney / McCreadie, McHugh
24	8	PL	H	Glentoran	D 1-1	Dyson / Cash
25	15	PL	A	Coleraine	L 1-2	McCourt / McCallion, Clanachan
26	18	Cas[1]	A	Portadown	L 2-4	Getty 2 / Arkins 2, Haylock, Woods
27	22	PL	H	Portadown	D 1-1	Dyson / Woods
28	25	PL	H	Crusaders	D 1-1	Getty / Morgan
29	29	PL	A	Glenavon	W 2-1	Getty, Collins / Ferguson
30	Dec 6	PL	H	Ballymena Utd.	W 2-1	Morrison, Getty / Muir
31	13	PL	H	Linfield	L 1-5	Hinds (pen) / Gorman, Beatty, Feeney, Larmour, Murphy
32	20	PL	A	Cliftonville	D 2-2	Morrison, McBride / O'Connor, Collins
33	27	PL	H	Omagh Town	L 1-2	McBride (pen) / Donaghey, Wilson
34	31	PL	A	Crusaders	L 0-1	/ Dornan
35	Jan 10	PL	H	Glenavon	W 1-0	Collins /
36	17	PL	A	Portadown	L 0-1	/ Smith
37	24	IC[5]	H	Institute	L 0-2	/ Deery, Maloney
38	27	MU[1]	H	AFC Craigavon	L[P] 2-2	Kerr 2 / Lavery, McConville
39	31	PL	H	Glenavon	D 1-1	Kerr / Grant
40	Feb 3	CCC[1]	H	Cliftonville	L 0-1	/ McCourt
41	7	PL	A	Ballymena Utd.	D 1-1	Bird / O'Connell
42	10	PL	A	Glentoran	L 0-2	/ Elliott, McBride
43	14	PL	A	Linfield	L 0-2	/ Beatty (pen), Kelly o.g.
44	28	PL	H	Cliftonville	D 1-1	Kerr / McCourt
45	Mar 21	PL	H	Crusaders	L 0-1	/ Morgan
46	28	PL	H	Glentoran	L 0-2	/ Mitchell, McBride
47	Apr 7	PL	A	Omagh Town	L 1-2	Prizeman (pen) / McHugh 2
48	11	PL	A	Coleraine	D 2-2	Kerr, Morgan / McAllister, McAllan
49	13	PL	H	Portadown	L 0-1	/ Arkins

50	18	PL	A	Glenavon	D 0-0		
51	25	PL	H	Ballymena Utd.	L 0-2	/ Muir, Loughery	

L^P = Lost on penalties

Final positions, season 1998-99

Division 1: 2nd	P 28	W 16	D 1	L 11	F 47	A 34	pts 49		
Ulster Cup: 2nd	P 7	W 4	D 0	L 3	F 14	A 10	pts 12		
Gold Cup: 3rd	P 5	W 2	D 1	L 2	F 6	A 10	pts 7		

	Date	Comp.	Venue	Opponents	Result	Goalscorers
1	Aug 15	UC	H	Bangor	W* 2-0	Morrison, Erskine /
2	22	UC	A	Limavady Utd.	L 0-1	/ Ferris
3	28	UC	A	Ballyclare Com.	L 3-4	Morrison, Dykes, McBride / McCrae 3, Johnston
4	Sept 5	UC	H	Carrick Rangers	W 3-1	Dykes 2, Prizeman / Crowe
5	8	GC	H	Omagh Town	W 3-0	Erskine 2, Beattie /
6	12	UC	A	Dungannon Sw.	W 3-2	Prizeman, Kerr, Erskine / Gough, Bates
7	19	UC	H	Distillery	W 1-0	Erskine /
8	22	GC	A	Portadown	L 0-3	/ Arkins 2, Hill
9	26	UC	A	Larne	W 4-1	Prizeman, Erskine, Kerr, Adair / McCormick
10	Oct 3	IL	H	Ballyclare Com.	W 2-1	Kerr, B. Martin o.g. / J. Martin
11	6	IL	A	Distillery	W 2-0	Adair, Dykes /
12	13	GC	H	Glentoran	L 0-5	/ McBride 2, Leeman, Kirk, Elliott
13	17	IL	A	Dungannon Sw.	L 1-2	Dykes / Bates, Robinson
14	27	GC	A	Ballyclare Com.	W 2-1	Erskine 2 / McCrystal
15	31	IL	A	Limavady Utd.	W 3-2	Beattie, Erskine (pen), Kerr / Curran, Love
16	Nov 3	IL	H	Carrick Rangers	W 1-0	Kerr /
17	7	IL	H	Bangor	W 2-0	Dykes, Kerr /
18	10	GC	H	Larne	D 1-1	Dykes / Withers
19	14	IL	A	Larne	W 2-0	Beggs 2 /
20	21	IL	A	Ballyclare Com.	W 5-2	Dykes 2, Erskine, Collins, Feeney / Owens, McCrystal
21	28	IL	H	Distillery	W 2-0	Prizeman, Erskine /
22	Dec 1	Cas[1]	H	Bangor	W^T 2-1	Morrison, Kerr / Crowe
23	5	IL	H	Dungannon Sw.	W 2-1	Beggs, C. Feeney / Montgomery (pen)
24	12	IL	A	Carrick Rangers	L 1-4	Dykes / Arthur 2, Murray, Sinclair
25	16	Cas[2]	A	Cliftonville	L 1-3	Tabb o.g. / Murray, Sliney, Scannell
26	19	IL	H	Limavady Utd.	W 3-0	Dykes, Morrison, Kerr /
27	30	IL	H	Larne	W 1-0	Dykes /
28	Jan 2	IL	A	Distillery	L 3-4	A. Campbell 2, Feeney / McDonagh, Clifford, Beggs o.g., Armour
29	9	IL	H	Ballyclare Com.	L 0-2	/ B. Martin, Picking
30	16	IL	A	Dungannon Sw.	W 2-1	Erskine, Adair / Gough
31	18	MU[1]	H	AFC Craigavon	W 7-0	Dykes 3, Adair 2, Collins, Morrison /
32	23	IC[5]	H	Ards Rangers	W 1-0	Adair /
33	26	IL	A	Bangor	L 0-1	/ Chapman

	Date	Comp.	Venue	Opponents	Result	Goalscorers
34	30	IL	H	Carrick Rangers	L 2-4	Prizeman, Beggs / Arthur 2 (1 pen), Dean, Trainor
35	Feb 3	CCC[1]	A	Bangor	W 4-3	Erskine (pen), Kerr, Collins, Reid / Surgeon, Cullen 2
36	9	MU[2]	H	Distillery	W^{T} 3-0	Dykes, Prizeman, Adair /
37	13	IL	H	Bangor	L 1-2	Erskine / Bailie, Surgeon (pen)
38	20	IC[6]	A	Carrick Rangers	L 0-2	/ Murray, Stevens
39	23	CCC[2]	A	Carrick Rangers	L 1-2	Ginty / Arthur, Armstrong
40	27	IL	A	Larne	W 2-0	Dykes, Adair /
41	Mar 6	IL	H	Distillery	L 0-2	/ Kelly, Armour
42	8	MC^{SF}	H	Portadown	W^{P} 2-2	Reid, Morrow / Arkins, McNamara
43	20	IL	A	Ballyclare Com.	L 0-2	/ Martin, Smith
44	23	IL	H	Dungannon Sw.	W 1-0	Ginty /
45	30	IL	A	Limavady Utd.	W 3-0	Beggs, Dykes, Beattie /
46	Apr 3	IL	A	Carrick Rangers	L 0-1	/ Armstrong
47	6	IL	H	Limavady Utd.	L 1-2	Beattie / McCallum, Calvin
48	13	MC^{F}	A	Glenavon	L 1-3	Ginty / McMenemy, Grant, Arthur (pen),
49	17	IL	A	Bangor	D 0-0	
50	24	IL	H	Larne	W 5-1	Morrison, Dykes, Kerr, D. McCourt 2 / Lowry
51	May 5	PLPO	H	Cliftonville	L 0-1	/ Withnell
52	8	PLPO	A	Cliftonville	L 2-4	Morrison 2 / Withnell 3, Flynn

W* = match awarded to Bangor 1-0
W^{T} = after extra time
W^{P} = won on penalties

Final positions, season 1999-2000

Division 1: 2nd   P 36   W 16 D 16 L 4   F 65   A 36   pts 64

	Date	Comp.	Venue	Opponents	Result	Goalscorers
1	Aug 14	IL	A	Dungannon Sw.	L 1-3	McQuillan (pen) / Robinson, McCann 2
2	21	IL	H	Institute	W 3-1	Shiels 2, Quigg o.g. / Cunning
3	27	IL	H	Bangor	D 1-1	Shiels / McBride o.g.
4	31	IL	A	Omagh Town	W 3-1	Peebles, Cleland, Collins / Wilson
5	Sept 7	IL	H	Armagh City	W 4-1	Shiels 2, Cleland, Haire o.g. / Murphy
6	11	IL	A	Larne	W 2-0	Kerr, McBride /
7	18	IL	H	Limavady Utd.	W 2-0	Collins, Magill /
8	21	GC[1]	A	Bangor	W 2-1	Kerr, McQuillan / Sliney
9	25	IL	A	Ballyclare Com.	D 2-2	Cleland 2 / Gibson, Kirk
10	Oct 2	IL	H	Carrick Rangers	W 2-1	Shiels 2 / Trueick
11	5	GC[2]	H	Glentoran	L 1-2	Shiels / Rainey 2
12	9	IL	H	Dungannon Sw.	D 0-0	
13	16	IL	A	Institute	D 0-0	
14	23	IL	A	Bangor	D 2-2	Shiels, Cleland / McKeown, Douglas
15	30	IL	H	Omagh Town	L 0-1	/ Henderson o.g.
16	Nov 6	IL	A	Armagh City	W 4-0	Young, Shiels 2, McBride /
17	12	IL	H	Larne	D 1-1	Kerr / Lowry
18	20	IL	A	Limavady Utd.	D 1-1	Young / Love

19	27	IL	H	Ballyclare Com.	W 4-0	McGrath, Beattie, Kerr, Cleland /
20	30	Cas[1]	A	Distillery	W 2-1	Curran, Cleland / McShane
21	Dec 4	IL	A	Carrick Rangers	D 0-0	
22	11	IL	A	Dungannon Sw.	D 2-2	Cleland, Shiels / Ruddy, Ritchie
23	14	Cas[2]	A	Carrick Rangers	W 5-1	Shiels, Kerr, Cleland, Beattie, Bailie / Hunter
24	18	IL	H	Institute	W 4-2	Young, Curran, Cleland 2 / Quigg, Coyle
25	27	IL	H	Bangor	D 1-1	Curran / MacPherson
26	Jan 3	IL	A	Omagh Town	W 2-1	Shiels, (pen), Cleland / Crilly
27	8	IL	H	Armagh City	D 1-1	Cleland / Walker
28	12	Cas[SF]	N	Glentoran	L 1-4	Kerr / Elliott, McCann, Young, Gilzean
29	15	IL	A	Larne	D 2-2	McQuillan, Beattie / Connolly, Storey
30	22	IC[5]	A	Dungannon Sw.	D 0-0	
31	25	IC[5R]	H	Dungannon Sw.	L 0-1	/ Gough
32	29	IL	H	Limavady Utd.	L 1-2	C. Feeney / Brown, McDowell
33	Feb 1	LC[1]	A	Cliftonville	L 2-5	Shiels, Cleland / Donnelly, McCallion 2, Scannell, Gribben
34	5	IL	A	Ballyclare Com.	D 2-2	McGrath, McQuillan / Hall, Kirk
35	11	IL	H	Carrick Rangers	W 3-0	Curran, Kerr, Shiels /
36	19	IL	H	Dungannon Sw.	D 2-2	McQuillan 2 / McCann 2
37	Mar 4	IL	A	Institute	W 2-0	McGrath 2 /
38	18	IL	A	Bangor	D 1-1	Cleland / Gorman
39	25	IL	H	Omagh Town	D 1-1	McQuillan / Boyle
40	Apr 1	IL	A	Armagh City	W 2-1	Bailie, Cleland / Murphy
41	15	IL	H	Larne	W 1-0	McQuillan /
42	22	IL	A	Limavady Utd.	L 0-1	/ Love
43	24	IL	H	Ballyclare Com.	W 2-1	C. Feeney, Bailie / Owens
44	29	IL	A	Carrick Rangers	W 4-1	McQuillan (pen), Collins, Kerr, Shiels / Murphy
45	May 2	PLPO	H	Cliftonville	L 0-2	/ Mulvenna, Scannell
46	4	PLPO	A	Cliftonville	L 0-1	/ Scannell

N = Seaview

Final positions, season 2000-01

Division 1: 1st   P 36   W 21   D 10   L 5   F 69   A 31   pts 73

	Date	Comp.	Venue	Opponents	Result	Goalscorers
1	Aug 12	IL	H	Carrick Rangers	W 2-0	O'Brien, McQuillan /
2	19	IL	A	Larne	W 3-0	Donaghy, Gorman, Bailie /
3	26	IL	H	Bangor	D 1-1	O'Brien / Millar
4	29	IL	A	Dungannon Sw	D 1-1	Gorman / Stevens (pen)
5	Sept 9	IL	H	Institute	W 2-0	Parker, Gorman /
6	16	IL	A	Ballyclare Com	W 3-1	Donaghy 2, O'Brien / Gray
7	21	GC[1]	A	Dungannon Sw	L 1-2	Gorman / Campbell, Forker
8	23	IL	H	Distillery	D 3-3	Bailie, Gorman, McQuillan / Martin, Bates 2
9	Oct 14	IL	A	Carrick Rangers	W 5-0	Gorman 2, McQuillan 2, McLean /
10	17	IL	A	Limavady Utd	W 2-0	Lowry, Gorman /
11	21	IL	H	Larne	D 1-1	Young o.g. / Bustard

12	28	IL	A	Bangor	W 2-0	McQuillan 2 (1 pen) /
13	Nov 4	IL	H	Dungannon Sw	W 3-1	McLean 2, McQuillan / Duke
14	11	IL	A	Institute	L 1-3	Gorman / Coyle, Doherty, Maloney
15	18	IL	H	Ballyclare Com	W 1-0	Bailie /
16	25	IL	A	Distillery	W 3-1	Curran 2, Gorman / Wray
17	Dec 2	IL	H	Limavady Utd	D 0-0	
18	5	Cas[1]	A	Glentoran	L 0-3	/ Smyth, McBride, Lockhart
19	9	IL	A	Armagh City	L 0-4	/ McKinstry 2, Gough 2
20	16	IL	H	Carrick Rangers	W 3-0	Divin 2, Reddish /
21	23	IL	A	Larne	W 3-0	McLean, Gorman, Reddish /
22	Jan 1	IL	H	Institute	D 1-1	Curran / Ross
23	6	IL	A	Ballyclare Com	W 4-0	Hall (pen), O'Brien, Reddish, McQuillan /
24	13	IL	H	Distillery	L 2-3	Parker, O'Brien / Bates, Curran o.g., Armour
25	16	LC[1]	A	Distillery	W 2-0	Gorman, O'Brien /
26	27	IL	A	Limavady Utd	D 2-2	Divin, Gorman / Devlin 2
27	30	IC[1]	H*	RUC	W 1-0	Gorman /
28	Feb 3	IL	H	Armagh City	D 2-2	Gorman, O'Brien / McKinstry, Morgan
29	6	LC[2]	A	Ballymena Utd	W 2-1	Gorman 2 / Loughran
30	10	IL	A	Carrick Rangers	W 3-0	Gorman 2, O'Brien /
31	17	IC[2]	A	Linfield	D 0-0	
32	20	IC[2R]	A	Linfield	L 0-5	/ Larmour, Ferguson 2, Morgan, Scates
33	24	IL	H	Larne	L 0-2	/ Murphy, Storey
34	Mar 15	IL	H	Dungannon Sw	W 1-0	Gorman /
35	17	LC[3]	A	Omagh Town	L[T] 0-2	/ Friel, Patton
36	31	IL	A	Institute	W 2-0	Moran 2 /
37	Apr 7	IL	H	Armagh City	W 2-1	Parker, Rainey / Morgan
38	10	IL	A	Dungannon Sw	W 2-1	Moran, McLean / Mercer
39	14	IL	H	Ballyclare Com	W 3-1	Gorman 2, Curran / McAtee
40	17	IL	A	Distillery	D 0-0	
41	21	IL	H	Limavady Utd	W 3-0	Curran, O'Brien, Rainey /
42	23	IL	A	Bangor	W 2-0	Gorman, Lowry /
43	26	IL	H	Bangor	D 0-0	
44	28	IL	A	Armagh City	L 1-2	Rainey / Walker, Hynds

H* = at Inver Park
L[T] = AET

Final positions, season 2001-02

League: 10th   P 36 W 6 D 9 L 21 F 30 A 71 pts 27
League Cup: 4th P 4 W 1 D 1 L 2 F 3 A 8 pts 4

	Date	Comp.	Venue	Opponents	Result	Goalscorers
1	Aug 11	PL	A	Omagh Town	L 0-1	/ McCann
2	18	PL	H	Linfield	L 2-4	Millar, Rainey / Larmour, Curran o.g., Ferguson, Murphy
3	28	LC	H	Linfield	L 0-4	/ Collier, Larmour 2, Hall o.g.
4	Sept 1	PL	A	Newry Town	W 1-0	Young /

5	8	PL	A	Portadown	L 1-2	Parker / McCann, Ogden
6	11	LC	H+	Distillery	D 0-0	
7	15	PL	H	Cliftonville	W 2-1	Rainey, Lowry / Curran o.g.
8	22	PL	A	Coleraine	W 2-1	Millar, Rainey / Tolan
9	25	LC	A	Glentoran	L 0-2	/ Hunter 2
10	29	PL	H	Crusaders	D 0-0	
11	Oct 6	PL	A	Glenavon	L 1-2	McLean / McMahon, O'Kane
12	9	LC	A	Bangor	W 3-2	Young, Larkin 2 / Adair, MacPherson
13	13	PL	A	Linfield	L 0-4	/ Ferguson, Morgan 2, Larmour
14	20	PL	H	Omagh Town	L 1-3	Divin / Patton, McCann, Sproule
15	27	PL	H	Newry Town	L 1-4	Lowry / Casey 3, Martin
16	Nov 3	PL	A	Glentoran	L 0-4	/ Lockhart, Haylock 2, Armour
17	6	Cas[1]	A	Carrick Rangers	W 1-0	Divin /
18	10	PL	H	Portadown	L 1-4	Sliney (pen) / Hamilton, Arkins 2, Feeney
19	17	PL	H	Cliftonville	D 0-0	
20	24	PL	H	Coleraine	L 1-2	Sliney / McHugh, McCoosh
21	Dec 1	PL	A	Crusaders	L 0-3	/ Campbell (pen), Magill, Bell
22	8	PL	H	Glenavon	D 0-0	
23	11	Cas[2]	A	Ballymena Utd.	L 1-2	Lowry / Withnell, Campbell
24	15	PL	H	Linfield	D 2-2	Morrow, Millar / Kelly 2
25	22	PL	A	Omagh Town	D 1-1	Millar / Crawford
26	26	PL	A	Newry Town	D 1-1	Sliney / Ward
27	29	PL	H	Glentoran	L 0-4	/ Hunter, McCann, Halliday 2
28	Jan 5	PL	A	Portadown	L 1-3	Elliott / Hamilton 2, Neill
29	8	PL	H*	Glentoran	D 0-0	
30	12	PL	A	Cliftonville	L 0-2	/ Scannell 2
31	30	IC[5]	A	Limavady Utd.	W 2-1	Bailie, O'Brien / Brown
32	Feb 2	PL	H*	Crusaders	W 2-1	Sliney (pen), Millar / Muir
33	5	PL	A	Coleraine	L 0-5	/ Armstrong 2, Tolan 2, Curran
34	9	PL	A	Glenavon	W 1-0	Rainey /
35	16	IC[6]	H*	Glentoran	L 0-5	/ Smyth, Halliday 2, Wright 2
36	23	PL	A	Linfield	L 1-2	Lowry / Morgan 2
37	Mar 2	PL	H*	Omagh Town	L 0-2	/ McCullagh, Patton (pen)
38	19	PL	H*	Newry Town	W 4-2	O'Brien, Rainey, Millar, Dickson / Arthur, Cleary
39	23	PL	A	Glentoran	D 1-1	Lowry / Walker (pen)
40	30	PL	H*	Portadown	L 0-2	/ Arkins 2 (1 pen)
41	Apr 2	PL	A	Cliftonville	L 0-1	/ Wall
42	13	PL	H*	Coleraine	L 1-4	McCracken (pen) / McCoosh, Curran, McHugh, Hamill
43	20	PL	A	Crusaders	D 1-1	Millar / Munster
44	25	PL	A	Glenavon	L 1-2	Curran / Smith, McCann

H+ = played at Clandeboye Park
H* = home fixture played away (no ground)

Final positions, season 2002-03

League: 7th   P 38   W 12   D 10   L16   F27   A 39   pts 46
League Cup: 4th   P 4   W 0   D 2   L 2   F 5   A 8   pts 2

	Date	Comp.	Venue	Opponents	Result	Goalscorers
1	Aug 10	PL	H	Crusaders	D 2-2	McCracken, Elliott / Marks 2
2	13	LC	A	L. Distillery	D 1-1	McCracken / Hunter
3	17	PL	A	L. Distillery	L 0-1	/ Prenter
4	24	PL	H	Newry Town	W 2-1	McCracken, Curran / Russell
5	27	LC	A	Bangor	D 0-0	
6	30	PL	A	Cliftonville	D 0-0	
7	Sept 7	PL	H	Portadown	L 0-2	/ Cleary o.g., Clarke
8	10	LC	H	Glentoran	L 1-3	McCracken / Smith 2, Halliday
9	14	PL	A	Linfield	L 1-3	Scullion / Feeney 2 (1 pen), Shaw
10	21	PL	A	Coleraine	L 0-2	/ Armstrong, McHugh
11	28	PL	H	Glentoran	L 1-2	Lowry / Halliday, Smith
12	Oct 5	PL	A	Omagh Town	W 1-0	Bailie /
13	8	LC	A	Linfield	L 3-4	Campbell, McCracken, Lowry / Feeney, McCann, Thompson, Morgan
14	12	PL	H	Institute	W 3-0	McCombe, Curran, McCracken /
15	19	PL	A	Glenavon	D 1-1	Reddish / McCargo
16	26	PL	A	Crusaders	W 2-0	Lowry, Young (pen) /
17	29	Cas[1]	A	Linfield	L 0-2	/ McBride, Shaw
18	Nov 9	PL	A	Newry Town	W 3-1	McCracken, Rainey, Lowry / McPhee
19	16	PL	A	Cliftonville	L 0-1	/ Tumilty
20	23	PL	A	Portadown	D 1-1	Reddish / McAreavey
21	Dec 7	PL	H	Coleraine	L 0-1	/ McCoosh
22	10	PL	H	L. Distillery	W 1-0	Rainey /
23	14	PL	A	Glentoran	L 0-3	/ Halliday 2, Armour
24	21	PL	H	Omagh Town	D 0-0	
25	26	PL	A	Institute	L 0-2	/ Deery, Parkhurst
26	28	PL	H	Glenavon	D 1-1	Cleary / McCann (pen)
27	Jan 18	IC[1]	A	Moyola Park	W 2-1	Haylock 2 / Hassan
28	21	PL	A	L. Distillery	W 1-0	McKeown /
29	28	PL	H	Linfield		
29	Feb 1	PL	H	Portadown	L 0-3	/ Hamilton, Fitzgerald, Neill
30	8	PL	A	Linfield	L 0-1	/ Feeney
31	15	IC[2]	H	Killyleagh YC	W 1-0	Rainey /
32	18	PL	H	Linfield	L 1-2	Rainey / Larmour, Ferguson (pen)
33	22	PL	A	Coleraine	L 1-3	Campbell / Tolan, Beatty, Hamill
34	25	PL	H	Cliftonville	D 0-0	
35	Mar 11	IC[3]	H	Glentoran	L 0-1	/ Smith
36	15	PL	A	Glenavon	L 0-3	/ Keenan, McCann 2
37	18	PL	H	Crusaders	D 0-0	
38	22	PL	H	Institute	W 1-0	Rainey /
39	25	PL	H	Glentoran	L 0-2	/ McCann, Halliday
40	27	PL	H	Newry Town	W 1-0	Haylock /
41	29	PL	A	Omagh Town	W 1-0	McCombe /

42	Apr 12	PL	H	L. Distillery	W 1-0	Kennedy /
43	19	PL	H	Cliftonville	D 0-0	
44	22	PL	H	Glenavon	W 1-0	Kennedy /
45	26	PL	A	Crusaders	D 0-0	
46	May 1	PL	A	Newry Town	L 0-1	/ Byrne

Final positions, season 2003-04

League: 8th   P 30   W 9   D 11   L 10   F 35   A 45   pts 38

League Cup: 3rd   P 6   W 3   D 1   L 2   F 8   A 8   pts 10

	Date	Comp.	Venue	Opponents	Result	Goalscorers
1	Aug 16	LC	H	Crusaders	W 1-0	Fitzgerald /
2	23	LC	A	Limavady Utd.	W 3-1	Fitzgerald 2, Scannell / McNerlin
3	Sept 2	LC	A	Coleraine	L 1-3	Cleary / Hamill, Tolan, Gorman
4	6	LC	A	Crusaders	D 0-0	
5	13	LC	H	Limavady Utd.	W 2-0	Fitzgerald , Lowry /
6	16	LC	H	Coleraine	L 1-4	O'Boyle / Tolan, Armstrong 2, McAuley
7	20	IPL	A	Newry Town	D 0-0	
8	27	IPL	H	Institute	D 2-2	Rainey, Fitzgerald / Parkhouse, McCann
9	Oct 4	IPL	A	Cliftonville	L 1-2	Fitzgerald / McMullan, McKeown o.g.
10	11	IPL	H	Coleraine	D 2-2	Kennedy, Williamson / Hamill 2
11	18	IPL	H	Linfield	L 0-4	/ Ferguson, Picking, Morgan 2
12	25	IPL	A	Limavady Utd.	W 1-0	Fitzgerald
13	28	Cas[1]	H	Carrick Rangers	W 4-1	Fitzgerald 2 (1 pen), Kennedy, Hunter / Moore
14	Nov 1	IPL	H	Crusaders	W 2-0	Feeney 2 (1 pen) /
15	8	IPL	H	Glenavon	L 2-4	Rainey, Batey o.g. / Smith, Hawe, Hamilton, McCracken
16	15	IPL	A	Omagh Town	W 4-1	Kennedy 3, Campbell / Crawford
17	18	Cas[2]	A	Ballyclare Com.	W 4-0	Kennedy, Rainey, Hunter, Fitzgerald /
18	22	IPL	A	Ballymena Utd.	L 0-1	/ Jemson
19	Dec 6	IPL	H	Glentoran	W 2-1	Feeney, Fitzgerald (pen) / McCann
20	13	IPL	A	Dungannon Sw.	D 2-2	Kennedy 2 / Slater, Topley
21	17	IPL	H	Distillery	D 1-1	Kennedy / Muir
22	20	IPL	H	Portadown	W 2-1	Fitzgerald, Rainey / Neill
23	26	IPL	A	Larne	L 1-5	Fitzgerald / Delaney 2, Parker 3
24	Jan 1	IPL	H	Newry Town	W 4-0	Hunter, Kennedy, Fitzgerald 2 /
25	3	IPL	A	Institute	W 1-0	Quinn /
26	10	IPL	H	Cliftonville	D 0-0	
27	19	IC[5]	H	Donard Hospital	W 10-0	Kennedy 3 (1 pen), Fitzgerald 5, Quinn, Lowry /
28	24	IPL	A	Coleraine	L 1-4	Rainey / Hamill (pen), Gaston, McHugh, Curran
29	Feb 3	Cas[SF]	N	Ballymena Utd.	W 1-0	Scannell /
30	7	IPL	H	Limavady Utd.	D 0-0	
31	16	IC[6]	H*	Ballyclare Com.	W 2-0	Kennedy, Gollogley /
32	21	IPL	A	Crusaders	D 0-0	
33	24	IPL	A	Linfield	D 2-2	Kennedy, Rainey / Picking, Ferguson
34	28	IPL	A	Glenavon	W 2-1	Quinn, Fitzgerald / Scullion
35	Mar 2	Cas[F]	N[2]	Linfield	L 0-2	/ Hunter o.g., Larmour

36	6	IC[7]	H	Omagh Town	L 1-2	Rainey / Fanthorpe, Sproule
37	13	IPL	H	Omagh Town	W 2-1	Kennedy, Rainey / Ward
38	27	IPL	A	Distillery	L 0-1	/ Downey
39	Apr 6	IPL	H	Ballymena Utd.	D 1-1	Kennedy / McBride (pen)
40	10	IPL	A	Glentoran	L 0-3	/ McCallion 2, Halliday
41	13	IPL	H	Dungannon Sw.	L 0-2	/ Coney, Forker
42	17	IPL	A	Portadown	L 0-4	/ Hamilton 2, McCann 2
43	24	IPL	H	Larne	D 1-1	Kennedy (pen) / McCloskey

N = Seaview
N[2] = Oval
H* = played at Ballyclare Showgrounds

Final positions, season 2004-05

League: 14th   P 30   W 6   D 8   L 16   F 33   A 54   pts 26
League Cup: 2nd   P 6   W 2   D 1   L 3   F 6   A 7   pts 7

	Date	Comp.	Venue	Opponents	Result	Goalscorers
1	Aug 14	LC	A	Linfield	D 0-0	
2	21	LC	H	Crusaders	W 3-2	Bailie, Reeves, Fitzgerald / Robinson, Munster
3	28	LC	H	Loughgall	W 2-0	Fitzgerald, Reeves (pen) /
4	Sept 11	LC	A	Loughgall	L 0-1	/ Percy
5	18	LC	A	Crusaders	L 0-2	/ Magill, Quinn o.g.
6	21	LC	H	Linfield	L 1-2	Rainey / McAreavy, Thompson
7	25	PL	A	Institute	D 1-1	Fitzgerald / McLaughlin
8	28	LC[QF]	A	Cliftonville	L[T] 1-2	Rainey / Scannell, Downey
9	Oct 2	PL	A	Cliftonville	W 3-0	Kennedy 3 /
10	9	PL	A	Coleraine	L 0-3	/ Carson, Moon, Armstrong
11	16	PL	H	Glentoran	L 0-3	/ Lockhart, Morgan, Halliday
12	23	PL	A	Crusaders	W 2-0	Reddish, Delaney /
13	26	Cas[1]	H	Dundela	W 2-1	Fitzgerald, Rainey / Parker
14	30	PL	H	Linfield	D 2-2	Kennedy, Fitzgerald / O'Kane, Larmour
15	Nov 6	PL	A	Limavady Utd.	W 1-0	Kennedy /
16	13	PL	A	Ballymena Utd.	D 2-2	Kennedy, Cleary / Simms, Smyth
17	20	PL	H	Omagh Town	W 2-0	Fitzgerald, Kennedy /
18	27	PL	H	Portadown	L 0-1	/ Neill
19	30	Cas[2]	A	Crusaders	L 0-3	/ Coates, Magill, Cleary o.g.
20	Dec 4	PL	A	Distillery	D 1-1	Kennedy / Mouncey (pen)
21	14	PL	H	Loughgall	D 0-0	
22	17	PL	A	Newry City	L 0-1	/ McCullagh
23	27	PL	H	Larne	L 0-3	/ Curran, Weir, Dickson
24	Jan 1	PL	A	Dungannon Sw.	L 0-7	/ Shaw 3, Adamson, Bownes, Scullion, Walker
25	8	PL	H	Cliftonville	L 1-3	Kennedy / McConnell 2, Mulvenna
26	15	IC[5]	H*	Ballyclare Com.	D 1-1	Fairclough / McRoberts
27	19	IC[5R]	A	Ballyclare Com.	W 1-0	Hunter /
28	22	PL	H	Coleraine	L 1-2	Fairclough / Tolan, Curran
29	29	PL	A	Glentoran	L 0-2	/ Lockhart, Morgan (pen)

30	Feb 1	PL	A	Institute	L 1-2	Ward / Porter, Whitehead
31	5	PL	H	Crusaders	D 2-2	Campbell (pen), Bailie / Dunne, Stirling
32	12	IC[6]	A	Institute	W 2-1	Kennedy 2 / Divin
33	19	PL	A	Linfield	L 0-3	/ Mouncey, Ferguson, O'Kane
34	26	PL	H	Limavady Utd.	L 0-1	/ Ramsey
35	Mar 5	IC[7]	H	Portadown	L 0-1	/ Arkins
36	12	PL	H	Ballymena Utd.	D 1-1	Rainey / Fitzgerald
37	19	PL	A	Omagh Town	L 1-2	Kennedy / Hamilton, Ward
38	25	PL	A	Portadown	W 3-2	Kennedy, Rainey, Waterworth / Arkins (pen), Lindsay
39	29	PL	H	Distillery	L 0-1	/ Martin
40	Apr 9	PL	A	Loughgall	L 1-3	Fairclough / Wilson, Harbinson, Percy
41	16	PL	H	Dungannon Sw.	L 1-3	Watson /
42	23	PL	A	Larne	D 2-2	Kennedy, Waterworth / Dickson (2 pens)
43	30	PL	P	Newry City	W 5-1	Kennedy 2, Rainey 3 / Curran (pen)

H* = played at Dixon Park, Ballyclare
L[T] = after extra time

Final positions, season 2005-06

League: 16th   P 30   W 6   D 2   L 22   F 31   A 62   pts 20
League Cup: 3rd   P 6   W 2   D1   L 3   F 6   A 12   pts 7

	Date	Comp.	Venue	Opponents	Result	Goalscorers
1	Aug 13	LC	A	Loughgall	W 3-1	Campbell, Hill, Waterworth / Guy
2	20	LC	H	Limavady Utd.	L 0-1	/ Semple
3	30	LC	A	Limavady Utd.	D 1-1	Hill / McIntyre
4	Sept 10	LC	H	Linfield	L 0-7	/ Kingsberry 2, Ferguson 2, Kearney, Thompson, McAreavy
5	13	LC	A	Linfield	L 0-1	/ Ferguson
6	17	PL	H	Cliftonville	L 0-1	/ Kennedy
7	20	LC	H	Loughgall	W 2-1	Hill 2 / Topley
8	24	PL	A	Glentoran	L 1-2	Hill / Nixon, Holmes
9	Oct 11	PL	H	Institute	L 1-4	Hegan / McCreadie, Ramsey 2, McCallion
10	15	PL	A	Glenavon	L 0-1	/ O'Connor
11	22	PL	A	Linfield	L 0-2	/ Mouncey, Thompson
12	25	Cas[1]	H	Ards Rangers	W 3-0	Knox, McGrath, Hill /
13	29	PL	H	Armagh City	L 0-2	/ Reilly, Ward
14	Nov 5	PL	A	Portadown	L 2-3	Hill, Hunter / McCann, Arkins, Kelly
15	12	PL	H	Ballymena Utd.	L 1-3	Jephcott / Youle, Haveron, Sweeney
16	19	PL	A	Distillery	L 0-1	/ McLaughlin
17	26	PL	H	Limavady Utd.	W 2-1	Jephcott, Hunter / Patrick
18	29	Cas[2]	H	Linfield	L 2-7	Waterworth 2 / O'Kane, Ferguson, Thompson 3, Kingsberry, Murphy
19	Dec 2	PL	A	Dungannon Sw.	L 2-4	Hill (pen), Waterworth / Ward 2, Fitzpatrick, Scullion

20	9	PL	A	Newry City	L 1-2	Tumelty / Crawford, Curran (pen)
21	17	PL	H	Loughgall	W 1-0	Waterworth /
22	26	PL	A	Larne	L 1-3	Jephcott / McCutcheon, Wilson, Dickson (pen)
23	31	PL	H	Coleraine	L 2-5	Hunter, Hill (pen) / Boyce, Anderson 2, Beatty, Neill
24	Jan 2	PL	A	Cliftonville	W 1-0	Waterworth /
25	7	PL	H	Glentoran	L 0-1	/ Browne
26	14	IC[5]	A	Glentoran	L 1-2	Waterworth / Nixon, Melaugh
27	21	PL	A	Institute	L 1-2	Moran / McLaughlin, Sproule
28	28	PL	H	Glenavon	L* 0-3	/ Verner 2 (1 pen), O'Connor
29	Feb 4	PL	H	Linfield	L 0-4	/ Thompson 2, Ferguson, Jephcott
30	18	PL	A	Armagh City	L 0-3	/ Meehan 2, Ward
31	25	PL	H	Portadown	L 1-2	McKee / McCann, Boyle
32	Mar 11	PL	A	Ballymena Utd.	D 1-1	Hill / Brown
33	18	PL	H	Distillery	L 0-1	/ Kilmartin (pen)
34	25	PL	A	Limavady Utd.	L 0-1	/ Cooke
35	Apr 1	PL	H	Dungannon Sw.	D 3-3	Campbell, Murray, Waterworth / Bulow 2, Adamson
36	15	PL	H	Larne	L 1-3	Davidson / Ward, McCutcheon, Foulton
37	18	PL	A	Loughgall	W 3-2	Hill, Ward, Hunter / Quilty, Coulter
38	22	PL	H	Newry City	L 1-3	McLaughlin o.g. / Willis, Feeney, Whitehead
39	29	PL	A	Coleraine	W 4-2	Hill, Sharratt, Magee, Waterworth / Ferry, Anderson

L* = Ards awarded 1-0 win

Final positions, season 2006-07

Division 1: 5th   P 22   W 11   D 5   L 6   F 42   A 25   Pts 38

League Cup: 4th   P 5   W 2   D 0   L 3   F 7   A 8   Pts 6

	Date	Comp.	Venue	Opponents	Result	Goalscorers
1	Aug 11	1LC	A	Portstewart	L 2-3	Rutherford, Tumelty / Parkhill, McAllister, Woods (pen)
2	19	1LC	H	Wakehurst	W 4-1	Tumelty 2, McKee, McCracken / Drummond
3	26	SSC[1]	A	Lisburn Rangers	W 1-0	McBride /
4	29	1LC	A	Carrick Rangers	L 0-3	/ Corr 2, Adams
5	Sept 9	SSC[2]	A*	Newcastle	W[P] 2-2	McKee, Neill / Allister, Doran
6	16	1LC	H	Oxford Utd Stars	W 1-0	Neill /
7	23	1LC	A	Lurgan Celtic	L 0-1	/ Hill
8	30	SSC[3]	A	Albert Foundry	W[P] 2-2	McGrath (pen), Magee / Doyle, Watters
9	Oct 7	IL	H	Ballinamallard U	W 2-1	McKee, Neill / McFarland
10	14	IL	A	Institute	L 0-2	/ Ramsey, Campbell
11	16	Cas[1]	A	Distillery	L 0-2	/ Verner, Armour
12	21	SSC[4]	H	Orangefield OB	W 3-0	Tumelty, McKee, Billing /
13	28	IL	H	Banbridge Town	W 2-0	Neill, McCracken /
14	Nov 4	INC	A*	Dollingstown	W 5-0	McBride 2, McCracken, Roy, Billing /

15	11	IL	A	H & W Welders	L 1-2	McKee / Bell, Hanna
16	18	IL	H	Carrick Rangers	L 1-3	Smith / Treanor 3
17	21	SSC[SF]	N	H & W Welders	L[T] 1-2	Neill / Craig, Taggart
18	25	INC[1]	H	Bangor	L 1-2	Ward / McDowell 2
19	Dec 9	IL	A	Tobermore Utd.	W 4-1	Roy, Neill, McBride, Billing / Owens
20	16	IL	H	Portstewart	D 2-2	McMillan, Roy / McAllister, Neill
21	26	IL	A	Bangor	W 3-1	Ward, Neill, Tumelty / Irvine
22	30	IL	A	Carrick Rangers	D 1-1	Roy / Corr
23	Jan 6	IL	A	Moyola Park	W 2-0	McMillan, Tumelty /
24	13	IC[5]	H	Dundela	D 1-1	McKee / Parker
25	16	IC[5R]	H*	Dundela	W 2-1	McBride, Roy / Murray
26	20	IL	A	Coagh United	W 1-0	McMillan /
27	27	IL	H	Institute	D 2-2	McBride 2 / Gill, Campbell
28	Feb 3	IL	A	Ballinamallard U	D 0-0	
29	10	IC[6]	H	Linfield	L 0-5	/ McAreavy, O'Kane, Thompson 2, McMillan o.g.
30	17	IL	H	Dundela	L 1-2	Burns / Burrows 2
31	Mar 3	IL	A	Banbridge Town	W 3-0	McMillan, Neill, McKee /
32	10	IL	H	Tobermore Utd.	W 4-1	McBride 2, McLaughlin o.g., Billing / Doherty
33	17	IL	H	Moyola Park	W 3-0	Billing, Burns, McBride /
34	24	IL	A	Dundela	D 1-1	Billing / Parker
35	31	IL	H	Coagh United	W 3-1	Billing, McMillan, Tumelty / McLernon
36	Apr 9	IL	H	Bangor	L 0-1	/ Melly
37	14	IL	A	Portstewart	L 2-3	McMillan, Billing / Kleczkowski 3
38	May 3	IL	H	H & W Welders	W 4-1	McBride, Billing 2, Pike (pen) / Hand

A* = Drawn at home but played away
H* = Opponents forfeited home advantage
W[P] = Won on penalties
L[T] = AET
N = New Grosvenor

EIGHTEEN

Bibliography

Malcolm Brodie *A History of Irish Soccer* Arrell Publications 1963

Malcolm Brodie (ed.) *Irish Football League 1890-1990* Universities Press 1990

Malcolm Brodie *Linfield – 100 Years* Linfield FAC 1985

Malcolm Brodie *Northern Ireland Soccer Yearbook* for various dates Howard Publications

Norman Clarke *The Ballymena Boy* Privately published 1997

Mike Collett *The Guinness Record of the FA Cup* Guinness Publishing 1993

George Eastham *Determined to Win* Sportsman's Book Club 1966

Cris Freddi *The England Football Factbook* Guinness Publishing 1991

Neal Garnham *Association Football and Society in Pre-partition Ireland* Ulster Historical Foundation 2004

Jimmy Hill *The Jimmy Hill Story* Hodder and Stoughton 1998

Barry J. Hugman (ed.) *The PFA Premier and Football League Players' Records* Queen Anne Press 1998

Robert Magee *Ards Football Club* Ulster Services 1988

Sean Ryan (ed.) *The Gillette History of the FAI Cup* Irish Soccer Co-op 1985

Jack/Glenda Rollin *Rothman's Football Yearbook* for various dates, Queen Anne Press / Headline

Belfast Newsletter

County Down Spectator

Ireland's Saturday Night

Irish News

Newtownards Chronicle

Newtownards Spectator

Northern Whig

Dear Reader

I hope you have enjoyed this publication from Ballyhay Books, an imprint of Laurel Cottage Ltd. We publish an eclectic mix of books, ranging from memoirs by Hugh Robinson, Aideen D'Arcy and Viv Gotto to local histories by John O'Sullivan and Harry Allen. Lovers of local music will enjoy Jackie Boyce's contribution of folk and traditional songs, while readers with an interest in poultry will find *Roosters and Hens for the Appreciative Eye* a most entertaining and informative read. *The Donegal Currachs* by Donál MacPolin is a recent addition to the Ballyhay Books catalogue, with Red and Blue Heaven the latest to join the collection.

To see details of these books as well as the beautifully illustrated books of our sister imprint, Cottage Publications, why not visit our website at **www.cottage-publications.com** or contact us at:–

Laurel Cottage
15 Ballyhay Rd
Donaghadee
Co. Down
N. Ireland
BT21 0NG

Tel: +44 (0)28 9188 8033

Timothy S Johnston

BALLYHAY BOOKS